THE ALPHA

Both those who run Alpha cou   ...ose who run away
from them will benefit from reading this book. It is constructive and clear-eyed. By reading it carefully the whole Church
can make better sense of the developing Alpha phenomenon,
and what it teaches us more widely about the mission of God,
across the UK and across the denominations.

Revd Paul Bayes,
National Mission and Evangelism Adviser
for the Archbishops' Council of the Church of England

Based on his own wide practical involvement in Alpha
Courses in several denominations, Andrew offers a book
which will stimulate discussion both in Alpha circles and
in the wider Church. Recognising that the Alpha Course
has made a significant contribution in furthering Christian
mission in a changing society, Andrew's gathering together
of reflections from theologians and mission practitioners
from across the Christian spectrum will help all of us to
evaluate our own commitment to mission. It is one of these
'not-to-be-missed' books!'

Revd Douglas Nicol,
Secretary, Mission and Discipleship Council, Church of Scotland.

Alpha has had huge impact and deserves to be well
understood and properly evaluated. There is much that can
be learned from it that will assist the church as a whole, and
not just Alpha enthusiasts, as we seek ever more effective
ways of communicating the Gospel. This book provides
an ideal opportunity to do this, helpful at both theological
and pastoral levels. It also reflects usefully on the nature
of Alpha's broad appeal across the denominations and its
ecumenical contribution with particular attention to an
examination of the interface between the 'Catholic' and
'Evangelical' worlds. With its impressively broad range of
contributors, this book should be of great value to both 'lay'
Christians as well as those theologically trained or engaged
in full-time pastoral ministry.

Mgr Keith Barltrop
Director, Catholic Agency to Support Evangelisation (CASE),
Bishops' Conference of England and Wales.

Alpha represents a significant gift to the churches. This book
represents a significant gift to Alpha. For all who want to
reflect on the Alpha phenomenon and, in particular, to see

how best to engage with it as our culture morphs, this book is a must.

Here is good critical engagement from some of Alpha's friends. It provides 360 degree insights on one of our best evangelism resources.

If you want to improve the effectiveness of Alpha, then reading and applying the insights from this book are vital steps to take.

Revd Dr David G Spriggs
Bible and Church Consultant, Bible Society.
Moderator, Group For Evangelisation, Churches Together in England.

Alpha is indeed a phenomenon but one that, until now, had received surprisingly little serious analysis. This detailed and thoughtful book rectifies that by looking at Alpha from many different angles in a sympathetic but clear-sighted way. It is empirically well-grounded, alert to the subtleties and complexities of Alpha and the social and cultural context in which the course evolved and now operates. But it is also – importantly – theologically well-considered, balancing its sociological analysis by paying careful attention to scriptural and ecclesial perspectives. Overall, it will interest not only those engaged with studying evangelism but also those curious about Alpha's success and the future of the Christian faith in Britain

Nick Spencer, Research Director,
London Institute for Contemporary Christianity (LICC)

The Alpha Phenomenon is the most comprehensive overview evaluating the influence of the Alpha Course upon the churches in the UK and Ireland I have seen. Alpha has inspired a multiplicity of entry courses to the Christian faith for enquirers. The thorough and balanced approach, insightful analysis and stimulating discussion of Alpha by Andrew Brookes is impressive and this is richly built on by the team of notable mission reflective-practitioners he has gathered together. This book is a timely encounter to review how our churches are engaging with Western culture today and will sharpen the reader's mission engagement for their own church's context. This book is essential reading for those tasked with leadership and are committed to thinking through how we engage as a mission church.'

Revd Terry Tennens
Director, 'Building Bridges of Hope' Mission Accompaniment process
Churches Together in Britain and Ireland

I know how fruitful Alpha can be when used in the right situation, so I welcome this very helpful book with its comprehensive, honest, and independent reflections on the Alpha Phenomenon.

I recommend *The Alpha Phenomenon* to all thinking Christians, whether you like or dislike Alpha, but particularly to those who have never considered using it. Here you will find a balanced perspective with some interesting ideas on how Alpha can help us face the challenges of the missionary mandate.

Charles Whitehead,
Chairman of Catholic Evangelisation Services and Chairman of the
International Charismatic Consultation on World Evangelisation.

This book offers a thorough, fair assessment of Alpha and important challenges to it. A number of the writers point towards depth of engagement with culture and society – as well as personal faith – as key issues for Christian formation today.'

Jonathan Bartley,
Co-Director, Ekklesia (Leading UK Christian Think Tank)

This book is an exciting analysis of an important way in which God is leading his people to explore and proclaim the Gospel. Andrew Brookes has given us a significant vision of the Kingdom and how God is at work in the Alpha phenomenon. I warmly commend it to all who are committed to the church and its mission today.

Dennis Wrigley,
Leader, The Maranatha Community.

Written by theologians and mission practitioners from across the Christian spectrum, the book examines the Alpha course in the context of Christian Mission and a changing Church, examining its use, fruit and the challenges and criticisms associated with it.

THE ALPHA PHENOMENON

Theology, Praxis and Challenges for Mission and Church Today

Edited by
Andrew Brookes

CHURCHES TOGETHER
IN BRITAIN AND IRELAND

Churches Together in Britain and Ireland
Bastille Court
2 Paris Garden
London SE1 8ND

www.ctbi.org.uk

ISBN 978-0-85169-331-6

First published 2007

Further copies are available from:
CTBI Publications, 4 John Wesley Road, Werrington,
Peterborough PE4 6ZP

Telephone: 01733 325002

Fax: 01733 384180

sales@mph.org.uk

Set in 9 on 11pt Utopia
Design and production by Makar Publishing Production, Edinburgh

Printed and bound by Cromwell Press

This book is dedicated to my Mum and Dad
who first introduced me to Jesus Christ
and his church and mission.
Thank you

Contents

Foreword

George Lings

Alpha – bad, mad or good?

I have met at least three very different views of *Alpha* which I will now outline. At some points I merely summarise, in others ringing phrases have stayed with me.

One exhibits unbridled confidence: 'Alpha is the best thing since Billy Graham. Any one from any background can come to a course and could well become a Christian. No church should be without it and it is our best hope, humanly speaking, for revival.'

Another is equally passionate but ideologically critical: 'Alpha is a dreadful proselytising sausage machine. It consumes the unwary and at best only turns out McDonaldised charismatic clones with fixed, narrow, opinions. At worst it damages people and destroys the very nature of faith.'

A different approach is more detached: 'Alpha is significantly effective for many existing church attendees. Some come to living faith for the first time, others go deeper and further, in renewal, knowledge and assurance. It works also for the open dechurched, or sometimes for those nonchurched who are more like pre-Christians but who have friends who are Christians. However it is not really appropriate for the non churched, who will make up the majority of those under 50 in the UK population. It has a sell by date.'

Where does the truth lie and what are its contours? Where does Andrew Brookes come from and what has he found? He brings to us the good gifts of theological rigour and depth engendered by years of Catholic seminary training and the practice of working widely with Alpha in different capacities as well as wider engagement in the fields of ecumenism and mission. That ecumenical and educational combination is itself typical of the unlikely but pleasant surprises that his closer inspection of Alpha reveals. We already have the external comments of the sociologist Steve Hunt, but this work builds on beyond that and is more like that of the mission companion/accompanier or critical friend.

Andrew offers his own careful and nuanced work in the first two thirds of the book, including bringing together different sources of statistics on who Alpha tends to work with, and for. Then he has assembled for us a commendable range of theological commentators, and some denominational strategists, to look widely but sharply at Alpha. Either offering on their own would be worth reading, but together there is a range of careful appraisal of the present content and dynamics, as well as exploration of the future that is important. Since Alpha is the best known of the process courses, though there are signs that its use in the UK has plateaued, it is essential that we have a well researched account of why and how it works and equally importantly who it works for and why. From there we will be better able to look beyond its likely 'best by date' and co-operate more closely with the God of mission who is always calling us beyond what is safe and predictable, into future discoveries in mission.

Mission, bridge-building and Alpha

I can picture the task of mission in the westernised world as like building a bridge to connect a post Christendom hill with the other side of a wide valley. On the hill are many people, deeply ignorant of the story and reality of Christ and how he transforms human beings, their relationships and contexts. At the other side there are communities of those who follow Jesus, still learning, but already living out that transformation for the benefit of others. How is that bridge to be made and what will it look like?

I regret that too many Christians, when they find something that at least half works, either want to invest all their energy in it, or alternatively want to criticise it for what it was not able to do. My take is that with Alpha, it is like those who come across a ruined viaduct of which there are still a couple of complete magnificent arches still standing. Those who want to embellish those arches miss the point that it doesn't span the entire space the original was supposed to cross. Others want to scorn what is left, but seem to have few ideas about a better alternative. The task before an engineer is how to work with the arches that do exist and how to build what could come before them and what could continue them to the other side. That broad task may well include creating different ways to cross; from making footpaths and rope bridges, to constructing a railway bridge as well as a road along the old arches enhanced by new arches. One way will not suit all journeys.

What are we about to receive?

This book is not afraid to be critical of hype, either the optimistic or critical kind. It knows the work of others who have already looked at Alpha, but it takes the doctrinal, ecclesiological and contextual

analysis further in creative ways, exposing its roots in such a cath-
olicity of sources as Lesslie Newbigin, Peter Hocken, John Wimber
and Richard Foster. I found among its fresh insights many indications
of what may still be needed as we take mission and church into the
future.

The unrepeatable social context of HTB with London drawing
many young people to it is acknowledged, Alpha's post-modern style
but modernist content is explored, the significance of pastorates
and continuing small groups for Alpha graduates is strategically
commended, as is synergy with cell church. What might be the areas
of content and style either side of Alpha are identified, the place of
experience is positively but not uncritically re-evaluated, as is the
deeper significance in the meal. Alpha will, surprisingly for some,
be seen as deeply ecclesial and positively ecumenical. In future,
connecting it more with a mystery that starts in God and heads toward
the mystery of how he will bring all things into Christ is a good catholic
comment as is the complementary exploration by Stuart Murray-
Williams and John Drane about mission after Christendom. The whole
work never falls into the traps of relying on Alpha alone or expecting it
to do what it was never designed for.

As a person who came with assumptions closest to the third view I
parodied at the start, I am glad to have found more nuanced evidence
to modify those opinions, and still more to have located depth of
analysis on roots, dynamics and ways forward than I was aware of. For
my own learning from Andrew and his team I am grateful and in that
spirit I warmly commend this book to the reader.

George Lings
Director of Sheffield Centre

Introduction

Why this book came to be written

As a relative newcomer to a parish in Dundee in 1997, I had no idea when my Parish Priest asked me if I would help running something called the Alpha Course that I would end up writing a book! Experience gained with Alpha in the parish led to me becoming an Alpha Adviser in 2000 and thus undertaking training and other advisory work in a variety of denominational settings in the UK, and then to working overseas with Alpha. I also spent a few weeks actually based at Holy Trinity Brompton itself. All of this was a rich experience.

Alongside all this, I was also working on a variety of projects in the field of evangelisation, often ecumenically. This gave me a fuller sense of what else was happening in mission at a practical level and in theological thinking about it, as well as gaining other perspectives and views on Alpha. I felt that, for the most part, the world of Alpha enthusiasts and the wider church worlds were separate and also that there was poor mutual understanding and often blatant misunderstanding. As a result, not much in-depth reflection or critical but balanced theological or pastoral appraisal of Alpha was happening, though Alpha was by any one's reckoning, a major church phenomenon.

'Why not try and plug these gaps by writing at length on Alpha?' others suggested, and then encouraged, assuring me I had the right sort of credentials. My own developing reflection, based on my broad experience of mission, was that Alpha and its underlying method were also more complex than was often indicated. I also felt that the Alpha phenomenon was so big, impacting so many church denominations and traditions as well as aspects of church and mission, that to do it full justice a team of writers with a variety of church backgrounds and academic specialisms would be needed to enrich and build on my more introductory analysis. Again, this idea was welcomed and I assembled a team. Churches Together in Britain and Ireland (CTBI) said they would publish, and writing began in earnest. (Some writings with more balanced presentations on Alpha have since been published and I am grateful to have been able to draw on these.)

Overall Approach

The overall approach adopted is one of 'critical solidarity' with Alpha. This means being appreciative of what Alpha has achieved but willing to look at issues, criticisms, gaps and to consider what else the church needs to develop to undertake effective mission. The reflection was to be theological but also pastoral, with an eye steadily on mission issues, since Alpha is identified as an evangelistic tool. We have sought to produce something of practical benefit to those engaged in mission and in developing local church life. As well as reviewing existing research findings, some contributors have also undertaken and reported new empirical research. The book should thus also be helpful to those conducting research and some suggestions for future research are included.

We have also been willing to ask questions and be original and creative in our thought, while also being factually accurate and rigorous but balanced in sustained evaluation. Nor have we shrunk from being challenging, though hopefully in ways that are respectful and sensitive. The broad range of writers and the fact that Alpha has a wide appeal across church traditions means that the book brings together a variety of approaches and sensibilities not usually found together. Hopefully this richness will suggest fresh Christian connections and stimulate further dialogue.

In a way this book and the wider project that formed it have been constructed by a methodology of open conversation between many participants. I, and others, have sought to draw the reader into this, not least by the use of questions in the text. I do not see the published book as the end of this conversation and hope it will stimulate still further constructive conversation and writing – with practical benefits, too.

Audience

The aim here is to make the main text as accessible as possible to 'thinking lay Christians', though there is also some material to give extra stimulation to the thoughts of more theologically-trained readers. In my sections I have done this by using endnotes, quite long sometimes, for deeper and more technical theological points as well as references and suggestions for further reading – these are placed at the end of each chapter. In the main body of the text I have tried to explain things more fully and simply. The 'general reader' can thus, if they wish, read the main text without being over-concerned with the endnotes. Most of the others contributors' material operates similarly, though it is more specialist, and there are some more technically difficult articles.

The book will hopefully be useful to anyone interested in Alpha (whether supportive or not), to those actually running it, to people using or developing other process courses of evangelism, and to those involved in taking forward mission or thinking about it more generally or just interested in contemporary church life. Though it focuses on Alpha in the UK most of it will be relevant to Alpha in other parts of the world.

The Writing Process

I wrote a first draft – of what is now Part One – and offered that to all other contributors as a factual foundation and first-level gathering and review of data, major opinions and questions on Alpha that they could then build on. I also incorporated a first-level of personal reflection on all of this to highlight issues that could helpfully be pursued in more depth. This was also to ensure that specialist contributors pushed reflection on Alpha to new levels.

Broad topics were originally suggested to the other contributors, then honed or even largely reworked in discussion them and others. No attempt was made by me to control or influence the conclusions each writer came to. Nor did I look to ensure that, overall, the writers agreed with each other – though I happen to think that broadly they do. This is so despite the fact that the contributors did not consult each other, as far as I know, or see each other's work.

Finally, I went through the first draft of my own material, and developed various points and also looked to ensure that the book as a whole was coherent and as comprehensive as possible.

Though initial ideas and preparation began earlier, the detailed project and writing team were largely put together in 2004. In practice most of the research and writing was undertaken in 2005. Updating, revised drafting and checking was undertaken in 2006 and the beginning of 2007.

The contents page indicates the overall structure and contents of the book. Since I have included a few paragraphs at the beginning of each section on its overall scope and function I shall not repeat these here.

Involvement of Holy Trinity Brompton/Alpha International

From the beginning, I also wanted to involve Holy Trinity Brompton (HTB), the 'home' of Alpha and Alpha International (AI) in the project as a dialogue partner. They warmly encouraged me to write and raised no objection to me drawing widely on my experience of Alpha and conversations with staff over the years. They have also wanted the book to be independent and emphatically did not want to interfere, or be seen to interfere, with it or its conclusions. As one staff member put it: 'We are really looking forward to this book since it is being written about us, rather than by us or for us.' Thus they have not put any pressure on me whatever regarding opinions. For these reasons, Nicky

Gumbel, the pioneer of Alpha, kindly agreed to give me an interview but did not want to see the draft book text as preparation. All this may surprise some!

AI/HTB kindly made available to me the most recent report which they have commissioned from Peter Brierley of Christian Research. These reports are usually kept confidential and I am grateful to them for this unique opportunity to use this research. Finally I was very keen to check facts. Thus I sent them a good draft of section one that covers the basic history of HTB and Alpha which Mark Elsdon-Dew, the Communications Director, kindly checked. Fortunately I had not made many errors!

They have seen a copy of John Griffith's chapter since this was written with their collaboration and data though the work and findings are entirely John's. By their own choice they have not seen the rest of the text though they also checked the transcript of Nicky's interview but requested no changes. As such Nicky's interview answers should be seen only as first thoughts on key issues as identified and raised by me. No doubt, more reflection on the book will be undertaken later by Alpha International. At other places I have referred to comments made by staff, particularly Nicky Gumbel and Sandy Millar and have made every effort to do so accurately though these have not been checked. Any mistakes here, though accidental, are my fault.

Language and Terminology
– and a challenge to our use of labels

Since I and other contributors have generally tried to make the book accessible to the general reader, technical vocabulary has been limited or explained where used. However, it will be helpful to readers if I outline here the meaning of a few terms used frequently in the book.

In relation to culture and society, I use '*postmodernity*' to refer to the recent changes in general culture that indicate we are moving out of the modern era and in which 'modern' is seen as exemplified by the Enlightenment emphasis on reason, objectivity, etc. By contrast, in postmodernity there is more emphasis on experience, opinion, etc. (when used, *postmodernism* refers to the philosophical reflection on this cultural shift – the adjective postmodern covers both!). Regarding specifically Christian aspects of culture and society, I use the term '*Post-Christendom*' to indicate the shift away from a society in which Christianity was strongly aligned with the major institutions of society and also its beliefs and values taken as normative in most of society.

I use the term '*dechurched*' to refer to those who have had a significant church connection/influence from Christianity but this has now been cut. The term '*nonchurched*' is being used to indicate the increasing number of those in society who never had such a connection. At times, where I lump these categories together or cannot distinguish between them, I use the more general term the '*unchurched*'.

Other contributors may have used the terms slightly differently, but, if so, this is specified in the relevant chapters.

Writing for as much of the Christian family as possible raises extra challenges since different traditions use different terminology, sometimes reflecting different theological approaches. I have tried to explain terms and also indicate parallel or similar terms and concepts in the text. Deeper discussion of some of the different theological approaches and terms is sometimes included. One particular term I will mention here is 'church'. Bearing in mind the broad uptake of Alpha and the ecumenical nature of this project, I have normally used the term to indicate the overall collectivity of Christians throughout the world. I have also used it to refer to local congregations. It is thus being used descriptively. I have not used it in a more specific theological sense or to distinguish between church and other ecclesial bodies. There is some discussion of these matters in Chapter 9.

Writing for a broad Christian audience also generates challenges and problems regarding labels for groups of Christians and what associations, simplifications, stereotypes and even false representations these labels and terms conjure up. Just referring to everyone or every group as Christian has some important merits but it is not a large enough vocabulary to tease out the richness and complexity of how being Christian has been worked out across time and space. For better or for worse there exist a variety of denominations and traditions. I have generally used the term 'tradition', or sometimes stream or churchmanship, for wider groupings, identified by common theological, spiritual and often practical and even broad organisational trends. 'Denomination' is used to refer to specific organisational and administrative units within or across these.

Labels for these broader groupings and traditions are problematic though without them, or any descriptive language, substantial communication would be impossible. Therefore I have sometimes used the terms 'Catholic', 'Protestant', 'Pentecostal', 'Orthodox' though I am conscious that each covers a diversity and that I am guilty of simplification. This may be particularly true with 'Protestant'. Categorisation makes us think in terms of sharp boundaries and it highlights differences, with the result we tend to neglect common features and connections. This book challenges all Christians to think outside these neat boxes.

Alpha is most commonly described as an 'Evangelical-Charismatic' course or coming from an 'Evangelical-Charismatic' church though Nicky Gumbel nowadays apparently prefers not to describe Alpha or Holy Trinity Brompton in such terms. I have taken up and used these terms – but not without reservations – and again the book indicates specific ways that their usage and assumptions need challenging. I am taking 'Charismatic' to indicate Christianity in which there is an emphasis on the gifts of the Holy Spirit as listed in 1 Cor 12:7–10 as well as a more general stress on the Holy Spirit in prayer, practice and theology. It is a term that some Christians from all of the types listed above apply to themselves. However, let me note here though that in my view most of these gifts also operate more widely in the church and well beyond those who would typically use 'Charismatic language' to describe them. Also the conviction that Christianity is in a fundamental way founded on gifts (the literal meaning of the Greek word translated as 'charism') is wider still and has many implications.

The term 'evangelical' is even more problematic. It is probably most commonly associated in the English speaking world with Protestants who place a certain emphasis on Scriptural authority, faith, personal conversion and proclamation of the Gospel – with other things often being treated as secondary. It is generally, but not always, seen as being expressed in theological terms coming from the Reformed (Calvinist) Tradition (though some Reformed Christians consider evangelicalism as distinct from that tradition if often influenced by it). I have accepted this use of the term as my starting point in the book though I think it needs challenging not least since it is also used by non-Protestant Christians. I have tended to use the term 'Conservative Evangelicals' to distinguish them from 'Charismatic Evangelicals' who place more emphasis on experience and less on dogma and generally hold less firm allegiance to certain theological positions long maintained in Protestant Evangelical circles. In many ways a significant undercurrent of the book is an examination and evaluation of how these labels work, especially the evangelical one, and the extent to which we need to rethink how each of us considers and connects with different Christian groups and traditions.

This is of course not just a matter of semantics. It indicates real shifts in how nowadays Christians put together and live out Christianity (forming a spirituality) and how they do or do not belong to local churches, networks and other groupings (forming an identity). It is about finding the most true and effective way(s) of being Christian in a changing world and how this is understood and expressed in language. Christianity in the UK and beyond is undergoing significant changes at present and Alpha and its broad appeal and impact are part of this. In an important way, Alpha (and this book) calls us to question what we mean by these labels and highlights problems with their use. I urge readers to be prepared to have their own use of these labels and their associations challenged! It may also manage to help people take significant steps towards new ways of understanding Christianity as well as living and sharing it.

Andrew Brookes
March 2007

Acknowledgements

I owe a debt of gratitude to a large number of people. Firstly, a big thank you to all the contributors both for their chapters and the foreword, for the generous and stimulating ways with which they undertook them and also other helpful comments and suggestions about my sections and the book more generally. It has been a joy to work with them all. I am very grateful to Charles Freebury for examining and commenting on a late draft of Chapter 7 and providing other data, and to Mark Elsdon-Dew who did the same for Chapters 1 and 2. I owe a particular debt to Anne Richards who took the time to read all of my material in late draft form and comment on it. Simon Barrow and David Spriggs have given valuable help at various points and I have also had useful conversations with Steve Hollinghurst, Mark Ireland and Terry Tennens, amongst others.

I am also grateful to my colleagues in the Mission Theological Advisory Group (MTAG) for the various ways they have stimulated my thinking about Alpha and mission in general, deepening and sharpening it, and their encouragement with this project. I am grateful to Maria Bartlett for transcribing Nicky Gumbel's interview, and to Catherine Brookes for reading and helpfully commenting on all my script. I remain responsible for the final text and its shortcomings.

I am grateful to all whom I have been involved with whilst working with Alpha. They have influenced and enriched me in all sorts of ways, and as such have contributed very significantly to this project. I simply cannot name everyone here. However, I would like to mention the Servite Parish of St Vincent's in Dundee and advisors I have worked closely with. Also a big thank you is due to the staff at Alpha International and Holy Trinity Brompton and to the congregation there too for the way they entered into the vision and spirit of this project. Along with their practical co-operation at various points, their openness, trust and encouragement has been impressive, and not without risks, and I hope that the book really is of help to them in their work and also helps build a bigger interface between Alpha and the wider church.

I am grateful to the staff of Churches Together in Britain and Ireland (CTBI) for their skill and support in publishing this book. CTBI also provided a grant from its Edinburgh Centenary Mission Fund to help meet some of my costs. Much appreciated financial support was also given by Robert Gamble from Poznan, Poland whom I got to know while promoting Alpha there. Almost finally, thanks to my friends, family and the Companions of Saints Margaret and Columba (COSMAC), for their encouragement and patience and various forms of practical support throughout the project.

Finally, thanks to God for calling us to share, in so many ways, in the Mission of God! I pray that this book enables the church, in the UK and also further afield, to do so still more effectively.

AB

List of Contributors

Simon Barrow is co-director of Ekklesia, the UK Christian think tank. He was formerly global mission secretary for Churches Together in Britain and Ireland, and has worked as a trainer and consultant on local church development. He is an Anglican with a strong affinity for the Mennonite peace church tradition.

Andrew Brookes is engaged full time in various projects in the fields of evangelisation and ecumenism. He has done voluntary work with Alpha across several denominations at local, regional, national and international levels. He is a Roman Catholic whose faith has been enriched by involvement with many other Christian traditions.

Helen Cameron is Visiting Research Fellow at the Wesley Centre, Westminster Institute of Education, Oxford Brookes University. She is Senior Tutor for the MA in Consultancy for Mission and Ministry at York St John University College. She is a member of The Salvation Army.

David Currie works as a Congregational Consultant for the Church of Scotland, primarily in the areas of faith–sharing, process evangelism courses (including Alpha), and emerging church issues. David has been a parish minister, served as Senior Adviser in Mission and Evangelism and has co-authored 'You're an Angel – Being yourself and sharing your faith'.

John Drane is co-chair of the Mission Theology Advisory Group of the Archbishops Council of the Church of England and of Churches Together in Britain and Ireland, and author of many books on church and culture as well as being a visiting professor at Spurgeon's College, London, and Fuller Seminary, California.

Charles Freebury is a Methodist in the charismatic evangelical tradition. Formerly a Director with PricewaterhouseCoopers, he holds a Cliff College MA in Evangelism Studies (with distinction), including specialist studies in process evangelism. A Circuit Missioner for 7 years until 2006, he is chairman of the Cliff College Committee and an Emmaus Course consultant. He is the author of *Alpha or Emmaus?* and other evangelism resources.

David Gordon is the National Mission Advisor for the Baptist Union of Scotland leading a team of ten 'networkers' whose primary role is to encourage the churches in holistic mission through networking, training, research and the development of new initiatives! He desires to see the growth of healthy churches reaching effectively into their communities with the Gospel of Christ.

John Griffiths has worked as an advertising/communications strategist and researcher with various companies since 1983. He has also worked regularly with churches and church organisations in the development of advertising campaigns and also serves on the board of trustees for the Christian Research Association. Now training as a layreader, he would describe himself as an evangelical in the technical rather than the subcultural sense!

Nicky Gumbel became a curate at Holy Trinity Brompton in 1986 after work as a barrister. He took over direction of the Alpha Course in 1990 and has since helped steer and support its uptake across the UK and world. He became the Vicar of HTB in 2005 and is the author of several books.

James Heard was originally from a Pentecostal (Assemblies of God) background, and went on to work at HTB for five years before training for the priesthood, in the Anglican Church, at Ridley Hall Cambridge, including PhD studies on Alpha. Following ordination as a deacon in July 2006 he has begun a curacy at All Saints Fulham.

George Lings was an Anglican vicar for twenty years before becoming the Director of Church Army's Sheffield Centre. Its story-based research into Fresh Expressions of Church, from all traditions, is published quarterly through the *Encounters on the Edge* series. He wrote the first draft of the 2004 report *Mission-Shaped Church*.

Dr Philip Meadows is an ordained presbyter in the British Methodist Church. He has worked as a lecturer in theology, religious studies, evangelism, missiology and Wesley Studies in Oxford, Chicago and now Cliff College. His research and publications seek to combine theology and discipleship in the Wesleyan tradition with the missionary challenges of contemporary culture.

Stuart Murray Williams is a trainer/consultant working with the Anabaptist Network and the director of Urban Expression, an urban church planting agency. Formerly a lecturer at Spurgeon's College, he has written several books on urban mission, church planting, contemporary missiology and the challenge of post-Christendom.

Anne Richards works for the Archbishops' Council of the Church of England as National Adviser: mission theology, alternative spiritualities and new religious movements. She is Secretary to the ecumenical Mission Theological Advisory Group, which looks at issues of mission affecting the whole Church, especially how the gospel relates to today's culture.

Rev Dr Philip Walker is an ordained minister and, until 2005, lecturer on mission issues with the Elim Pentecostal Church and is the founder of Healthy Church UK – the Natural Church Development (NCD) partner for the UK and Ireland. He edits 'Healthy Church Magazine', concentrating on the health of local churches through telling stories and reflecting on best practice.

Abbreviations

AB
Andrew Brookes, author and genral editor of this book.

AI
'Alpha International', the charitable company set up by HTB to promote Alpha and associated ministries.

AI/HTB
I have used the formula 'AI/HTB' where it is difficult to make a very clear distinction between the role or impact of HTB and AI (or where the impact of both have been important over time). In reality there has over time been a swing, regarding impact on and responsibility for Alpha, from HTB towards AI as the latter has developed.

AIC
'Alpha International Campus', new building complex being developed to take forward the work of AI.

CRA
Christian Research Association, based in UK, directed by Peter Brierley.

HTB
'Holy Trinity Brompton', Anglican church in London which developed the Alpha Course.

NG
Nicky Gumbel, current Vicar of HTB, pioneer of Alpha's wider use.

SM
Sandy Millar, Vicar of HTB from 1985–2005.

RCIA
'Rite for the Christian Initiation of Adults'. The process and set of liturgies commonly used for people becoming Christians in the Roman Catholic Tradition.

PART ONE

THE ALPHA PHENOMENON: EXPLANATIONS AND ANALYSIS

The aim of this part is to give a full and accurate account and explanation of Alpha with a first level of analysis and reflection on issues already associated with it. Section 1 provides a solid factual platform of facts about Alpha and HTB. The Alpha course as such is then analysed and discussed in depth in Section 2. In Section 3 I examine issues arising out of its impact (Chapter 7), namely how effective is it, how well does it respond to features of our changing culture (Chapter 8), what impact is it having on ecumenism and the church more generally (Chapter 9) and how effective are the strategies of AI/HTB (Chapter 10).

This presentation and analysis draws on my own experience with Alpha and mission/church more widely, research and reflection by others on Alpha, and my own reflections on all of this.

AB

SECTION 1

The Development, Spread and Promotion of the Alpha Course

The aim of this section is to give an overview of the history, development and spread of the Alpha Course. This is placed in the context of wider developments at Holy Trinity Brompton (HTB) which produced it. This account relies largely on information made available from HTB in different forms – albeit in a piecemeal fashion – and picked up during my own involvement with the course and a number of conversations with their personnel. It is generally a descriptive account laying out the facts about Alpha and HTB and is intended as a foundation on which further analysis, reflection and discussion can then be securely built in subsequent chapters. However, some comments on factors effecting the development of both HTB and Alpha that most appropriately belong in this section. Chapter 1 focuses on HTB and the early development of Alpha until 1992. Chapter 2 deals with events and developments after 1993 and includes the establishment of Alpha International (AI), the emergence of other ministries and courses and the very recent announcement of the establishment of the Alpha International Campus (AIC).

AB

Holy Trinity Brompton and the Formation of Alpha

Andrew Brookes

Why Provide A Profile of Holy Trinity Brompton, the home of Alpha?

The Alpha Course was developed by a local church community, Holy Trinity Brompton (HTB) in west central London, over a number of years. Some commentators view these features – a slow thoughtful development and a local setting – as being foundational, even vital, to its subsequent huge impact. Nicky Gumbel (NG) points out, 'I did not invent Alpha', and he adds that it is precisely this fact that makes it easier for him to devote much of his time to promoting it. He sees it as a useful evangelistic tool through which God has blessed their own church, and he along with his long-time Vicar, Sandy Millar (SM), and the rest of the church have been happy to offer it to the church more widely – with very significant results! This has changed many churches and had broader impacts on our approaches to and appetite and confidence for evangelism and mission as well as other aspects of church life. It has affected huge numbers of individual lives. All this has impacted the local church that produced it. It is said that Alpha is part of the DNA of HTB. Thus, it is not really possible to get a full picture or appreciation of the Alpha Course without first having an overview of this local church, along with its values and some of the developments that have occurred there during the period in which Alpha was developed and has since been exported around the world. It is the purpose of this chapter to provide such an overview.

Setting

HTB is an Anglican church, located in Kensington in busy west central London, close to Harrods on the one side and to the Victoria and Albert and Natural History Museums on the other. Politically, the constituency in which it is located is regarded as a very safe Conservative seat. The church building, dating from the Victorian era, is in a neo-Gothic style, replete with organ, stained-glass windows and substantial pillars, designed with a substantial sanctuary area with choir stalls beyond. It has its own pleasant grassed grounds, which have the feel of an oasis in modern, noisy and frenetic central London with its predominance of stone, concrete and tarmac. Central London is very expensive to live in and the congregation coming to HTB is often described as 'well-heeled' though the impact of Alpha and other initiatives have broadened this. Certainly HTB attracts many from the professions who work in the city in various capacities. It has also attracted large numbers of recent, and thus young, Christian graduates who often come to London for a period of professional training and/or work for a number of years early in their careers. This creates a good age range and a certain mobility and turnover in part of the congregation. It also helped generate the so-called 'HTB Diaspora', made up of friends of HTB now re-located elsewhere in the country or beyond. The congregation is getting increasingly younger over time.

Since the mid 1970s HTB and its clergy have had a close association with the nearby Anglican church and parish of St Paul's Onslow Square. The two were first linked under the care of Rev Raymond Turvey. Since then various ways of organising this relationship have been adopted, along with various uses being made of its buildings and land.

Historically, HTB belonged to the 'evangelical wing' of the Church of England. This included elements of traditional worship. SM refers, in conference talks, to the traditional nature of the worship and the robed choir during his early time as a curate. At that time people still sat in pews. SM also often tells the story that once, while leading a traditional service in his earlier days on the staff, he saw a young person come in, look around while trying to make some sense of things, shrug his shoulders and walk out. This – and perhaps other incidents or converging factors – convinced Sandy that things had to change to attract younger generations, or HTB was doomed to become an increasingly ageing congregation and then to die. Since the 1970s there had also been a regular charismatic prayer group led by one of the staff members and linked to the church though not visibly central to its life. It has been commented that this helped prepare for what was to happen later in the 1980s and since. Raymond Turvey, Vicar from 1975–80, also had well known 'Charismatic' speakers like Jackie Pullinger come and lead days on charismatic gifts etc. From 1978 informal worship was introduced to the evening services led by their own worship band 'Cloud'. In 1980 John Collins, well known as a Charismatic Evangelical Anglican, was appointed Vicar, remaining in that position until 1985. The church became increasingly charismatic during this period. An emphasis on and development of house groups with an evangelistic edge dates from 1981.

Friends of mine went to HTB as young graduates in the early 1980's and I would sometimes visit. There was an emphasis on clear Bible-based teaching in the Evangelical theological tradition and mould.

C. S. Lewis, John Stott, David Watson and Michael Green were among authors commonly cited as being worth reading in their church circles.[1] I once heard a sermon there on the unity that Christ brings which included a reference to this meaning no Pope and no Mass – quite a change from their present ecumenical openness. During and since the 1970s, people had joined mid-week house groups where people met for bible study, prayer and fellowship. There was a marked emphasis on undertaking personal evangelism and the importance of personal conversion was stressed. An outreach course they ran called 'Alpha' was on occasions mentioned to me! Nicky Gumbel reminisces that at the first house group meeting he went to, led by Sandy Millar, Sandy preached with the conviction of Billy Graham to the handful of people present![2]

Staff

There has been a remarkable stability in many of the key clergy and other staff and members during the years of the development and spread of Alpha. Sandy Millar has been involved with HTB throughout this period. He is Scottish and of Presbyterian stock, coming to personal and committed faith as an adult in 1967 (aged 28). In fact he came to HTB as a member and practising barrister in 1968. He conveys the sense of being significantly formed by and at home within Anglicanism. After marrying Annette (1971) and training for church ministry he joined the staff as a curate with a 'charismatic interest' in 1976. He became the Vicar in 1985 and remained in that post until his retirement in the summer of 2005, having reached his 65th birthday in 2004. In July 2004, in announcing his planned retirement, Sandy said he would stay on the staff of HTB, be based at St Mark's Tollington Park, London and continue to serve the church more widely. The Bishop of London, Richard Chartres, then hinted strongly that this would include using his wisdom and expertise in the area of church-planting. Sandy himself noted he wanted to contribute to this and to work for the poor. In October, 2005 it was announced that Sandy would become an Assistant Bishop in London (though consecrated by the Archbishop of Kampala, Uganda) in the hope that he would contribute to attempts to build a mission-shaped church. Sandy and his wife Annette have thus been at the centre during all of the Alpha and associated developments and at the helm for most of this period. Many point to his overall sense of vision and leadership as being central to the developments at HTB.

There has also been a remarkable stability amongst many other key staff members with many of them being associated with HTB for all or most of SM's years as Vicar. Nicky Gumbel is from a secular Jewish background on his father's side of the family. His mother's family come from a Christian background and he was baptised and confirmed while growing up and learned about Christianity while at school at Eton. Describing himself as fluctuating between being an atheist and an agnostic around this time, he decided Christianity was untrue. He had a strong personal conversion to Christianity as a student at Cambridge in 1974, becoming active in the evangelical Christian Union and associated ministries. He first came to HTB and met Sandy in 1976 shortly after Sandy started as a curate. Married to Pippa, NG was an active member of the church whilst working as a barrister in London and after training for church ministry at Wycliffe Hall in Oxford, joined the staff as a curate in 1986. NG took over as Vicar of HTB in July, 2005.

Nicky Lee (a university friend of NG) and his wife Sila, and also Ken Costa came to the church shortly after NG in 1976. Nicky Lee also went on to become a curate (1985) and has been on the staff for a long time. He and Sila have since been responsible for developing the Marriage Course. Ken works in the city and is Churchwarden and Chair on the Alpha Board amongst other things. Other long term staff members include Jeremy Jennings and his family – an accountant and parishioner who again became a minister and has developed many facets of HTB's prayer life, and Emmy Wilson who pioneered much of the prison work and still works on this closely with Paul Cowley. Many of the other administrative staff have been very faithful too and bring much more than just their professional skills to the work and life of HTB. It would take too long to name them all, enough to say that teamwork is a hallmark of HTB! I think it is fair to note that it must take something quite significant to persuade very talented people to stay together for that length of time. Indeed this stability and the friendship, unity and loyalty between staff – along with their gifts, faith and love – has made possible much of what has happened at and through HTB. Other key long serving staff members have been home-grown and/or emerged through Alpha and its use and spread. Tricia Neill, now Executive Director of Alpha International, is perhaps the most well-known and influential. She has done much to cultivate efficient professional working practices. SM places huge value on the church staff, even joking to visitors that they can help themselves to anything that might help them in their own church life but asking them please to leave the staff behind! In passing, it is true to note that many of the clergy were educated in public schools with Oxbridge as a finishing school and that they worked in a profession before training for church ministry. It is also true that the wives of the clergy are clearly heavily involved in the life of the church and very much part of the ministry of their respective husbands, something that the clergy often give thanks for publicly.

The Influence of John Wimber

At the beginning of the 1980s a handful of influential Anglican Charismatic leaders invited John Wimber to England from America. He led a number of big conferences and also worked more closely with a few specific congregations. Most notable amongst these (with hindsight) are probably St Andrew's Chorley Wood, near Watford, which under David Pytches' leadership went on to develop the New Wine Network and various associated Ministries, and HTB. It is quite clear listening to more than a few talks by SM or NG that John Wimber had a huge impact and influence on them personally, and on how HTB and thus Alpha developed. A study and comparison of John Wimber's materials with the training and other material produced by AI/HTB supports this view too.

John Wimber was from California and by his own reckoning brought up in a secular environment. Born in 1937, and having taken up a career as a professional musician, which met with significant success, he converted to Christianity in 1963. Always passionate about sharing his faith with others he entered full-time church ministry. After periods as a pastor and Bible teacher, he worked as a consultant in church growth, connected to the Fuller seminary. He moved from a faith that was initially broadly conservative evangelical to one that embraced more charismatic and Pentecostal elements as well. He and his wife Carol were forced out of their own church and then started leading their own fellowship that has grown rapidly into the worldwide network of Vineyard Churches. In this connection he travelled extensively. Drawing on his musical gifts he composed worship songs and helped bring contemporary and more intimate devotional worship music to new levels of skill, creativity and professionalism. A major part of his ministry in the later years of his life was organising conferences and other training events in various aspects of church life and ministry. Typically – and HTB follows this in its own work – these follow a three stage pattern of theological basis, model and practice. He died of cancer in 1997. He is remembered for his contribution to charismatic Christianity – with its focus on the person and work of the Holy Spirit – linking this to an evangelical outlook. He developed ministries linked to the charismatic gifts as listed in 1 Cor 12:8–11 including prophecy, healing and deliverance. He also sought to bring together in closer co-operation and unity the different strands of charismatic Christianity, seeking to break down walls of hostility, suspicion and independence that often prevailed between these groups and their leaders. As well as some from the historic Protestant traditions and more recent independent Pentecostal and Charismatic streams, he managed to include some Roman Catholics in this work too. As part of this he looked at new expressions and formulations of doctrine and biblical exposition, more consciously bringing in and weaving together insights from different traditions and denominations that were historically kept apart, and usually still are.

In talks, Sandy frequently recounts the first time John Wimber came in 1982, at the invitation of John Collins, and led evenings in the Church house for clergy and house-group leaders. It marked a very significant watershed for many individuals and for HTB as a whole, if one that was approached and crossed with significant anxiety by both SM (then a curate) and NG (still a practising barrister), based on the accounts they both give of it. For SM this concerned the challenge that if the charismatic gifts really were still operating in the church today through the power of the Holy Spirit, then they ought to be used by the local church in a way that was central and integral to its life. This included HTB – but how? He has also commented that it marked a certain coming of age in the church, since its members began honestly to name their inner pains and struggles in front of others and still be accepted. This followed a situation in which individuals actually ident-ified themselves in response to various prophetic words that John and his team gave, about various health problems existing in the relatively small group present. Significant healings followed this and later also followed their own early attempts to pray for people's healing. The occasion of this announcement of human ailments by John Wimber also impacted NG. Reluctant to be prayed for concerning his athlete's foot, he was prayed over in more general terms. This resulted in him shaking on the floor and John Wimber declaring that he was at that time being given gifts to equip him for evangelism that would result in him reaching thousands with the gospel. It was not long after this that NG began to train for church ministry.

Deep friendships were formed and close working relationships and associations between their churches began. It was not at that time John's intention to establish Vineyard Churches in the U.K,[3] but to work with local churches for their own renewal. John invited HTB staff to pay visits to his California base and to pick up and learn what would be useful in their own setting. SM, and others, made several visits. HTB, under SM's leadership has maintained its Anglican identity but it has been profoundly influenced by John Wimber's ministry and the life of the Vineyard Movement that he established.[4] SM has commented that he felt John Wimber did more to renew the Anglican Church than anyone since John Wesley. While HTB is usually seen as having kept both an Anglican ethos and the broadly evangelical theology and outlook that had marked it hitherto, after this date it became increasingly charis-matic – and in ways more visible and central to its life.[5] Alongside this, T.V. and other screens came in (early 1980s), pews were taken out (1993), attention was give to a friendly relaxed setting in tune with the perceived tastes of the dechurched or nonchurched, especially the young. Worship became more flexible, devotional and intimate with increasing use of guitars and other contemporary instruments. However, they still use a variety of musical styles and employ an organist. HTB retained a stress on Biblical teaching too, but any reservations more typical of conservative evangelicals about an emphasis on the Holy Spirit and the so-called charismatic gifts have been shed. Indeed, HTB in general, and Alpha in particular, has received some of its sharpest criticism from more conservative evangelicals.

Pastorates, Planting and Prayer

I need to look briefly at three other aspects in the life and development of HTB which give important insights into aspects of its life, spiritual energy and commitment to mission, and also affect Alpha, before returning to the development and spread of Alpha itself. Conveniently, these all begin with the letter 'P'! They are Pastorates, Planting and Prayer.

Pastorates

An important feature of the life of HTB that SM and other staff developed and has significance for Alpha and other things are what they describe as 'pastorates' which have been a feature of the life of HTB since around 1982.[6] Until that time people met in small mid-week groups of around six to eight people for bible study, prayer and fellowship. Sandy has commented to me that the needs that these groups meet and their dynamic are such that they tend to stabilise in membership and become inward looking. Neither of these features facilitates outreach, the welcome of newcomers and their growth, or makes it easy for people to be trained in new gifts and ministries, all these being facets that Sandy considers vital to church life. It was also noted as a church begins to grow that having significantly larger numbers than 40 at any Sunday service changed its dynamic, with both gains and losses in what can be effectively done and which needs of people can be met or not met. HTB thus started combining three or four small groups together and creating larger groups. These are sometimes described as 'congregational sized groups' and at HTB are called 'pastorates'. A different set of dynamics operates in these ultimately larger groups and they can serve different functions in the overall life of the church.

HTB defines a pastorate as 'a congregational-sized gathering of between 25–35 people who meet fortnightly on a midweek evening or morning to worship, pray, learn and share a meal together'.[7] Typically they begin with a meal, then welcomes and notices, followed by worship (i.e. praise and thanksgiving), a short talk and a discussion of it, prayer ministry usually in smaller groups with a definite end time.[8] The sorts of numbers involved in pastorates and the values of hospitality they practice make it easier for members to invite friends. Pastorates serve as a means to foster solid Christian friendships,[9] provide discipleship and give people an opportunity in a safe and relaxed setting to train in and begin to exercise spiritual gifts and other ministries. HTB considers them the best way to invite newcomers (new Christians or others) to the life of the church. Pastorates typically begin with small numbers gathered around a leader and a leadership team, none of whom are full-time paid members of church staff. When the numbers reach around 25 or the venue is at 85% capacity it is time to start thinking about establishing a new pastorate. The leader will typically emerge from the existing leadership group. However, all leadership appointments are made or at least confirmed by HTB's full-time staff. The role of the clergy and any other paid pastoral assistants is to select, train, communicate with, support and pray for pastorate leaders. The pastorate leaders are then given a good deal of autonomy and flexibility regarding the week to week running of the pastorate.

An outward focus is considered very valuable to maintain the pastorate's vitality and it also deepens members' understanding and participation in the mission of Christ. Often this takes the form of a regular engagement in a local social action project. Some members of each pastorate are also frequently invited to help on each Alpha course. Often they form the leaders and helpers for a particular small group on Alpha. In these cases those guests who complete Alpha in this small group and want to get more involved in the church tend to go to this pastorate – at least as the first port of call. Pastorate members are also welcome to form themselves into small groups of around six – eight people for more intimate prayer, bible study and fellowship which typically meet on the weeks when pastorates do not happen. These groups can be stable and long-term. Thus pastorates are vital to the life and work of HTB and also intrinsic to the way HTB runs Alpha, concerning both the finding of teams and the integration of guests into the wider life of the church. Just how integral is this link is not really spelt out as much as it could be to churches thinking of running Alpha. I strongly suspect that often other churches struggle to integrate Alpha into their church life and deal adequately with guests, precisely because they do not have something similar to pastorates operating in their own church.[10]

Planting New Churches

Much has been written on church planting and there are many variations on the ground but in general the aim of church plants is to bring the church to where people are, rather than expecting the people to travel or to change their culture in order to join the church. Typically, they are led by a minister together with a core group from an existing church. Over the years HTB has kept growing to such an extent that this has been an option – but only when combined with a willingness on their part to send out some of its most talented and generous members. Clearly the compactness of London, the number of church buildings held by the Church of England (and the near emptiness of some) and the fact that people travel into HTB from a wide area, have all also helped to make this possible. These 'church plants' have happened when part of the congregation, typically between 50–100 people led by a minister on the staff at HTB, move to, integrate with and lead, in consultation with the local bishop, the running of a local but small church congregation usually characterised as struggling, failing or even dying. They have gone to inject new life into the church and to bring Christ' s presence and mission nearer to the people of the area. The first took place in 1985 under John Irvine. HTB have successfully undertaken a number of such plants, managing to build up self-supporting local churches in different areas. Sometimes HTB have taken on a member of the clergy as part of their staff on the understanding that they will in due course lead a church plant. At the time of writing, HTB has made 8 church plants, some of which have planted themselves. They tend to carry much of HTB's DNA with them and operate with a significant overlap of values and pastoral practices. Supporters argue that all of this shows a great commitment to mission and to think beyond the confines of HTB to the good of the wider (Anglican) church and for the sake of Christ's work in London. However, the strategy has not been without its problems and critics. There have been concerns about how effective it is to introduce a church group from one area and background into another set up and situation, and also concerns about respect for the territorial nature and jurisdiction of other parishes and dioceses.[11] It has even been described as empire building by HTB rather than really building local church though it has also had warm endorsements and praise from bishops.

Prayer

Alpha stresses the importance of prayer but if you get to know HTB better you will quickly discover that this is part of a much bigger emphasis on prayer that is expressed in a real and practical commitment to it running through the life of the church. This includes both worship (praise and thanksgiving which also encourages intimacy with God) and intercessory prayer. They also train and encourage people actually to pray for each other in prayer ministry and provide training and guidelines for this. There is a deeply held conviction that nothing very worthwhile will happen unless it is founded and surrounded in intercessory prayer.

It would appear that this conviction about prayer goes back a long way at HTB and is well-bedded down. Mandy Patterson, the wife of Charles Patterson who was a curate at HTB in the early 1970s, reported to a friend of mine that HTB had intercessory prayer groups running behind the scenes from the 1920s. Mandy Patterson indicated that such groups have met since that time in one form or another, often praying specifically for healings and miracles to emerge at and from HTB. She joined one such group in the 1970s and commented that she had never experienced people pray with such conviction and power. She added that she feels sure that this habit and practice of saturating all events in significant amounts of prayer before they even occur, lies at the heart of the huge impact of Alpha.

They have devoted much time, under Jeremy Jenning's supervision, to finding different ways to do this and, alongside the prayer of individuals and informal groups, build prayer into the weekly and longer timetable of the church. Often this is early in the morning. Again, they have begun running conferences on how to foster 'dynamic' prayer in local churches. While it may be difficult scientifically to assess the effectiveness of prayer, there can be little doubt that this lies behind the impact of Alpha and other aspects of the ministry of HTB.

Early Development and the Basic Structure of Alpha

The early development of Alpha can now be set against this backdrop. It has had quite a long evolution with many people involved and led by a succession of ministers. The Alpha Course was started by Charles Marnham, a curate at HTB, in October, 1977. It began as a four week course for new Christians and also other Christians new to their church. From the beginning it was located in a person's house, beginning with a relaxing meal and with a discussion after the talk.[12] This remains the core structure. Over the years the content was changed and added to. John Irvine took on the course in 1981 and lengthened it to ten weeks, adding the weekend away with teaching on the Holy Spirit.[13] Nicky Gumbel credits John with substantially determining and ordering the (still largely current) teaching content of the course. Nicky Lee ran the course from 1985 to 1990, average numbers per course increasing from 35 to well over 100. Nicky Gumbel then took charge. It was he who shifted Alpha's focus to those outside the church. This was partly because he observed that many non-Christians were attending the course. Their evening course now runs three times a year, with well over 500 attending each course (including the team).

The name 'Alpha' has persisted but has had different connotations and operates at several levels with different meanings. It would appear some of these were added or developed at different phases of the course's history! At the beginning it was the first of a series of courses the church ran: it was called Alpha, the second Beta, etc. It then became part of a more structured set of teaching material – including several courses – run over a two year period. It came first;

the others had names reflecting their content. The use of 'A.L.P.H.A.' as an acronym summarising key features of the course was a relatively late development. Thus it became A ~ anyone can come; L ~ learning and laughter; P ~ pasta; H ~ help each other; A ~ ask anything. This is the use and meaning of the name 'Alpha' that most people would be aware of nowadays. Throughout, it can be argued it has a certain allusion to Christ who is described as the Alpha and Omega (Rev 1:8, 21:6, 22:13) – though I have not heard them make much of this.

In essence the Alpha Course can now be summarised as follows: Alpha is a ten week practical introduction to Christianity, presented in a lively and engaging way. It is designed principally for non-Christians or new Christians – though it also serves well as a refresher course. Each session begins with a meal and throughout runs on a host-guest model of relationships between 'Christian team' and attending 'non-Christians'. A caring pastoral attitude and respect for all are stressed throughout the course. The meal is followed by a talk which combines well-illustrated bible teaching, accompanied by a good deal of testimony, all peppered with humour. Participation in small 'sharing' groups rounds off the evening. Here the emphasis is on respect and openness within a setting of trust and confidentiality; guests are encouraged, though not pressurised, to say exactly what they think and feel and to ask anything! Approximately half way through the course is a day or preferably a weekend away together with a focus on the Holy Spirit and extended opportunity for teaching, prayer, fellowship and recreation together. The course is intended to be run in a roll-on manner, with (converted) guests on one course both helping to lead the next one and also inviting their own friends to attend. To this end a celebratory supper with a talk and testimonies is scheduled which marks the end of one course and introduces the next one.

The titles of the 15 talks, each one lasting for approximately 45 minutes at HTB and on video, are as follows:

Week 1: Who is Jesus?
Week 2: Why Did Jesus Die?
Week 3: How Can I be sure of my Faith?
Week 4; Why and How should I read the Bible?
Week 5: Why and How should I Pray?
Week 6: How does God Guide Us?
During the Day or Weekend Away:
Who is the Holy Spirit?
What does the Holy Spirit Do?
How can I be Filled with the Spirit?
How can I make the most of the rest of my life?
Week 7: How can I resist Evil?
Week 8: Why and How should we tell Others?

Week 9:   Does God Heal Today?
Week 10: What about the Church?
          Celebratory Supper:
          Christianity: Boring, Untrue and Irrelevant?

It was in this form and stage of development that the Alpha Course was made available outside HTB in 1993. We shall follow developments since then in Chapter 2.

The Key Values and Spiritual Ethos of HTB

Before we engage with these I think it is necessary to complete this introductory chapter by looking at some of the key values and spiritual attitudes that have informed and underpinned HTB – and therefore Alpha – during all these years and since then up to the present. An appreciation of them greatly helps in understanding the course and wider Alpha phenomenon. My own view is that these should be spelt out more fully than they generally are by AI/HTB.

Alpha is often presumed by critics and others to conform to a certain evangelical stereotype, and claimed to be only concerned with individualistic conversion. SM consistently states that conversion involves three moments/dynamics which he calls a triple conversion, all conveniently beginning with 'C'. Thus there is: conversion to Christ; conversion to Christ's church; and conversion to Christ's cause.[14] All three are important. A close analysis of Alpha supports this claim. Clearly it calls for personal conversion. It certainly asks for church involvement; indeed, the whole course has an ecclesial setting, being located in the concrete setting of the local church. What exactly is the nature of the church and how this is expressed in worship, sacraments and other pastoral activities is a different matter! It certainly calls the individual into active discipleship and to an active and lively, committed participation in the mission of Christ too – Christ's cause. Indeed, the active participation of all is a feature of HTB. Although what this is understood to include may be more contentious to some. These are all really part of one overall conversion, but highlighting the distinct elements can be useful pastorally as well as for others doing an audit or review of their own church life and formation processes. It also reduces the chance of any one of these being overlooked or taken for granted and indeed indicates that 'conversion' may be needed to enter effectively into any or all of them.

What sort of church does this triple conversion involve one in? Using an acronym, SM says that he thinks we should aspire to a church that G.L.O.W.S. (glows)![15] In this acronym, 'G' means a church that grows, 'L' is a church that loves. 'O' indicates a church that obeys. This refers firstly to obedience to God's Revelation and commands as well as to good order in church life and to proper leadership. 'W' indicates a church that worships. SM stresses the primacy of this above all else and says he would have used an acronym beginning with 'W' if he could have thought of one. 'S' indicates a church that serves. My own expansion and linking of these core points is as follows. God is central and the full response to God is that of worship. The call to love, obey and serve him flows from whom God is – and how God is encountered in worship. It is precisely this encounter that inspires and leads people to love, obey and serve each other in and for God. This is not to be kept within the Christian body but offered to others in evangelism, in an attitude of love and service, and this will lead to growth if obediently and faithfully carried out. Growth also calls for an outward and flexible attitude. Each of these values implies certain virtues and attitudes to make them a reality. The truth of Christian Revelation is taken seriously, as is God's holiness, but also his mercy and closeness to humankind.

This has been further articulated in the core values of the church.[16] Here, worship is listed first. This includes a longing for Spirit-Enabled worship in a style that is intimate, dynamic, culturally acceptable and life-changing. None of this necessarily precludes a central place for sacramental celebrations and liturgical rites but they are not generally stressed by HTB staff. They do have Communion services one Sunday each month. Preaching and teaching based on the Word of God is the second value. The third is fellowship which includes cultivating friendships that are intimate, real and enabling. Thus there is stress both on relationship with God and others, both of which are intimate. The fourth value is ministry: and specifically that all are called to serve Christ in the power of the Holy Spirit.[17] The following examples are given: preaching, persuading people to repent and believe in Jesus, healing, care of poor and needy, counselling with God's wisdom, teaching Christian truth to believers, training Christians to serve, giving resources to the work of Christ. The fifth value is training. I consider that realising the centrality of training is vital to understanding how HTB operates, and crucial to running Alpha well there or elsewhere. They state that they 'believe that all Christians should be trained to do the ministry of Christ'. This is implemented comprehensively. I am also struck on visits by the quality of encouragement and willingness to let people have a go that pervades the church community and fosters both the involvement in ministry by all, and their training to do this effectively. They are 'committed to the 'show and tell' model of on the job training' and 'aim to provide training for every aspect of responsible Christian life and training'. (Many other churches do not match this and flounder with Alpha.) The sixth value reflects HTB's apostolic outlook and sense of commitment to the wider church. It is summarised as 'Sending' and states HTB's aim to renew and refresh existing churches by sending out trained personnel on short-term ministry trips, and also to building up the church by sending out trained personnel to plant churches.

Set alongside these values it is interesting to dwell briefly on their understanding of what faith is, a touchstone word vital in Protestant-ism and central in all Christian circles. It is clear that they are excited by big conversion stories but recognise that for many it is a gradual journey without clear moments of conversion or 'being saved'.[18] Faith is seen as a journey or process towards spiritual maturity. Thus a person journeys from being a non-believer to a convert to a disciple to a worker to a leader. There is always room for growth. I find the comparison of immature and mature faith given below by Sandy Millar full of insight and also challenging.[19] Certainly it would be unfair to assume or even expect such faith of all HTB's members but I think we can take it as what its leadership tries to live and in which it tries to form others. It is one that challenges any simple attempts at describing HTB as insular and fundamentalist. It ought also to be considered when evaluating the criticisms and at times fierce accusations of some Christians that Alpha mainly and even excessively presents the Gospel as being about meeting our felt needs and God as being loving in a way that is soft on sin.

IMMATURE FAITH	MATURE FAITH
• Good Christians don't have pain or disappointment.	• God uses our pain and disappointment to make us better Christians.
• God died to make us happy.	• God wants to make us into the image of Jesus.
• Faith will enable us to explain what God is doing.	• Faith helps us understand God's sovereignty even when we have no idea what God is doing.
• The closer we get to God the more perfect we become.	• The closer we get to God, the more aware we become of our sinfulness.
• Mature Christians have answers	• Mature Christians can wrestle with tough questions because we trust that God has the answers.
• Good Christians are always strong.	• Our strength is in admitting our weakness
• We go to church because our friends are there, we have great leaders and we get something out of it.	• We go to church because we belong to the Body of Christ.

It will be well to hold on to a sense of these core values, convic-tions and principles. Certainly, they are ideals to be aimed at, but HTB makes a very serious effort to implement them. When people try to describe Alpha and HTB more generally, and to categorise them in terms of theology and churchmanship, these values ought to be considered and taken seriously. The following is my own summary of what has been happening and has emerged at HTB over the period of SM's ministry there, as these values have emerged, been articulated and applied. These formulations that I have drawn on here, by Sandy, come in his mature years and after a long period of living them and reflecting on them. I would imagine it has not always felt as clear as these printed summaries might suggest!

To summarise, HTB has moved from having worship and a general approach that were formal and traditional to a notably Charismatic, but informal and relaxed, style. The sense is gained of a church that longs for a real sense of God at its centre and one based on solid Christian Revelation and truth. It has developed its own 'School of Theology' providing more in-depth lectures and courses in Biblical and theological topics. It is aware of the importance of Christian friendship and 'belonging' and it is encouraging, hospitable and caring, and presents a sense of God as compassionate and merciful. Throughout all these developments it has continued to stress the importance of personal conversion and the call to discipleship, holiness, evangelism and adherence to 'Biblical truth', all of which provide grounds to describe it as 'evangelical'. Accompanying this, and especially in recent years, there has been an increasing interest in issues of social justice and poverty with many projects in these fields springing up. It has retained its place and roots within the Church of England and Anglican Communion although some characterise it as being more like a Vineyard Church in terms of how it operates.[20] Alongside all this it has been increasingly ecumenically open through the wide uptake of Alpha and the desire to find practical ways of working alongside other denominations etc. It is a church where all are encouraged and trained to use their gifts, time and money in Christian ministry. Over the years the average age of the congregation has come down and it now sees itself mainly as a church for students, young professionals and others starting out in adult life. It still has a large congregation though a high turnover of members as people relocate or move with a church plant. Even allowing for these factors the Sunday attendance has grown from around 1,200 in 1985 to around 3,200 in 2005. HTB has sought to be pastorally flexible. It is a church willing to change and grow in order to be a more effective instrument for the building of God's Kingdom, one humble and faithful enough to rely on God in prayer, and honest enough to seek to give him the glory for the results.[21]

Now let us look at developments since HTB made Alpha available for wider church use in 1993.

Notes

[1] Many of these authors are quoted in the Alpha Course materials.

[2] *Alpha News*, June 2004.

[3] This later happened under the leadership of (former Anglicans) John and Eleanor Mumford.

[4] In my view, nearly all the aspects of his work have had an impact on HTB or been utilised in Alpha either during its formation or to facilitate its spread or deal with issues arising from this.

[5] There was already a certain openness to charismatic Christianity at HTB as noted earlier.

[6] The basic understanding and practice for pastorates was developed in 1982–3. Training for Pastorate leaders started in 1986. Since originally writing these pages based on discussions and conference notes, AI have made available a short booklet on Pastorates (available from Alpha Publications).

[7] For those familiar with them, the theory and practice of pastorates has similarities with the theory and practice of both cell groups/cell church and also basic ecclesial communities (BECs). However, some authors (for example Mike Booker in *Evangelism – Which Way Now?*, by Mike Booker and Mark Ireland, Church House Publishing, p. 200) regard these as having different dynamics; cell groups being generally 'top down' while BEC's are 'bottom up'. HTB's pastorates have their own features too. Although HTB makes reference to them being for 'congregational' groups, this should not be taken to imply it is part of a church organisation, authority and polity as practised by what are known as 'Congregational' Churches or Denominations. Some Alpha critics have wrongly assumed this.

[8] The similarity with the structure of an Alpha evening will be apparent.

[9] It is often stated that people become Christians for many reasons but need to develop a significant number of Christian friendships to stay Christian.

[10] To an extent this has been corrected in the development of the new conference: 'Building a 21st Century [or Growing] Church' which HTB/Alpha International has started running since 2002.

[11] The Church of England commissioned a working group to look at church planting as a result of the first plant made by HTB which was seen by some as 'illegal'. The resulting report *'Breaking New Ground – Church Planting in the Church of England* (Church House Publishing, 1994) explored the issues and gave guidance on how planting should be organised. The working group that produced *'Mission Shaped Church* (Church House Publishing, 2004) was originally set up to look afresh at church planting but decided to move on to fresh and wider issues in mission.

[12] I am told that starting (evening) events with a meal was very much local custom rather than a deliberately thought-out strategy.

[13] In actual fact, it grew to six weeks under Charles Marnham in 1979, and John Irvine first increased it to eight weeks (1982) before arriving at the ten-week version.

[14] I am informed that John Wimber used this terminology before SM.

[15] From talk 'Integrating Alpha into the Church' and accompanying conference notes from '(How to Run) Alpha Conference.

[16] I have made these summary points based on talks given at the 'Building a 21st Century Church' Conference (2002) led by HTB and the associated notes given out.

[17] SM tends to stress the priesthood of all believers but this can be understood at least broadly – for instance in Catholic theology – as exercise of the grace of baptism. In fact, Catholic teaching on the graces and calling of baptism asserts not just the *priesthood* of all baptised believers but the prophetic and kingly

ministries and roles shared by all too! HTB's approach can be squared with a distinct sacrament of Holy Orders, though HTB do not stress or explicitly teach this.

[18] Beyond talking about faith journeys, they do not go so far as to stress generally that faith should not be viewed as static, private or a once-and-for-all fact.

[19] Building a 21st Century Church Conference, 2002.

[20] Interestingly Vineyard is said to operate with an Episcopal, rather than Congregational or Presbyterian approach.

[21] None of this is to suggest it is perfect or has not made mistakes or that there are not other valid and indeed complementary and even essential ways of being church and fulfilling its calling. Nor is it to say that they are right on all matters of Christian truth and in the interpretation or understanding of Revelation. Also, none of this is to suggest that Alpha is perfect or even the best tool in evangelism or even that its main success has been to reach unbelievers and bring them to initial Christian conversion.

CHAPTER 2

The Spread and Promotion of Alpha

Andrew Brookes

Alpha Beyond HTB: 1993 onwards

By 1992 five churches were running the Alpha Course – all church plants from HTB in London or closely linked churches, and all within the Church of England.

After enquiries and encouragement to do so from other churches, the leadership of HTB decided to make the Alpha Course more available for use by other churches. The first Alpha Conference was held in 1993. That year saw 200 churches taking up the course. 2,500 churches had taken it up by 1995, 10,500 by 1998 and over 16,000 by 2000. The global figure stood (at the end of 2005) at around 31,000 churches registered as running the course in a total of around 150 countries right round the world. The course and training material had been translated into over 50 languages. These are phenomenal figures but they are worthy of more analysis. Whatever other causes can be seriously put forward, the involvement of the grace of God should not be discounted either!

An indication of attendees through to 2005 is given below, though it does not give a breakdown of the figures into team/Christians/non-Christians or how many convert or even benefit.[1]

YEAR	COURSES (World)	ATTENDEES (cumulative)
1992	5	
1993	200	4,600
1994	750	25,000
1995	2,500	100,000
1996	5,000	400,000
1997	6,500	800,000
1998	10,500	1.3 M
1999	14,200	2 M
2000	17,000	2.8 M
2001	19,800	3.8 M
2002	24,400	4.7 M
2003	27,340	5.7 M
2004	29.051	6.8 M (est)
2005	31,167	8.0 M (est)

A promotional DVD from early 2007 indicated just under 33,000 courses are registered as running across 161 nations, with an accumulative total of approximately 9 million guests. The material had now been translated into 88 languages. This shows that worldwide growth is still happening at a significant rate.

Alpha Across Britain

Alpha spread rapidly to British churches and these must have been responsible for the bulk of the numerical growth in the early years. British churches accounted for most of the 6,000 or so courses running by 1997 though the British figure did not later rise much beyond 7,000 churches. This rate of uptake was very fast. It is worth pausing to look at some of the reasons why this may have happened. A number of factors were present and came together to help drive this high rate of uptake. These include the emergence of nurture groups, research on the nature of conversion, the decade of evangelism, HTB's profile, professionalism and marketing, and the Toronto Blessing.

Firstly, Nurture Groups (i.e. small groups for faith sharing and then also enquiring about the faith) were forming in a number of settings in the UK in the 1980s. Seeing the evangelistic potential in these, some other courses were also being developed, used and then quite widely made available before Alpha was given its big launch in 1993. 'Saints Alive!' and 'Good News Down Your Street' were already available. Others continued to be developed alongside Alpha and these others have since come onto the market. These have included 'Emmaus' and 'Christianity Explored'.[2] The Catholic Church had done similar work through its R.C.I.A. process, launched internationally in 1972. John Finney did extensive research on how people come to faith. Published in 1992,[3] it drew attention to the idea that conversion was usually a process amongst other things. Thus when Alpha was made available, it found an audience of church leaders already familiar with many of the ideas behind it.

The decade of Evangelisation, originally announced by Pope John Paul II as a preparation for the Millennium, was taken up by many denominations. In England, a joint ecumenical co-ordinating team, the 'Group for Evangelisation (GfE)' was set up. They decided that the nurture groups should be its mainstay and not the big stadium events and national campaigns used hitherto. Such campaigns used very early in the decade did not have a great impact. Local churches were thus encouraged to set up such groups and run courses to draw in those outside the church. By now local churches were looking around for ideas and help with this.[4]

Alpha, described as 'a tool for local churches to do evangelism', was launched around this time, and may have been seen by many churches across the denominational spectrum as a way of taking up the challenge of the Decade of Evangelism. HTB was clearly seen to be a growing church with relatively young people involved. The well-thought out and tried approach in Alpha, along with the provision of good resources and training conferences from the beginning, made it attractive to many clergy/churches who were looking for good resources. HTB was already well-networked with many other churches and Christian movements.

Also, in 1994 HTB became one of the major UK churches at the centre of the Toronto Blessing.[5] This is most closely associated with the Toronto Airport Vineyard Fellowship, Canada, led by John Arnott. It 'started' there in January 1994, rapidly attracting huge attention from around the world. Eli Mumford, wife of British Vineyard pastor John Mumford, visited the Toronto Vineyard in May and on her return was invited to speak at the Sunday Services at HTB. As elsewhere with this phenomenon, extraordinary scenes happened. This had both exterior and interior elements to it. The exterior aspects included people shaking, falling over and then sometimes resting on the floor – often for long periods, weeping, laughing and groaning. Interior aspects seem to include inner (emotional) healing and renewed conversion in persons; in general these seem to be linked with a strong sense of the love of God. These are, by believers, attributed to the powerful action of the grace of God usually expressed as the work of the Holy Spirit. The Toronto Blessing is closely linked with spiritual activity and ministry interpreted as using the spiritual or charismatic gifts of the Holy Spirit, as listed, for example in 1 Cor 12:8–10. There have been debates about how much of this phenomenon is of human origin and how much is divine, with some claiming that demonic influences were at work.[6]

The Toronto Blessing and HTB attracted huge interest from right across the country and from the media too. People travelled long distances to come to HTB. Very long queues formed to get into services and extra services were put on. It raised the profile of HTB and its various activities, including Alpha, still higher. While this may have attracted some to use Alpha, it also put some off or at least made them nervous. Other factors, perhaps with links to Toronto, such as long-term hopes for revival linked to prophecies about Britain may have drawn interest from some quarters.

Once the rapid uptake began, further interest, if also criticism in some quarters, was generated and still more started the course. The initial impression people got of Alpha and its materials was good; HTB's reputation grew along with the list of endorsements from church leaders and celebrities, and still more interest and excitement were generated. It became very much 'in vogue' with people keen to jump on the bandwagon, at least for a time anyway. By the time Toronto 'quietened down' in the UK, Alpha was well established and has kept up at least some of its momentum.

Stephen Hunt[7] argues that the Toronto Blessing was the crucial factor and that Alpha has only really been adopted by Charismatic Churches already committed to such things and has generally only impacted people who were already Charismatic Christians. While it is certainly true that Toronto had an impact, I think it is important to give due weight to other issues connected with the change in the understanding of evangelism/conversion and its application, and the decade of evangelism itself. Toronto put a good number of people off Alpha. It is clear that early on many people avoided running the Holy Spirit weekend and downplayed Charismatic parts of the course generally, so the idea that the course was run almost entirely by Charismatic Churches does not stand up. Certainly many Charismatics ran Alpha. However, many people tried it from beyond this background and in spite of, and not because Alpha had charismatic elements.

The rapid uptake of Alpha in the UK, drew attention from all over the world and acted as the springboard for Alpha spreading right round the globe. This analysis of factors that may have influenced the interest in and uptake of Alpha is not intended to suggest that God has not been at work in the midst of this, operating through these channels and others.

However, by the year 2000, the figure for British churches registered with HTB as running Alpha had plateaued at between 7,000 and 7,500. This was and remains the slightly changing figure as a few new churches continue to register and old ones decide to come off the Alpha Register.[8] The number only rose in 2001 by around 200, despite the substantial exposure given to the Course by the ITV television series *'Alpha: can it change their lives?'*, hosted by Sir David Frost. Along with background material and supporting interviews, this used a reality television approach, in which a small group of guests was followed through the Alpha course at HTB. All this suggests to some that the potential market of British churches that might consider running Alpha has been fully tapped. Alternative courses are now readily available. However, new churches do continue to register and people still come to Alpha Conferences in the UK for the first time. Certainly the rapid growth seems to be over and the emphasis has changed to bedding these courses down and, from AI/HTB's perspective, providing material and training to help local churches run the course more effectively.

Some of these features are highlighted in a form of analysis and presentation undertaken by Charles Freebury to track numbers of Alpha Courses in relative terms over time.[9] Freebury has expressed the headline figures for total numbers of registered courses as percentage changes compared to the previous year's total. For example, no change would give a figure of 0%. This allows relative growth or decline from year to year to be easily observed.

Alpha UK number of courses year-on-year rate of change

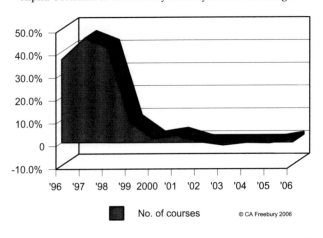

No. of courses   © CA Freebury 2006

This representation points to the big growth in the mid-1990s associated with the impact of the Toronto Blessing and the positive reception of John Finney's research etc. Slower increases continued into the first two national Alpha Initiatives of 1998 and 1999. (These are described later in this chapter.) However, since 2000, there has been a virtual plateaux. Freebury has pointed out that this is now about half of Alpha's public life. It emphasises the view that Alpha is now not likely to end up being run in so many UK churches that it (and AI/HTB) 'take over', though Alpha is still very influential. This representation of the data supports the view that the advertising campaigns (apart from the first one arguably, though this rise may have been based on momentum already generated), and the ITV series have not had much impact on expansion. (They may have prevented decline but this cannot be proven.)[10] Drawing on his experience of the business world, Freebury comments that such a fall-off curve is typical of businesses that are riding a popular crest but then fail to invest in ongoing development for new and significant innovations and eventually end up beached.[11]

Is it fair to apply such comments to Alpha? The graph represents Alpha courses in the UK only. It does not consider Alpha elsewhere in the world; here new courses have continued to register and the 'Alpha Movement' is thus still expanding. And, as I shall soon describe, AI/HTB have started developing other Alpha Course variations and quite different new ministries, with more in the pipeline, though currently these only make up a small fraction of the total number of registered Alpha courses. Freebury may be right about Alpha in the UK, and be flagging up real concerns, threats and challenges facing the Alpha Course which may indicate the possibility of it having a limited life, at least in the UK. (It would be interesting to see similar graphs for other specific countries/regions of the world.) However, AI may be doing enough to ensure a wider Alpha Movement continues. Thus AI may have brighter future prospects than the actual Alpha Course in the UK. A further point is that this graph is based on overall headline figures, and as such does not consider if there is a significant turnover of courses. As I shall explore in Chapter 7 there has been some turnover, indicating that there are both dynamics of growth and decline hidden in what looks like an overall plateau. Nonetheless, complacency is not recommended. Freebury's suggestion that the course may well need a major overhaul (not just relatively minor changes to adapt it to different settings) if it is not to become outdated is worth taking seriously. (In fact, it is considered at various points of this book.)

The figure of just over 7,000 churches is said to approximate to around 25% of the actual churches that exist in Britain.[12] The course has spread to virtually all of the denominations present in Britain, including Anglicans, Methodists, Baptists, Congregationalists, Presbyterians, Roman Catholics, Salvation Army and Pentecostal and Independent and House churches. It has crossed class, social (city centre, suburbs, town, rural) and age boundaries too. In these cases it is fair to say that there has not always been an uptake or fruitfulness that proportionately reflects the presence of these denominations or groupings in the total of British society.[13]

Alpha Around the World

In recent years most numerical growth in Alpha has been outside the UK though the UK still makes up around 25% of the churches registered. The figures outside Britain do not show an even distribution. Much effort has been put into promoting Alpha in the USA, both by Americans and HTB, who have considered this an important zone. As a result 36% of the non-British courses are run there. A further 36% are run in countries which were part of the 'old' Commonwealth – Australia, Canada, New Zealand and South Africa.[14] These are principally all English speaking. There has been significant interest from across Commonwealth more generally.[15]

Other countries may develop more slowly or at least differently. They are less influenced by British culture and history and less likely to look to Britain or to the wider Anglican Communion of churches for a lead or help with aspects of their lives. Still, there are some interesting stories developing. It is not difficult to see that a course with a 'meal–talk–discussion' structure run over several weeks might well be attractive and workable in different cultural settings around the world. As in the UK, there is evidence Alpha can cross cultural boundaries of all sorts. However, merely listing the countries where Alpha runs, or even giving a simple list of the numbers, while it gives a first impression, does not tell the whole story or allow any real analysis of what is happening, how well, and why or why not. Also these countries reflect a whole range of variations in denominational mix, and the size, ethos and vigour of the church and its state of development. Additionally, the countries have different histories, interactions with Christianity and other cultural factors. All this has been compounded by specific organisations and publishing houses as well as individuals that HTB has chosen to take the lead in developing Alpha in other countries and broader language groups. Sometimes the arrangements have worked well, and sometimes they have caused local suspicion or rejection on the part of major denominations/traditions and thus restricted Alpha's uptake. When I raised this with Mark Elsdon-Dew, AI/HTB's Communications Director, he commented that, apart from some initial problems in some countries associated with lack of familiarity of particular issues, he felt Alpha generally has been well-received.

Alpha Course Variations – for specific settings and groupings

The course, originally developed for use in a parish setting, also found itself being taken up in other more specialised settings. Under the co-ordination of Paul Cowley and Emmy Wilson, the course has been taken into British prisons on a very large scale. It is currently registered as running in around 80% of British prisons and an increasing number of prisons overseas. It is, I feel, significant that HTB have really given a great deal of attention not just to adapting Alpha for use in prisons but especially to fostering the overall pastoral care of prisoners before and especially after their release and in addressing the underlying causes of why people offend/re-offend. They have addressed the issues facing a local church in welcoming an ex-offender as part of the congregation in practical and realistic ways, involving amongst other things the use of contracts. HTB have welcomed some ex-offenders themselves using these methods. HTB have developed materials and courses for 'Caring for ex-Offenders' and 'Breaking the cycle of Crime' as part of this.

Alpha was recognised as clearly having potential for evangelising students. Stereotypically, many of them will be interested in a free meal, are used to long talks/lectures and are often keen to discuss the meaning of life and related issues well into the night! Currently students are sometimes characterised as belonging to the 'Friends Generation', that is to say that forming relationships, which is part of Alpha, is important to them. Attention has been given to understanding the issues of campus life, the student mindset and examining how to adapt the course to fit the restrictions of university terms and student budgets. It is now running in more than 80 British universities. Again HTB has begun working closely with other Christian organisations with student ministries, not least with a view to addressing in an integrated way the overall pastoral care of Christian students and equipping them more generally for mission and making an impact in society. Though it is too soon too tell what the results of this will be, an increased uptake of and attendance at student courses has been reported by HTB in 2004–5.

The Alpha Course was designed for adults and HTB had little experience in the early years of its expansion of using it with youth. (They have always been reluctant to promote versions of the course widely where they have not already seen good working models first.) Youth versions of the handbooks, with cartoons but few other changes were available. More recently, following collaboration with people with youth ministry experience, newer and more extensive youth resources have been made available. Alongside this, work to promote Youth Alpha has been undertaken since around 2003 on a larger scale and in association with other student Christian ministries and agencies. These materials show a marked adaptation and encourage a more flexible use of the standard adult format for the course. AI/HTB show they have responded to many criticisms of the 45 minutes lecture style regarding its pedagogy and educational level. These new resources show a greater variation in how the content can be presented, along with additional interactive activities. The youth material is available in three streams. 'Tech' is nearest the adult course in academic content and argument but with lots of suggestions for video and other IT inputs. 'Active' has less teaching content (and less intellectual coherence too) and uses lots of games and other hands on activities. 'Lite' is designed to fit the course into sessions of around 30 minutes or so and uses a story format to cover the content. It is suggested the meal is often downplayed or replaced or combined with games etc to help young people get to know each other. All three have a weekend or day away and the decision has been made to cover the material in the same blocks over 10 weeks rather than spread the content over a longer time period. The Charismatic elements are still flagged up. It remains clear that it is an adaptation of an adult course rather than something created from scratch for youth. These are good resources that may well find lots of applications – and not just on Alpha courses. People have already commented to me on the potential of using them with groups other than those who could be honestly described as 'youth'.[16] There is some use of Alpha in schools, typically as an extra-curricular activity, though even as part of some R.E. courses. Here the 'lite' version is suggested.

Again it is too soon to tell what the impact will be but initial uptake has been impressive. The new youth manual notes that courses can be used for non-mission purposes, i.e. just to disciple existing Christians/those coming to Christian youth groups, so it is not clear, if it is mainly being used for these purposes, how much evangelistic impact the courses will actually have. In fact, the guidelines indicate that it is not best to use the course simultaneously for both discipleship and outreach purposes and also that it may well be difficult to move it from discipleship to mission with the same group of people. (One may well wonder to what extent this happens in non-youth courses too!)

Course variations and/or additional support materials for running the course with people working in the Forces (i.e. on military bases) have taken place. The same has happened more recently for older people and is now marketed as Senior Alpha. Its materials use large print for the short-sighted, and are ring-bound to help those with arthritis. Alpha has also been used in workplaces, typically being run as a lunch time course. Originally referred to as Business Alpha, this is now marketed as 'Alpha in the Workplace'. Following the 'piloting/ assessing' of a successful version in Canada this adaptation is being more extensively promoted. AI reported in 2005 that it currently has the fastest uptake among the Alpha products. One particular problem in this setting is the length of the video talks. AI/HTB have now produced edited versions of the normal adult video talks which last for around 25 minutes, called 'Alpha Express'. Many people have wanted a shorter version of the talks for some time and it is easy to see how, even if these short talks are only officially marketed for workplace Alpha, that they will find themselves used in many other settings. Many of these variations have a good initial uptake. This is not entirely surprising considering the high profile Alpha enjoys and the networking and marketing that are built on top of this. It remains to be seen what their evangelistic and pastoral impact will be, and indeed, what their longevity will be. In all cases the content is still based closely on NG's book, *Questions of Life*, though often more selectively, but still reflecting the balance and flow of its contents. Although this change has not been flagged up by HTB, the copyright statement has been amended, with the word 'all' being omitted from the phrase 'Courses must be based on [all] the content of *Questions of Life*'.

The developments of all of these course variations has led to adaptations in the standard product. With it AI/HTB have thus introduced some flexibility, perhaps more than they once encouraged. This ought to be borne in mind when considering claims and weighing arguments about HTB's alleged lack of flexibility and use of copyright. At the same time, the key features have stayed constant: meal or alternative socialising opportunity, material based on *Questions of Life* as input, sharing of reactions to this; a 10 week duration and a day or weekend on the Holy Spirit, though this has had to be adapted on occasions (such as prison). In a way these elements make up the Alpha Brand. The cultivation and profile of this help existing and new products to be promoted, but retaining the integrity and distinctiveness of the brand puts limits on how far things can be adapted and respond to changing challenges in culture and mission and still be called 'Alpha'. All this will be discussed more fully in Chapters 8 and 10. Also, the original idea and much of the initial development/evolution of a good model and practice has often been undertaken outside HTB and sometimes the UK. AI/HTB have been partners in facilitating, encouraging and finally resourcing such developments rather than always being the orginators and trail blazers.

Support for Running Alpha

The spread of Alpha has involved proactive and reactive elements. It is clear that HTB is a large talented church with a big vision and this is expressed proactively in Alpha and many other things it does. At the same time they have been genuinely surprised by the interest in Alpha, the spread of Alpha and the speed and scale of this. They have tried to support this, helping local churches to run it. Much of this has been a reactive process as problems, needs and possibilities have arisen as Alpha has spread across UK and around the world. Mistakes have been made, new insights and a deeper understanding gained, networks formed and a large set of resources and supporting infrastructure developed. This leads people to ask – with various mixes of anxiety, interest and excitement – if Alpha is just as a tool for local churches or something more? Some see Alpha as a multi-national company or as a mass movement or as a new and special intervention of God in history by the Holy Spirit, and this may even be linked to seeing it as God's chosen instrument for a special – and even final – missionary outreach. To come to any conclusions about these issues it is necessary to know more about what support is available for Alpha and how it is organised.

Materials and the 'Alpha Conference'

In preparation for the original Alpha Conferences begun in 1993, NG wrote up what was then the current theory and practice of Alpha, developed over several years at HTB. The book-length publications were published by Kingsway, and various training booklets by HTB themselves. The book *Questions of Life* contains the content of the 15 talks that make up the course – without most of the jokes and some of the testimonies. It is often referred to as the textbook of the course. First published in 1993, it has been successively altered in more recent editions, after various consultations, to make it more ecumenical in flavour. This refers both to some of the theology, or at least the theological terms used, as well as to drawing testimony examples (historic and contemporary) and illustrative quotes and anecdotes from across as much of the Christian spectrum as possible. Kingsway then published *Telling Others* and *Searching Issues*, both by NG, in 1994. With *Questions of Life* these make up the essential reading resources for the course. *Telling Others* deals with the principles and practicalities of running an Alpha Course (including pastoral care, leading small groups, prayer ministry and giving talks. This broadly corresponds to what is covered in the typical two day Alpha training Conference. *Searching Issues* deals with what NG considers the seven most common questions that unbelievers ask about Christianity. These are: suffering, other religions, sex before marriage, the New Age, homosexuality, Science and Christianity, and the Trinity.[17] The book is recommended to small-group leaders and helpers so that they can deal with these questions when they come up.[18] It may also be used as material for follow-up course to an Alpha Course. Kingsway have also published other books by NG that were at that time part of the two year programme HTB had developed for new Christians. These were: *A Life worth Living* (1994), a study based on St Paul's Letter to the Philippians; *Challenging Lifestyle* (1996), based on the Sermon on the Mount; and *The Heart of Revival* (1997) drawing on Isaiah 40–66. Many of these books have been reprinted or come out in new editions or with different covers in the following years.

The two day 'Alpha Conference' developed and has been delivered in a settled format for a number of years. The content of the main sessions covers principles and practicalities of Alpha on Day One followed by various seminars covering administration, prayer, worship and some of the specialist varieties of Alpha. This is rounded off with a typical Alpha evening – well, sort of. There is a supper followed by the talk on 'How to be Filled with the Holy Spirit?' followed by a period of ministry led from the front and followed by individual prayer ministry for those wishing it. Day Two often begins with an early and optional intercessory prayer session. Then there are talks on pastoral care, leading small groups and prayer ministry. After a question and answer session, things are rounded off, if a suitable speaker is available, with a talk on integration of Alpha into wider church life. NG and SM say they choose to deal with the talk on 'Being Filled with the Holy Spirit' and subsequent ministry at conferences, since this is the part of the course that causes most confusion (and controversy) and thus the part it is most important to teach and model.[19] As well as the content, the conference team model and cultivate the practices, attitudes and ethos that ought to be part of each Alpha Course. The conferences are thus experiential, as well as cerebral, learning encounters.

Originally held in HTB, other venues were soon also used. Local teams, from various churches working together, now organise them in different locations, HTB then sending a team of speakers and other personnel actually to deliver the conference. In this way conferences have been held throughout the UK and now right across the world. NG and SM were for a long time the main conference speakers. Demand and workload has meant that other speakers are increasingly being used, either HTB staff, members of their pastorates or other people (not members of HTB) with suitable Alpha experience. Training is provided. To go with the conferences HTB produced and published since 1993 various conference notes as well as booklets and taped talks.

Despite all the help provided, Alpha is quite a complex tool to use and is labour intensive. People asked for help with the talks. At first audio-tapes were made available and then videos. These have been frequently updated and are now available on DVD too. Some people assume that Alpha was conceived as a video based course but this is not true. HTB advise that the best option is to use a good local speaker – who can customise and inculturate the material effectively. The worst option is a bad local speaker and the use of the videos falls between these options. Evidence suggests that around one third of courses run entirely with local speakers. Some use a mixture of speakers and videos (in different proportions) and the remaining 40% use the videos entirely. Many courses start with the videos when they are just being established and then move onto a live speaker format, perhaps progressively. It is important not just to understand the content of the talks when doing this but also the style and mood. In fact, the videos are very straightforward, consisting almost entirely of a 'talking head' of Nicky Gumbel[20] – with a few cuts to the congregation and some headings and scripture quotes 'pasted on' – for 45-minutes duration. These have been criticised for their simplicity by some, though this does give a straightforward proclamation of that part of the Gospel message, and the lack of 'special effects' may encourage churches to give their own talks. Videos of training talks and other presentations are also available. The number and nature of all these resources has mushroomed over the years. There are now over 150 items listed in the UK Alpha Publications catalogue, covering everything from videos and worship CDs to cookery books and beer mats. SM has sought to resist the developments of products that do not have a direct use in running or promoting the course.

Alongside these is the regular production and free distribution of *Alpha News* which initally came out three times a year in a tabloid newspaper format (from 2006 it has been produced twice a year.) It is edited by Mark Elsdon-Dew, who previously worked in Fleet Street and now has a British circulation of 250,000 to say nothing of its distribution overseas. It is packed with news about Alpha and its spread, celebrity and church leader endorsements, helpful information and contact numbers. Each issue also carries a number of testimonies, usually dramatic ones, about individual conversions or churches that have seen significant growth through using Alpha. It is intended to encourage readers to try or persist with Alpha and is deliberately upbeat. Some people have commented to me that they wonder how really representative it is; others that the concentration on big 'success' stories can actually discourage or alienate churches who are struggling, just plodding along or even ticking over with small but undramatic conversions or individual or corporate growth. I did hear NG comment once that he knows there are problems out there and that if the problem stories and discouraging situations were written up and all published it could create a newspaper much much longer in length just by themselves. Yet, a more balanced set of stories, including the more 'ordinary' action of God, might appeal to and connect with still more people.

From the very beginning of its more public use, HTB has collected and publicised endorsements from church leaders from across the Christian spectrum and from right round the world, and also from celebrities. Good photo opportunities are eagerly seized too! Also present from the beginning was the increasingly well-known Alpha logo: the cartoon character in yellow t-shirt and blue trousers struggling to carry a large red question mark, with the word 'Alpha' written beneath.

Personnel – Paid and Voluntary – and the establishment of 'Alpha International'

By average church standards, HTB already had a large staff, both of clergy and other paid personnel, in 1993. However, this was no way near enough to cope with the huge interest, requests and advice being sought after that year from all over the country and then the world. More and more staff were taken on. There are now about 140 paid staff, mostly full-time. Beyond being Christians, people are generally recruited for their professional skills relevant to each specific remit, typically learned and transferred from other non-church environments, rather than a detailed knowledge of Alpha, or other church matters, as such. Most notably Tricia Neill, herself a convert from an HTB Alpha course, and with senior management experience in the media world, was brought in to organise and run the church office. This experience and her well organised, professional approach and realistic pragmatic attitude have been very influential – even vital – in many ways as the Course spread and grew. Clear job and role descriptions, prioritising, record keeping, good communications, attention to detail and accountability are all features of work at Alpha Headquarters. Hard work is also expected! At the same time, several mornings each week time is scheduled for a collective period of biblical teaching and prayer. I have always found staff friendly, polite and helpful. One aspect of this work is that HTB have often sought to get quantitative and qualitative feed-back from Alpha courses around the country and use this in the planning of the support they develop. Beyond this there is a huge number of volunteers drawn from the congregation who help out in many ways.

At first all the support provided was run from within the HTB set up itself. Indeed, it was largely funded by the congregation too. In this and other ways the church has looked well beyond its own needs and advantage to the larger needs of Christ's church and mission. The scale of Alpha became such that eventually the finances and other aspects of Alpha needed to be separated from HTB. In 2001 'Alpha International' was established as a company limited by guarantee and registered as a charity. The vision of Alpha International is 'the (re)evangelisation of the nation(s) and the transformation of society'. This clearly goes beyond just 'saving souls' or personal conversion of individuals to a much broader vision and application of the gospel and its power. Nonetheless, the statement strongly indicates, what appears to be HTB's view, that the transformation of society, while important, is linked to and indeed flows from the conversion of individuals. The conversion of individuals is thus a central priority. AI has the remit of 'promoting the Alpha Course and ancillary ministries throughout the world'. (I shall touch on some of these 'ancillary ministries' later.) AI is not part of HTB or the Anglican church as such though there is an overlap in the roles held by some people. The Alpha International (AI) staff is now generally housed at the near-by church of St Paul's, Onslow Square which has been specially fitted with office space. There is still a very close co-operation between the two entities and HTB is still seen very much as the 'home' of Alpha.[21] The financial scale of what AI undertakes has kept growing. AI's Annual Review for 2004 gives the (un-audited) expenditure for that year as £4,348,000.

As mentioned, the congregation of HTB has been very generous in helping to fund Alpha. Other benefactors have also contributed. There is now a scheme called 'Alpha Partners' to foster financial giving, especially from the affluent. The videos and other Alpha resources generate income too. While being a well-off congregation has undoubtedly helped support Alpha' s spread, it cannot really be given as the main reason for it. In fact, when AI/HTB work out their annual strategy, priorities, plans and projects they do not start from a knowledge of how much money they have or know they can easily obtain. They assess what is happening pastorally, pray, listen to the Lord and discern in the light of their vision, and then make detailed plans including a costing exercise. How to get the money is then looked at. After review, they then start work in faith, and also bring the money in both through specific 'fund raising' activities and through prayer.

Beyond its base in central London, HTB soon began appointing local Alpha Advisers. These are people who are recognised as having experience and competence in running Alpha locally and who are willing to offer advice and often more concrete help (resources, training, speaking etc) to others in their area who are running or wish to start Alpha. Appointed by AI/HTB, these people are volunteers though they often put in a considerable number of hours. Since the areas to be covered as well as the range of help needed can be so vast AI/HTB has and is generally moving from a pattern of 'lone rangers' to 'Regional Teams'. These comprise several advisers and others with specific relevant skills or competence, and ideally include people from a range of church denominations/streams and those with expertise in the more specialist courses such as students, prisons and youth etc. These teams help build a local network and often organise ecumenical training days, prayer events and some joint invitational suppers to launch courses and also encourage churches to pool resources on advertising and help with contacts with the media generally. Other promotional and taster events are also organised. Also a Regional Team may organise a major two day Alpha Conference or other event in conjunction with a team from AI/HTB. These include running the one-day 'Equip and Refresh Days' based on the Alpha training materials. All this is proving an interesting development in local grassroots ecumenism, sometimes building on ecumenical links already established in some cases, and, in other cases, building them from scratch. In this way sometimes they are bringing together churches or individuals from parts of the Christian spectrum that were previously unacquainted for various reasons. It has often provided a good united witness to the gospel that has had an impact on guests.

AI/HTB are also beginning to identify some churches scattered around the country that run Alpha well and are large and are active and big enough to be able to offer resources and help to that region. They are being appointed as 'Resource Churches'. AI is now beginning to open Regional Offices across the UK In 2004 the first two were opened in the North of England and in Scotland. More are planned. It is said that these will allow Alpha and its promotion/support to be better tailored to local conditions. In its first year of operation the Scottish Office has focused on forming or building up geographically smaller and more local Regional Teams involving more people each with a smaller remit. They have also seen roughly 65 new courses (which is approximately a 10% increase in the number of courses), though not all these are based in churches as such.[22]

As Alpha has taken root in other countries similar strategies are being followed regarding advisers and regional and national teams. Often a National Office, closely linked to AI is also established. Some of these have several paid employees too. Publication of translated Alpha materials is typically organised by these national offices and/or co-ordinators. National Offices also often produce their own version of '*Alpha News*'.

Other Developments
The Alpha Copyright

At first, as Alpha spread, HTB allowed and even encouraged local congregations to adapt the 'Alpha course package' to their own setting.

People then contacted HTB with questions about problems they were encountering and it soon became apparent that largely this was due to people not just tweaking the course for local use but changing it wholesale. HTB then – with some reluctance I am told – introduced the copyright statement. The very exhaustive legally worded statement includes the following: 'Holy Trinity Brompton accepts that minor adaptations to the Alpha Course may occasionally be desirable. These should only concern the length of the talks or the number of sessions. In each case the essential character of the course must be retained. Alpha is a series of about fifteen talks, given over a period of time, including a weekend or day away, with teaching based on all the material in *'Questions of Life'.*[23] Otherwise people are asked not to call their course by the name of Alpha. The world-wide spread of Alpha, the proliferation of its resources, concern about quality control which is itself linked to the large scale promotion and advertising of Alpha, have all been given as supporting reasons for this copyright policy. HTB also argue that people who recommend the course to their friends in other parts of the country or world want to know that they will get what they themselves expect, i.e. they want to know that Alpha is a uniform package no matter where it is run. NG explains and justifies this by using an analogy with McDonald's multinational fast-food chain: a person can only recommend McDonald's burgers to friends in other places if they know the food will be exactly the same in all the outlets.[24] The copyright policy and the connected impression of control, and even uniformity, has often been criticised and is even seen as controversial. (These issues will be discussed in more detail in Chapter 10.)

Follow the recipe

The reasons given for introducing the copyright make it very clear that there have been all sort of departures from the course as HTB run it. Cataloguing and analysing these, AI/HTB have come up with booklets based on the seven most common mistakes and also 15 ways to attract more guests onto your course. I will reflect on some of these and the issues and insights they raise in Chapter 10. In short, the advice is to follow the recipe! AI has highlighted the need for proper and on-going training to run Alpha well. AI/HTB have continued to do this through their busy schedule of conferences. In many ways this has been a new emphasis in the strategy used to promote Alpha, with increasingly more attention being given to the quality of courses, and not just the quantity of them. Recently (2004) they have introduced a new twin-track conference: while newcomers attend the original sessions, experienced Alpha and conference delegates can go to sessions dedicated to looking at these issues of common mistakes and how to avoid them and how to get more people onto courses. Some local Alpha advisers and regional teams have also devoted considerable time and effort to addressing these issues, sometimes in quite creative ways.

The National Alpha Initiative/Invitation

In September of 1998, i.e. before the beginning of the autumn Alpha courses, HTB ran its first 'Alpha Initiative'. It consisted of a period of heavy public advertising of Alpha on a national scale, using billboard posters and a huge array of other products and media channels to promote Alpha. Local churches were invited to sign up for and participate in this in a special way. It was considered successful and has been run each year since on increasing scales. (A participation fee was only asked for in the first year of operation.) Since 2000, part of the strategy has been to invite the nation to supper – the supper being modelled on the Alpha celebration/introduction evening. Each year sees new poster designs; in 2004 it was renamed the 'Alpha Invitation'. Posters can now be found on buses in various places too. Cinema advertising was introduced in 2005. (See Chapter 19, and the back of the book, for reproductions of these advertising campaigns and a wider discussion of them.) Alpha advisers organise local events, including large scale multi-church 'Guest Suppers' to coincide with this. Since 1999 AI/HTB have co-ordinated and provided resources for a series of Alpha prayer evenings as part of this initiative, these again being organised locally and ecumenically by local Alpha advisers. These now run all over the country too. It is emphasised that prayer is vital to the 'success' of Alpha. All of this is very expensive but has definitely increased the public profile of Alpha.

Since 1999 a Mori Poll has been undertaken after each Alpha Initiative to see what is the recognition of Alpha by the general public.

Public awareness of Alpha (% of adult population that know Alpha is a Christian Course)

1999	9%
2000	9%
2001	16%
2002	17%
2003	20%
2004	19.5%
2005	22%
2006	23%

Figures from Alpha News.

Questions have been asked about this use of money and how far it is effective in really promoting the Gospel. AI/HTB consider it as supplementary to and supportive of the need for individual local churches and individual Christians to personally invite people to courses. At the same time there are accounts of people turning up at courses largely or initially due to the publicity campaigns – and the ability to access details of local Alpha courses from the Alpha website/ other directories. At the same time it has estimated that perhaps only a few guests (generally figures put it between 2–5% and at most 10%) come on the course based on advertising alone. Personal invitation – and relationship evangelism more generally – remains the most important factor here.

National Initiatives have also started running in other countries where Alpha is well established. These have included New Zealand (where one third of churches are registered as running Alpha), Canada, Norway, Switzerland, Singapore Hong Kong. Without a good percentage of churches running Alpha a national distribution of these, use of such a strategy is not recommended.

Associated courses and Ministries

Over recent years AI/HTB have developed other courses more or less closely connected with Alpha. These have included 'The Marriage Course'. This is a series of eight sessions designed to help any married couple strengthen their relationship. It covers: building strong foundations, the art of communication, resolving conflict, the power of forgiveness, parents and in-laws, good sex and love in action. 'The Marriage Preparation Course' is a series of five sessions designed to help any engaged couple develop strong foundations for a lasting marriage. This course covers: communication, commitment, resolving conflict, keeping love alive, and shared goals and values. The aim of both courses is to help couples build a healthy marriage that lasts a lifetime. The courses provide them with practical tools to strengthen their relationship and it gives them the time and space to discuss any difficult issues. The hope is it will help them to break bad habits and create good ones to enable their marriage to grow. The aim is that it won't just attract those in crisis but that it will be an opportunity for any couple to invest in their marriage. It is not necessary to be Christians to do the courses. They are proving very popular and their use is spreading.

It is my view that Alpha has to be seen in the context of the fuller life of HTB. Therefore, these are not disconnected though they are bearing fruit in their own right. At HTB and elsewhere, they actually have been used to help Alpha, and attract guests. Conferences have been developed to promote these and other aspects of the life and ministry of HTB. These include conferences on dynamic prayer, worship, building a 21st Century Church. A third stream to the Alpha Conference was announced in 2007 specifically for senior church leaders to look at broader issues of linking Alpha with wider church life. Other courses are offered in partnership with other church agencies. Some of these have now been run in places other than HTB too. The Marriage Course has attracted the most interest and a Marriage Preparation Course now sits alongside this.

Alpha International Campus

Shortly before completing this book, AI announced that it is undertaking a large building project on the site occupied by St Paul's Onslow Square which will then locate the 'Alpha International Campus (AIC)'.[25] It will become the new international headquarters of AI and aims to provide training facilities to the world-wide church. It will cost several million pounds and will take two years to complete, with work scheduled to start in November 2006.

Nicky Gumbel recognises that supporting the world-wide scale of Alpha has outstripped the present structural facilities available in their present buildings. But the plan goes beyond this. To quote Gumbel: 'The vision is to create a multipurpose Christian campus in central London which will serve the worldwide Christian community through training leaders, supplying resources of a high standard, and offering Christian teaching using the most up to date technology.' In this AI hopes to play its part in reversing the decline in Christianity.

The new site will be the first phase of the AIC. Plans include:

- A worship centre with seating for 1,400 people.
- A theological centre with opportunities for full-time and part-time courses.
- A centre for church planting.
- A family life centre.
- A centre for the transformation of society with opportunities to learn about urban mission and to participate in a variety of projects.
- A school of worship including training.
- Cutting-edge broadcasting capabilities to enable teaching to be communicated around the world.

In many ways, I suspect, such an AIC may bring together many of the different developments, ministries and strands that have been emerging out of HTB, Alpha and AI. (Both Nicky Gumbel and Ken Costa indicate that they have had this project in mind for some considerable time.) It may help give more overall coherence to all this work and also provide a platform and opportunity for further development. It is to be hoped AI will also undertake some reappraisal of where things have got to so that the most is made of such a project.

Since this news has only just been announced as this book was being completed neither I nor other contributors have written with it in mind. (I have included a few comments on it at the end of Chapter 10 and in my closing remarks in Chapter 24.) However, I hope that what we have written will help as these plans are taken forward.

There have been many developments and different emphases at different points since Alpha was made more generally available. There have been setbacks and disappointments and what are probably mistakes too. Yet clearly the whole Alpha enterprise has not run out of steam yet, though it has changed in many ways and will probably keep on changing.

Taking Stock and Moving on

It is difficult to imagine that when HTB planned their first Alpha Conference in 1993 they could have guessed all that would follow. A lot of energy and effort has gone into promoting and supporting Alpha. There have been proactive and reactive elements affecting it and it is clear that there is still energy in the Alpha Movement. Exterior factors have influenced developments as well as factors and decisions internal to AI/HTB who have chosen to retain not just oversight but a good measure of ownership and control of Alpha. There has been a trend – a drive, some would say – towards standardisation and what could be described as 'centralisation'. A humble tool for local churches has become part of a large corporate organisation with national strategies and a lot of business thinking to support it. AI/HTB have, until now, focused most of their attention on the Alpha course itself, rather than the wider issues of integration and local church development.

The impact of Alpha, and the accompanying enthusiasm, was such, especially in the mid-to-late 1990s, that people wondered just how far it would spread. People talked of Alpha as a 'one-size-fits–all' evangelistic tool that might suit all denominations and social settings etc. I am not sure from where these ideas originated. Certainly some of the Alpha promotional material of that time pointed out the wide set of situations and denominations in which it was being used and apparently working. Such thoughts may also have influenced AI/HTB's later strategy decisions. The interest in Alpha and the reputation it gained in these years all helped to create the platform from which Alpha has become a truly global phenomenon. All of this has brought reactions and criticisms of various sorts. Initially mainly about the content and theology of the course they have gone on to look at its method and overall effectiveness.

There have been criticisms even from among those broadly supportive of Alpha. If these strategy and policy decisions had been different – and alternatives were available – might things have worked out differently? Would that have been better and more fruitful is another question as is the time scale over which fruitfulness is measured. Could things be changed radically now, or is the direction of development that Alpha will follow very much fixed? Ought it to change as the culture and society in which it operates continues to change?

Building on Part 1, I will now proceed to look at the nature of the Alpha course itself in more detail (Part 1 Section 2) and then issues around its impact and effectiveness (Part 1 Section 3), in both cases looking at criticisms and providing critiques.

Notes

[1] *Source: Alpha News* May–November, 2006.

[2] See appendix for more information.

[3] The popular version was called *Finding Faith Today* (Bible Society, 1992)

[4] John Finney in his *Emerging Evangelism* (DLT, 2004) provides some extra detail on the development of Nurture Groups and the Decade of Evangelism. See Ch. 5 where he also assesses their effectiveness.

[5] Apparently NG now prefers to call what happened at HTB in these years simply as a 'move of God'. This is discussed more fully in Chapter 10.

[6] For a helpful introduction and wide discussion see Anne Richards, *The Toronto Experience – an exploration of the issues*, Church House Publishing, 1997. 31 pages.

[7] This is a major argument in both his books on Alpha. See Stephen Hunt *Anyone for Alpha? Evangelism in a Post-Christian Society*, DLT, 2001 and *The Alpha Enterprise – Evangelism in a Post-Christian Era*, Ashgate, 2004. I provide a fuller overview of these texts in Chapter 7.

[8] The Alpha Register lists all the churches that want to be named on the register as running Alpha. This information is available on the website to help potential guests find a course.

[9] This form of analysis was developed and first presented by Charles Freebury in *Alpha or Emmaus?*, 2005 (updated version), 103 pages. It is available free on CD in pdf format from the author. For more details on the work of Charles Freebury, see Chapter 7, especially footnote 12. Charles very kindly updated the graph and made it specially available for this book. Charles can be contacted as follows: Address – 89, Hermitage Street, Crewkerne, TA18 8EX. Tel – 01460 78501. Email – charles.freebury@tiscali.co.uk.

[10] A similar analysis presented in Chapter 7 on the total number of guests attending Alpha, suggests a similar limited impact of advertising on the number of guests – though it may well have helped *sustain* the numbers at a high level.

[11] For more of Freebury's analysis see *Alpha or Emmaus?*, p. 10 and p. 40ff.

[12] It is difficult to put an exact figure on this since not all denominations count local churches in the same way and by no means all small house churches or fellowships are registered on central directories.

[13] An analysis of this distribution will be undertaken in Chapter 7. In Part 2 (Section 4) of this book various authors will analyse and reflect on the uptake and effectiveness of Alpha as well as reactions to it in their own particular denominations or church streams.

[14] From *Alpha News*. June 2004.

[15] Mark Ireland asks if this, with firm copyright application etc, could (perhaps unwittingly) become a new form of the Victorian missionary effort across the British Empire when the gospel was carried along with a lot of British culture and

imposed without regard to or appreciation of the local culture and what it had to offer. See Mike Booker and Mark Ireland *Evangelism – Which Way Now?*, 2nd ed, Church House Publishing, 2005

[16] Typically this would be for guest groups perceived as less academic than the graduates that typically make up a substantial part of HTB's clientele. People working with such groups may also be interested in the development of shorter videos, officially as part of Alpha in the Workplace.

[17] Independent research strongly supports the first two of these as indeed being the most important questions that non-Christians wish to ask Christians about.

[18] As such this advice may sometimes – if interpreted as meaning the leaders and helpers jump in with quick ready-made answers – conflict with the general advice not to answer the questions of guest themselves but rather to throw the issue back to the body of the group for further exploration. Reading the book is likely to provide the leaders with material to bolster their own faith and prevent it being 'confused' by difficult questions. Although not stated explicitly, this may be a significant reason for recommending the book and one that is compatible with still allowing a free-flowing discussion of the issue in the small group. The book can be recommended to those who ask about and wish to explore further the topic raised.

[19] Thus while it could be said such emphasis on the Holy Spirit is talked up on the conference it is recommended to talk it down to guests during the early part of the course as it can cause anxiety or false expectations.

[20] HTB had considered using a variety of speakers but were advised that using the medium of video it takes longer to establish connection and trust with the viewer and one speaker would accelerate this process. The live course at HTB does use several speakers.

[21] I shall generally refer hereafter to Alpha International as AI. Where there is clearly a strong partnership with HTB I shall group the two together and use the collective abbreviation AI/HTB.

[22] Data supplied to me by Scottish Alpha Office, January, 2006.

[23] Gumbel, *Telling Others*, Kingsway 2001, p. 224.

[24] This example has been given at some Alpha Conferences. Mark Ireland also cites it from an interview he conducted with NG. (See *Evangelism – Which Way Now?*, 2nd Ed pp. 20–1). Mark Elsdon-Dew commented to me that NG has since had reservations about the comparison since it suggests Alpha may be bland.

[25] *Alpha News*, May–November, 2006, p. 9.

SECTION 2

The Nature of the Alpha Course

In this section I will look more deeply at the course, explaining and reflecting on its nature and how it functions. I will also review objections to it relating to immediate issues of the nature course itself, some of the responses typically made by AI/HTB to these and then provide further overall critique. I will use information from AI/HTB sources/publications and draw on my own and others experience working with the course.

A first impression of Alpha may be that it is straightforward. The meal–talk–small group for discussion and possibly prayer/bible study format seems simple enough! At one level it is. However, Alpha is a complex course and is not easy to fully understand. Nicky Gumbel often says that a church will need to run it up to eight or nine times just to 'de-bug' it. To deal with the complexity and try to make it accessible I intend to approach the course from three angles: from the content of the course (Chapter 3), the principles behind the course (Chapter 4) and the method of the course (Chapter 5). Many criticisms focus on only one or other of these aspects and thus often fail to get or critique an overall sense of what is really involved. I will then provide some more general reflections that arise out of, and build on, the first level of description and analysis (Chapter 6).

In Chapters 3 and 4, I have used 'summary' sections to express the thought of Nicky Gumbel and/or the standard Alpha publications and then 'comments and critiques' sections to express and then discuss various comments, qualifications, and concerns. I also flag up issues and raise questions more generally about Alpha, usually in regard to other evangelistic themes, many of which will not be answered immediately but will be addressed in later chapters by myself and by other contributors.

AB

CHAPTER 3

The Content of Alpha

Andrew Brookes

The Content of *Questions of Life* and Alpha Videos

The content of the Alpha Course is contained in Nicky Gumbel's book, *Questions of Life*, which he and others describe as the textbook of Alpha. The videos cover most of the same material with some omissions but more jokes. The Alpha copyright statement makes clear that for a course to be called Alpha it has to be based on all of the material in *Questions of Life*. Thus an assessment of this is a fair way of looking at the official content of Alpha.

It is an intriguing combination of topics and materials that have led to many different responses and criticisms: some are theological, others are missiological, and others still are more practical or pastoral. The course and HTB have had a long and changing history leading up to the publication on *Questions of Life* in 1993. The text reflects this history and development as well as the different uses/audiences it has been geared towards at various points. Since 1993 further relatively small changes have been made, these being introduced principally in response to the ecumenical use of Alpha. These have consisted in a broadening of the illustrations and testimonial examples to embrace a wide range of the Christian family. Again the selection of cited authors has similarly been extended. Also, and after careful consultations, some other changes have been made in response to some theological problems and criticisms, again in an attempt to make the course as usable as possible by as many denominations/traditions as possible. Perhaps the biggest set of such changes followed a serious and relatively high level consultation with the Catholic Bishops in France around 2001.[1]

In many ways I think it is fair and helpful to see it as comprising a number of sections or elements – though these are my own divisions, not official ones of AI/HTB. I shall outline these including a brief synopsis of the material covered in each with some comments.

A basic introduction to Christianity intended to bring a person to understand Christ, the Cross and Conversion
(Introductory/Celebratory supper and Weeks 1–3)

The course is Christocentric and starts with a presentation of who Jesus is. The celebration supper, to which prospective guests are invited, likewise has a talk that answers the title question 'Christianity: Boring, Untrue and Irrelevant?' It does this by presenting Jesus as the Way – not boring, Truth – not untrue, and the Life – not irrelevant (Jn 14:6).

Who is Jesus?

Summary

The course proper begins by introducing the figure of Jesus and establishing his divinity. It does this by an argument that firstly gives evidence for his historical existence and the reliability of the New Testament documents. It is then argued that Jesus clearly claimed to be divine. Supporting evidence is then given through Jesus' depth of teaching, works and wonders, character, fulfilment of Old Testament prophecy and the evidence for his Resurrection. Listeners are then presented with three options: Jesus is either mad for thinking he was God, or bad for deceiving people with this claim, or God since the other options don't seem likely.

Comments and Critique

All this is done in 45 minutes. This is a lot of ground to cover. Much of it assumes a familiarity with the basic story of Jesus and a broader knowledge of the Bible and accompanying history if the argument is to be properly followed. What sorts of people have this familiarity nowadays? Of those that do, how many can follow the argument in 45 minutes? Even if people think it unlikely Jesus is mad or bad, it is a big jump to affirm he is God. God sometimes grants this grace and inner knowledge of an illumination of Christian Truth 'in an instant'. However, normally it happens over time and thus the starting point of contemporary people needs to be considered since grace typically works with reason, and this talk is a reasoned argument. The term 'God' means lots of different things to different people nowadays. Without a specific prior understanding of/familiarity with the Trinity and Incarnation, what sort of God are people identifying Jesus as? (This will be considered further in Chapter 8.) Little external evidence for Christianity is covered after this point.

Why did Jesus die?

Summary

Participants then look at humanity's sin and need of forgiveness and the divine solution given in the death of Jesus who died in the place of each of us. For the most part it is assumed we already or will quickly recognise we are sinners and feel a sense of guilt about this. In this sense sin is also presented as objectively wrong.

An understanding of the problem of sin is then developed under the headings of the pollution, power, penalty and partition of sin, using Biblical data. Jesus' death is then presented as the solution: God has reconciled us to himself by the self-substitution of Christ who bore our sins, dying in our place. Having alluded in literally less than one paragraph to other aspects of the fruit of the cross, NG describes the results of Christ's death under four images that correspond with his earlier characterisation of the problems of sin. Firstly, the law court is used. We have been found guilty and sentenced but Jesus received the punishment in our place and thus removes the penalty of sin. (The term 'justification' is used in this explanation.) Secondly, the market place and its slave trade are invoked and it is explained that Jesus paid the ransom price to set us free. (He does not explain in terms of salvation, who the ransom is paid to – something of large theological significance.) This makes us free and breaks the power of sin, we are told. Thirdly, he draws on Jewish temple worship and the animal sacrifices for sin. Christ is the perfect sacrifice since he did not sin; he died in our place, our substitute, and thus purifies us from all sin, removing the pollution of sin. Fourthly, he refers to the home. He argues that since it is God the Son that reconciles us to God the Father, again through God's self-substitution, that we can know God as a Father again, thus destroying the partition of sin.

After giving an account of John Wimber's conversion, the talk ends with a chance for those who feel they have never 'really believed in Jesus' to say a prayer which allows them to start a Christian life and receive 'all the benefits which Christ died to make possible'.

Comments and Critique

This material has attracted considerable attention and merits further comment here. The talk is essentially a version of a format used in the classical evangelistic talk, also published in numerous pamphlets and tracts. Like them it ends in a prayer for conversion of the form: 'Sorry, I have sinned, thank you for dying for me, please come into my life.' (Such prayers are often referred to as the sinner's prayer.) These talks typically assert that:(1) God made us and wants a relationship with us; (2) we sinned and have incurred his displeasure making the desired relationship impossible; (3) Jesus came and died to remove the problem and barrier of sin; (4) faith in Jesus and inviting him into our lives establishes a relationship with God. Hence the final prayer. Put in broad terms, such as these, all (or most) Christians would affirm them, but in the telling of them or fleshing out of them, big differences and then disagreements occur. NG does avoid the crudest versions of such talks and tracts that present Jesus as taking a beating from an angry and bad-tempered God who had to get this hostility out of his system so he could love us intimately again – or just to love us at all. NG is aware of this and much more nuanced, but it does not follow that live local versions of the talk will be.

It is generally thought that NG's talk was originally based on, or is at least adapted from, a presentation of the atonement (that is, how God reconciles us to himself or, more generally, what is the meaning of the death of Jesus) based on the theology of substitution and in particular, penal substitution.[2] Such presentations have come under a lot of scrutiny. There is not an issue in saying that Jesus died for us – that is clearly Scriptural. However, expressing this as *penal* substitution is hugely problematic to many Christians, including an increasing number of Evangelicals.[3] The problems seem to increase when the idea of penal substitution becomes more central to and even the exclusive way of explaining the cross.[4] Even if a carefully nuanced form of penal substitution, explicitly placed in a wider theological framework, can be formulated which is compatible with Christian Revelation, it does not follow that it is wise to use it – largely stripped of wider teaching – as the centre piece of evangelistic talks, which of their nature have to simplify and summarise. Is penal substitution so central to Biblical teaching on atonement, which uses a rich variety of images and expositions on this topic, that it is sensible to use it evangelistically to represent the Good News as such? Many would argue it is not.

Evangelistic talks that centre on penal substitution may initially appear as though God is offering people a great deal, and thus really be good news, but they tend to carry all sorts of issues with them for those who care to think more deeply. First, typically we are introduced to God as a loving Father by being told how he is angry and required the violent death of his son. We are then asked if we want to be his adopted child. Such a person would not be allowed to adopt 'physically' in the UK today yet many do not see or are happy to live with the tensions – many would say contradictions – and sign up to be his adopted 'spiritual' children. One also wonders what, if any, theology of the Trinity and of the relationship between God the Father and God the Son underlies this. In fact, does it play off an angry and perhaps demanding overbearing Father against a tolerant and merciful gentle Son?

Such a view is not scriptural and hardly permits any sense to be made of Jesus' often repeated assertion that to have seen him is to have seen the Father (e.g. John 14:9). The truth is that Jesus is as just as his Father and the Father as merciful as his Son, Jesus. However, at their worst such presentations result in it looking as though Jesus is saving us *from* (a wrathful angry) God, not *for* God. They can also end up suggesting a sort of 'Divine schizophrenia' in which two different and contrasting divine personalities, wrestling with each other, exist in hopeless degenerative tension. Far from pointing to faith in the Trinity, such talks can end up nurturing a faith that is implicitly, if not explicitly, dualistic in which a kind God saves us from an angry God. Just briefly referring to the 'self-substitution of God' does not overcome these problems unless what this means –in Trinitarian terms – is carefully explained.

In societies such as ours where so many have poor, or no, experience of father figures – and this is what they bring to Christian talks – these considerations are not just about truth and abstract theological interest. There can be real practical benefits for people if God's fatherhood is presented well but also a reinforcement of wounds of various sorts if presented badly. A strength of the official Alpha text and video on this topic, and the course more generally, is that it does recognise the importance of presenting us with God as a loving Father. In fact NG makes several references to God as a loving Father throughout the course. A good case can be made for saying this is the principal way he presents the first person of the Trinity.[5]

Serious questions can also be asked about what such presentations communicate about how just God is – punishing someone who is innocent – and how violent God is if the suffering of Christ is seen as directly organised or even required by God? Such talks often contain other difficulties in presenting God as just. What credible modern legal system would knowingly allow an innocent person to suffer a penalty for a guilty one? If such a miscarriage of justice had been committed, reputable legal systems would then re-open the case to find and deal with the really guilty party. It is hardly surprising if people do not see an immediate link between the death of Jesus (understood like this) and going out and building a just world. Further, we are called to imitate and be formed in the likeness of God. So what if we have, at least implicitly, taught or been persuaded that this God is violent and retributive? Many Christian thinkers are increasingly questioning whether such presentations and the theology behind them lead to, or at least support, the violence and repression used by Christians both historically and currently, including that of 'Christian states and governments'.[6] Some question whether these theologies are Biblical at all.

However, these problems do not entitle us to ignore any of the Biblical imagery about the death of Christ. Legal metaphors are found there. Certainly reflection on the cross has to consider how Jesus 'bore our sins' etc. It also needs to take seriously God's holiness and sense of justice. It needs to consider sin as not merely subjective, but as objective as well. It needs to stress the free and merciful initiative taken by God who loved us first and while we were sinners, and our reliance on what God does (cf Romans 5:6–8 and I John 4:10). These elements are present in theologies of penal substitution but can also be found in other 'objective' theories.

Such detached objectivity does not exhaust the Biblical data. As the objective view began to gain ascendancy with Anselm, an alternative 'subjective' approach was also developed that places the stress on how much God has done to forgive us – even to the extent of sacrificing his Son.[7] The appeal to conversion is then based on how much God loves us, rather than the objective seriousness of sin and justice and the wrath of God; we should love him in return, giving him our lives, part of which means turning from sin to him. Again, support for this can be found in Scripture (eg Romans 5:11 and 1 John 4:15–16). The perceived weakness to this approach is that Jesus can end up just being presented as a loving person of integrity who has left us a moral example, but did not really change the spiritual state of humanity before God.

Where do Alpha and NG fit into this pattern and debate? NG is aware of at least some of these issues and in many ways NG tries to combine these two (objective and subjective) approaches. He includes a variety of scriptural images about the cross though the overall structure follows that of a classical talk on penal substitution. Close examination of different editions of *Questions of Life* indicates less prominence given to legal/punitive language and images over time. (By implication this may suggest less support for penal substitution.) Whether this reflects personal changes in NG's own theology or responses to criticisms and ecumenical considerations, or a combination, is another matter. Whether what we now have, or ever had, in Alpha works as a synthesis or is just a muddle of bits and pieces and Bible quotes is still another matter.

People from many different theological perspectives have asked if NG's approach is intellectually rigorous and theologically coherent and even if it uses Scriptural data properly.[8] Many Conservative/Reformed Evangelicals have roundly condemned it for not taking sin or God's wrath or holiness seriously.[9] For some it so distorts Biblical Revelation that it is quite simply heretical. Others ask if it places too much stress on sin. Gumbel is happy to cite the criticisms of one group to the other in both directions and hold a position somewhere in the middle. It is also fair to ask if what may be regarded as a compromise text results in local speakers taking lines that are very different and even sharply at odds with each other. In such cases are they really giving the same talk or conveying the same message?

An alternative evangelistic presentation to that which relies centrally on penal substitution could be developed that used very centrally the theme of 'exchange' as developed by, or building on, the early Church Fathers who in turn draw on Biblical texts. This looks at the way Christ takes on our human nature and life so we can take on his divine life.[8A] It is God who takes the initiative in Christ that makes this possible. It is rooted in the Incarnation as well as the cross and glorification of Christ. The Son of God, temporarily, exchanges life in

Heaven for human life on earth, emptying himself of Divine heavenly glory (Philippians 2:6–11). From his baptism onwards he increasingly identifies with, and takes on, our sin (Matthew 3:13–17; John 1:29–34), this finding its full expression on the cross when he offers it to his Father so we can exchange our sinful life for new life in Christ (1 Peter 2:21–5 and others). We thus put off our sinful humanity and by the power of his grace at work in us, grow into Christ, effectively putting on his divine humanity. In something that embraces aspects of decisive event and ongoing process, we exchange our autonomous sinful existence for godly righteousness as God's sons and daughters.

In many ways Nicky Gumbel – implicitly perhaps – already draws on this exchange concept. His presentation is already wider than the normal penal substitution talk. The exchange theme can easily take up the images that NG develops in his material: thus we exchange condemnation due to sin for divine mercy and forgiveness; slavery to sin for graced freedom; the pollution of sin is exchanged for the purity of grace; separation from God is exchanged for intimacy with God. Rooting and framing his presentation here – and it could be done more explicitly than it currently is – may provide it with more theological coherence and robustness and a better defence against those who assail it from various sides as a (poor) presentation of penal substitution. Of course, those Christians who are strongly wedded to penal substitution, or to the appearance of the motif of penal substitution in evangelism talks even if it is not well expressed, would probably regard such moves with concern.

It is also true to say that the course does not relate the death of Christ to his life or to his Resurrection and Ascension.[10] All of this has theological implications that most Alpha commentators have not picked up or at least developed. *Both* the main two approaches that NG uses focus on the individual before God. Sin and the death of Jesus are treated in personal and individual terms. I think a good case could be made for broadening this and looking at atonement as liberation from all oppression (political, social, religious, personal etc, understood collectively as sinful) and to look at the *whole of* Jesus' life, death and resurrection in this light.[11] Such a presentation calls for a personal response and recognition of personal involvement in this sin. Thus conversion is still called for: a conversion that affects *all* areas of our lives. In addressing poverty, this means not only providing for people's needs, but also addressing and trying to remove the causes of poverty.[12] It thus links the work of Jesus and our personal conversion intrinsically to the agenda of social-justice and the environment, areas where Alpha is often considered weak. More generally, it could also similarly establish better links between Jesus' saving work and the world of human work.

Let me seek to sum this up in more pastoral and practical terms. It is a commonly held conviction among those who work as evangelists to help bring about personal conversions that it is essential to convey and emphasise that, whatever else Jesus died to achieve in terms of bringing in social justice, restoring creation etc, he died for each of us personally. This is typically covered by saying 'he died in my/your place.' Such presentations have clearly been effective in bringing many people to a significant conversion and focus on Jesus as their saviour.[13] NG, and therefore Alpha in general, use this approach too. Such presentations typically draw on the language and thus theologies of 'substitution'. There is perhaps a need for a greater dialogue between theologians and evangelists. It would be helpful if theologians apply more thought to these important pastoral concerns of evangelists. It would also help evangelists ensure that evangelism is theologically sound and balanced and evangelists do not give seriously unbalanced or ultimately misrepresentative presentations.

The course is also sometimes criticised for covering all this material, especially sin, far too quickly and thus superficially.[14] For some the lack of sense of sin which is very prevalent nowadays makes it a hard topic to deal with, especially this early in a course for non-Christians. These may also be pastoral and educational concerns, rather than the more theological ones noted above though these often interact. Is it reasonable to assume that most Non-Christians nowadays have such a sense of sin? Or if not, that they can be very quickly taught it or brought to a realisation of it? In fact, a sense of sin, as opposed to just a sense of our inadequacy or failure, requires some sense of God and his goodness and holiness.

Others say that the life, death and resurrection of Jesus should be more related to issues of meaning, purpose and hope and not just dealing with guilt. (Some of these ideas are related to how we present the unchanging Gospel in a changing culture and will be explored in more depth in Chapter 8.) The atonement is currently a topic of debate that is lively and also sharply contested. It would be impossible for Alpha to please everyone in such a situation and many will be happy with at least some of what Alpha covers. However, perhaps a new approach that looks at the topic more broadly and widely would provide a way forward.

How can I be sure of my faith?

Summary

Having already invited people to make a commitment of faith, the nature of this faith is explained. It is not just subjective experience but based on the historic events of Jesus; this faith fulfils and is in accord with Biblical promises and data; and it is also a result of the action of the Holy Spirit.[15] This is what is referred to in some circles, including classical Protestant evangelical ones, as a talk on assurance.

NG affirms that people can enter into committed faith gradually – and even from childhood – or it can be more dramatic with people knowing the time and place. For NG, the important thing is not the past (with any issues of how and when a person became a Christian) but that a person has faith now and is a Christian now. Central to and characteristic of this is a 'living relationship with Jesus' or 'knowing Jesus' now. There is relatively little attention given to the future aspects of faith on Alpha either. NG has broadened the terminology he uses to describe all this to include phrases acceptable and used by as many denominations and theological schools as possible. He thus brackets together expressions such as 'becoming a Christian', 'coming to faith', 'coming to the Lord', 'being converted', 'being saved', 'being born again', 'having one's faith come alive/switched on spiritually', 'faith becoming personal', 'knowing God/Jesus personally' – and others together. NG does not deal explicitly with, or propose a clear view on, the issue of an individual's absolute guarantee and sense of certainty of full and lasting personal salvation, or the lack of it.

Comments and Critique

The Alpha materials avoid addressing the point directly of when a person is saved or fully saved. The overall nature of the course amongst other things suggests to me, at any rate, that HTB do not hold that just saying a prayer, or just having a certain experience (or both), are necessarily sufficient. However, saying such prayers from the heart have often been the real turning point in people's lives and God certainly takes note of us when we really turn to him in humility, trust and surrender. God does use experiences to change people and bring real and lasting spiritual changes about. HTB stress the importance of an ongoing life of discipleship which is, of course, a life of faith, only made possible by God's grace and mercy. They stress that what we do is always a response to what God has done and this is received fundamentally as a gift.

The authority of the Bible is assumed in this talk. The stress falls on the individual and his faith as affirmed by the Bible. Much more could be made of the living and ongoing testimony of the living community of believers across space and time as affirming and interpreting the search and experience of the new believer. This would draw on and could even introduce the church as a community of faith existing across space and time in continuity with Jesus and the apostles.[16] It is through this community that God 'produced' the Bible and any local Alpha course meets in continuity with this larger church community. These church communities are vital in helping people come to faith and recognising and understanding that faith as Christian.

What God offers, through his love, is seen as a gift that we are free to receive: faith is receiving what God offers through Jesus Christ in the

Holy Spirit. This Christocentric gift-response dynamic, energised by the Holy Spirit, is central to the whole course.

Whether this presentation conveys an adequate understanding of faith is contended by critics from various parts of the denominational and theological spectrum. For some it is seriously flawed and inadequate. For others it is fine. Some may judge it as incomplete but pastorally adequate for a person near the beginning of their faith journey.

It is worth noting that by the logic of the *material alone*, a person ought to be a Christian by now and the rest of the content, on the face of it, builds on this supposition, being about discipleship and growth.

Introduction to some basic points of discipleship
(mainly weeks 4–6)

Why and How should I read the bible ~ Why and How should I pray? ~ How does God guide us?

Summary
Practical talks are now given on how to read the Bible (talk 4) and how to pray (talk 5). Each has some material explaining *why* pray and *why* read the Bible, the latter including some material on the inspiration of Scripture and on the Bible, science and reason. This is followed by the talk on guidance (which used to be done later on the course) that covers different aspects of life and how God provides guidance for them.[17] More aspects of life and how to live them as a Christian are covered in 'How can I make the most the rest of my life?' (classified as talk 15) which normally comes at the end of the weekend/day away.

Comments and Critique
This material all provides a basic introduction to Christian life, discipleship and personal spiritual life. It is worth noting that, having treated sin and redemption as mainly personal, the areas of discipleship it generally focuses on are ones that affect individuals and their immediate situations. More such material is included in other areas of the course, for instance on ways to evangelise. This section of the course has attracted relatively little controversy.

Since it is an issue of current debate it may be as well to summarise the course' s position on sex and particularly homosexuality. All people are to be treated with respect. Sex is good and is for (heterosexual) marriage. Homosexuality is not treated explicitly in Questions of Life – but is covered with a whole chapter in *Searching Issues*. People are not to be judged or condemned for their sexual orientation. A homosexually orientated person who is Christian ought to be celibate unless God heals them is such a way to allow them to form heterosexual relationships and marry a person of the opposite sex.

Life in the Power of the Holy Spirit
(Day or weekend away and week 7)

Who is the Holy Spirit? ~What does the Holy Spirit Do?
~ How can I be Filled with the Spirit? ~ How can I make the most of the
rest of my life? ~ How can I resist Evil?

Summary
This section introduces people, by teaching and experience, to the work of the Holy Spirit. The aims are that guests be filled with the Spirit, experiencing God's love and power and begin to use the charismatic gifts of the Spirit, though these are not taught as essential to being a Christian as such but as very worthwhile. The talks cover what is felt to be the necessary Biblical/doctrinal and spiritual preparation.

The basic pattern is to recap the general aspects of Christian life, Jesus, faith and repentance and to see the crucial role of the Holy Spirit in all this. (Talk 7 and 8. 'Who is the Holy Spirit?' And 'What Does the Holy Spirit Do?'). These also introduce the more charismatic aspects of the Holy Spirit's action, including the so-called charismatic gifts (see 1 Cor 12: 8–10), and also point out and comment on the experiential (emotional) effects that can accompany the Spirit's action in individual lives. There is no specific teaching on the charismatic gifts other than speaking in tongues. Teaching on tongues is given as Charismatics consider that it is often the first gift to be received, that it requires faith to be exercised and it often appears to be the gateway to receiving other gifts. The course manuals ask small group leaders to explain the other gifts (though no material is provided) since they may be in evidence later in ministry time and in various ways are presupposed by some later parts of the course. Talk 9 ('How Can I be filled with the Spirit?') is still more practical with content on how to be open to the action of God's Spirit, how to spiritually prepare, what to expect and not to expect. It addresses issues of fear, doubt and unworthiness and is followed by an opportunity and encouragement to 'be filled' both by a corporate prayer and more individual prayer time.

This material on the Holy Spirit, and any experience a person has had, is directed towards the context of a life of active Christian discipleship with the talk 'What shall I do with the rest of my life?' on aspects of discipleship. Though this is supposed to round off the weekend/day, time is often tight and it often tends to get truncated in various ways.

These talks are all done on the Holy Spirit Day or Weekend. This takes place in a more relaxed setting away from the hassles and distractions of everyday life. Time is allowed for relaxation, entertainment and getting to know each other better. As such it draws on the general Christian practice of retreats/house parties which have long been known to facilitate openness to God. They also allow non-Christians to be with

Christians for longer and thus hopefully be more relaxed and open. HTB also include a Communion Service on the weekend version.

It is the common understanding and experience of practitioners of Charismatic Christianity that such an experience of the Holy Spirit may well be followed by doubts and/or increased tension which is ascribed in part, at least to Satan and/or other evil spirits. Counsel, and if necessary teaching, on spiritual warfare usually follows to equip the person to understand and deal with this. NG has given a whole talk to this topic (Talk 10: 'How do I resist Evil?') a few days after the day/ weekend away.

Comments and Critique

This material has attracted a lot of comment – mainly about whether it has the right amount of stress on the Holy Spirit – as well as some more specific points. In very general terms comments vary from 'There is far too much emphasis on the Holy Spirit', 'It is just about right, balanced and well–explained' to 'There is not enough'. Much depends on a person's starting point. I have developed more detailed reflection on the Holy Spirit in Alpha and HTB in Chapter 4 (from Principle 4 'Wonders' to the end of the chapter) and would direct readers there for a wider discussion of these issues.

The content of this section is not dissimilar to various other courses developed by sections of Charismatic Renewal designed to introduce people to the life and gifts of the Holy Spirit. Indeed, as such it is not very original though does have its own features, especially when these are seen within the wider functioning of the whole Alpha course.[18] Some have criticised AI/HTB for presuming competence in other churches to undertake the work of explaining the various gifts of the Holy Spirit, other than tongues, without any material resources or help. In general, HTB have increasingly invited other churches to join their own weekend away to learn how to effectively present all this material and lead the linked ministry. This highlights just how challenging it is to many churches. It may also suggest that the way HTB does this is quite specific and that something similar, though not identical, needs to be followed elsewhere if Alpha is to be effective. Just doing any sort of 'Charismatic event' may not be appropriate.

Some have concerns that the attention to Satan (talk 10 on resisting evil) encourages a form of dualism, which may be practical rather than essentially doctrinal. Certainly some Christians, including some Alpha graduates, seem to see Satan very directly involved in just about everything that they are not absolutely sure that God is fully behind. Such Christians give little attention to the complexities of 'the flesh' and 'the world' as causal forces or agencies to be considered. Overestimating, or 'talking up', the power of Satan and evil powers can lead to spiritual, emotional and other problems just as under-estimating them can. Different denominations and specific local churches within them running Alpha will have different perspectives and outlooks on this area. These will affect how Alpha is actually run and the effects of it on people doing the course there.[19]

The talk on resisting evil is thus quite specific in context and is not a general introduction to morality as some might suppose. The presentation given may also encourage too superficial an appreciation and evaluation of our contemporary culture, a proper evaluation of which is vital for effective mission. Too simplistic or inclusive a view of what is definitely of the devil (and as such bad, to be avoided and disapproved of) also runs risk of missing opportunities to connect effectively with 'spiritual seekers' and other contemporaries. Such people may well have experimented with all manner of 'spiritual practices' during their searching and need a sensitive and nuanced approach to explore and evaluate these and Christian claims about the Holy Spirit. For others, a stark presentation of spiritual evil, and a contrast with good spiritual realities, may be helpful and effective.

Participation in the mission of Jesus and life of the Church
(weeks 8–10)
Why and How should we tell Others? ~ Does God heal Today?
~ What about the Church?

Summary
The final section is about witnessing to Christian faith and considering actual involvement in the local church. Again the talks have a strong practical application. With the end of the course in sight, attention is now focused on preparing for life after the Alpha course and for getting new guests, often friends of existing participants, on to the next course as well as selecting any suitable guests as team members for that course. All this may partly explain the order of talks within this section. There are two talks linked to evangelism. The first ('Why and how should we tell others?') covers the topic in general, under the headings presence (including works i.e. social action), persuasion, proclamation, power and prayer. The second ('Does God Heal Today?') focuses on healing and is really a look at power evangelism in more detail and gives the chance to actually take part in this. The small discussion groups are replaced by a healing service where all can be involved using spiritual gifts, including prophetic words of knowledge about people's health problems, and praying for others and/or being prayed with.

Lastly (in 'What about the Church?'), people are invited to get involved in church since they – believers – *are* the church. They are advised to join a good local vibrant church. The church is considered as the People of God, the family of God, the Body of Christ, a Holy Temple and the Bride of Christ, all biblical images used to describe facets of the church. In reality, stress is placed throughout on the church comprising the body of Christians living in good relationships, as friends, with each other as they share in the life of God, Father, Son and Holy Spirit. Church organisation is mentioned in terms of the pastoral practice operated at HTB and implicitly encouraged elsewhere: small stable prayer groups or cells, larger pastorates and Sunday congregations, all linking size and function.

Comments and Critique

This material is practical in tone and it aims at getting guests practically and very actively involved in living out their faith. Witnessing to one's (new) faith is recognised as a very good way of helping it to bed down. Ideally the healing talk involves guests in doing the healing prayer. A good response to these talks assumes a rapid and keen beginning to the life of any Christians. This, in turn, may depend on what has happened up to that point on the course and especially on the weekend/day away. One wonders what happens in churches where this is not the case, though I do know of other effective ways of conducting a healing service within Alpha. Some feel the healing talk makes light of suffering in the lives of people. Material has been added to try and address this concern. However, it is still intended that the talk will build an expectant faith that God heals – and that he may actually heal people that very evening.

Does treating the church last mean treating it least too? Some think so! Others say that unchurched (Post-modern) people are so suspicious of church it is best to leave it to the end when they are more at ease. (As we shall see in chapters 5 and 6 the course has an 'ecclesial setting' throughout which partly offsets this.) Does the treatment of church have denominational bias? In reality, beyond broad themes and Biblical imagery of church, much of the practical application refers to practical and pastoral organisation (cells/pastorates etc): these insights could be fitted into different ecclesiological understandings.

It is particularly difficult to get the teaching content on church right and worded to suit all or any denomination since the splits of the Reformation period, and many subsequent ones, were linked specifically to ecclesial issues. This means that no one is really happy with what is there, except perhaps those with a very minimalist sense of church and perhaps also a general lack of ecclesiology. This material has been changed over the years to make it as ecumenically inclusive as possible. (This has pared down the material even further.) Only certain points, that are deemed to be held commonly and even then have been carefully worded, are included on the sacraments. (HTB have even reduced what they would like to present as Anglicans to accommodate others.) Baptism and Eucharist are mentioned specifically. There have been many critiques of the course, from many denominational standpoints, on these topics. HTB accept and are happy to advise churches to add any extra material (on this or any topic) they see fit or necessary for their own denomination, but in sessions *after* the Alpha Course but *not during it*. Some do so. How much the Alpha material gets slanted during the course and especially in live local talks is a matter of speculation.[20]

This talk could possibly introduce more basic ideas behind the sacramental principle since they are Biblical and tied to the Incarnational economy itself. Thus in sacraments the invisible grace, action and presence of God operates through created material signs and actions. This happens throughout Salvation History as recorded in the Bible. The material points beyond itself – to God and his action. And God's grace, the power and love of the Holy Spirit, accomplishes what is pointed to, though this requires faith to be effective. All of this is Biblical and, for instance, HTB do advocate the laying on of hands in prayer ministry. Fundamentally, Christ is the sacrament of God and Church is basic sacrament of Christ. This sacramental principle can be extended further to specific sacraments and even beyond that. The Word of God, written or proclaimed, can be considered as a kind of sacrament of the Divine and pre-existent Word who was with God in the beginning, is God and through whom all was made.[21]

Other Aspects of Content

Follow up Content

HTB used to stress they ran Alpha as the first module in an overall programme for new Christians lasting two years. They appear now to place greater stress on getting newcomers happily into pastorates and then look at what doctrinal/sacramental formation they need. This indicates a recognition of the importance of 'belonging'. Both strategies also indicate they do not regard Alpha as a complete course in Christianity or as an adequate formation for new Christians. Other churches may or may not follow these views and practices. Some other denominations/churches have done different things regarding extra, often quite specific, content. Baptists have been known to add, after the course, their own material on adult baptism. Catholics have added material of various lengths and weeks on a fuller treatment of the church, sacraments and church authority and sometimes other issues too. Catholics sometimes run Alpha at the beginning of R.C.I.A.(Rites for the Christian Initiation of Adults) which is the process, content and rites recommended to be followed for people becoming Catholics.

Some other General Comments on Course Content

The Alpha Course contains and sets out elements of Divine Revelation expressed in Biblical language and/or in fairly accessible, non-technical, terms from the history of Christian doctrine. It is a selection, made on the grounds of what it was felt, in part at least, new Christians need to know. It reflects the Evangelical-Charismatic tradition but the language has been adapted to make it as usable as possible by as many Christian denominations and traditions as possible. It is Christ-centred, with a focus on his saving death, has a pneumatological approach (i.e. it is concerned with the Holy Spirit) and is underpinned by a Trinitarian perspective. Beginning and/or deepening an ongoing personal relationship with Christ as Saviour and Lord and linking this to participation in Christ's church and mission is at the heart of what the course presents. As such it treats of common Christian themes.

Yet often it has surprised Christians to discover that other denominations hold these beliefs in common and have found the same course effective! Such is the level of ignorance and even suspicion that still divides parts of the Christian family. Alpha has helped in breaking some of these down.[22] It expresses the Biblical basis of doctrine rather than doctrine as such. In this sense it is a foundation for more doctrinal teaching, of whatever sort. It sets out to be substantial enough to stimulate and be able to respond to questions, sensitive enough not to offend unnecessarily and robust and attractive enough to invite a response of faith or further enquiry.

Where is authority located in the course? A substantial authority for the Bible is assumed throughout. Exactly how much authority is not stated, nor is its relation to other sources of authority in different denominations. At least this appears to be the case in the current material though earlier versions were less ecumenically nuanced. This is too little for some. There is also an appeal to experience and testimony. The focus on and appeal to experience as a source of insight worries some; indeed, some consider this as the major source of authority and yardstick of judgement used on the course. For people of such views, Scripture or other formulations of Christian truths are judged to be just religious glosses. NG also draws on arguments and testimony from the history and ongoing witness of the church, something that could be seen as acknowledgement of, and even the beginnings of an argument from 'tradition'.

Suggestions for Additions or Changes and a Note on Omissions

Some other specific points or suggestions about content keep coming up in my experience, discussion and research. 'More is needed on the life and person of Jesus!' suggest some. The nature of conversion, repentance and even the after-life merit more attention for some. The theology behind the course is Trinitarian but some feel the Trinity needs a more explicit treatment. Others want, and have sometimes introduced, material on other world religions/New Age and suffering early on, sometimes drawing on NG's material in Searching Issues. Some feel there is too much emphasis on faith as individualistic, interior and affective, and that other aspects should have more attention. For example, some would include more on the Christian's duties in and for society and creation generally.

How much selection and tweaking goes on in live versions, changing the balance – or even rendering it denominationally specific and exclusive rather than ecumenically inclusive – is impossible to tell. Do all, or even most, local course leaders, speakers and even ministers see and understand all the issues and textual subtleties involved here? Shorter talks will be even more selective and potentially less balanced. At what point 'local adaptation' distorts the course or the ethos underlining it is questionable but important if, as AI/HTB claim, people should have confidence in a uniform product so that they can suggest their friends go to any Alpha Course in any church. Course uniformity is also presupposed if national advertisement claims on behalf of courses everywhere are to be taken seriously.

No course can cover everything, certainly not a ten weeks introduction. Some specific concerns about gaps have already been mentioned. However, by way of observation, rather than criticism, it may be worth ending this section on Alpha's content by noting what common Christian material is not present or only briefly mentioned and not a focus or substantially explained. I am not suggesting that these topics are not held or taught at HTB but just drawing attention to what a person will and will not learn just by following Alpha. It is only a tool, after all, and other material can be added elsewhere.

There is no proper treatment of Jesus' teaching on the Kingdom of God and his parables or indeed an account of the development of his life and public ministry. Although the Resurrection is covered (and used apologetically as evidence for Jesus' Divinity) its link to the cross and death of Jesus when dealing with how God redeems and saves us is not developed. The Ascension is hardly mentioned and not explained. Little mention is made of Heaven (or Hell) or the after life, Christ's Second Coming and the resurrection of the dead, the New Heaven and New Earth. As such there is little attention to the future and eschatological aspects (dealing with the final end of things) of faith. Christian hope and endurance are closely linked to these perspectives. In our current era with its marked sense of despair and lack of hope, or at least a somewhat short termist view of reality, this may well be worth attention. On Alpha, there is, rather, an emphasis on what Jesus can do for me here and now in this world, how he meets my needs and helps me live, especially in terms of my personal life and relationships.

Is Alpha Basic Christianity? If so, what sort?

Again, presumptions or deductions of how complete a Christian course Alpha is supposed to be have set off a whole set of criticisms. It claims only to be an introduction – which is fair – but this does beg the question about how comprehensive and full an introduction it is. It is described as dealing in 'Basic Christianity' but what does this concept mean and include and exclude? These questions may not have been difficult for HTB to answer when the course was designed and run just for them and possibly other Anglican churches. However, these questions become a good deal more complex now that the course has been adjusted to make it as accessible and usable as possible by as many denominations and streams as possible. It should also be noted that most renewal movements in the church tend to see themselves as returning to basic aspects at the heart of Christianity. Alpha may simply be seen as falling into this pattern in its self-understanding and talk of basic Biblical Christianity.

Nonetheless, it is now claimed to cover basic material common to all (or most) denominations yet this has been contested from all parts of the Christian spectrum. 'Basic' has many connotations. Here does 'basic' mean 'essential', implying other doctrines are non-essential or less true? Is there an inference that this is the kind of material that must be covered first with new Christians? Does the presentation given to these basic Christian truths skew other ones or make them seem secondary and as such disposable or at least debatable? Is there an underlying theology, or set of doctrines that are inseparable from the course, that favour one form or denomination or broader school or tradition of Christianity over others?

Some think so, usually regarding it as fundamentally, and perhaps exclusively, evangelical-charismatic and, more generally, specifically Protestant. For some, the spread of the course across denominations is an attempt to spread Evangelical-Charismatic Christianity within the church. Yet it has been severely criticised by Evangelicals too, normally those of a more Conservative outlook. This highlights the problems and ambiguities in using such terms as 'evangelical'. Compounding this still further, Catholics use the word 'evangelical' though often principally to refer to explicitly Gospel-centred, and possibly mission-ary, features and attitudes of Christian life. Understood this way, many Catholics would consider Alpha as evangelical, unless they judge that some of its content or the doctrinal presuppositions explicit or implicit in its presentations subvert the true Gospel message.

Alpha is clearly a selection: a look at the omissions ought to convince any Christian of that! Further it was developed by one local church of an Evangelical-Charismatic type within the Church of England. None of this has ever been denied or hidden by AI/HTB. It was not devised for broad church use *a priori*. In reality they have amended its content to broaden it and make it more usable by others. A case could be made that it is no longer dependent on the theology of English Evangelicalism as it has emerged and developed since the 18th Century and indeed of Protestant Theology more generally. It has been considered to be a betrayal of either Evangelicalism or Protestantism or both, and thus far from authentically promoting them. Perhaps a case could even be made for looking to establish a still broader theological base, while keeping features that give it a significant evangelical-charismatic spirituality. Some might wish to say that in doing this they are drawing on the understanding of the Church of England and wider Anglican Communion to be some sort of middle path, the *via media*, between Protestantism and Roman Catholicism. Evangelicals in the Church of England tend to highlight their Protestant credentials though. However, other motivations and concerns might also be involved. (I will take up and develop all these ideas further in Chapter 9.) It is worth noting that AI/HTB have been more concerned to retain the emphasis and quality of the ('charismatic') action of the Holy Spirit than with any particular approach to evangelical identity.

Some Suggested Evaluation Criteria for Deciding whether to Run Alpha

The content of Alpha, especially in the mid to late 1990s attracted a lot of interest. The analysis and discussion in this chapter indicates Alpha's content and these debates are quite complex. So how does a church decide, on the criterion of content, if it should approve of or run Alpha?

I would suggest that a denomination and/or a local church have to ask themselves a version of the following sets of questions.

- Do we accept the truth of *Questions of Life*? Can the selection and formulation, allowing for local adaptation, be fitted into our own overall understanding of Revelation and Christianity? As such can we, in theory, use it as an introduction to the Christian faith?
- Does its use by other Christian groups cause a threat and potential misunderstandings to things we hold essential and as defining of what is church and more fundamentally of what is Christian and genuinely of God? That is, does Alpha cause confusion and misunderstanding (deliberately or accidentally)? Does Alpha give a misleading view of ecumenical co-operation and what is sensible or possible?[23]

Different people will come to different conclusions on these questions. These will help determine whether they will use or avoid Alpha.

However, the issue of content is not the end of the matter. There are then a range of other questions and factors to be considered. These will make more sense in the light of the following two chapters but I will include them here for convenience and completion and as a link to what follows.

- There are questions about Alpha's ethos and style – its spirituality – and if this is compatible with the local church considering running it.
- There are pastoral questions and issues about the method and about integrating it into the life of the local church. This includes considering how much the local church is willing to change to really accommodate Alpha and those people brought to faith or significantly enlivened by it.
- There are evangelistic ones about its appropriateness for those whom the church wants to reach out to, and practical questions about running it and having enough, or any, suitable personnel.
- In more theological terms, does the understanding and scope of mission and evangelism/evangelisation as put forward in Alpha fit with that of the church or group thinking of running it?

Light will hopefully be cast on these in the next two chapters!

Notes

[1] When studying early articles critiquing Alpha on theological grounds, relating to its content, it is important to realise that many of these critiques are based on versions of the text that have now been superseded (partly in response to these issues raised). Depending on print runs and other publishing factors, it can take some time for alterations to get into copies available in bookshops. These delays can be even more exacerbated in foreign language versions. Of course, changes to the text may be too late from HTB's perspective to undo the conclusions people have already come to about the content of the course.

[2] A notable emphasis on and application of legal (forensic) imagery to the ways God deals with humanity, including penal substitution, was developed by Martin Luther (1483–1546) and especially John Calvin (1509–64) who introduced a legal and with it a punitive tone to much of his theology and reform. Many of their followers accented these elements still further. Penal substitution is considered to have been put in a very full version of its modern form by Charles Hodge (1797–1878) in his *Systematic Theology* of 1872–3. Versions of penal substitution still abound with popular versions taught to children and used extensively in short evangelistic presentations in certain Christian circles and traditions. In short, God's wrath is only satisfied by the death of his innocent Son. Some one had to be punished and Jesus accepted this instead of us – i.e. he was a penal substitution for us. This means that God the Father can have a relationship with us again.

A very influential theology of substitution in which Jesus dies to satisfy God's honour had been developed by Anselm of Canterbury (1033–1109) in *Cur Deus Homo?*. Nowadays Anselm is often criticised for being too selective in his use of scriptural images and relying on an appreciation of feudal society for his argument to hold. As such, some point to Anselm's theology as starting the path that led via Calvin to Hodge. Others think this is unfair on Anselm whose theology, though adapted to the culture of his day, also picks up on earlier themes and is close to the mentality of the Biblical writers on many points including his appreciation of the corporate understanding of being human and the centrality of shame and honour in sin and redemption.

In reality, successive thinkers have taken up legal imagery from Scripture and tried to relate it to the legal understanding and judicial systems of their day (sometimes building on the work of previous thinkers) and have probably strayed from the original largely Jewish understanding of law and justice which were linked to covenant and the importance of restoration respectively. This may well have led to a distortion of our picture of God as such and not just of redemption.

The New Testament writers felt the need to use a variety of images to try and express what God had done. The Jewish understanding of covenant and sacrifice is central to this and to any proper understanding of how Jesus represents or substitutes for us on the cross. Increasingly relying on just legal and penal imagery will distort this balance and so will using modern understandings of justice, law, crime and punishment. Anselm may have inadvertently started such a process and it was speeded up by the Protestant Reformers and has been exacerbated since.

Theologians are increasingly calling for all this to be re-appraised and a more balanced theology of atonement articulated. Interestingly, after Anselm and before the Protestant Reformation, a more balanced approach – drawing together a fuller range of Scriptural images and teaching was expressed by Thomas Aquinas (1225–74) in his *Summa Theologiae* Pt III q 46–50 though this has been given little attention by the historians of theology of the atonement. Interestingly, Aquinas also synthesised objective and subjective approaches and indicated links to the life and resurrection of Christ. (See the ongoing argument in the main text of my chapter and footnotes 10–12.)

[3] For instance in 2004 Steve Chalke wrote a book – *The Lost Message of Jesus* – in which he said that penal substitution was tantamount to child abuse. This caused a furore within evangelical circles and the Evangelical Alliance itself. (See Steve Chalke with Alan Mann, *The Lost Message of Jesus*, Zondervan, 2004.) The Evangelical Alliance held various meetings and consultations to discuss the issues raised by Chalke and atonement more generally. Some details of these can be found on their website www.eauk.org under theology. For a commentary on this debate and other perspectives see the Anabaptist Network website, www.anabaptistnetwork.com

[4] Jesus' solidarity with us, and his capacity to represent us before his Father in his death relies for its effectiveness more on an understanding of Jewish understanding of priesthood and sacrifice – linked to covenant. However all this is usually not explained, and often not mentioned, in such talks that reduce everything to penal substitution. Certainly substitution is found in the Bible. So is the idea of representation. The idea of Jesus *representing* us before his Heavenly Father may be worth exploring as a better a central idea of atonement than substitution (even with its penal elements reduced, refined or removed).

[5] It may well be more than a co-incidence that commentators sympathetic to the Toronto Blessing, which had a big impact on HTB, argue that at its core this Blessing is about a re-discovery of the loving heart of God the Father.

[6] For a good introduction to these themes see the collection of essays on the death of Jesus edited by Simon Barrow and Jonathan Bartley, *Consuming Passion (Why the Killing of Jesus Really Matters)*, DLT, 2005. It includes a piece by Steve Chalke reflecting further on some of the material in his book *The Lost Message of Jesus* and the reaction to it. An ongoing concern of many of these contributors is that the death (and indeed life and resurrection of Jesus) are not linked to a practical commitment to justice by his followers. The emphasis has been placed on salvation as largely or entirely private. These points may thus link up with and be

relevant to the perceived concerns about Alpha and its alleged position on social care and the pursuit of justice as evangelistic.

[7] This was first put forward by Peter Abelard (1079–1142) and considered a subjective theory of moral influence and persuasion – by comparison with (penal) substitution.

[8] Broadly, in the history of Christian theology, it is accepted that the atonement is, in part at least, a real mystery, something revealed and accepted in faith and then reflected on, but something that we cannot fully understand or explain in fully rational terms. Our reflection on it ought to be balanced, based on Scripture used in context and reflect the overall range of Scriptural data, while accepting the limits of our intellect. A good theology should aim to do all this and hopefully to connect with the mind-set, cultures and issues of the age for which it is written. The reader can decide how close NG comes to this.

[8A] In classical Theology, this is often referred to as the "admirabile commercium" or the "wonderful exchange". The church fathers, especially the eastern ones, often use the phrase "God became man so that man could become God" to sum up the theme. The term "Divinisation" explores what this means and how it can happen.

[9] Probably the fullest and best-known version of this criticism is found in *Falling Short? The Alpha Course Examined* by Chris Hand (Epsom: Day One Publications, 1998). He also articulates most of the other concerns of Conservative Evangelicals about Alpha.

[10] It seems to me that many of the problems of penal substitution expositions of the atonement – and especially of evangelistic talks based on them – arise precisely since they treat Jesus' death in isolation. It is not related to his life and resurrection; and it is not treated historically. Rather the individual addressed is related to Christ's death with no bearing to Christ's or the individual's social and historic situation. (Often, a convert from such an address tends to see salvation in similar terms.) It then relies almost exclusively on (biblical and other) imagery of law, crime, punishment and even wrath. NG addresses, or at least attempts to address some, but not all, of these problems.

[11] Expressed well, such a presentation can combine the historic and eschatological dimensions as well as address objective and subjective concerns.

[12] Again see *Consuming Passion (Why the Killing of Jesus matters)*, edited by S.Barrow and J. Bartley, DLT, 2005 for a development of some of these ideas. For a good and broad treatment of many of the issues about the theology of the Cross I have raised here see Joel Green and Mark Baker, *Recovering the Scandal of the Cross*. Paternoster Press, 2000.

[13] Many do not give adequate treatment on the need to accept and follow Christ as Lord too. NG's talk certainly stresses Christ as Saviour more than as Lord – though this is addressed elsewhere in the course.

[14] As already noted, doing the course 'Exploring Christianity' is a solution for some. It develops the themes of sin and conversion much more fully than Alpha though within the scope of what could be described as Protestant Reformed Evangelical theology.

[15] NG ascribes the Biblical promises to God the Father, the historical work of Jesus to God the Son and the testimony in experience to God the Holy Spirit. Personally I do not find this attribution of parts of his argument to different specific Persons of the Trinity entirely clear or convincing. There is much more overlap and co-operation between the work of the Divine Persons. For instance, it is the Son who is the Word of God, declaring the promises of God.

[16] This Christian community (the Church), with the Jewish community before and in continuity with it, are in fact recipients of Divine Revelation and are the historic instruments in the production of the Biblical texts. It is they who, through the authority of their leadership, recognised what now constitutes the Bible and

identified it as divinely inspired. (The relationship and ongoing interplay of the Church with the Written Word of God (Bible) and how the latter is interpreted by the former are more denominationally contentious issues, to put it mildly!)

[17] NG notes that it is good to consult other Christians and church leadership in matters of guidance.

[18] For example, while other courses also exist, 'Life in the Spirit Seminars' is a very commonly available course and a few notes comparing them may be helpful. Life in the Spirit is typically run in seven sessions over seven weeks with communal worship followed by a talk with testimonies and then small groups whose purpose is to discuss and pray. Alpha is more fraternal through the inclusion of a meal. It is more flexible or at least less programmatic in that Life in the Spirit expects a commitment to attend all the sessions and quite clear indications are given on what spiritual progress is expected by each point. Also the gift of tongues is insisted on more. Alpha makes fewer assumptions about prior Christian knowledge, faith and commitment i.e. Alpha starts further back on the journey into faith and is more flexible in dealing with its participants. In many ways Life in the Spirit is, I think, aimed at renewing or deepening the faith of people already at church and who can be expected to make a commitment to follow the course from the outset. It has effectively introduced many thousands of such people to a more personal and charismatic faith. Alpha may be more appropriate for those who are more lapsed from faith/dechurched, but have some familiarity with Christianity. Alpha may well take people further forward too by the end of the course, by looking more fully at how to live and to apply graces given by Holy Spirit. Other factors concerning follow up/after care also need to be considered.

(These are generalised and personal comments and there are lots of local variations on how both courses are run. Also, while 'Life in the Spirit' seminars may be the best known course of its type, others have been developed, often starting from this basic model.)

[19] NG is orthodox as opposed to dualist, I think, but he focuses on supernatural evil and as a consequence perhaps does not really draw out the ideas and issues of opposition to the Christian life from the flesh and the world.

[20] There is no mention made of an opinion on women priests. In practice HTB work with churches that hold all positions on this issue and with women priests and ministers. At HTB there are a lot of women active in the church and in positions of responsibility and often with leading pastoral roles. Many are paid and often in full-time church employment with HTB or AI. However (at the time of writing) there are no ordained female staff at HTB.

[21] In a similar way, the Eastern Orthodox refer to the Bible as 'the Audible Icon'.

[22] After reviewing the content of Alpha and critiques of it, Stephen Hunt concludes that it does not really contain anything that has not passed for sometime as mainstream Christianity. See *The Alpha Enterprise*, p. 89.

[23] Some of these issues will be discussed more fully in Chapter 9.

CHAPTER 4

The Principles behind Alpha

Andrew Brookes

Alpha slowly developed into an evangelistic course at HTB. In fact, its evangelistic fruitfulness was *first* empirically discovered and *then* reflected upon. The first major, publicly available, version of these reflections is what is called the 'Principles of the Alpha Course'. They make up the first talk at the Alpha Conference (since 1993) and are published in book form as Chapter 1 of *Telling Others* by Nicky Gumbel (1994). Thus they record the thinking of NG at around that time and they have not really changed significantly since. They attempt to give a reflection on the foundations behind Alpha and to link it to other thinking about evangelism, evangelisation and mission at that time. As far as I know they have not been scrutinised anything like as fully as the content though some of the more general concerns about Alpha fit naturally into a discussion of the principles. I will attempt to do that here, by summarising the principles, reviewing and comment-ing on concerns already recognised, and also adding further notes of concern and thoughts about the extent of the principles' applicability and thus the extent of the usefulness of Alpha itself. Other evangelistic issues and themes connected with missiology will be raised too. This chapter also builds on the spiritual and pastoral profile and values of HTB presented in Chapter 1. Through all this, a fuller understanding of the effectiveness and also the limitations of Alpha should begin to emerge.

NG says that he thinks that the reason for the wide use of Alpha around the world is that 'Alpha is based on six New Testament principles' of evangelism.[1] They are:

1. evangelism is most effective through the local Church;
2. evangelism is a process;
3. evangelism involves the whole person;
4. models of evangelism in the New Testament include classical, holistic and power evangelism;

5. evangelism in the power of the Holy Spirit is both dynamic and effective;
6. effective evangelism requires the filling and refilling of the Holy Spirit.

1. Evangelism is most effective through the local Church

Summary

This means that each local congregation can be effective in evangelism and should engage in it. Also it means that each person in the congregation has talents that can be used, be they hospitality, administration, intercession and cooking as well as the more obvious skills of giving talks or leading small groups. This amounts to creating evangelising communities where mission is a focus for all the church does and to which all are committed. The church as a whole will be most effective at evangelism if all local congregations competently engage in it. During the process of undertaking such an evangelistic course, guests will gain a sense of what the local church is like, one in which they might subsequently get involved. Thus if evangelism is linked to the life and ethos of a local church it makes it more likely that 'converts' will smoothly become active in the local church themselves rather than be 'lost' again. Much evangelism is based on Christians building relationships and forming friendships with non-believers and then being able to invite them to 'come and see'. A good local church and one with competent evangelistic practices is essential if this friendship, and invitational, evangelism is to be confidently and competently undertaken by parishioners.

Comments and Critique

The importance of the local church (and not just special crusades and guest speakers etc) in evangelism, was being flagged up in a number of ways around the time Alpha was publicly launched. This principle is key to Alpha, which was developed by a local church – HTB – as a means of evangelism. The 'local church' lies at the heart of the vision of Alpha and is generally the focus of the work of Alpha International. It is difficult to disagree that all local congregations should engage in evangelism. It is healthy to see it as an activity that should be integrated with the overall life of the church and one that all parishioners should to varying degrees feel involved with and responsible for. HTB does have great skill in drawing many individuals into evangelistic work, whatever their gifts and temperament.

But an important question is does it work in *any* local church? How effectively can a course designed by and suited to one congregation in one denomination in one country with its own culture and religious/secular setting be transferred to and really bed down in others?

Certainly many have tried it. There are good examples across the denominations of it bedding down and helping the community in the long term and not just the short term. But there are also many stories of it being tried and quickly dropped, or petering out, or causing actual problems – and sometimes serious divisions. Sometimes it has been run by a minority group in the parish and has sat just on the fringe of parish life; it may have been allowed to survive because of this arrangement but will probably not have really grown.

The spread of Alpha has encouraged some local churches to become more evangelistic. However, in the context of mission it is worth noting the strength and the limitation of this. It is important for local churches to have an eye for and make a priority of evangelism, to become more hospitable and welcoming and to reach out and say 'Come and See!' Alpha can do this effectively if it is owned by the local church. However, saying 'Come and See!' means that fundamentally we are inviting others to come and see us on our terms as we are and how we do things. This will be effective for some people – probably mainly those already at home with, or at least able to make a bridge between, where they are at in terms of life style and even attitudes and where those in the specific local church are at.

Mission also more radically involves a call to 'Go and Tell' or put more fully 'Go to others, live and be among them and witness there'. This type of mission is becoming increasingly necessary in Britain as the country and its people and culture drift further from its Christian roots. Alpha was not really designed for this aspect of mission though helpfully AI/HTB do advocate running Alpha in 'secular' (non-church) settings. Nonetheless, other strategies are needed alongside that of existing churches more effectively opening their doors. A focus on Alpha, and other process courses, should not distract Christians from these wider challenges.

In short, Alpha has helped some local churches more effectively engage in evangelism. But it is not effective for all local churches and there are other aspects of mission that Christians and local churches need to address.

2. Evangelism is a process
Summary

AI/HTB consider it vital to see a person's entry into Christian faith as a journey or process. That is why they run the course over 10 weeks rather than just doing evangelism as single events. While they acknowledge that 'Damascus Road style' conversions do occur they stress that even these are part of a longer process or journey. Birth –and, by analogy, spiritual rebirth – is preceded by a long pregnancy and followed by even longer after-care. In part the duration of the course is now intended to give time for certain factors, helpful and possibly essential to conversion, to grow. Week by week, an overall picture of Christian truth, its accompanying worldview ('meta-narrative') and what it is practically like to be and live as a Christian are built up. Time also allows a sense of belonging to develop as well for friendship and a sense of trust to form. If the person commits to Christianity before or early in the course, an actual sense of practical participation in the community can also begin. All of these allow the person to gradually open up spiritually before others, themselves and hopefully God.

Comments and Critique

At conferences AI/HTB usually acknowledge that this principle is an insight for which they are grateful to Roman Catholicism and say that for this reason they prefer to use the term 'evangelisation' rather than 'evangelism' concerning Alpha since the former implies a process.[2] It is certainly true that Catholics have long since seen the spiritual life as a journey or process and would even talk about on-going conversion, though there is an understanding that decisive moments of conversion and experiential breakthroughs happen too.[3] The Protestant world also has thinkers who by this time had been arguing for seeing conversion as a journey.[4]

This insight, that conversion takes time and that it is important to make provision for a structured process and time frame, has contributed much to the fruitfulness of Alpha. In fact, it is a principle that has been taken up by many other courses in evangelism/evangelisation too, many developed since Alpha and selectively drawing from it the insights and features the designers find attractive, while leaving out or modifying other aspects.[5] It is thus a principle that is broadly and increasingly accepted nowadays

However, the question has to be asked if 10 weeks is generally an appropriate period to allow someone to make a journey into faith. More and more people in Britain are less and less familiar with church life and the practice of the Christian faith and increasingly less familiar too with the general truths or claims of Christianity.[6] Basic ideas on the historic existence of Jesus, why the Bible consists of an Old and New Testament cannot be assumed even among relatively well educated people of the younger generations. These phenomena are all part of what is generally referred to as secularisation and, for some, what is now referred to as a 'Post-Christian' society. Some say this now means we have entered, or are entering, a Post-Christendom era.[7] It is said that one major reason evangelistic crusades, like those led by Billy Graham were so successful was that there was a still a strong connection with Christianity among those not at church; in fact many were only one good sermon away from conversion or re-conversion.

Nowadays, many more people are not just dechurched but completely nonchurched, not just 'lapsed' from Christian and church practice but not ever really converted or part of the flock in the first place. For such people, is a 10 weeks course time enough to overcome their fears and suspicions and foster an adequate sense of belonging to bring them into meaningful Christian faith and practice? Much may depend on how much work has been done beforehand and how much Christian/church contact they already have. Finney's research at the beginning of the 1990s indicated that the average time for a gradual conversion was four years.[8] The early church took two – three years to form people, where people had no significant knowledge of Christianity.

NG acknowledges that people don't even listen – that is begin to take in – the content of the talks until they are relaxed and have a basic trust and this typically takes three to four weeks. By this time the course has already presented all the material on who is Jesus, why he died and what is the nature of faith! Though some will think that this does not really matter very much, it certainly raises concerns for those who wish to use Alpha as a basic, or even quite full, teaching course systematically presenting Christian doctrine. It is also a concern to those who use Alpha evangelistically, with many having concerns that the course does not make adequate provision to deal with this basic material and the steps involved in bringing people to 'real' conversion.[9] If Alpha is used evangelistically, measures may well be needed to ensure that this content be adequately recapped for those who later make conversions at subsequent points on the course.

The insight about conversion and faith as a journey has been important and helpful to Alpha but needs to be applied still more thoroughly if we are to keep finding effective supports to bring contemporary people into faith and into participation in church life and mission. For a variety of reasons, and for an increasing number of people in Britain, it is simply not enough time. For those who wish to persist with Alpha, there already is a pressing need – and one that I feel will increase – to look at what a church does 'Pre-Alpha' to facilitate people's early journey towards Christian faith. This could take many forms, some more structured than others, some about method and relationship, others about belonging, others about listening, discussing, sharing but with a content more adapted to the really nonchurched and more consciously starting from their agenda – not that of the churches. Participation in social care projects might help some. There is already evidence of this being looked at by some Alpha course leaders and others in mission. (I will look at issues of where people start, and how much time they need to journey, in more detail in Chapters 7 and 8.)

3. Evangelism involves the whole person

Summary

Alpha claims to make an appeal to head, heart, conscience and will. It looks at people holistically and integrates these appeals.

Comments and Critique

It is fair to say that Apha attempts all four – and this is a strength for many.[10] However, it has been criticised from various and different quarters for how well it does each of them and in what relative proportions, and as a consequence it has also been argued that it does not do any of them well. I will comment on each in turn.

There is some intellectual content, though this includes testimony, illustration and application as well as doctrine and biblical citation/explanation. NG himself advises people to construct talks using a point, then illustration, then application (and then next point etc) structure.[11] Opinions of the videos vary. Many view NG's summaries of Christian teaching and practice as clear and helpful. Others feel he assumes too much background Christian knowledge and sheer intelligence in his audience (or at least audiences other than those like the largely middle class graduate one at HTB) as well as expecting a long concentration span, if a 45 minutes video or talk is to be presented. Some find his treatment of topics simplistic. Still others, and these are not likely to run the course at all, feel the content is substantially experiential and practical and just hung around traditional Christian themes with the Bible merely used to provide proof texts. Some feel that this is OK if the course is a practical introduction to Christian life while others are unhappy about what the underlying theological implications and suppositions of this are. Opinions vary enormously on how well NG's clean cut image and public school accent, and the talk illustrations that accompany this particular background, go down in different social settings. All of these concerns and critiques have to be set against the purpose and intended audience for the course, and also the fact that people are free to give live talks of shorter length, adapted with illustrations to suit the specific audience and social setting. They still have to follow the 'doctrinal' content in roughly the same number of weeks! However, there is scarcely time to fill out the doctrine more fully within the scope of the course, and arguably not within its ethos, or copyright criteria, either.

There is certainly an appeal to the heart, both its deeper longings and perhaps also emotional needs and issues nearer to the surface of the human psyche. This comes through the practical nature of the content and the use of testimony, as well as the opportunity in small groups to share and discuss how they *feel* about the talk, the course in general and their own spiritual search. Some critics state that there is too much attention to emotion, and that prayer time focuses on such issues and can even be suggestive and 'leading'.

At various points the course asks for conversion and makes it clear this involves moral conversion; some elements are spelt out, others just alluded to or omitted, though guests can bring them up if they wish. It is expected that much will be learned from the example of those on the course. It seems to me that HTB applies the pastoral principle common to many churches, that, once converted and 'in Christ' and aware of God's love for them, many moral issues can be dealt with later and progressively as a person gets established and grows in their faith. While a potential convert needs to be aware of their own responsibility for sin and therefore need for forgiveness, it is felt not right to deter them from approaching and accepting God's mercy until they have dealt with *all* moral issues in their lives. They feel God will make them aware of sins when they need to be and when they can realistically be dealt with, and not before. My understanding is that HTB while not attempting to catalogue all possible sins, would not deny something was a sin, as they understand it, if directly asked by a guest etc, and would advise those running the course to do the same. They would argue that Jesus came in compassion to save us and not condemn us. It is fear and doubt about being forgiven and accepted by God and the church that can keep people away as much as, if not more than, a refusal to see certain things as morally wrong and sinful. Some time is given to explaining that people should pay attention to their conscience and recognise the need to be instructed in how to do this. Some critics hold that more instruction should be given on these matters and on certain aspects of sin, especially in a culture as morally relativistic and permissive as ours. In short, some see Alpha as being soft on sin and over optimistic about an individual's ability to tell what is sinful.

Conversion is seen in principally in terms of coming into a relationship with Jesus Christ and thus God the Father. This is achieved through the action of the Holy Spirit who comes to dwell within a person. The stress is on faith as relationship with God and as personal and intimate, 'interior'. It is about trust. People have to be individually sorry for their sins, grateful that Jesus died for them, and want to have God, through his Spirit, at the centre of their lives. This is expressed in NG's version of the Sinner's prayer that he structures around the words 'Sorry...Thank you...Please'. 'Converts' are advised to begin a life of discipleship (prayer, bible reading etc) and to join a lively church. That faith involves others and church is covered to an extent, but in ways that build on and follow from a personal faith and relationship with Jesus, which is central and even crucial.

The course stresses the need not to pressurise people into making commitments they are not ready for. Persuasion in the form of discussion or 'argument' should fall short of being rude to or offending guests. Guests are encouraged to give their opinions and these are to be respected. People are not asked to make public commitments or to come forward etc; they are only asked to make a silent 'Amen' in their heart to a prayer read out from the front if they feel it is right to do so. They are then advised to make this known to a team member they trust since this will help in providing appropriate pastoral follow-up. Such prayers can be offered at any stage of the course when the leaders/speakers judge it may be appropriate. At least, this is the HTB model. It is not clear how other churches apply or express this. This approach has led some critics to accuse Alpha of not preparing people adequately to make an informed commitment. For others it shows gentleness, and respects guests and a sense of their privacy, and their needs for personal space and time.

While the appeal is holistic, its focus is mainly on the individual, with little attention to a still more holistic approach to being human, that embraces relationships and wider communal, social, global and ecological responsibilities and aspects of being human. All of these need transforming by the Gospel and are valid 'targets' for evangelisation. To be human and Christian is not to be isolated or locked within the physical frame we call our body.

4. Models of evangelism include classical, holistic and power evangelism[12]

Summary

This principle outlines NG's and AI's vision of the overall scope of evangelism. It is claimed to involve classical evangelism, i.e. proclamation of the core Gospel message in words; holistic evangelism, which NG takes to mean social care and transformation; and power evangelism, used to describe evangelism reliant on or closely linked explicitly to the charismatic gifts of the Holy Spirit. This principle is sometimes paraphrased as evangelism through 'words, works and wonders'. All three are claimed to be part of the Alpha course.

Comments and Critique

It is fair to say that all three are advocated on Alpha but is it fair to say that all three are intrinsic to the course or presupposed as principles behind it? The extent to which each is stressed has been the source of debate and criticism. Some claim no or little emphasis is given to the social responsibilities of Christians, this often being linked to claims that the course is individualistic and inward-looking in focus. Others argue that far too much attention is given to power evangelism at the expense of the other forms, some questioning the validity and authenticity of this at all. Again, these specific claims raise more general questions about the relative balance of the three models/forms on the course, and the balance and indeed priority and inter-relationship these ought to have in more general Christian and church life and mission. Specific questions are also asked about the actual way each 'model' is used on Alpha. I will now reflect on these issues more deeply.

Words

'Classical' evangelism – the term itself indicates a certain tradition in churchmanship and theology with a stress of the proclamation of God's Word – is given through the talks, done live or by video. How central and crucial God's Word is to the talks has been disputed with some asking if Alpha amounts to a real proclamation of God's Word? The course certainly has a good deal of Biblical material and the Bible is taken, indeed more or less presumed, to be an authoritative text from the outset. The main developed argument given to support this is the large number of nearly identical New Testament texts produced relatively quickly in the early centuries of the Church. Some other comments on Biblical inspiration are given in the talk on reading the Bible in Week 4. It is fair to say that the talks are not long expositions on specific scriptural passages; but then, they are not part of a course in biblical or dogmatic theology but an attempt to reach non-Christians or new believers. It should also be remembered that Scripture has a power to affect and influence people that goes beyond the exact use to which it is put or the genre in which it is located.

It is worth pausing to ask what sort of talks they are. Are they mainly an announcement of the core Gospel kerygma? Many Christians, and especially 'Evangelicals', would summarise this along these following lines. Namely, God made us for him, we sinned, Jesus was sent by God and died for our sins, and we are now called to repent, believe and be baptised so that we can have a relationship with God and others through the Holy Spirit. These are often called the four spiritual laws. Well, these points are covered: this is the essence of Talk 2 'Why did Jesus die?' though it does not discuss baptism. However, the course goes much beyond this.

Is it mainly apologetic,[13] dealing through the use of reason with objections to the Christian faith and thus paving a way for a person to hear and respond positively to the kerygma? Well, not very much actually. Some of the evidence for Jesus is covered in Talk 1 'Who is Jesus?' Other bits of supporting argumentation are included here and there but it is hardly comprehensive or robust.

Others see the course as offering basic teaching to get new Christians established in the practice of their faith. Most of the content fits this model or hypothesis. As such it attracts criticism for what it includes and more especially excludes as introductory. Most or all of the material from Week 4 onwards can be considered as a discipleship course, or a course in catechesis, both of which presume faith in the recipients, preceded by a review of an understanding of what underlies faith in Weeks 1–3. Again this reflects well the course content and the actual history of the course at HTB.

If this is so, can the entire course be called evangelistic as such and if so how? NG claims the entire course is evangelistic and that people come to faith at points right through it. As such the course addresses the unconverted each week from the standpoint 'If you were to become a Christian, this is how it would work ...'. More specifically, 'This is how you would read the bible', 'This is how you would pray', 'This is how you could receive guidance', etc.'[14] Guests can then test what is proposed in the talk against what they see around them and in the lives of team members. Recognising there are many mixed populations with many dechurched people in traditionally Christian countries and cultures and, familiar in a superficial way with Christian truths and life, but not wholeheartedly converted or believing, the *General Directory on Catechesis* talks of a need to develop forms of 'kerygmatic catechesis'.[15] This has much to commend it as a good description of Alpha.

Many academics and others maintain that we are in the transition from a modern culture with its emphasis on reason and truth and proof to a new one, currently referred to commonly as a post-modern period which has more emphasis on practicality and affectivity and relativism.[16] Viewed this way, the course addresses and speaks to the post-modern mindset which is more pre-occupied with the question 'Does it work?' rather than the modern mindset question 'Is it true?' So what appears to have been designed as discipleship teaching for a modern generation can become, with a few alterations, more explanation and practical illustrations, an evangelistic presentation for at least some people in a post-modern generation. In some respects the course straddles the modern and post-modern cultures.[17] Whether this means it meets the needs of both or falls between stools or will soon be outdated even as a transitional course is, again, subject to question. Most Christians would agree that the selection of material for proclamation and the style of presentation must suit the age, mindset and culture to which it is addressed – though the content of Revelation does not change as such. Does this make Alpha a clever evangelistic proclamation or is it a course that is unsure of who it is really trying to reach? Is it one that has managed to keep adapting as its audience and their culture has kept changing? If so, for how long can it be expected to manage this, especially given the constraints now imposed upon itself by its own copyright? An assessment of these questions has to consider not just the modern to post-modern shift but the shift from a Christian culture with a churched population to a 'Post-Christendom culture' with a totally nonchurched, not just dechurched, population.[18]

Works

By works NG says he recognises that Christians have social responsibilities for the world. This is certainly mentioned in Alpha – and the references have been increased partly in the light of criticisms. The references are to people with excellent records of social care as much if not more than those involved in political campaigning and protests, and NG is careful to select people who to current audiences are of broad appeal and relatively non-controversial. They are always individuals noted also for a clear and personal relationship with Jesus. He sees the evangelistic potential and connection of such work but does not reflect on or clarify the relation of such care and action to the work of bringing people to personal conversion.[19] Is it just a means to a more important end or something of absolute or intrinsic value in itself?

Suspicions remain in some Christian circles that Alpha and HTB do not place great store on such social and political action – at least when compared to bringing people to knowing Jesus personally.[20] It may be worthwhile exploring what may lie behind this. It is true that while Alpha to an extent does mention such caring work it does not model it during the course, or expose guests to it, something it does do with 'word' and 'wonders' evangelism. It is also true that the immediate focus and aim of the course is to bring people to a personal relationship with Jesus and as part of that to introduce them into some aspects of church life. There is a primary focus of trying to invite friends onto the next course, along with a concern to identify and keep good guests as leaders and helpers of subsequent Alpha courses, and all this can, perhaps unfairly, infer such 'evangelism' has a priority over social care work. HTB does engage and encourage social care for its congregation and I think this is something that has grown in recent years.[21] That is not to say that all other churches running Alpha do the same or that it is the main reason why guests come to Alpha at HTB or elsewhere. Social care work invites or inclines people to go outside their social grouping (especially if they are middle or upper class) whereas friendship evangelism, like Alpha, typically means people invite friends of their own social/work background.

The interaction between social and political work and kerygmatic proclamation is multi-faceted and complex. Indeed, it is part of a bigger debate about how different components of what can broadly be called mission are prioritised, integrated and implemented. Although NG espouses the value of such work and would link it to evangelisation the lack of more developed thought leaves lots of questions and room, perhaps unfairly, for criticisms.[22] Mission is approached differently by various Christians and groups, and indeed whole schools of theology, spirituality and praxis. As such this concern about Alpha touches on wider tensions and issues within the Christian family. Probably diversity and debate about these broader factors helps explain why such criticisms of Alpha persist and why some Christians are suspicious about the style of Christianity and Christian worldview and engagement with the world that Alpha promotes.

Debate about Alpha's promotion of works has tended to focus on social care. It is worth briefly considering a wider characterisation of what Christian Mission is viewed as entailing and seeing how Alpha matches up. The Lambeth Conference of the Church of England in 1988 produced 'Five Marks of Mission'. These, or close variations of them, have been adopted by many denominations. They are: (1) Proclaiming the Good News of the Kingdom; (2) Teaching, baptising and nurturing new believers; (3) Responding to human need by loving service; (4) Seeking to transform unjust structures of society; (5) Safeguarding the integrity of creation and sustaining and renewing the life of the earth. Rather than just discuss to what extent Alpha promotes social care it may be more fruitful to consider it within this wider framework. Alpha could be considered to be good at Marks 1 and 2 and to encourage 3 to an extent. There is less evidence of it actively promoting Mark 4, though AI/HTB did recently support 'Make Poverty History' though not really as pace-setters, and less evidence still about Mark 5 (that I am aware of).

Wonders

This and indeed the remaining two principles are concerned with clear and supernatural action by God. They are identified in the Alpha/HTB literature and elsewhere with the person and action of the Holy Spirit. In short, it is argued that it is crucial that a demonstration of the Spirit's power (i.e. wonders) goes hand in hand with the verbal proclamation (words) of the Gospel. It is argued that this was the pattern of the ministry of Jesus and of the Apostles after him.[23] The training material indicates that word and wonder go together to make evangelism dynamic and effective.

Their main source for this is John Wimber, especially as taught in his various courses and conferences and as summarised in his book *Power Evangelism* and evidenced in his ministry, which HTB frequently acknowledges. In essence, power evangelism means that God continues to act now as he did in the New Testament period as recorded in Scripture. This includes healings, exorcisms and deliverance, as well as preaching, forming holiness and bringing believers into conformity with Christ crucified (i.e. by persecution). All this is possible through the power of the Holy Spirit and his action and gifts (including the charismatic gifts as listed in 1 Cor 12:8–10 etc.) These are available to all believers. Through all this, the Kingdom of God is a present reality now and not just a future expectation. It is such signs and action of the Holy Spirit that made evangelism effective then, and caused the church to grow and will do so now, it is claimed. On Alpha this is highlighted in the emphasis given to the Holy Spirit: topics, that could be treated differently, refer to the Holy Spirit as their major focus – and what could be called a weekend or day retreat is called the 'Holy Spirit weekend'.

The role of the Holy Spirit in evangelism is developed further in Principles 5 and 6. Yet in essence all this forms part of one argument and principle which I will summarise as follows. 'The power of God/supernatural wonders are part of God's strategy to establish his Kingdom. It is these that have made and make evangelism effective. This happens through the Holy Spirit who is also available to us in an ongoing way now if we ask the Spirit to keep filling us.' I think it is fair to say that the last two principles are devoted to drawing this point out!

Critics, commentators and others have wondered why NG/HTB have decided they need two and a third principles to cover this ground and suggest it indicates a clear bias or preference for 'Power evangelism' over the other two forms. It is argued that this is evidence Alpha has a clear preference for 'Charismatic Christianity'. Others have gone further and suggested or claimed that the stress on the Holy Spirit, accompanied by a lack of specific treatment on the Trinity within the course, misrepresents, and even misunderstands, the Christian understanding of God, as a unity of Father, Son and Holy Spirit. The standard reply from NG/AI on this point states that they say that they value all three forms of evangelism, thus defending Principle 4. However, they state that there is broad consent and little controversy in Christian circles about words and works, but, since there is much more debate and even misunderstanding of wonders and the role of the Holy Spirit, they feel this needs to be given more attention.[24] They affirm that the understanding of God that underlies the whole course is an orthodox Trinitarian one. The role ascribed to the Holy Spirit within Alpha, and the extent to which the whole course is Charismatic or more broadly pneumatological, are some of the most contentious issues that have accompanied Alpha's use.[25]

5. Evangelism in the power of the Holy Spirit is both dynamic and effective

Summary

Continuing from Principle 4, NG argues from the Scriptural record (almost entirely from the Acts of the Apostles) that such power evangelism, now explicitly ascribed to the Holy Spirit, is crucial to and indeed an essential cause of effective evangelism and church growth.[26] Though hardly stated at all, it is also vital to NG's argument that God has not ceased to act in this way, but that he acts in this way in the contemporary period too.[27]

Comments and Critiques (of both Principles 5 and 6)

Please see notes under wonders (Principle 4 above, p. 75) and in the section below on Holy Spirit.

6. Effective evangelism requires the filling and refilling of the Holy Spirit

Summary

The point and aim here is to stress that participants have to go beyond theology and theory and actually be open to 'being filled with the Holy Spirit'. This section consists entirely of accounts from the lives of a variety of Christians over the ages who are noted for evangelistic work. It narrates clear and relatively dramatic experiential conversions or accounts of a deepening experience of God that made their evangelistic work more fruitful, all of which are ascribed specifically by NG to the Holy Spirit. Being filled with the Holy Spirit is an ongoing reality, according to NG and being open to being filled with the Spirit is vital to the success of Alpha too:

> 'One of the keys to Alpha is having a team of Spirit-filled people using every gift they possess to lead others to Christ. Those who come to Christ on the course know that a radical change has occurred in their lives because they have been filled with the Holy Spirit. This experience of God gives them the stimulus and power to invite their friends to the next Alpha.'[28]

At conferences, this point ends the talk on Alpha Principles and runs immediately into a time of prayer ministry and a chance for people to be prayed with/be filled with the Spirit again or even for the first time.

The Holy Spirit and Ministry on Alpha

This is as good a place as any to provide some information on HTB's general ideas on how the action and power of the Holy Spirit is part of their church life and in particular how this is expressed in prayer ministry in general and specifically on Alpha.

In HTB's view, such an interaction as this with the Holy Spirit is a normal, and ongoing, part of Christian life. Indeed, they teach and apply the general position of most denominations that the Holy Spirit is active and responsible for bringing us to personal holiness including conversion, to gathering us into the unity of a holy people, and to accomplish, often through human agency, the work of mission. Specific gifts and ministries are given to fulfil these roles, though, in some respects, debate around certain gifts of the Spirit and religious experience distracts people from these more fundamental points.

However, on Alpha they are careful to avoid the use of specific theological terms or explanations, such as 'baptism in the Spirit' or a 'second anointing' etc, that tend to interpret it as a specific and essential part of becoming a Christian. They prefer the much less contentious, more general and denominationally more inclusive phrase 'filled with the Holy Spirit' and most frequently cite Eph 5:18, stressing the Greek 'present continuous' tense, and thus translating it: 'Go on being filled with the Holy Spirit!'

The experiences associated with these different terminologies have much in common, based on the evidence of peoples' various testimonies. Perhaps the appeal to be filled with the Holy Spirit even becomes synonymous with, or very similar to, simply encouraging someone to enter fully into the life of grace. Neither do AI/HTB see the reception and demonstration of certain gifts of the Spirit as essential to prove that a person has become a Christian in the first place, or that this proves a person has been filled with the Spirit. (Often, in Charismatic or Pentecostal circles, speaking in tongues or sometimes prophecy, is seen as essential evidence of this.) However, Alpha does teach on tongues and encourage the use of this and other charismatic gifts of the Holy Spirit. Receiving/using the gift of tongues is often seen, in practical terms, as the gateway to receiving other gifts. It involves stepping out in a certain form of faith.

Being filled and refilled with the Spirit is viewed as being about experiencing God's love for you personally and intimately. This could bring a person to conversion in the first place. God's Holy Spirit is seen, in HTB's and charismatic theology generally, as the agent for bringing this about. It can happen in a variety of ways and settings, a common one used on the course and at training and conferences being during 'ministry time' when the leader asks the Holy Spirit to come and touch all present and people wait openly and responsively for whatever happens. Discernment or various words or prophecies or guidance may be publicly given to help people understand, open up and respond more fully to what appears to be happening. Another opportunity is individual prayer ministry where an individual is prayed with by one or two trained church members, and during which they typically open up and share specific details or situations in their lives. Often the two are combined, corporate ministry time being followed by individual prayer ministry for those wishing it. The training conferences give several opportunities for this. On the Alpha course the day or weekend away have such opportunities, and others may come later in the course, especially after the talk on healing. Others can be informally added.

During the Alpha Course, HTB are careful to preface such ministry time with clear teaching on the Christian understanding that underpins it. This is to try and ensure that it is grounded and founded in faith and in responsiveness and openness to God rather than emotion and self-suggestion/introspection. In reality, there is always a risk of the latter at this time and, indeed, throughout any Christian life, however mature, and care needs to be taken to help people to grow in discernment in relation to both self-knowledge and the things and ways of God. HTB try to avoid fostering emotional intensity and discourage the team, or others present, from being eccentric in any way. People are exhorted to be 'supernaturally natural and naturally supernatural'.[29] They stress both the person's freedom to be open when, and to the extent to which, they feel ready. They also stress God's respect for this and their decisions and assent to his action in their lives. God, it is pointed out, is truly good and would not do anything to harm anyone. Confidentiality is stressed too. Some might think that this reduces it all to a human technique. God is often able to act best and most effectively and clearly supernaturally when humans are just natural, open and themselves; more natural but no less supernatural for that! Indeed it can thus be more supernatural. They point out that God's action need not be dramatic though it might be; it, or its effects, might well be felt but might not be felt at all since it is fundamentally of faith. God's gifts are received in faith and exercised in obedience – with gratitude.

All of this advice and practice shows wisdom in the ways of God and of people. I have had enough contact with HTB to know they apply these insights to a high and consistent level themselves. That does not mean that all other churches running Alpha do![30] The amount of time and emphasis that HTB devote to these matters in training conferences suggests that they too are aware of this as a problem. It can arise from churches that are sceptical or simply uninformed about such 'Holy Spirit Ministry', and also from ones that are over zealous or intense or otherwise immature in attempting it.

So how charismatic are Alpha and HTB?

Should Alpha and HTB be labelled as charismatic? They prefer not to be. I think this is on grounds that such a label suggests a form of church life that is specialist and distinct from what is considered normal by most. Being labelled charismatic might also mean being considered odd or having a superior or exclusive attitude. These associations may not be fair but I suspect HTB accept the real power in them.

For many people, a specific focus on the gifts of the Holy Spirit listed in 1 Cor 12: 8–10 lies at the heart of a definition of Charismatic Christianity and makes it distinct. Yet HTB would argue that these gifts of the Holy Spirit should be a normal part of all church life. As such, HTB considers it is normal – not distinct or unusual – to be open to them and to have forms of worship and ministry that use them. They do not make all of this obligatory for being a Christian, and consciously put these gifts and ministries at the service of others and mission. Thus they are not ends in themselves. All this is done whilst cultivating cultural and emotional/psychological normality too – or at least avoiding obvious eccentricity, as they perceive it, and fostering a community marked by love and aspiring to holiness. For all these reasons HTB does not want its way of living, moving and ministering in the Holy Spirit to be seen as making them distinct from the aspirations of 'most Christian churches'.[31] They just see it as normal Christianity though one that is animated by these particular ways in which the Holy Spirit works.

HTB wants these ways and gifts to be available and effective in the lives of more individuals and churches. Yet HTB feels that this only too often does not happen. So they end up having two and a third principles to flag it up, as well as flagging up the role of the Holy Spirit on the course itself. This indicates just how hard many other churches still find this! Effective pastoral approaches have to consider theological and human factors and it may be that HTB have genuine insights in these Holy Spirit matters that can benefit other sectors of the church. Some claim that one of the main impacts of Alpha is spreading 'Charismatic Christianity' even if it is usually accepted that their version is less dramatic and distinct than some versions. Some see this as a dilution and compromise of the original vigour and even Divine impulse behind the Pentecostal and Charismatic Movements. Others would see it as very worthwhile and a plus, since it means this type of action of the Holy Spirit moves into more of Christianity, has more impact and is seen increasingly as normal.

AI/HTB clearly know the advantages in promotional and pastoral terms of being regarded as 'normal' meaning 'not odd', though they do not want 'normal' to imply 'bland'. What is normal can be assessed on theological grounds, criteria of human health, psychology and behaviour, or on statistical grounds of frequency. The word normal is thus ambiguous and so are assessments of Alpha and HTB regarding its approach to the Holy Spirit and 'charismatic status'. HTB's approach to the Holy Spirit is more humanly attuned and theologically open and flexible than many approaches. Alpha has spread this further afield. Whether HTB and Alpha's approach should be seen as the yardstick for 'normal' is something about which debate will continue – not least since having 'normal' status means so much!

Closing Remarks

The articulated principles behind Alpha are broad ones. They give some indications of the interfaces between the understanding of Alpha developed at HTB by 1992 and more general Christian thinking on evangelisation. Though there is a clear emphasis on the Holy Spirit these principles do combine insights drawn from across a wide spectrum of

Christian thought, and are much broader than a 'Protestant Evangelical' stereotype. This range perhaps helps explain the wide interest and respect for Alpha from across much of the Christian family.

Given the long and changing history of Alpha at HTB, it would be interesting to know at what stage these six principles were consciously recognised as important and were used to inform their pastoral planning. They do show how NG attempted to think through and explain how a local discipleship course was being fruitful evangelistically – as appeared to be happening locally at HTB. While these principles can genuinely be applied to Alpha, it does not follow that Alpha fulfils them as completely as some might like to think. For example, local churches should evangelise but Alpha, though designed for local church use, may not suit many of them. Also, parts of these perhaps express the vision and scope of the wider work of AI/HTB rather than the specific impact of Alpha. For example, this may be true of the value ascribed to social care and the promotion of justice. AI/HTB also need to be assiduous in making sure that Alpha continues to fulfil these principles adequately as culture changes, and mission challenges change with it. This is very relevant, for example, when seeing coming to faith as a journey. Realism is needed in using these as criteria to discern whether to run Alpha in other churches/settings. It is not true that just because another church affirms these principles that it will find Alpha effective if used. Other factors come into play. Having noted some restrictions, it is important to note that all these principles have broader applications to evangelisation more generally. For instance, some or all of them can be, and have been, used to generate other process courses.

Whenever and why they were developed, they do inform the course, but other factors – not specified in presentations of these six Principles – also do and are important to a proper understanding of Alpha. In many ways I feel quite a big mental jump is required in moving from the presentation of these very broad principles, to the very practical presentations that follow this, in both *Telling Others* and at Alpha Conferences. This gap could perhaps be bridged with inclusion of more of these specific explanations/reflections on Alpha's method. I shall try and contribute to this by developing some thoughts on the method of Alpha in Chapter 5 and some more general considerations in Chapter 6. These may contribute to a still more informed, less robotic, use of Alpha than sometimes appears to happen.

Notes

[1] *Telling Others*, p. 22.

[2] In fact Catholic Church teaching considers it a process within a bigger process/multi-faceted reality. My own summary/definition is as follows. 'Evangelisation announces the Kingdom of God and makes it a reality in our midst. It brings the presence of Jesus into every human situation and life, aiming at the

conversion and formation of individuals, the building up of Christian communities that in turn can evangelise, and the permeation and transformation of societies and cultures with gospel values – making all creation new.' This all happens in a still bigger perspective. All these evangelistic activities are instruments of, and a participation in, the mission of God which is the source, inspiration, heart and motor of all evangelisation. In this divine mission the Father sends the Son and the Spirit out into the world to save it and fulfil all God's plans for it and its peoples.

It is understood that this is a process involving many complementary steps. These include witness of life, listening, dialogue, proclamation, basic conversion, teaching (catechesis), sacramental initiation and life, promotion of social justice and peace, inculturation. It all has to be undergirded by prayer. It is principally a work of God – through the Holy Spirit – but one in which all Christians (whatever their specific vocation) are called to have a co-operative role. Thus Catholic and Alpha terminology would perhaps be more fully correlated thus: Evangelisation (R.C.) = evangelism + social transformation. This wider understanding is also similar to what some other Christian groups now call 'whole body ministry' and is consonant with the attempts of Mark Greene and others at the London Institute of Contemporary Christianity (LICC) to look seriously at how Christians impact the world of work and more generally overcome the sacred-secular divide.

To return to the journey of each individual it would be as well to add the following clarification of the Catholic position. After initial conversion, faith is a process or journey of deepening growth in God, involving ongoing conversion and it is part of what God wants and needs to achieve in us. This journey is always a life of faith, and dependent on grace; though it is one that needs humility and our ongoing assent of will.

[3] The 'Rite for Christian Initiation of Adults (RCIA) is the official process and liturgical rites accompanying it, re-instated in 1972, and based on the practice of the church in the earliest centuries for adults wishing to journey into Christian faith and full participation in the life of the Catholic Church. It has similarities with Alpha's approach and principles. Phase 1 insists a person comes to basic conversion to Christ as their Lord and begins a life of prayer and discipleship and becomes familiar and connected with the Christian community. Some have used Alpha to help deliver this phase.

Sandy Millar has commented on the problems he faced as a younger Christian helping at mission events when people were presented with the gospel in such a way that they were required to opt in then and there, or often made to feel they had rejected the Gospel forever. He felt that some may have been interested but simply not ready at that point to make a substantial commitment. He sees this as associated with certain styles, and theological understandings, of evangelism; and he thus came to prefer the journey approach and Catholic terminology.

Interestingly some Catholics choose to use the term 'evangelism' (rather than the broader evangelisation) to indicate an involvement in the work of bringing people to initial conversion and/or knowing Jesus personally. This is often seen to be brought about by a decisive decision that too much emphasis on process can obscure. Such Catholics often look to Evangelical Protestant models and resources for help. Overall these trends may indicate a convergence in theological understandings and pastoral/evangelistic practice. (They also highlight the limitations and problems of terminology!)

[4] Something of the same has been articulated in Evangelical circles through James Engel and his Engel's scale which articulates a journey of steps – marked by issues of cognitive understanding – that a person might be expected to follow on a journey towards and into Christian faith. This too will probably have been known at HTB via John Wimber if not through other sources. (It is treated in his Book, *Power Evangelism* written with Kevin Springer. Hodder and Stoughton,

1985, updated in 1992.) The ideas in Engel's scale are useful though other factors, other than these cognitive ones, also mark a person's journey towards and into faith, for example affectivity, morality and belonging, to name but some. The journey nature of conversion was also highlighted in John Finney's research published in *Finding Faith Today* (1992).

[5] See Chapter 3 and Booker and Ireland, *Evangelism – which way now?*

[6] It is reckoned that only 4 in 100 young people of around student age go to church regularly.

[7] At the same time huge generalisations are often made about what life – and importantly religious practice and understanding – were like in the so-called era of Christendom. In short, there was more variation in understanding and less practice than is often suggested. Suppositions about high levels of practice have led some to exaggerate the extent of secularisation and misjudge some of its causes. Is 'Christendom' to be identified with a dominant Christian culture or with a close relationship between church and state, or both. Christendom is often dated from the time when the Roman Emperor Constantine first made Christianity legal and then the official religion of the Empire, yet in other parts of Europe Christians were still persecuted. There are and have been significant variations in church-state relations and these have often been used by some Christians against others. Certainly the church has been profoundly influenced by state protection and even patronage and has also been impoverished by being too closely linked with the State, with many injustices being committed by Christians through this connection. Involvement by Christians in all spheres of life, including the political realm remains important to most denominations and traditions.

(Stuart Murray reflects on this Post-Christian understanding of society and its implications for how we undertake mission in Chapter 21)

[8] See John Finney, *Emerging Evangelism*, DLT, 2004, ch. 5, footnote 5, p. 166.

[9] Some prefer to use 'Christianity Explored' which focuses more on the nature of conversion and specifically on the deliberate decision involved. Some have proposed running it before Alpha which would then be more of a discipleship course (and introduction to Charismatic Christianity.)

[10] I am grateful to Helen Cameron of the Salvation Army for pointing out to me that in meeting people's physical needs through provision of a meal, that Alpha in a way evangelises our bodies too.

[11] See *Telling Others*, p. 121.

[12] I prefer the word 'forms' to 'models' on the whole in this context, since Gumbel is referring to actual practice rather than an abstraction or theory for the most part. Alternatively, as I shall consider, it could be said that NG/HTB advocate all three *models* on Alpha but only practically use 2 *forms* during the course: classical and power evangelism.

[13] I use the term here in its classical sense of utilising reason and trying to arrive at firm conclusions and proofs. In our post-modern era, other less rational and more sensual and experiential forms of apologetic are being considered. (For example, see the forthcoming publication, *Sense Making Faith* ed Anne Richards, CTBI Press, 2007. This was written by the Mission Theological Advisory Group (MTAG).)

[14] I do know of someone who became a Christian after the talk on evangelism since she maintained that unless they really believed it was true, they would not go to so much trouble and take so many risks to witness to it. She felt this must be because Christianity was true and committed her life to God. Relatively soon afterward she was in full time Christian work herself.

[15] Published by the Vatican in 1993

[16] It is also altogether more sceptical about the power of the human intellect and claims to absolute truth. It is also more suspicious of big institutions and

authority in general.

[17] NG observes at conferences that the earlier, more modern, parts of the course tend to appeal to older guests brought up in this mindset while younger generations tend to find the later parts (and especially the Holy Spirit weekend etc) more interesting and appealing with its greater stress on affectivity and a demonstration of God clearly at work.

[18] I treat all these issues more fully in Chapter 8. John Drane and Stuart Murray treat them in still greater depth in Chapters 20 and 21

[19] The Alpha International vision statement distinguishes but combines the expressions 'Evangelisation (evangelism)' and 'social transformation'. This would suggest one cannot be a substitute for the other though both are important. Where is the greater primacy? Conversion is mentioned first. Traditionally, most Evangelicals put priority and stress on personal conversion and view all else as flowing from this. Is HTB evangelical in this sense? Official Catholic teaching also stresses that nothing else can, or should, take away from our personal responsibility and response to God.

[20] Peter Brierley's research on church life in Scotland showed that churches running Alpha were more likely to be also engaged in 'community service' (68%) than those that did not (52%). See Peter Brierley, *Turning the Tide (Report of 2002 census)*, Christian Research/Church of Scotland, 2003 p. 118.

[21] The 'Besom' Project which encourages and helps Christians to give time and resources to help other less well off in their communities, was and is fundamentally a separate and distinct project started, on his own initiative, by a member of the congregation, James Odgers. It has expanded and involved, amongst others, many members of HTB. The link between the two groups has grown, and been mutually supportive, but Besom remains an independent organisation. HTB often hosts Besom conferences/seminars.

Many other projects connected with social care and the poor have emerged from HTB. Details of current ones are provided on their website www.htb.org. uk. These have increased in recent years though they have had specific commitments to work with the poor/in poor areas going back to at least the 1980s, for example the Earl's Court Project and later the 'Regeneration Trust' based in the World's End Estate. Mark Perrott who led the latter is involved in setting up AI/HTB's School of Urban Mission.

[22] This series of concerns and questions include the following. Does Alpha see such social and even political work as being as important a part of the life of a Christian as explicit kerygmatic proclamation? What sort of faith, worldview and engagement with the world does Alpha foster and form people in? In comparison to advocating a personal and interior sense of knowing Jesus, how much should the church preach a conversion aimed specifically towards caring about and working for people's physical welfare and about justice in the world – not to mention ecological issues and the integrity of creation? How should such an interest in the complexities, pains and ambiguities of the outer world be balanced with, or set against, a concern for the inner world of people's souls and a focus on the world to come? Does Alpha encourage a response and quality of faith that engages in the world as it is, or does it simplify things and even generate a form of escapism? Might opening one's heart to the complex problems of the world be seen as threatening and even destroying the inner peace of knowing Jesus and what are felt to be strong but simple faith convictions that accompany this and, some feel, may even be necessary to make it possible? Is a strong personal faith vital to making a real Christian contribution to such issues and situations? How does such a person keep faith replenished/renewed? Is the way Alpha presents Jesus and his death and resurrection the most appropriate one if we are also trying to promote work with the poor and for social justice?

Christianity is not political idealism and cannot be identified with any one form of political ideology or party. There are no easy answers to these points but they are ones that Christians need to address and wrestle with broadly and not only, or even mainly, just in terms of Alpha. There are signs that HTB, at least, are increasingly grappling with them.

[23] NG is fond of quoting 1 Cor 2: 1–5 in this regard. No short Biblical text is likely to cover everything and NG's use of this text should not have too much read into it – but some might well ask 'Where are 'works' in this schema?'

[24] Many thinkers from many (Western) denominations – not just Charismatics – think that there had been a neglect of the person of the Holy Spirit and there has, as a corrective, been more attention given to the Spirit in 20th century theological thought. In Eastern (Orthodox) Christianity the Holy Spirit has always had a more central place in their theological thought.

[25] Philip Walker reflects on some of these issues in Chapter 16.

[26] Although this is not explicitly developed, this principle stresses the view that charismatic gifts, and the Holy Spirit's action more generally, are to be linked to and put at the service of the Church's mission, and not mainly be seen in terms of personal fulfillment. In general terms it seems best to place NG's approach to the Holy Spirit within what is called 'The Third Wave'. In this schema, used to classify Pentecostal/Charismatic Christianity, the first wave is the emergence of Pentecostal denominations at the beginning of the 20th century. The Second Wave is the renewal of faith brought to many in mainline denominations in Charismatic Renewal since the 1950s. In both cases the acquisition and manifestation of gifts of the Holy Spirit tended to be linked to Christian initiation/coming into a new depth of conversion. The Third Wave, most especially associated with the work of John Wimber from around the 1980s, placed the emphasis on the action and gifts of the Holy Spirit as being for mission (rather than a concern about their link to stages of initiation). Hence, the development of the term and idea of 'power evangelism'.

[27] The contrary view is prevalent amongst certain Christian groups (typically Protestant of various shades of evangelical and liberal outlook). They either dispute the miraculous ever happened at all or teach that they ceased at the end of the era of the original Apostles (cessationism).

[28] Gumbel, *Telling Others*, p.42

[29] This strikes me as a good application of the principle of Christian life and spirituality that grace builds on and perfects nature. Grace and nature are distinct (metaphysically and theologically) yet existentially very often commingled.

[30] Hunt gives accounts of some concerns on this and connected points. See *The Alpha Enterprise*, ch. 14.

[31] They would also endorse and live out a spiritual attitude that sees Christian life as a response to Divine initiative and gifts. The Greek for gift is 'charisma' meaning in a more general way, all of Christianity (at least that which gives grace a central place) can be seen as charismatic.

CHAPTER 5

The Method of Alpha

Andrew Brookes

The teaching content of Alpha is substantial and attracts a lot of attention yet, I think too close a concentration on and examination of the content can be a distraction at times to seeing what Alpha is really about and where its effectiveness really lies. Nor does an appreciation of the principles enunciated as being behind fully explain how Alpha works. Thus here I intend to examine and reflect on Alpha's method as such. Again I will evaluate and raise questions as well as explain.

Alpha is not simply, or mainly, a vehicle to communicate Christian teaching. It seeks to be formative and also evangelistic. That is presumably why it is called 'a *practical* introduction to Christianity' (my italics). Indeed, titling it 'a practical introduction to Christian *life*' might be more accurate still. It takes a person right into a living Christian community where the guests can see Christianity lived and have the opportunity to form relationships with Christians. All this also allows the guests to ask questions of why Christians do what they do, and explore their own possible connection, and even involvement, with it all. I will make a number of points about aspects of the course method, some of which are more obviously treated by HTB than others. In training resources, AI/HTB do not really focus on the method as such though they do sometimes, and often only tangentially, refer to aspects of it. (In more general terms still, it is interesting what they assume, pass over or stress in their training and other materials!)

A Process and Ecclesial approach to Mission: Getting alongside People and staying there

I have already noted that Alpha is based on the conviction that conversion is a process and thus evangelism/evangelisation has to be too. The choice of a 10-week period for the course is determined in part, at least, by the view that this allows people time to make a commitment. It also allows HTB, and others following their model completely, to run three courses back to back in a year. NG feels you need this turnover to build momentum and create a dynamism that keeps things moving and new people moving through.[1]

Many feel this is too much for their human resources and run fewer courses than this. More fundamentally, many find that 10 weeks is not sufficient time for many of their guests to come to conversion and/or a level of discipleship and ministry skills to be able to help on a new course immediately. Such leaders feel that more attention needs to be paid first to these guests' ongoing journey. This raises questions about who the course is really effective for, and what starting position it assumes in guests. All of this raises further questions about how realistic it is to expect the course designed by one church for one setting to be fully transferable, and thus also asks questions about how effective it can really be in other settings. In short, is Alpha transferable, when, where and for whom? (I address these questions in chapters 7 and 8, and other contributors also examine them.)

If the content has a mainly individual focus, though it does look at and introduces bigger themes, the method and setting for the course are profoundly relational, friendship-based and communal. In a general sense this makes it ecclesial. It is true that church is not addressed as a topic until the last week – when it almost looks as though it might have been forgotten and is just tagged on, but it is introduced existentially from the minute guests step through the door on week one. For HTB, church is a community, even a family, of people who love God and each other and want to share that with others while loving and respecting and being genuinely interested in them. Being church and doing mission go hand in hand. Any church of whatever denomination can share this vision; it is Biblical and is hardly doctrinally controversial. This is the womb and environment from which and in which the course is run. Guests are introduced to and experience many aspects of church life and given the chance to commit and participate at their own speed. Worship is introduced along with prayer, reading and sharing around the Bible and prayer ministry. HTB includes a Communion service on its weekend. At the end of the course, people are invited to bring guests (i.e. to evangelise) and to join house groups. Throughout the course people seek to get to know guests, to socialise with them and to develop friendships.

It is relationship, or friendship-based, evangelism. People invite their friends to come on the course. For all the advertising and posters[2], HTB knows and states this is the main source for new guests. It seeks to create a setting and the possibility for these friendships to grow and for new ones with other Christians to be formed. They know and cite the dictum: 'People become Christians for many reasons; they stay Christian for only one – if they know and benefit from a number of Christian friendships'. This is seen, by many writers and pastors, as vital to an individual's Christian life and growth – and to initial conversion bedding down.

Belonging, Believing and Behaving

More deeply though, all this raises deeper issues about what is involved in conversion and discipleship. Is the forming of Christian friendships and belonging to church that comes with it just a matrix supporting the essential business between the individual and God or is there more to it? Recent writing reaffirms that believing, behaving and belonging are all seen as important elements in the life of a Christian. But which comes first? Or do they come together? How do they operate on Alpha?

Traditional models of evangelism – ones that could at least broadly be classed as Protestant/Evangelical at any rate – consider that first a person comes to believe and then to belong. Behaving (repentance) is typically put alongside believing as part of basic conversion. 'Repent and Believe!'[3] Belonging is helpful and should follow! But now belonging is increasingly being discovered in such circles as vital to the whole process of helping someone come to believe, and also to behave, in the first place.[4] Much evidence supports this. Nowadays it is often seen that it is after a person feels they belong they will want to commit and accept the belief system (meta-narrative) of the group and its norms, i.e. start to behave in a way the group expects. I have put this in slightly sociologically terms here but the point is clear and has big pastoral implications.

All this is highly relevant for modern society where people feel increasingly rootless for various reasons and there is a high conscious stress on individualism. People are looking for a place to belong – not just physically, but at many levels of life including a spiritual sense. Also they still search for a general outlook on life beyond themselves to plug into, even if they insist on shopping around for this and not having it imposed on them. The Church can provide all of this. Yet at the same time many feel alienated from the church.[5]

The general understanding of how Alpha works is that belonging will now accompany and often precede believing.[6] Behaving will accompany and sometimes follow belonging and believing. Often these latter two, and the pastoral support and grace that go with them, will enable behaviour issues to be dealt with in ways that were not possible before.[7]

Host-guest model

So how do we help people belong? In everyday contexts we would do this by a combination of some or all of practising hospitality, welcoming people, showing genuine interest, giving time and effort. On Alpha, and at HTB generally, these practices are implemented extensively and, in my view, sincerely. In fact, significantly and, I think very importantly, they characterise the relationship of Alpha team to its participants as a host-guest relationship. I feel that this is often quickly passed over, even by people running courses, partly because it sounds easy to understand and we take it for granted that as Christians, or just decent people, we do this.

But do we really practise hospitality in our churches and general church life? How far do we go to welcome people? To make them feel at home? To accept them as they are? It is important that we do this as being worthwhile in itself and not just a means to an end. All of this will tend to build an environment in which they can share and will in time want to share things that matter to them and are more personal, deeper and even spiritual. This in turn allows us to share aspects of our own life stories relating to these issues. We may even then have the opportunity to show links to our beliefs and the God who sustains it all. As all this happens, they may want to journey further into our faith world with us.

In a sense this is the dynamic that is applied and used on Alpha. It provides an underlying integrity of approach that runs from the meal and its dynamics right through to the approach and dynamic expected in the small groups. I don't think it is taught as clearly as it could be and understood less well by many courses and also critics. Churches might also benefit enormously by applying it to other aspects of church life. Interestingly, the HTB Marriage course has basically the same dynamic except people discuss things as a couple (not a small group) in the more exclusive and intimate setting provided at their attractively set meal tables.

In more detail, how then is it possible to see such a host-guest model being applied and operating on Alpha? Firstly, it is a matter of a caring loving attitude and a willingness to help guests, serve them and be interested in them. It is also necessary to respect their freedom and privacy and be sensitive. Such pastoral care is taught and is essential to any course that expects to bear fruit. It needs to be authentic. It is important to realise how apprehensive non-Christians are about entering church and so try to use a setting that is easy for secularised people to enter. AI/HTB advise homes or non-church buildings. HTB only resorted to running it in the church (worshipping space) itself when they no longer had any other rooms big enough to cope with the numbers of guests. They advise making an effort over setting, environment, and food. The issue here is not whether it is pasta or pies that are served and whether it is flowers or posters that are used for décor but that it will all help the guests in that particular environment feel at home, relaxed, and valued as persons. Clearly the meal, or simpler provision of snacks and drinks depending on timing and setting, is vital. The New Testament records that Jesus frequently attended meals; indeed, shared meals were an important part of the life of the early church too. Non-religious conversation is advised. It is important that populist and media-fuelled suspicions about Christians being manipulative or weird are overcome if a guest is to journey further. It is a chance to get to know people and allow them to relax and open up. In reality this is essential if the talks and small group discussions are to bear much fruit. NG says they do not listen properly to the talks until relaxed, which he says does not happen until around Weeks 3–4 or so. It is also why the weekend is not done any earlier than after Weeks 5 or 6.

Small groups can be likened to relaxed conversation that follows dinner and after-dinner speeches, the latter made up of the talk or video. Their openness and effectiveness is greatly improved by the shared meal and relaxed friendly atmosphere.

Dialogue or Proclamation? Or – who sets the Agenda?

The host–guest model encourages mutual respect and sharing. In this sense could Alpha be described as being about dialogue as much as proclamation? This is an important question since evangelism is typically seen as being principally about proclamation and the accompanying call to conversion. The answer is: 'To an extent, yes!' Though since there is a talk which conditions and shapes the 'after dinner conversation in small groups' it is not a shapeless conversation or one in which the guests set the agenda. Though they are supposed to be given substantial freedom in it, it remains a response to what has been presented in the company of at least some Christians who are hosts. It has also been commented that the custom of a host-guest relationship does mean that the guests are respectful of their host's sensibilities too – and this may put some pressure on what is said or done by them at Alpha.

Those concerned about who sets the agenda and how much listening happens, could push the equilibrium point nearer to that of the guests. Alpha's official timetable balances a 45-minute talk with the same amount of time to discuss it etc. Some other process courses (for example 'Emmaus') have mixtures with relatively less input by Christians and relatively more opportunity for guests to discuss, explore, share and take issue. Other courses or one off events could use the host –guest model and allow the guests to set more of the agenda and even topics. Seekers' Evenings or sessions for 'Agnostics Anonymous' can be run but organisers will have to decide how long to offer them for. Alpha or other courses, where topics are looked at more clearly from a believing Christian's perspective, could be made available to those who wish to move on to them.

AI/HTB have been asked about why they do not include at least some of the content of *Searching Issues* within Alpha or just before it begins. Apparently they had tried a version of this. However, NG reported that Christians were not able to give very convincing answers – since these are difficult issues and all people struggle with them, including Christians – and so it did not move people forward. HTB came to the conclusion that it was best to start with good solid presentations of Jesus, the Cross etc. NG/HTB felt it was better to lead with subjects and presentations that give a more compelling and credible account of Christianity than those that Christians and others struggle with. Clearly it is felt this approach, and the content on these topics, will better foster belief. In other words, NG feels there are 'good' objections to Christianity (or at least ones that people consider to have real merit) so his advice is along the lines of 'Let's not look at them unless we have to and, instead, get on with giving our account'. NG has used a cricketing metaphor, saying that his preferred option is to choose to go into bat and get some runs on the board! This clearly indicates that there are limits to how dialogical AI/HTB think they should be in presenting the Gospel. In this sense there is a clear priority given to proclamation. The talk is not sprung on people – they know it is part of the evening. People may ask anything (as the advertising states), but only in this context. They do not set the agenda – or in cricketing terms get first use of the wicket. Whether this is too much Christianity, being presented too assertively, too soon, for some guests and potential-guests, is an issue I will return to in Chapter 8. Even NG has commented to advisers that the major drop off in attendance by guests is in the first three weeks or so. It is precisely in these weeks that the facts about who Christ is, our sinful nature and need of forgiveness, and what is faith are presented in rational categorical terms.

In this sense Alpha does not advocate as much dialogue as is possible with a host-guest model. It occurs to me that it could also be compared to a tennis match where the one player insists on serving in each game, rather than alternating! Full authentic dialogue needs to give everyone a good chance to air views and ask questions; it requires respect and listening but does not have to presume a relativist or agnostic position about the possibility of there being Real objective Truth (and by implication error). Nonetheless, there are elements of real conversation and sharing on Alpha and, depending on how the course actually operates on the ground, these can be very genuine. For other guests, HTB's approach may well – and clearly sometimes does – all smack of agenda setting, control, imposition and even fundamentalism.[8]

Dialogue and proclamation are both part of the bigger process of evangelisation. In fact dialogue and proclamation are closely related and in a way overlap. This is because of the nature of Truth. I am reminded of an insight gained from Pope John Paul II who noted that any authentic proclamation can only propose, and must not impose, Christian Truth. This, he argued, is both out of respect for human freedom and for the nature of Truth itself. Premature or inappropriate proclamation may result in a rejection of the Gospel when more dialogue, preceding actual proclamation, may have resulted in its acceptance. Neither should esteem for dialogue prevent us presenting the challenge of the Gospel, or be overcome by fear lest it be rejected. Timothy Radcliffe, OP, notes that we need to speak and proclaim the truth with both confidence and humility. We need confidence that what we speak is really revealed and true and has transforming power. We need humility to know that how we put it does not exhaust the reality and mystery of God, and also the humility to listen to what truth God may be speaking to us through others.[9] This seems good advice but I do not know how far it resonates and operates across Alpha Courses!

Small Groups

A key aspect of Alpha is the small groups. NG lists them as having six functions: to discuss, to model Bible study, to learn to pray together, to develop lasting functions in the Body of Christ, to learn to minister to one another, to train others to lead. All of these are part of the overall aim to 'help to bring people into a relationship with Jesus Christ'.[10] Many though not all of these happen sequentially. Everything is to be done openly and well-explained with the intention not to spring anything on a guest and to keep all the guests at their ease. For instance, leaders should not ask a guest to lead a prayer without advance warning and without also explaining this to the whole group. Also, things are only taken forward at the pace of the slowest. Thus, for as long as there are non-Christians present the discussion of the talk remains the first and central concern. NG accepts that with mainly non-Christian guests things may not move beyond this discussion stage. He notes that this is now typical at the courses run at HTB. Small groups need to be marked from the outset by mutual respect, non-judgement (at least by the team) and confidentiality. Providing encouragement and confidence is essential. Giving people permission to say what matters to them is vital.

Regarding discussion, the Alpha small group has its particular style and ethos and method. It appears simple but is quite sophisticated. In my experience and in discussions with other course leaders, it is often poorly understood and thus poorly implemented. What is it not? It is not to be a monologue: a chance for leaders or helpers to do their own version of the talk, whether repeating, augmenting or correcting the video. Nor is it intended to be entirely dominated by any one guest. Neither is it ideally a question and answer session where everything is directed to an expert or experts – the leader and possibly also the helpers. This can happen at first but the leaders' aim is to seek to draw in as many guests as possible.

Instead it is a conversation where the lead in conversation is freely and naturally passed from one person to another as ideas and opinions and experiences are exchanged directly between the guests. The leaders just seek to get things going, involve as many people as possible, keep the principles and mood of respect operating, perhaps give a gentle steer if things wander too far from the subject and only answer any really technical questions if required.[11] Fundamentally they only have to ask two basic questions: 'What do you think? What do you feel?' Leaders and especially helpers are asked not to rush to give their opinions. They should do so only when persistently asked – and after the guests have given theirs – and helpers in particular should be willing not to speak at all. The role of the team is to listen and to facilitate the group, helping the guests share views and ideas and questions. NG anticipates that as a course goes on the guests will relax and increasingly want to know what the Christian team think, feel and live. They will then consider this Christian testimony as material for their own exploration and it may be used to point to a solution for them. This testimony and apologetic should not be imposed or given until freely sought. Otherwise the group and conversation assumes a Christian consensus on issues from the outset. In this way it is thought they can explore the topic and come to their own conclusions regarding whether the Christian faith makes any sense and might answer their questions and fulfil their deep yearnings. The team should be on hand to provide suitable follow up and pastoral care to each guest as seems appropriate, though this may be done outside the actual group session.

Is this effective? The team need to understand the method well and have good discernment and pastoral skills as well as being good group leaders/facilitators. People have very different personalities and bring these to it. The 'collective personality', sensibilities and 'outlook' of whole congregations or denominations can also affect how all this happens. These variations can customise it, enrich it, or distort the essential functions. Some of the best listeners might not ever suggest or invite a person to make a commitment they are longing to make, while some zealous evangelists jump in, not listening, and scare people away just before they would have taken the plunge anyway. Some groups may enjoy and even prefer things to be open-ended with everything always contestable; others convey fear or disapproval about the articulation of any view not understood by their church to be divinely revealed.

There are lots of pitfalls. In my experience the approach is often misunderstood and its actual performance variable – to say the least.[12] It is unpredictable, not clear-cut and can be messy. People come on Alpha from all manner of life journeys and often with all sorts of issues and problems. Such is work with real people and their inner journeys! The leaders need to be flexible. When it is done well, it can be very effective. In my experience, it is often the part of the evening new guests most dread, yet by end of course it is the section they most appreciate and want more of in some form. Why? How? Partly, it just gives people a chance to talk and reflect about themselves, especially on spiritual matters. More and more research shows people have what they identify as spiritual experiences.[13] How many opportunities do people normally get in life to share these and reflect on them?

How can and does this help produce faith? I think it may be helpful to compare it with spiritual direction, and especially its more non-directional styles where the stress is on allowing the recipient time to learn, to explore, and to articulate his/her own views, feelings, issues and concerns. This itself can lead to clarification and a decision as to what a person's next step is. The facilitator listens and may feed back what is heard, and may assist the search for meaning and purpose by asking gentle open questions. As they speak out what is within them, guests can listen to themselves and judge their own comments for how well they really resonate with what is within. They can also listen to what others say and see if that helps them and how well it resonates, and whether it casts additional light or shadow on their spirit and path. It is about looking for authenticity. All of this is food for a spiritual journey. The interpretation of experience in terms of the Christian Gospel is integral to a journey into Christian faith. The small groups provide such an opportunity. Conversion, initial or ongoing, is linked to a new and fuller integration of a person's head, heart, conscience and will with the Gospel. All of this needs to be infused and inspired by the grace of God made visible in Christ and working in us by the Holy Spirit.

Pastoral Care and Ministry

It should be clear by now that Alpha's method is complex and multifaceted. Certain skills must be learned regarding leading people to Jesus and helping them make basic conversion, either initial or renewed. How to follow this up is also required. The team – or some of them – need to know how to pray with people appropriately. Leading or helping in small groups needs to be taught. It is important that the team know how to get alongside non-Christians and new Christians and how to build relationships with them without being possessive or suffocating. Other skills and attitudes are vital such as love, service, being an encourager and community-builder and also a bridge-builder and even peacemaker if required. Ongoing prayer and faith are crucial. It all takes time and effort, so commitment and reliability also matter. Specialist skills concerning administration are important. Having good local speakers and musicians (worship leaders) – and also cooks – helps!

All of this may put potential adopters of Alpha off. I feel, therefore, that it is important to stress that it is possible to start small. A couple of people in their living room with a TV and video have often run very fruitful courses having invited a few friends round. On this or larger scales, if the team really love and listen and respect the guests and pray, people will benefit, with you seeing spiritual growth in them whatever form that takes. Organisers can learn the rest as they go along, but should not underestimate just how much 'the rest' is! Regular team training is recommended by HTB to help master and keep refreshed in all this – but often omitted by many Alpha courses. Selecting the team carefully is also considered very important. Mistakes, having serious consequences, are often made through poor team selection. AI/HTB advocate selecting the team after prayer rather than just asking for volunteers.

And afterwards? Life beyond Alpha

It is very important that a church running Alpha makes provision for those guests who have 'stayed the course' and are interested in journeying further with the church in one or several ways. Much depends on what each individual wants or needs and can do. Equally while it is necessary to be flexible much can be anticipated and has to be thought of and planned for, probably and preferably before the Alpha course even begins. This may mean starting something for this purpose. If the Alpha environment, style and ethos have helped them grow it makes sense to continue it. More specifically, if people have had a good experience of the small group they will probably want to go on meeting. HTB offers them the chance to join a pastorate.[14] Outlined in Chapter 1, they follow roughly the same pattern as an Alpha evening but take people further into the Christian life. To aid this transition further, a pastorate will often supply the entire team to lead and help with a new Alpha group. On alternate weeks, when pastorates do not meet, these new members can take part in small groups, perhaps if they wish with some of the people they met on Alpha. Participation in these groups helps them build friendships, put down roots and belong. Participation at Sunday worship and other church activities can be incorporated when each person is ready.[15] All this indicates that Alpha is very well integrated into the overall life of HTB.

In my view churches that run Alpha need to think about the follow-up before they begin. Running Alpha long-term will, I feel, almost inevitably mean setting up some sort of house group/cell/pastorate/ basic ecclesial community system. Not all churches want to do this for various reasons but it can be fitted into the theology of most denominations. Churches who wish to run Alpha effectively long term will have some other serious choices to make. Either they will already have and approve of many of the values of HTB and its ethos – in a sense its 'spirituality' – or they will have to want to move in that direction or at least be honestly open to the possibility. If not, there will be disappointments or even problems of one sort or another.[16] It is worth noting, and probably not co-incidental, that a high number of cell churches run Alpha. This can be a two-way synergistic relationship. Cell groups provide a destination for Alpha guests, and running Alpha is a very suitable outreach activity for a cell group to organise. If Alpha is run on a separate night to the normal cell meeting, this overcomes the problem often faced by cell church of trying to combine ongoing discipleship of current members with the basic evangelism of potential new ones.[17]

Some guests want to repeat Alpha. HTB has a firm rule that a person can only do the course once as a guest. This rule is designed to stop the tendency for courses to get gummed up with believers, cliquish, and lose their outward focus and evangelistic momentum. Being willing to be on the team, and being invited to do so, is the way to get on to subsequent Alpha courses. People are invited to invite their friends on to the next course. They would then typically come with them and be on the team. HTB has more recently started finding there are guests who do the course, are still interested in Christianity but not yet committed and want to go further. What they have started doing to address this, without breaking their rule, is to allow them to come back to Alpha as helpers.[18] NG says they often make commitments early in their second course. (HTB runs Alpha three times a year. If other churches run it much less frequently this may not be a realistic option.) It is now thus considered that the role of the helper can be carried out by people sympathetic to Alpha but who are not yet committed Christians. The role of small-group leader could not! NG reckons that fairly new Christians, who still remember what it is like not to be a Christian, very often make the best team members anyway.

The issues of Post-Alpha follow up and how to integrate Alpha into each local church are very important and often not sufficiently considered. Introducing change into a congregation's life is not easy or straightforward. Becoming a mission-shaped church is not easy either. Alpha is not the only option. HTB have tended to package Alpha as a 'tool' and while they give some indications of what to do – for instance, the training conference talk 'Integrating Alpha into the Church' – they do not lay anything down. I expect this is because all situations are different and also that they do not want to be too imposing or be seen to want to take over. However, it is an area where many churches fall down and long-term fruit is not achieved. The suitability of a local church for running Alpha long-term does not depend fundamentally on denomination/tradition. There are successful long term Alpha courses run in churches right across the Christian spectrum though some denominations may find a greater number of congregations/leadership teams with the appropriate ethos, spirituality and missionary sense than others. Such local churches could be developed in most denominations and could certainly become more common than at present. But, for this to happen, more practical help with integrating Alpha, and more generally orientating the local church towards mission, as well as towards the other values and features of HTB (or similar ones), is probably needed.

The Need for training

I think the above explanation of Alpha makes clear that it is complex and sophisticated. That is why, HTB strongly advise local churches to follow the recipe carefully until they have properly understood it. They suggest that it is after this point that adaptations can be effectively made, if necessary. It is also why they stress the importance of coming to a training conference where, along with the actual information communicated, they also try to model and convey the ethos of the course. Further, they strongly advise regular local training. It is very interesting how often none, or not much, of this advice is followed. Too often it is seen as a quick fix, a product that can be used 'straight off the shelf' like instant pre-prepared food. Quite possibly, the manner in which AI/HTB have promoted and especially advertised the course encouraged this sort of thinking, or at least plays on such a mindset already well-established in people by our consumer society.

Closing Remarks

The method of Alpha and its insights, many of which have transferable and broader uses, may well be the main part of its legacy. At least they may have more long-term relevance and date less quickly than the content of the course. Much of what is written here is true of other process courses too and explains their large impact. I think a focus on Alpha's method gives some real insights into what is really happening on the course. I want to take some of the insights here and, along with others, develop them more in the next chapter into a fuller and more synthetic reflection on the course and how I think that God works through it.

Notes

[1] Nor should it be forgotten the pragmatic fact that when he took on oversight of the Alpha Course at HTB, NG inherited what was already a 10 weeks course and one that he observed was bringing people to faith.

[2] It has been estimated that it may be only 2% (or at any rate not many more than 5%) of guests come on the course directly through such advertising.

[3] While Jesus proclaimed this message from the beginning of this ministry (Mk 1:15), the church (after Pentecost) following Jesus' instructions (Mt 28:19) preached 'Repent and be Baptised (Acts 2:38)'. The Apostles clearly understood faith in Jesus to be part of this. Baptism has always been regarded as an act of the church, bringing people into the Body of Christ.

[4] For example, see Finney, *Finding Faith Today*. Also Booker and Ireland, *Evangelism – which way now?*

[5] Some important early reflection on belonging and believing and how the church might respond was reported in *The Search for Faith and the Witness of the Church* by the Misison Theologicial Advisory Group, Church House Publishing, 1996.

[6] For example, see Booker and Ireland, *Evangelism – Which Way Now?* Ch. 2.

[7] See Stuart Murray, *Church After Christendom*, Paternoster Press, 2004, Chapter 1 for a still more nuanced treatment of the variations and combinations of believing, belonging and behaving.

[8] Perhaps of most interest, and even concern, in this regard is that HTB use, and at training conferences suggest to others, coded comments in the small groups to warn Christians in the know if guests are talking heresy etc. The leader will respond to such views with something like 'Mmmm, very interesting! Thank you for that comment. I have not heard that before!' There is a clear concern about a risk of Christians getting confused about their faith.

[9] Timothy Radcliffe, OP, *I Call You Friends*, 2001, Continuum, esp. 'Truth' and 'Mission to a Runaway World'. Confidence and humility are not opposites and need not be at odds with each other. Both can be founded on and grow out of a life founded on the transcendent Truth and Love of God – provided we resist the temptation to accommodate both God's Truth and Love to categories and formula and boundaries that make us secure, and give us control and even power. God's Truth and Love hold and define us. We do not hold and define them. We are to be given over to them and open to their still greater depths rather than them given over to us as our property or for our convenience and ease.

[10] Alpha Conference Speaker Notes. 'Leading Small Groups'.

[11] *Searching Issues* was written by NG and recommended as preparatory reading material for group leaders.

[12] The groups and their conversation can be much more closed than open, with Christians ready with set answers rather than a listening heart.

[13] For instance, see the research of David Hay and Kate Hunt, *The Spirituality of People who Don't Go to Church*, University of Nottingham, 2000.

[14] They now regard this as a greater pastoral priority than putting people through content-based courses for new Christians.

[15] Convention and traditional wisdom is that a person first gets involved on Sunday. Those that are keen can come mid-week. This practice which other new and emerging churches follow reverses this. Yet these churches are growing! It may well be all the more necessary to do this if the style and even purpose of the Sunday worship is different from that on Alpha, and especially if it is too complex for, or presumes too much of, very new Christians. Another practical, if regrettable, reason for this is that people nowadays have many other competing commitments scheduled on Sundays.

[16] Mark Ireland cites Robert Warren as saying that the easiest way of creating division in a local church is through spirituality. (*Evangelism – Which Way Now?* p.31)

[17] Mark Ireland also develops this point in *Evangelism – which way now?*, Chapter 10 on cell church. He observes that the main weakness facing UK cell churches is witness or outreach. Running Alpha (or another process course) alongside cell meetings – rather than within them – could be a good answer. (It is difficult for the same meeting to fulfil a discipleship and evangelism function.) In many ways, this is similar to the pattern HTB operate where pastorates meet and also provide teams for Alpha courses.

[18] This phenomenon, of more people now coming off Alpha interested but not converted, may well indicate that people are starting the course further from Christianity and any suppositions the course makes, than was the case earlier in the course's history when its format was more or less fixed. Prioritising getting people into pastorates before putting them through systematic courses may indi-

cate something similar; or a greater variation in the needs of people for systematic formation (and thus greater difficulty in providing 'one size fits all' courses) or an increased recognition of the importance of belonging. It may also result from a combination of these and perhaps other factors.

CHAPTER 6

Some Theological and other Reflections on the Nature of Alpha

Andrew Brookes

Introduction

I hope the reader will now be appreciating that along with a type of simplicity, there is also a lot of complexity in Alpha. The simple 'meal-talk – discussion' formula turns out to involve a complex interaction based on the principles, method, content, ethos and other factors. The range of things that guests are exposed to, and variously influenced by, on an Alpha Course has led me to ask, and then ponder, important questions. How is the Gospel actually communicated on Alpha, and, more importantly, what sort of God and Christian spirituality is presented? What type of faith or Christian spirituality is being formed *in* guests? Linked to this, *how* is grace acting and forming people?

I would contend all this is more complex than it appears at a first glance, and indeed commonly tends to be assumed, even by the advocates of Alpha. Again, AI/HTB have not provided much public reflection on this. Alpha training materials provide a few clues but I suspect that even these, and the language they use, indicate, at best, a loose and tentative grasp of what is really happening, and as such the guidelines are at times not that well fitted to the reality. What follows is very much my own exploration of these questions, building on the last three chapters. I am not laying any claim to AI/HTB agreeing with these reflections, wholly or in part. They are generally more theological than what has gone before and attempt to push further into new ground. Trying to understand Alpha's processes of learning, Christian formation and conversion in more depth, and thus hopefully but respectfully gaining a deeper sense of how God might be acting in and through the course, are important since they help people co-operate more in the process and even to improve it.

Alpha's Development Reconstructed

I have decided to begin by sharing some ideas and reflections on how the Course in its present form developed and was put together. I have decided to include it because it throws extra light on the aims of HTB at various points, the pastoral needs they sought to address, and how they tried to do this. As such I think it provides a fuller foundation for the discussion that follows and is developed further in other parts of this book. This is my own re-construction and, as such, I am not guaranteeing it is entirely factual, though it does fit with information publicly available from HTB and also with anecdotal recollections some people have shared with me. I do feel it makes broad sense, even if it is not right in every detail. (In outlining this reconstruction I have put in brackets the 15 Chapter headings from *Questions of Life* that *mainly* cover the themes referred to. Most of the themes or points on Alpha *now* get a whole talk, though some are spread more widely, especially general discipleship issues.)

Alpha started off as a course for new Christians in an evangelically-minded church. How then did the course begin to take shape and select its content? Let's compare the process with what happens at and after an evangelistic rally or event or just mission talk, such as those led by Billy Graham and others. Inspiration and ideas for Alpha may well have been taken from what happens at, and especially immediately after, such evangelistic talks. A talk is given presenting our need for God and forgiveness, and why Jesus died, and people are then asked or challenged to convert. People who have made commitments are given 'counselling'. A number of things will be recommended during this, and relevant literature may be given on them. They are told to read the bible (Chapter 5) and to pray (Chapter 6). They are encouraged to tell others about their faith (Chapter 12) and to get involved in a local 'good' church (Chapter 14). They may first be given more 'assurance' and explanation on what faith is (Chapter 4). In addition to these fairly standard 'crusade counselling' items, practical help and guidance with getting started with Christian discipleship may need providing (Chapters 7 and 15). I would guess that this type of material is broadly what made up the original four weeks course as devised by Charles Marnham (1977–81) and as expanded by him to six weeks in 1979. From the outset it was decided to run the course in someone's house, thus establishing the crucial host-guest relationship and meal–talk–group to share and pray format from the beginning. This also introduced the elements of belonging and relationship building.

As time went on, two major blocks were added. John Irvine, who led the course from 1981–5, is credited with extending it first to eight and then ten weeks and adding the weekend on the Holy Spirit. I would suggest the first block came at the beginning of the course as HTB discovered, became concerned about, and sought to address the growing ignorance of Christian knowledge among those on the course (reflecting shifts to a more secularised society at that time). It was probably discovered that people were not even sure about 'having faith' (resulting in more attention being given to assurance, Chapter 4). More fundamentally still, it was discovered that guests were not really sure about the Gospel kerygma on which faith is based, for a variety of reasons. Thus the course was extended earlier into the journey into faith, to look at (or revise) the cross of Jesus (Chapter 3), material covered in a typical evangelistic sermon. Then, since people had uncertainties about Jesus himself, it was extended still earlier into Christian doctrine with material on who Jesus is (Chapter 2) being added.

The second block would have resulted as a result of HTB's powerful encounter with John Wimber (from 1982). All the material connected with a life lived in the power of the Spirit was then added, and mostly delivered in the form of a weekend away (Chapters 8–11 and 15). The talk on evangelism was augmented by one on power evangelism, i.e. healing (Chapter 13). Other material may also have been added throughout (perhaps to cover the gaps in people's knowledge etc) and the full material spread over the 15-session, 10-week course. As NG points out, he inherited the present teaching content from John Irvine and the 10-week plus weekend structure. At this stage all the material would almost certainly have been arranged and presented with an audience of Christians in view or, if not, people who were at the fringes of church and thought they were Christians, or wanted to brush up or re-engage with their faith. Thus a basic 'assumption' and starting point was made in the presentations about the audience having some background knowledge about the Christian faith, and especially that they were sympathetic to it.

Nicky Lee ran the course from 1985–90. HTB was growing as a whole at this time. Pastorates had already been introduced and the numbers on the course continued to grow. The numbers of those attending who were on the edge of the church grew and, as noticed by Nicky Gumbel (1990–), included non-Christians. The content and method of the course was such that at least some of these became Christians during the course, although originally it was not designed for them. NG now saw this as an evangelistic opportunity and recast the material[1] with more explanations of *why* Christians do things, as well as how, in an attempt to address both non-Christians and new Christians. The course continued to grow. When the celebratory supper was added an introductory talk with an evangelistic edge was included (Chapter 1). Training was worked on throughout. This is the course that was written up and launched in 1993, along with the, until then, in-house training materials.

Since then relatively small changes have been made and these were done to broaden its ecumenical appeal/usability. For reasons already explained HTB soon also introduced a copyright, which along with the heavy branding and promotional work, will make it harder, even for

HTB, to change things very much and still call a course 'Alpha'. This means there may well be limits to how much more it can change.[2] Yet the starting point of the audience in terms of culture and mind-set, has continued to change. Alpha changed to suit the starting point of the audience, as it developed between 1977 and 1992, but has it done so since then? Since then it has changed mainly to suit different church users. AI/HTB have attempted to address non-Church goers through its advertising campaigns. These appear to be aimed at non-Christians with slogans such as '9–5: is there more to life than this?' Even the invitation 'A chance to explore the meaning of life?' does not state that Alpha covers Christian content although it does say it is being run at a church near you! Yet on the course the talks, with the probable exception of the celebratory supper and Week 1 tend to answer questions that only Christians or people very near to becoming Christian would naturally ask. Many of these Non-Christian people have other questions, and also may need longer journey time.

I would like to introduce here the issue of when conversion happens, or is thought to happen on Alpha. HTB would originally have expected people to have faith when they started the course, and then by the end of Week 3 (How can I be sure of my faith?). On the basis of content, though not necessarily the presentation as it is given *now*, all that follows this is about how Christians are called to live. Then HTB found that conversion could happen later and indeed at any point on the Course. The weekend away is still a crucial time for many. I think this is partly because of when it comes in the course, and its relaxed setting/retreat structure, as much as the specific content covered. Although looked at through the prism of the Holy Spirit it does in fact recap much about general Christian faith and life that has already been covered.[3] Now people are getting to the end of the Course, still interested, and not converted.[4] Why? I would suggest that a major reason is that their starting point (and background knowledge) is less and less Christian. This may also help to explain the large drop out in the first few weeks, estimated at around 30% at HTB. These 'dropouts' may well be real and genuine seekers but sense they are just not getting what they need at that stage. The material/presentation may be 'too Christian' for them (i.e. assume too much Christian knowledge or interest).

Alpha, after evolving a lot while being used internally at HTB, has stayed relatively fixed for a long time. Will Alpha soon be outdated? Is it already? Will it need supplementing? Does it already? Does it need a radical overhaul? Can it receive one, given the copyright, branding and publicity that surrounds the present format? Will churches need to devise and run Pre-Alpha packages or strategies, as much as Alpha and Post-Alpha ones? These are important questions that need addressing. (I will begin to open up some of these issues in Section 3 of this book.)

NG talks about HTB *discovering* the evangelistic potential of Alpha rather than inventing it. Such comments support my view that the development of Alpha was piecemeal and somewhat 'accidental' (humanly speaking), rather than it being coherently and systematically planned from principles clearly grasped from the outset. If the development has been 'accidental' in this sense, it highlights the importance of proper analysis and reflection on Alpha to grasp better what its real operational features are, and how these ought to be understood theologically. Such work ought to assist any further evolution of Alpha or development of other courses or pastoral approaches.

Whether or not the reader accepts these ideas about the development of Alpha, let us now look at how the interaction of the different facets of the course might be better understood.

Learning Styles and Educational Elements of Formation on Alpha

There are lots of educational theories that study how people teach and particularly how they learn. Many of these approaches and insights may have relevance to understanding Alpha and I will briefly outline and apply some of these.

Some theories look at the variety of learning styles. Different people have different preferences. For example, one classification of learning styles considers people as activists, reflectors, theorists and pragmatics. Actually Alpha combines several of these elements. Using a different classification, didactic, reflective, discursive and kinetic (practical 'hands on' learning) elements and phases are all present. Yet again, some parts of Alpha are more individual-based, for example the talk/video and any private follow-up reading. In contrast, some parts are more social in nature, such as the meal and small groups. There is also a constant interplay between theory (Biblical/Christian ideas) and experience, either through reported testimony or what participants actually share. This mixture on Alpha may help explain its broad appeal.

Testimonies and stories on Alpha are generally seen as a form of illustration. However, they may have more educational use and potential than that. In short, do folk learn better from concepts (about ideas that may be true) or stories (about people and how they live)? It may well depend on who you are! Some theorists consider that, in general terms, the latter are more suited to the so-called 'feminine' mind (not necessarily belonging to females), and some link it to the post-modern psyche and personality. Whether or not such classifications are accurate or helpful, the use of testimony may be of a directly educational value, and not be '*mere* illustration'. This point was brought home to me by a middle-aged woman with no formal theological education who commented (a little apologetically) to me about Alpha 'I find it easier to learn from stories about people than just ideas.' I am reminded too that Jesus' main teaching approach was to tell stories.

Alpha does encourage questioning, something that may have seriously opened up some people and even whole congregations.[5] This will have seriously changed the attitudes of some, opening them up to new possibilities. However, there are legitimate questions about how open Alpha really is.

More broadly, different elements of Alpha may well appeal to different personality types too, thus giving it a wide range of appeal – though these claims should not be extended too far. Alpha is hardly the 'one size fits all personalities' solution to the extent that some, including Michael Green,[6] suggest or claim. If it has elements that appeal to all, it will also have elements that put off many, separately or in accumulation. John Finney, an enthusiast for process courses, has noted their common limitations and faults. Firstly they are made up of artificial groups. Finney says we need to learn how to 'gossip' the gospel in general non-church situations. Groups do not suit all sorts of people. They do suit some backgrounds and temperaments better than others. Thus they suit the gregarious, the curious, the articulate and generally educated too. By implication they will not suit others as much and alternative strategies are needed to reach them.[7]

God works in various ways. Other approaches are nourishing people in faith and also attracting them to it. Icons, pictures, candles and the use of ritual are finding renewed appeal. So is meditation. The sense of silence found in cathedrals and other old churches, or newer ones that have been well designed, is attractive to many nowadays, especially when there is no congregation present! The sense of history and rootedness provided by old buildings also seems important to some. In some respects, HTB consciously moved away from some of these approaches to become more Charismatic and informal in the 1980s.

No single approach, or course, will please everyone. Even though it may have a broad appeal, Alpha will not suit everyone's learning style and some will leave, or gain very little, as a result. The wider variety of methods now offered for Youth Alpha increases the learning styles, and perhaps could be helpfully applied to more adult audiences as well. However, churches should not come to the conclusion that Alpha, or process courses more generally, are all they need to use to attract and form people in faith. Nonetheless, educationally, the Alpha method and overall synthesis are worth reflecting on and learning from[8] – even if the course is not adopted.[9]

Alpha is unlikely to have been designed, or to have evolved, with educational ideas to the fore, yet it does include a variety of approaches. What is less clear is how well these combine or even more importantly, how well they are integrated. This matters because it significantly determines the overall formation that a person receives on Alpha. Perhaps more attention needs to be given to all this. As well as educational scrutiny, it is capable of theological scrutiny as well.

Christian Formation in Faith on Alpha: the Ecclesial Dimension

Learning and thus overall human formation take place through what is encountered – and God works through all this. This is far more than just through the teaching content. The space and atmosphere that guests encounter impact them. The setting and surroundings, the atmosphere and ethos, all matter. People are encountered and relationships, and even friendships, form. All of this is not just about cultivating relaxation, familiarity and a sense of belonging. It goes beyond that. It speaks of, and expresses, a corporate reality. This corporate reality is *church* – or at least a local expression of it. The local church is an assembly of believers, part of the Body of Christ in which God is alive, present and working. The guests encounter the church[10] and God's presence *and action* in a number of ways.

God is present in the midst of our relationships, not just within each person but *between* them, so to speak. Hospitality is fundamentally about being available and welcoming, much more so than about the menu. This says and expresses something of the nature and love of God. There is a quality and spirit present, which may in time be sensed and named as divine. People have commented on the quasi-sacramental nature of the meal.[11] It may also resonate with the practice of the early Christians to celebrate 'Agape meals', the sharing of food in a loving setting. Corporate worship and shared prayer, though they need to be handled sensitively and explained to non-believers, are nonetheless part of a full Alpha Course.[12] These are explicitly directed at God 'in Heaven', and they articulate convictions about God's reality and presence, and they also seek communion, or fellowship, with God who is present among them.

The guests encounter all this. Not only that, it is bound to affect them. Often it opens them up to more of God's presence, grace and action, which form them, even if at times this seems sub-conscious and imperceptible. The elements of this may include a sense of spiritual hunger, a curiosity, a sense of disquiet with how things are, a sense of new depths, a desire for healing or help with a problem. These may need addressing and sensitive handling but a sense of feeling safe, being at ease and then increasingly being helped and spiritually fed, and belonging may well also develop. What do they sense and belong to? Both to the church and to God present and at work in it.

Certainly the Word of God is proclaimed and the Holy Spirit is invoked to come and work powerfully and clearly. But the light of the Word and the power of the Spirit work in this setting, and it is this setting that undoubtedly helps, even ensures, that they produce fruit.[13] In actual fact the Word is proclaimed by the church, and the

Spirit invoked by it – since the church is present and acts through its members (whether officially or unofficially). The setting is the church. As such it is the medium through which, and in which, the Gospel is announced and people brought to and formed in faith. At one and the same time, God's presence and action are mediated through the church and sensed immediately ('directly') by each person. These two features complement and should not be played off against each other: both are facets of God's work.

For these reasons it can be asserted that Alpha is strongly ecclesial in nature, even if some would rather ignore, or are uncomfortable with, this pastoral and theological reality. This church environment is crucial. It is like a womb that forms believers and nourishes the life that guests, implanted there, begin to receive. In some sense, the course is a mother, as the church is a mother. The application of feminine and maternal imagery to the church is found in Scripture (for example Eph 5, Rev 12, Jn 19) and the early Church Fathers, even if it is nowadays used by some denominations more than others. I am reminded of the words of St Augustine. 'If you would have God for your Father, you must also have the church for your mother.' Perhaps God is also calling us back to a fuller appreciation of the role of the church in evangelisation, and of how fundamental evangelisation (or mission) is to the true identity and purpose of the church, and also to the feminine and maternal features within this?

How does Christian Formation and Conversion really take place on Alpha?

Is it possible to say more about how specifically Christian formation and conversion takes place within this ecclesial setting? Significant human formation takes place on an Alpha Course. It is a result of the combination and interaction of the elements referred to already. Learning is linked to formation and, in turn, this is linked to how grace acts or is obstructed.

Although I do not think HTB designed the course with a set of 'educational' or even 'formative' principles worked out in advance, examination of the course indicates elements that were consciously introduced for specific reasons at different phases. Early on, it was fundamentally a teaching course conveying Christian content that was then discussed and prayed about. (Probably the meal was not methodologically central to proceedings at that stage but it did express welcome and fostered belonging.) After the initial impact of John Wimber on HTB, more experiential and practical ways of learning were introduced. People need to use the spiritual gifts they receive so ways were found of facilitating this, and more generally allowing people, in non-threatening ways, to participate in church life, actually doing things Christian do. All this was aimed at Christians. It then started having a very positive impact on non-Christians who happened to be on the course. Why and how then did it start to work effectively to help people actually become Christians and get actively involved in church? Which bits help? How is God working? Quite probably NG and HTB were not entirely sure but, seeing that God was at work, NG tweaked the content to make it more accessible to non-churched people, but fundamentally carried on with what was working.

Since then, an appreciation of the importance of hospitality, belonging, relationships, process and journey time, experience, a chance to explore and ask questions have all been increasingly highlighted in thinking about mission/evangelism and it is easy to see that Alpha already had these in place. But this does not fully answer the question of how formation and conversion happens, and is to be understood theologically. Because of the 'Evangelical-Charismatic' background people have tended to use popular and theological terms from these traditions but these may well not really be as appropriate as some might think. Let us explore a little more.

A number of factors (channels through which God can work) converge and hopefully work together. God is not typically met as the conclusion of an argument and certainly things cannot well be left at such a place. God is also and most importantly a presence that we sense and respond to. We, and guests on Alpha, sense and approach God through our minds in truth, through our hearts' deep yearnings, through a sense of goodness and its opposite, and through a search for purpose/direction and something to which we commit our will. All this may seem spiritual (in the abstract sense), but our physical nature is affirmed through eating, this social activity also meeting our concrete need to connect and relate with other people. In all this God can become relevant and present, even if sometimes in an illusive way. Worship and prayer point people beyond themselves. These may thus elicit curiosity about other dimensions, and even wonder or a sense of peace. In this way God is sensed as real, as present, but as a Mystery. We know but in part. We sense and feel 'something' but sense this is not everything. Confidence is gained and we open ourselves up to the possibility of God existing and being able to touch us. Being able, in what feels a direct way, to sense God, to be touched by him, to 'hear' him and to 'know' him become plausible and even likely. We come to realise we are called beyond this tangible (finite) something to the 'more' of (infinite) reality; beyond this natural reality to supernatural reality.[14]

Christianity, understood as a multi-dimensional reality, makes more and more impact on a person. A certain weight of evidence, experience and conviction build up, and at a certain stage, which may or may not be dramatic, and sometimes may not be obviously perceptible, the person identifies herself or himself as Christian. Some images may help. In effect a 'critical mass' has been achieved, and a (nuclear) reaction happens which brings about and sustains 'conversion'. Or again, our evidence and experience accumulate producing weight, and the 'spiritual see-saw' moves and then resolutely tips from a position of unbelief to a position of belief. Or, put another way, enough strands have formed, come together and been connected and tied up, creating a Christian fabric (or rope) strong enough for someone to risk their weight and life on it in faith. Each person is different but I would suggest that this may form a broadly true and useful template. Having such a general sense of what God is really up to may make it much easier for the team to co-operate as 'spiritual midwives'.[15]

This has a number of important implications, firstly about how appropriate it is to uncritically label Alpha as an evangelistic tool. Alpha on the ground may well not follow the conventional ('Protestant-Evangelical') logic of how this should work. The *content* of Alpha suggests conversion and then discipleship is all very orderly and logical. People first believe that Jesus is God, then accept they are sinners and that Jesus died for them, then they start to pray and read the Bible and then are filled by the Holy Spirit. This leads them into active evangelism and church participation. This is what is expected from just examining the course content. Yet the testimonies show clearly this is not the pattern most of the time. For a lot of people on Alpha in the last 15 years the 'critical mass' is reached during the weekend away. Yet this is not always the case and conversions have been noted at all points of the course. It appears to be increasingly the case that people have been taken forward on a spiritual and specifically Christian journey during Alpha but are not yet Christians at the end of it. How should a church treat people who have apparently heard the Gospel but not responded favourably?

The frequent discrepancy between the content of Alpha and the point at which conversions actually take place also raises an important question about the relationship between evangelism (with its focus on initial conversion) and discipleship. Typically the two are seen as distinct with the former taking place *before* the latter. Perhaps what is happening on Alpha calls for this to be rethought. Perhaps conversion (and thus evangelism) should be seen more as something that happens *within* a wider process of discipleship. Alpha was originally designed as a discipleship course and perhaps it should still be seen that way though one with significant evangelistic potential. As a discipleship course it not only explains basic ways of being Christian within church but also begins to teach and equip people for service and witness outside the church. In all of this it has a practical approach with a releasing ethos. Conversions happen while all this is going on. Part of Alpha's contribution to mission may be to help us rethink how conversion relates to discipleship and its methods. In fact a good case can be made for saying that Jesus operated such a process on earth, with conversion taking place within people's formation as disciples and after it had begun. For instance, at what point during his life as a disciple did Peter come to conversion? At the beginning when he left everything to follow Jesus (Mk 1:16–18)? When he realised he was a sinner (Lk 5:1–11)? When he realised Jesus was the Messiah and Son of God (Mt 16:13–17) though he clearly still had problems with what this really meant (Mt 16:21–3)? When he experienced the Risen Lord and received forgiveness (Jn 20–1)? When he received the Holy Spirit and witnessed publicly to his faith (Acts 2)? Interestingly in the great commission Jesus instructs his apostles 'to go and *make disciples* of all the nations, teaching and baptising (Mt 28:19)'. He does not specifically highlight evangelism as distinct from that. While real and decisive conversion, including repentance, matters and should not be ignored, perhaps the church should focus more on a comprehensive process of discipleship that is open to, and encouraging of, bringing people to clear and also ever fuller conversion within that. Is this what HTB rediscovered through Alpha?

The Impact of Alpha on Nonchurched Guests

The fluidity and even (apparent) randomness of conversion needs to be recognised and taken seriously, especially if Alpha teams are to co-operate more effectively with how God is really working. This is particularly important in the case of nonchurched guests. I will now look at this in more detail. Accepting that there are big individual variations, I would suggest the interaction of experience/reaction/formation/conversion that happens during an Alpha Course is something like this for nonchurched guests.

However nervous or sceptical nonchurhced guests are on arriving, they feel welcomed, valued and listened to. They begin to form relationships, and begin to belong. They see that for these Christians, God is real and relevant and that their faith in Jesus matters. They begin to become familiar with bits of the Christian story, outlook and life. They begin to see that the substance of Christianity is plausible and worthy of serious consideration. These Christians have something – a different quality – that resonates with them and suggests itself as an answer to their own search for meaning, peace, love, forgiveness, and as a way of living. They become more 'spiritually sensitised' and hungry. At the same time they begin to trust and open up more, even to the possibility of God/Jesus actually wanting to come close and affect them.

By or during the day or weekend away they may well be sufficiently interested and open, and say, in a variety of ways, that they want God, if he exists, to be real to them. (It may happen later than this in the course or even well after it has ended.) Corporate and individual prayer ministry fundamentally involves asking the Holy Spirit to come and be present.

Whether or not guests are 'filled with Holy Spirit', many feel touched by God, sensed variously as 'Love', 'Holy', 'Other', and either as transcendent or immanent – or a combination. They may want to name this as 'God' or they may at least sense something significant even if they are not sure how to name it.[16] Many sense something new, or deeper or more peaceful, perhaps even something stronger.[17] A new awareness or appreciation of Christianity, or a deep, spiritual and possibly mystical experience then needs to be variously 'held', pondered, deepened, explored, sensitively interpreted through the Christian faith.[18]

Exploration thus continues during the rest of the course. Belonging grows deeper and stronger, and a Christian interpretation of their experience and life makes more and more sense. Clear belief begins to form in them and at some point a conscious deliberate commitment is made, or they realise they have moved in small steps, or even imperceptibly, into a committed and increasingly public faith. They continue to grow by putting down roots and the Gospel challenges more and more areas of their life style.

There is nothing inevitable or imposed about this and people can and do take time out, or walk away completely at any stage in the process. There are various stimuli that help nudge a person along this journey, though the speed and direction ultimately needs to be decided between each individual and God. It can take a very variable period of time, longer or shorter than the 10 weeks of the course. Although I have outlined this process as a smooth progression, there will often be clear breakthrough moments when a person, by grace, moves forward a lot in a short space of time, almost 'at once'.

In this model, experience has a central place. This experience, as already noted, is multi-faceted and, handled properly, is not reduced to shallow emotions. Human experience becomes seen as spiritual and even as religious experience, or at least the spiritual and religious dimensions are drawn out, named and clarified.[19] The talks are important to help fulfil this role with the Scripture and other elements of the talks casting light on what is happening in a person's experience. Scripture and Christian teaching are thus offered as much to help interpret experience *after or sometimes while* it happens, as beforehand, when they operate to 'create the conditions' in which the experience can happen in the first place.

I would contend that something like this is essentially what is happening for the dechurched and completely nonchuurched guests. If the course is being aimed specifically at them as an evangelistic tool then the material, that is the teaching content, probably needs adjusting so that it accompanies their real journeys, and effectively casts light on their experience, offering meaningful Christian interpretation. The issue is not just content, but importantly also the style, tone and mood with which it if presented. Imposing the content heavily and, worse, in an overbearing way, will very probably not be helpful! Offering it in a polite and respectful manner will probably open more doors. (A polite offer need not imply a lack of authority.) As things stand, even if I am only partially right in my assessment of what is happening formatively, the teaching is currently largely or significantly out of step with the experience of guests, before and after the weekend. Instead of being helpful, it may well on occasions be a real hindrance and even cause some guests to drop out.

This would not have been the case when the course was run for Christians or relatively recently 'lapsed Christians'. This model of how Alpha works suggests Alpha will manage to function with dechurched guests who have had a Christian upbringing or are in some other way broadly familiar with the ideas being presented. Some other very well-disposed guests might persevere. However, for most of those further away (i.e. nonchurched), the content will not help much and will probably get in the way. As society becomes increasingly de-Christianised this will be a more and more serious problem. The window of opportunity for Alpha, in its present form, to be specifically and genuinely and effectively evangelistic (i.e. of real benefit to the nonchurched) may be limited.

Experience, Truth and Love – as Constituents of Christian Faith

Is this suggesting that Christian faith can be reduced to, or is merely about, feelings? That is not my intention. However, many people, from doctrinal positions right across the spectrum of Christian denominations, have criticised, and often condemned, Alpha on these grounds. An examination of what 'experience' can mean may thus be helpful in this context.

In the first place, experience is much richer and fuller than what is commonly understood or 'experienced' as feelings. Thinking is an experience; consciousness, at its various levels, is experienced. Is the human spirit, and even the Divine Spirit, experienced? This depends on a person's specific understanding of how humans are put together but I would say it is clear that directly or indirectly the human spirit and Divine Spirit make their presence and action felt, known and experienced.

Intellect and will are typically seen as the key powers of the human spirit, the source of our spiritual dimension. They give shape to our experience. They permeate and work through experience and yet transcend it. Intellect, and the knowledge it furnishes, provides structure for experience. Will, and its application in decisions, gives dynamism and movement to experience and life as such. Something similar can be said of God, his Spirit, and his impact on us. God, and his grace, impacts our experience and our soul. God comes as Truth and Love which in a way correspond to our intellect and will.[20] They transcend us and yet penetrate us, and are thus sensed within as well as beyond us. God is deeply connected with us – yet distinct. We need both truth and love. Love without truth is blind. Truth without love is cold. When Love and Truth come together a fire is set alight which gives light and warmth. This takes us into the heart of God's life. Of course, whatever formal distinctions we make, in practice all this works holistically. Looked at like this, and this holistic approach is the one used generally in the Bible, everything is part of experience. We are to love God with all our heart and mind and soul (Mt 22:37).

Is faith then just about good experience, about a deep feeling of well-being and even confidence, optimism and inner peace? No! A sense of God's absence can also be our experience. This can be for several reasons. It can be because we have turned our back on God deliberately, but it can also be part of a search for God and can also occur within faith. Here it can bring spiritual good. It develops our longing for God, making us long for God more. It purifies our desire to do God's will without obvious benefit or enjoyment, making, or encouraging, us to want God in and for himself. This is a purer love and builds a more freeing love. In God's absence we find his presence in a deeper way, in a 'dark' way – less obviously perceptible, at least at first, but still 'experienced'.[21] The same goes for an actual sense of feeling forsaken, or spiritually anguished. It is enough to appreciate that Christ, who is God, experienced this in his passion (Mt 27:40–50 amongst others) for us to know that God is, or can be, present in such (or approximately similar) spiritual experiences of our own. Thus the possibility is created for us to feel, through faith, united to God while feeling, at other levels, forsaken by him. Since the spiritual anguish of Jesus is part of the act by which God redeemed us, we can have confidence that he can powerfully and fruitfully use experiences we have of spiritual anguish too. (For example, see 2 Cor 4:8–18.) Thus, they are part of the mystery of his love by which he makes our obedience perfect and fruitful. All of this can be held within the experience of Christian faith – or, more accurately and fully, within Christian faith, hope and love. The Bible is full of very rich accounts and deep appreciation of a vast gamut of experience, yet this is does not mean the Bible is short on faith, hope and love!

The question of whether Alpha is mainly about feelings, or is too experience based, does come up often enough. The fuller scope of experience just outlined may allay the concerns of some. Valid concerns can still be raised. Some critics judge it too subjective and light on truth, playing it down. Certainly, Truth cannot be ignored and there are dangers if experience is allowed to be entirely self-verifying. This can give it an 'authority' that can be disproportionate and dangerous, not least since humans have capacities for poor self-knowledge, self-deception and also for being self-serving. All these need guarding against. It is not experience as such that is objectively true and capable of carrying authority in itself, but it is true and carries weight and is true in as much as God in Christ is clearly present and acting in it. The interpretation and understanding of experience are thus vital. Christian Revelation provides the light for this. Bringing and subjecting individual experience to this Revelation, and also bringing it to the Christian community and following practices of Christian discipline and practical service are very likely to reduce the dangers to a person from self-absorption and deception. It can be argued that this does, or can, happen on Alpha. However, the extent to which it does may vary a lot and be dependent on good pastoral leadership. On some occasions it may be seriously lacking. Perhaps AI should flag this up more.

It is long recognised that faith journeys often begin with strong experiences, pleasant at least in part. There is evidence of this on Alpha. Certainly churches need to take people beyond any 'honeymoon period' of initial faith into mature discipleship, and Alpha ought not to give a false impression of the costs, as well as the benefits, involved in this. Perhaps these issues also need more stress.

However, I think these question about Alpha and experience also pick up on and reflect a deep tension between the intellectual and affective parts of faith. This 'split' is something very typical of Western religion of the modern period, and is connected with and more generally rooted in modern Western culture and thus the modern Western mind's approach to being human. It very probably affects how people assess Alpha, and much else. It is not something that would have bothered the Jewish person at the time of Christ. What is its origin?

Western, and especially European, thought (traced back to the powerful influence of ancient Greek culture and philosophy) has forged a large dichotomy between truth and knowledge on the one hand and love and feelings on the other. It has been particularly marked since the emergence of the Enlightenment culture in the 18th century with its emphasis on the mind and rationality, but also the presence alongside it, as a shadow or undercurrent, of the Romantic movement with its focus on the heart, feelings and spontaneity. But there was a real sense of fracture between the two, fostering dualist tendencies. People's Christian experience, and reflection on it, has also been very influenced by this fracture and dualism. This is not found in the Hebraic and thus Biblical approach. There, love and knowledge are much more deeply connected. Also they are both linked to relationship.[22]

We have made truth something much more abstract and derivative. Statements are true when they correspond with reality. And what is reality? This is true when it clearly and authentically reveals itself, rather than pretends or is false or illusionary. And what is the yardstick of authenticity or revelation? For the Jew, ultimate knowledge – Truth as such – is rooted in and founded on the experience of encounter with God. God is the creator, sustaining the universe and who reveals himself. The root meaning of the Jewish word for truth (*aman*) is 'to be reliable, certain, worthy of confidence'. Thus in the Bible truth indicates that something or someone has the qualities of being stable, proven and reliable. Applied to God or people it means 'trustworthiness' and as such elicits confidence. This is how it is used to refer to God and his actions. It is best to understand the usage of the term in the New Testament, especially in the Pauline and Johannine writings, as fundamentally in this Jewish tradition, rather than the Greek one.

This also connects with the theme of wisdom. Jewish wisdom is both about knowledge and insight, but it also embraces moral principles and practical advice about life. It addresses and comments on what are now seen as distinct, and even opposed, questions: 'Is it true?' (seen as a typically modern question) and 'Does it work?' (seen as typically post-modern). The 'Jewish' synthesis unites the two in a fruitful way. On the one hand, it 'prevents' (or reduces) the scope for truth to veer off into irrelevant abstractions. On the other hand, it prevents the assessment of practical function (i.e. if a thing works) being reduced to crude utilitarianism and the end justifying the means. Biblical Truth unites both of these and they both flow from the experience of an encounter with God. Jesus then is the fullness of the truth and wisdom of God. (1Cor 1:18–31). Even the most 'foolish' thing that God did in Christ, the death of Jesus by crucifixion, is wiser than the wisdom of men: it is full of revelation – full of truth and love – and has untold practical benefits too!

Truth is about, and perhaps nowadays well-expressed as, reality and authenticity and the freedom that goes with that. In this sense, truth as reality has to be experienced, known and reflected on, loved and lived. Where is it to be found ultimately? Jesus claims to be ultimate reality. Jesus claims to be 'the Way, the Truth and the Life (Jn 14:6)', to be 'the Truth that sets us free (Jn 8:32)', to be the invisible God made visible, one with the Eternal Father (Jn 14:10–11). Who he was, what he said and claimed, and what he did all fitted together: he was, and is, authentic. If Jesus is authentic reality, he too has to be encountered and experienced so that he can be both known and loved. Knowing and loving interact and attract each other. Thus we tend towards loving who and what we know to be true, and getting to know who and what we love. Thus we grow in both love and knowledge as they feed each other. In the case of Jesus, all of this can be endlessly deepened, since the riches of God and encountering God can never be exhausted. Encountering the reality of God also makes us more real if we allow the reality of God to transform us, also changing what we do.[23]

Truth then is not just about careful use of language. However true our language, it simply cannot do full justice to God. Making true statements about God, Jesus and Revelation does matter and is of value.

Nonetheless, to reduce God, Jesus or Revelation to a series of statements, however many and detailed, or to seek to contain, and restrain or exhaust these Divine realities within these statements, is to miss the point and can ultimately be unfaithful to God. (It starts down a road that can lead to making faith into an ideology and a fundamentalist one at that.) Faith is not just affirming or even understanding a set of creedal statements – true and important though they may be. Truth, real knowledge of God, has to be centred on an encounter with God, a profound experience and one of immense and increasing depth over time. Eternal life is to know the one true God and Jesus Christ whom he has sent – and this Jesus is a living person (Jn 17:3). He must be loved with all our heart, mind, soul, will and strength.

True statements, lots of them, can be made, but they will not exhaust the Truth of God but only touch its edges, the 'hem of its cloak', for at the heart of God, and all persons, is a mystery that is known through love.[24] Indeed, 'mystery' is the theological term used to express this idea that God is a personal reality which can only be known in part – and that largely because it has chosen to make itself known (i.e. to reveal itself). Rather than reducing the scope of faith, embracing God as mystery makes for a more whole and holistic faith and appreciation of experience. It allows such faith to flourish. It brings together and unites truth, love, experience (including difficulty and darkness) and faith. Faith is not static; it is dynamic, relational and capable of growth. It longs for its fulfillment and is thus also linked to hope.

The idea of an encounter with Divine Reality answering both the questions 'Is it true?' and 'Does it work?' gives us confidence that the God of Jesus Christ can happily address us in both the modern and post-modern era and in the current transition. Indeed, each era just highlights different facets of God and the richness of the Christian faith.[25] All of this may well help to explain the attraction, usefulness and significance of Alpha as a way of presenting the Gospel at this point in our history and cultural journey.

Truth as an experience of encounter with God may also cast light on why Nicky Gumbel and others stress the value of a period of worship in each Alpha session. In worship we come into God's presence. We affirm the truth of God and try to relate to God as God really is. God is the end and centre of worship, not us. This focus on God and affirmation of God is particularly marked when we give thanks and praise to God. (Indeed confession and petition should flow from this to be most effective and fruitful.) Such praise and thanksgiving is advocated for inclusion on Alpha. The musical style and choice of songs is very secondary and only a means to an end. Such worship (praise and thanksgiving) puts us into an attitude of being able to encounter God and be transformed by God. The structure and inner dynamic of worship times is such that they end in prayerful silence, that is in adoration, surrender and listening, and all this should then be applied as obedience in our daily lives. Participating in this, or just being present as a witness, must surely increase the likelihood that the whole Alpha evening, and all the activities and attitudes that make it up, becomes an encounter with God, and one that calls for a response from those present. As such, worship is linked to conversion, and this can have implications for evangelism.[26]

The value of worship also underlines another important point about experience. It is very important that a person's focus ultimately is on God and not on her or his own experience. Is God the end a person seeks, to serve and give glory to, or does a person seek her/his own autonomy and self-satisfaction? Focussing on God and surrendering to God in humble and generous obedience will lead to a life founded on God and full of 'Christ-esteem' and an experience of God marked by peace and contentment will follow. Focus on oneself (selfishly) and a search for pleasurable (self-indulgent) experience will probably result in a person seeing a mirage, not reality, experiencing shifting emotional sands and not secure peace, and a life founded at best on self-esteem but one without God to underwrite and define it. We best know we are getting this choice, focus and response right if we increasingly love our brothers, sisters and neighbours in concrete ways (1 Jn 3:11–24, Mt 25:31–46). As it happens Alpha seeks to model this on the Course, and encourages its practice outside the course schedule as well.

One final comment in this reflection on experience. The overall effectiveness of Alpha may well consist in giving people lots of opportunities, ways and experiences to be open to the presence of God. It may consist in the particular combination of these opportunities and perhaps also in the way guests are prepared for this Divine encounter and transformation, even if things were not consciously or deliberately planned that way. Alpha may be a very good milieu in which people can be well prepared to meet God, and thus one in which God can make himself, and so much of his richness and mystery, present in so many ways.

Alpha: An Encounter with The Mysterious Presence and Action of God?

If formation and the way grace acts on Alpha are both multi-faceted, then so is the faith (and more generally the participation in a life of grace) that is formed. Faith is not fundamentally a formula and neither can the God it points to be reduced to one. People are not saved by a formula – or, by extension, a technique or method – but by an ongoing encounter with the Living God. God is not an idea, formula or definition, though these can usefully be pointers, but a presence, a mystery which our words and even true definitions and doctrines just touch the edge of. I think that Alpha challenges us to see and enter into faith, and the life of grace, more generally as an encounter with mystery. A better appreciation of mystery as linked to God and faith may facilitate a fuller understanding of what happens on Alpha, and give its practitioners insights into how to co-operate better with God's presence and action there.

The idea of mystery is poorly understood and often maligned, especially in modern scientific culture. Teasing out some of its facets, and the issues it raises, in a bit more detail may therefore be of real value. Our minds have often been trained scientifically and rationally to dismiss mystery or treat it as something to be overcome. Words themselves and definitions mount up in an attempt to explain everything. Less space and time are found for silence and wonder. This outlook has even influenced our faith that as a result is often presented and defended using certain forms of reason and philosophy that may tend to skew it. This impact is subtle but strong. Hence I will map out in some detail how making mystery more central to our perspective can change and nurture our faith, and how we share that with others, or try to support their journey to faith on Alpha or elsewhere.

Although mystery seems abstract and remote, it is all around us, as real as ordinary facts or things. We meet – we experience – God who is a Mystery that touches us and all our faculties, yet is not contained by any of them. Certainly Biblical truth and good doctrine accurately describe God and point to him, but they do not contain or in any way exhaust the reality of God. In fact, in the Old Testament the admonitions against idolatry were to prevent God's people tying down too closely who they thought God was or how God could be represented. God chose to be named somewhat enigmatically as 'I am who am' (Ex 3:14). God identifies himself as a mysterious personal presence! He also makes clear that there is a mystery through which he will fulfil his plan of salvation. This Mystery became flesh! Visible, audible, touchable, within and yet beyond these human dimensions, Jesus of Nazareth is Divine, communing with the fullness of the Godhead and bringing Divine life and even a sense of future Divine glory (1 Jn 1:1–4 and Jn 1:1–18). God is made knowable and intelligible through Jesus Christ, the Word made flesh, but as a Mystery to be encountered, pondered, received, yielded to and loved, entered into and communicated, and not a fact to be memorised or fully understood.

As Risen Lord, he is mysteriously with us still, his Spirit poured out and at work. Our encounter and interaction with this mystery extend to the church community we are part of and the mission we share in. We encounter this Divine Mystery in all these ways yet, as mystery, God is hidden as well as revealed, grasped but not fully grasped. The Mystery of God is set forth in Christ (Eph 1:9), yet in Christ are hid all the treasure and wisdom of God (Col 2:3). God is a reality – the reality

– to be grown into slowly as we journey in faith, hope and love, but one we will never come to the end of or exhaust. God is mysteriously within us, around us and beyond us, at hand and yet beyond. In fact we can only end up responding in love, wonder, adoration, silence and obedience.

Faith that is aware of its object as Mystery is able to hold together reason and experience. It is able to hold a middle position between rationalism, that inflates the role of the mind and ignores experience and trust, and fideism, that downplays this and focuses on faith almost exclusively as trust and can even tend to reduce it to feelings. It can hold together and befriend both clarity (that is, light) and darkness. As such it sits with a theology that accepts both what we can affirm of God (kataphatic theology) and also recognises that there are large areas where God is unknowable (apophatic theology). It allows the mind to engage with and be held, through God's grace, by the Truth of Divine Revelation yet be open to new depths and insights – thus avoiding fundamentalism and ideology. At the same time it does not have to state the answer to everything and can be peaceful, even joyously free, in that.

Taking seriously such a sense of the Mystery of God, and how it is held and responded to, affects our Christian spirituality, i.e. how we relate to God and live out our faith. This may be challenging! For example, faith is typically identified with certainty and absolute clarity, and seen as opposed to doubt. Faith rightly does affirm some things as true but certainty is, or can be, as much the enemy of faith as doubt, cutting us off from the growth in Christ that God wants for us. God, like the Apostle Paul, wants us to move from milk to solid food in our appreciation of his Revelation (cf 1 Cor 3:1–4). God wants us to live increasingly by spiritual, not natural inclinations. Here we find that God is both grasped and hidden by faith. God is so immense that faith is hearing but also not hearing everything, seeing and not seeing, touching and not touching, experiencing and not experiencing, knowing and not knowing. This is the case since God has revealed himself and is always with us, but also is always 'more'. True knowledge and wisdom cast light on mystery but they do not remove it. Faith is reasonable but goes beyond reason to love, hope and obedience. Faith affirms God as a mysterious presence who calls us forth – always. His presence and nature gives us assurance but also challenges us.

Many see our societies as increasingly spiritual, or at least see many people in them as increasingly searching for something beyond the rational, material and instantly pleasurable. They look for something beyond what appears superficial and often actually sense a deeper, if more mysterious and even paradoxical, dimension that they want to affirm and explore. Rather than see mystery as a problem or something for Christian experts, perhaps we should face and name it from the outset and address and embrace it in evangelisation? Why not see God as a mystery made visible, though not removed or overcome, in Christ? For some people, coming to faith, as well as growing in it, may actually be helped by accepting and affirming mystery. With this can come an affirmation of the mystery of God in Christ and of God's dealings in all of creation and with each of us. An appreciation of mystery probably makes it easier, not harder, to affirm God as Father, Son and Holy Spirit and to become attuned to their presence and action in the world. People can thus find faith in yielding to mystery, giving in to it, even committing to it, rather than in seeking to deny it, to overcome or conquer it or argue past or round it or completely rationalise it.

Neither does the journey end with 'conversion' but rather it is ongoing since it is the mysterious God whom we now journey with. We encounter and enter into Mystery – the Mystery of Christ. Mystery is not about vagueness and still less about a lack of confidence in Divine Revelation. Rather, it is about realising that there are limits to our knowledge and that even any intellectual understanding of God and even Jesus, while it can eliminate certain falsehoods, is still limited. The Spirit leads us to God and into the mysterious depths of God, though we will never exhaust them (1 Cor 2:6–16). Let us be willing to follow where the Spirit would lead! However much difficulty there is on our journey, we have a sure hope and a confident longing for God since the Spirit poured into our hearts gives us assurance and intercedes for us, even in unutterable groans (cf Rom 8:26–7).

Is this the sort of faith that is formed, or at least begun, on Alpha? Sometimes, yes![27] I do think it is the sort of faith that sits best with what is actually happening on the course and the way God seems to be acting in the wider movement that has emerged around it.[28] It is not, of course, by any means unique to Alpha and many times such faith will be resisted on Alpha for various reasons. It is a faith that challenges us, often to move beyond boundaries we have set for ourselves, or had set for us, by our theologies/Christian ideologies. Perhaps some of the material on Alpha could usefully be realigned to better nurture a journey into such faith – if this is first seen as desirable. Having a good sense of the sort of faith, and a radically Biblical vision of the life of grace that God wants to call us into, helps us respond fully. It is a deeper faith that may speak more to the emerging deep spiritual awareness of our age. As such mystery ought to be considered more by those engaged in evangelisation and mission.

Following God into new ways of Mission

Clearly Alpha has been, and to a degree remains, fruitful evangelistically. Fundamentally evangelisation depends on the belief and fact that God is already present and at work, drawing people to Himself, to conversion, to fellowship and communion in the Church. This is expressed by the idea of the *Missio Dei* ('Mission of God'). God is the chief evangeliser and goes ahead of us. We are asked to co-operate with him as his instruments. To do this most effectively we have first to see clearly what he is doing, how and where. What we then do is not so different from the advice sometimes given to people engaging in prayer ministry. 'See what God does and bless it!' More specifically in a mission context, this might be paraphrased as 'See what God does and follow him!' We need to see and keep following our Missionary God! It could be argued that NG and HTB saw what God was doing evangelistically and went with it. He may continue to surprise us and do new things! It requires open eyes, ears and hearts, good discernment but also flexibility on our part and even a willingness to be challenged. The Scriptures make all these points clear on numerous occasions.[29]

I would like to end this chapter by briefly mentioning two aspects that strike me about mission and evangelisation on Alpha in all this. Firstly, Alpha has put a focus on the role of the Holy Spirit in mission. In a way, the Spirit seems to have got ahead of what HTB had expected and 'allowed' in terms of their understanding and teaching. This is an example of how, more widely, the Spirit goes ahead and makes God's presence felt in various ways. The Spirit acts in people's experience. This points them towards looking at the real possibility of the Supernatural and its relevance to them, and to want to understand it. The Word then establishes its power and truth by interpreting and informing this, and also points to and leads a person to name God as Father and become his child. The Father is seen as having sent both the Son (Word) and Spirit. Meaning and purpose in life begin to emerge. Discipleship begins. A sense of God's goodness, holiness and otherness emerges. This highlights our sin, prompting people to ask for mercy at some point in this process. All this happens in the environment and womb of the church. All of it is linked to and facilitates conversion, both initial and ongoing. In a sense there is a Trinitarian procession here, though we should be careful of separating out and 'isolating' the work of each person of the Trinity due to the intrinsic unity and profound co-operation between them. This sequence (Spirit–Son–Father) may have relevance to aspects of mission in an age that is seen as increasingly spiritual but is also tired of words and suspicious of Christian ones.

The second point is linked to the fact that what the Holy Spirit does fundamentally is to make God present (or make people aware of God's presence). Some will see this as part of 'power evangelism'. There is some truth in this. In power evangelism the emphasis tends to be on clear, preferably dramatic, charismatic actions of God. However, what the Spirit is doing, at the deepest and most pervasive way, goes beyond the use of identified gifts and the demonstration of power. It is more about making God real as a mysterious but real loving presence than about demonstrations of unusual power. It is about people opening up to this in an ongoing way, rather than about repeated dramatic powerful actions and deeds of God. People, especially some Pentecostals and Charismatics, may well be inclined to overlook God's presence and treat it as a kind of bonus prize or consolation if the Charismatic gifts and unusual signs are not in evidence. Yet I would suggest that these gifts are (adopting the use of the term in John's Gospel for Jesus' miracles) signs that point to Christ, to who he is, to God dwelling among people, being present with us. What we may have here is 'Presence evangelism' where 'presence' does not just mean our silent witness but the active and truly powerful presence of God. In actual fact this is directly linked to the Risen and Ascended Lord Jesus whose presence, power and influence now fills all of creation and which is brought to us in a special way by the Holy Spirit, the pouring out of whom is made possible by Christ's Resurrection and Ascension (e.g Jn 14:12–21, 16:5–15 and Eph 4:7–13) and the new covenant which this Passover of Christ establishes (Jer 31:31–4 and Heb 10:11–25). This Divine Presence calls us to be present to him, to sense him in the depth of our being as well as filling the universe, and to respond in contemplation and silent adoration as much as with words and action. It then calls us to be really present to others by the gift of ourselves in love. Again this is present but not that explicit on Alpha. It could perhaps be acknowledged and flagged up more. Worship, which is included on Alpha, is seen as bringing us into the presence of God (and often focuses on the Risen and Ascended Lord worshipped in Heaven). This awareness of Divine presence may also point to aspects of mission that generally need to be given more attention by the church.

This chapter has tried to make clear that the Alpha Course operates in ways that are more complex than usually indicated. I hope it has also cast some extra light on the true nature of Alpha as well as stimulating further questions, and giving practitioners suggestions on how to better co-operate with the work of God on Alpha or other process courses. It has been a chance to step back and reflect on the course as such. In Section 3 I will engage with issues raised by the impact of the course.

Notes

[1] I would suggest this is all he did for the most part since he has often said that the basic teaching content was put together by John Irvine.

[2] It would be hard but it may be possible! I consider the content more likely to date than the method. It might be possible to introduce a new text – or a seriously reworked version of the present one – though in part that would be a *policy* decision for AI.

[3] I do, however, think there is some, even important, significance in the emphasis on the person and work of the Holy Spirit.

[4] Some of the testimonies published in *Alpha News* follow this pattern. It is also happening elsewhere.

[5] I know of cases where people have felt free to ask questions for the first time at church. In a way, this is a sad reflection on the churches concerned.

[6] Michael Green, *After Alpha*. Kingsway, 2nd ed 2001 (First edition was 1998). See 'Tailpiece (For the Culture Vultures)'. Green is very enthusiastic in his defence of Alpha; in fact, he is zealous in promoting it. His detailed understanding and application of the personality types underpinning the Myers-Briggs Personality test (p. 250–2) to Alpha is also enthusiastic, though I think Green's application of the Myers-Briggs Personality Types Indicators to Alpha is superficial and problematic.

The Myers-Briggs analysis of personality works on a theory of how individuals relate to and draw energy from the 'outer' world to the 'inner' world (being extrovert or introvert); how they construct knowledge and meaning (being sensate or intuitive); how they determine value (thinking or feeling); and how they take decisions/organise their lives (judging or perceiving). Each of these functions is classified as operating in one of two ways, (as indicated above) though the terms are defined in quite specific ways, not entirely in line with their everyday use. The overall personality of a person is a *combination of the interaction* of the features found in them, giving 16 broad personality types. However, Green takes each personality feature in *isolation* from the others – and presents them out of order too – while the creation of personality types in the Myers-Briggs approach is dependent on the interaction of these different features. Further, he then describes each feature in very broad terms, perhaps broader than the scope of the original theory. Alpha is then trawled for features that will appeal to these generalised, abstracted, and possibly enlarged, features considered as psychological entities/personality types in their own right. His argument for the attraction of 'perceivers' to Alpha is probably the most far-fetched of all. He invokes 'sheer curiosity' as the attraction when this personality trait is marked by spontaneity and flexibility! Common ground between many of these personality traits and Alpha can certainly be found, but looking at the 16 Myers Briggs personality types as such, I think some will have much more affinity with Alpha than others.

[7] See John Finney, *Emerging Evangelism*, pp. 86–7.

[8] Charles Freebury suggests that Alpha follows a cyclical model of learning as described by Anton Baumohl. In this, information and experience are received, reflected on, existing concepts are then updated, and new learning put into practice. He feels the supply of information is somewhat more linear and fixed than newer and younger generations would expect from being able to use the web to zoom around texts and links, following their own interest and whim rather than following the original article they started with. (See Charles Freebury, *Alpha or Emmaus?*, 2005, p. 44, available as pdf file. For details on other resources available from Charles and how to get them please see Chapter 7, footnote 12, or the Appendix.)

[9] Several other process courses (either evangelistic or more generally formative) have been developed that have clearly studied Alpha and learned from it, even if the final product is for various reasons then presented as an alternative to Alpha. Some will be commented on briefly in Ch.8. For further information see appendix. (See also Mark.Ireland's chapters in *Evangelism – Which Way Now?* for more details and evaluation)

[10] The focus here is not church buildings (though they can have an impact) but the community of people.

[11] See Chapter 12, 'Eating Alpha' by Anne Richards for a development of this.

[12] Nicky Gumbel has cited accounts of people who have been converted during Communion Services.

[13] In combining these three elements it is similar to a whole series of evangelistic courses developed in the Catholic church. Their approach and method is summarised as ke-ka-ko where ke is kerygmatic, ka is charismatic and ko is community. (The originals were not in English!) It is the integrated combination that is effective.

[14] How is this possible? Christian theology insists that though God has planted the desire for God in our hearts, it is dependent on free Divine initiative. It is only because the Supernatural Reality has become part or our natural reality, acting in it and ultimately becoming human, thus allowing us to grasp and know and love God in terms of our own existence and way of living. Humanity is then caught up into divine life by Jesus' death and resurrection into new life of human nature first achieved by God's Son and offered to us in the gift of his Spirit. The Supernatural (Divine) nature takes on the natural (human) nature so that the human can take on Divine nature. Not just humanity but all of creation in renewed as part of this Divine work.

[15] However, the Spirit blows where it wills and our God is a God of surprises. Unexpected moments of grace, small or life-changing, happen when God wills and at levels that even they may not understand, if a person's heart is open. However, useful they may be, it is foolish to try and restrict God to our understanding and models of what he should do!

[16] In technical terms, this is often referred to as a sense of the 'numinous'. There may also be a sense of God as 'Truth' or 'Reality'.

[17] Some testimonies indicate there may be a significant resistance to or difficulty with all of this and even an immediate and strong repulsion. Handling this requires good, wise and sensitive pastoral experience but a person can be helped to explore these 'difficulties' in ways that cast light on them and do take such a person forward spiritually. Clearly, this may not happen immediately or even quickly.

[18] People's testimonies (through Alpha) do not tend to be expressed in cold dogmatic tones but in language that is much more about an immediate encounter with God. This may be dismissed as pure emotion – and may sometimes be this – but it may go much deeper and be a type, perhaps only an 'introductory' type, of mystical experience. Though difficult to define, mysticism is commonly considered as 'loving knowledge of the Divine' and 'intimate union with God'. Examination and reflection on the Christian mystical tradition may prove profitable in order to understand what is involved, at least sometimes. It may also help significant connections be seen and made with experiences which a lot of (not necessarily religious) people nowadays describe as being 'spiritual', though careful discernment is needed in such work.

[19] Even here it can be multi-faceted and can be mainly cognitive, emotional or volitional, or about conscience or be various combinations of these.

[20] Perhaps something similar, or analogous, could be said about conscience as a spiritual function, or capability, in humans and the impact on it of God as Holiness and sheer Goodness. However, conscience may also be viewed as a specific interaction of intellect and will.

[21] The action of God in such situations and experiences (sometimes called trials or even dark nights or purifications) should not be discounted or resisted. In these, patience and character are formed and hope grown and expressed, hope's fulfilment assured by the gift of the Spirit, poured into our hearts. (Rom 5:1–5).

[22] The Bible describes sexual union as a person 'having knowledge of' (or 'knowing') their spouse. Modern Western culture often refers to such an act as 'making love'. These idioms point to both knowledge (truth) and love (appreciation) being rooted in the encounter between persons. (If both idioms are taken, at their core, as expressing something valuable and of dignity, then truth and love are connected and humans yearn for both. The complementary insights of,

and thus deep connection between, these idioms, deriving from very different cultures, may give us hope that a healthier more integrated understanding of the connection between love and knowledge [and goodness and truth] may yet be developed and, more importantly still, be practiced.)

[23] It will have to purify us in the process. Our understanding of truth needs to be purified and transformed by Divine Truth; so must love, so must our sense of goodness, and thus justice. Likewise, our sense and living of relationships must be re-visioned and practically transformed by encountering God who is Father, Son and Holy Spirit in a perfect unity (which is the model of all community).

[24] Indeed, the Bible often uses paradoxical language – that specifically defies the use of neat definitions of words and their 'logical' connection to express this encounter with God. Thus 'He who would save his life must lose it (Mk 8:35)' etc. This language expresses the logic of faith and love and the coherence of God's Providence, grace and ways of working with us.

[25] However, we do need to be careful not to get too fixed in the cultural and epistemological premises of either culture but to transform both with the Reality, the mystery, of Christ.

[26] Having written this material on worship I chatted with a friend originally from the North of Scotland and the Reformed (Presbyterian) tradition. He remarked that the centrality of worship and a clear focus and presentation of Christ lies at the heart of their Christianity. Indeed, conversion (and thus evangelism and even 'revival') would be seen as flowing out of it, and as a consequence of it.

Such traditions are cautious about stressing the role of man or placing too much emphasis on strategies of mission. Rather let the focus be on God and then his grace can achieve what only it can do! I have heard, and on occasions witnessed, accounts of conversions happening when people encounter Christians worshipping God in other traditions and liturgical styles including sacramental and formal ones. Ministers in these traditions have sometimes made quite similar remarks to my friend from the Reformed Tradition though this tradition is normally seen to be at odds with the Catholic/Orthodox Traditions. Whether 'high' or 'low' in terms of liturgy, perhaps such people share a high theology of grace in many ways.

[27] It sits fairly well with some of the qualities of mature faith outlined in the table comparing the qualities and outlook of mature and immature faith towards the end of Chapter 1.

[28] It sits with the multi-faceted formation of faith proposed in this chapter. It may appear to jar with some aspects of the talks (though that depends on how the content is delivered) but does seem sit well with the stated open exploratory purpose of the small groups. It may even help generate a situation where the small groups become spaces where mutual listening and learning more naturally happens.

[29] For just one example see Acts 10. Peter is 'converted' on seeing how God had converted Cornelius. The result was the church's commitment to mission to the Gentiles!

SECTION 3

Issues arising from the impact of Alpha

Alpha has had a big impact and also enjoyed a high profile. This has made it the topic of research and many articles – as well as conversations. These are very varied and often partisan and not always well-informed and often cover similar ground. It is my intention in this section to review and critique this work and begin to build on it too. In this way I hope to take the level of thinking forward and make it more informed, thus providing a good platform for any future discussion.

I have done this in four chapters. The first (Chapter 7) overviews research surveys to look at what is actually been happening with Alpha in practice. In some ways the other three chapters build on these findings – though it is not necessary to grasp all the numerical detail and analysis presented in Chapter 7 to understand these other three chapters. A brief summary of these findings is placed at the end of the chapter. I look at Alpha specifically in the context of mission and the changing culture in the UK (Chapter 8) though it ought to have wider geographical relevance too. Alpha has had a broad appeal that has raised various questions and possibilities for ecumenism and Christian unity. These issues and some others about how church is changing are discussed in Chapter 9. Lastly, questions have been asked about the strategies used to promote Alpha, what the long-term hopes and aims of AI/HTB are and how effective the strategies used to implement these are and what else might be tried. In a way this brings together all the previous work and rounds of this section and part of the book (Chapter 10).

AB

CHAPTER 7

Alpha on the Ground
An Overview based on Major Surveys and Reports

Andrew Brookes

Introduction: Aims and Approach

Alpha is described as a tool for evangelisation – for outreach to those not at church. 'Running in more than 7,000 churches of all denominations across the UK' is the bright heading printed across *Alpha News* for many years, similar wording being used elsewhere. These are the basic statistics and impression that are probably most commonly known and held about Alpha. More grandly, the impression has sometimes been gained, if not intentionally given, that Alpha is a 'one size fits all' product and even a special answer to the church's problems. It is sometimes viewed as a course so 'blessed' or 'anointed' that it will always work whenever, wherever it is used and just running it repeatedly will turn around the churches and nations. It is the intention of this chapter to examine to what extent all these claims are true, or not, and thus also lay a firm foundation for chapters which follow.

I do not doubt at all that attending Alpha courses has changed many lives for the better. Frankly, I do not have to be convinced of this. I have been directly involved with courses where people have become Christians or returned to church practice after many years away. I have seen people significantly deepen an existing Christian life and some get much more involved in local church activity too. I have seen people healed both physically and in more inner (emotional) ways too. I do not hesitate to say that I have seen God at work in all this. I have heard many other such testimonies. I am sure there are local churches that have run Alpha frequently and seen considerable growth; Alpha is very probably a factor in this growth, though it would be interesting to delve further and see how it and other factors interacted. Yet all this is not the whole story. I have also seen people finish courses relatively unchanged or walk away much earlier. I have seen churches take it up and put it down again. I have seen courses struggle to really get outsiders to come at all or simply not attract significant numbers. I have seen tensions in local congregations over the use and wider impact of Alpha. I also know these observations are not unique to me. Alpha can work but how well, where and how often? Where does it not work and why? Has it reached its sell by date or at least its best before date? Why or why not? I have already hinted at some of the factors that go to answering these questions. We will now build on this much more fully. In short, this chapter sets out to look at empirical evidence to see how Alpha is working on the ground.

To do this I do not intend to use testimonies or endorsements – AI/HTB are very good at this – but to try and look at the broader picture and general trends here. That inevitably means drawing on surveys and statistics collected by others. Some of these question the claims made by, on behalf of, or about Alpha and what the real effect is that Alpha is having. Some have produced findings more supportive of Alpha. Other 'Alpha watchers' have raised concerns about reported findings from some research, though this appears to be especially about the interpretation given to data rather than generally about the data itself (though this too may be seen to be limited). There have also been concerns about headlines and summary articles published without giving the full data or even much indication of it. These are, of course, from a scientific perspective fair concerns. Researchers have their own angles of approach, their own agenda, convictions and suppositions which will tend to come into play, especially when it comes to interpretation. Often the data is open to more than just the interpretation given. Sometimes research has left important questions unanswered. Large scale generalised and clumped statistics, while they may sound impressive, often hide as much as they reveal, if not more. Articles written for the wider market may be intended to be more about promoting or debunking Alpha than about reporting research, though the reader may not see it this way.

How should all this data be handled and these concerns responded to? My aim here is to draw together major research findings within one chapter, something that I do not think has been previously done on this scale. Secondly, I intend, where possible, to see how well these corroborate each other, i.e. how consistent the data are. Where this is not possible I have looked to see how the different research findings may complement each other to build a more complete picture of the use and impact of Alpha than has hitherto been compiled. Thirdly, I will offer some comments and interpretation based on my own experience of Alpha through running courses, and offering training and advice to others doing so in a number of settings. Again this makes this study different to most of the major ones published since they (most notably work by Brierley and Hunt) are not carried out by Alpha practitioners. Though familiar with Alpha I am not being paid by AI (or anybody else) – and indeed have been encouraged by AI to write independently. My publisher also encouraged an independent and fair approach. I will also draw on the comments given me by other Alpha practition-ers and advisers, as well as others working in the field of mission as evangelists, mission consultants and mission enablers. I have tried to comment on and also address concerns raised about data too, since most of it has been contested by various people. Throughout I shall endeavour to carefully separate and distinguish the data from the interpretation given it by their respective authors, others and, indeed, by myself. For all these reasons I believe that this reflective review is an original contribution, though I realise it would not be possible without the research of others and is also enriched by the comments of others working in this field. For all this I am most grateful. At the same time I am aware that it does not address all issues adequately. Gaps remain which others are welcome to fill, but hopefully it is helpful.

One of the aims of this book is to stimulate a realistic and well-informed debate about Alpha. For these reasons I have structured my presentation around the sort of questions and issues that people either tend to raise about Alpha or, on occasions, perhaps ought to be asked more often. Another hope is to provide a good accurate foundation for further research. Thus I have also sought to give some indications of how and in what directions any debate and also research and devel-opment could move in the future. Some original research has been conducted by authors in Section 4 of this book, carried out and written up on the basis of the first draft of my material.

Some introductory notes about sources

I think it will be helpful to gather here a few introductory comments about some of my major sources and to raise a few general concerns I and others have about them. First a general note on sample sizes and their importance. It is a rule of thumb in such research that to be confi-dent of making generalised 'national' conclusions a sample size of 1,000 or more is needed. Many Alpha research projects do not actually manage this. With smaller projects, it may be important to examine the results and correlate them with the results of bigger experimental sets. When issuing questionnaires to 'cold' audiences a return rate of anything over 10% is better than average according to normal market research. Obviously when dealing with a questionnaire about church to church groups, or specifically about Alpha to churches registered as running it, a higher return rate would be expected. This proves to be the case in these studies. The bigger the percentage return, the smaller the percentage error in findings. It is also worth noting that those who are particularly enthusiastic about Alpha might be more likely to return forms. This ought to be born in mind when scaling up sample results.

Peter Brierley (Christian Research Association)

Peter Brierley is the Executive Director of Christian Research Associ-ation, committed to undertaking major research for Trinitarian churches. This involves collecting data about church life and inter-preting it and suggesting action so that the Kingdom of God may grow. Various projects it undertakes are sponsored by different church groups or combinations of groups. Christian Research has published a large number of papers and bigger publications. Although very widely used, the work of Christian Research Association is not without its critics. A concern that has been brought to my attention is about assumptions made and procedures followed to scale up sample sizes to give overall national figures. Also recipients of reports have noted a certain (under-standable) tendency to write up reports such that generally things are put in favourable terms to the sponsoring organisation, though Brierley does make criticisms too. Brierley has been commissioned by AI to do research but I shall treat this under the heading of AI. Brierley has also included questions about Alpha in a number of surveys. The ones I have drawn on most heavily are as follows.

Turning the Tide: the Challenge Ahead

This is the Report of the 2002 Scottish Church Census.[1] This was an extensive survey across all the denominations. Forms were sent out to as many churches as could be identified through collaboration with national leaders. Responses were received from 52% of the churches they were sent to. By my calculation this meant that the data came from 2,132 different congregations with a good spread across the denomi-nations. As such it can be confidently scaled up to give a national Scot-tish picture. However, it should be remembered that church life and especially the distribution of denominations shows marked differ-ences across England, Scotland, Wales and Ireland and thus some figures cannot so easily be applied to other nations. It asked a number of questions about Alpha.

Research Commissioned by 'Springboard'

Springboard was an Evangelism Initiative of the Archbishops of Canterbury and York in the Church of England. In March 2000 Peter Brierley conducted research for Springboard, looking at patterns of growth or decline in all churches running Alpha (as listed in succes-sive editions of *Alpha News*) against national statistics on growth and decline over the period 1989–98 (based on the data from the English Church Attendance Survey).[2] 8,700 churches took part in the surveys of 1989 and 1998 making this a large survey.

Research on Church Growth commissioned by the Salvation Army

Peter Brierley/Christian Research UK were commissioned in 2002 by the Northern Division of the Salvation Army to undertake research on factors that had helped churches in England grow in the 1990s. Starting from a data base of 8,700 churches whose numbers were known in 1994 and 2002, a random list of 2,900 were approached, the selection ensuring a variety of patterns in growth and decline. The result was a study of 1,125 churches (i.e. a response rate of 38%). This was thus a very large study. The Salvation Army kindly allowed some of the data to be published as *Leadership, Vision and Growing Churches*.[3] It undertook research on the use of Alpha and other process courses.

Christian Research has also been sponsored by AI/HTB to undertake an annual study of Alpha each year since 2001. I shall discuss this under the heading of AI/HTB below. However, from time to time Brierley (with permission) writes articles in which he uses some of this data and makes generally favourable comments about the progress and impact of Alpha. These really need to be taken with some caution since the full data is not given. Some commentators have expressed very real concerns to me about these articles and especially their headlines and summaries! Indeed, some feel he is generally upbeat about Alpha to a degree that the evidence does not fully justify. (However, see also my comments on the full AI reports below.)

My overall view of Brierley's research on Alpha is that the data are very helpful in building up a picture of what is happening with Alpha. However, different interpretations to those that Brierley gives can sometimes be posited. Much as I value, respect and use Brierley's work, I have on occasions noted what I feel to be a tendency to comment on statistics in ways favourable to Alpha, where the actual data is, of itself, more ambiguous. Also he has sometimes tended to adopt uncritically AI/HTB generated statements on what Alpha is doing/how it works and to use these for interpretation.[4]

Stephen Hunt

I shall also draw significantly on the research of Stephen Hunt. A sociologist of religion, Hunt has researched Alpha empirically. After a pilot study involving four churches (400 questionnaires with a 76% return) from one area in south England in 1999–2000,[5] he undertook a much more substantial study on Alpha. It was based on a random and national sample right across England and Wales, starting by approaching every 50th church listed in the Alpha Directory. From this 31 were eventually selected, providing a sample from across the denominations and independent churches, regions, social background etc. Between summer of 2001 and the end of 2002, some 1,500 questionnaires were administered and 839 returned, a response rate of 55%.[6] Fifty interviews were also conducted (from 113 volunteers who returned the questionnaires) and separate research conducted on Alpha in prisons (11 prisons of various sorts), seven universities and colleges and four youth courses.[7] Written up as *The Alpha Enterprise*,[8] it makes for interesting reading. Well-informed on Christianity and broadly sympathetic to both Christianity and Alpha, Hunt is not a Christian but is described in the introduction by Martyn Percy as a 'seeker'.

Hunt's research focuses on the guests who attend Alpha while most other research is addressed to, and the forms filled in by, church leaders. It is thus a very helpful complement to the work of Brierley and others. His pilot study is small and cannot be used to make more general conclusions. The central plank of his main study consisted in interviews with 839 people from a range of churches originally on a random basis. Although this falls a little short of the 1,000 regarded as a big enough sample size to make national generalisations, it is still large (and larger than most Alpha samples) and thus some more general conclusions can be drawn from it though with some caution. Generalisations can not so readily be drawn, if at all, from his smaller studies of specialised Alpha courses.

The chief model he uses to approach religion, and Alpha in partic-ular, is that of a producer: consumer interaction. His approach and critque to Christianity in general and Alpha in particular uses the paradigm of an increasingly consumer society (which has been gener-ated in the West by increased material provision and comfort) marked by choice and in which religions, Christian churches and particular Christian products have to compete. There is some validity in this model and approach though it is, in my view, not a complete under-standing of the religious situation and has its limitations in analysis. He sees value in religion though struggles to see direct agency for God or the supernatural. Charismatic Christianity is viewed principally as addressing emotional needs and therapeutic issues. He thinks that Christianity, faced with the current and ongoing erosion in church attendance, Christian belief and values, has a huge and uphill task if it is not to continue to decline (by traditional measures and in its trad-itional forms at least) in the foreseeable future. He thinks that Alpha's main impact has been on those already at church, spreading Evan-gelical-Charismatic Christianity, with some impact on others beyond that but concludes it has had limited overall impact and is unlikely to reverse this general decline. Not directly theological or pastoral he is humanly sensitive, respectful and practical. I do not agree with every-thing he says or with all his interpretation but he provides helpful insights that, he thinks, largely confirm his views expressed in the pilot study, though he has modified these in places. His data, which can be used without accepting all of his interpretative framework, provide a picture of Alpha more mixed than the one that readily emanates from HTB and especially from *Alpha News*.

Alpha International/Holy Trinity Brompton

a) Research

AI/HTB have conducted some of their own research – in detail on the courses at HTB – and, especially in the 1990s, through questionnaires sent to churches running Alpha. They have increasingly relied on research commissioned annually for a number of years (since 2001) and undertaken by the 'Christian Research Association' directed by Peter Brierley. They do not make these reports publicly available, as is their right. They did however, very kindly make a full copy of the 2005 Report available to me for this book. This report gives summaries of previous reports on a number of points too. This has greatly added to the conviction with which I have been able to draw conclusions. It also allows more sense and realistic weight to be given to summary use of these statistics in *Alpha News* and by Peter Brierley elsewhere.

Some general background on these reports may be helpful. Brierley is given access to the addresses of all course administrators on the Alpha registers. A random selection is made, with care made not to survey churches in two successive years. New registrations are included in that year's survey. The different Alpha specialisms are also taken into consideration as separate entries. In this way, for example, the subset that was mailed the questionnaire towards the end of 2005 consisted of 5,098 courses. Of these, 915 returned the form by the deadline, and a few afterwards. This is a response rate of 23%. This compares with a response rate (with presumably not very different mailing list subsets) of 30% in 2001, 38% in 2002, 31% in 2003 and 29% in 2004. Brierley comments that such a downward trend is typical of survey responses generally, but may be worth future attention. He also notes that the market research industry today would still regard a 23% response rate as good. It is a large body of data and, in fact, is a bigger sample size than any other that I have come across in specific studies on Alpha, though questions on Alpha have been included in other large surveys. For all these reasons, it seems fair to regard Brierley's data presented in these reports for AI as reliable though I shall make some comments later on its use, interpretation and scaling up process. In general, it seems fair to ask if it is likely that courses committed to Alpha will be proportionately more likely to return questionnaires than those that are not very active or not very successful. Thus, do the figures, most probably accurate and useful in themselves, give an over-indication of Alpha activity if scaled up in a linear manner?

b) Other Information

AI/HTB, usually through *Alpha News*, release certain statistics about Alpha. These include the reports they commission from Christian Research and also other reports that are given to them. The promotional aims of *Alpha News* need to be remembered in interpreting these since all material used aims to present a positive picture of Alpha. In doing this, AI is operating no differently to any other business and most Christian organisations. Despite *Alpha News'* populist, almost tabloid, style, I think its writers use language very carefully and precisely, a lot of care going into ensuring literal accuracy. (The same is true of other information coming out of AI for public consumption.) In fact, having had access to a full Alpha annual report I am more confident than before that they are and have been conscientious about information released being as accurate as possible. A selection of favourable figures is used, as should be expected. They are no different to other groups in doing this. In fact, it could be argued they have released more data than they have to, and more than most Christian organisations.

The public use by AI of statistics and other claims are quite limited. In fact, scouring the pages of *Alpha News* and other AI publications with a critical eye and researcher's intent, it is very difficult to get anything like a full picture of what is really happening with Alpha.[9] They do from time to time produce articles with some statistics, and occasionally packed full of them. As a researcher, one should read them carefully and be cautious about drawing conclusions and determining causal links between them. In my experience a very careful reading of such articles, paying attention to what is said, how it is said, and also what is not said, can furnish useful information though conclusions can only be drawn from such inferences with a good deal of caution.

AI does not obstruct or discourage research and, indeed, they are helpful to researchers and authors.[10] AI is also keen to get and receive accurate research on Alpha.

Other Studies by Denominations, Church Agencies and Individual Researchers

A number of other studies have been undertaken, some of them quite large or at least fairly comprehensive within the specific group of churches being investigated.

Baptist Union of Great Britain

I have been given a copy of research for the Baptist Union of Great Britain (not including Scotland) by Darrell Jackson and Beth Johnson.[11] This was carried out in 1999 and written up in 2002. The annual returns included some questions on Alpha. Out of 2,120 churches in the Union, 1,754 returned a completed form (83%) and of these 857 had used Alpha. This makes it a helpful study and it has some very helpful data and perceptive interpretation.

—

Others that I have drawn on are as follows. The Evangelical Alliance conducted research on Alpha in 1998 among its member churches and a selection of other churches in 1996. This totalled 442 churches, including 300 of its member churches. Forms were returned from 46% (i.e. 192 churches) of which 69% has used Alpha. Research is reported by the Anglican Diocese of Lichfield undertaken in 1999 amongst 426 parishes. Mark Ireland undertook and wrote this up and I am glad to draw on his findings in 'Evangelism – which way now?' and on other information he reports there and questions he raises. St Alban's Anglican diocese conducted research in 2001 on people who had attended courses over the previous five years and this has also been drawn on. Research undertaken by the Church of Scotland and reported to its General Assembly, the Roman Catholic Church in England and Wales (by the Catholic Missionary Society), and amongst Methodists and the Salvation Army has been covered in section 4 along with the reports of new findings.

Finally I am indebted to the work of Charles Freebury. He has undertaken a significant gathering of information on Alpha (including smaller studies) as well doing as his own research and analysis. Until recently he worked as a lay Missioner in his Methodist Circuit and has a good grasp of the issues facing local churches when they engage with mission. His work on Alpha and Emmaus is respected by many including Mark Ireland and John Finney. I am grateful to have been able to draw on and ponder his work, including summaries of other studies, and also to discuss it and my own work with him. He has also produced other resources to supplement Alpha and other process courses.[12]

Numerous studies by students have been undertaken, of variable quality, but collecting and analysing these would be far too big a task.

Research on Specialist Alpha Courses
– and Concerns about Amalgamated Data

Most of the data and my comments focus on the normal (adult) course as designed and promoted for use in local churches. It has been available since 1993 and there is most information available about this. Many of the other versions have only been marketed recently, though I have made some comments where appropriate. Indeed, the advent of these other courses makes it harder to interpret aggregated statistics. What looks like overall growth in uptake may be attributable to an enthusiastic use of new versions (and probably with mainly Christian guests) while numbers attending the standard course, and actual numbers of these courses running, may be falling. To follow the effective development and real evangelistic (i.e. outreach) effectiveness of each version it is necessary to keep the statistics separate.

How many local churches actually run Alpha, how often and how well?

Hunt presents brief 'biopic' summaries of what has actually happened with Alpha in the churches in his major study – and it is very variable. He approached every fiftieth church in the first 7,000 churches listed in the Alpha register (which I calculate at 140 churches) and drew up his experimental set from these. Some run it regularly, a few of these more than once a year, some have tried it and are no longer active. Some are not running it all. It includes churches that only ran it once, and ones that ran it very few times and did not really get guests beyond the church. Not many were running it repeatedly and getting many non-Christian guests.[13] These are all churches in the Alpha register – and sent enough returned questionnaires to be included in the write up! Of the churches he originally approached, 26 felt they could not contribute because they had not run the course for some time (and sometimes for several years), four said they had never run it, and 20 could not be contacted by phone or other means.[14]

This is quite a variable pattern of usage and non-usage. How does it compare with any other records or observations? It is fair to say that it sits reasonably well with what I have encountered on the ground as an advisor. Other advisors I have chatted with also report variable frequency of use and persistence with Alpha. Advisers readily accepted that by no means all those registered were running all the time or even each year. Advisers have cited to me a fairly wide range of estimates on what fraction of registered courses might actually be running at any time, though it is clear that this changes a good deal, and ultimately reflects lots of very local factors and decisions. Beyond those factors within a specific congregation, there are likely to be variations stimulated by the arrival of new Alpha products/course variations as well as the appeal of any particular Annual Invitation. The vitality and effectiveness of the local Alpha regional team of advisers at any time is very important and I suspect that the most accurate Register figures correspond to places where the Regional team of advisers have good contacts with local churches and have managed to feed-back data to AI. Additionally, there are some courses running who choose not to register for various reasons.

Mark Ireland has undertaken a survey by phoning churches on the register in his home town of Walsall. Thirteen Courses were registered. It turned out that five had stopped running Alpha. Two had only starting running it recently and three were well established. Ireland felt that a further one course was an odd-ball with no clear correspondence to Alpha. Two churches could not be contacted due to inaccurate phone numbers being given. Ireland also found a further course not registered.[15] This is a small sample but again indicates the complex reality on the ground, and is not dissimilar to what advisers have reported to me.

Are there any other sources of more accurate figures? Brierley's reports for AI do reveal some figures collated since churches were asked to indicate how often and when they had run Alpha in each year they were surveyed. In 2005, 21% of responding churches did not run an Alpha Course in that year. This compared with 25% in 2004, 30% in 2003 and 28% in 2002.[16] This variable pattern appears to be broadly in line with Hunt's findings though the figures are towards the top end of the wide range of guestimates – admittedly anecdotal – given to me by Alpha Advisers. It is legitimate to ask if scaling up from these sample figures to national figures is entirely fair and accurate since relatively active churches may respond more frequently to the questionnaire than inactive ones.[17] Nonetheless, Brierley comments that this 'reflects both the accuracy of the Alpha register and the commitment of those churches on the list to the Alpha vision' (p. 14). It might be strictly more correct to say that the Register is about 75% accurate based on his findings. Brierley's data indicates that in recent years, at any rate, the percentage of active churches seems to have held up well. In my view there are likely to be variations across regions of the country and even denominations/churchmanship with some showing more persistence than others, and other denominational initiatives also impacting on what energy is focussed on Alpha.

How often do these churches run Alpha? My own anecdotal evidence suggests that most run in the Autumn term, often linked to the Annual Invitation that takes place each September. Many in fact only run once a year. Some run it a second time and relatively few run it three times. Churches may also run other course variations, or the adult course during the day, which will enhance the overall statistics. This pattern is supported by the findings in the AI reports from Peter Brierley. Over the years 2003–2005 around 40% ran one course per year, around 20% ran two courses, and around 7.5% ran three with around 2.5% running four and 2.5% running more. (Those running none fell from 30% in 2003 to 21% in 2005 – see above).[18] This research also showed that (in 2004 and 2005) around 15% of courses ran in the daytime with the rest in the evening. In 2005 57% ran in the Autumn term (53% in 2004) and 30% in the Spring (33% in 2004) and 13% (14% in 2004) in the summer. Again, this conforms well with my own anecdotal observations.

The Alpha Register

So what should we make of the Alpha Register, its accuracy and statistics based on it? The Alpha Register groups together all churches that wish to remain on the register as running Alpha. It does not indicate how often they run it. It is also one means of attracting guests to your course. Churches are encouraged by AI/HTB to register when they first start a course (or thereafter if they not already done so). Being on the register means AI/HTB keeps the church on the mailing list which means *Alpha News* is regularly sent along free with information about forthcoming conferences and other training events and resources. People, other than those actually running course, clearly choose to stay on the Alpha Register for a variety of reasons! Many may well hold some hope of running Alpha again in the future. Others, perhaps, just wish to keep receiving *Alpha News* and other HTB publications and brochures that come free to those on the register. This information along with enquiries from potential guests made precisely because a church is registered may sometimes stimulate a church into offering Alpha again. Some may just not get round to de-registering, though this will be confusing for potential guests who may contact them looking for a course. These factors might suggest that churches are more likely to register than de-register. It has been commented to me that perhaps this idea should be combined with the overall registered figures to conclude that actual Alpha use has been in decline since around 2000 as more and more churches stop using it and no more are added. Certainly there is a rate of drop-off over time but as we shall see there is also evidence that the overall use of Alpha is more complex than that in reality.

Do AI/HTB know that not all courses registered are actually running? Yes, I think they do – though quite possibly they do not know what the accurate figure for active courses is. Are they being deliberately dishonest with the register? No – their use of language is accurate. It is interesting to note that the phrase 'now running in 7,000 churches of all denominations across the UK' that used to appear very visibly on front of *Alpha News* no longer does so.[19] Also their literature now tends to use the phrase 'Alpha is *registered as running* in xx no of churches/ prisons etc'. This subtle change in language is more accurate and its introduction follows on from the research they commissioned by Peter Brierley, though its implications, I suspect, tend to be overlooked. AI/ HTB have always maintained that there are some courses that run and choose not to register, though it is difficult to know if these make up for the number of 'sleepers' on the register. Some supporters of Alpha might find the real figures dispiriting! Some have suggested the register now reflects little more than a pool of interested and sympathetic churches, and thus ones that can be informed of new developments and versions of courses etc. This seems very unfair since the majority run at least one course a year and the accumulated total of courses is higher than the total number of registered churches. This total number has fluctuated between 8,540 and 10,090 in the period from 2002–5.[20]

Brierley's work for AI suggests the register is around 75% accurate though this figure may be too high if active Alpha churches have preferentially returned more completed questionnaires than inactive ones. The work of Hunt and Ireland suggest it may well be lower – though these are much smaller samples. I suspect there are significant regional variations. Rounded up statistics ought to consider all this. They also need to consider that not all churches running Alpha bother to register. It is very hard to put a figure on these. The only hard data I am aware of on this comes from the Baptist Study of 1999. The annual returns indicated that 857 Baptist churches had used Alpha. However, Jackson and Johnson were only able to find 401 of these on the Alpha register. This is a huge discrepancy, potentially indicating that the register underestimates the number of registered courses by over 50%! The authors indicate they had a personal conversation with Peter Brierley who is reported as indicating that this is not too different from Brierley's findings when engaged with AI. Jackson and Johnson concur that such discrepencies could lead to a major underestimation of UK and world totals for number of courses and participants.[21] This may indicate why Brierley is happy to regard around 25% sleepers as cancelled out and thus to use the total on the register as accurate for rounding up purposes. Has this pattern of non-registration changed over time and are Baptist registration patterns typical of other denominations? It may have come down over time as AI has established itself more in the public eye and is seen to have more to offer local churches. However, all this certainly suggests that the real situation on the ground is far more complex and fluid than the figures for overall total number of registered courses might suggest. Caution is required when using the Alpha register for statistical purposes and it cannot be easily taken uncritically at face value.

One could ask if AI should do more to make the register accurate. I recently asked AI about this. They point out that each mailing to registered churches (till now there have been three every year) asks churches to update registration details and only stay on the register if they are running or intend to run a course relatively soon. It is felt, fairly, to be unreasonable for a church to register and de-register more than once a year. I was told it was not in anyone's interests for the register to be inaccurate. They also said that the register is publicly available on the website and that if errors are spotted and reported they will be dealt with.[22] They have alluded to the administrative time that reviews would take and that since they are seriously stretched with other work, making time for this (or justifying it as a priority) is difficult. However, from time to time and for various reasons, they, or even local regional teams, do pro-actively check out some of their figures. From information made available to me as an adviser, questions appear to be asked and data collated in such a way as to combine and keep on the register 'those who are running now with those who hope to run it again in the future'. Again this new wording allows a fair degree of latitude. It is understandable that AI do not wish to alienate people who are well disposed to Alpha and aggressively de-register churches which may then start running again. I also reckon that, encountering on the phone a friendly and polite Alpha adviser, most churches who are unsure of their intentions will tend to decide to stay on![23] However, inaccuracies are far from helpful to the potential guest for whom the register is supposedly intended to help find a course that is actually running. Quite possibly, some give up, disillusioned, after contacting inactive 'Alpha churches'.[24]

The Alpha Register was established to help people find an Alpha Course and it also allows Alpha churches to keep in touch with each other and with Advisers. Its purpose is thus practical and pastoral and it was not primarily set up to aid research! It is reasonable to conclude that AI/HTB have made some provision to keep the register accurate and at the same time have sought to maintain contact with interested churches and to give them a point of contact with the wider public.

Quality

A few other words should be mentioned about the register. It would be wrong to assume equal quality of courses. Of those that run, some do not really follow the recipe well and a smaller number clearly and deliberately make changes in breach of the copyright. There are a few incidences of thoroughly rogue registrations where churches admit they register in case it attracts enquirers but then run their own distinct course, though I do not think that this is frequent. People have been asked to de-register who are known to do this. Relatively few run the course three times a year in a roll-on manner as recommended. Those that do continue to run are generally running it better, or at least more closely in line with AI/HTB guidelines. Training issues will be considered in Chapter 10.

Turnover

Total numbers on the register do not give any real idea of what is the turnover of churches registering as running Alpha. The overall number of registrations has been fairly static since 2000, fluctuating between roughly 7,000 and 7,300 courses. This may suggest that the market of potential of 'Alpha Churches' has been exhausted, but that registered Alpha churches are staying loyal. However, it may just mean that new registrations and de-registrations are fairly evenly matched. This is an important issue and has a number of implications. For example, it raises the question of how many times any local church actually runs the course before becoming a latent Alpha church or de-registering. More fundamentally this then raises the question as to why this happens. In fact, Brierley's research for AI does cast some light on this. Churches were asked when they first ran Alpha. In 2005 the average was 5.5 years ago.[25] This suggests there is in fact quite a big turnover in churches adopting, using and stopping Alpha. His 2005 data also casts some light on the scale of this. Of the 915 responses to questionnaires, that year about 140 ran their first course that year. All new registrations were sent a questionnaire and, as Brierley notes, these churches may have been more enthusiastic than others in sending back the questionnaire. However, some scaling up can be attempted. The 915 responses represent 21%.[26] Although it may be a slight overestimation, this suggests about 700 (i.e. 140×5) new churches (or other institutions) started Alpha that year. This is approximately 10% of the overall total. This is a high figure.[26A] The high number of new registrations may have been influenced by the arrival and initial impact of new versions of the Alpha course, with workplaces, old peoples' homes and various youth institutions (including some schools) registering.[27] It is encouraging that new churches, and other institutions, are still starting Alpha but discouraging (from AI's perspective) that they are also stopping. I shall return to this later when I consider the long term use and impact of Alpha. Any significant turnover complicates attempts to calculate the overall number of churches that have run Alpha at some point. It is also possible that some churches might re-register after a gap, perhaps with the arrival of a new minister.

Implications for undertaking and reporting research

An appreciation of the complex reality that lies behind the overall list of registrations matters and it has many implications. A simple straightforward use of these overall numbers will not give a full or entirely realistic view of the use, frequency and vibrancy of Alpha courses around the country. Research needs to take this into consideration and not assume it is running evenly across the board. The scaling up of figures, and determination of numbers of attendees, based on samples could end up being quite spurious. More detailed data is needed to give a meaningful picture of what is actually happening. Questionnaires to local churches need to ask more than 'Have you run Alpha?' since lots of churches have! 'How many?' is still not very helpful by itself: a church may have run Alpha five times, but stopped using it by 1998 (or earlier)! 'How often, and when, have you run it?' would be much more helpful. 'When?' could usefully request information if the courses were run/are running in Autumn and/or Spring and/or Summer. I was interested to discover that the research commissioned by AI does in fact address these questions although their summary reports and use of the statistics do not reflect this. Other research needs to be at least as accurate and varied in its approach if it is to cast much light on what is actually happening. It would also be very helpful to know accurate information about numbers of unregistered courses and how they fare.

Lumping together statistics from different versions of the course will also tend to cause confusion, though it might look good at first, since it will make it difficult to see, beyond initial interest and uptake, how well particular versions are bedding down and becoming evangelistic. Also, in the last three years or so they have put new versions of the course (Youth, Workplace, Senior, Forces) onto the market, and made a bigger push with students. Counting, or just presenting, the figures for all these in together will result in difficulties when interpreting the results. Geographic and other variations should also make researchers cautious about scaling-up local results to give an overall national picture.

Some reasons for variable uptake and persistence with Alpha

The analysis of the course in Section Two furnishes a number of reasons for this variable pattern of actual uptake and sustained use of Alpha. Some have used it, persevered, and had clear success. Some questions come to mind about this. How close to HTB's pattern of church life and its values were these churches at the time of taking up Alpha? Such churches could be expected to take it up and integrate it smoothly and relatively easily. How keen or at least willing and open were they to change and adopt more of this total 'church' package in order to integrate Alpha effectively into the life of their local church? How crucial was this to its long-term success? What other factors were involved in their church growth and how significant was Alpha within these?

Questions can be asked of less successful usage too. How often, have people taken up some of it but left out other parts? How often have people felt that there are elements of theology they don't like and perhaps changed bits? Even if this is not so, how often has there been a strong feeling and unease that their own local church's ethos and emphases – its 'spirituality' if you like – is not the same as that of HTB and thus transmitted by Alpha? How willing has the church been to engage in real outreach and what awareness does it already have of what this might involve? Has outreach with Alpha been tried and just not worked? If so, why? Does Alpha, in fact have a restricted missional range across the population? Or has it only been used 'in-house' for Christians or perhaps the immediate fringe-attenders? Any of these factors can result in Alpha being tried and then dropped or remaining marginal to the congregation life, or in members of the congregation not feeling confident to invite their friends. Worse, it can cause tensions and even divisions in a congregation.

What is the Variation in Use across Denominations and Churchmanship styles?

The analysis and reflection above raises questions about how much of the church spectrum Alpha is really suited to. Let us look at this in more detail.

It is claimed that Alpha has been used – and works – right across the denominational range in the UK. Literally speaking this is probably true. However, I strongly suspect that the spread among denominations is not even, or proportionate to their share of the Christian family, and the percentage that 'tried it and dropped it' is not consistent across denominations either.[28] It has had a much better uptake in some denominations than others. Further, some have proved more effective at persisting with it, integrating it into their church life and actually attracting non-church guests. Variations can happen for a number of reasons, operating either singly or in combination. These include specifically denominational reasons (organisational/theological); the presence of an Evangelical-Charismatic spirituality (which finds expression across lots of denominations, but to varying degrees); the pastoral support and follow-up required or at least desirable. Cell churches (or churches in whatever denomination with similar groups) very often run it as an outreach programme. The relative importance of these is worth reflection by the wider church.

Brierley's research on church life in Scotland investigated aspects of Alpha and casts light on this issue.[29] He found that 27% of churches in Scotland had run Alpha at some point. The breakdown both as a percentage of each denomination and a churchmanship profile are given below.

Churches Running Alpha as a % of each Denomination [30]

Church of Scotland	29
Roman Catholic	8
Independent	31
Baptist	58
Episcopal	16
Smaller denominations	32
Other Presbyterians	11

Churches running Alpha by % of each type of Churchmanship [31]

Broad	23
Catholic	9
Evangelical-Charismatic	69
Evangelical-Mainstream	34
Evangelical-Reformed	52
Liberal	14
Low Church	35
Reformed	25

Ministers were asked to identify their church using up to 3 categories. 'Evangelical' was originally one category, but, on reviewing the first set of responses, this was then sub-divided into the 3 more detailed categories indicated in the table and the question asked again.

It is worth noting that the largest correlation is with an 'Evangelical-Charismatic' churchmanship. This will not surprise many. The course is frequently described as 'Evangelical-Charismatic'. At the same time the breadth of (a lower) appeal across the spectrum is of note.[32] This pattern is likely to be similar in England and Wales.

Brierley also looked at geographical location, social environment and other factors. He affirmed that the closest correlation as to who runs Alpha is with churchmanship but there was a wide spread here too. He commented that local factors in the leadership were particularly crucial to the decision to run it and could override all other factors. Brierley also discovered that most ran it once a year and on average had run it for 3 years.[33]

The appeal of Alpha to the Evangelical constituency is supported by other findings. The (relatively early) 1998 survey by the Evangelical Alliance indicated 69% of those questioned (mainly its members) were running Alpha. (This report popularised and possibly coined the term 'Alpha Churches' too.) The Research by the Baptist Union of Great Britain (in practice excluding Scotland, undertaken in 1999) cites 48.9% of their member churches as running Alpha (in 1999).[34] This relatively high figure can perhaps be attributed to their largely evangelical constituency. At the same time it should not be forgotten that some of the sternest criticism of Alpha has come from Evangelicals, typically those who would describe themselves as Reformed or Conservative Evangelical.

If the turnover in courses noted in the section above is true, it is reasonable to think that the early adopters of Alpha would have been mainly by churches of an 'Evangelical-Charismatic' approach but that churches of other less obviously Evangelical-Charismatic approaches have increasingly taken it up since. This may be happening based on the profile and reputation that Alpha has established now over a number of years. Such churches may face a different set of challenges to effectively run Alpha and integrate it into their wider church life than the Evangelical-Charismatic ones and this may have implications for what training and other support AI develops and offers.

Who attends Alpha and Why?

Total Numbers

Overall figures are from time to time published in *Alpha News*, and for the most part have been provided from the research commissioned by them and undertaken by Christian Reseasrch. Brierley, using data from his various reports, wrote an article on Alpha in the Quadrant (March 2006) giving the full set of his figures. The UK figures are given below. For interest, I have also included figures for the rest of the world, which Brierley also researches for AI, though I am not commenting on them here. (Brierley does note that about half the total is made up from North America.)

Total attendance at Alpha course per year (to nearest 1000)[35]

Year	UK	Outside UK
1994	25,000*	0
1995	67,000	13,000
1996	129,000	126,000
1997	181,000	225,000
1998	228,000	319,000
1999	253,000	440,000
2000	238,000	583,000
2001	190,000	733,000
2002	153,000	758,000
2003	147,000	886,000
2004	175,000	936,000
2005	182,000	950,000
TOTAL	1,968,000	5,969,000

OVERALL WORLD TOTAL: 7,937,000

This figure is the combined total of 1993 and 1994 (as explained in AI Report, 2005)

These figures, Brierley notes, involve some rounding up and gener-alised assumptions. The most recent figures are based on detailed analysis of the autumnal courses and extrapolation from these. It is assumed that non-Autumnal courses have 80% attendance of the autumnal courses. Consideration is also given to the (relatively small) numerical contribution of specialist courses. It seems to me that an additional assumption has been made about the set of returned ques-tionnaires (915 in 2005 which was down on previous years) being truly representative of all of the registered courses. Also, putting these figures together accumulatively, it appears to be assumed that people do not attend more than once. This is not true. People do for various reasons. Some do so in ways approved by AI, for instance, by 'progress-ing' from being a guest to a helper to a leader. In fact, some churches allow people to repeat the course as guests too. Finally none of these figures seem to indicate how much of the course people attend: does attendance infer all, most, part or even just one session of the course? This matters. Elsewhere, HTB have been cited as reporting the drop out as around 30%, mainly in the first few weeks.[36]

However, some features can be detected in the UK figures above. They point to the rapid rise in the mid 1990s. This corresponds with the impact of the 'Toronto Blessing' at HTB (1994–7), as well as the impact of the publication of John Finney's *Finding Faith Today* (1992).[37] The biggest years of total attendance were 1998–2000, pointing to the ongoing rising momentum and also the impact of the first two Alpha

Initiatives (1998 and 1999). Since then there has been a significant decline which has been slightly reversed in 2004 and 2005. This corresponds with the arrival of new course variations. (I am not saying that these 'correspondences' definitely amount to complete causes, but I suspect they have been influential factors.)

It is worth considering the *relative* changes in these numbers over time. For this publication, Charles Freebury has kindly determined the relative rate of growth each year by expressing each year's figures as a percentage increase, or decrease on the figures of the previous year. These results are expressed in graphical form below.

Relative Change in numbers of Guests at UK Alpha Courses over time.

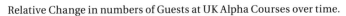

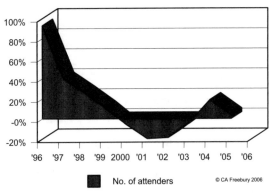

No. of attenders   © CA Freebury 2006

By this analysis the rate of growth has been falling since 1996. Between 2000 and 2003 there was real shrinkage, year on year. Very recent years have seen the decline stopped but not turned into a significant rise again. In broad terms, things have been relatively static for half of Alpha's 'public' life. This pattern of growth and decline does not really point to Alpha relentlessly gaining momentum and so achieving the evangelisation of the country all by itself. It also points to the National advertising campaigns having had, at best, a limited impact, though there is no way of determining what might have happened to the figures in their absence. (I shall explore these themes in more detail in Chapter 10.)

Nonetheless, even if the absolute figures in some respects should be revised downwards, or at least qualified in various ways, they still indicate that a large number of people are still attending Alpha and being impacted by it. Even though there was a dip (and even here figures were still around 150,000 per year), the attendance at Alpha courses has remained high, even after the excitement and public attention of the Toronto Blessing period had faded. Whatever, the means, AI/HTB have sustained good overall numbers. These figures (even if moderated) do indicate that Alpha is still having a big impact. At the same time it is important to take seriously that the numbers per year appear to have plateaued. Will another assent happen if more and more churches run Alpha well and break into real outreach, or will the plateau turn into descent and decline as more and more churches just give up? It is difficult to tell and may depend on where AI places its energy, money and what support strategies it develops and applies.

Social background, Gender and Ethnicity of Participants

What more detailed data do we have on what types of people attend Alpha? Hunt has investigated this but his data (based on churches in England and Wales) can be usefully introduced and complemented by data from Brierley on Scotland regarding the social environment of churches running Alpha.

Churches holding Alpha by proportion of Environment (%) [38]

City centre	38
Urban priority centre	24
Housing scheme	38
Suburban	51
Town	44
New Town	20
Rural: Dormitory	33
Rural: Other	25

Hunt's research showed that the background, regarding occupation, education of all those attending Alpha reflected the average patterns for church-goers as revealed in Brierley's research published as Christian England in 1992.[39] Thus, a large majority of people attending were of lower professional or clerical/administrative occupational background. Skilled, semi-skilled or manual workers were underrepresented. Hunt points out that these categories of Alpha participation correspond well with those categories of people already at church and specifically those who look for Evangelical-Charismatic spiritualities and the chance to join discussion/faith sharing groups. By implication, Hunt asks if Alpha is changing these trends and effectively reaching beyond these groups or just reinforcing and extending them. Hunt states that his research shows that a relatively high percentage of people attending were not in paid employment, and suggests this may mean they have more free time which may be crucial to them committing to and completing a course that is relatively demanding in time. The male (37%) and females (67%)ratio reflected that in churches generally.[40]

Ethnicity did not reflect the general patterns in society or church and relatively few non-White churches have endorsed it, especially in its early years. Thus the ethnic origins of Alpha guests were: White – 86.2%, Black – 6.2%, Asian – 2.2%, and Other – 5.2%. (total: 100%).[41]

Age of Participants

Age, according to Hunt, showed a large range from 16–85 with the peak in the 30–40 category. This is older than HTB's own relatively young profile but does still indicate a significant interest from younger generations. This is shown in more detail below:

Alpha Guests by Age categories (%)[42]

– 20	6.4
21 – 30	7.8
31 – 40	35.1
41 – 50	20.0
51 – 60	17.5
61 – 70	11.4
70 +	2.5
	100

Since Hunt's research was conducted, AI have produced new versions, or at least packaging, of the course and actively promoted them. Many are aimed at different age groups: specifically senior, student and youth Alpha. Initial interest in repromoted student and new youth Alpha seems high. *Alpha News* reports a fall in the age of people attending the course. 59% of all guests are now under 40 and 29% under 30.[43] Whether these changes will be sustained, or just reflect initial interest in a new product, remains to be seen. The Alpha Invitation Report of 2005 gives more detail still as indicated below:

Average Age of Non-Churchgoing and Churchgoing Guests[44]

Type of Guest	2002	2003	2004	2005
Non-churhgoers	41	40	39	37
Churchgoers	44	44	45	43

Brierley also categorised guests by age. In each of the categories under 40 (i.e. under 20s, 20–29, 30–39) the non-churchgoers were represented significantly more than churchgoers. The reverse happened with all the older age categories. An identical pattern happened in 2003 and 2004. Brierley notes that this means that Alpha does have the capacity to appeal to younger Postmodern people. He also notes that since most churches have rapidly ageing populations this may create a problem in effectively integrating any young converts into churches after Alpha.

Church Background of People Taking Alpha

Church background of people taking Alpha is a very important indicator of who it attracts and who benefits. People can be classified in different ways – with a more differentiated classification giving poten-tially more useful information. Both AI's commissioned research and Hunt have looked at it. Brierley just asked churches to classify their guests as churchgoers or non-churchgoers – a relatively simplistic division – though he does also usefully ask for numbers of helpers and leaders (i.e. team members) too. The findings are given below.

Breakdown of Numbers and Types of Guests attending Alpha[45]

% Autumn Attendees who were:	2002	2003	2004	2005
% Churchgoing guests	37%	39%	34%	38%
% Non-churchgoing Guests	38%	33%	35%	32%
% Helpers/leaders	25%	28%	31%	30%
Total of Non-Churchgoing guests	58,100	48,400	61,400	58,100
% change on previous year	+17%	–17%	+27%	–5%

The % of different sorts of guests is based on the autumn courses of each year.

Hunt obtained more information on the religious background of people at the time of attending Alpha that provides a sense of who is going.

Church Background at time of Taking Alpha Course (%)[46]

Already in church which is running course*	57.8
On fringes of church which is running course	13.6
Agnostics with some experience of church life	16.3
No church experience, non-believers	8.0
Belonging to other churches	4.3
TOTAL	100

* I presume this category includes the team running the course.
The total number of churched guests here is 57.8 + 4.3 = 62.1%

Actually the data of Brierley and Hunt show close agreement. Brier-ley has the percentage of non-churchgoing guests averaging at about 35% over 4 years while Hunt puts it at 38% in 2001–2. (In fact for that year Brierley records 38% too!)

Brierley's reports for AI also indicate that the number of helpers has been rising. This may reflect an increased spread and use of a prac-tice, which HTB has sometimes followed, of allowing certain guests to come back as helpers, especially if they are not fully converted after the first course but still open.

It is worth noting just how many course participants are already involved in church. 62.1% appear to belong to churches already with a further 13.6% on the fringe of the church running the course. A further 16.3% have some church experience, though they do not describe themselves as believers.

These figures sit very well with the pattern Hunt found when he asked people why they attended the course. Those attending Alpha as a refresher course (51.1%) or as team members (5%) can be regarded as Christians already. Even some of the others may well have church connections of varying degrees: for instance, some of those wanting company or some of those invited by family.

Why did you join Alpha? (%)[47]

Refresher Course/spiritual development	51.1
Spiritual searching	14.4
Invited/persuaded by friends/family	13.9
Wanted to join 'something'/hospitality/ company	11.8
Running the Course	5.0
Advised by Church leaders	3.8
TOTAL	100

These figures indicate very clearly that Alpha is mainly functioning as a refresher or even a 'going deeper' course for existing Christians, who make up more than 50% of participants. However, it does have some outreach appeal. This appears to be highest among those who are on the fringes of church or who have, or have had, some church connection. Knowing someone in the church increases the likelihood of people attending Alpha. Nonetheless, the total numbers of unchurched guests still give Alpha a significant evangelistic dimension across the country.

It is worth noting that there are other ways of profiling people in contemporary society that may be helpful indices when it comes to interpreting and responding to religious, spiritual and other trends. The Church of England Report *Mission-Shaped Church* uses a classification which is becoming increasingly used: churched, fringe, open dechurched, closed dechurched. Stuart Murray has further subdivided people in his *Church after Christendom*.[48]

In his *The McDonaldisation of the Church?* John Drane describes a different approach with seven such categories at some length. They are the desperate poor, the hedonists, the traditionalists, the spiritual searchers, the corporate achievers, the secularists, the apathetic.[49] This approach has been well-received by many commentators and may be of significant value in relation to understanding who Alpha does and does not reach.[50]

Conversions on or through Alpha
Who and How Many are Converted?

Alpha is explicitly promoted as being a tool for outreach. So how effective is Alpha in reaching those not already at church? AI do not print any such figures in *Alpha News*. They have commented to me that they accept that conversion is difficult to measure and do not want to make misleading claims. Defining or characterising conversion creates difficulties and challenges to theologians resulting in a plurality of stances), but also to empirical researchers – be they religious or secular – resulting in a variation in measures. I shall return to this but first let us look at what data is available.

Though they do not measure or publish figures on conversions, the research undertaken for AI by Peter Brierley does look at the impact of Alpha. Course administrators were asked: 'In total, how many people do you estimate now attend services or a mid-week group at your church at least once a month as a result of attending an Alpha Course?'[51] The approach here is looking for hard evidence but also clearly implies an understanding of conversion as a journey. The broad measure, with its relatively low change in church involvement, indicates here they are counting all who take the next step which may well in many cases still be prior to 'full conversion'. Apparently, it does not (or should not) include any who were already churchgoers who are considered, or consider themselves, as having come to faith on Alpha, and as a result attend church more often. The results are shown below.

Newcomers attending church as a result of Alpha (expressed in blocks of churches as % of total number of churches in sample)[52]

Newcomers at church	2004	**2005**
None	9%	8%
Up to 10	42%	48%
10–19	22%	20%
20 or more	27%	24%

Brierley acknowledges that there is some approximation evident in the way people have given their figures.

A significant number – nearly 10% – had none. Nearly half the churches have 1–9 newcomers. This is reflected well in the median figure that was 8 in 2004 and 7 in 2005. (This means that half the churches had more than this number and half had less.) The mean averages were 13.8 in 2005, 15.3 in 2004 and 11.8 in 2003. These figures include a few churches with very many which when omitted bring down to 11.2 in 2005 and 13.8 in 2004. The failure of these figures to rise from 2004 to 2005 is hardly evidence that Alpha is becoming increasingly effective at bringing the unchurched into church over time, though this statistic may be a 'victim' of aggregating figures from new and well-established courses together, especially if there were a lot of new courses in 2005.

How many is this per course? Brierley does not calculate this but elsewhere does give the average number of total courses per church (in the samples) as 7.9 in 2004 and 7.6 in 2005. Using these figures the average number of newcomers per course comes out as follows.

'Newcomers' at church per Alpha course run.

	2004 data	2005 data
Including all churches	1.94	1.82
Excluding very big courses	1.75*	1.47*

*I do not have figures for the adjusted average number of courses excluding
very large users – and have thus used the total average which will be higher
thus giving a under-calculation of the number per course.*

The figures work out at between 1–2 newcomers per course. In 2005, the average course had 21 participants in total so this works out as 8.7%. The percentage of non-churchgoers in attendance at Autumn courses in 2005 was calculated at 32% so this suggests that 27.1% of these end up coming to church events at least once a month. Based on my own conversations with people who have run Alpha over a significant period, not all with persist through to a bedded-down 'conversion' or to full membership; some later lapse as well. However, if a church runs it regularly, Alpha is a good source of new members or at least participants. I shall return to the long-term impact of Alpha below.

Again Hunt has some figures on conversions, but what is his understanding and measure of conversion? In his first book *Anyone for Alpha?* Hunt reduces his figure on conversions from approximately 17% to 3–4% 'true conversions' on the grounds that many of them were already church attenders and therefore not real conversions by his reckoning.[53] He does not explicitly state that he has done the same in the second book but does say that his conclusions are broadly similar to the first small pilot study, suggesting he may have.[54] In his second book, Hunt does not give his definition of conversion though he usefully discusses and critiques several approaches. Neither does he provide the reader with his full research questionnaire or with any accompanying notes that may have been sent out to explain how terms such as 'conversion' are to be applied. As shown in the table immediately below, his research on conversions indicates previous church background and since he can account for all his converts using background rather than current church practice this may again well support the view that any church converts have been excluded from his (published) statistics.

Church Background of those claiming Conversion[55]

None	11
Anglican	11
Baptist	10
Pentecostal	6
Roman Catholic	2
Methodist	2
Other	5
TOTAL	47*

* Out of a total number of 837 respondents. This is 5.6%.

The most striking figure is that the vast majority of converts had a church background of some sort. Put another way only 23.4% did not. (We shall return to the significance of this again.) Of those with a church background, 17 had attended as a child and the rest during a period as an adult. The table does not indicate that such guests converted within/to or away from their background church. However, it is worth noting that Anglican and Baptist churches (and Evangelical-Charismatics within them) are noted for having made substantial use of Alpha. They may well be attracting former members or those at church as children back.

Age of those claiming conversion[56]

– 20	4
21– 30	11
31–40	12
41–50	13
51–60	5
61–70	2
70 +	0

This age profile is higher than the one at HTB itself. Again Hunt points out that there is good evidence of Alpha having an appeal to those in 'middle age' who are re-appraising life and re-examining a previous (now lapsed) religious commitment.

In Hunt's sample, 17 males and 30 females claimed conversion (p. 188). This reflects well the overall ratio of males:females attending. All respondents (including team members and existing Christians, and any who had dropped out) were asked to comment on two further questions. The results[57] were as follows:

	Has Alpha changed your view of Christianity? %	Has Alpha influenced your Spiritual life? %
Yes	38.2	55.5
No	58.6	32.1
Unsure	1.5	12.4
	100	100

Those 'unsure' are likely to be those who had more recently finished a course and therefore had a chance to really assess its impact on them.

Hunt points out that a change in view about Christianity could be positive or negative and that 'spiritual influences' cover many things. I agree with Hunt that spiritual influence, and even 'spiritual growth', can cover a wide range of things. Indeed, in line with my description of how Alpha really operates formatively (see Chapter 6), we should expect a large variation in what might be called a spiritual benefit, even a positive one. As noted, people's spiritual journeys are complex and often long, both before, during and even after active commitment to Christianity. Some of those influenced spiritually may well go on to fuller involvement and even conversion later, perhaps much later.

Two Anglican dioceses have researched conversion on Alpha and other process courses and both gave roughly the same findings. Lichfield conducted research in 1999 on Alpha and other courses, reporting (in 2000) that 4,687 people attending Alpha, 992 (21%) were described as 'new Christians'. Here the definition was that in the view of the priest they had 'come to Christian faith, commitment or confirmation' during (or presumably as a direct result of) the course.[58] St Alban's diocese conducted research in 2001 on people who had attended courses over the previous five years. Of 6,307 people who had attended Alpha, 1,010 were described as 'conversions' (16%) and of these, 597 went on to confirmation.[59]

The (UK) Evangelical Alliance conducted research in 1998 on a total of 442 churches including 300 of its member churches and other selected churches). 69% had run Alpha, many repeatedly. 97% reported success and conversions were calculated at between 11–15% of participants. (This would have been relatively early in the use of the course by churches when it could be expected that many of the guests would have been churched. See below.) Even so, this conversion rate for 'confessing' evangelical churches may surprise some for how low it is!

Hunt's main research found that of the 837 respondents (from across all denominations and regions), fortyseven (5.6%) claimed to have 'become a Christian as a result of taking Alpha'.[60] He notes that most of the churches assess conversion by baptism and church attendance, though adds it is a 'slippery and broader term' than these criteria suggest. Hunt goes on to describe and assess a number of approaches to analysing and measuring conversion.[61] However, he does not state, as far as I can see, what criteria he actually uses himself or what, if any, guidelines or specifications he gives to those completing this part of his questionnaire. Others may well have benefited but already been Christian or were still not Christian.

Alpha in comparison with other Process Courses

Peter Brierley/Christian Research UK's research for the Salvation Army on factors effecting growth in churches asked about Alpha and other process courses.[62] The summary booklet gives data is on conversions.

With reference to Alpha, the balance of church attenders to non-church attenders was 69% to 31%[63]—figures not dissimilar to those found by Hunt and AI's reports. There were 3.5 converts per Alpha course, that is 25% of the attendees, split very evenly between those that were

Comparative Process Course conversion

Type of course	Alpha	Emmaus	Y course	Good news	Christianity explored	Credo	*Overall*
Courses held	3	3	4	6	3	2	3
Church people per course	10	9	7	6	6	11	10
% faith commitments	17	38	18	24	22	38	24
% non-church people per course	4	3	4	3	5	4	4
% faith commitments	45	50	38	50	27	57	46
% non-church people making a commitment in church 6 months later	100	100	83	88	100	100	91
Ever held course (at least once)	69%	16%	8%	5%	5%	1%	104%

(The figures are medians for the number of courses ran). I note that no further information on what is a faith commitment, when it was made and if the converts themselves were consulted is given. Various people have commented to me that the 100% figure for 'converts' staying in church seems very high. Additional data is given below as reported by Freebury. Whatever, the exact figures, Alpha and process courses in general are very good at helping seekers and converts integrate into church.

previously churched (12.1%) and those that were unchurched (12.9%). Thus proportionately more unchurched people converted, though we are not given more information on any previous Christian experience they may have had in the past. However, a very significant number of church people were claimed to have made conversions. The percentage of the unchurched claimed as converts (45%) is higher than the percentage of unchurched guests claimed as attending church more often (27.1%), based on Brierley's studies for Alpha International. This raises some interesting questions on what is conversion. At the very least they have started a journey and have some familiarity with Christian life and ideas. They could be said already to 'belong' and even to understand at least some 'beliefs'. At what point a person moves into faith is hard to assess; some of these may in fact just be deepening what is a already a commitment.

It is also worth noting how Alpha compares with other courses. Based on these data, it is less effective than most at bringing to conversion those already in church but about average when used as an instrument of conversion with the unchurched. Emmaus appears better with both categories. Christianity Explored is markedly weak with the unchurched. The course with the 'best statistics' – Credo – had the lowest usage! Lacking anything like the same publicity as Alpha, have these other courses been chosen and run after more thoughtful discernment as to the local suitability by the local church leadership team?[64] Is this also because the other courses are more effective because they can be adapted locally. This may imply that people should be more discerning and explore the market more thoroughly before running Alpha. All of this sits with the data of Ireland[65] and also Groundsel.[66] Both show Emmaus to be more effective than Alpha. The number of newcomers going onto confirmation was 57.3% for Emmaus and 21.9% for Alpha. The number of newcomers attending church was 75.3% for Emmaus and 59.9% for Alpha. Both Ireland and Groundsel report that home-grown courses produce the highest convert rates of all. Groudsel's respective figures for home-grown courses were 97.4% and 88.9% respectively. Such courses require more effort and commitment and even skill but are likely to be very much better contextualised. It is fair to ask how many in church ministry have such skills, commitment and time. However, at the same time, all this raises the question of whether Alpha's copyright policy impedes its local effectiveness, at least in part. Is this likely to increase with increasing cultural changes over time? It should also be noted, however, that the sheer scale on which Alpha is used in comparison with other courses means overall, it has more impact.

Finally it is worth noting that this table is based on data collected in the 1990s. Will conversion rates as a result of running Alpha fall or rise with time and an even more changed cultural situation from the one Alpha was set up to meet? It is also worth noting that a median of 3 Alpha courses per church over a potential of 8–9 years strongly suggests a lack of sustained use of the course by many churches. Other data – already referred to – suggests this is happening too. Why is this? I shall take up some possible angles on this in my examination of the long-term effects of running Alpha below.

Overall Impact of Alpha in terms of Conversions

What are we to make of all this? Can it be put together in a meaningful way? The diversity of approaches, measures and findings here may well emphasis the wisdom of AI's decision not to publish figures on conversions! However if we look at coming into and growing in faith as a journey we can, in fact, see something of a more coherent pattern. Organising and summarising the major findings in a sequence that moves from the broadest spiritual impact of Alpha to conversions of unchurched people we get the following pattern (figures are given as percentage of total participants):

- Alpha has had spiritual impact on 56% of participants (Hunt);
- 38% say Alpha has changed their view of Christianity (Hunt);
- Conversion varies from around 25% – half were already churched prior to doing Alpha – [Brierley for Northern Division of Salvation Army] to around 21% in Anglicn diocese of Lichfield

and 16% in Anglican diocese of St Albans; to around 11–15% in a Evangelical Alliance survey. Hunt's research variously gives 17% (downgraded to 3–4% true conversions in his smaller study) or 6% (larger study – precise definition of conversion not given but likely to exclude those already churched – see below);

- Where researched, it is evident that many of these converts were already churched. Brierley puts the ratio of churched: unchurched converts at 1:1 (research for Salvation Army but across many denominations);

- Alpha has an impact on the unchurched at the time of doing Alpha as follows. Brierley's 2005 data for AI suggest that 8.7% of guests attend church events at least once a month afterwards – though not all are (yet) converts. Hunt calculates conversion at 5.6%;

- Of those that were unchurched at the time of doing Alpha, Hunt's data suggests that most had a previous experience of Christianity: around 23.4% had no church background; 36.2% had attended church as children and the rest (40.4%) for a period thereafter. The latter two groups would be categorised by Richter and Francis as dechurched;

- The vast majority of converts appear to have stayed involved with church.

There is a clear progression here, and a broadly coherent one. I will discuss further issues on how conversion is defined and measured below but first let us attempt to quantify what this means in terms of converts.

Whilst noting problems in rounded up figures let us use the figure (determined by Peter Brierley) of 182,000 attendees at Alpha courses in 2005. The number of converts in 2005 works out as follows:

At 25% conversion rate:	45,500 converts
At 15% conversion rate:	27,300 converts
At 5% conversion rate:	9,100 converts

Using the middle figure of 15% and applying it to the aggregated total number of Alpha participants since 1993, we get a figure of 295,200 converts, though I should stress this is approximate and does not consider many variables more evident over such a time frame and other complicating factors. It may well be broadly accurate to split this figure almost evenly between those who were already attending church at the time of doing Alpha and those that were not, and to remember that some conversions may have occurred after Alpha had actually finished. This would put approximately 13,700 into each sub-category for 2005 or 147,500 in total for the UK.

We ought to be very grateful for any conversion and especially for these sorts of numbers. Clearly Alpha is producing conversions, and many are staying in the church where the course was run, though there is some suggestion that these are not evenly distributed across denominations/ churchmanship or even the country. Most converts have already had significant contact with Christianity prior to coming on Alpha. It is also not at all clear that conversions are happening uniformly across social background or age. However, they also need to be put in perspective. By way of comparison, it was estimated by Richter and Francis[67] that 1,500 Christians just leave church each week – not including deaths or church transfers. This is 78,000 per year.[68] This helps us see why despite Alpha and other courses and initiatives, overall church attendance is still declining in the UK. Nonetheless, the rate of decline would be significantly worse without the impact of Alpha and other process courses.

Discrepancies in Defining and Measuring Conversion

The discrepancy in conversion rates, is quite large and it would be worth investigating and reflecting on. For example, the research in the Anglican dioceses suggests around 15–20% of guests come to faith during Alpha. Hunt's research puts the figure at 5.6%. Does it mean that Alpha is more effective as an outreach tool in some denominations, including Anglicans, than others and Hunt has picked up the average? There may be some truth in this, though its effectiveness is likely to vary within denominations as well as across them. Is Hunt's figure brought down by the fact that his survey includes a lot of churches who did not run Alpha often and thus probably had mainly Christians on them? As mentioned earlier, in his first book 'Anyone for Alpha?' Hunt reduces his figure on conversions from approximately 17% to 3–4% 'true conversions' on the grounds that many of them were already church attenders and therefore not real conversions (by his reckoning).[69] Freebury has noted and commented on this. He feels that Hunt has misunderstood, or underestimated, the importance of belonging happening before believing. Thus the suggestion is that Hunt factors out those who already belong whereas Freebury (and possibly others) would include them if they do not yet really believe or act in a committed manner. If Hunt has made a similar reduction in his major study report, his figures come into close line with those of the Anglican dioceses and Brierley's research for AI.[70] In fact, it is the research for the North Division of the Salvation Army that then appears to give least congruent conversion statistics.

This discussion of Hunt's data naturally leads me to ask what definition of conversion has been used in these studies. Is it the same? This is unlikely. Has a clear definition been communicated by the researcher or even implied in more subtle ways to those asked to fill in forms. This matters because people filling in forms tend to respond to the expectations of the researcher (unless they are carefully guided not to). The concerns, motivation, self-consciousness, vulnerability and even the honesty of people responding also comes into play. Do they want to report conversions or their lack; are they inclined to see any/some/ a lot of spiritual progress as conversion? All these factors and indeed ambiguities can operate with a good degree of integrity in the context of questionnaires, conversations and research. Thoroughness and an examination of assumptions are what are required if really good data and meaningful comparisons are to be gained.

This would include scrutinising a variety of issues about what conversion is understood as anyway. Does it include movement from one denomination to another? When this happens, does the receiving church regard the original denomination as generally Christian anyway? Even if some basic faith (and baptism) is recognised, if confirmation of other initiatory acts or declarations are received or made, many will then count such people as converts. What is meant by 'New Christians' or 'becoming a Christian'? Some, even some Alpha activists, distinguish between being religious and having personal faith in Jesus. Sometimes this may be valid, but by no means always. I know all this from a long interaction with people from other denominations to my own. It may be useful for a church-goer to look at a presentation of the faith that sees it as a very personal encounter with Jesus – and there is a real grace in the discovery of this. However, it does not necessarily mean that the person who did not, and may not still, express their spiritual outlook in such terms does not in fact already have Christian faith.[71] Alpha may then help people come to a new discovery within faith – and it can be very helpful in this – but I feel this ought to be distinguished from outreach as such. Whether it is part of evangelism or evangelisation depends on what your definition of what such activities are and who they can be legitimately aimed at.

Further, how people describe their faith journey, and any key moments or phases in it, is often strongly influenced by how the church to which they belong or wish to join expects them to express it, consciously or unconsciously. Whether a person brought up within a significantly Christian environment has to leave behind 'dead religion' to become a Christian or just grow it into a more 'personal and committed reality in their lives' is often a matter of perspective. In the Catholic tradition, it is sometimes asserted that most people are rarely fully evangelised and we are all in need on ongoing conversion and growth anyway! Others will say that a person is not fully converted until they have left the Catholic church. Other examples from other denominations could be supplied.

Uptake and Conversions among 'Specialist Groups'

Data on courses and Alpha specialisms other than the standard adult course is much scantier – not least because many of these are run on a much smaller scale or have only been available for a relatively short time. I think it is important to note these statistics against course developments and other strategy developments at AI, and in association with other organisations. What follows is very patchy but may be of some use.

The Alpha Invitation 2005 Report counts the number of specialist courses as follows:[72]

2002	2003	2004	2005
9.1%	8.9% (est)	9.7%	8.9%

One piece of text refers to these as youth and student courses.
(Students are concentrated in a very few courses.)

Alpha News reported that churches involved in Youth Alpha rose by 42% between 2003 and 2004[73] while churches involved in Alpha for students rose by 160% in the same period. It also cites Peter Brierley as saying 'This is highly significant'.[74] It so happens that these increased figures for younger people followed big pushes by HTB to launch better youth materials and work in partnership with other Christian youth agencies. Similarly they have gone into partnership with several Christian Ministries for students and young people. If there has been a collective push by all these groups to get courses started then it is good if it has worked but not proof that the courses are full of non-Christians; it tends to be Christians that initially attend new courses. Even if a significant number of these guests are non-Christian friends, we have no data provided on how the course affected them.[75] (No actual numbers were given, so the reader did not know what significance to attach to these percentages.)

At the UK Alpha Strategy Day in February 2006 various presentations gave additional and updated figures. Thus there are now around 1500 Youth Alpha courses registered, and 40 or so youth advisers appointed. Alpha in the workplace course numbers have risen from 31 in July 2004 to 45 in March 2005 to 75 in February 2006. Senior Alpha had 60 courses registered by February 2006.

How are these courses working? Stephen Hunt conducted some (relatively small scale) research (2001–2). His research on prisons and universities showed that the uptake and, indeed effective implementation of Alpha at all, had been patchy. Data on the number of converts in both institutions was poor, and HTB has not really produced much either beyond the list of numbers of institutions running it. Hunt's interviews suggested it had only limited success and that there were all sorts of organisational problems to be overcome to effectively run it. Indeed, the course had to be so adapted for prisons, one wonders whether it is really and essentially using the same method. Some conversions were reported but the impact was limited and prisoners have very particular problems that need to be carefully addressed.

Although a (free) meal–talk–discussion format ought to appeal to students there were problems getting it going here too, partly linked to transient student populations. Hunt reported that it was commented that Alpha often assumed a far greater understanding of Christianity to follow the course arguments than most young people now have.

What is the Long term Effect of Alpha in Churches that Run it?

AI's Model for the Long-term Use of Alpha

AI/HTB have for some time proposed a model curve of guests numbers on Alpha over time and repeated runs of the course to help people understand what happens. They recognise that when a church first runs Alpha it may well open it up to the existing congregation and that many of the guests may be from this group. This does have the advantage of making the church familiar with and hopefully still more supportive of Alpha. In the next few courses the number of church guests will decline – perhaps sharply – as the source of guests in the existing congregation dries up. HTB estimates this typically happens after about three courses, but it will depend on the size of the congregation etc. The temptation is to stop running at this point as numbers fall, but AI/HTB stress that it is crucial to carry on since as an outreach tool, the course may well not even have really begun. Those attending so far, thus, are not generally 'real guests'. Members of the church may invite others on the fringe of church life and Alpha may renew them and bring them into the centre of church life. They may invite friends even more marginal to church. Hopefully, from the beginning there will have been at least a few non-Christians. As they convert they will bring their non-Christians friends. It is non-Christians who have more non-Christian friends than most Christians, especially those who have been Christian for some time. In this way, and through other sources of 'real guests', the trickle of guests does not dry up, and the course will, having bottomed out numerically then continue and then see more and more growth.

How well does the model work? Is it reasonable to expect many churches to follow it all the way into real numerical growth through non-Christian converts? I think the first part of the model 'works', i.e. can be applied well. How many churches continue after the drop is unclear and it is also unclear to me how long churches may have to persist at the bottom of the graph, without dramatic growth, or much growth at all. Alpha is not a quick fix! Nor do I think is it just a matter of keep running Alpha. If the course is to be fruitful long-term, churches will have to find ways (compatible with the experience and ethos of Alpha) to take forward the spiritual journeys of these 'real guests' and integrate them into overall church life. This, as I have indicated, involves lots of factors and challenges. To be really effective, Alpha must be part of a long-term overall church strategy. It is not the equivalent of fast-food evangelism. Those that have taken it up like this are likely to be disappointed.

Empirical Evidence about the Long-term use of Running Alpha on churches

a) Evidence Generated Outside Alpha International

Hunt's stories of local churches support this. As do anecdotal evidence and comments I have received from Alpha Advisers etc. Implicitly, AI/HTB's strategies on how to improve Alpha and the effort they put into them, give some support to this interpretation too. However, it is fair to ask if AI have done enough to stress the full range of factors involved. Their focus is for churches to run Alpha and keep running it. Is their focus too narrow?

Clearly conversions are happening (see above) but how long do churches persist in running Alpha and what is the impact of Alpha on the overall growth of churches? There is now some independent evidence on this.

Peter Brierley's research in March 2000 (for Springboard) looked at patterns of growth or decline in all churches running Alpha (as listed in successive editions of *Alpha News*) against national statistics on growth and decline over the period 1989–98 (based on the data from the English Church Attendance Survey).[76] 8,700 churches took part in the surveys of 1989 and 1998. Of these 22% grew by more than 10%; 14% remained static (+/– 9%) and 64% declined by 10% or more. Of Churches listed as running Alpha, 43% did not decline (compared to 36% national average). The figure increased with the length of time Alpha had been running. Thus 51% of churches that had been running Alpha for more than 6 years did not decline. This data does not look at why these churches are growing and what is happening on Alpha as such, and what the connection is. However, this has been interpreted to mean that churches running Alpha for 3 years or more were more likely to grow (than those that ran it for less or not at all). Brierley argues that by this time they will have no longer be filling Alpha with their own congregation so this must be real outreach growth due to new members, i.e. Alpha works at bringing people in. The survey report claims to give 'statistical evidence that Alpha Courses help congregations to grow.'[77] The conclusion taken from this (by HTB at any rate) is to keep running Alpha![78] More accurately, it is fair to say that Alpha may often accompany and even be associated with church growth but it is much more difficult to determine that it has caused it, or does cause it.

I respect Peter Brierley and value his research but other interpretations of this overall church growth, or merely lack of decline, are possible. Are these people coming in already Christians from other churches – i.e. just transfers, drawn to what is probably a substantial church that is more attractive as an overall package than the one they hitherto attended? I certainly know of cases where this has happened. People have said they want something livelier, friendlier, or more 'charismatic', or they want a church with house groups etc. Sometimes it has been in indirect effect – and not directly to do with Alpha – in that they want a church with good facilities for their own young families or youth. Such denominational transfers may be motivated by deeper theological and spiritual issues, though one would think that Alpha in its ecumenically inclusive format would be unlikely to specifically promote these. On any of these occasions, if joining the new church included a change of denomination and completion of initiation rites/ membership ceremonies then such individuals could and sometimes are referred to as converts. Many of the 1,500 Christians who just leave church each week, still believing but no longer belonging for various reasons, depending on their reasons, ought to be relatively easy targets and sources of growth. Also I know of courses that were still attracting their own members or allowing them to attend more than once after more than two years of running Alpha.

Further these statistics can be looked at from the other perspectives. The majority of churches running Alpha will continue to decline even if they have run it for as long as 5 years. Secondly, as Freebury notes from the Christian Research Survey, three in four Alpha churches were not growing. One in two churches still declined despite running Alpha repeatedly.[79] How crucial is Alpha then?

The research done by Brierley for the Salvation Army is for the 1990s. Already summarised above, it is worth further comment in this context. Brierley points out that 73% of growing churches are likely to have held an Alpha course but so do 64% of declining churches.[80] Further, he draws the following conclusion: 'Does holding specific mission or evangelism events help a church grow? YES in the sense that such add to the overall numbers but as such events are equally held by growing and declining churches, the overall answer is NO!'[81] The key factors for growth he identifies are leadership and vision. Peter Brierley would appear to have modified somewhat his earlier conclusions on the evidence for Alpha being *the cause* of local church growth.

Other data are available too. Jackson and Johnson's research on the impact of Alpha in Baptist churches along with some very pertinent comments is very helpful. They found that more than half the churches running Alpha said their Sunday congregations had increased, a quarter claiming to be up by 10%. 67% of all baptisms were from churches running Alpha (though it is not stated how many were attributable to Alpha).[82] The report points out that overall many other strategies were being used as well, including in this order, meals, musical events, door to door work, the Jesus video, open air services, seeker services, street work – and the accumulative numbers of these far outweighed Alpha. To put it mildly it would be difficult to regard or prove that Alpha was the critical factor and better to see it as one among many good influences. Further (not reported in headline articles at the time but in the report) a slightly greater percentage of declining churches were using Alpha compared with those that were not. This may indicate that declining churches are hoping for growth from Alpha but it does not support the idea that Alpha works in all cases – and certainly not quickly.[83] Closer analysis of those registered as running Alpha indicated that 31.8% could show evidence of growth in membership after implementing Alpha. However, 10% had seen previous growth reversed, becoming static or actually declining after introducing Alpha.[84] The situations are indeed complex and Jackson and Johnson stress that many factors are involved and crediting Alpha as the main cause of growth is difficult. They call for more research.

The Baptists are noted in many church circles for having started very early to address dangers of long term decline, and to have made serious attempts to prioritise mission throughout their structures and life. They are thus seen to be 'ahead of the game', though statistically only just about preventing overall decline. We might well then expect them to have better figures for the long term use of Alpha – and to have integrated it better with other tools – than most other denominations.

b) Evidence emerging from Alpha International

Resource Churches
Alpha News does not frequently report stories of growing churches, which may be revealing – though there are some. Do they hint at this model for the use of Alpha being realistic and bedding down through other data, directly or indirectly? AI appoint some churches as 'Resource Churches'. These are described as 'a church of any denomination that has run Alpha successfully over a number of years and has grown as a consequence.' Their task is to support other churches in their area running or starting Alpha. By the end of 2004 they had appointed 60.[85] Details are not given on what exact role Alpha played in their growth. However, this is some evidence of growth although 60 out of over 7,000 registered churches is not many! *Alpha News* of November 2005–February 2006 listed 70 'Resource churches' though its description of them makes fewer claims. It says 'they run "come and see" courses for those interested in seeing how Alpha is run in practice and may also be able to send teams to help local courses with Alpha weekends and team training.'[86] Clearly this should not be seen as an exhaustive list of growing churches.

Size of Courses over time
The size of courses may be an indication. At the launch of the Alpha Scotland Office in April 2005 a presentation was made using some of

Peter Brierley's data on this point. These figures were repeated and updated in this year's report. The average course size had grown from about 11 in 1997 fairly steadily to 21 in 2005 (with the exception of 1998 when the figure jumped to 17.5 and then fell back to 13 in 1999.[87] In itself this seems encouraging though the changes are not big. However, the percentage of churchgoers has gone up since 2004 – and held at about the same level since 2002 and the percentage of non-churchgoers has declined over that time.[88] The size of courses appears to have been increased mainly by more helpers/leaders. Interpretation of these figures could also be complicated since they are overall averages. Thus they include new courses and new specialisms of Alpha both of which will initially tend to have mainly church members. So it is difficult to interpret these increases in course numbers as clear evidence that AI's model is operating accurately.

New Church attenders as a percentage of total congregational size
Brierley, in his research for AI, asks churches to express the number of people attending church (at least once a month) as a percentage of overall church size (i.e. congregational numbers). These figures work out at a mean average of around 10% (or a median of 9%) over the years 2003–5.[89] I must admit that I am not sure how meaningful these particular figures are – and I also have reservations about how full a picture they paint. They do not indicate overall growth in the congregation, and do not ask about this either. In fact it might be falling while this is happening. Also the figure is very dependent on the actual size of church.[90] There is probably a need for meaningful case studies to supplement and replace some of these more superficial statistical approaches if we are to really gain a proper understanding of how Alpha interacts with a local church over time. These figures do show that if a church keeps running Alpha the percentage of those in the congregation who have done Alpha will rise. (Including figures of those who were already churched and did Alpha will put this figure up a lot more.) This is hardly surprising[91] but, if a church leader is hoping to change his entire church over time (and its ethos, values and spirituality) with the help of Alpha, then this may be significant. This may in turn have other long-term effects including some for evangelism and overall growth.

The persistence of churches in running Alpha
Some helpful data is available in the Alpha Invitation Report 2005. Administrators were asked 'When did your church hold its first Alpha Course?' The average answer was 5.5 years ago. This suggests a significant turnover of courses with many eventually de-registering, i.e. not persevering with long-term use. In the sample of 915, about 40 had run their first course before or during 1994. The number starting each

year then rises to about 70 and after that fluctuates around about 65 starting each year thereafter until 2003,after which fluctuations due to the sampling method kick in. Administrators were also asked 'How many courses the church had run in total?' The answers suggest some rounding up to multiples of five, typical of surveys but these figures cast more light on perseverance. It emerged that 50% had held 1–5 courses; 28% had held between 6–10 courses; 22% had held more than 10, and the number ranged up to those who had done more than 30. These total numbers of courses may well include specialisms such as youth or even student courses as well, with these needing to be tracked as separate 'curves'. Daytime courses may follow their own curve too.

Thus only about half the churches seem to persist long enough to really test AI's model. Many may well take AI at their word that it will decline until about the third course – and then pick up as guests come in. I wonder if they feel that after about 5–6 courses they are not getting enough guests and decide to give up. This issue of long-term persistence is, I think, one that could do with more attention from those who support Alpha and seek to help it integrate into local churches and produce long-term fruit. Is attention being directed to the most critical issues?

Other Data
Is other data available on the long term use and effect of Alpha? Brierley reports in *Turning the Tide* that on average there were 11 people per course and an average accumulative total of 40 per church – data collected in 2002. This works out as 0.9% of the Scottish population.[92] Brierley suggests that many may have started after the first September Initiative in 1998 and inferring that this figure of 3.7 courses over 4 years for churches still running Alpha. In this case further growth might be expected. He did not ask for dates when the courses ran. His figure of an average of just over one course a year (4 courses in 3 years) cannot reliably be taken to indicate ongoing use. Many may well have run the course 3 or 4 times and then stopped. In fact, since that is the average and there were already around 500 courses registered by 1998 it is almost certainly the case that many had stopped running it – at least regularly. 51% of churches had only run Alpha once or twice. Far from supporting the model of the fruitful ongoing use of Alpha, this tends to undermine it, with churches seeing they are not getting growth and giving up, though there might be other contributory reasons for giving up. At the very least, these figures presumably indicate that many churches are not convinced it is worth persevering. They have not been convinced by AI/HTB's model.

Drawing some conclusions on Alpha long-term

I would like to draw together some conclusions and comments on this section. Some churches have persisted in the use of Alpha, integrated it well into their overall life and seen ongoing growth. At least sometimes this will be real growth through addition of new members who were previously not churched, though probably mainly these are dechurched rather than completely nonchurched. However, clearly just running Alpha repeatedly does not guarantee church growth. Most churches (to date) do not get overall growth through keeping running Alpha. Many continue to shrink. Thus Alpha's model on the effects of running Alpha long-term does not hold up in the majority of churches. Even in those churches that do grow, several other factors will have been involved in the growth, though AI/HTB do not focus on these or spell them out very fully. It is clear that most churches do not persist in running the course regularly, despite the fact that people do convert on Alpha. This also raises all sorts of questions about what it is realistic for Alpha to achieve away from the church where it was produced and especially when one moves away from settings and churchmanship similar to these. It also raises questions about the obvious difficulty that many churches – and thus especially its ordinary members – have in attracting guests (other than members or those already on the margins of the church.) This would appear to be something of a bottleneck. Why is this? Is it because they are simply not into evangelism? Are these church members awkward about raising the issue with friends? Do they feel they, as a local church, really own Alpha, or that it is not really part of their church? Do they feel, without perhaps knowing why, that it is just not suitable or the best thing for many of their friends? This area is, I feel, worthy of further research.[93]

It also raises questions about what is the best way of promoting Alpha or supporting its use in local churches around the country. I think AI are right to see – and respond to – the need to train people to run Alpha well but I suspect this is not the complete answer to the long-term effectiveness of Alpha. Clearly many churches (around 50% it would appear) do not run more than about 5 courses. Is this a measure of Alpha fatigue setting in? Are their expectations of what Alpha can do, and do easily, simply too high? Have these hopes been unfairly raised? Do churches feel they cannot keep up with what might seem, rightly or wrongly, like the pace setting emanating from AI/HTB? Is a more radical rethink of Alpha and how it is promoted, supported and developed now needed? I shall explore this more in the following chapters, especially Chapter 10 on strategies and hopes.

What is the real influence of the
National Initiative/Alpha Invitation?

When it comes to discussing how Alpha is promoted and supported it is important to give some attention to the Alpha Initiative/Invitation and its role and impact. How effective is it? AI puts a lot of energy into the Annual Invitation – is it increasingly becoming a rallying point? For some time, I have increasingly suspected that most churches that do now run, do so starting in the early autumn after the high profile advertising campaign. Are 'Alpha churches' flagging and increasingly having to be enthused by AI and the annual National Initiative, financially costly though that is? What impact does it have on the unchurched and dechurched and on their attendance at courses that run on the back of the Invitation?

Data already made publicly available by AI (and now confirmed in more detail by the access I was kindly given to the Alpha Invitation 2005 Report) certainly highlight the impact the Invitation has. In fact, Brierley's research is conducted soon after the Invitation with a lot of focus on it and so is of particular interest and detailed accuracy on this aspect of Alpha.

The annual Invitation attracts a lot of support from churches on the Alpha register as indicated in the table below.[94]

% of 'churches' on AI data base involved in the Alpha Initiative/Invitation.

2001	2002	2003	2004	2005
69%	72%	68%	60%	60%

Churches here includes some other institutions too that run Alpha. During this time the number of churches on the data base each October varied from 7,194 to 7,313.

This decline somewhat undermines my comment about it being a focus, though the decline may reflect less overall activity from some churches on the register.

Brierley also looked at how each church is involved in more detail.

Method of involvement (% of churches involved in Initiative/Invitation).[95]

Method	2002	2003	2004	2005
Hosted a Supper to launch their own Autumn course	68%	56%	73%	69%
Joined with another church rather than host their own event	7%	11%	12%	12%
Hosted an evangelistic event which was not a supper	8%	7%	12%	10%
Not involved in one of these ways	17%	26%	3%	9%

In 2001, 81% of churches used a supper to launch their Autumn course.

In some regions, often where there is a strong Regional Alpha Team or a suitable sponsor, churches work together to put on a large supper, often accompanied by a lot of local shared publicity too. It is interesting to note that many people, through these supports and also through local creativity and attention to their own local situation and mission challenges, choose to put on a different event. These range from taking part in civic/wider community events to holiday events to parties, film events, barn dances, open air services, healing services, music events and more besides. These tend to require more effort and people in the planning and delivery but also, on average, attract more guests. This independence, and perhaps creativity, is also evidenced in the numbers that used AI's promotional material each year.

Use of AI's Promotional Material.

2002	2003	2004	2005
63%	76%	86%	75%

Figures are percentage of churches taking part in Initiative/Invitation who answered this question.
In 2005 this was only 60%. Brierley notes that this presumably means the rest did not use it.
75% of 60% is only 45% of the total taking part in the Invitation which is only 60%
of those registered, i.e. 27%.

Prayer meetings (often held jointly by several churches) are the other main feature of the Invitation. In 2005, about 20% of all churches taking part in the Invitation positively affirmed that they had held a prayer meeting. Average attendance was 25, or 20 if some very big meetings are excluded. About half the events involved more than one church and the ecumenical mixture varied a lot but averaged at only 2.1 per meeting, though again there were a few with in excess of 15 denominations present.

All of this indicates that each local church is in fact quite selective about the extent to which it gets involved in the Invitation – if it gets involved at all. What does this reflect? Is it local scepticism about certain elements of the Invitation or about their suitability to a particular church's situation? (The extent of this could vary from year to year depending on the exact products available.) Is it just an affirmation and statement about the local autonomy of the local church and a wish not to be subsumed into something big and perhaps more faceless? Does it reflect local dynamism that sense better or more adapted ways of doing things? Or is it other factors? It appears difficult to assess clear trends or reasons for some of the annual fluctuations. The overall variations in participation hardly support the view that AI is creating church clones and mindless subservient ones at that!

This variation in response will no doubt encourage some and discourage others. However when this involvement is translated into national figures of actual involvement the scale is not to be underestimated. Concentrated into about 1 week the number of people praying is not insignificant.

National Involvement in Prayer Meetings.[96]

	Total Number of churches	Total number of participants
2003	1,270	Not given
2004	1,775	59,700
2005	1,449	36,200

What about the Invitation itself?

Average number attending an Introductory Alpha Supper.[97]

2001	2002	2003	2004	2005
29	25	23	27	28

What follows is a table summarising the calculations and results and giving overall figures for involvement.

Total Numbers attending Suppers and other Launch events (2001–5)[98]

	2001	2002	2003	2004	2005
Total attendance at suppers and other launch events	145,200	121,300	87,700	115,400	111,700
No of helpers at events	N/a	N/a	9,300 (est)	14,900	19,700
Total attendance of nonchurchgoers at events	62,400	52,300	37,500	49,500	42,400
Nonchurchgoers as % of total no of guests	43%	43%	43%	43%	38%

The biggest difference is the increasing rise in the number of helpers – which helps to force the percentage of nonchurched guests down. Apart from this feature, there has been an approximate ratio of 1:1 for churched to unchurched guests.

These are good numbers. When the Initiative was first launched in 1998 major hope was that it would help bring more 'Non-Christians' on to the course. What impact does the supper and other events have on guests? After the first Initiative HTB organised its own survey. This found that approximately 26,000 unchurched guests attended the Initiative and that the ratio of unchurched guests to churched guests on subsequent Alpha courses rose from 2.7 to 3.5 for every 10 churched guests. On repeated courses it rose from 3.5 to 4 for each 10.[99] This helped persuade them to continue the Initiative on an annual basis. Has this trend repeated? It appears to have variable impact. Between 2003 and 2004 course attendance rose by only 17%, compared to the 32% rise in supper attendance and during this year (2004) when there would also have been significant impact on accumulative attendance of the recent launch of new versions of the course (workplace, senior) and the repackaging of youth Alpha and the re-strategising of Student Alpha. Unfortunately Brierley's research does not indicate if these guests had previous church experience. We are not given conversion figures or, indeed, an idea of how long these guests persisted with the course. It would be interesting to know if guests, who have been befriended over time and possibly even introduced to aspects of Christianity in conversation and even in practice prior to attending a launch supper and course, persist more and find the course more fruitful than ones who just turn up by themselves.

What impact does the public advertising have on all this? Many praise it for its quality of advertising and use of the media and even general creativity. However, within the bigger aim contained in AI's mission statement to evangelise the whole nation, how effective is it really? I will evaluate this more in Chapter 10 on strategy and the theme is also taken up in more detail still by John Griffiths (Chapter 19). However, it is interesting to note here that the recognition by the public of Alpha as a Christian course fell slightly between 2003 and 2004 while attendance at Invitation events rose markedly so this may indicate that public advertising is not the main factor in attracting people.

The impact of the Autumn Invitation is felt in other ways too. Data for 2004 and 2005 indicate that 53–7% of courses run in the Autumn.[100] When a church first starts Alpha, between 52–4% of churches do so in September (the next highest month being January with 14%).[101] The Alpha Invitation thus has a significant impact on how and when Alpha is organised locally in churches even if a significant number opt out or use it selectively. It has a wider impact too. But, while the Alpha Invitation is a national event of some size, what is its missional impact? Can it help bring about a (mass) revival? Will it contribute significantly to forming long-term growing churches? Does it ultimately have more glitter than substance? Is it the best way of spending the substantial sums of money involved in putting it on? Is it really leading to more non-Christians attending *and* being converted on Alpha? Does it distract from the real issues now facing AI and the church more generally, even if it may give a short term 'feel good' factor? These are strategic and missional questions and I will consider them in next three chapters, which examine and evaluate hopes and strategies for Alpha and the challenges facing mission and being church of a changing British culture.

Overall Summary

All of this suggests a much more mixed picture than one might have originally thought! *Alpha News* headlines highlight certain positive features and their highlighting use of statistics again hides as well as reveals what is going on. This is typical of the use of headlines, publicity and statistics by any organisation. Their use of figures, testimonies and statistics does seem honest and accurate. Their willingness to make information available for this book is further proof of this. Hopefully this analysis has provided a fuller picture. I hope it is accurate and also helpful. It is intended to be anyway. Although it may present a 'warts and all' picture it is still clear that there is a good deal of evidence to back up the impact of Alpha and that there is still significant energy and life in the wider Alpha Movement.

Alpha is not a 'one size fits all' solution to the challenges facing the church in the UK. Its uptake by churches shows significant variation across denominations and especially in correlation to churchmanship, though the breadth of its appeal may well be increasing with time. It is more commonly used among some social groups than others.

Alpha has had a big impact and it works in a number of ways bearing beneficial fruit for many. Many of these are already churchgoers and most of those brought to faith and church involvement have had significant prior church connections. Given the overall numbers of churches running Alpha round the country and the total number of guests attending, these numbers should not be trivialised. In evaluating this, nor should we forget the words of Jesus that there is more rejoicing in Heaven over one sinner who repents than over 99 who have no need to repent (Lk 15:7). Most of these 'Alpha converts' appear to stay involved in church. The later impact of these converted people on church life and beyond it is not easily measured but may well prove to be very significant. At the same time, it is evident that Alpha is not (yet) reversing the overall decline in church attendance in the UK, though statistically it has reduced it. The lesson drawn here ought not be to 'blame Alpha' but to see and commit to whatever needs doing to undertake mission more effectively.

Perhaps we should not be surprised if most churches just run it a few times and stop and that it is mainly Christians who attend. It was designed by HTB for Christians anyway. It does to some extent work evangelistically, though this is limited. However, having much evangelistic appeal in a local church may depend on factors other than just running Alpha – and be more to do with the whole church life (and leadership) and also the social setting of the church. More detailed research, even looking at individual case studies (especially of growing Alpha Churches), would, I suspect, be very helpful and supplement what can be learned from large scale questionnaires and statistical approaches. It would also be useful to distinguish within unchurched guests (in Brierley's/AI's terminology) between those who had had significant church/Christian experience in the past (dechurched) and those that have not (nonchurched).

Although there is still significant energy, fresh ideas and forward momentum within the Alpha Movement there are also signs of people/

churches trying it and after a time stopping it. What the implications of all this are for Alpha's longevity remain to be seen, but we shall explore some of the factors affecting this later in this book.

Hopefully this analysis gives a fuller picture of the impact of Alpha, and from this a clearer sense of its real strengths, limitations as well as the opportunities it presents to local churches (if also the threats) begins to emerge. Better use of, and support for, Alpha, may develop from this.

Notes

[1] Peter Brierley, *Turning the Tide: the Challenge Ahead*, 2003, co-published by Christian Research and the Church of Scotland.

[2] It is reported in 'Church Growth in the Nineties', Christian Research, London, 2000 – and summaries are found elsewhere.

[3] Published by Christian Research Association, 2003 as 'Leadership, Vision and Growing Churches' by Peter Brierley.

[4] Having read his full 2006 report on Alpha in 2005, I feel his presentation there is 'sober'. Perhaps in some other articles he is just keen to convey to a wider public what he feels to be the overall positive sense in the data emerging from his research for HTB and to encourage its continued use and support for it?

[5] This was written up in book form as *Anyone for Alpha?*, DLT, 2001, (127 pages).

[6] See Stephen Hunt, *The Alpha Enterprise*, pp. 92–3.

[7] AI has released new youth materials since this research was done.

[8] *The Alpha Enterprise*, Ashgate, 2004.

[9] John Griffiths comments in his chapter that not making too many specific claims is useful, and prevents them being the bearers of false claims and broken promises.

[10] John Griffiths, in order to produce accurate research for his chapter on Alpha's advertising campaign, requested and was also given access to various information, and granted an interview with Tricia Neill (AI's Executive Director) and Mark Elsdon-Dew (its Communications Director).

[11] Darrell Jackson and Beth Johnson, *The Impact of Alpha on Baptist Churches*, 2002 (research undertaken in 1999).

[12] Charles Freebury, *Alpha or Emmaus?* 2005 (updated version). This is available and kindly supplied on CD-Rom without charge from the author. It comes together with other relevant Alpha titles such as *FAQs* (2004 add on course dealing with 'God and Suffering' and 'God and Other Religions'; *Stepping Stones* (2005 – a pre-Alpha Course designed to help church leaders and helpers develop their external relationships [i.e. those with non-Christians]); and *Creative Worship* (2006, a post-Alpha course to help churches adapt their worship to new situations. All these titles come on CD and are in Acrobat format and/or Powerpoint presentations. Charles can be contacted as follows: Address – 89, Hermitage Street, Crewkerne, TA18 8EX. Tel – 01460 78501. Email – charles.freebury@tiscali. co.uk.

[13] These features of courses should be remembered when analysing the figures Hunt produced on who attends the course and what effect it had on them. See *The Alpha Enterprise* and later in this chapter. Unfortunately Hunt's research does not test the claim and question 'Does Alpha, when it is kept running by the method for a long time, produce converts? If so, and factoring in all the things this entails, how many churches [on or off the register] can realistically achieve this?'

[14] See Hunt, '*The Alpha Enterprise* Chapter 6, 'The Survey in the Churches' for details. (pp. 91–105)

[15] See *Evangelism – which way now?* 2nd ed., p. 14

[16] Alpha Invitation 2005 Report, p. 14. Used with permission.

[17] This gives added weight to concerns about the problems of accurately scaling up from this sample. It is perhaps fair to comment that the sampling technique and linear scaling up may enhance the actual percentage participation to a degree. Newly registered churches (which will tend to run Alpha that year), though probably now a small percentage of the total, are always sampled in that year. (These made up 140 out of 915 in 2005.) Scaling up also assumes that the questionnaires returned are representative of the entire register. However, might it be that active Alpha churches are disproportionately more likely to return forms? (I have no hard evidence to confirm or deny this latter point.)

[18] *Alpha Invitation 2005 Report*, p. 14. Used with permission.

[19] It last appeared on the November 2002–February 2003 edition.

[20] *Alpha Invitation 2005 Report*, p. 14. Used with permission.

[21] Darrell Jackson and Beth Johnson, *The Impact of Alpha on Baptist Churches*, 2002. p. 2.

[22] Mark Ireland suggests that a facility on the Alpha website by which churches could de-register themselves might help. See *Evangelism – which Way now* (2nd ed) p. 14.

[23] A full review of Scottish courses was undertaken by the new Alpha Scotland Office in 2005. Although a significant drop had been expected and feared only 10 out of around 600 courses did in fact re-register. During this period around 65 new courses also registered. This is indicative of the good initial impact the Scotland Office has made. When a similar review was conducted of Catholic registrations (when the Alpha for Catholics Department was set up) the number fell from around 400 to 150 and the register was adjusted accordingly.

[24] An alternative approach would be to inform all churches to register each time they actually intend to run and to back this up by automatically wiping clean the register once a year (perhaps at the end of July). AI could well choose to keep another list of interested churches, and those that want to receive *Alpha News* and other literature; churches should be informed of this to help them make choices about being on the register. However such a strategy could well result in many courses just not registering and losing a connection with AI and the general Alpha Movement. As such a significant amount of the energy in the Alpha Movement might be lost.

[25] *Alpha Invitation 2005 Report*, p. 25. Used with permission.

[26] *Alpha Invitation 2005 Report*, p. 25. Used with permission. Data obtained from fig 3.1 and scaled up using other data in report.

[26A] As this book was being finalised *Alpha News* (No. 40, November, 2006) reported figures from the latest English Church Census, conducted by Peter Brierley, on the number of English churches who have done Alpha. (As reported in *Alpha News*, the question is about past and current use of Alpha, not just current use.) The total was recorded as 14,250 churches (38%). *Alpha News* quotes its head of Alpha UK, Rebecca Stewart, as saying this indicates that "there are also many more churches running Alpha than we supposed" (p. 1). Doubtless, there have been and still are some unregistered courses running – but probably not twice the number of registered courses. This 14,250 figure may in fact mainly point to, and give further evidence of, a high turnover of churches running Alpha, one unusual feature of which is the fact that new and cancelled registrations have very much kept pace with each other.

[27] However, the overall number of specialist courses (including students and some other specialisms that have been running for some time) only amount to 8.9% of the overall total registrations in 2005, a figure down on 2004's 9.7%. (*Alpha Invitation 2005 Report*, p. 18, Table 2.7. Used with permission.)

[28] HTB recently contacted, or tried to contact, all the Roman Catholic Courses on the UK register as part of its work to promote Alpha among Catholics. The

register has now been revised down from *c.*400 to *c.*150. (There are just under 3,000 Catholic parishes in England/Wales and around 450 in Scotland.) This new figure includes both those churches that run it currently – I presume that means at least once a year – and those that hope to run it again. It was also found that not all those running it fully 'follow the recipe'. See my article in Part 2 for more details of Alpha's impact on Catholics. Such research would be interesting for the full register and with denominational and other breakdowns of figures.

[29] Peter Brierley, *Turning the Tide: the Challenge Ahead*, 2003, co-published by Christian Research and the Church of Scotland.

[30] Adapted from Table 8.1, *Turning the Tide*, p. 110.

[31] Adapted from Table 8.2, *Turning the Tide*, p. 111.

[32] This somewhat undermines Hunt's theory of near exclusive Evangelical-Charismatic usage of Alpha. Hunt goes so far as to actually suggest that the number of courses registered corresponds almost exactly – and thus may well be linked – with what he reports as the total number of Evangelical-Charismatic churches in UK! There may be a better correspondence between churches that have persisted with Alpha and Evangelical-Charismatic churchmanship, however. This has not yet been tested empirically as far as I know.

[33] Brierley's research did not ask for, or at least record, which years it had run and if it was still running. However, some of his analysis tends to assume ongoing use (and even a start date in 1998). My own information (obtained previously from HTB) indicates that the uptake of Alpha in Scotland started earlier and rose steadily, with around 500 courses registered by 1998. (That rise has largely levelled off with current numbers registered being around 600 with a recent increase following the establishment of the Alpha Scotland Office.)

[34] Darrell Jackson and Beth Johnson, *The Impact of Alpha on Baptist Churches*, 2002 (research undertaken in 1999), p. 1.

[35] This full set of figures is taken from an article in the *Quadrant*, March 2006, 'Alpha UK and Worldwide' by Peter Breirely. (He acknowledges the figures come from his private reports for AI, used with permission.)

[36] For example, see Hunt, *Anyone for Alpha*, p. 116. I suspect the dropout rate tends to be higher when genuinely unchurched guests are invited.

[37] I have discussed the significance and interaction of this and other factors in Chapter 2 (under the uptake of the course across the UK) and will return to it again in Chapter 10.

[38] Adapted from Brierley, *Turning the Tide*, Table 8.3, p. 111.

[39] Hunt., *The Alpha Enterprise* p. 160, and Table 10.1.

[40] Hunt, *The Alpha Enterprise*, p. 167–8 and Table 10.6.

[41] Hunt, *The Alpha Enterprise*, p. 169 and Table 10.7.

[42] Hunt, *The Alpha Enterprise*, p. 165–7 and Table 10.5.

[43] *Alpha News*, March – June 2005, p. 4.

[44] *Alpha Invitation 2005 Report*, p. 21, Table 2.12. Used with permission.

[45] *Alpha Invitation 2005 Report*, p. 21, Table 2.11. Used with permission.

[46] Hunt, *The Alpha Enterprise*, pp. 169–71 and Table 10.8.

[47] Hunt, *The Alpha Enterprise*, pp. 181–4 and Table 11.7.

[48] See chapter 8, footnote 11, for more detail on how this was devised by Georege Lings, building on the research findings of Philip Richter and Lesely Francis. See Stuart Murray's more detailed classification, see *Church after Christendom* (Paternoster press, 2004, C1and 2)

[49] For more details, see John Drane *The McDonaldisation of the Church*, Chapter 4, 'Who are We Trying To Reach?', pp. 55–84.

[50] John Drane outlines such an application in his article in this book. See Chapter 21.

[51] *Alpha Invitation Report*, Questionnaire, Q. 10. Used with permission.

[52] *Alpha Invitation Report 2005*, p. 27. Used with permission.

[53] Hunt, *Anyone for Alpha?*, p. 97–8. His sample size here was 99.

[54] In fact, he accepts that the first book did not take sufficient account of, or measure, the fact that a well established course will tend to attract more unchurched guests over time and that this may have had some impact, as shown in his bigger study. This would sit with the 'conversions' figure rising from 3–4% to 5.6%. If the total number of churched and unchurched converts had really fallen from 17% to 5.6% it is difficult to believe Hunt would have said the second study broadly replicated the findings of the pilot. Indeed, it is highly likely he would have made a lot of such a change.

[55] Hunt, *The Alpha Enterprise*, p. 187, Table 11.9. I shall return to Hunt's understanding of conversion later.

[56] Hunt, *The Alpha Enterprise*, p. 188, Table 11.10.

[57] Collated from Hunt, *The Alpha Enterprise*, Tables 11.12 and 11.13 on p. 193.

[58] *Evangelism – which way now?* pp. 15, 35. Mark Ireland points out that the 21% figure was almost identical to that for 'Emmaus' and 'Good News Down the Street' Courses, and less than that for smaller courses and home-grown courses (27%).

[59] Hunt. *The Alpha Enterprise*, p. 186.

[60] Hunt. *The Alpha Enterprise*, p. 187.

[61] Hunt, *The Alpha Enterprise*, pp. 187–91.

[62] Published by Christian Research Association, 2003 as *Leadership, Vision and Growing Churches* by Peter Brierley.

[63] These are Brierley's summary figures. My calculator produced 71% and 29% respectively, though he may have used more exact figures for his calculation. I used his averages from the table.

[64] At times this may in fact amount to no more than having the impression that Alpha will not suit them, and going for the process course portrayed as being better suited to their churchmanship/spirituality. Thus Conservative/reformed evangelicals will tend to go for Christianity Explored, Anglicans for Emmaus, Catholics for CaFE, and Anglo-Catholics for Credo. I am grateful to Charles Freebury for pointing this out (in a personal communication).

[65] *Evangelism: which way now*? p. 15.

[66] A study by Melanie Groundsel on128 churches in the diocese of Guildford in 2002. As reported by Freebury, *Alpha or Emmaus?*, p. 13.

[67] Philip Richter and Leslie Francis, *Gone but not Forgotten*, DLT, 1998, p. 2. I shall examine their work more fully in Chapter 9.

[68] This comparison is not intended to compare one local church directly with another – some are clearly growing consistently, though others are declining markedly – but to give an overall picture at a national level. As such this does not discount the overall positive impact of Alpha on *some* local churches.

[69] Hunt, *Anyone for Alpha?*, pp. 97–8. His sample size here was 99.

[70] See C. Freebury, *Alpha or Emmaus?* 2005 edition. PDF file, p. 59.

[71] Something similar can be said for people who are made aware of/come into a closer co-operation with the work of the Holy Spirit through Alpha.

[72] *Alpha Invitation 2005 Report* p. 18. From Table 2.7.

[73] The new course manuals for Youth Alpha recognise and even approve of Alpha being used with existing Christians. They note that if it is started like this, it is unlikely to make a transition into an outreach course.

[74] From 'Exceptional: Report on 2004 Initiative' in *Alpha News*, March 2005.

[75] Research has shown that an alarmingly large number of young people who attend church while at school and home give up during the transition to university. Ministries such as 'Fusion' who are working with AI are seeking to help young Christians make this transitions and stay involved with their faith and church. This is commendable and to be encouraged. (How the results of this work should or should not show up in Alpha statistics is another issue.)

[76] It is reported in *Church Growth in the Nineties*, Christian Research, London, 2000. I have here cited it from *Evangelism: which way now?*, first edition (2003), p. 16.

[77] P. Brierley, *Church Growth in the Nineties*, p. 5. (Cited in, and taken from, Freebury, p. 83.)

[78] This research and findings were also reported in *Alpha News*, March – June 2002. Brierley acknowledges it is open to other interpretations in *Turning the Tide*, 2003, though he does not spell out what I have gone on to note above about sources of growth.

[79] C. Freebury, *Alpha or Emmaus*, p. 80.

[80] Brierley, *Leadership, Vision and Growing Churches*, p. 18.

[81] Brierley, *Leadership, Vision and Growing Churches*, p. 20.

[82] Darrell Jackson and Beth Johnson, *The Impact of Alpha on Baptist Churches*, 2002 (research undertaken in 1999). p. 3.

[83] Jackson and Johnson, p. 4.

[84] Jackson and Johnson, p. 6.

[85] Alpha International Review 2004–5, p. 5.

[86] *Alpha News*, November 2005–February 2006, p. 26

[87] AI/HTB have reported what is, broadly speaking, a fairly steady rate of rise of the total number of Alpha guests over time in the UK. If the size of courses has got bigger (×2) this suggests strongly that the number of courses running has gone down by about the same factor (i.e. it has halved). There will have been some turnover of churches on the Register (and complications to the statistics due to new versions of the course coming out, though most will be run by existing Alpha churches/outlets), but all this again suggests to me a reduction in the number of churches running Alpha (and/or the number of courses that each runs), despite a nearly constant number registered.

[88] *Alpha Invitation 2005 Report* Table 2.11 – and as reported earlier in this chapter. Used with permission.

[89] Alpha Invitation Report 2005, p. 28. Used with permission.

[90] Most courses result in 1–2 new people attending church or 13.8 in total. If the church has only 50 members this is a 27.6 %. If the church has 250 members this is only 5.5%. In other words these statistics may tell us more about the size of churches running Alpha – rather than about numerical growth of church members.

[91] The rise in these percentages over time is hardly surprising either. The small rises over time can hardly be seen as giving proof of significantly accelerated growth as a result of continuous use of Alpha.

[92] Brierley, *Turning the Tide*, pp. 118–19.

[93] Charles Freebury has commented to me (personal communication) that his formal and informal research indicates that churches that have an outreach culture, and are up to speed on relational evangelism, are able to make Alpha work long-term. (I presume that is if it suits their churchmanship too!) Others, he observes, will always struggle with this. His popular 'Stepping Stones' programme is designed to help address these issues. It looks at how to move from social encounter with people, to spiritual engagement, to actual (and natural) invitation to a process course or other church event. AI certainly also think that the outreach culture and issues of relational evangelism are important since they highlight 15 ways of inviting more guests on to Alpha in the booklet *Maximising the Potential of Alpha*. I suspect that these, though helpful, are not always complete answers.

[94] Information taken from *Alpha Invitation 2005 Report*, p. 4, Table 1.1. Used with permission.

[95] *Alpha Invitation 2005 Report*, p. 5, Table 1.2. Used with permission.

[96] Constructed from Information on p. 11 of *Alpha Invitation 2005 Report*. Used

with permission.

[97] From *Alpha Invitation 2005 Report 2005*, p. 7, Table 1.5. Used with permission.

[98] Adapted from *Alpha Invitation 2005 Report*, p. 10, Table 1.8. Used with permission.

[99] As reported by Stephen Hunt in the Appendix of *The Alpha Enterprise*, pp. 257–8. He was given a copy of this report.

[100] *Alpha Invitation 2005 Report*, p. 15, Table 2.3. Used with permission.

[101] *Alpha Invitation 2005 Report*, p. 26, Table 3.2. Used with permission.

CHAPTER 8

Alpha and the Challenges of Mission in a Changing Culture (an Introduction)

Andrew Brookes

Alpha is claimed to be a tool for evangelisation, or, in other words, for mission. It is my aim here to lay some foundations for reflecting on and assessing how effectively it is able to contribute to contemporary mission, and begin to look at whether its effectiveness has changed and will change over time. This means looking at, appreciating and evaluating cultural shifts. Other contributors will take up aspects of this in their own work. What follows is an introduction, a platform on which others can build, with some thoughts, suggestions and questions to which others can respond.

Mission is about the impact in and on society and its people of the Gospel and church that bears it. Though 'Jesus Christ is the same, yesterday, today and forever' (Hebrews 13:8) we have to find appropriate and effective ways of communicating Christ, who is also 'ever ancient and ever new', to each generation and culture. Truth does not change yet the language we express it in may change. Divine Revelation or Truth is so rich that any one set of words (or even any one theology) will not exhaust it either. New situations and cultural challenges face us with new questions. Taking these to God in prayer, God's Spirit shows us new depths, insights and riches, yet these are still parts of the mystery and wisdom of Christ and his Revelation. These may profoundly challenge us and much we have taken for granted – and even hold dear. At heart, mission is the work of God (the *Missio Dei*) who goes ahead of us in his Spirit. It is also for us to see what he is doing as a missionary God and then co-operate, if needs be, moving out of our comfortable familiarities, settings and slogans and adopting new approaches and methods.

Society and its outlook, values and attitudes – its overall culture – change over time for various reasons. Being aware of and interacting appropriately with these changing trends is vital to all attempts at Christian mission. Let us look very briefly indeed, at some of the changes that have swept through and shaped our culture. Here I can do little more than introduce in very general lay terms, a few ideas that keep coming up as people have reflected on and analysed society and culture.

Throughout the next few sections, before I treat Alpha specifically, I have inserted some questions about Alpha – highlighted with a bullet point thus ℘ – to get the reader thinking. Most of these points will be addressed specifically in the second half of the chapter.

An Overview of Cultural and Religious Changes in Britain (and beyond)

The 20th Century saw many changes in the British religious scene. The country would have been considered thoroughly Christian at its beginning, its dominantly Protestant Christianity very much part of the fabric of society, its institutions, and values and outlook. Nearly all people would have said they were Christian and church attendance was relatively high. Britain, made rich on the back of the Industrial Revolution and proud developers of the Enlightenment had a global Empire and a major world role. It epitomised what is called the Modern Era. But how did we get there?

This is seen as first emerging from Medieval Culture after the Humanist Renaissance of the 15th and 16th Centuries that, with other changes, brought about the emergence of Nation states and Protestantism in its various forms.[1] More and more attention was given to the use of human reason and its autonomy and authority (in contrast to religious authority), as well as stress on the individual. Culturally and philosophically these found their clearest expression in what is called the Enlightenment.[2] Its values are now regarded as typical – quintessential even – of what is called the modern period. These brought about significant developments in science and a lot of technological innovation. The Agricultural and Industrial Revolutions followed. They brought much prosperity to some but poverty to others and also led to the migration of many to the emerging cities, all this leading to the disruption of traditional life, including its religious dimension and practices. Britain led the way in these trends and it paved the way for the expansion of the British Empire.

However, in many ways there were already signs of less and less religious influence in society. Christianity and its status was tarnished by the long period of religious wars fought between and within nations in the Early Modern Period. The churches struggled to deal with the issues created by the Industrial Revolution and the disruption to traditional religious life. Increasingly the local church was less at the centre of local community and people looked increasingly less to it for their needs to be met. State hospitals and state schooling emerged. State welfare systems came in too. Atheistic ideologies accompanied these. All of this has been assumed under what is called 'secularisation'. It refers to the reduction of religious influence in the life, beliefs, practices and institutions of society. (In this country that is taken to mean less *Christian* influence.) People actually began to attend church less often too. This decline became increasingly marked since the end of World War II, and especially since the 1960s. (The two world wars themselves left many people questioning their religious commitments and beliefs.) Other outlets increasingly provided people with entertainment and leisure and the church became still more peripheral to the lives of many people. Although changing more slowly than actual church attendance, people began to hold Christian beliefs with less conviction, with actual knowledge of the faith also diminishing. These trends have continued steadily and constantly to the present with barely 10% of the population now attending church each week, though this is still more than do any other activity, including football.

Further cultural and philosophical shifts accompanied all this. Other non-Christian religious groups came to stay in this country and British people travelled, especially to the East. Our culture became multi-religious, and more generally pluralistic, and it was realised that there were serious alternative overall religious beliefs and world-views (meta-narratives) to the Christian one. To an extent it was also seen that there were different moral values too, or at least different reasons that could be given for holding moral positions. Tolerance was seen to be very important. Confidence in the ability of human reason to arrive at a definitive version of truth diminished and was philosophically challenged in many ways. We are now much more pragmatic: 'if something works' is generally seen to be of greater primary importance than 'if it is true'. The Enlightenment consensus, and presumptions, had been broken (at least intellectually). Relativism came into more and more of our ways of viewing and judging the world. Confidence in all institutions and in external authority of any sort has diminished considerably. These cultural shifts are commonly now described as Post-Modernity. The accompanying philosophical stance describing it as Post-modernism.[3]

The stress on the individual has grown, with his or her freedom and rights. Consumerism has accompanied and further fuelled this. Fulfilment matters and is closely linked with experience and affectivity. This was and still is seen by many in material, and often sexual, terms. However, increasingly so in recent years, more people are coming to look elsewhere, to their inner self, to meditation, relaxation, even to religious resources of various origins; in short, to what is increasingly and generically called the spiritual realm. Spirituality is in, not usually as something abstract, but seen in a holistic and integrating way, people being seen as a body-mind-spirit reality.[4] Words and ideas as mediators of knowledge and insight are being replaced or at least complemented by the visual realm, in icons and symbols, and by a general material mediation through all the senses.[5] In the consumerist and autonomous ethos of our age, people look around, explore and pick'n'mix from what is out there in our supermarket of spiritualities etc, looking for authenticity. Although it is a very loose term, the phrase 'New Age' is used to describe much of this. People insist on being able to explore, to decide for themselves. They look for respect and still value authenticity and integrity in others.

Since the 1970s, roughly,[6] still more changes have occurred. Technological innovations have continued apace. The development of IT and with it the revolution in communications and storage and use of information, alongside other ones which include quicker transport have made the world smaller and more accessible. There are closer links between us all; we are more connected and interconnected than ever before, and conscious of it. We live in a global village. This trend is called 'globalisation'. With it comes a sense of greater uniformity and, for some at least, the suffocation and even suppression of local identities, communities and cultures. In part, this, together with a more general availability of media technology etc, has led to local or ethnic or religious identities being strongly re-asserted in the face of faceless globalisation. This emergence of local and specific identities threatens what was previously thought of as cohesion based on nationality. National identity is also squeezed from the other side by international globalisation.[6A] Many of these technological and industrial changes, ever since the Industrial Revolution that began the Modern Period, have used up resources and caused pollution, leaving more and more serious questions about the environmental sustainability of it all. These have highlighted and, in some ways at least, increased greater disparity between rich and poor, both locally and globally.

Optimism and confidence in progress are diminishing. Many people are fearful, lack direction and purpose. Many feel increasingly isolated and rootless in their individualism and sense a new desire for community and a sense of belonging again. Here there is generally a shift from a sense of hierarchy and even authoritarianism to a sense of participation by all and even co-responsibility. Some have looked deeper, often within, for spiritual help.[7] Some have looked for a clearer code of right and wrong, truth and error, sometimes embracing clear 'fundamentalist creeds' of various sorts. Others are inclined just to live for today in a nihilistic and hedonistic way. The extent to which people keep moving job and physical location has added to all this and also threatens or poses serious challenges to family life and to a wider sense of local geographically-defined community. The desire to assert a personal identity has links with the emergence of branding, which in turn links to consumerism and what is seen as freedom of choice, since these facilitate the creation of a personal identity of one's own choosing.

We are thus going through a period of dramatic cultural changes across a whole range of issues. It has been speeding up and shows no sign of stopping. It is not clear where it is all heading. The extent of the changes persuades many that we are in what is historically a major period of transition. How to name and understand all this is more problematic. It depends on which of the trends outlined above are thought to be the most significant ones, and the ones that are seen more as causes than effects and how individual thinkers then steer a course through all the other cultural phenomena. I will briefly refer to some of the most common categorisations below. Of course, it is possible to combine some, or hold several to have some validity at the same time. All labels using the prefix 'post' infer we have a sense where we have moved from but that we have less clarity about where we have moved to, or, given that we are still in transition, where we are moving to.

Many say that the classical modern period is over or that, at least we are leaving it. 'Post-modernity' (or versions of this) is a common term. Some feel that what is happening is a result of the operation of the major forces and principles that characterise modernity, and that these are still operating. They recognise that there is a shift going on. Some see the shift as happening within modernity. One assessment describes the present reality as 'liquid modernity' (as opposed to 'solid modernity) since there is more fluidity in the present situation and more stress on relationships, networking and process rather than structure, plant and product.[8] Others look at the more spiritual dimensions. For some the phrase 'New Age' is apposite which (with or without a cosmological and astrological framework) infers a whole new spiritual era with different operating values. These include intuition (rather than logic), feelings rather than facts, feminine (rather than masculine) etc. Looked at specifically from a Christian perspective, some see us entering a new era where Christianity is no longer the dominant cultural force and where Christian beliefs and even values cannot be taken for granted. Christians will increasingly find themselves as marginal to society, one group among many. People debate whether this is good or bad or just different but many insist it means rethinking how we are church and do mission. This is often referred to as ' 'Post-Christendom' or sometimes a 'Post-Christian Society'. Post-Christendom is probably the more useful term and refers to us moving out of a period (referred to as Christendom) in Western Europe when Christianity was central to the institutions, values and outlook of the whole of society and powerful as a result.[9]

All these cultural and societal changes have multiple impacts on Christian/church life and mission. It is worth remembering that Alpha first started in 1977 and had reached its present form by 1992 – yet these changes are still ongoing.

೧ What particular features does Alpha best address? What ones is it less well suited to respond to? How will this change over time and as more cultural changes occur?

Religious and Spiritual Profiles and Perspectives on the British Population

Before examining the impact of all this for and on Alpha, we will look in more detail at how these changes have shaped Christian practice, belief and more general spirituality since this is our immediate focus.

Believing but not Belonging

Church attendance – on Sundays – has been falling for much of the 20th century, especially since the 1960s. In broad terms, it is now reckoned that about 7% of the population come each week (to one denomination or another) with about another 7% coming up to once a month. All these figures show a continued decline up to the present. What does it mean and what about the rest of the population? How non-Christian are they really?

It is a common concept, flowing in part from the research of Grace Davie in 1994,[10] that many people do still 'believe and not belong'. Her research suggests a latent and even personal spirituality which is no longer connected with corporate involvement in the life of any church institution. In this, it is argued, church attendance has fallen in the same way that membership of other institutions has in recent years. There is still a large number of Christians who just give up going to church. A recent ICM poll (November, 2005 – i.e. after the London tube bombings) updates yet broadly confirms these findings. 67% said they were Christians. Only 17% of these (11% of the total population) went to church at least monthly. Of those claiming to be Christian, 57% said they knew a lot about Christianity while 43% said they only knew a little. Of the 67% claiming to be Christian, 84% said they thought Christian values were important for Britain as a whole – compared with 72% of the overall population and 50% of people of other faiths. I will now explore these features in more detail.

The Churched, the Dechurched and the Nonchurched

Philip Richter and Leslie Francis investigated church attendance/non-attendance in more detail. [11] George Lings then came up with a more specific classification of people intended to give due weight to the Post-Christendom reality, thus exposing what he felt was unhelpful Christendom thinking.[12] He then applied it to the data of Richter and Francis, and it has become increasingly used since. It is one I have used here and throughout this book. A useful summary can also be found in the very influential Church of England report *Mission-Shaped*

Church which build on their findings (and of which George Lings wrote the first draft).[13]

Richter and Frances (using Ling's classification) analysed the population like this.

- Regular attenders: Roughly 10%, across the denominational spectrum, attend church perhaps 5–8 times in a two month period.
- Fringe attenders: Roughly 10% may attend church 1–3 times in a two month period.
- Open dechurched: 20%. At some point in their life attended church and are open to return if suitably contacted an invited.
- Closed dechurched: 20%. Attended church at some point in their life but were damaged or disillusioned, and have no intention of returning.
- Nonchurched: 40%. Have never been to church, except perhaps for the funeral or wedding of a friend or relation. (This 40% figure is a national average. In some urban areas it may soar to 80%.)

In reality, there is a continuity of trends within and between categories. The group of nonchurched is growing rapidly. Less and less people have been involved with church or church-related activities as children yet in the past the main churches relied on these people returning later in life. Francis and Richter also found that across the UK about 1,500 people per week just gave up going to church.[14] This figure does not include deaths. A variety of reasons have been suggested including moving house, falling out with church personnel, or needing to leave to keep their personal faith or spirituality alive. This is, or ought to be, very challenging to those in church ministry!

What follows is a summary of some of the *Mission-shaped Church Report* conclusions. These categories all need different pastoral approaches. Most conventional mission is aimed at those on the fringe or those who are open dechurched. The closed dechurched are probably the most resistant to church, having had a significant experience of it and walked – or felt pushed – away. The nonchurched vary enormously but their distance from and unfamiliarity with church and Christianity in general should not be under-estimated. For many it is all just completely weird. They will tend to take seriously media presentations of church, however unfair Christians feel these are. At the same time they may well have no negative attitude to church/Christianity and be willing to explore – if Christians get alongside them in the right way which means on their cultural terms. It is likely to take time. It is less a matter of 'Come and see us' (initially anyway) but feeling commissioned by Christ to 'Go and be with them!'

૯૪ Most of our evangelism has been geared at the dechurched. Now we need to look at nonchurched. What does Alpha realistically do?

Changes over Generations and Time

The boundaries between these categories are open and there is a dynamic process going on – with changes over time. Most of it is currently from churched to dechurched to nonchurched. Finney succinctly describes the most common pattern over time, even if it is a generalisation.

> *Generation 1:* Parents and children attend church. All have some knowledge of the faith.
>
> *Generation 2:* The children now grown up do not go to church, but send their children to church or at least to some church-based group or religious school. All have some knowledge of faith, though this is decreasing.
>
> *Generation 3:* Those children when they grow up do not send their children to church. Only the parents have some, now vague, knowledge of faith.
>
> *Generation 4:* The next generation have no contact with the church whatsoever, apart from an occasional funeral or wedding. None have any significant knowledge of the faith.[15]

This shows that having a real and visible church presence in the community and keeping a link with its people are important. Most people will not just arrive at Christian faith, or sustain faith, in the privacy of their own house.

It is worth looking at group dynamics too and the influence of dominant culture. Whereas a few atheists or devout sceptics or agnostics will tend to be swept along by the Christian majority, for instance around 1950 (and thus not radically shape the overall culture), they will not be swept along by the weaker Christian presence in Generation 4, i.e. nowadays. Indeed, to the contrary, a person of 'weak' or struggling Christian faith is likely to be swept away from this faith and church involvement by the non-Christian culture of Generation 4. This suggests Christian culture will erode at a more rapid rate from the public space or 'national scene' as these generations pass, and if the trends continue. Again most of our evangelism is pitched at Generations 2 and 3 and is reliant on, or at least supported by, elements of Christian culture that offers them some support.[16]

℘ Which generation(s) might Alpha address effectively?

Research has also made it clear that the extent to which they were familiar with the Christian faith as children has had a significant effect on their religious outlook as adults.

'Faith' in two Groups of non churchgoers: % who agree with each statement[17]

	Non-churchgoers as children (unchurched) [n = 126]	Weekly churchgoers as children (dechurched) [n=274]
'I don't believe in God now and I never have.'	40	6
'I believe in God now and I always have.'	11	39
Never pray	70	41
Pray at least every fortnight	6	13
Strongly agree/agree that there is a God who concerns himself with every human being	4	18
Definitely/probably believe in		
Life after death	31	35
Heaven	22	40
Hell	12	16
The Devil	10	17
Religious miracles	12	26
Some faith healers	25	42

This shows that church going/contact does help to maintain belief; church leaving diminishes it or makes it less 'orthodox'. Also people are selective in what they choose to believe, and becoming increasingly so. They have less grasp, or even familiarity, with the overall Christian story or 'meta-narrative', or even of the life of Jesus. Nor does what they select necessarily fit into any systematic theology or even into a logical or coherent pattern. In this study more believe in Heaven than in life after death! Some beliefs persist better than others. In this study more believe in God than the Devil. However, other detailed studies reveal that 'God' comes to mean a variety of things from a personal transcendent being to an immanent force present in all of us to something still less definable. There are relatively few ardent atheists around.[18]

Similar trends, perhaps more alarmingly, occur in questionnaires among people who identify themselves as Christians. These throw up sharp questions about what is meant by 'Christian'. Depending on the questions asked in surveys, many people will say they are Christian but will then not believe in a personal God, or if this is the case do not believe in an after life, but may well believe in Heaven, though only more rarely in Hell. Many do not accept any sense of objective moral right and wrong and may be quite sure Jesus was only a good bloke, or sometimes just a bloke. In other words their beliefs do not fit into a coherent pattern of Christian belief. Elements of Christian belief will often be found in a syncretic mix with elements of other religions or philosophies, even if the person is not aware of the specific sources.

Attitudes to morality are much more piecemeal and selective. People vary enormously over what areas of life and conduct they now feel it is appropriate to talk of in terms of right and wrong: some highlight issues of social justice, poverty and the environment; some sexual matters; or again financial matters or some other area. Some emphasise some of these, in varying combinations, some all, some none. Generally people make less appeal to external authorities for their moral code which is often expressed as avoiding deliberate harm to others but in which the details are judged personally on a situational basis.

ᘓ A course like Alpha presumes a good background knowledge of the Christian faith if the arguments are to be followed properly. Which group – dechurched or nonchurched – are best equipped to follow Alpha's arguments?

A new sense of Spirituality

People tend not to describe themselves as religious unless they have some actual contact and involvement with Church activities. This is largely due to 'religion' mainly having bland or negative connotations in popular culture. Nonetheless, many still say they are Christian, though it does depend on the context in which they are asked, and polls show a consistent decline in numbers of 'Christians'. Yet more and more say they are spiritual. Some authors see this as an important part of the shift from modern to post-modern culture.[19] 'Spiritual/spirituality' have become very loose and broad words but ones that are being used increasingly. More and more 'body – mind-spirit' sections in bookshops, courses and fairs are devoted to it. The research of David Hay and Kate Hunt is very often quoted.

Frequency of report of religious or spiritual experience in Britain for years 1987 and 2000.[20]

	1987	2000	% increase
A patterning of events/transcendent providence	29%	55%	90%
Awareness of the presence of God	27%	38%	41%
Awareness of prayer being answered	25%	37%	48%
Awareness of a sacred presence in nature	16%	29%	81%
Awareness of the presence of the dead	18%	25%	39%
Awareness of an evil presence	12%	25%	108%
CUMULATIVE TOTAL	48% *	76%	

* This includes totals for respondents to 2 additional questions asked in 1987 (but not in 2000) about 'a presence not called god' (22%) and 'awareness that all things are One' (5%). This means the 76% accumulative total for the year 2000 is likely to be an underestimate, relatively speaking.

It is not clear whether this means spiritual experiences as such are more common. It may well mean that a change in cultural perspective and new vocabulary more popularly available has led more people to recognise, name and talk about them. Nonetheless, these findings and the sheer scale of them are quite staggering. 'Body-mind-spirit' sections of bookshops attract a lot of interest (much more so than the religion section), spirituality fairs and festivals abound and it is now becoming a thriving lucrative business too, for some anyway. Some put more effort into their non-religious spirituality than many Christians and church congregations put into theirs.

The church needs to sit up, pay attention and work out how to connect with this spirituality. However, enthusiasm needs balancing with good discernment and with a few words of caution.[21] 'More spiritual' does not necessarily mean 'more religious'. Specifically it does not necessarily mean 'more Christian' or even open to Christianity. Sometimes it will, but often in our culture, rightly or wrongly, Christianity still has a lot of negative associations. Also some people specifically leave church because it is not spiritual enough![22] We may have to make our Christianity more spiritual if it is to hold on to current Christians and to reach out to spiritual seekers. Many are very genuine and sincere in their search, wherever it has actually taken them.

More and more people will admit to having what they know to be a spiritual experience – and being open to such experiences. I know of occasions where a person will happily be prayed with, or admit to praying, while in the previous sentence say they don' t believe in God or are fairly unsure about God's nature anyway. Jesus as a person still attracts respect and interest, and he is often seen as a spiritual guru, though people may still be very cautious about getting too close – and being too challenged. People may well be willing to check Christianity out or even give it a go if they can fit it into their schedule between the gym, night club or zen (or other) meditation.

'Spiritual' tends to imply something not well-defined, sometimes deliberately vague and often lacking specific moral aspects. This is probably how it tends to be used in 'New Age' literature. As such 'more spiritual' does not necessarily mean 'more moral'. This general spirituality is changing in some quarters. An aspect of this, viewable as both a development of and reaction against this spiritual and moral vagueness, is the emergence of Neo-paganism which has a much more specific moral concerns and a more specific, though still relatively broad, set of beliefs. Here spirituality has taken on a relatively specific religious form.

ᴄⱭ How well does Alpha connect with this open spiritual attitude and search for depth in experience? How open is Alpha? Is it too directive? How spiritual is Alpha, and how much real depth does it have? Does it express the appropriate link between spirituality and morality?

Facing up to the dynamic interactions of these features
– and resultant large variations

I have looked at aspects of belonging, believing, behaving and spiritual experience. These should not be seen in isolation. Clearly these overlap and interconnect though in complex ways.[23] The situation is dynamic and constantly changing, with many cultural variations. Even if, as described previously, belonging typically happens now before believing, once belonging has stopped, the nature and content of belief does not stay static. It tends to decline and become less 'orthodox', less coherent, more selective and religiously syncretic or an even wider pick 'n' mix. Probably relatively few leave church as a result chiefly of a crisis in belief as such. Some may leave for moral reasons. Work and other pressures on people and many aspects of contemporary life, including the transformation in how Sunday is seen and used, do not facilitate church involvement as it is traditionally and still normally organised. It is a matter of profound concern that people actually give up going to church in order to keep their inner faith alive; clearly there is a profound lack of deeper appropriate spirituality and also other aspects of formation in many congregations. However, many leave and become less spiritual too, as well as less religious. Modern spiritual searchers and consumers may well have no background connection with church or any familiarity with its ideas or story. They may well be keen to try out many 'products' but keep moving on and not stick with anything. Belonging can help people put down deeper roots. Belief, or at least good use of the Christian tradition, can provide effective means to help interpret, deepen and sustain people's spiritual experiences and new spiritual life.

No two individuals are the same. In fact people vary a great deal.[24] This then is the situation we must conduct Christian mission in. Nearly all evangelism in the last hundred years in Britain (and in fact for much longer) has addressed the dechurched, assuming a good background of Christian knowledge and even familiarity with church. There are still people – a reducing number – who fit this category. However, Christians also have to address the nonchurched and all those cultures where Christianity has had no significant positive memory and impact. In fact, it may, rightly or wrongly, have a bad reputation. This amounts to cross-cultural mission which needs to draw on principles similar to those in what are traditionally called 'overseas missions'.

ᔕᔕ How does Alpha fit into this situation? Is it addressed mainly to the dechurched or nonchurched? How does it address and use these dynamics?

How does Alpha Fare? An overview

There is clearly a wide range of people who attend Alpha. Since the course is multi-faceted it can have a 'spiritual impact' on a variety of types of people. However, what impact does it have on those not already active in church?[25] This will give a measure of Alpha's success as an evangelistic (outreach) tool. Certainly there are some converts during the course and many who have been helped on their spiritual journey. Some of these later convert/become active in church. All of these outcomes can be regarded as positive evangelistic outcomes. Some have a negative experience and some drop out. The timing and situation in their life may just not be right. HTB estimates the drop out rate at 30%, most in the early part of the course, i.e. chiefly in the first three weeks.[26] Some may actively be put off. It is important to try and gain a sense of why this is happening too. Hunt indicates that, by far, the most common criticism of the course (43.8% of all asked)[27] is the length of each session and the overall length of the course. Many just could not keep going after a long day and trying to juggle other commitments. It has been commented to me that this is harder still for people from poor backgrounds and very pressurised personal situations.

What is also worth reflecting on is the religious/church background of those who come to faith on Alpha. Hunt's research suggests that a lot of those attending Alpha who are not currently in the congregation are already on the fringes of church or have been involved with church at some point in their life. Are those coming (back) to active faith mainly from these groupings or from people with no prior Christian background or experience whatever? Hunt indicates it is mainly the former by a ratio of roughly 3:1. He further points to the main age group of 'converts' and suggests that they are 'adult returners', spread evenly across the 21–50 age range.

Certainly my own experience, and conversations with many others, indicate that even where the person (or their minister) considers they have come to actual faith (often characterised as 'knowing Jesus') for the first time, that they have had a background familiarity with Christianity, and often a strong and well-informed one. Sometimes this had previously not made sense, or not seemed relevant or it had not been a personal priority and may have been imposed or even damaging. They may just have been to church as a habit or custom, and not felt they saw Christians who did otherwise, i.e. for whom faith really mattered. People, who had a relatively authoritarian religious upbringing, often say they never got to ask questions or to express their own views and feelings and come to a personal commitment. There may be hurt or suspicion and fear to be overcome. Alpha's whole approach may well suit people from such backgrounds. Indeed it may be much better suited to them than to people coming to Alpha with no Christian/ church background prior to Alpha, or, if this is not the case, without having made significant contact with Christians prior to coming on Alpha. (For some, put off or stifled by an 'evangelical' approach to faith/church in childhood, adolescence or early adulthood, Alpha may be completely the wrong option, if Alpha causes these painful memories to resurface.) At the same time, I know *of some* stories where people from completely nonchurched backgrounds have come to faith during an Alpha course. If a person is open and their heart is ready, God can, and clearly sometimes does, act very powerfully. (There is also clear evidence, not least in testimonies published in *Alpha News*, of conversions in people from such backgrounds happening well after Alpha was attended and due to multiple influences.) God is not restricted by our sociological trends, though we would do well to learn from them, and grace does tend to build on nature and in a way that includes culture too. More data on this whole area would be helpful.

All this suggests that Alpha does have a part to play in outreach to non-attenders at church though these are likely to be mainly people at its fringes or those with a previous church connection. Since many local churches are still poor at this or don't do it at all, there is an ongoing scope for Alpha and similar courses. When used by a local church, the impact will depend in large measure on how well the course is run and how much effort is put into reaching out to the fringe and open dechurched and any others too. However, a course that can work well with some fringe people may not, because of its style and approach resonate well with the fringe of all denominations: it may strike some as alien or confusing, putting them off rather than helping them come home. Equally Alpha may not sit with the fringe of some local churches understood in terms of their social background or 'spiritual temperament'.

I am not aware of any local church that matches the size of course run by HTB itself. Very few if any have such a young age profile of guests too. In significant part, this is because the course was specifically designed for their situation. Although it is clearly transferable and has worked elsewhere, the scale of the fruitfulness of this is likely to be closely linked with how similar the church or immediate surroundings are to HTB and how willing the local church is to become like HTB. Also, being located in central London means HTB has a very large pool of people within travelling distance, a fact augmented by the large turnover of new graduates and young professionals spending time in London at the beginning of a career. Again these features are not reproduced on the same scale in many, if any, other places, though of course, to take advantage of this, the church, as HTB has done, must find ways to build up a nucleus of young people to begin with. HTB's big reputation also attracts further interest.

It can, as noted, also help churches begin to move, in more general terms, from being maintenance to mission orientated. Also Alpha, and HTB's overall approach and values can be learned from even if a church does not then use Alpha.

By this analysis Alpha is likely to have less and less impact, or be relevant and effective with less and less of the population over time. Increasingly Alpha is not even in the situation of being a complete evangelistic (outreach) strategy by itself but must be integrated with other activities, running as both pre-Alpha and post-Alpha, or along-side it. It is seen increasingly as only part of a much bigger interaction of elements of evangelism, discipleship and release into ministry, all of which need to be connected to a process that creates affective belonging. If this is how it is now being used, then a review of it to see to what extent each of its constituent elements really helps or hinders in this bigger process may be helpful.

Can Alpha be used effectively in a Post-modern and Post-Christendom Society?

Let us now look more specifically at how well Alpha is suited to the changing features of British culture as described above. This will provide further clues about the present and future effectiveness of Alpha and give some valuable clues about the issues and challenges for present and future mission in the UK and beyond.

How does Alpha fit with, and respond to, all these phenomena and changes in society and in the religious and spiritual make-up of the country? It is worth noting that it has developed over a significant period of time since its inception in1977. The current length of the course and the theological content was determined between 1981–6. The material was made more accessible to the 'unchurched' around 1990 and since 1993 the only changes have been to broaden its ecumenical appeal. There have been huge societal, cultural changes in that time and it is fair to ask if Alpha has kept up with them. In more popular terms at least, the whole debate about post-modernity and post-Christendom has taken place since Alpha began and largely since Alpha's length and general content was fixed in the early to mid 1980s. Let us look at a few of the cultural indicators outlined above with respect to Alpha.

General Course Content, mood and style

Certainly an approach that looks at 'Does it (Christianity) work?', which much of Alpha effectively does, appeals more to the post-modern than 'Is it true?', used by Alpha mainly in the first three weeks. The examination of experience and the generally holistic appeal along with the opportunity to explore values and share experiences and test authenticity, if well handled, may all suit the post-modern as well. The focus on actually having experience itself appeals to the Post-modern too. So may the relaxed unpressurised style, but do note my earlier comments under 'Dialogue or Proclamation?' (see Chapter 7) about Alpha still setting the agenda through the talk. Interestingly, Hunt reports that far more people found Alpha beneficial for reasons that fit a post-modern agenda than a modern one. Thus when asked for the perceived advantage of Alpha, the two largest responses were that it was 'good for spiritual development (27.8%) and 'allows a discussion of faith' (25.7%). A 'Non-threatening environment' came third. 'Provides knowledge of the faith' came fifth with only 7.9% though this may have been in part because only 12.1% thought its main attraction was that it was easy to understand.[28] (It should be remembered, in this context, that where there are a large number of Christians present they tend to find the content too elementary.)

Belonging

People still crave, and need, to belong even, and perhaps especially, in our strongly individualistic age. It could be said that the transition from modernity to post-modernity, which at least is a dissatisfaction with and questioning of the values of modernity, is partly a transition from individualism and personal freedom from constraint to a search for community and belonging. (However, individualism remains strong and while people want to relate and belong they want to choose how, when, where and with whom they do this.) Alpha can help people see if they belong in a (particular) church community. Various commentators have pointed out that many churches are using the insight that many people prefer to journey towards belonging before coming to believe and make this a major plank of their evangelistic strategies. This also picks up on the conscious desires of seekers who want to taste and see Christianity at work before committing to it. Process courses, including Alpha can be considered in this light.

Branding

AI/HTB have made heavy use of branding, of the media and specifically advertising in promoting the Alpha Course. In this it has hooked very deeply into modern consumerism. Arguably consumerism belongs to both modern and post-modern phases and in a sense helps generate the trends that are going on. We choose, we buy, we throw away, we largely create our own identity. People pick'n'mix their lives and explicitly their own spirituality too. Adopting and wearing certain labels, and spurning others, is part of this. Things become fashionable and then unfashionable very quickly. People find a product, and especially a well-branded one, something they can choose and that they can decide upon in their own terms. There seem to be fewer strings attached. Consumer power means they have more influence over it.

The implications of consumerism and thus branding for Christianity and the response of Churches and individual Christians to it are less clear. How is a Christian brand or product viewed? Christianity as a historic tradition, and especially church as a long-established institution, are treated with suspicion at the very least. However, Jesus is still regarded generally as a good and fascinating guy.

The language and attitudes of the consumer and branding are the mindset and milieu of many today so by using branding and advertising, Alpha may actually be making Christianity (or at least that part of Christianity and its message that it contains) accessible and attractive and even 'credible'. This is likely to be especially so for younger generations more influenced by these trends. Also, Alpha's advertising has, if anything, targeted younger generations, seeking to make Alpha look like something younger people do. *Alpha News* reports increasing interest in Alpha from younger generations so there may be something in this.[29] But the specificity involved in branding can be double–edged. The presentation of Alpha/Christianity as a successful brand (and even a brand *for* the successful) may appeal to some in society, especially the relatively successful or those who aspire to be. But it may also put off others, specifically the less successful, oppressed or those not convinced or critical of the value of obvious success.

Consumerism

For some Christians, use of consumerist strategies is odd, distasteful and even wrong – and even a betrayal of the Gospel in moral, theological and prophetic terms. Some counter this, arguing that we need to start where people are at even if we intend not to leave them there. In my view, at the very least, we need to be careful that the packaging for promoting the Gospel does not become the package and the message itself. Even if this is not intended it may be how it is perceived. Are we communicating the message that God/Jesus is a product/service provider, someone there to meet our needs? Never mind its branding and advertising, much of the content of Alpha looks at how God addresses and meets our needs, how Christian faith is of benefit to us here and now. Of course, it is true that God does meet our needs but that is not the whole Gospel by any stretch. God is certainly our saviour – the ultimate needs provider! – but he is also our Lord. What about taking up our cross daily and denying ourselves? What about being happy to suffer for the sake of justice? Does a Christianity that only stresses how God is our saviour distort the Gospel and also the process of conversion and discipleship and the cost and sacrifice involved in this? I think the answer to this is 'Yes!' Others can debate whether or how close Alpha (its content and also its promotional strategy) comes to this!

Christendom and Post-Christendom Audiences

All the above are indications of how Alpha *may* be seen as address-ing and appealing to the post-modern. It could be argued that Alpha picked up on these trends early and that is why it has had such appeal. Others may argue that it does not get very far into these cultural shifts or that it only addresses some of them. Yet when we look at the content we get a different sense. Although framed as questions, the material in the course follows an agenda that addresses questions that Christians or those already very sympathetic to it, would ask. As argued previ-ously the material assumes a certain journey to conversion and on into individual discipleship and finally church involvement. Truth claims are made early on and the intellectual coherence of the course relies on these being accepted and built on. The choice and also order of topics suits the modern and Christian mindset. (How many non-Chris-tians are deeply troubled by the question 'Why did Jesus die?'). The material assumes a good familiarity with Christian truth and bibli-cal stories if it is to be followed. However much the course may have negotiated the passage from modern to post-modern is it floundering in the transition from a Christendom society to a Post-Christendom one? If this is a problem, then can we as Christians change what we present as the Gospel or must we present what we (think we) have always presented?[30] In a society that increasingly describes itself as spiritual but not religious does Alpha offer appropriate spiritual food and insight, substantial enough to make searchers think that religion or at least Jesus and Christianity is really spiritual? These are perhaps bigger questions and challenges. I shall look at them a little below.

Michael Green, John Finney and Nicky Gumbel on Alpha, Post-Modernity and Post-Christendom

How do other authors assess Alpha in this context? Michael Green (in work first published in 1998) describes Alpha as thoroughly post-modern and regards this as a major factor in its rapid spread and fruitfulness.[31] In my opinion, John Finney (in work published in 2004) commented with more perception that process courses in general are post-modern in method but modern in content.[32] His book (which also gives some attention to Post-Christendom factors) begins to point towards how we may have to draw on different aspects of Christian Revelation if we are to convey the Gospel in a meaningful way that really connects with people today. He is well aware this will raise more than a few eyebrows, not least in the Evangelical camp (in which he has largely operated himself). In actual fact Green highlights aspects of Alpha's method and ethos in declaring it post-modern. He does not address issues of content at all.

What about Nicky Gumbel? At various conferences and days for Alpha Advisers he has commented on the issue of Alpha's appeal to those on the Modern and Post-Modern axis. He is aware of the course's long gestation. His view is that there are elements that appeal to the older, more modern generations, and also elements that appeal to the younger more Post-modern generations. He argues this mainly with regard to the content of the course though also with regard to aspects of its method. He thinks that the first part of the course mainly deals with issues of the truth of Christianity and is an appeal to the head. This he says appeals generally to older guests; younger ones often struggling noticeably. The course, and especially the day/weekend away, then goes on to look at things more experientially and looks at how Christianity works. This appeals to younger people. Older people have more apprehension about the day away, NG has commented. In the small groups, asking 'What do you think?' will appeal to the modern generation, and 'What do you feel?' to the post-modern, it is claimed. (This is a somewhat simplistic division, I feel.) However, NG considers that this combination of elements means that Alpha is well-suited to the current period which marks the end of the modern era and beginning of a new era. He also considers that the format of the course with its emphasis on eating and sharing together is well-suited to the younger people, of the so-called (Post-modern) 'friends generation'.

This appears to put him between the positions of Green and Finney! I am not aware of NG commenting on the Post-Christendom issues in terms of what people know about the Gospel, and if and how the actual content of it needs to be adjusted to deal with this. (Green does not address this either.) Nicky Gumbel and Sandy Millar refer to the fact that the gospel does not change but the packaging can. In using this analogy do they regard the packaging as the method and consider that the content is substantially unchangeable anyway? Copyrighting the content and length of the course (rather than its method) perhaps lends support to this view. Do they think the content can be much changed?

Are the Post-modern, rather than Post-Christendom, factors and analysis the more pertinent ones here? Freebury observes that all generations are permeated with post-modern attitudes and sensibilities nowadays. NG has commented that drop-out is highest in the early part of the course, reaching as high as 30%. Perhaps we, and NG, should look more to Post-Christendom phenomena to explain the difficulties younger people have with the early part of the course. Is the issue sheer ignorance of the Gospel and problems with what is presented as well as how? Older people have more (residual) knowledge of Christianity and more of them were actually involved in church related activities when younger. It may suit some to interpret the difficulties of younger (Post-Christendom) guests as indicating their lack of openness to the Gospel. However, it may be that we are just not presenting the Gospel effectively and as a result pushing away people who do have a genuine interest. This could do serious damage in the long and short-term.

By deliberate design, good and gifted pastoral gifting or just sheer providence, there are good arguments that Alpha has been able to help the church and some of its ministries transition at least part of the way through the change from a modern and Christendom culture. It seems to me that it does this best with reference to the post-modernity shift rather than the post-Christendom shift. Also it appears that it is the method, more than the content, that has enabled it to be used with some effectiveness up to this point. However, how much longer will it be really effective in responding to the continued change into Post-modernity and Post-Christendom? Again, it may well be the specific content of Alpha, not the Gospel as such, that may be the weakest link in this regard. Let us explore these issues further and in more depth, an exploration that ought to have relevance far beyond Alpha.

The Challenges of presenting the Gospel in Post-Modernity and Post-Christendom

In this context it is the subject matter of the first three weeks, or how they are presented that is most obviously modern and perhaps the most problematic for both younger and increasingly Post-modern and Post–Christendom guests. The sheer logic of the course content is that a person is a Christian by the end of Week 3. The style of argument especially in week 1 is very much a modern, and not post-modern approach as well as one that sits with a predominantly and substantially Christian culture. I will look at this in detail and then more briefly at weeks 2 and 3.[33] As well as content, the 'tone' of all these three sessions is very much a modern one, that is categorical, assertive and intellectually up front. Post-moderns prefer something more subtle, less direct, more open and discursive, more suggestive and invitational. A more narrative form of presenting Christianity may have appeal and be (seen as) less authoritarian and dogmatic while having real substance. This can seem like surrender and a form of weakness but much of the Bible is narrative, and telling stories and offering 'puzzling riddles' were central to Jesus' own ministry.

Talk 1: Who is Jesus?

As already pointed out, the presentations make certain assumptions about Christianity. It is not really a course in apologetics, building up a series of arguments as to why Christianity is true. Such presentations would have been typical in the modern era with its emphasis on the mind, rationality and truth. It is the first talk 'Who is Jesus?' that presents the clearest and fullest sustained argument. Because it covers so much ground, it alludes to and skims over areas very quickly and lightly that someone without a significant Christian background will struggle to understand or process. It ends by presenting the option that Jesus is either bad, mad or God. In my view, this argument also presumes (and originally was set in) a Christian culture wrestling with issues of historicity and using rational argument against predominantly rational atheistic secularists. This is no longer our predominant setting nowadays or the starting point of most people.

Also many enquirers may be attracted to the person of Jesus and be willing to think it unlikely he is either bad or mad. They may well sense there is something unusual and even extraordinary about Jesus, something 'more' that means he does not fit into normal categories – but they may not wish, or feel able to, conclude immediately that he is God. The Apostles were with Jesus for all his public ministry and it still took them till after the Resurrection to get a real and lasting hold on this. Also the term 'God' means lots of different things to different people nowadays. What sort of understanding of who or what 'god' is might guests be bringing to this talk? Gone are the days when it can be assumed that there is a basic familiarity with the Christian teachings about Incarnation and Trinity. A number of philosophical or religious or spiritual approaches can be used to consider what 'God' means/is.[34] God could be a force or just the spiritual part of all of us. Influenced by New Age thinking, some would affirm we are all divine. Then there are the views of other religions. Some Hindus, for instance, would happily affirm Jesus as being divine but not in the same unique way that orthodox Christianity does. Muslims regard him as a prophet (neither mad, bad or divine) who ascended to Heaven and will return. In reality, Jesus can only be properly understood as God within a framework and understanding of the Trinity and Incarnation. None of this is explained in this talk. C. S. Lewis who is cited on the 'Mad, bad, God' argument, wrote in the 1950s[35] to a much more Christian culture and one with significantly fewer other world religious groups or views, or New Age thinking, present. It would have been much more easily convincing then![36]

For the first disciples the issue and nature of Jesus' divinity was not principally the conclusion of an intellectual argument, however reasonable. Less still was it an interesting idea or hypothesis. They met, encountered, befriended, saw, listened to, and touched a real person. Jesus was – and is – a real person, a person so striking that, by grace, people felt they were literally in the presence of the Divine (1 Jn 1:1-4). His own teaching and actions pointed to the same conclusion. And also the manner of his death and what happened afterwards – the empty tomb, the apparitions, Pentecost. Certainly all this needs explaining and I have no doubt that the orthodox Christian one is correct but it is worth giving properly and in terms suited to the mindset and questions of each age.[37] If not we are likely to be called fundamentalist and be accused of over-simplifying things.

The case can be made for saying that a full intellectual presentation of Incarnation and Trinity can wait, and later flow out of a fuller presentation of who Jesus is, what he was like, taught and did. None of this can be grasped with the mind alone; grace is needed. Understanding Jesus goes beyond reason and is an encounter with Divine Mystery, one to be drawn into and encountered, not just thought through in relatively simple logical terms. Indeed, through encountering the Mystery of Jesus we will experience and contemplate God as Father, Son and Spirit, another and arguably still bigger mystery. Seeing Truth and knowledge as affirming and leading us towards and into mystery is not to deny the value of the intellect and reason, but to see their limitations and boundaries (and, paradoxically perhaps, establish their proper use). It helps us to see, value, be comfortable with and freed by what cannot be said and defined as well as what can.[38] Faith is thus midway between rationalism and fideism.

Faith comes from an encounter with Jesus. We hear about and encounter the historical Jesus but (and this is a major part of Alpha) we also meet him risen, alive and at work today. This double encounter quickly or slowly casts light on peoples' objections, be they intellectual, emotional, moral etc, and can (if not resisted) overcome them. Confidence is gained, decisions are taken and we begin to follow, connecting with Jesus/God through faith, hope and love. Nowadays, where and how do we encounter this Jesus? In Scripture certainly; and through prayer; with Christians and on our own; in our need for forgiveness; through the powerful and tender action of his Holy Spirit; in sickness and in health; in the poor and needy and in working for justice and peace; in searching for meaning and truth; in witnessing to the Truth and obeying our conscience; and in the church through the ages despite all her weaknesses and faults; in the sacraments, liturgy and worship; in creation and in our hearts; in love and in faith; in word and in silence; in darkness as well as in light, in life and in death.[39] These are all things that are to varying degrees dealt with on Alpha, though how it looks at them may need to be recast. There is a lot of variation in the time people need to spend with Jesus, journeying with him and perhaps with others, before they see him clearly, hear him surely, and arrive at trust and belief in him and commit to following him. It may all take longer than an Alpha course, or it may take less time. Perhaps we should more explicitly aim to keep guests interested and 'exposed' to Jesus for as long as we can and let Jesus work on them at his and their speed rather than leave them feeling from Week one onwards that only one conclusion is reasonable.

Talk 2: Why Jesus Died? (Or: Why Jesus Lived, Died and Rose Again?)

Let us look at some of the issues presumed in the presentation of the meaning of the death of Jesus in Talk 2. I have already discussed some of the theological issues around Alpha's presentation of the death of Jesus and atonement. I will not repeat them here but will draw on the argument and some of its implications. Alpha presents the cross in isolation from both the life and Resurrection/Glorification of Jesus, though these have been introduced the previous week. However, it is highly unlikely that seriously nonchurched guests will have picked up enough knowledge to put the death of Jesus, along with the issues of religion, politics and justice that led up to it, in this context. No significant introduction is given to eschatological elements or perspectives either in Week 1 or 2.

Basically we are told that Jesus died so that each individual could be forgiven for their sins and thus have a personal relationship now with God through Jesus. Though some indications are given of how sin affects us, very largely it is assumed that guests have a knowledge of what sin is and that they are sinners. In some cases, Week 2 may be too early to confront people with sin – and thus put them off. For such people Alpha's approach may be too direct. For others Alpha's approach may assume too many religious and specifically Christian sensibilities. The evidence is that for many people a sense of sin is lacking. A sense of moral ambiguity and personal failing and even the potential for doing bad things may be present and recognised. However, it only really becomes *seen as sin* when we see all this in the perspective of a just and good God. Commonly this is not the case, since it supposes a sense of God and at that, one typically within the Judeo-Christian tradition, though similar senses of what is supernaturally wrong are found in other religious traditions too.

So again, is Alpha starting at the right place? Is it setting and using the right tone too? Alpha places the emphasis on personal sin. Replacing the word 'sin' with a word like 'abuse', 'damage' or 'wounding', both received and given, may help but still not fully connect. Various opinion polls and other research indicate that many people are much more convinced of social, global and ecological problems and the dimension of moral right and wrong within them than they are in more personal spheres, including matters of relationships, sex, honesty, how they spend their time. (Look at the huge popular support for the 'Make Poverty History' and 'Live 8' campaigns, as well as for ecological and peace issues.) In these former areas, there is often a sense of corporate and even personal implication and involvement in the 'crime' or 'abuse' or 'wounding' that occurs. This will often be accompanied by a sense of hopelessness and even despair but often too by a desire to want to do something about it. The latter 'personal' areas are typically regarded as amoral matters of private choice.

Why not start with this sense of moral awareness as a way into looking at sin? This would include examining what the Bible/Gospel says about it and looking at the life, teaching, death and resurrection of Jesus in this light. I am not, for a minute, saying that we should just make sin into a social and institutional reality that does not affect us personally or call for personal response. Far from it! Such an approach can lead us to see that it not only affects us personally, but that ultimately it starts in the disordered and confused and selfish desires in our own hearts. Looking for a way to understand this takes us to the teaching and truth of Jesus. Looking for a way to deal with it then takes us to look to God and his Kingdom, to his grace and forgiveness and to appreciate what the cross and resurrection are all about. In fact, it will also tend to help us to see that all people are made in the image of God and to be respected equally because of this, and thus that relationships and (traditional) family life and education are all part of the picture too. Thus the full range of Christian morality (and therefore sin) is brought into the picture, but in a different order to that followed conventionally. Of course, some people will follow their journey into an appreciation of sin and forgiveness by many other routes, including the more traditional 'interior and personal' one.

One reason, we tend not to adopt such an approach to sin, redemption and justice – and may regard it with suspicion – is precisely because of the way we so often introduce presentations on the death of Jesus. It is not linked to his life, his teaching about the Kingdom of God, or to the controversies about matters of justice that he stirred up, but is presented in isolation and with a view to removing personal guilt and giving an interior sense of fellowship with God. I do not wish to downplay the importance of these but they are not the full picture and can make us spiritually short-sighted, even tending to inner blindness. The Gospel challenges us to see the full scope of sin, the full scope of Christ's redemption and the full extent of God's Kingdom that we are to build as God's instruments. It goes beyond the individual. Extending our gaze so that we offer practical help to those in need is very important. But it is not enough. We have to examine and address and seek to remove the roots and causes of such poverty and injustice too. All of this involves a challenge to our lifestyle.[40] At the same time reducing Redemption to political action to be played out exclusively in the social and historic arena is deficient too. The vision of God's future, anticipated and begun in Christ's Resurrection, and the fuller eschatological dimension need to be firmly presented and held on to. However, this has broken into this world and the work of transformation, achieved in the power of the Spirit, has begun. Let us contribute to it: this is the message that Jesus brought and died and rose for![40a] Could Alpha be adjusted to bring out these themes more fully? It may prove very fruitful to do so.

And what of individuals praying a version of 'the sinner's prayer', expressing sorrow, faith in Christ and asking for forgiveness? I think HTB generally has a good approach to this. It should be used as and when appropriate, though its scope and the content of any explanatory booklet may want to be expanded. At the end of the day it is the Holy Spirit who convicts us of sin (Jn 16:8–11) and this Spirit blows where he wills (Jn 3:8), bringing conversion and growth in different ways, how and when God wills and we respond. Sensitivity, flexibility and discernment are what are asked of us as spiritual midwives.

One other point worth mentioning in this regard is that despite conventional wisdom and a certain stereotyping of people's conversions, research shows that a sense of forgiveness for personal sin is often not the main element in a person's journey into faith. Other elements are as important, if not more so. These prominently include a sense of God's love and particular Bible passages.[41]

Talk 3: How Can I be Sure of my Faith?
(Or perhaps 'How can I connect with Jesus today?'
or even 'What is Christian spirituality all about?')

This is fundamentally a talk about what faith is and is a talk designed to give assurance to a new Christian. Whatever the original theological position of HTB on these issues, the current format in *Questions of Life* is broader than traditional Evangelical Protestant presentations on this topic. Nonetheless, this remains a talk that states what faith is. It is directive in stating how people should interpret their experience and constructs its argument using Scriptural texts, relying on, and even assuming, the authority and credibility of the Bible. This may well be a valid approach to help someone recently but genuinely converted, though even then it will not appeal to all. Its impact on unconverted Post-modern Post-Christendom people attending their third session on Christianity is likely to be quite different. (Remember, most nonchurched and even dechurched guests do not convert this early on courses nowadays.) It may well be far too assertive and be seen as very directional. An approach that is broader and more exploratory might be more appropriate.

Interestingly Alpha asserts that faith is founded on facts and needs to look to facts rather than feelings. This has much to commend it but this is a strongly modern approach to truth, feelings and experience. Why these particular facts anyway? The talk aims to remove doubt. What if guests are not ready to come to faith at this stage? Do they receive the message that simple acceptance of the Christian facts as explained is the only way forward? Is their search – which may contain a lot of 'doubt' – made to look like as simple lack of faith? What experience are they generally bringing to the talk anyway? Some may have deep spiritualities or spiritual understandings of their own; these are not addressed. It might be better to gently propose or just suggest these Christian insights as a way to understand or shape their experience and to deepen or change their own spirituality. Rather than stimulate spiritual life, the talk could, unwittingly perhaps, stifle it for many.

There is a virtually exclusive focus on faith in this talk. If the talk is seen more as a very general introduction to how Christians deal with experience, and interpret life and look for inspiration and motivation – something lots of seekers would be interested to hear about – then it might make sense to broaden the content. What Christianity offers, looked at it under the headings of faith, hope and love, all of which are deeply Biblical and have long been seen as foundational aspects of grace-filled Christian life, may be more rounded and fruitful. Other aspects could be included too. An examination of experience and spirituality in more general terms could perhaps introduce or be related to this.

I shall resist the temptation to go through the whole course like this! It is worth noting though, that some churches, and I am told HTB, now do the talk on how to pray before the talk on how to read the Bible, owing to the increased appetite for spirituality and meditation techniques, etc.

All this does highlight the challenges we face with a changing culture and it requires us to look seriously at the way we select and present the Gospel and what theological suppositions are tied up in old and new ways of doing this. It will make, and has already made, people ask if Alpha, especially in its content, is past its 'sell-by' date, or at least its 'best before' date. Let us look at the implications of all of this.

Exploring the Implications: Pre-Alpha, Amended Alpha, Extended Alpha in Modules or Something Different or New?

Putting all this together it is not difficult to see why many people drop out, especially during the first three weeks.[42] Many may have a genuine interest that could have been better nurtured using a different combination of tone, format and content. (Of course, there will be other reasons why people drop out.) Nonetheless this issue of where people start from and the mis-match with where Alpha starts from is leading increasingly more people to ask about what needs to happen before Alpha. Specifically 'Pre-Alpha' courses are discussed and proposed. Some of the other process courses already developed seem to be able to address some of the issues raised. Not all would see these courses as Pre-Alpha. Some see themselves as alternatives or would recommend other follow-up in preference to Alpha.

The eight week 'Y course' looks much more specifically at questions it thinks non-Christians ask such as 'Can anyone know what god is like?', 'Why so much suffering and so many religions?', and 'Is there really life after death?'. Other questions set up an obvious presentation of the Gospel. It has an Evangelical theology and is less experiential than Alpha. How far it really goes to addressing the real and full Post-Modern and Post-Christendom agenda is not clear. 'Start!', devised by the Church Pastoral Aid Society (CPAS) has six sessions, which are less high-brow, more explorative and try to start further back than Alpha and have a variety of activities. Local adaptation is encouraged. 'Essence', pioneered by Rob Frost, really tries to grasp and address the issue of New Age and the new search for spirituality. Again it runs over six weeks looking at themes of our journey, identity, the environment, pain and healing, prayer and lastly the future (dreams, life after death). It is very experiential, practical and open-ended with the leaders being open to receiving and discovering as much as the guests.[43] Still other courses have been made available and no doubt many more have been developed and used locally. Courses on prayer, that have been devised as discipleship material in various denominations, might have good use (possibly with small adaptations) as courses for spiritual seekers who are not signed-up Christians at all.

Can Alpha adapt itself? Is a substantial rewrite desirable, required – and possible? Well, within the ten week period it specifies for the course there are limits to what it can realistically cover. Most would argue that it is, if anything, top heavy on content already. If it changes the content much there is a risk that it will upset at least some of its client base. (The present version of *Questions of Life* has already been pulled, pushed, and tweaked a good deal to maximise its appeal within its original scope. Pulling it further may just not work and end up pulling it apart.) Alpha's copyright statement and policy, defining the course as based on (all of) *Questions of Life* and running over ten weeks may put further limits on how far the present course can be further developed under the name 'Alpha'. Building on this copyright policy, they have developed a brand and then advertised it heavily and run national campaigns and invitations building on this (apparent) standardisation. All this may have advantages but it makes further development difficult. Unwittingly perhaps, adopting these business and commercial strategies may have resulted in Alpha having a certain 'built in obsolescence', which ironically is another feature of our modern commercial and consumer world. In its present form Alpha may have a best before date. Some use may well even then persist but Alpha's principles and method and ethos may well prove more durable than its content and thus than the current overall Alpha course itself. If the content is the limiting factor it may well be worth looking at a serious update, and then facing up to any resulting copyright and branding issues.

Most of what I have suggested above for the first three chapters could possibly result in each of these becoming a mini-module in its own right. Such development and recasting could go well beyond what some may feel to be non-negotiable theological and spiritual premises and foundations of Alpha – though an introduction may be achievable in three weeks. Others may feel something else can be done by AI, and even HTB. Interestingly, the most recent trend with AI resources is to produce shorter talks (for 'Alpha in the Workplace' – but they will most probably be used elsewhere) and specialist youth materials in which the content is also reduced anyway. This loss of content and with it intellectual coherence will bother some, but appeal to others. It responds to what Hunt found to be the biggest weakness of the course – the length of the sessions. Will it, accidentally or otherwise, produce a less coherent course and a more simplistic and even fundamentalist one? In the future, the key may be for churches to have a pallet of resources (including home-grown ones), most of which can be run as short modules, and to use them flexibly, tailoring them to the local situation and each audience.

Linked to this discussion is the length of time people need to come to faith and how long they need to be in basic discipleship formation after that. Ten weeks is increasingly seen as insufficient on average. NG has remarked on unconverted guests returning to help on subsequent courses. Most churches only run Alpha once a year making this less practicable. I know pastors who do this deliberately because they think they need at least this long to properly follow-up and form guests, before they can help on another course. Even testimonies from *Alpha News* indicate that conversion can take much longer then attendance at the course and involve other significant factors. Post-Alpha courses have long been talked about. In the early church it took up to three years to form people who came from completely nonchurched backgrounds to a point of full Church participation. We may well be heading toward the same sort to time-scale again.

Bearing all this in mind, what might be the future of Alpha? It may just try and cover too much too quickly for most situations and most sorts of people now. It is interesting that what was devised as a discipleship course found an evangelistic purpose and even more intriguing why it was then mainly promoted as a chiefly evangelistic tool. It may tend to revert to its former use or be broken down into component parts that can then be adapted more freely.

Laurence Singlehurst has a model that it may be helpful to apply here. Singlehurst looks at evangelistic strategies as a sequence of sowing–reaping–keeping.[44] It is probably true that the original four weeks Alpha course were about 'keeping'. It then moved into both reaping and still initial stages of keeping. It was probably felt it could handle all of sowing and reaping but in fact most and even all of the sowing, especially with the nonchurched (and closed dechurched), needs to be done before Alpha if Alpha is to be most effective. It may well end up doing little keeping if conversions happen late on the course. Suitable Post-Alpha groups and activities then become even more important. On other occasions, it will just move a person forward on a spiritual journey, that may well leave them more open to the possibility of Christian commitment at a later stage in life. All such outcomes can be regarded as being part of effective evangelism.

All this suggests strongly that Alpha in its present form increasingly cannot often, if at all, be used as a 'stand alone' course or strategy. Churches will need to understand the overall process of evangelisation better as well as the contemporary and changing culture, the particular situations of the people they wish to reach and then plan and act accordingly. Certainly Alpha is worth looking at and learning from as part of this bigger task.

Other Challenges for Contemporary Mission

The church needs to direct far more attention to this Post-Christendom reality that has emerged and is growing. In short, we need to become missionary in our own country. This needs more than a strategy of geographically evenly distributed parish churches whose main concern is the pastoral care of those who choose to *come to us*. We need to *go to them, to all;* to get alongside them on their terms and in their settings and cultures and grow forms of Christian lifestyle, service and community there. This needs new pastoral, missionary or evangelistic strategies – or whatever anyone cares to call them. It can and has been referred to by different denominations and traditions as being about 'new forms or fresh expressions of church', 'emerging church', 'mission-shaped church', 'a new evangelisation, new in scope, methods and ardour'. Whatever the terminology, the same challenge faces all Christians!

Alpha emerged from an existing local church that adapted itself, but people were still being invited in to meet and join with what was already there. Alpha has adapted to a degree over time and is looking at, with varying success so far, if it can be run in some of these new cultures and settings, for instance in prisons, in universities, in business settings. How effective Alpha will be in such more obviously post-Christian settings remains to be seen. It may only be effective if used as part of a much bigger well-integrated strategy and if and when this is already well-developed and locally bedded down. Such new 'emerging churches' may have to develop out of these new environments and cultures, something variously described as a process of 'contextualisation', 'inculturation' or 'incarnation'.[45] Here, Alpha may (sometimes at least) be too unwieldy and modern to be used as it is. If so, some of its insights, principles may still usefully be applied and elements used.

In closing this section on current and future trends I will briefly mention some more facets of contemporary Britain that need to be faced by Alpha and the churches in general. Firstly we live in an increasingly Multi-Faith society. This means that people have a lot more questions about other religions and religious pluralism than in the past – including their views on and about Christianity. Secondly many of our perspectives are changing in the new world order and outlook brought in since 9/11 and the war on terror.[46] The latter has focussed attention on the former, on what is done in the name of religion and on the interaction of religion and state, on what are our common values and where they come from in new ways. It calls for new inter-religious dialogue, and will affect people's starting points regarding religion and therefore our evangelistic work. It has also produced a new anxiety, and perhaps pessimism about the future generally. War and peace loom large again; so does the nuclear issue. The ecological issues and those of world poverty are also very much on people's minds. All of these need to be addressed by Christians. None of these are major features of the Alpha course; nor are they really developed in *Searching Issues* either.

In the midst of all this, spiritual searching goes on, taking on ever new forms and combinations. Christians may need to rethink their whole approach to this spiritual consciousness and hunger that people have.[47] There are shifts within New Age spiritualities and how they are interpreted. One feature of this is what some call Neo-Paganism which some now see as a distinct religion. Though it has connections with New Age in many ways it is distinct and even consciously set apart from and opposed to some of what New Age typically stands for. It is a fast growing religious group – though commentators dispute what should define it and therefore how many adherents it has. Some claim its growth outstrips that of Islam and that it already has more adherents than the Baptist Union and its numbers exceed those who on a weekly basis attend either the National Church of Scotland or the Catholic Church in Scotland. Whatever the figures and its status as a religion, it needs to be taken seriously.[48]

We may be seeing a new cultural and thus mission challenge with contemporary youth. It is not yet clear if the present generation of young people (i.e. those born after about 1980 – and sometimes called Generation Y), and especially those under 20, will be similarly interested in spirituality like the generation before them. Research by Bob Mayo suggests they are much more focussed on the present moment and immediate concerns. Thus they have less expectation of a big metanarrative of any sort and do state an interest in explicit spirituality. They appear to be concerned to enjoy themselves and to be concerned about the welfare of their immediate circle of family and friends. With narrower concerns and less anxiety about meaning and deeper issues, they want to be happy and find pleasure. In a way they are a 'now' generation. Some would describe this as more hedonistic. (They have been described as having a happy midi-narrative.) Other academics have expressed real concerns to me about the validity of these findings due to Mayo's choice of sample and method.[49]

This chapter's comments on Post-modern and Post-Christian society and their relation to mission have referred specifically to the British context. The influence of these in other parts of the world varies, as does the general size, vigour and development of church life and its denominational mix. Alpha could have very different patterns of uptake, fruitfulness and longevity in other places. In some it may have much more impact than in Britain. Possibly the USA that has a much stronger Christian culture, or at least identity at any rate, is one such example.

Looking Towards the Shape of Mission in the Future...

It is clear that Christians face many challenges to engage in effective mission in the UK. These are not likely to decrease in the future. The church and its mission underwent huge changes entering into and throughout the Modern Era; it is likely to have to change as much if we are really entering into a major new era. These changes will be magnified still more regarding major shifts in Christendom. None of this will be easy, especially as specific churches have identified themselves with the values of these eras – and all, to a significant degree, have done so.

It is relatively easy to point out the limitations in what we currently do. It is far harder to indicate accurately what we need to be doing next. Yet to do the former without the latter can lead to despondency rather than hope. In the briefest of outlines I would like to end this chapter by giving some indications of shifts and developments that I think need to happen in mission – and thus in the churches since it is churches that undertake mission, having received this mandate from Christ. I am conscious of struggling to find the best descriptive terms and aware that I cannot develop them here. My language is thus somewhat tentative though I think and hope that what it refers to has some substance and relevance. However, this should not be seen as comprehensive.

Mission/church needs to become more spiritual. (An alternative word might be mystical.) It needs to take experience seriously but look for and develop depth in it. Without a clear appreciation of, and hunger for, the Spirit of God, and without an awareness of our spiritual poverty we will not get far. It can draw on the traditions of Christian spirituality. It can take on the better elements and insights of Charismatic Christianity but it needs contemplative depth and stillness to root all this. This contemplative depth brings consistency, real listening, discernment, insight and the resources that will better speak to those who are spiritually hungry today.

Mission/church needs to become more evangelical, but in a more radical way than the common use of this word normally implies. Christians need to see clearly what the modern era and the Enlightenment have done to shape our understanding of 'evangelical' and go beyond these limits. More radically still, they may have to critique it in terms of the whole of the Christendom legacy. Christians need to go back to our Biblical sources (including their Jewish roots) and read them anew and find out how to proclaim them in true, meaningful and relevant ways, and have a passion, albeit a humble sensitive one, to proclaim it. They need to rediscover a deeper and more pervasive Christ-centredness.

Mission/church needs to be more fully earthed again, aware of our bodily dimension and how this, and indeed all matter, is taken up into God's plans and blessed. It needs to affirm God as Creator and Redeemer and embraces fully the Incarnation. In a way this means a deeper appreciation of our own bodies, of community, of the church in a corporate enfleshed way. Christians make up, and are, the Body of Christ. It means a (re)discovery of the sacramental economy by which God uses matter to bless and sanctify us.

Mission/church needs to develop, live, proclaim and work for a compassionate, prophetic and liberating righteousness. This is about a comprehensive morality but one founded on the Kingdom of God. It includes all people, from the womb to the tomb. It embraces our personal lives, family, society, economy, justice, environment and peace. It has to be lived, but in this we rely on the grace of God, and aim to have God reproduce the life and Paschal mystery of Christ in our lives. It is a gift but one to be co-operated with, and this will be costly but rewarding. It is to be lived in solidarity with others, attentive to them, since they are all our neighbours, mindful also of the weakness in which all people share. It is challenging. It needs to be culturally sensitive but also prophetically counter-cultural when this is required. In all these ways it is authentic righteousness but a real witness and compassionate, liberating and transforming one.

Christians, and people more generally, also need to find better ways to bring together and deal with the past, present and future, finding attitudes that help us to deal with the problems and fears of each, but also their riches and promise too. People need healing and hope.

In many ways these goals are a development of present features of church and mission; as such they are a fruit of our co-operation with the Mission of God which is ongoing. The task of Christians is to try and keep up and be useful instruments! The challenge is to develop these features – and others, no doubt – and also to integrate them more completely. I suspect that parts of the church, and perhaps also mission agencies/projects, would probably be best advised to develop areas where they are weakest, which might mean learning from others. None of this may sound dramatic but I would suggest that few local churches or missionary projects embrace all these, and less still do so in a vibrant and integrated manner.

HTB is just one example among many of churches trying to engage seriously with mission. I have pointed out many of the limitations of Alpha. Yet it does actually embrace to a significant degree many of these elements and in an integrated manner. It is not complete and there is much else to be done by all Christians and church communities. I will begin to explore further the links of mission and church and how we co-operate and learn from each other in the next chapter. However, in ending this one let us remember that our Missionary God is with us always and let us be grateful for the progress that is being made in our times, as well as being aware of the challenges that lie ahead.

Notes

[1] The period from around 1500 to around 1750 is referred to as the Early Modern Period. The Modern (or later Modern) period as such is dated from around 1750.

[2] There was also a somewhat contrasting movement, perhaps epitomised in the Romantic Movement, that emphasised feeling, creativity, nature and spontaneity. It was real but an undercurrent to the stronger and more obviously dominant rationalist values of the Enlightenment.

[3] The German thinker, Frederick Nietzsche (1844–1900) is often seen as a forerunner to this school of thought.

[4] People's use of the word spirituality is often intended to distinguish it from Religion which is generally viewed negatively.

[5] Another word for this, in a religious context at least, would be 'sacramental'.

[6] It is from this period that Alpha began to develop at HTB.

[6A] The communications and travel boons that have led to globalisation could become opportunities for the human family to come together and co-operate more, our interdependence more clearly recognised. Depending on how this is done, it could be a real opportunity for Christians to preach and implement the Gospel with its message of reconciliation and justice for all. As such globalisation could be an opportunity, rather than a threat.

[7] There are also new forms of ritual emerging ('secular' and 'religious') and some people want to insert themselves into, or associate themselves with, some sort of overall spiritual rhythm (on a daily, weekly or annual basis).

[8] See Pete Ward, *Liquid Church*, Paternoster press, 2002. I shall examine this in Chapter 10.

[9] See Stuart Murray, *Post-Christendom*, Paternoster press, 2004, for an informed and sensitive introduction.

[10] Grace Davie, *Religion in Britain since 1945: Believing without Belonging* (Blackwell, Oxford, 1994).

[11] Philip Richter and Leslie Francis, *Gone but not Forgotten*, DLT, 1998. Research was conducted in England in 1996.

[12] George Lings explained the process to me in a personal note: 'The language 'dechurched' and 'nonchurched' (to differentiate for more general unchurched) first appeared in print in my *Encounters on the Edge No 1 Living Proof*: 1999 Church Army: pp. 13–14. I then met the Richter and Francis work – see esp pp xii and p138 – which gave me the additional insight that I should add the terms of open and closed, as subsets of these broader categories; I also took on board their surveyed view of the percentages involved.'

[13] *Mission-shaped Church*, A report by the Church of England's Mission and Public Affairs Council, Church House Publishing, 2004. See especially pp. 36–9.

[14] Richter and Francis, *Gone but not Forgotten* p. 2. This figure does not include deaths or transfers.

[15] Slightly adapted from Finney, *Emerging Evangelism*, p. 78. The acceptance of this model and its reality in parts of the country persuaded Finney, and the diocese of Wakefield, that a 10 or 15 session course was not enough to evangelise this fourth generation. This led to the development of the Emmaus Course. It has a 'nurture' unit, with significant similarity to Alpha but also some differences. It then has about 15 other courses (with a total of 64 sessions) that can be used flexibly afterwards over a long period of time. This process is accompanied by an attempt to keep them within the supportive fellowship of a group. (See appendix for more information.) It can be used flexibly and adapted locally. It has now gone round the world. Freebury compares it with Alpha in his *Alpha or Emmaus?*

[16] I am grateful to Steve Hollinghurst (Researcher with Church Army) for his insights on this point.

[17] Data originally from R. Gill, *Churchgoing and Christian Ethics*, Cambridge University Press, 1999 (pp. 132–3). Cited in, and here reproduced from, Bob Mayo with Sara Savage and Sylvie Collins, *Ambiguous Evangelism*. SPCK, 2004, p. 22.

[18] In a recent radio programme, sympathetic to them, a commentator described them as 'muscular atheists'.

[19] This is a major part of the recent work of John Drane – see his chapter in this book. In Grace Davie's 1994 work, she suggests that the switch from modernism to post-modernity marks a shift from secularisation to a culture that gives permission and space to explore issues of self-fulfilment and to have 'a sacred space'.

[20] David Hay and Kate Hunt, *The Spirituality of People who Don't Go to Church*, University of Nottingham, 2000. The figures are a percentage of the sample interviewed (less than 200). However the sample was chosen to be representative of wider trends giving it added significance.

[21] This involves avoiding being too keen to embrace all forms of spirituality immediately and wholeheartedly, but also avoiding rushing to dismiss all of it as superficial froth or malevolent evil, though elements of these may be present.

[22] Lack of spirituality is sometimes associated with lack of intellectual depth and an inability to connect effectively with contemporary issues. Faith and reason are thus not seen as operating symbiotically.

[23] See Stuart Murray, *Church after Christendom*, Paternoster press, 2004, Chapter 1 for a detailed treatment of these interactions. Chapter 2 looks at reasons for comings and goings to and from church. He points out that as we move further into a Post-Christendom culture, terms like dechurched and unchurched will not be adequate or even appropriate forms of description.

[24] The work of Nick Spencer, based on detailed long interviews is valuable in helping Christians understand where people are really at and in making suggestions as to how Christians can connect with it. See *Beyond Belief? (Barriers and Bridges to Faith Today)*, LICC, 2003. And *Beyond the Fringe – researching a Spiritual Age*, Cliff College Publishing, 2005. For example, The *Beyond the Fringe* research indicated that the following are still big issues among the unchurched:.destiny (What happens after we die?); purpose (What is the point of life?); the universe (Is it designed?); God (What is he, she or it like?); the spiritual realm (What form does it take?); suffering (Why is there so much of it? What can be done about it?). Jesus is still a respected figure who commands a mixture of interest, respect and fascination. Biblical knowledge is poor. The church struggles to overcome how it is seen stereotypically though individual Christians are often respected. People value their freedom and do not like being told what to do.

[25] My impression is that in the research done by/for HTB and AI all these people are classified as 'unchurched'; the helpful distinction between dechurched and nonchurched (or further subdivisions) not, I suspect, being used.

[26] Hunt, *The Alpha Enterprise*, p. 184. Participants at courses there have verbally

given me estimates of 25–33%.

[27] Hunt, *The Alpha Enterprise*, p. 179.

[28] Hunt, *The Alpha Enterprise*, from Table11.3, p. 177.

[29] However, other factors may have influenced this increased interest from younger generations (new products, new working partnerships with other Christian agencies) and it remains to be seen how satisfied (and converted) these younger folk will be, and, as a result, if this more 'post-modern' interest will be sustained.

[30] Although we talk of an unchanging Gospel and eternal truth, it is simply not true that even in the Acts of the Apostles the exact same Gospel content was preached. It was not. The Apostles selected and shaped the material to suit each audience. (For example, comparing Acts 2, Acts 13 and Acts 17 indicates common elements but also marked adaptation and selection for each audience and attention to specifics in the situation.)

[31] Michael Green, *After Alpha*, Tailpiece, pp. 231–52.

[32] John Finney, *Emerging Evangelism*, p. 187.

[33] The reader may wish to refer back to Chapter 3 where I summarise and comment on the content of the course. I will apply and develop those points here. *Questions of Life* by Nicky Gumbel may also be consulted for further details if required.

[34] Alpha/NG choose not to use any arguments from philosophy about God – and scarcely anything from religion as a whole, but to rely entirely on a presentation of Jesus. This has major strengths but also some weaknesses.

[35] *Mere Christianity*, 1952. *Surprised by Joy*, 1955. (Various publishers)

[36] I know and appreciate the basic validity of the 'Mad, Bad, God' argument. Here I am highlighting how many additional premises it supposes, and which are not here, or usually, fully developed. I am also pointing out its lack of connection with the issues facing the contemporary post-modern, post-Christendom, multi-religious and generally spiritual culture and mind-set. As such I am questioning its apologetic and evangelistic use, or at least looking at limitations in this. In my view, the quartet, 'legend, lunatic, liar or Lord?' gives more scope but still needs careful (additional) groundwork. Fundamentally, it will still have to be explained that Lord means and implies God. These are thus both variations on a simple argument from elimination based on the claim that Jesus claimed to be God. We have to be able to deal with, or at least explore, the question of what sort of God he meant. (Ultimately this means looking at the Incarnation and Trinity – teachings directly dependent on and implicitly part of the Revelation of God given in Jesus. In his own day, despite the Scriptures Jesus himself pointed to and argued from, most Jews felt his claims went against their conventional understanding of God and were as such blasphemous.) If not we are likely to lead people into a form of fundamentalism, or at any rate be *proposing* Christianity as a form of fundamentalism, or at the very least, fideism.

Interestingly, Will Vaus in his book on the thought of C. S. Lewis, *Mere Theology* (IVP, 2004) makes the point that Lewis' presentation of the 'mad, bad or God' alternatives come after he has argued against and dismissed other forms of religion (pantheism, dualism, atheistic materialism etc). The argument then carries weight when, and if, one accepts the Jewish understanding of a world with one transcendent God, and thus the charge of blasphemy that Jesus was bringing on himself if he was lying. (See pp. 29–31.) This appears to support my point here.

[37] The New Testament is actually both subtle and very rich in how it explores and expresses who Jesus is, and who he is not. It strives to find a new vocabulary and also makes a rich use of Jewish religious language to express his divine consciousness. It related him and his actions to what God had promised to do in their own Scriptures. It needed to wrestle with his self-emptying and death as well as his pre-existence and relationship to what he called his Father in Heaven,

and also to the Spirit of the Lord. His identity as being both divine and human in one person is thus explored from many angles and expressed in a variety of ways. Christian Tradition and theology have added to these.

Just jumping from Jesus not definitely being mad or bad to God, and by this implicitly having to accept all or most of the Christian metanarrative and beliefs there and then, can leave us open to simplifying things or encouraging a certain form of fundamentalism. I do not think Alpha is generally fundamentalist by intention but it does open itself up to the charge of being simplistic to the contemporary mind. Fundamentalism, in its various religious and specifically Christian forms, tends to result from an over-defensive and inappropriate over-reliance on certain forms of reason to combat a culture that itself elevates and heavily relies on reason. Even after we have established that he worked miracles, gave profound moral teaching, that he had an attractive and extraordinary character and deep integrity and goodness – and all this while claiming in some sense to be God – we must still do more. Jesus lived in a religious Jewish environment and he and his disciples framed their discourse in terms of this. Whilst drawing on and in a profound way relying on what is revealed, we need to listen to and address the views of other world religions and New Age, and even some atheistic secularists, about God to adequately fill out and convincingly present Jesus' claim to be Divine.

[38] Negative (apophatic) theology is a vital part of the Christian tradition and theology as much as positive (kataphatic) theology. We have tried to address the enlightenment culture with its emphasis on reason with a focus on the positive use of reason. (At times we now seem to be left clinging onto a God of the gaps in knowledge and in a situation where these continue to recede.) Negative theology has been played down and may need to be given more attention nowadays. An interest in such approaches to mystery and philosophy is what attracts many to the Eastern religions, spiritualities and philosophies.

[39] This potentially provides connections with science, the arts, politics, philosophy and religion more broadly.

[40] It is interesting to note developments within the work emerging from 'The Besom' project in this regard. It was set up to operate within a consumer society and seeks to help recycle and redistribute the surplus goods from those who have and often have too much, or wish to replace/upgrade, to those who do not have. This is very well worthwhile, but does not address or deal with more fundamental issues of the causes of justice and inequality. Getting alongside people in need may stimulate such questions and result in action to address these root causes. If so, this is good. In this connection, a very worthwhile aspect of Besom is where people commit time and not just their (spare) material assets to those in need. Christians need to move from a position of condescension (even a well-intentioned and generous one) to one of real solidarity and fraternity with others who are less materially well-endowed, aware of our own poverty and what we can receive from them. Jesus' approach to life and death exemplifies all this. Clearly this challenge is one for all Christians and not just those at HTB or involved in the Besom.

All this challenges how we live ourselves. This can leave us feeling helplessly complicit in our Western societies. Besom, having lived with these issues, have now devised a very good well structured practical 10-week course for small discussion groups looking at issues such as the use of time and wealth and the environment, and looking at the value of simplicity, community and work. It is called *Simplicity, Love and Justice – a discussion course* by James Odgers published by Alpha International in 2004. This direction of the movement is very encouraging.

[40A] Such expositions could take up and develop the theme of 'Christ the Victor' (Christus Victor) as found in some of the Church Fathers, especially those writing before the Roman Emperor Constantine legalised Christianity.

[41] See the work of John Finney. A summary on this point is provided in his *Emerging Evangelism*, pp. 69–91. He points out that only a total of 21% of respondents cited either forgiveness of the death of Jesus as particularly appealing in them 'turning to God'. This was based on research conducted at the beginning of the 1990s and contained a lot of 'Evangelical Christians'. 61% said they felt no sense of guilt when they came to faith. Rather than conclude that it is not that important to talk about the death of Christ, I think this may mean that as well as broadening the content of what we present we need to talk of the death of Christ in other, more meaningful terms than those conventionally used.

[42] At an Alpha event in 2006, NG commented that the small group discussion at HTB in these three weeks tends to wander all over the place and not stay on the topic – but after that it tends to become more focussed. This would suggest to me that guests really struggle to engage with the material as presented.

[43] For further information see appendix. Also see Ireland and Booker's 'Evangelism – which way now?' for more introductory information on these and other courses and some critique.

[44] Laurence Swinglehurst, *Sowing, Reaping, Keeping (People-sensitive evangelism)*, 1995, Crossway Books.

[45] For introductions to some of this work, for example, see Steven Croft, *Transforming Communities*, DLT, 2002; Stuart Murray, *Church in Post-Christendom*, Paternoster Press, 2004; Michael Moynagh, *Emergingchurch.intro*, Monarch Books, 2004. Many more are available!

[46] In fact, this issue was already present well before then. 9/11 brought it to everyone's attention. Highlighting 9/11 has meant it has tended (in the West, or at least Britain and America) to be presented as a problem created by Fundamentalist Islam, when, in fact, there are deeper causes, and other parties who need to give a fuller account of themselves and examine their past, present and future contribution.

[47] Recent resources produced to address the increased sense of spirituality among non-church goers are an encouraging and, I think, significant development. These include *Equipping Your Church in A Spiritual Age (A resource workbook for local churches)*, GfE publishing, 2005. Also *Evangelism in a Spiritual Age: communicating faith in a changing culture*, various authors, Church House Publishing, 2005. See also Nick Spencer's research findings. Road tours to venues to unpack explain 'Equipping your Church in a Spiritual Age' have been undertaken in 2005, organised by the 'Group for Evangelisation (GfE)', and a website has been set up – www.ciasa.org.uk.

[48] For an introduction to it and how to respond to it as Christians see, Steve Hollinghurst, *New Age, Paganism and Christian Mission*, Grove Evangelism Series no. 64, 2003. (Ridley Hall, Cambridge.)

[49] See Bob Mayo with Sara Savage and Sylvie Collins, *Ambiguous Evangelism*, SPCK, 2004, especially Chapter 2, 'Generation Y'. Some other researchers have expressed concerns to me about how this research was conducted. Many agree that more research on young people is needed.

Mayo suggests that the lack of interest in spirituality in Generation Y is a result in part at least from an over ubiquitous use of this term by which it means little more than personal experience. The term has become so broad as to be virtually meaningless. Also this generation has even less latent religious language to give it an appreciation of spirituality that has any link with what others would call Christian or theological spirituality.

This seems not unreasonable to me. The previous generation or two rejected religious practice but kept spirituality or at least felt a hunger for it. This generation has moved away even from this, at least as a conscious feature of life that can be articulated and ought to be addressed. Now people just want to be 'happy' and to 'have friends', trying to have 'kind relationships' with them. (Perhaps with more effort and help they would articulate similar spiritual attitudes to those older than them – though their inclination/capacity not to do so, if confirmed, has to be taken seriously.) In some ways, the rapid emergence of Neo-paganism can be seen as an alternative reaction to what is seen as the over-use of self-fulfilling and introspective personal spirituality of the New Age.

All of this has serious implications for evangelism. All of this may imply Generation Y are even further away from a conscious interest in the Gospel, but it no doubt has points of connection with certain aspects of the Gospel message and to certain forms of Christianity. Oddly, an effective form of Youth Alpha may have some appeal to the sort of people outlined by Bob Mayo, though whether this reduces God and the Gospel to someone/something that makes us happy and gives us friends ought to be a serious concern. Some will argue it could be a good start. It is probably more accurate to claim that Alpha has elements that could be usefully taken up in developing evangelism for this generation. As a short cut it could be very fundamentalist. Teaching and accepting any old belief as long as you are happy/secure and have friends is the method cults are regularly accused of using! I have already pointed out that, if anything, these people need more journey time, not less. Mayo concurs with this – and argues for new approaches too. The Alpha package may have some useful insights for approaches to discipleship with this generation.

CHAPTER 9

Alpha, Ecumenism
and a Changing Church

Andrew Brookes

I want to devote some space to reflecting on Alpha's impact on the church and in particular its ecumenical dimension. Church and ecumenism/unity are themes that are sometimes sharply disconnected from mission by some groups of Christians. However, I would maintain that both church and unity (and thus ecumenism, which aims to restore, maintain and deepen unity) are profoundly linked with mission. I would further suggest that what has happened with and through Alpha may be significant and give some indications of deeper shifts in how we live out and also understand these facets of Christianity. I intend to introduce and describe Alpha's involvement in these areas and then introduce some reflection on the strengths and weaknesses of all this and what it may indicate for what may lie ahead in the light of the current situation facing Christians in the UK.

Sandy Millar and Nicky Gumbel, and their collaborators, chose to respond to the broader interest in Alpha and thus embarked on an ecumenical journey. In fact, they probably found themselves joining a journey that others were already on and glad to find ideas, advice and help from them. In part they have been playing catch-up. In part they have been fellow-pilgrims. In part they have been trail-blazers, bringing new perspectives and possibilities to this ecumenical entourage and also new practical expressions of local ecumenical collaboration which, given the sheer scale of Alpha, have been significant in quantity as well as quality. The simple fact is that Alpha has much broader appeal than nearly any other initiative or course. This and its focus on local church use means it is still changing attitudes and, with its large impact, is opening up still other possibilities. Let us explore the extent to which the Alpha phenomenon represents and offers a new approach and impetus for ecumenism.

A Brief Outline of Alpha's Embrace of Ecumenism

Notwithstanding the various sharp criticisms made of Alpha from various quarters of the church[1] and any reservations that may continue to emerge about its limitations in effective outreach, Alpha has had a huge appeal and impact across a very large section of the church. It has been used in all the major denominations and traditions in this country and many abroad.[2] The uptake has not been even across them but this breadth is still significant. Looked at in terms of churchmanship, it has been used by more than those that would automatically or readily describe themselves as Evangelical-Charismatic though churches that would be relatively happy with this (self) description make up the bulk of churches running Alpha. This has led to various new links, friendships and even practical co-operation between individuals and whole churches who would not previously have thought of it, or even have known much about the other and perhaps sometimes respected them even less.

NG has commented that when HTB first made Alpha generally available he thought it might have some appeal beyond the Church of England, perhaps to some Methodists and even Baptists – but not much more than that. The scale and width of the interest has genuinely surprised them. Not all denominations or traditions came at once.[3] AI/HTB have gone to a lot of effort to try and accommodate each one, making a number of changes to the content, in response to points raised, to facilitate its use across an increasingly broad spectrum of Christianity. This has partly been done by avoiding certain issues and at times changing theological and other terms and, being honest and frank, at times too employing clever turns of phrase, ambiguity, fudges and vagueness. More fundamentally, the text largely uses biblical expressions when treating religious matters and has content in line with Apostolic and Nicene Creeds – accepting there is a breadth of interpretation of these by denominations anyway.[4]

At conferences they sensitively draw attention to the denominational breadth of participants. Again the conference talks are carefully constructed to deal with ecumenical sensitivities – and speakers are briefed on these issues. They use a certain amount of humour to try and defuse some tensions. When these cannot, in their view, be avoided, they try to balance things off by offending the sensibilities of one denomination and then another in roughly equal measure! They refer to the benefits of local co-operation at the level of training and intercessory prayer and sharing of other resources, linking all this to building regional ecumenical Alpha Teams. This demonstration of practical co-operation amongst Christian groups all adds to the credibility of the Gospel and enhances its impact on a sceptical and cynical world.[5] However, they do not generally encourage actual ecumenical courses as this makes it harder to integrate guests into specific churches afterwards, though some such courses do run. (I have heard a number of good reports about such ecumenical courses, especially in villages and other relatively small population centres.)

As I see it, they have over time increasingly flagged up the ecumenical import of Alpha as being not just accidental but actually integral to what God is doing in and through Alpha.

NG has said that God has given AI/HTB a love for all the churches and it is hard to doubt the sincerity of this claim. Given their evangelical influences and history, it is perhaps surprising. Evangelicals have traditionally had little to do with the official ecumenical bodies in this country, regarding them as theologically suspect and liberal, and talking shops that achieve little except use up resources and time, distracting people from more important issues and action. The very word 'ecumenism' is still a bogus word in many such circles.[6] Neither have Charismatic/Pentecostal Churches or groupings generally had much influence or participation in these *official* ecumenical bodies, though Charismatic Renewal has, since the 1960s, built many cross-denominational links, networks and friendships due to what it seen by its participants as a common work of the Holy Spirit. Yet, directly and indirectly, AI/HTB have drawn on the work and findings and experience of people engaged in such ecumenical work to find ways ahead through the challenges that cross-church work has brought to them. However naïve or inexperienced AI/HTB may have been – and they have also made mistakes along the way in these areas – they are making a significant contribution to fulfilling Christ's desire and prayer that we be one that the world may believe.[7]

What Characterises the Ecumenism within Alpha and the wider Alpha Movement?

There are many different approaches and motivations to ecumenism and emphases within it.[8] What has brought AI/HTB to their ecumenical position? I think it springs from others coming to them from these different traditions and denominations and them being moved to respond positively and to keep doing so. Lessons have been learned along the way – and no doubt, a price paid in criticism received from certain quarters too. They admit and stress that it amounts to being willing to see and accept the grace of God at work in all who believe in Christ. They point out that this may mean having to repent of past attitudes.[9] They sometimes frankly and publicly admit they themselves had to repent of their attitude to Roman Catholics in the past. They cite John Wimber's inclusive attitude to Christians – one that he came to through a process of challenge to and repentance from his previous attitudes too. With their stress on the Holy Spirit and participation in the growing Charismatic networks, I think they often see this as a major, common point and stimulus for their ecumenical impulse. For example, NG writes as follows:

If people have the Spirit of God living in them, they are Christians, and our brothers and sisters. It is a tremendous privilege
to be part of this huge family; one of the great joys of coming
to Christ is to experience this unity. There is a closeness and
depth of relationship in the Christian church which I have
never found outside it. We must make every effort to keep
the unity of the Spirit at every level: in our small groups,
congregations, local church and world wide church.[10]

What else characterises it? The Alpha material is rooted in biblical
texts and language. It is Christ-centred and has a strong sense of the
Trinity running through it. It emphasises the cross and resurrection
of Christ (his Paschal Mystery) which resulted in the gift of the Spirit
and the birth of the church. The Alpha course and wider movement
is about mission[11] and is, while stressing prayer (including common
prayer and worship), focussed on action (including shared action). It
is about a Christ-centred unity in spirit and purpose. This is nourished
by love and respect that avoid criticism and rivalry.

Does the course trivialise Christian Truth and important issues that
divide Christians? What is AI/HTB's and in particular NG's and SM's
attitude to Christian truth and what is their deeper understanding of
ecumenism and of the church that underlies this and their approach
on Alpha now, if not at the beginning? What evidence and clues can
be found in the course materials? They state that truth matters and
acknowledge the need for proper theological conversations to resolve
differences.[12] Do they operate the principle common among Protestant Evangelicals of first order and second order truths?[13] I am not
aware that they have explicitly stated this, or that there is much hard
evidence to support the view that they do. However, it is fair to note
that many involved with Alpha do hold such a view or follow such a
modus operandi. Is the Catholic principle of the Hierarchy of Truths
nearer to the position adopted and strategy followed by NG and SM?[14]
Do they follow a different approach to both of these?

NG goes further in clarifying his position:

The Incarnation demands a visible expression of our invisible unity. Of course, this unity should not be achieved at
the expense of truth but as the medieval writer Rupertus
Meldenius puts it, 'On the necessary points, unity; on the
questionable points liberty; in everything, love.'[15]

This points to the physical fleshy reality of the church as a community of people and the Body of Christ being important for NG and SM.
Further this is not just at the local level but at the worldwide level and,
by implication, through time. They draw their illustrations on Alpha
from across the history of the church as well as its breadth. While they

accept, as part of work for unity, the need for theologians to work to come to a better mutual understanding and to overcome our differences, they do call for mutual love, shared prayer and practical co-operation in various ways too. Truth is not the only factor in their ecumenical approach. Practical co-operation in and for mission must be undertaken.

What deeper understanding of the church underlies this ecumenical position?

As more and more denominations have taken a serious interest in Alpha, AI/HTB have undertaken these practical steps. However, I think they have also been stimulated, and perhaps profoundly challenged, to reflect on their attitude to other denominations and thus to ecumenism itself and also to ponder their deeper understanding of church and its relation to mission. I strongly suspect that this has happened 'on the hoof' as Alpha has spread rather than having been thought out before hand, though they may have been prepared in part by previous influences. For instance, John Wimber had already tried to break down barriers between denominations. I also think that these ideas and their application are both ongoing, very much a work in process. Nonetheless, I think they now have a sort of road map, if not perhaps one with all the details marked out. Listening to conference talks, and being at other Alpha gatherings and HTB events, provides many strong indications and other clues as to what some of these other influences are. It is worthwhile looking at this and offering some comments. Since AI/HTB have not clearly enunciated these positions it may be all the more valuable to attempt do so – both for supporters, enquirers and critics of Alpha. Since they do not publicly state their position in a formal way, it should be stressed that what follows is my own 'construction' of it and only an introduction at that, but one I am confident has very significant bearings on reality.

The thought of Lesslie Newbigin

What deeper understanding of the church now underlies Alpha? Gumbel and Millar are very impressed by and guided by the work of Lesslie Newbigin, even if they do not follow its every detail. Both Millar and Gumbel often publicly acknowledge their friendship with Newbigin and the help he gave them in understanding and taking forward their work. Particularly pertinent here, is an understanding of the worldwide church first put forward by Lesslie Newbigin in *The Household of God* in 1953. I have good reasons to believe they do take this very seriously.[16] Newbigin, although not generally describing himself as an Evangelical or Charismatic, very much made HTB his home in the last few years of his life in the early 1990s. This was precisely the time when, with Alpha impacting the wider church, it is easy to imagine HTB's leadership reflecting on and seeking to under-stand/position this theologically and practically. (The extent to which the rest of Newbigin's thought has influenced the ideas, vision and policy of Alpha and its implementers is also worthy of reflection.)

I cannot do justice to the richness and complexity of the thought in Newbigin's book here.[17] I will attempt a very brief and inadequate summary and apologise for its deficiencies. In short Newbigin insists the church is formed in and by the Word which it also proclaims – typi-cally seen as the essence of being 'Protestant'. It also has to be phys-ical, incarnational, sacramental and in 'bodily' continuity with Christ and the apostles – typically seen as 'Catholic'. It has to be filled and led by the Holy Spirit and his gifts and action – typically seen as 'Pente-costal'.[18] At the same time the church, now understood collectively as the synthesis/integration of these three traditions, has to be orientated towards and profoundly influenced by the eschatological perspective and focus on and hope in Christ's return. This needs to be recovered more fully. Finally the church has to be committed to mission, for which purpose it exists. In some way these five features or elements, which embrace the breadth of Christianity as well as its orientation to time and space, need integrating in a healthy and balanced way for the church to be fully alive and to fulfil what God calls it to be. I will expand on this a little, focussing on the 'Catholic', 'Protestant' and 'Pentecostal' dimensions, though the others are vital too.

Newbigin holds that the church – the household of God – is to be incarnated and be a real tangible people in continuity with the Jews, gathered around Jesus at its centre to receive there, from him, forgive-ness and salvation. The church is in continuity with the apostles and receives and expresses its life in Christ in the sacraments.[19] The church is under the Word of God which constantly challenges it to be all that God has revealed and wills. It is also filled with and animated by the Holy Spirit. He accepts that the church originally had all three dimen-sions. However, the growth of the church, perhaps accompanied by a neglect of the Word or Spirit, can mean that the church as a body and 'institution' focuses in on itself and can even become, at least in prac-tical terms, an end in and for itself.

It needs to be vigilant about being under the Word of God. However, when a 'reform' focuses in on one particular aspect of Revelation in the Word (which may well need highlighting) it should aim to reform the whole from within. When the reforming impulse based on a particu-lar emphasis then leads to a fracture or split that becomes a church in its own right (or claims to be), there is a real danger that it is now not founded on the whole Christian truth and life in a full and balanced way. According to Newbigin, such a church, while having a recognis-ably distinct character, tends also to have deficiencies or gaps too, thus being skewed or unbalanced in other ways. If later splits come from it, through attempted reforms or similar dynamics, they will likely be even more skewed. This marks much of the history of the Protestant reformation and subsequent multiplication of splits. Newbigin does not doubt the presence of God's grace in such movements and church bodies – the more so when there is a real reforming motivation involved.

The church is to be filled and moved by the Holy Spirit who brings us the grace and experience of salvation and equips and motivates us for mission. This counter-balances a danger in Word-based Christianity which, by its focus on truth, becomes over–intellectual, cerebral and dry.

The church is all these things as a sign and instrument of the Kingdom of God and it is given over to mission (that is, to fuller realisation of God's Kingdom) as its fundamental calling and something at the core of its identity. In all this, the church (the Bride of Christ) looks to Christ, the head of the church, to be her guide and fulfilment knowing everything can only be done in God's grace. She knows ultimately that all God intends can only be fulfilled by His Return and for this she earnestly desires and prepares for. In Newbigins's view the church needs to be focussed on her mission and be keenly aware of its eschatological dimension and setting if it is to find the right balance for its life of being a corporate sacramental body, under the Word and animated by the Spirit.

Now for a few of my own comments! It is a crude and distorting simplification to segregate out elements of God's economy in the church to various denominations. It is wrong to say that Catholicism ignores the Word and Spirit or that Protestantism ignores sacraments and Spirit or that Pentecostalism is not interested in the Word or more incarnational/sacramental elements of Christianity. Newbigin notes that this is not the case and is aware of the danger of such generalisations. Yet, in general terms, since the 16th century attempts at reformation, the resulting blocks of divided Christians have defined themselves and their communities as much by what they are not as much as what they are and have lived consciously segregated lives as Christians, if not mutually hostile ones. At the lived level, practically and pastorally, certain mutual impoverishment has happened. This has reinforced the identity and boundaries of each group, and often fuelled further suspicion, prejudice and disunity. Many would now argue that through this wounding there has been a certain partitioning of the riches and gifts Christ intends for his Bride, and with it a diminution of the vigour of the life He intends to flow into and through his body – at least in practical terms. All of this has implications and challenges for Christian mission and church unity at all sorts of levels.[20]

Newbigin was more interested in the broad theological perspective/mood and resulting spirituality and lived attitudes than in the details of dogma. He draws out in one relatively short book the strengths and weaknesses of the theological and more practical outlook of each of these broad Christian blocks and their consequences for spirituality and lived pastoral and mission practice of Christianity – especially when this includes diminishing one or more of the others. Writing in 1953 (when the Catholic, Protestant and Pentecostal worlds were each self-contained and not very open to each other, if not down-right hostile), it is clear that for Newbigin, the church (the household of God) includes all of them. Further he sensed there is a real need to reconnect these Christian blocks so that they mutually enrich each other – within and for the sake of mission given by God and with a renewed and vital sense of the eschatological setting. He was well aware that disunity of Christianity hampered mission.[21]

He did not develop these thoughts systematically in later works. In many ways they were modelled (at least in part) by the Church of South India of which Newbigin was Bishop. (Some points are developed in his written papers and correspondence.) Even at the time of original publication of *The Household of God* weaknesses were recognised. More consideration too needs to be given to the Orthodox Churches and traditions.[22] though they would fit into this broad vision and bring many riches and insights to all three strands described. More explicitly Jewish forms of Christianity, emerging relatively recently, also need consideration. Nonetheless, what it aspired to may have seemed no more than wishful or even dangerous thinking but much has happened since it was written.

Since the original publication of this book by Newbigin, major developments in the church world have seen a convergence of these major Christian blocks. For Newbigin, a principal weakness of Catholic position (in 1953) was that it regarded itself exclusively as the Church of Christ, and was thus not able to affirm Christian life outside it. Vatican II with its decree on Ecumenism (1964) and statement (amongst others) that the Church of Christ subsists in the Roman Catholic Church changed this. The Roman Catholic Church also became much more deliberately conscious and explicit about its dependence on the Word of God and Holy Spirit. The type of experience that was foundational to the Pentecostal movements and denominations spread to the mainstream denominations in the 1950s and 1960s through the Charismatic Movement and later moves (Third Wave etc) and links have been built between Pentecostal denominations and Charismatic groupings within both Protestant and Catholic denominations. There is, more recently still, an increased interest in many aspects of Catholic (and Orthodox) life, spirituality, liturgy and teaching from many in both the Protestant and Pentecostal world – and from Evangelicals as well as High Church traditionalists. Alongside all this there has been theological dialogue and interactions and other links. The morphology of the Christianity is constantly changing and there are nowadays various ways the Christian family can be categorised and divided and many approaches to looking at similarities and themes. In many respects common theological, spiritual or pastoral approaches nowadays go across denominations rather than within them. (I shall look at some of these below.) However, these three blocks still indicate one approach and one that in many respects is embedded in our cultures and has a significant hold on the minds and attitudes of Christians.

The Newbigin model, vision and understanding of church certainly has had a major impact and has significant influence on thought of highest leaders of Alpha, that is SM and NG, even if to some extent it is dated. I will analyse the extent to which it has been put into practice later. However, it seems worthwhile briefly outlining two other approaches to understanding the breadth of the Christian family that have emerged, that NG and SM are familiar with and have probably to some degree influenced them.

Peter Hocken

The first is that developed by Fr Peter Hocken, an English Catholic priest. He spent many years living as part of an ecumenical (Catholic-Protestant) Charismatic Community in USA, with a common life based on the common heritage of the Word (Scripture) and the charismatic gifts and action of the Holy Spirit. A noted church historian of the Charismatic Movement he is also a theologian. He has worked extensively in ecumenical circles and Charismatic networks and is frequently consulted on such matters. As such he has written on Alpha, promoting its use among Catholics. He is known to HTB because of this range of work.

His wider understanding/model for how God is at work in the church focuses on what he calls 'streams' of renewal and their impact for the 'church' understood in more corporate, bodily terms.[23] He certainly thinks that the Catholic and Orthodox traditions have most to bring to the ongoing corporate reality of the church and are most closely identified with it, but includes the 'historic' or 'established' Protestant churches here in his treatment too.[24] He identifies 4 major streams (or moves) of the Holy Spirit in recent centuries. These are the Evangelical Stream (from around 1750) followed by the Holiness Stream (19th century), the Pentecostal Stream (from around 1900) and then most recently the Charismatic Stream (since the 1950s). He generally sees the first three as broad moves by the Holy Spirit in the non-Catholic world. He does not focus on denominations here though he accepts that these moves of the Spirit have become concretised in various denominations, church agencies and other (para-church) organisations. However, he sees a different set of functional dynamics and emphases at work in the churches to that present in the streams.

Each has its own strengths and also weaknesses. What is distinctive about the Charismatic Stream is that fundamentally it is a bringing of the graces and dynamics of the Pentecostal Stream into the mainline churches. He regards this as very significant.

He wants to see a much fuller integration of the other streams into the life of the churches too so that there will be a sharing of the strengths of each with the other. He sees their strengths as broadly complementary and thus sees this coming together as strengthening and enriching the whole Body of Christ. Conscious of its divisions, his vision is thus one for the unity of the Body of Christ, the Church. It is a theology with a marked sense of the Holy Spirit and the Spirit's work in history. It also has a marked eschatological emphasis with a strong sense of the Coming of the Lord as a reality we should be much more conscious of and shaped by. In some of his writings he has also stressed the importance of all Christians recovering their shared Jewish heritage; in connection with this he is interested in the various groups of Messianic Jews who believe in Jesus as the Messiah while living as Jews.

His writings look extensively at the interface between the churches and the streams, their mindsets and attitudes to each other and at what needs to be addressed to bring them to integration and unity. His thought and vision is more dynamic, historically rooted, and practical than that of Newbigin which, by contrast is theological in a more systematically dogmatic and also structural way, though it is very spiritual too. Though he is rooted in the Roman Catholic Tradition, Hocken's thought and vision is markedly cross-denominational. It does not regard denominations or (at least some of them) as the most pertinent way of viewing what God is doing with his people, preferring the language of streams, though each of these can be clearly characterised.

Richard Foster

The second approach I want to outline is still more cross-denominational in character and again it uses the imagery and language of streams (though the term 'traditions' is more deeply written into his thought and work). This is the work of Richard Foster, described in his book *Stream of Living Water*.[25] Foster is an American Quaker and has pastored Evangelical Friends churches. He has developed a much broader approach to Christianity and appreciation of the width and historic depth of the Christian Tradition. He was already very well-known for his *Celebration of Discipline* when *Streams of Living Water* came out in 1998. This developed the ideas behind the earlier book, painting them on a broader canvas. In 2000, he visited HTB and, after a warm introduction from Sandy Millar, addressed their congregation, their bookshop well-stocked with this, his latest book.

Foster has studied and trawled through the entire width of the Christian family and also its historic length and has described the life embodied and lived by Jesus Christ as lived out in six major streams or traditions of grace. Christ is their source as both exemplar and giver of grace. These traditions or streams are concrete forms of spirituality, ways of living out the calling to follow Christ and share in his grace that have been followed down the centuries.

The six he identifies and then characterises are:

- The Contemplative Tradition – in which people discover the prayer-filled life;
- The Holiness Tradition – in which people discover the virtuous life;
- The Charismatic Tradition – in which people discover the Spirit-Empowered life;
- The Social-Justice Tradition – in which people discover the compassionate life;
- The Evangelical Tradition – in which people discover the Word-Centred life;
- The Incarnational Tradition – in which people discover the Sacramental life.

Each has a recognisable and describable set of characteristics and dynamics. These give strengths but also weaknesses especially if too much focus is given to that steam or approach alone. As such the traditions should mutually enrich and balance each other. He considers that in the present age Christians are being challenged to integrate all six streams into their own lives – and presumably that of their churches too. Foster's aim is to help people live out a complete and balanced spirituality in which they are rooted in, able to draw on and learn from the life of the church in all its traditions/streams. He founded and leads the Renovare Movement to encourage this.

Foster is very clearly and quite intentionally encouraging people to think outside the tramlines of any specific denomination. And not only to think this way but to be enriched in prayer, outlook and concrete action by this approach too. It is a form of very full and concrete spiritual ecumenism, one that enriches but also challenges narrow denominational exclusivity and narrowness.[26] Compared to Hocken there is a still greater focus and emphasis on spirituality and on a fluid approach that is even more thoroughly cross-denominational across all of Christian history.[27] One might almost describe it as non-denominational. There is less focus on theology as dogma or truth or on the church in structural terms. I am not aware that Foster spells out explicitly what he sees as the implications for the life, structure and mission of the church of this approach, though it is difficult to believe he does not have some thoughts on these. He considers it as vital for us to recover this sense of wholeness. It is my guess that he thinks we have tended to lose it by parcelling it out to different denominations or specialist groups within a denomination.

Towards an overall integrated foundation...

All three of these authors are concerned about the unity of the church. They also sense the value and even importance of mutual enrichment between the 'parts' of Christ's body/or groupings who are, in some sense, 'in Christ' to use a still more general term. Each of the three has an interest in mission, the church and its unity and spiritual vitality. However, they do, I think, have different emphases and even starting points and principal concerns. Thus Newbigin is concerned with mission/missiology and relatively dogmatic or systematic theological categories. Hocken is more focused on ecclesiology with particular attention to pneumatolgy and the interaction of the charismatic (i.e. freely inspired) moves and gifts of God's grace and the interaction of these with the more ongoing corporate and even institutional elements of church. Foster's main interest is Christian spirituality, hoping for the interaction of themes or traditions that he identifies in thematic terms that run across all denominations and time periods since Christ. There are potential applications and practical dimensions to all three.[28]

How we see church and the interconnection of those groups who call themselves Christian varies and changes over time. Without pushing this too far, it may be fair to say we see a broad progression in the direction from modern to more post-modern modes and preferences of thought in the work, attitudes and overall 'models' moving from Newbigin to Hocken and on to Foster. The approach, language and building blocks of the arguments move from those of the relatively abstract themes of dogma and church blocks through to those of relationally and hopefully organically linked movements and bodies and then on to those of spirituality and practical Christian living. Still other approaches are being developed.

An application of this in practical terms within Alpha and AI with analysis and reflections

How does all this work out in more concrete terms? In practice I think SM, NG and others at AI/HTB have drawn heavily on Newbigin in a key, and even foundational, way and been enriched by these others – and probably more besides. The points at which these influences arrived relative to other developments with Alpha and Alpha International need to be considered closely too. Apart from some (relatively minor) changes to make the text ecumenically broader and more considerate the actual Alpha course was already fixed before any of this happened. As such it was formed in a quite specifically, and relatively insular, Evangelical-Charismatic environment, and a Protestant and specifically Anglican one at that. Further, its rapid uptake, with all that flowed from that, was already significantly underway.

This resulted in the initial uptake being by Christians and churches with an Evangelical-Charismatic theology and spirituality. They still predominate. This has, I suspect, also resulted in AI moving less slowly away from conventionally Evangelical positions than its senior leadership might want; in short, others involved in significant ways in promoting Alpha are less 'ecumenically inclined' or 'converted'. This Evangelical predominance has happened not just in the UK but overseas too. Individuals and Christian Agencies were appointed and deals done with various publishing houses, nearly all of whom were from Protestant Evangelical-Charismatic backgrounds. Much of this was done very early before the wider appeal of Alpha was even recognised or seen as significant. When this has happened in countries and language groups where such Christians are a clear minority, and additionally when they lack broad ecumenical appeal and especially where tensions exist with other groups, this has had an impact on the perception and uptake of Alpha.[29] All this has led many to see Alpha – and Alpha International and the broader 'Alpha Movement' as fundamentally a means of spreading Evangelical-Charismatic Christianity. Some see its ecumenical claims as just sheep's clothing under which a devouring Evangelical-Charismatic wolf hides – and a specifically Protestant one at that. Is Alpha, as some claim, fundamentally Protestant? This has been claimed by some Catholics but also by some Protestants.[30]

We should not underestimate the Evangelical-Charismatic nature of Alpha or of the church leaders who developed and then made it available, and thus still lead the wider Alpha International and others who have influence in the wider Alpha Movement. Each person has a history and each form of churchmanship has a characteristic mindset and key attitudes. Underpinning these are certain presuppositions[31] –which may even be a kind of ideology – and these are usually so pervasive and deep that most adherents are not clearly aware of them. (Meeting Christians from other traditions can be a powerful challenge to these ideological elements.) This is true of Evangelicalism and Pentecostalism and, though it is a more recent development and thus less fixed, Evangelical-Charismatic Christianity too.[32] In a way John Wimber, amongst others, had challenged some of these presuppositions and probably helped to give Alpha its ecumenical foothold. That said, it is important to remember that the Alpha Course was not designed for broad ecumenical use or even for different social settings. It was a specific course for a specific local church in a specific social and cultural setting. It is very probably true to say that it still works best there too – something that contains many lessons. In this regard it is interesting that it has found any fruitful application beyond situations comparable to it in its essential features, however limited this has been.

Let us look at this in terms of the Catholic –Protestant interface in a bit more detail.[33] A quick look at the content and what is clearly included and not included makes the course look more completely Protestant than Catholic. However, as already indicated in Chapter 4 on course content, the approach to these topics as not now 'stereotypically or classically Protestant'. It is not clear that a specific denominational theology now underlies it. Whether any or all groups feel they can take what is there and integrate it into their theological and pastoral strategies is the practical issue. Perhaps Catholics will generally have to do more to achieve this than Protestants.

Alpha does reflect the Anglican origin of the course and of Evangelical-Charismatic Christianity within that. However, this has been broadened – some would say diluted – as subsequent editions of the resources have been produced. Is AI trying to make Catholicism Protestant? They have gone to a lot of effort to get Catholics to use the course, and taken a lot of criticism for it. In 2003 they even set up an 'Alpha for Catholics' department within AI, employing practising Catholics, to promote this. At the same time this suggests other aspects of their assessment. Thus, the fact that they feel they need to treat Catholics (but not different Protestant denominations) as a special group with its own department is highly indicative that they feel the course as originally set up is less easy for Catholics to use. It is also probably reflects an awareness of the issues and problems of prejudice (personal and historic) that still mark the Catholic-Protestant divide. It is my guess that, if the Eastern Orthodox, show sufficient interest in Alpha, AI would probably look at creating a similar set of arrangements for similar reasons.

It is also fair to ask just how far they have moved from the 'evangelical heartland' in doing all this. For Conservative or Reformed Evangelicals, the incorporation of an experiential and Charismatic element was already a betrayal of the core 'evangelical' identity. There are many (Protestant) Evangelical-Charismatics who would regard the opening up of this to Catholics, and the use of typically Catholic theological and spiritual insights, as now going too far. The constitutions of many 'Evangelical' groups and organisations that have a doctrinal basis use wording specifically designed to exclude Catholic positions. How many people of such groups are uncomfortable with where Alpha has moved to, possibly having already got involved with it? Some might well prefer that Alpha no longer be described as 'evangelical' at all. Much may depend on how 'evangelical' is defined and on whether the definition is more concerned with core central values or with a clear boundary (that both excludes as well as includes). Linked to this, it is important what historic period it regards as inspirational and foundational or whether it takes a much broader view, perhaps somewhat along the lines of Foster though other alternatives come to mind too. Interestingly I am told by Mark Elsdon-Dew that Nicky Gumbel no longer likes to describe himself, Alpha or HTB as 'evangelical'. Neither, I was told, does he like the label 'charismatic'. He apparently prefers simply to use the word 'Christian'. Some will argue that it is not that easy for a leopard to change its spots, and that identity and history have deep influences on us (individually and communally) that need to be acknowledged and owned whatever labels we use or discard. Nonetheless it indicates a deepening breadth of vision and approach and probably a realisation that labels can restrict and impoverish us.

Let us examine some more integrated approaches, which may be what has moved NG to prefer the simple term 'Christian'. Far from seeing it in specifically evangelical terms, the course can also, and perhaps better, be seen as a combination of elements from the three main traditions identified by Newbigin. If we allow ourselves to accept or at least work with the simplification that major traditions or blocks can be summarised in one or two elements, it is possible to say that Alpha brings together – even relies on – key aspects of each tradition. Thus it has an ecclesial setting. It proclaims the Word and it relies in a clear way on the power of the Holy Spirit. It integrates these elements and is fruitful through the synthesis of all of them.[34]

Another example is how it treats conversion.[35] These major church groupings or traditions also often see faith and conversion differently in terms of it being mainly about continuity and discontinuity of life. It can be seen as an ongoing part of a spiritual journey in life, including ongoing conversion, or as a radical new birth and beginning, conversion marking the transition between two sharply differentiated life phases. Both models have Scriptural roots, and have strengths and weaknesses regarding pastoral care. The former has tended to be identified with Catholics and the latter with Protestant Evangelicals, though this compartmentalisation is breaking down. In reality both elements and dynamics happen and it is helpful to recognise this to facilitate conversions, ongoing pastoral care and spiritual maturity. The Alpha Course values and applies both these elements and additionally brings the power and work of the Holy Spirit and the dimension of experience. Other writers and evangelists are integrating all these elements as well. It is worth quoting some of Pope John Paul II's summary of conversion to illustrate this further.

> The proclamation of the Word of God has Christian conversion as its aim: a complete and sincere adherence to Christ and his Gospel through faith. Conversion is a gift of God, a work of the Blessed Trinity. It is the Spirit who open's people's

hearts so that they can believe in Christ and 'confess him' (cf 1 Cor 12:3); of those who draw near to him through faith Jesus says: 'No one can come to me unless the Father who sent me draws him' (Jn 6:44).

From the outset, conversion is expressed in faith which is total and radical, and which neither limits nor hinders God's gift. At the same time, it gives rise to a lifelong process which demands a continual turning away from 'life according to the flesh' to 'life according to the Spirit' (cf Rom 8:3–13). Conversion means accepting, by a personal decision, the saving sovereignty of Christ and becoming his disciple.[36]

Catholic and Evangelical Shifts...and Connections?

So, rather than Alpha being about the export of evangelical Protestantism, should all this be taken as indicative of a 'Catholic shift' in evangelism? AI/HTB do draw on Catholic theology to explain parts of the thinking behind Alpha, even preferring to talk of evangelisation, rather than evangelism.[37] There may, in fact, be some truth in such a 'catholic shift'! It is something that others have commented on, and whilst viewing developments more broadly than Alpha. Anglican Bishop and evangelist John Finney, in his book on emerging evangelism writes the following: 'From his evangelical background, Canon Robert Warren is able to say: "The Future of worship belongs to the Catholic tradition".'[38] He cites this in connection with the development of alternative worship, its use of candles, images, incense and ritual and sees this as an awareness of mystery and all this as a consequence of the shift from a modern to post-modern culture. It is quite clear that Finney thinks this 'Catholic shift' has implications and lessons for evangelism too. He is not alone. For example, Steven Hunt refers to Andrew Walker commenting about a 'Catholic turn'.[39]

Before Protestant Evangelicals get too alarmed let me point out a different trend or shift that is also occurring. An 'evangelical shift' has been identified as taking place within Roman Catholicism. Cardinal Avery Dulles comments: 'The evangelical shift brought about by Vatican II, Paul VI and the present pope [John Paul II] is one of the most dramatic developments in modern Catholicism.'[40] To what is this seen as referring? In brief, it is seen to include a renewed Christ-centredness, a more prominent interest in Scripture and thirst for it, a much stronger commitment to mission or evangelisation, one that is seen as the fundamental identity and purpose of the church and to involve all its members. It is marked by a desire for people to know Christ personally through both initial and ongoing conversion.

This has gone alongside an increased commitment to ecumenism. Dulles points out that it has happened so quickly (relatively speaking) and is so significant that it is taking time for the teaching to be absorbed and fully practised by Catholics around the world.

It hardly needs saying that this language – and much more so the reality behind the words – is challenging. It will challenge many of those who describe themselves as either 'Evangelical' or 'Catholic' though there are more and more exceptions. To undertake the 'shifts' or 'turns' involves facing up to our stereotypes, presuppositions (about ourselves as well as others) and even our prejudices and fears. It means being prepared to move out of the comfort zones (that have been created for us, and that we have absorbed and even added to) of familiar self-understandings reinforced by clear boundaries and a strong received view of what lies beyond in 'them'! It is about reconciliation and this is a multi-faceted process and one that takes time to come to maturity. Yet the Gospel we proclaim – the centre of our mission – is one of reconciliation so it is vital. (For example, see Eph 2:11–3:2). Repentance may be required, even in an ongoing way. Building mutual understanding and trust is a slow process but one that needs to precede or at least accompany, practical co-operation in aspects of mission. There is evidence of this at various levels and on occasions within the movement that Alpha has spawned. At the same time it needs to be ongoing. (As with other groupings, people have all sorts of different starting positions within Alpha with some less sure than others on how far the course and wider movement should be opened up.)

So, putting these two shifts together – if they are both real and sustained – we may see significant convergence and mutual enrichment. A shift towards greater emphasis on the Holy Spirit and pneumatology is also recognised by many as a major feature of the 20th century. This is seen as ongoing by many, especially the need to assimilate and reflect fully on it. It needs to be seen more widely and deeply than Pentecostal and Charismatic renewal. Indeed, it could, and perhaps should, be still more clearly linked or at least explored along with the focus on spirituality and 'mystical' experience within and beyond the church.

These should not mainly be seen as an introspective discussion amongst churched people or as an exercise in ephemeral spiritual stargazing. There may well be benefits for mission. Indeed, some authors flag up these 'shifts' or 'turns' with a specific eye on mission. Alpha (and mission more generally) flows into wider currents and moves of God and in part influences them.[41] It is also worth bearing in mind the ongoing shift towards a post-modernity and post-Christedom society and culture and the implications of this for church, ecumenism and theology as well as for mission. We live amidst ongoing changing and interacting realities on all these fronts.

*From Theology and Spirituality to organisations,
networks and structures*

How helpful and theologically sound is such an 'ecumenical vision' and how far this can be realised is open to debate and reflection by others. It would perhaps be helpful if AI articulated its own reflections on this important aspect of the impact of Alpha. This may be of practical help to Alpha practitioners. At any rate, Alpha is contributing to ecumenism and has given some clues and glimpses of unity being nearer to reality. Nor is this only about theological reflection or agreed joint statements. It is an ecumenism that is mission-inspired and for the most part is local, relational, practical 'bottom-up' co-operation. In a period where the energy and direction seems to have been lost from much other ecumenical work, people could do with looking at what can be learned here for the future direction of ecumenism as well as mission.

Alpha and AI/HTB did not set out to generate ecumenical reflections. The ecumenical dimension came from its practical involvement with different churches and Christian organisations and of them with it. This operates locally and at the level of central and national leadership contacts. Certain 'policy' or 'strategy' imperatives no doubt guide it. Let us now look at this in the more concrete, practical and organisational aspects of its interaction with churches.

Alpha: tools, movements and changing patterns and ways of being church

Alpha as a tool, a movement and an organisation

Fundamentally, HTB started out as a local church offering a course they developed there to other local churches. As such, AI/HTB have always marketed Alpha as a 'tool' (specifically, an evangelistic tool) to be used by local churches and left things at that. They have affirmed it is only one tool among others. They have sought to encourage people to use Alpha within their own local churches and they have cultivated links with the leadership of denominations when possible. They have made a point of encouraging people to work closely with the leadership in their church, whatever form that takes. In this sense they have accepted the existing structures at all levels and tried to work with them. As such they recognise denominations and the integrity of these but work directly with local churches. At this level they offered a tool with back-up service mainly for existing churches.[42] However, there are a few instances of people running Alpha and then for various reasons starting a small local, usually house, church based around it.

Alpha generated enthusiasm and links between churches using it. Certainly significant bonds of friendship and co-operation have grown up between people using Alpha from right across the Christian church.

The extent of Alpha's appeal and uptake[43] along with the formation of local teams of volunteers (with their strong sense of identity and commitment to the course) to promote Alpha and the general approach to Christianity all this reflects, has led many to wonder, and some to fear, where it is all going. People have for sometime talked of an 'Alpha Movement'. Some talk of 'Alpha churches' and some want the course to be so standardised that they can have confidence in sending their friends to any such church anywhere. Is this all part of a deliberate strategy emanating first from HTB and now from AI? Do they intend to establish a new 'denomination', helping to shape it through copyright and conferences? Are they well on the way to this, no matter what is officially intended? Michael Moynagh identifies 'brand churches' as an example of emerging church and cites HTB as an example. He says that in a choice-fatigued age clear brands with a good reputation are attractive to the public. He says that such churches do not just have a product but a set of values and a particular tale and way of telling the Christian story. It is this combination that, clearly branded, appeals to people who are now consumers in a choice-fatigued age. Interestingly he observes that such church brands appeal to specific groups of Christians or lapsed Christians, but not yet to specific groups of the unchurched.[44] I suspect HTB and AI's leadership would dispute this interpretation of their intentions, but it may, of course, still turn out to be true. In Moynagh's analysis much depends on the choices of the consuming public.

Is Alpha a movement? 'Movement' is a loose word to describe any spiritually animated strategy or group with a popular base and appeal. It seems reasonably fair to use such a label in regard to Alpha. In this sense Alpha is a movement that sees itself as concerned with the renewal and equipping of the church for the work of evangelisation. It has certain religious qualities and values that undergird this.[45] It has also helped nurture better relations and practical co-operative unity amongst Christians. None of this ought to be feared and it is indeed difficult to raise objections. However, the Alpha Movement is one that even from early on had a significant structure to co-ordinate it (in the shape of HTB) and, linked in part to this, was able to raise significant funds. This has been significant in its development, as has the business expertise available in the HTB congregation and drawn from, and also imported from elsewhere, to manage Alpha. As well as admiration this generates more questions about what it all means. What is its structure and what sort of organisation is it becoming as it evolves? It is said to be the biggest and most financially well-off Anglican parish in the country.[46] Its size and turnover makes it bigger than some entire denominations. HTB's success may well make others feel ineffective and unsuccessful and this may sometimes spill over into fear, suspicion and jealousy – not least because, while HTB and AI are growing, most denominations are declining and some facing crisis and even collapse. It has a direct influence on many local churches. Does this undermine confidence in their own national structures, even if this is not intended?

Let us analyse and assess the structure or AI and the wider Alpha Movement in a little more detail, though this remains very introductory. HTB employs a large number of people and – as a local church – has more structure, activities and products than many church agencies and even denominations. The same can now be said of Alpha International as a distinct entity. Indeed, this is a parachuch organisation itself, and a large international one at that. With such a large structure it has taken on many of the qualities of an institution or business and its decisions and planning simply have to take into consideration its overheads, employees and much else. Put simply, Alpha is now big business. This is all largely at the central level. Beyond its head quarters, the scale of Alpha should not be overstated. However, they are producing still more National Offices overseas.[47]

Let us focus on the UK. Their regional offices in the UK mean they employ around four people outside London, though the funding of the offices is supposed to be increasingly developed and then maintained in each of the regions in due course. They do have hopes for more regional offices in the UK. Everyone else involved is a volunteer! In reality Alpha regional teams vary enormously in their strength. Some are just extensions of pre-existing local church partnerships though some have come into being through Alpha. In some places they are almost non-existent. Most probably, less than the 7,000 registered churches actually run Alpha. As I have indicated, it is unrealistic to suppose that an Alpha course will be identical wherever it is run – and naïve to think that churches running Alpha see eye to eye on nearly all things or even on Alpha. For all these reasons it is probably best not to see it as an emerging denomination (though members of a denomination rarely see eye to eye on all or even most things either!). It may be better to see the Alpha Movement as a network, and a means for mutual support and the sharing of resources, rather than anything more formal or structured.

The Denominational Nature of Christianity and issues facing it

Some of the hard pressed folk responsible for many denominations may be relieved to hear these conclusions about the 'Alpha Movement' but we need to put them in the context of the state and future of a denominational basis and approach to Christianity. What if denominations, in structural terms, are largely replaced by networks? Could Alpha then be seen as helping to pioneer a new form of church to replace the denominational model?

We live in an era when people's allegiance to, and understand of, any particular denomination (especially within what can broadly be described as Protestantism)[48] is declining. Generally it is less important, especially in younger generations, than just finding a local church of any denomination where they are comfortable with its broad approach and feel it provides for their needs and those of their family. In a way this reflects the shift to post-modernity and also our consumer and increasingly mobile and rootless society. People want a church that 'works for them'. The doctrinal issues that led to the splits that produced many of these denominations are simply not important to most people nowadays, even within the churches. Some people operate a kind of 'portfolio membership' of churches, attaching or hooking into different churches or Christian groupings for different facets of their Christian life and service. Some, in increasing numbers, do not look for a church that has a fundamentally geographic identity either: work churches or clubbing churches or surfing churches are emerging. It is easy to see that those who do have strong denominational loyalty and leaders with denominational oversight at various levels might feel apprehensive. What constitutes a person's Christian identity and loyalty? Is it their denomination, or Alpha or something else or a combination? Some will argue it hardly matters as long as the Kingdom of God is being built up, but such talk can be become an excuse to avoid us facing issues of concrete and responsible involvement with other Christians that is earthed in a local setting.

Further, and perhaps linked to this, many denominations face uncertain futures as structures and institutions. We live in an era when most well-established denominations feel threatened by all or at least significant number of the following: falling attendance and participation, rising costs and often increasingly acute financial crises, shortage of ministers/priests and an ageing clergy, threats of internal splits over certain doctrinal issues. Maintenance of their status quo way of living and operating is not possible. It is likely that most will significantly shrink and change their structures and that some will merge or disappear. This need not be seen as tragic. Communities and institutions, like individuals, can be life-giving and inspiring in their deaths.[49] Taking a long historical perspective, patterns and forms of church life (understood as systems of organisation and administration) and their spiritual and evangelistic approaches have kept changing, punctuated with periods of sharp upheaval. Such a long view ought to give some encouragement, though it should not be a cause for complacency.

I think there is much for saying that denominations are a particularly, even characteristically, modern way of looking at and thinking, being, doing and organising church. Moving beyond the period of Roman Catholic Christendom to the National Churches of the emerging nations of the early modern period,[50] the emergence of (tolerated) denominations and then their increasingly rapid multiplication happened in the 'high modern era' marked by the Enlightenment and Industrialisation. Nonetheless they built on what these two previous phases had created, and on some of their presuppositions. In a way, they are – or can be viewed and analysed as – kinds of industries (regional, national or multi-national) each with a distinct identity and relatively sharp boundaries. In a way each demonstrated early forms of branding, even if it was all done in the name of truth and theology and correct worship and discipline. As such each turned out a product, constructing local plant (buildings) and developing structures and jobs (forms of ministry) to administer it and deliver it. Aspects of this approach can be identified in AI and Alpha.

Yet people now suggest that these threats to denominations mean we are entering a period of Post-Denominational Christianity. This is often linked to wider cultural shifts in society away from classical or high modern and largely Christian society. Let's examine and apply some more insights on this and also see if and where Alpha and AI fit into these models.

Liquid – and Solid – Church

I think that the analysis of Pete Ward may help cast light on this phenomenon or critique.[51] He characterises the present cultural shift as one from solid modernity to one of liquid modernity. Amongst other things he sees a shift from a settled to a mobile population. He also draws on industrial imagery, seeing the Fordist factory system princi-ples as characterising solid modernity. Size, plant, boundaries, norms, rules, expansion are what matter in this. People are largely told what they need and it is then (mass-)produced for them. Belonging and confidence are related to these with attention to size and numbers. He now sees a shift in emphasis happening from production to consump-tion. Here there is more stress on what the consumer actually wants: this means listening more; people want variation and authenticity. This means they want more depth and quality too, though in reality they want a combination of the profound and also accessible. It is more about desires than prescribed needs. Along with this is more stress on creativity, relationship, and participation. Commitment is more important than attendance. There is a shift form a hierarchical and paternalistic and condescending approach and style of leadership to one that is humbler, gets alongside, co-journeys, collaborates, enables, and even releases and gives permission. Applied to Christianity, he talks of solid church and liquid church.[52]

All of this provides much promise for the church and mission. It could be argued that the inability to see this change and thus to respond to it has contributed significantly to the decline of involvement in denominations and thus such measures of church life as attendance at Sunday worship. It is easy to see much of the mindset and practice of solid modernity in our denominations. Ward sees the emerging liquid church as one that stresses relationship and network far more. It is about connection, community and common cause and desires, but will hopefully move people out, beyond itself, into the social landscape. Networking matters and the common 'meeting ground' can be a shared feature of culture or an interest and even work rather than a geographic one.

Ward anticipates these forms of church will grow. He suggests it may replace Sunday worship and geographic congregations almost entirely. Others are less convinced that the shift will go that far.[53] It is very likely, that we will still need and retain elements of the more geographically defined church too – though probably more thinly distributed. Nonetheless, there does seem to be a good deal of truth in his analysis. He sees many denominations having to reduce in size and structure and some becoming and operating like networks anyway. (Many networks are growing among Christians and Christian groups anyway. People can be in several networks and they inter-connect in various ways.) All of this is a challenge to denominations. We could already be part of a major transition to a new way of thinking, being, doing and organising church – one that, in effect, will largely be post-denominational. In a way this can be seen, not so much as a death (i.e. oblivion), as a metamorphosis (a translation from one form of life to another) though the difficulties in making this transformation should not be underestimated. A new form of organisation like this means a new form of ecumenism and a new possibilities for – and challenges to – unity among Christians.

How will AI cope? It has elements of network and liquid life and may well cope better than many denominations. At the same time, it has many elements of solid church and will face challenges if it is to continue effectively into a still more liquid future.

'Emerging Church' and inherited church

Another way of viewing church is more explicitly connected with an increasing realisation that we need to commit to mission. This uses the language of inherited church and emerging church. This has come about in part from the increasingly conscious move into a Post-modern and Post-Christendom culture and its implications for mission and church. In this model Alpha, along with other relatively traditional forms of evangelism, would typically be viewed as attempting to do mission by helping existing or inherited churches say 'Come and see!' It uses content that is fairly solidly rooted in the modern era and for people who ideally have a fairly good background of Christianity. However, the gap between existing or inherited church culture and wider culture, which is increasingly seen as a patchwork of many cultures, is now recognised as so large that we need to go out, live in these cultures forming relationships there and building local churches (i.e. Christian communities) there. Such churches emerge and are profoundly linked to and shaped by these cultures with all their dynamics, values and forms of expression etc. These are described as 'fresh expressions of church' or 'emerging church'.[54] Such expressions of church are already with us. Some denominations are actively and vigorously encouraging people to 'plant' more.[55] Elsewhere Christians are just going ahead and doing it. Interestingly they also borrow elements of spirituality and worship and ritual and other pastoral practices and insights from different Christian traditions and denominations very freely.[56]

The contrast between inherited and emerging church should not be overstated. Every generation builds on what has gone before it even if this building involves reappraisal and some reaction. It involves a constant interaction with a changing culture too. In the midst of all this some elements of church stay the same. The phrase 'fresh expressions of church' perhaps catches both the idea of continuity and newness. There is also continuity in the movement from one to the other even in present strategies. Different denominations label and handle this differently but a model of progression can be outlined.[57] Firstly, new local church communities can be established or planted within a present denominational or similar structure – with broadly similar structures and approaches to the parent (sponsoring) body. Secondly, such a parent body may look to pioneer and establish new forms of local church at the edge of its present forms and structures but with links to them but also importantly shaped by the demands and possibilities of the new cultural situation. (The link to a parent body may come from those doing the pioneering as much as the other way round.) Thirdly, new forms of church community can be grown in new situations beyond and without formal links to any denominational structure – though often even these look to some body or network for support. (These have most freedom to be creative but also less support. As they develop they may choose to develop links with other existing groups and even denominations.) All of these take us beyond a static church model with the assumption that people will just come. The amount of change from the received way of doing things is likely to increase through the models in the order outlined but this need not always be the case. It may also depend how well relationships, and also accountability, are handled with those in more established forms of church and how much freedom but also support is given to attempt new pastoral and missiological experiments.[58] All of this is happening in real life and only then being theorised about. Thus considerable variations around these models as well as new approaches and interesting continuities and connections are currently being generated.

Recalling the complex development of HTB itself, its involvement in church planting, and now the many versions and uses of Alpha that have been developed, as well as some of the other initiatives that are linked with AI/HTB is a looser way, it is fair to say that the Alpha phenomenon cannot be rigidly classified as only being part of inherited church.

Is the Approach and Structure of the Alpha Movement Modern, Post-modern or Transitional?

Where do Alpha and AI fit into all this and how can they contribute? The 'Alpha Movement' seems to have elements of both solid and liquid church. Thus, it may be better placed than some denominations to transition further. However, it is more difficult to see how the Alpha Course can be used to establish or grow these new emerging churches though it does have some potential for this. The ordinary Alpha course and, even more so, some of its specialist forms (workplace, forces, senior) could if run fruitfully in a specific cultural setting result in a new Christian community forming around them. More general things could probably be learned from Alpha. Alpha looks quite conservative, even tame and dated in comparison to some of these new ventures, though it does share some of the traits that these emerging churches have taken still further, with others features added in besides. If these trends continue, Alpha may well end up looking like a transitional product, i.e. a bridge between where we have come from and where we are going.

In the meantime there is still a pool of people Alpha can help and a number of inherited churches that are using it and others that could be helped to use it still more effectively. There are others that are not engaged in mission at all that could possibly still use it or learn from it. This situation which combines inherited and emerging churches has been referred to as a 'mixed economy'.[59] They have much to teach each other and hopefully will live together symbiotically. If cohesion and even glue is needed within such a mixed economy then AI/HTB may be of help since they do seem to have some elements of both inherited and emerging church attitudes and practices. They have already started doing significant collaborative work with different forms of church (old and new) and cross-fertilised with networks. Differences provide the opportunity for mutual learning and enrichment. Stuart Murray has commented:

> Hope for the future of the church in Western Culture does not lie with the inherited church. Nor does it lie with the emerging church. It lies in conversations between inherited and emerging churches that enable each to learn from the other and together find fresh ways of incarnating the Gospel in a changing and diverse culture.[60]

Though it may no longer be 'cutting edge', Alpha may have a significant role to play for some time yet. However, it is important AI and church leaders more generally, see clearly what Alpha can and cannot do and what else needs to be done. Also, AI may yet develop new resources and courses that make significant contributions to the ways we will do mission and be church in the future. In all this, it is also important that AI gives thought to the consequences and implications of its policies – even if these are not directly intended.

———

To conclude, Alpha has had a big impact on church, and how we envision it and live it, in all sorts of ways and levels. This is likely to continue for some time, even with the present resources of AI. May be the focus will move beyond the present form of Alpha to wider and different applications of the core insights that have shaped HTB, Alpha and AI? The Alpha Movement cannot afford to stand still in a changing world and church. Vision and strategy matter. We will now go on in Chapter 10 and look at how AI/HTB have developed vision and devised and applied strategies on their journey so far, and look at what their underlying hopes and aspirations might be.

Notes

[1] Very often, these have just been re-runs of pre-existent arguments or controversies over various doctrinal or other issues, now applied to the high-profile Alpha Course. Such axes had been seriously sharpened long before Alpha came along!

[2] To the best of my knowledge it has not been used yet very much by the Orthodox traditions though there has been some interest in it. However, significant links are now being forged in Russia and Eastern Europe and AI are due to give their first Alpha Conference in close collaboration with the Russian Orthodox Church in Moscow in 2006. This could be a very significant breakthrough.

[3] For example, Catholics first approached HTB in 1996 though some Catholics had done courses at other churches by this time and were then beginning to start their own.

[4] Much the same pattern happens in other forms of ecumenical discourse and in joint ecumenical statements.

[5] Cf John 17:21.

[6] I have many 'evangelical' friends, including church ministers, who assure me they are not ecumenical but are happy to pray and work with other Christians to build the Kingdom of God. Many others would say this was a very good definition of what ecumenism is, or ought to be, about.

[7] Jesus' priestly prayer in John 17 explicitly links the themes of unity and mission through the impact of unity (or disunity) on the credibility of the Gospel message.

[8] These include approaches that focus on elements of common heritage and life: for instance a sharing of Scripture or of life in the Holy Spirit and his gifts. Some are based on looking for visible and organic, sacramental and structural unity. Some are based on an exploration of theology and ideas more generally. Some are based on practical co-operation – often local – in aspects of witness, service and mission. Others again focus more on shared prayer, sometimes with atten-

tion to the overcoming of mutual hostility through confession of and lament for past and present sins against other Christians, and positive reconciliation and healing. (This latter approach is often called spiritual ecumenism.) These approaches are not mutually exclusive and can be combined in various ways. Others may be thought of, or even develop. Attention could usefully be given also to their interaction.

[9] Pope John Paul II, in *Ut Unam Sint* (1995) and elsewhere, has stressed the need for such repentance as being essential to progress in ecumenical work and Christian unity. He flagged up spiritual ecumenism in general.

[10] Nicky Gumbel, *Questions of Life*, Chapter 9: What Does the Holy Spirit Do?, pp. 152–3. This whole section on unity in the family fills this out more.

[11] Its ecumenism stems from its interest in mission. The modern ecumenical movement, usually dated from the Edinburgh Missionary Conference in 1910 was also motivated by missionary concerns.

[12] Nicky Gumbel, *Questions of Life*, p. 234.

[13] This means that first order truths are more important and clearly revealed. They are capable of a fairly, or very, definite understanding and are seen as non-negotiable. They form a consensus around which Evangelicals can agree and form associations, and on the basis of which they can work together. Belief in them may be considered essential for salvation. Second order truths are ones that are less important and are doctrines on which they do not all agree. They agree to disagree. Sometimes these (or some of them) come to be regarded as personal interpretations or little more than opinions, and, by implication, dispensable and not really true or revealed.

[14] The Catholic approach to Revealed Truth has similarities with the Protestant Evangelical approach but also differences. It is based on the principle of there being a hierarchy of truths among what is revealed, when this is considered as doctrine. In fact, fundamentally it is the Person(s) and mystery of God who is revealed (not primarily ideas), and this especially through the Incarnation (i.e. *the person* of Jesus). Some truths are nearer to the centre of what God has revealed than others, and touch on what it is more essential to understand so as to consciously enter into the grace of Christ. These include beliefs about Christ, and his Paschal Mystery, and the Trinity. Others follow from them and intellectually are dependent on them. For instance the nature of the church and, dependent on all of this, an understanding of specific sacraments and ministries etc. However, all are held to be revealed and true and helpful for our salvation. Catholicism also teaches that the content of Divine Revelation can be expressed in different language(s) at different times and that we can grow in our understanding of what God has revealed over centuries as well as in our own lives. Belief in the Trinity is one such example: the term is not used in Scripture at all. Also different parts of Revelation are better understood or gain more emphasis at certain times, and in different cultures/situations, and by individuals. In part, this means that what appears to divide Christians may in part at least, be different but complementary understandings of Divine Revelation, though there may also be distortions. All this means we can and should seek to learn from each other.

[15] *Questions of Life*, p. 234. (What about the Church?). But who decides what is necessary? This is a big issue! The 'what' in part depends on the context and purpose/situation. What is necessary in order to pray together may be different from what is necessary to serve our neighbours, or even to proclaim Christ together, which may be different again from what is necessary to have full sacramental communion.

[16] Newbiggin's teaching at HTB's School of Theology in 1994–5 has since been published in 2003 by HTB/Alpha International as *Discovering Truth in a Changing World* and *Living Hope in a Changing World*. In his forward to *Discovering Truth* Sandy Millar comments: There was certainly a prophetic anointing on him …

And I think it extraordinary to think that in *The Household of God* he so clearly identified the major streams of Christianity – the Catholic, Protestant and Charismatic – so far ahead of time.' (p.vi). When 'The Household of God' was re-issued by Paternoster Press in 1998 Nicky Gumbel is quoted on the back cover: 'Lesslie Newbigin was one of the greatest thinkers and theologians of the twentieth century. Of all his wonderful books, this is my personal favourite.'

[17] A shorter and more selective, if clear, version is given in *Discovering Truth in a Changing World*, Chapter 5.

[18] His chapter headings for these are 'The Congregation of the Faithful', 'The Body of Christ' and 'The Community of the Holy Spirit'. Actually, he links the administration of the sacraments to the Protestant tradition too, but is emphatic that they have an inadequate ecclesiology.

[19] Newbigin views sacraments as objective actions of grace. In this he is close to the Catholic position though he accepts the validity of sacramental ministry in other denominations not considered by Catholics as valid, though on different grounds.

[20] I am aware that at a doctrinal level all this also asks some very serious questions of how we fundamentally understand the church and in what – and where – its fullness exists. These are very important issues, though ones that I simply cannot do justice to within the format, scope, approach and remit of this book. I have taken this decision in order not to trivialise them but in view of their importance.

[21] It was this concern that had first stimulated the modern Ecumenical Movement at the beginning of the Twentieth century.

[22] Newbigin readily concedes this. See *The Household of God*, Preface. p. xii. Paternoster Press, 2002.

[23] These ideas are most fully worked out in *The Strategy of the Spirit?* (Eagle, Guildford, Surrey, 1996). *The Glory and the Shame* (Eagle, Guildford, Surrey, 1994) uses a similar approach but only addresses the 20th century Pentecostal and Charismatic Streams. He prefers the imagery and language of streams and renewal to that of waves and revival. He feels the graces are more continuously present and active even after their first impact and that the former vocabulary better expresses this reality.

[24] He is ecumenically very well-informed, sensitive, respectful and open but he is quite clear about his own convictions and theological formation. He is up front about being a 'convinced committed Catholic'. Interestingly he has been criticised by some Catholics for making too much of a distinction and contrast between what he sees God as doing in the churches and what God does in the streams/movements. (For some, this is seen to imply a serious depletion of grace, and fullness, in the church. Thus, they argue, the extent to which the church needs to receive the graces of the streams/movements to become complete or full is overstated. All this may then imply the church has less and is less than Christ intended, which may imply inadequacy on the part of Christ.) Like Newbigin he acknowledges that he has not developed much thought on the Orthodox Traditions.

[25] Richard Foster, *Streams of Living Water (Celebrating the Great Traditions of Christian Faith)*, Harper Collins, 1998 (1999 in UK).

[26] In this sense it goes beyond the bounds of the normal sense of 'spiritual ecumenism in which participants interact with a relatively clear sense of their 'denominational' identity and home. This has led to criticism of Foster. He has been severely criticised in some circles, notably Conservative Evangelical ones – for not relying appropriately on the Bible and drawing in practices from outside that tradition, most especially from Catholicism and also from mysticism in general.

[27] Appendix A of *Streams of Living Water* outlines church history. He regards

the main three strands of Christianity as Roman Catholicism, Eastern Orthodoxy and Protestantism. He sees all his 'traditions' – including (yet as distinct) the evangelical and Charismatic ones) as running across all of these. Appendix B (pp. 304–78) provides brief biographies of examples of each tradition drawn from right across the Christian spectrum and history. In these points he differs from both Newbigin and Hocken.

[28] To an extent, and understandably and properly so, they each reflect the personal history of each author and the time in which they were developed and then written and the immediate issues facing them. (Newbigin wrote more than 40 years before the other two!)

[29] Some of these situations have more recently been changed, often with these individuals or groups volunteering to work with other Denominations or even hand over the lead role to them. The generosity and at times courage this requires should not be under-estimated. In this way, it has led to some interesting reconciliations and partnerships. The fault for such underlying tensions cannot all be put at the door of Evangelicals by any means. All Christians need to examine their attitudes to other Christians. Building mutual understanding and trust is a slow process but one that need to precede or at least accompany, practical co-operation in aspects of mission. Repentance may be required – even in an ongoing way.

[30] Hunt cites an example of this. See *The Alpha Enterprise* p. 155. I know of others. Indeed, some really only accept and view Catholics as Christians if they are clearly Evangelical-Charismatic in their spirituality and vocabulary. Some would say (and certainly think) they are, in these cases, Christian *in spite of* being Catholic and not *because of* it. Mind, some Catholics hold similar attitudes to others too!

[31] David Bebbington, a Protestant Evangelical, characterises Evangelicalism as being conversion centred, cross centred, Bible centred and marked by activism. (See *Evangelicalism in Modern Britain*, Unwin, 1989, p. 3).

[32] It is taken as generally and almost normatively true that this means it is Protestant too. However, there are Catholics who would happily also describe their Christianity as 'Evangelical-Charismatic' (if not always with deep theological understanding).

[33] I realise it is a gross simplification and even a distortion to group all non-(Roman) Catholics together and that many have their own specific issues[34] with Alpha. I do not mean to trivialise these or dismiss them either. However, for the purposes of examining the ecumenical usability of Alpha I will concentrate on its interface with Roman Catholicism.

[35] Those who would put forward this as reflecting the persons of the Trinity (working together) ascribe the ecclesial setting to God the Father. Thus, an ecclesial setting implies being at the heart of the Christian community or family; each family has a Father – in this case God the Father. In this sense we go beyond the Word (alone) based approach and even beyond the Word-Spirit approach to a full Trinitarian model and understanding of God's action.

[36] Amongst others, these ideas has been put forward by Peter Hocken. For example, see *Blazing the Trail*, (Bible Alive Publishing, 2001), Chapter 3.

[37] John Paul II, *Redemptoris Missio* (The Mission of the Redeemer), n.46, 1990. He goes on to look at the sacramental and ecclesial dimension.

[38] Nicky Gumbel has gone so far as to comment publicly (at Home Focus, 2002) that changes made to the content of *Questions of Life* as a result of conversations with Catholic Bishops and theologians, were not just better for Catholics but better for Alpha itself.

[39] J. Finney, *Emerging Evangelism*, p. 137.

[40] See S. Hunt, *The Alpha Enterprise*, pp. 252–3.

[41] From his article in *Pope John Paul II and the New Evangelisation* ed by Ralph

Martin and Peter Williamson, Ignatius Press, 1995. p. 32.

[42] It might even be worth considering these shifts alongside the missionary 'shifts' or marks I identified at the end of Chapter 8. (There are significant connections and overlap in the ideas.)

[43] 'Inherited' churches is a term that is now often used to distinguish these from 'emerging churches' or 'fresh expressions of church'. (See below for more details on this.)

[44] Especially in the mid-1990s when this uptake was very rapid.

[45] See Michael Moynagh, *Emergingchurch.info*, Monarch, 2004, pp. 79–80.

[46] These could be expressed as an ethos, spirituality and even a theological outline, but I do not think any of this has formally, or at any rate definitively, been done. HTB as a local church does have statements on these areas.

[47] S. Hunt, *The Alpha Enterprise*, p. 15.

[48] These vary hugely in size, from ones with several employees to ones that are essentially a few volunteers.

[49] There is also much more cross-fertilisation across the Catholic-Protestant boundary than previously.

[50] The life-giving death of Jesus is central and foundational to Christianity. How Christians handle death and loss at all levels can and ought to be a very important testimony to the truth of Christianity. (Of course, this is easier said than done!)

[51] In this period, people were largely expected to adopt and follow the religion chosen by the monarch.

[52] See especially *Liquid Church*, Paternoster press, 2002, though he has also written shorter accounts elsewhere.

[53] The perception and comparison of solid and liquid church is perhaps fundamentally to do with the sociology and practical organisation of church, though it has theological, pastoral and missiological implications and should be reflected on from these angles.

[54] Some churches may be able to combine elements of solid and liquid church life. In some respects this has happened in the Catholic Church with the rapid development of 'new communities and movements' largely since Vatican II in the 1960s though some were earlier. Most have a clear missional/evangelistic dimension. They currently sit alongside older, more solid, forms, though there have been tensions and serious problems too. In the UK these movements are very marginal still, with there being much more emphasis on maintaining a system of parishes and dioceses. In fact, new communities are often seen as a threat to this. The establishment of CASE – Catholic Agency to Support Evangelisation (in 2003) may bring in some changes and help a broadening of approach and better integration too. (This model of solid and liquid church, especially if it is seen as a mixed economy operating in communion, may be a helpful model for Catholics and others to understand these shifts. The Church of England is looking at similar processes in its report *A Mission-Shaped Church*.)

[55] Their emergence is – or ought to ask – some serious questions about our basic understanding of church and its link to mission or even its missional identity, but also its unity and sense of inner cohesion or communion. How this is approached and addressed will vary depending on denominational background. Such reflection may throw up some interesting ecumenical convergence on the understanding of church; equally we may get a greater (theological and practical) fragmentation still.

[56] The Church of England has started such a initiative, under the co-ordination of Steven Croft. In this they are working closely with the Methodists. The groundwork was prepared by the report *A Mission-shaped Church – church planting and fresh expressions of church in a changing context* which is proving of great value within, but also significantly beyond, the Church of England.

[57] For a good introduction to Emerging church, and some of the issues it raises, see Michael Moynagh, *Emergingchurch.into.* (It also has contributions from George Lings, Stuart Murray and Howard Worsley.) Also just published as this book goes to press is *Changing Mission: Learning from the Newer Churches* by Stuart Murray (CTBI publications, 2006).

[58] These three models are based on a presentation given by Bishop Graham Cray at a 'Mission 21' Conference (looking at ways of doing mission/church planting in the 21st century).

[59] All of these developments could further fragment the church with all sorts of consequences. Is this the price that has to be made for realistic cultural engagement and effective mission? Again, although they cannot be explored here at length, it is worth noting that all this raises profound questions about the nature and unity of the church and many practical challenges too. How does the identity of the church relate to its core missionary function? Is there more to the church than this? What about belonging? Because of our physical dimension this will always involve a physical dimension, which again takes us onto church as a corporate fleshy reality. How we belong then matters. Is it just fellowship or practical co-operation or sacramental or creedal? Even pioneers are actually part of a bigger whole. What about being in continuity with those who have gone before us, passing the faith on to us, so we in turn can pass it on to others?

In some circles mission is popularly seen as opposed to tradition, a word that is given conservative, and even reactionary, associations and identified with maintenance of the status quo. In actual fact the word tradition is fundamentally about the passing on of faith from one person to another, from one generation to another. It is about transmission. As such it both looks forward and back, and also around. It is not about death, decay and being old-fashioned but about life, vitality, urgency and creativity as well as wisdom and experience.

All this matters if we preach that Christ came to gather all people into one body and family – the church. How do all missionary projects, agencies and groups fit together and participate in the life of the church? What sort of integration, and even accountability and authorisation, is needed? In many ways this brings us back to some fundamental themes in a theology of the church. Whatever else is involved, surely this has to be about unity in diversity – about communion of parts within a body – rather than uniformity? Attention could be given to this and how it operates in practice and in what ways. Attention could also be given to a fresh look and deeper understanding of the church as one, holy, catholic and apostolic. How in the midst of all this do we retain respect, love and tolerance, a missionary impulse, flexibility and a real openness to the Spirit? The answer, theoretically and practically, to this would involve a lot of faith, hope, love, and grace!

[60] I first heard the phrase in conversation with George Lings of the Sheffield Centre.

[61] In Michael Moynagh, *Emergingchurch.intro*, p. 153.

CHAPTER 10

Strategies for Promoting Alpha:
An Initial Exploration

Andrew Brookes

I intend to complete this section of the book by drawing on the findings and reflections of the last three chapters and look in more detail at how AI/HTB have chosen to promote and support the wider use of Alpha beyond their own congregation. I will also attempt some introductory evaluation (to be built on by other authors) and give some suggestions as to what else might be tried. Beyond that I hope to raise issues and ask questions that will stimulate readers and help them come to their own informed assessment.

An Overview of Changing Strategies

Early Days and the First Approach: 'Adapt Alpha to your Situation!'

HTB did not anticipate or plan for the actual level of interest in Alpha achieved when it was first launched. It was offered as a tool to help local churches to engage in evangelism. Initially they encouraged churches to adapt it to their own local circumstances. Looking back they were probably very optimistic – naïve perhaps – about how easily other churches would pick it up and what wider resources skills and features of church life they already had in place to facilitate effective and sustained use of Alpha. The reality was that most churches were not just like HTB or, indeed, anything like HTB. These problems and the gap in church culture and practice were made worse by the rapid interest in and uptake of the course by churches from a very wide range of denominations and social settings following the dramatic impact of the 'Toronto Blessing' at HTB from May 1994. By then about 2–300 churches were running Alpha. By the end of 1995 the figure was 2,500 and this figure doubled again to 5,000 by the end of 1996.

All this called for a response and a change in strategy resulted. HTB had produced some resources that others considered good and helpful. They were asked for more. They delivered. This dynamic of request and supply of resources has gone on and on, with AI/HTB becoming proactive at some points too. HTB soon discovered that local adaptation was undertaken so extensively that it resulted in the course not functioning at all or at least not being recognisable as the original. This local variation and interest from the public was such that they introduced the copyright statement and policy. It required and asked for a high measure of standardisation. It may well have helped courses run better. It also helped AI/HTB keep some sort of control on developments. Intentionally or not, it resulted in a certain centralisation and AI/HTB became more powerful and influential. It also meant that local churches had less authority and scope to adapt things to their local situation or especially to adapt Alpha to fit into their own pattern and even theology and spirituality of church life.

'Follow the Recipe!'

HTB focussed its help on the Alpha course itself. Emphasis was given increasingly to running Alpha after the model established by practice at HTB. This remains the case. 'Follow the recipe' is the mantra that emerges from many conferences and other training days. Initially they had to stress the importance of including the Holy Spirit Day/ Weekend, and specifically Charismatic elements more generally. Nowadays they say this is less of an issue. However, other issues have arisen, been identified and addressed.

In fact, AI/HTB are well aware of many problems that churches face in running Alpha. They have analysed feed-back and published materials describing the most common mistakes and ways of improving Alpha. These seven mistakes, formulated here as the corrective action[1], are worth listing since they give indications of the issues facing local churches and their general mindset. Some brief explanations or comments are appended.

- *Don't drive without taking lessons.* Go to an Alpha conference.
- *Carefully choose the right team.* This includes delegating to it and renewing it, by a rollover of personnel, to avoid burnout.
- *Stay in training.* Ideally train all of the team each time the course is run; this includes the principles (i.e. why-s) as well as how-s and what-s.
- *Follow the recipe.* Fundamentally include meal–talk–small group and do them well.
- *Don't forget to go away.* That is, go away for at least a day together and preferably for a weekend.
- *Plan the talks.* It is best to have a good live speaker(s).
- *Keep Alpha rolling.* To keep momentum going. Alpha is a long-term strategy.

In fact, the use of conferences by local churches and the attention they give to training is somewhat patchy. The percentage of churches with at least one team member who has attended the two-day Alpha

Conference has consistently fluctuated between 53–59% for 2001–2005. Using a similar criterion, only 21% of churches had sent someone to an 'Equip and Refresh (training) Day in 2005, half of these having sent someone to a full conference. [2] The amount of local training is indicated below. It highlights that AI is right to stress it and to put on events. It also shows that churches are slow to take up training opportunities. Is this laziness, time pressure or a desire not to be too influenced by AI? It also suggests that there will, as a result be quite a variation in how closely courses do in fact follow the recommended model.

Alpha Team Training (% of churches in sample)[3]

Training?	2001	2002	2003	2004	2005
Yes, before every course	41	36	35	41	36
Yes, but not before every course	34	36	36	36	36
No	25	28	30	23	28

The *Maximising the Potential* booklet also has a section covering and stressing the importance of local prayer being vital if Alpha is to be fruitful. The reason AI emphasises this may well be that a significant number of churches think Alpha is just a magic technique or quick fix that works automatically or easily or without grace.

The booklet, and other resources, then gives a section covering 15 ways to attract more (non Christian) guests onto the course. This clearly indicates that many churches have a problem doing this. This is a real challenge to them and also AI/HTB since they specifically claim that Alpha is an evangelistic (i.e. outreach) course. A failure to attract guests from beyond the worshipping community is likely to result in Alpha not being run long-term in a church. Surveys indicate that, in fact, many churches do not persist with Alpha.

An Expanding Vision and Evolving Strategies

To address all these issues AI/HTB have generated more and firmer guidelines, rules, resources and services including the national Annual Initiative/Invitation. For some, all this is seen as requiring, and even being driven by a desire for, standardisation and control, something many see epitomised by the McDonald fast food chain. This has led to the description of Alpha as a form of religious 'McDonald-ization' a sociological concept (explained below). This has practical but serious pastoral implications (again discussed below). NG actually refers to McDonalds and compares Alpha to it and in some ways wishes to emulate it, since Alpha, like McDonalds, needs to be a standard product so people can have confidence in it, and feel able to invite their friends to an Alpha Course running anywhere.[4] This has now become very much part of their strategy. It is perhaps unlikely that this strategy would have been followed in quite this way without there already being a large scale of adoption and interest in Alpha but in the UK this was judged to exist and to present new possibilities. However, this is quite different to what appears to have been the earliest idea of just offering the course and then providing support for local churches that could freely adapt the course.

The next clear step up in explicitly stated vision and strategy came with the beginning of the National Advertising Campaigns in1998. This was soon followed (in 2000) by the decision to augment this with the National Initiative/Invitation to invite the whole nation to supper while, or just after, the Advertising Campaign was running. This continues and is supported by the organisation of large numbers of ecumenical prayer meetings around the same time. Also around 2000 Alpha International was formally established as a charity and company limited by guarantee with the vision/aim of 'the (re)evangelisation of the nation(s) and the transformation of society'. This was connected to the problem of holding development within HTB itself (including the financial implications of this) and also to overseas developments with Alpha. Nonetheless, it indicates a still bigger vision, the creation of an independent company to implement and run it also opening up all sorts of new strategy possibilities.

These have now included new versions of Alpha, tailored to specific people groups or environments. Other courses and ministries are also being promoted. Plans for the new Alpha International Campus (AIC) could open up a whole new phase and set of strategies. This again could be very significant.

NG clearly has a passion for evangelism and an eye for opportunities to undertake it. He and others at HTB think big, too! Perhaps without this, Alpha would not have become the phenomenon that it has. However, all of these developments do stimulate questions about the extent to which their vision is achievable. Just how much evangelistic potential does NG see in Alpha? Just how much impact can Alpha have on the country as a whole? Are the right approaches being used to promote and support it? Are there any unfortunate side effects of all this? It is my aim now to evaluate these strategies and address the questions raised here and some others ones.

Alpha – a form of religious McDonaldisation? Is this effective for mission?

What is McDonaldization?

George Ritzer used the term McDonaldisation to denote global patterns of consumption and consumerism as typified by McDonalds,[5] the American and now global fast-food company. He sees this as part of a process of rationalisation. This builds on the work on Max Weber in the early 20th century who saw the development of bureaucracy as governed by an over-arching rationalisation. A bureaucracy involves and includes clearly defined goals and methods, strict rules and regulations to be applied in certain conditions, as well as specific roles and appropriate training. It is argued that McDonalds have applied this to the world of food, both as a producer and vendor but also by exploiting such a 'rationalised and bureaucratic mentality' in the mind and psyche of the consumer. It represents standardisation (rather than variation, local adaptation and creativity) as being good and aims at a near market monopoly. Predictability is a virtue. This approach and mentality – ethos – has been applied beyond the food industry to many areas of life including education, politics, health care, travel and leisure.

Ritzer considers McDonaldization under four categories: efficiency (but in such ways that just make people cogs in a machine, that is uncreative automatons); calculability (including the elevation of quantity over quality); predictability (including security that comes from formalisation and routine but can lead to dispirited mediocrity); and control (which stems from a desire for power and restricts the freedom, action and responsibility of sub-groups or individuals). Through them, this process is leading to humanity being systemised and dehumanised – constricted – in an 'iron cage of rationality'. It can be traced back to the Enlightenment emphasis on the mind and power of reason though there is debate about its relation to the modern/post modern paradigms.

This concept has been applied to Alpha by Ward and Hunt and this application commented on by Phil Meadows and Mark Ireland.[6] The general view is that Alpha shows signs of encouraging and using aspects of McDonaldization though it is accepted that there are limits to how far it can be applied to the theory and practice of Alpha. The concept was applied more generally and comprehensively to the church by John Drane.[7] He thinks it has a considerable and deep, and often subtle, influence on much of church life. He is concerned it has seriously stifled our spirituality and creativity, concerns that are heightened by the church now needing to respond increasingly more often to a rapidly changing world in which more people are openly spiritual and seeking spiritual depth. At the same time he notes that aspects of it are acceptable, good and welcome. I think that discussions about how much of the reactions to and by Alpha/AI ought to be set in the context of just how much this mind-set has *already* entered the church, and not see it principally as being *introduced* by Alpha.

Assessing Alpha for the Components of McDonaldisation

The immediate similarities between Alpha and the McDonaldization process and components are obvious enough. AI/HTB are well run and efficient and undoubtedly adopt many insights and practices from the business world. They have developed a product that has its own logo and branding and is well marketed with good advertising. Lots of resources are available. There was a hope and desire (originating from outside HTB) that the course would be the same everywhere.[8] A copyright policy has been developed, training is made available and people are increasingly encouraged to follow all the guidelines if they want results and also to be entitled to the benefits of registering with the organisation. Models exist to predict what will happen with Alpha over time. Statistics – quantities – are used to demonstrate the success of the course.

Some people see this as AI/HTB trying to take over local churches and perhaps bigger church organisational groups, stifling their individuality and trying to build some sort of monopoly. More credibly, it has been noted that in getting and holding on to as large a share in the religious consumer market as possible, AI may squeeze other smaller process courses out of existence. For others, it is viewed as spreading a certain type of Christianity across all the church under the cover of supporting mission for all.[9] Although AI would deny these intentions, some of these may be unintended consequences of Alpha's huge profile and promotion. The following questions do merit attention. Has the scale of investment in Alpha forced other useful initiatives out of business? Do most churches even know about other initiatives? By putting this amount of effort into Alpha, what is the wider church not looking at?

The huge rush by so much of the church to use Alpha may well be, in part anyway, an indication of just how McDonaldised, how lacking in creativity and effective evangelism it had already become in its approach to its life and mission. An alternative, and perhaps complementary way, of looking at this is to conclude that the large uptake of Alpha reflects just how many local congregations knew they needed help with evangelism/evangelisation, and were more than happy to use even a pre-packaged product if this got them started and made a difference. Taking up Alpha, at least meant they were doing something to take their evangelistic responsibilities seriously!

As I have indicated HTB's motivation in first making Alpha available, and then in developing support etc, was pastoral and generally in response to the requests of others both to use Alpha and then to have support for 'running it well'. It was such people who wanted courses to be uniform – like McDonald's restaurants and food. This suggests a church population and mindset already significantly penetrated by a consumer mentality for 'off the shelf' ready-made products and easily and swayed by branding, advertising and celebrity endorsements. It makes it hard to assess the extent to which AI/HTB have just been keen to help, though they have certainly plugged into these mentalities.

Assessing Alpha and AI for the impact of McDonaldization

Many see a contrast between the local level, where Alpha was a tool for local use (and one that at HTB kept developing for some time), and the national and international level, where Alpha is now a big organisation with a standardised product, with local churches being asked to participate in strategies and initiatives emerging from there. There has clearly been a shift in this direction. Some development of central staff and plant has been inevitable given the scale of Alpha. However, it is important that AI are aware of its downside too. There is so much activity happening with Alpha world-wide that it is easy for AI to be insulated from and overlook problems areas. Even the overall attractiveness of HTB as a local church can mean that issues facing many other local churches running Alpha are not felt so keenly by NG *et al* and again, may not be given the attention they deserve.

Standardisation is necessary if the national campaigns and advertising are to have any credible foundation. Branding is linked to this and this can have a very significant impact. Freebury reports a major study in which 76% of 38,000 respondents say they would be likely to buy a brand they had heard of but not tried. This compares to 90% if they have been introduced to it by a friend and only 23% if they have not heard of it at all.[10] Thus, all of these elements are linked. Such a strategy has further implications for standardisation. If AI promote the course through a national initiative, saying it is 'running at a church near you', then they should make more effort to undertake quality control and to see that registered courses are actually running Alpha. A concern to do this may well have made guidelines still more rigid and pastorally inflexible.

Providing training is worthwhile – especially if the principles behind it are explained – and in general very needed in church circles for most laity and even some clergy. In my view, a good deal of this has been very helpful because the course is sophisticated and much is involved in running it well: most local congregations do not pick up all of this immediately. However, following routines and instructions – especially if this becomes mechanical – can risk reducing or stifling spiritual depth and creativity in individuals and whole congregations. Other ways of helping local congregations become missionary exist, even with pre-existing tools.[11]

Issues about mission also need to be considered in making an evaluation. Is it reasonable to expect, or even want, courses to be the same everywhere, even if this does reflect common church practice in such area as liturgy etc? Mission theology and practice advocates the importance of responding to the local culture and situation, a process typically called inculturation by Catholics and contextualisation by Evangelicals. This results in allowing the form of church life and even how the Gospel is presented to be influenced by local factors, values, ways of thinking, questions and needs. It does not mean changing the absolute core of the Gospel but it does take the principle of Incarnation (by which God adapted himself to human ways and Jewish Palestinian ways specifically) seriously. Thus, the Gospel is both incarnated and shaped by the culture and also challenges, transforms and shapes it. (This two-way interaction is sometimes called inter-culturation.)[12] Does the course have to inculturate (be locally contextualised) more than a beef burger – to really be effective? Some commentators suggest that it does and that its standardisation, far from extending and promoting good evangelistic practice, is stifling it.[13] (Mark Ireland's work suggests that local courses do have the best conversion rates. Run at HTB, Alpha is one such example!)

Clearly there are risks and pitfalls with attempts at inculturation and it requires gifted practitioners to do it well. Much can be learned from first studying effective tools. It is also true that AI allow some local adaptation in examples, setting, talk length etc. Whether AI has got the right balance between top-down standardisation of a tested method and local bottom-up adaptation is likely to be an ongoing debate and it may well depend on how far the cultural situation is really removed from the original one at HTB. Could an approach by which churches are encouraged to learn from Alpha and perhaps adapt it to their circumstances more radically than at present be developed? This might entail them selecting what is appropriate for their circumstanes while accepting help from Alpha 'consultants' who might advise and work with them over time. This would probably result in the production of similar but not identical courses – but these could still be linked in a wider Alpha family or movement. It is probably the specific talk content rather than the method that would be altered.[14] It might not be desirable if national advertising of an allegedly standard course is a priority.

What wider message does all this send to the public? Being efficient and well-organised is commendable, but this should not be an end in itself and needs a bigger Gospel picture and deeper spiritual motivation. It is important it does not indicate an unthinking capitulation to worldly consumerism. Nor should it stop at promoting God as someone who is principally a supplier of people's needs.

People vary in their opinions and conclusions about Alpha and McDonaldization and the extent to which AI has got these balances and its strategy to support and promote Alpha right. Quite probably there are some positives and negatives. Other process courses have not gone down the same track – nor have they become so big. They have generally allowed greater freedom for local adaptation. May be now they are seeing the benefits with higher conversion rates (and lower central running costs). It would be interesting to know the extent to which AI has reflected on all these issues and any impact it is – deliberately or otherwise – having on such an 'iron cage' developing around their clients and, indeed, them too.

What role can a National advertising campaign play in evangelising the entire nation?

What impact has the campaign had and can it be expected to have, bearing in mind the current spiritual profile of the nation and what has so far happened with Alpha? Can it deliver national wholesale evangelism?

The Alpha Initiative/Invitation has run each September since 1998. Since 2000 a major element has been to 'invite the nation to supper', especially to big events, which function as the introductory night to the Alpha course. It has used posters on prominent public billboards and other aspects of advertising each year and is thus one of the longest running, and some say most effective, Christian advertising campaigns ever mounted (see Chapter 19). The style of the posters has remained very consistent. After cartoon posters featuring slogans with the Alpha Logo in the first two years, the next four years featured faces of people – relaxed, vivacious, smiling, 'with it' but normal and approachable. There is the Alpha Logo and the strap line 'An opportunity to explore the meaning of life. The Alpha Course – starting at a church near you'. These convey the sense that Christians are normal and indeed contented happy people (and by implication that Christianity/church is normal and happy too) and that it is an OK, not wacky, thing to explore spiritual issues. In the last two years there has been a more direct attempt to challenge non-believers and their satisfaction, or its lack, with their own lives. The happy people have been replaced in 2004 with a mobile phone and in 2005 with a computer screen, and on both occasions with the caption 'Is there more to life than this?' The other features of the poster have remained the same. In 2004, the picture of the mobile phone with its text message was accompanied by an intensive campaign of sending text messages. Cinema adverts have been used for the first time in 2005, featuring young successful Christians who have been on Alpha and are Christians. (Illustrations of these posters can be found in Chapter 19 by John Griffiths, and on the book's back cover.) Who do these posters impact most and why do AI/HTB keep spending large sums of money on such campaigns?

AI/HTB state that they are to encourage Christians actually to get out there and invite friends on the course. They do this in two ways. Firstly, they put Christianity into the public arena, dragging it out of the silent zone of private faith. In this they reinforce what Christians know but may feel inadequate about – that they are called to witness to their faith by talking about it and by inviting others to explore it. Secondly they legitimise the making of invitations and the accepting of them. They do this by planting the following thought: 'A course that has the money to advertise itself nationally and to a high quality must be good, or it would not have sufficient backers/supporters in the first place!' In short, Christians will feel good about and have confidence in the faith, church and Alpha and will invite friends to come to Alpha. (Of course, they may also still keep quiet but decide to go to Alpha themselves at a local church that is running it.) For both these functions, the posters are actually mainly aimed at motivating Christians, despite the content.

What message do they convey to the dechurched and nonchurched? The posters say virtually nothing about the content of Christianity. It is not obvious that smiling faces or the word 'Alpha' or a man holding a large question mark have anything to do with Christianity or religion. The only clue about Christianity in the poster itself is the reference to the course being run at a local church. This may be an attempt to suggest that the course does not impose religion on people and that Christians are nice interesting people to hang about with. It may well speak to people who have had a Christian connection in the past and indeed may want to go back by encouraging these thoughts, giving the assurance this is a good idea and that at least some Christians are welcoming and friendly. (As I have noted, the actual content of the course, may well be suited to these type of people.) Thus the posters may serve a purpose for this 'in-shore fishing', but how good are they for 'off-shore fishing', that is 'how well do they communicate with the really nonchurched?' Do they scratch where these people itch? How well do they get people interested in the gospel? What do they say to the non-believer? It is no wonder that it is taking time for the population at large both to recognise the logo and get to know that Alpha is a Christian course. However, even if they know this, will they know what sort of Christian course it is and what it aims to do? Will they have any real idea if this has any relevance to the itch they sense they have?

These questions matter. For advertising to sell a product potential consumers have to meet three conditions: 1) they need to know what the product is; 2) they need to know that the product is good, i.e. to know and have confidence in the manufacturer/supplier and brand name; 3) they need to have a reason to want/buy/use the product. It is not at all clear that the style of advertising used by Alpha, combined with the present state of most of the population will result in many direct sales, so to speak (and this only means people initially turning up at courses or looking up further details – rather than actual conversions). The posters may also stimulate non-Christians to ask Christian friends (if they have any) what the poster is all about, thus providing the Christian with the opportunity to explain it and invite people along. However, merely knowing what Alpha represents is still only one of the 3 factors that need to be met. Despite decreasing knowledge of Christianity, most of the population know that Jesus is a figure associated with Christianity but most do not seek to be his disciples. Most know the Bible is a Christian book but most do not read it. Just knowing Alpha is a Christian course, does not mean people will go on it. Hunt found that 5% of attendees decided to come on Alpha through advertising and a further 5% through the media.[15] I have heard estimates from AI/HTB as low as 2%.

HTB point out that the numbers of people who recognise the logo as Christian is rising,[16] and they are encouraged to think – and have expressed the hope – that if this continues, the figure will reach 'the tipping point'.[17] According to certain sociological and marketing theories (backed by evidence) after the tipping point is reached a product will then move rapidly through most of the rest of the population. This has happened with many household brands and products. The tipping point theory is based on a particular understanding of and profiling of the population. In this model (and other similar ones) the population is seen as being distributed like a bell shape.[18] Small numbers of innovators (9% of the total population) are followed by a rising number of early adopters (15%) and then by the early majority in the middle (30%). The curve falls away with the late majority (30%) with the laggards (16%) bringing up the rear – and some hardly getting there at all. The 'Tipping Point Theory', although largely couched in different (more inspirational) terms, says that the uptake of products follows this curve – or that it does in some cases. It argues that the majority, while more cautious, can and will see this benefit of what the innovators and then early adopters have and want it. Thus, after slowish rates of uptake amongst early adopters the main body of the population follows suit and this is shown by a rapid increase in numbers, uptake or sales or whatever the appropriate measure is. Eventually enough people have confidence in it and seeing that it works and seeing a need for it, most take it up.

Can this be applied to an interest in/conscious need for Alpha or Christianity more generally? How will most of the population respond to the posters/wider national campaigns? If they see no need for the product (the Gospel) then they will not follow those designated as early adopters. I have already argued that the spiritual state and latent familiarity with the Gospel in Britain is probably such that this is likely to be the case. The majority just sense no need or interest in Christianity. They are happy enough as they are and don't look to interpret any gap as related to God or at least the Christian God. In reality it may very well be the wrong model to apply to how interest in the gospel/uptake of Alpha occurs and thus of how advertising can be used or what it can be expected to achieve. The so-called early adopters may prove (in percentage terms) to be the main group of adopters with a dwindling tail behind them. They may well be churched and 'open dechurched', these groups having markedly different spiritual profiles (and thus 'spiritual buying or consumer habits') to the rest of the population. Even if secularised non-Christians know that Alpha is a Christian course, do they know what to expect from it, and if so, will the local church they go to deliver what they expect? Spiritual search and process courses are not exact fits and putting nonchurched people straight onto Alpha may well not be the right approach to take forward their spiritual journey. Indeed, it may put many off.

Though substantial numbers of people still do Alpha each year the uptake per year has fluctuated over the years and has not again risen to the numbers doing it between 1998–2000. It has not actually produced even linear growth let alone a growth pattern that fits well with the curve expected from the tipping point theory. (It should be remembered that these numbers include guests from different versions of Alpha, thus complicating interpretation. The majority of initial guests on these new courses are probably Christians or at least churched people.) By 2001 41% of the adult population already knew someone who had done the course.[19] This figure ought to have risen by now. However, this high 'familiarity', which is much higher than those people who know Alpha is a Christian course, does not seem to be translating into higher attendance at the course. Again this suggests it is not very appropriate to apply the tipping point theory and associated profile of the total population to uptake of Alpha.

The tipping point and especially the patterns of adoption that underlie it may well be more relevant to an understanding of how local churches have chosen to run Alpha rather than how the general public have chosen to come on the course. Thus an initial slow beginning was followed by a huge surge of interest (ca 1994 – 1998). (This corresponds with the immediate impact of the Toronto Blessing/time of refreshment which may well have introduced other factors into the pattern of adoption.) Since then there has been a much slower rate of interest but some churches are still adopting Alpha for the first time. Looked at this way, whatever the exact sociological dynamic, the advertising campaigns may well have been most effective by persuading local churches and their leaders that Alpha is still around and can make a difference. People, originally cautious, are still being persuaded to give it a go. Clearly not all churches will try Alpha and an increasing range of alternative courses will probably limit the market for expansion. Another major concern is that, even having tried it, most churches only run Alpha about five times before stopping. NG has commented that, while in the mid-1990s there were expectations of a very high overall number of churches running Alpha, AI/HTB have now revised their expectations downwards. AI has also adapted its strategy with more focus on improving the quality of these courses.

What other impact might AI's poster campaign have? It is worth pondering what else the posters may – unintentionally – convey about Christianity. A number of questions can be raised that may help indicate the limited impact of the poster campaigns. Are the faces of people used (all of whom are actual 'Alpha graduates') too middle class or ethnically narrow to connect with much of the population or indeed the congregations of many local churches? Do they convey a sense that Christianity is a middle class pastime for people who want to engage in self-improvement and a bit of spiritual enhancement? Do the posters convey the sense Alpha is mainly about an (intellectual) search for meaning? How important is 'meaning' to most people? Is it a middle-class thing for the most part? Is it where most people consciously itch? What about justice? Or peace? Or fellowship or love? Or reconciliation (of various sorts)? What about just avoiding violence and getting meals, clothes and a roof to live under? All these issues are also important to many people. Thus, it may well be that these posters simply do not connect with large parts of the population. There is also the possibility that the advertising conveys the message that Christianity is just another part of the consumer world, using its methods to advertise and recruit. Advertising may help Alpha reach some but it may actually prevent it reaching others or it may even put some others off who are looking for the meaning of life and much more in the Gospel of Jesus Christ.

To conclude, national advertising has had positive effects but these are limited and have probably not achieved all that has been hoped of it. It is also costly and pursuing it tends to shut out other strategic options that could be taken. These might require less standardisation and also on grounds of limited finances. Again it is a matter of ongoing debate whether AI is following the best tactic and for how long it should be continued.[20] However, it is important that Christians take seriously the media and advertising since they are very powerful in shaping opinion and minds in today's world and much can probably be learned from this campaign by other Christian groups.

Is having the Main Focus on the direct evangelistic use of Alpha the Right one?

AI/HTB has placed a lot of focus on using Alpha as a tool for outreach. At the same time, it is clear, as already noted, that many churches find this difficult to do, especially in a sustained way. It is thus well worth pondering if this focus is the right one, and, if it is, if it has been pursued the best way.

'Just Keep Running Alpha – and you will see the fruit!' Or will you?

Part of the strategy of AI is to focus on Alpha and to encourage other churches to focus on Alpha, and especially to focus on it as a tool specifically for outreach. The advice from AI/HTB is often reduced to 'just keep running it: after three times you will (probably) be into outreach!' This may not seem odd – but perhaps it is.

Actually HTB ran it many many more times, adapting it and integrating it and its underlying values with their overall church life. Indeed, it may well be much truer to say Alpha grew out of HTB's church life and values. Only then, was its outreach potential and fruitfulness seen. And this happened accidentally. Why do they then expect real outreach to occur for other churches after as few as three attempts with an imported course? Why expect its main impact to be outreach and numerical growth anyway?

The Brierley research cited in Chapter 7 on Alpha's impact over time (in England and Wales) was conducted with Bob Jackson and Robert Warren of Springboard (the Archbishop of Canterbury and York's Initiative in Evangelism). They wrote it up for *Alpha News*. It is worth quoting the conclusions of the *Alpha News* article at length.

> The results show that Alpha by itself does not reverse overall decline, but it does slow down decline significantly. Alpha is not the only answer to decline but it is one highly important one. There is some evidence that other 'process evangelism' courses are similarly effective in sharing the faith. Also there are several other key factors which led to growth. *Alpha may not reverse decline by itself, but using it in combination with other measures may generate growth.*[21]

I think all of this is significant and was possibly even prescient back then. I have highlighted the last sentence because the *Alpha News* article next to this one ends by saying: 'It was these statistics that led the authors to conclude, 'This might be summarised, 'Alpha is good for you. Have it again and again'.[22] Has AI narrowed its focus too much just on Alpha? There are a number of reasons to think this might be the case.

Firstly, there are some pastoral factors, concerned with the guests and team on Alpha courses. For a long time AI/HTB have advocated churches try and run the course three times a year as a rolling programme. It is claimed this is the best way to build up momentum and a good inward flow of guests. It is also a good way to burn out your team; most churches simply do not have the number of staff and suitable volunteers to do what HTB do. More than that, a number of church ministers I have spoken to, and who understand Alpha and run it well, think they need much longer than ten weeks to adequately form disciples enough to have them help on the next course. A good number feel it much more effective to run just one course a year and integrate it with other discipling work and aspects of church life.

Secondly, there are factors that have come to light from those who have studied elements that make up a healthy and/or growing church. Several studies and surveys indicate that several features operate in tandem (in an organic living way) to produce vibrant and growing churches. The various lists depend in part on what premises and basic convictions the developer of the model begins with. There is not space here to review them but it is clear that there is a large overlap in the features identified, whether or not the terminology exactly matches. One such researcher is Christian Scwharz of 'Natural Church Development'.[23] He argues that it is a serious mistake to view any course or programme as a solution for church growth in isolation; he argues the church needs to look at its overall life in a number of key areas if it is to find and sustain real growth. He warns: 'Whenever a 'successful' programme is automatically presumed to be a church growth principle – a widespread Christian pastime – it causes tremendous confusion.'[24]

AI has, in effect, sought to drive renewal/growth of congregations by telling them first to focus on mission and this through use of one course. Has this in reality been a good strategy? The data reviewed in Chapter 7 suggests that this had only limited benefits. Many churches have struggled to invite many previously nonchurched or dechurched guests. Many have given up running Alpha after a few attempts. This may well be because they actually need to give attention to other aspects of their church life as a greater priority than fine-tuning their outreach course. It might be right for many churches to focus more attention on proclamation outreach – and Alpha may help them with this – but AI's emphasis on this may actually move some other churches to a less healthy form of church. Mission is certainly central to the identity and life of churches, and as such needs to be flagged up, but more generally unhealthy churches are unlikely to engage well in mission in the long run.

The work of researchers in church growth suggests that the journey to become a long-term growing missionary congregation is more complex than just running a course that happens to be effective elsewhere. AI may have underestimated this complexity – at least in their resources and public advice. (As a local congregation HTB appears to appreciate, or at least follow, these factors most often identified as necessary for growth.) Further, in as much as AI has raised expectations of relatively quick success, they may actually have done damage since such expectations can easily and quickly translate into disillusionment and abandonment of a plan or course or outreach more generally. AI might be well advised to look at developing resources, conferences or training advisers to appreciate these broader factors and to be able to work with local churches more flexibly to bring about long-term growth.[25] A detailed study of Alpha Resource Churches (and others that have actually grown significantly while using Alpha) might yield some helpful findings that could be applied here.

Alpha's impact on existing Christians: an overlooked Cinderella?

This marked emphasis on outreach means, unintentionally perhaps, that everything else tends to be perceived as somewhat secondary. It means that allowing existing Christians to do Alpha and the benefits they receive from this are not regarded as significant and are overlooked and almost dismissed. But does this attitude overlook and even fail to build with what could be very important?

Spiritual growth is usually reported, whether or not this actually results in 'conversions' or 'new Christians'. Spiritual growth on Alpha among existing Christians comes in various types. These include a more conscious focus on the person of Jesus and devotion to him, deeper personal prayer, more hunger for Scripture, a deeper awareness of the work and gifts of the Holy Spirit, greater appreciation of types of group prayer and worship, a commitment to various church ministries and a desire to witness – even if they are not sure how. This should be harnessed rather than overlooked. An appreciation of and desire to take part in small groups (be they house groups, cells, pastorates or some other variation) often emerges. New attitudes and perspectives begin to permeate the congregation through those who have done Alpha, or, if present already, permeate it more fully. A greater spirit of participation, collaboration, hospitality and the permission to ask questions as Christians are all things I have also seen and can be built on. Also this source of renewal could be the beginning of a much deeper change in the congregation and one that leads to far more effective outreach in the long-term. However, this will take time and may not be dramatic. It will involve more than just running Alpha.

This was in fact the case at HTB. A whole set of changes were introduced over time and integrated with each other. It was the overall synthesis that resulted in a growing church. Its vibrant life drew people to it. In point of fact, it happened on such a scale that a discipleship course started working evangelistically. Why did NG and HTB then take this discipleship course and promote it in isolation from its natural environment as an evangelistic tool? Despite AI/HTB's best efforts to get people to view and use it evangelistically, most people persist in seeing and using Alpha as HTB used it for many years – as a course for Christians! It is perhaps not surprising that so many churches use it mainly as a refresher course and that so many Christians attend it – well over half the guests in most surveys. Yet, rather than be seen as an inconvenience, embarrassment or failure, this could be seen as an opportunity to help churches begin a more fundamental transition and one that could result in the congregation, like HTB, eventually growing significantly.

For example, running an Alpha Course, even when it is mainly attended by Christians, introduces many experiences and skills, insights and perspectives into a Christian community. It gets Christians talking and sharing about their faith and spiritual and more general life experience. It allows them to ask questions. It allows them, without fear or castigation, to express doubts. They can experience and value hospitality, small-group dynamics, collaborative ministry and teamwork, or at least evaluate these. They can see how all sorts of people can contribute to church life and to evangelism in such a team approach. Mission itself can be reflected on better and more fully on the basis of such experiences. All of these (and others too) are rich in potential and suitably used, could take a church forward in many ways and into more effective mission – whatever 'Alpha statistics' it produces.

Mission programmes/process courses are unlikely to work very well or bed down long term if they are just bolt-ons to the rest of the life of the church and especially if the one chosen is at odds with some of its key values and spirituality. Mission may, or may not be the right place to begin and it is certainly not the only place that typically needs attention. Alpha's impact on existing Christians could in some cases be the beginning of changes in a congregation that bring a more long-term missionary shift in the congregation. Long-term that may or may not involve Alpha courses.

It is increasingly clear that many factors are involved in why certain churches grow and more generally transition from maintenance to mission and engage with the contemporary and changing social and cultural scene. Many factors are also involved in why certain churches decline.[26] It is also becoming increasingly clear among those who work to support transitions in churches and especially that 'from maintenance to mission' that outside help from a well-informed, listening and supportive 'mission companion' who journeys with them is very valuable. Various models are increasingly emerging for how to do this. The process is now generally being called 'mission accompaniment' and most of the core values and skills are agreed on, though identified and developed independently by different denominations and church agencies. Mission companions or accompaniers, who facilitate this process, should not drive change – this must be locally owned – and certainly not impose solutions. They should listen, encourage, provide insights, resources, experience and wisdom and even raise difficult questions and lighten up local blind spots. It increasingly appears that this needs to happen over a significant period of time.[27] In significant part this tends to contrast with what is seen as the centralised and standardised top-down approach of AI, though there is some significant overlap and AI could conceivably develop means of support for churches closer to this in nature and mood, drawing from its insights.

To what Extent have thinking and hopes of Revival influenced Alpha and its promotion?

The period between 1994 and 1997 was marked by some intense and unusual religious experiences and events at HTB. I think it is fair to say that this period was in many ways crucial to the whole impact of Alpha. At the beginning of it there were only 200 or so churches running Alpha. By the end of it (1997) there were around 6,500 and HTB and Alpha had a much bigger public profile. All this had major implications for Alpha and strategies to promote it. Firstly there were enough courses running in the UK for HTB to consider national advertising of Alpha worthwhile. It also resulted in interest from around the world that has resulted in Alpha becoming a truly global phenomenon. The sheer scale of this made the development of Alpha International a sensible and, in some ways, a necessary step to take. Combined with other courses and ministries that have been developed, all of this in turn has led to the proposal to form an Alpha International Campus. I am not saying that everything in that period was of God but it is hard to deny a significant Divine action in the midst of it. Its impact on uptake and influence of Alpha was consider-able – though this was linked to other factors such as the call for a decade of evangelisation and the findings of John Finney as reported in *Finding Faith Today*.

There was talk of revival during those heady years.[28] SM, NG and others preferred to regard it as 'a time of refreshing' since it was mainly impacting Christians but there were hopes that it could lead to revival – if the graces were nurtured and a commitment to outreach was made and sustained. If not, NG feared the graces would dry up or be with-drawn. This may well go a long way to explain NG's and AI's focus on presenting Alpha as an evangelistic tool to reach the unchurched. Ideas and hopes for revival have persisted and, I suspect, influenced thinking and strategising about Alpha in various ways though not all of this may have been helpful.

Revival means a lot of different things to different people.[29] At its heart is a sovereign act of God coming in a dramatic, powerful and often unusual way. This brings about a variety of responses from people impacted by it. These too can often by striking. For some revival is looked to as a quick if dramatic fix by which God restores the fortunes of the church. It has been observed that revivals often happen in situa-tions with a significant Christian culture – if one where there has been backsliding too. The act of God revives this faith. Some commenta-tors consider that it is not an appropriate way to look at the challenges that face us since we no longer live in a country or culture where there are enough people with a latent Christian faith or background knowl-edge such that this can be relatively easily reignited to reverse overall church decline and influence on society. It is argued that hoping for revival, whilst not looking to change any church or missionary practices, may in fact be a distraction. Certainly the church still depends on God's powerful grace but it also needs to reshape itself more radically and re-engage with a de-christianised culture more seriously and do all this over the longer term to see lasting renewal. It may continue to shrink in the meantime. (Of course, such a long-term renewal may still be described as revival by those committed to the term.)

NG's book The Heart of Revival was published in 1997. It attempts to give a very broad understanding of how God's grace can impact Christians and of a wide response to such grace including proclamation, social care and social transformation. It was written in this period of optimism. Drawing on Isaiah 40 –66, he sees the church (and nation) as being like ancient Israel, about to emerge from a period of exile and re-enter the promised land, renewing it. Is the current British situation that simple? NG does not give much cultural analysis but may in fact have underestimated the problems in the church as a whole as well as the nation, and the sheer scale of the cultural issues that need some response. To pick up further on Biblical exile imagery and setting, our reasons for being in exile, the cultural dissonance and new challenges it involves may be more serious than NG anticipated. Thus the length of exile and our current position in such a process (if this is what it turns out to be) may all present bigger challenges and need more radical solutions, meaning a quick return to familiar homeland is not possible.[30]

I was recently (in 2006) told by Mark Elsdon-Dew, that nowadays NG prefers to describe the events of 1994–1997 at HTB as 'a move of God' and prefers it not to be linked formally with the Toronto Blessing. This may reflect a desire to allow the graces of that period (as effecting HTB and Alpha more widely) to be evaluated in their own right. Does it also reflect a more sober view of just how much is required of the church to bring about the re-evangelisation of the nation and the transformation of society, the vision of AI? None of this is to say that HTB and then AI have not responded well to the graces of that period. There are clear indications of fruitfulness, even if detailed strategising may need re-appraisal.[31] After all, planning around a large sovereign act of God is almost a contradiction in terms – since such sovereign acts are freely initiated on God's part. All anyone can do is try and respond using the light they have and trusting that God has put them there for a purpose, having prepared them in advance by his wisdom. Not all of this may be evident at the time to participants and even to leaders who also walk by faith. (Leaders also have to work with the expectations, views and interpretations of others, whether they are helpful or not.)

It seems to me that God may have used that period to sow the seeds of Alpha's ecumenical impact and fruit. A significant part of the graces of those years was that it drew in people from right across the denominational spectrum. People also often testified to receiving a deeper appreciation of the church as such and a love for the whole church. Barriers came down. Christians have been encouraged to appreciate and learn from each other's traditions. All this may well have been one of the more important, and ongoing legacies, of this move of God.

Many Alpha enthusiasts did, and some still do, see Alpha as anointed as such, something God more or less automatically blesses. (It is easy to see how such views can lead people to strongly advocate standardisation, copyright and national advertising.) SM uses more cautious language, typically saying that it seems that 'God has adopted Alpha'. There is also an acknowledgement that this might not be permanent and they hope to have the humility to move on when and if God does. Mixed with a sense of urgency, HTB's leaders also give a sense of being committed for the long haul. They still hope and pray for revival and encourage others to do the same. But there is also present a sense of realism, perhaps something that has grown over the years, though I do not think it has dimmed their overall vision. There may still be some interesting developments and contributions to be made by the Alpha Movement.

Alpha International Campus:
the formation of technicians or apprentices?

Again the graces of 1994–97 were seen by many as God flagging up the Alpha Course as such. They perhaps ought to be seen as God flagging up the wider way that HTB do church and mission (and other associated ministries) as a whole. Perhaps more attention needs to be given to the overall package and its underlying values and spiritual disciplines. If I am right, this may be something that AI needs to pay attention to as well as the wider church public.

The focus on Alpha as such has tended to end up with AI presenting it as a technique and alongside this there has been a certain tendency to produce relatively robotic technicians to run it. Replication has been seen by many as a high priority. This could happen with their other materials and courses too. The challenge may be to develop and give a deeper training that really helps people to grasp the key principles and then give them more scope to experiment so they can really find a suitable tool for their own church and locality. This means that people will be more like apprentices who learn and then apply a craft with AI having a mentoring role as a 'master craftsman'.[32] Resulting courses may still be in the tradition of Alpha if not obvious carbon copies, though they may be better contextualised too and fruitful as a result. This may well mean changing some current 'policies' and would perhaps pull against some of their own tendencies and attitudes perhaps– as well as a McDonaldized mentality and technological mindset in contemporary culture, including the church. Interestingly, based on personal observation, they seem to encourage greater scope for initiative and experimentation within HTB itself. So why not extend this? Jesus himself prioritised training and releasing people over creating products and programmes. AI has a reputation for producing good quality resources. Can it match these with the quality of its training? In developing the Alpha International Campus (AIC) and its various ministries it is something that it might be well worth aiming at. The scale of the vision and range of ministries and training being planned for AIC suggest it is possible.

Notes

[1] From *Maximising the Potential of your Alpha Course*, Alpha Publications. Now also presented as part of the new twin track Alpha conference.

[2] *Alpha Invitation 2005 Report*, Tables 3.8 and 3.9, p. 29.

[3] *Alpha Invitation 2005 Report*, Table 3.7, p. 28.

[4] For example, see the report of interviews of Nicky Gumbel and Sandy Millar with Mark Ireland in *Evangelism: Which Way now?* Chapter 2. Unless I am very much mistaken, NG has also used the McDonalds' illustration to explain the copyright policy at Alpha Conferences. Whether or not NG and others at AI intend to highlight the comparison by this use of McDonalds, the analysis of Alpha in terms of what is now called McDonaldization is an entirely valid venture and line of enquiry.

[5] George Ritzer, *The McDonaldization of Society*, Thousand Oaks CA: Pine Forge Press, 1993, 2nd expanded ed, 1996.

[6] P. Ward, 'Alpha – The McDonaldization of Religion?,' *Anvil*, 15:4 (1998), pp. 279–86. (1998) and Hunt in both *Anyone for Alpha?* (DLT, 2001) and *The Alpha Enterprise* (Ashgate, 2004). See *Evangelism: which way now?*, ch. 2 and Philip R. Meadows, 'The Alpha Course', in: W. Stephen Gunter and Elaine Robinson, *Considering the Great Commission: Evangelism and Mission in the Wesleyan Spirit* (Abingdon Press, 2005), chapter 18, pp. 269–91.

[7] John Drane, *The McDonaldization of the Church*, DLT, 2000.

[8] As noted, NG has specifically used the analogy with McDonalds when explaining and justifying this. If he is aware of – or concerned about – these critiques this is a surprising choice to make for an illustration. Mark Elsdon-Dew recently told me that NG has concerns about it on the grounds that it makes Alpha seem bland.

[9] For example, see Stephen Brian, *The Alpha Course: an analysis of its claim to offer an educational course on 'the meaning of life,* (Ph D Thesis, University of Surrey, 2003). He argues it is recycling believers and making them more Charismatic in outlook. For a comment see Booker and Ireland, *Evangelism, Which Way now?*, 2nd Edition, p. 17.

[10] See Charles Freebury, *Alpha or Emmaus?*, p. 42.

[11] See rest of this chapter and also Chapter 22 by Phil Meadows in this volume who develops some of these issues.

[12] John Drane considers aspects of contextualisation in Chapter 20.

[13] Should it be a cause of concern that AI/HTB invite and encourage Local Advisers to get in teams from HTB to lead local training 'Equip and Refresh' Days? Does this stifle local wisdom, even if unintentionally so?

[14] Helpful lessons may be learned from looking at the evolution of the 'Cursillo' course and associated courses. Cursillo (literally 'short course') was developed in

the 1940s and it is intended to evangelise/renew people in faith and equip them to evangelise. Run over three full days, it consists of talks, small-group sharing, shared and personal prayer and times to eat together, socialise and build friendships, It is referred to as a tool, offers ongoing support and as a result is referred to as a wider movement. Does all this sound familiar?! It is still run today right round the world. The original course was devised by Catholics for Catholic use. Other denominations have wanted to use it but to change bits to suit them. Cursillo leaders allowed this but asked them to change the name to reflect this. Usually these names show a clear connection with the original course and there are very close bonds of friendship, prayer and fellowship between their promoters in the wider Cursillo family/movement. Other adaptations and applications of the course have also occurred. (It was, for instance, a major influence on the 'Life in the Spirit' seminars and course materials.) Cursillo has a less rigid policy in these regards than the one followed by AI, though this is probably affected by the branding, advertising, range of resources available and the generally more substantial and pro-active approach used to support and promote Alpha. Perhaps AI should reflect on this model, especially if the time comes when it feels it should end the national advertising campaigns? Variations need not follow denominational lines.

[15] See S. Hunt, *The Alpha Enterprise*, p. 176.

[16] In actual fact it has not changed very much for the last four years. (Thus: 2003 – 20%; 2004 – 19.5%; 2005 – 22%; 2006 – 23%.) Also I think it is reasonable to assume that Christians make up a fraction of this number that is disproportionately high compared to their numbers in the total population. For instance, as reported in Alpha News in November 2006, the English Church Survey of 2006 found that more than 99% of church ministers and priests have heard of Alpha. It may be very reasonable to assume that nearly all the 7% of the population that go to church every week know Alpha is a Christian course. If not all, most probably will. That does not, of course, mean they have done it, approve of it, or would recommend it to their friends. Approximately another 8% go to church up to once a month. If a significant number of these also know Alpha is a Christian course, then the remaining group of unchurched (dechurched and nonchurched) people who recognise it is not huge – but it is still significant. Also, Alpha would be of significant benefit to, and could well be effective with, occasional, even monthly attenders. Most statistics indicate that Alpha guests typically include a range of churched and unchurched guests and HTB have always recognised it serves as a refresher course, a course for new Christians, as well as having some evangelistic potential.

[17] Malcolm Gladwell, *The Tipping Point*, Abacus 2002. (The ideas were known about and in circulation before this book was published.)

[18] The bell curve is officially called Roger's diffusion of innovation.

[19] From *Alpha News*, November 2001–February, 2002.

[20] John Griffiths analyses the advertising campaign in more detail in Chapter 19.

[21] *Alpha News*, March–June 2001, 'The facts: what our research revealed', p. 4. My italics.

[22] *Alpha News*, March–June 2001, 'Independent Surveys show 'Alpha is good for churches'' p. 4 (no author given). I cannot find these exact words in the other article though they do encourage churches to 'keep on plugging away year after year'.

[23] In the UK this is promoted by 'Healthy Church UK' See the website www. healthychurch.co.uk for more info.

[24] Christian Schwarz, *Natural Church Development Handbook* p. 34. (British Church Growth Association, 3rd edition, 1998. His eight quality indicators are: empowering leadership, gift-orientated ministry, passionate spirituality, func-

tional structures, inspiring worship services, holistic small groups, need-orientated evangelism, loving relationships. Schwarz argues that all of these must be present.

In actual fact I think that an examination of the overall life of HTB would indicate it has all of the ones identified by Schwarz. Also Alpha, if it is run well, does actually draw on several of them and it presupposes the capacity of the church to bring many of them to bear on Alpha and in following up guests who want to get involved in church afterwards.

Robert Warren has produced a different, but similar, list of quality characteristics in *The Healthy Churches Handbook* (Church House Publishing, 2004). Thus, healthy churches: are energised by faith; have an outward-looking focus; seek to find out what God wants; face the cost of growth and change; operate as a community; make room for all; do a few things and do them well.

For an introduction to overall church health, see Booker and Ireland, *Evangelism – which way now?*, Chapter 9.

[25] Charles Freebury provides a useful and fuller discussion of the interaction of Alpha with other features of church life and health. See *Alpha or Emmaus?*, Chapter 7 'Impact'.

As the publishing process of the current book was being completed, AI released the short book *From Vision to Action* by Tricia Neill in 2006. It is described as a practical and encouraging 'how to' for turning vision into reality and managing church growth. (Some of these ideas are related to how we present the unchanging Gospel in a changing culture and are explored in more depth in Chapter 8.) It draws very heavily on her experience at HTB and the set-up there and focuses on church management. It goes some way to addressing these wider church issues.

AI announced a one-day Stream 3 to the Alpha Conference for first time in February 2007, for major church leaders to attend, looking at wider issues of Alpha and church life. As we go to press, it has not yet happened so I cannot comment further on it.

[26] Brierley's list of what church activities are and are not (statistically) associated with growth makes for interesting reading. Leadership is vital and should be sustained over a number of years. Team leadership is effective and all members should be encouraged to take responsibility. A vision and strategic thinking also matters. A church community that is well integrated into its area, knows local needs and responds, was also effective. Being hospitable and welcoming – with a specific team to do this well – also makes a difference. Church activities that meet pastoral/spiritual needs of people at particular times or events in their lives (births/baptisms, marriages, deaths) were well attended and could well lead to new members. Attention to the young families and the elderly was also associated with growth. Other factors showed a correlation with growing churches too. (See the booklet *Leadership, Vision and Growing Churches* for more details.) Of course, numerical growth is not the only indicator of the real spiritual health of a congregation. I also suspect that in the end detailed case studies may have to replace (or at least build on) generalised statistics if we are to understand these issues properly.

[27] An introduction to mission accompaniment is due to he published by Churches Together in Britain and Ireland later in 2007 called *Journey into Growth (Introducing Mission Accompaniment and its Core Values)*. It has also established a 'Centre for Mission Accompaniment' and various networks are being established to support such work. This particular approach, developed by the Building Bridges of Hope Project, links the skills and attitudes of 'the companion' to core values of church growth identified as promoting mission.

[28] Many helpful insights from this period can be gained from a series of six tapes called *Times of Refreshing* (HTB Publications with Alpha Resources, 1995). They consist of various talks given at HTB at various points in the first 18 months of

this phenomenon. The speakers are Eleanor Mumford, John Wimber, Patrick Dixon, Sandy Millar and Nicky Gumbel.

[29] Revival, and especially the term 'revival', are most typically perhaps associated with Evangelicals and Pentecostals and most books on it reflect this and use their theologies to understand and interpret it and then to try and prepare for it too. Its theological roots probably come mainly from the Reformed (Calvinist) tradition. (The term 'revival' arose out of the American Awakenings in the 18th and 19th centuries.) For some the mark of revival is the renewed life of believers on a scale that means churches actually grow. Lapsed Christians come back to a vigorous faith and effective outreach to the really unchurched may also occur – though this is less common on a large scale. 'Renewal' or 'refreshment' are sometimes used as terms to describe still more local, and small scale, effects of a work of God. If the impact of what God is doing is such that it flows out beyond churches into all the population and affects social life, community relations, justice and peace then the term 'awakening' is sometimes used.

In fact similar phenomena are described in other forms of Christianity and predating the rise of modern Evangelical and Pentecostal Christianity. They have been written about within these other theologies too, sometimes using different terminology often with wider use of the term 'renewal'. Some attempts at ecumenical correlation and synthesis have been attempted too. Because of the problems of terminology and of classifying God's action some find it easier to talk of moves of God and times of blessing, the resultant fruit often called movements. Again moves of God have been variously categorised as waves (implying discreet graces that tend to have definite endings) and streams that imply ongoing effects even after the major – or initial – impact has been seen. (In general, 'waves' tend to be used by writers more influenced by Protestant theology and ecclesiology and 'streams' by those more influenced by Catholic thought.)

[30] Exilic imagery has been developed and applied by many contemporary church commentators in various ways. Stuart Murray takes it up in Chapter 21.

[31] There is a tendency for Christians, as individuals or communities, to focus in on themselves during 'times of refreshing' or 'moves of God' rather than grow in their commitment to service and mission. Some feel this introspection, which may well be self-centred and selfish, tends to dry up the flow of God's grace. Whatever the limitations of the ways Alpha was presented as an evangelistic tool, the sheer fact of challenging Christians to translate their experiences of God's grace into active service and mission may well have had very positive effects and greatly increased the fruitfulness, and even the length and actual grace, of this 'move of God'.

[32] This is the line of argument developed at length by Philip Meadows in Chapter 22.

PART TWO

SECTION 4

Alpha in Specific Church Settings

Section 4 consists of a closer examination of Alpha in specific denominations by members of those denominations who have a close interest and expertise in mission. The choice of denominations was partly intended to reflect the spectrum of the wide Christian family, and it also more pragmatically reflects who could be persuaded to write in the time frame of the book. There are lots of gaps and please do not feel offended if your denomination is not included! Authors either conducted their own original research or gained access to data held within their denomination and not generally available (or both), commented on how and why Alpha had impacted their denomination and on any wider reactions and issues. This section thus fills out what is currently known and indicate differences across the denominations and traditions within them.

AB

CHAPTER 11

'Alpha' and the Scottish Baptists

David Gordon

> 'First and foremost Alpha has brought people to a personal
> faith in Christ – that would be fundamental. Secondly, but
> also very importantly, is that Alpha has involved many more
> people in the church...there's that sense of serving that has
> come through it. The church has grown probably four-fold in
> the last four years and Alpha has been very, very significant
> in terms of that growth.'
>
> Colin Mutch, Pastor, Southside Christian Fellowship, Ayr

The story of this Baptist church in Ayrshire is tremendously encouraging, and it is interesting to note from the outset that the pastor
identifies a clear link between the use of Alpha and the growth of his
congregation. If there were no other stories to tell, the Baptist family
in Scotland can give thanks to God for how this 'programme' has been
used by Him to bring a significant number of people in this one area to
a living faith in Jesus Christ as Saviour and Lord.

The Baptist Union of Scotland was formed in 1869, and presently
consists of 176 churches with approximately 14,000 members. With
a regular church attendance, however, of nearer 25,000, it is possibly
the largest Christian grouping in Scotland outside the Church of Scotland and the Roman Catholic church. Historically, Baptists have stood
within the Evangelical tradition, and have always been committed to
evangelism. One of only three statements in the Declaration of Principle of the Union is 'that it is the duty of every disciple to bear witness to
the Gospel of Jesus Christ and to take part in the evangelisation of the
world.' It would be surprising, therefore, if Baptist churches throughout Scotland had not considered Alpha as a possible tool within their
overall mission strategy!

The **8 key findings** in this chapter have been produced as a result of
a questionnaire sent to Baptist churches within two distinct geographical areas:

Glasgow (G) – including the wider urban area;
Inverness (I) – including the Moray coast and the Orkneys;

There was approximately a 50% return rate within each area.

1. Deployment within Baptist churches

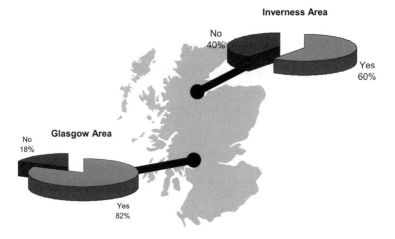

These figures suggest that the percentage of Baptist churches using Alpha could be considerably higher than the 58% indicated in the Scottish Church Census of 2002.[1] It is possible, of course, that church leaders with a positive experience of Alpha may simply have been more inclined to complete the questionnaire! It is more likely, however, that the differential can be understood by the fact that the collected data is an accumulated total of those that have ever run Alpha. This is in line with our research which indicates that almost 50% of those churches responding from within the Inverness area only started using Alpha within the last three to four years! The significant regional variation may also caution against an over optimistic interpretation. Having said that, the national profile of Alpha, particularly within the large urban conurbations has increased considerably in recent years, and this may help to explain the apparent increase in 'take-up' within Glasgow.

Even though our research does not identify the precise number of churches that are currently using Alpha, I would suggest from personal contact with most of the churches responding that as many as 70% have conducted Alpha in the last twelve month period.

There has been very little usage of prison, student or senior Alpha although there has been some take-up of youth Alpha mainly within the larger suburban churches.

The most popular alternative used by Baptist churches is Christianity Explored, and in the Inverness area, it appears to be just as popular as Alpha.

2.   What type of Baptist churches are using Alpha?

- It is difficult to be precise, but in general terms there appears to be a greater usage of Alpha among those churches that describe themselves as 'evangelical charismatic'. Generally speaking our 'northern' churches would be less open to charismatic influences, and this is highlighted by their comments that suggest very clearly that the charismatic emphasis within Alpha is the primary reason for not using the material.
- Even though there is a considerable regional variation, Alpha is being used in all kinds of church environment (city centre; housing scheme; island; suburban etc) within each area.
- There appears to be no variation on the take-up of Alpha by Baptist churches on the basis of their size.

3.   What is the nature of the relationship with Alpha, UK?

- It is interesting to note that especially within Glasgow, almost every church using Alpha had registered with the Alpha office. This contrasts sharply with the research done in 1999 among Baptist churches in England and Wales[2] where less than 50% of churches using Alpha had registered! Even though the materials can still be purchased from any Christian bookshop, it is an encouraging sign from Alpha's perspective that their ongoing encouragement in this area is now paying dividends.
- It is also pertinent to note that only three Baptist churches indicated that they had ever made contact with the Alpha Scotland office, and none of these were from the Inverness area.
- There is also evidence suggesting that those churches further north are less likely to send people on Alpha training courses especially if they are located in London or even the Central Belt of Scotland.

4.   How many times have churches held Alpha courses?

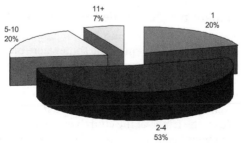

- It would appear that 80% of our churches that have used Alpha have conducted more than one course. This seems to suggest a confidence in the programme itself.

- The average number of courses held by Scottish Baptist churches is **4.9.** Even if this figure is adjusted because of the distortion caused by one church hosting over 30 courses, the average figure per church is still **3.**
- The vast majority of churches run one course per year and this is normally held in September/October to coincide with the 'national initiative'.
- Even though the 'pattern of frequency' will in reality be much more difficult to interpret than the simple pie chart illustrates it does appear that most of our churches who have commenced using Alpha continue to do so on a regular basis. For example, out of the 53% who have run courses on 2-4 occasions, most have only started using Alpha in the last five years! In other words, the numbers who have ditched Alpha after one or two courses appears to be quite small!
- These figures are in keeping with the observations by Peter Brierley that 'perserverance pays off', and that the longer Alpha is sustained the more likely the church is to experience numerical growth.[3]

5. Did the church incorporate a 'Holy Spirit' weekend?

- It is clear that most churches did incorporate an away weekend into their programme, but in some cases this was reduced to a day and held on the church premises.
- It is interesting that every church describing itself as 'evangelical charismatic' incorporated a special weekend away.
- There appears to be no direct correlation between the number of people coming to faith and the existence/nature of a 'weekend away'!
- There appears to be no correlation between churches sending representatives to Alpha training events and the incorporation of a weekend away.

6. How many people attended and who were they?

It is difficult to ascertain the exact numbers of people attending each course, but the average figure seems to be somewhere between 10 and 20. Of those attending, approximately 40% had not previously been attending the church. In some situations, people have simply turned up on the 'opening night' as a result of information gleaned either from church notice boards or via the internet. The vast majority, however, have been people on the fringe of the church or friends and colleagues of existing church members. We have no way of ascertaining to what extent these people had any previous church connection!

Almost every church leader hosting Alpha has indicated that people have been 'helped on their journey to faith' as a result of attending. In general terms, those churches attracting a higher proportion of 'outsiders' to Alpha have indicated larger numbers of people. The figures given by church leaders are, however, so varied that they are impossible to analyse satisfactorily. I suspect the variation has more to do with their understanding of the 'nature of conversion' than with the effectiveness of the course itself! In some situations, only people who have had a traditional evangelical 'conversion experience' will have been included, but in other situations where 'salvation' is understood more as a 'process' or a 'journey' then the question will have been answered very differently.

7. What most attracted churches to Alpha?

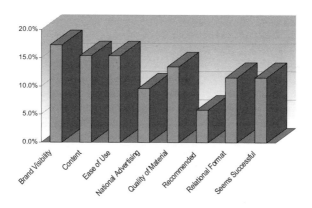

- It would appear that Alpha's high profile (national advertising combined with brand visibility and stories of success) is the most significant factor in church leaders opting to use the Alpha material.
- The content and quality of the material together with its 'easy to use' format is also important.
- Even though the 'relational format' is still a selling point, it appears to be not the most significant factor presumably because there are an increasing number of other 'process evangelism' alternatives on the market.

8. What impact has Alpha had on Baptist churches?

It is tremendously difficult to assess the overall impact of Alpha within our family of churches, but the following graphs (overleaf) depict the typical patterns of decline and growth in churches that have implemented Alpha. Once again, it needs to be recognised that these figures are based upon the responses obtained from pastors, and not from raw data!

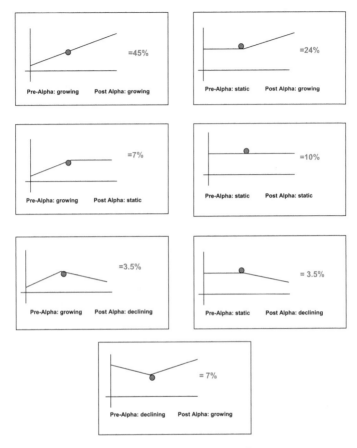

The following five observations can me made.

1) *Before embarking on the Alpha programme the majority of churches indicated that they were already experiencing growth*

These graphs do not permit the assertion in a simplistic fashion that the implementation of Alpha is responsible for the patterns of either growth or decline. They probably reflect the fact that 'growing' churches are much more likely to be engaged in evangelistic programmes in the first place, and are more open to explore new initiatives. It can not be denied that where churches are using Alpha there is a greater likelihood of such churches reporting increases in membership and attendances at worship. It is claiming too much, however, to suggest that Alpha was *the* factor resulting in the ongoing growth of these churches!

In particular it may be that churches who recognise the changing culture in which mission occurs, and the changing context in which people come to faith (the move from event to process) are much likely to opt for any one of the courses built around a relational evangelistic approach. For example, research comparing the effectiveness of 'process evangelism courses' shows that the number of people coming to faith is remarkably similar whatever the programme![4]

On a cautionary note, it would also appear from personal knowledge of and involvement within the churches that the perception of some pastors is different from the reality! From 1995 to 2005, a significant number of churches described as 'growing' have actually declined significantly either in membership or attendance or both!

2) *It is nevertheless true from the overall returns received that churches not using Alpha are more likely to be in decline!*
As with the above comments there is no direct causal relationship between the 'lack of Alpha' and the decline, but rather an indication that the church is probably not engaging in mission at any level.

3) *The most encouraging result is the number of churches previously static who experienced growth following Alpha.*
The percentage of Scottish Baptist churches using Alpha is almost double that of the Church of Scotland and the percentage difference is even greater when compared to the Episcopal or Roman Catholic churches. Between 1994 and 2002 when all the major denominations in Scotland experienced considerable ongoing decline, it is interesting to note that the Baptists experienced a small increase, albeit by only 1%. Even though there can be no simple relationship between the two, it is encouraging that after many years of decline some of our 'static' congregations are rediscovering a 'mission' dimension, and if Alpha has played even a little part in that, thanks be to God!

4) *There were also a number of churches who either were growing or static prior to using Alpha that have since declined or saw no change!*
This clearly demonstrates that Alpha is not a panacea for all ills, but is a further reminder that the use of Alpha or any other programme will probably not be effective unless it is accompanied by a corresponding change of ethos and outlook by the wider congregation. It would appear that some churches have used Alpha as a 'bolt-on' without thinking about the values that underlie it.

There is clearly a wide variation in the response to Alpha even from 'similar' churches in 'similar' areas, and this may suggest in addition to the above that there were other factors present. Based purely on personal involvement in a number of Alpha courses within Scottish Baptist churches, there is considerable variation in the quality of the 'Alpha event' being offered. Such factors range from the quality of food and the ambience of the location to the nature and quality of the presentation (live speaker V video).

In some situations the Alpha material and format has been adapted and the overall 'package' has suffered as a result.

5) *Even though the numbers are very small it is interesting that each declining church experienced some measure of growth after using Alpha!*

This should be an encouragement for any church 'in decline' – it is possible to turn things around! Even though these churches are often small, Alpha provides an easy to use, 'off the shelf' programme that is likely to be effective when combined with a renewed desire to reach out to friends and neighbours with the gospel.

—

In conclusion, Alpha has been used by churches of all shapes and sizes within the Scottish Baptist family. In spite of the reservations that some of our ministers have about certain aspects of the 'course' (too charismatic; little emphasis on sin and repentance; baptism ignored) it has, generally speaking, been not only warmly welcomed, but also put to good use! So let me tell you about Donna...

She went to Alpha at the invitation of her friend Kathleen and became a Christian. At the end of the Alpha Away Day she said a prayer and asked Jesus to come into her life. 'I now have a personal relationship with Jesus and I pray every day. Christianity is now my whole way of life. Now I'm on this mission to get everybody converted and have what I've got.' So she invited her friend Margot, who brought her partner Inglis. They became Christians. Then Donna invited her friend Tom, her sister Karen and another friend Simon. All are now Christians. To be continued...

Notes

[1] Peter Brierly, *Turning the Tide, Report of the 2002 Scottish Church Census*, Christian Research, London, 2003

[2] Darrell Jackson, *The impact of Alpha on Baptist churches,* an unpublished report for the Baptist Union of Great Britain, 2002

[3] Peter Brierley, *Church Growth in the 1990's,* Christian Research, 2000.

[4] Mark Ireland, *A study of the effectiveness of Process Evangelism Courses in the Diocese of Lichfield, with special reference to Alpha,* dissertation in part-fulfilment for MA in Evangelism Studies, University of Sheffield at Cliff College, 2000.

CHAPTER 12

Belonging then Believing:
Alpha and The Salvation Army

*Dr Helen Cameron**

Introduction

In this chapter, I analyse the statistical information available about the take up of Alpha in The Salvation Army in the UK and supplement it with data from sixteen telephone interviews with leaders of corps (the term for local churches). As a sociologist, I feel that comparisons generate valuable debate even if they don't offer firm conclusions and so I have also collected data about open air evangelistic services and the provision of meals in luncheon clubs. The chapter seeks to ident-ify some issues both practical and more theological in the implement-ation of Alpha.

The take up of Alpha

It is not possible to establish the exact take up of Alpha in The Salvation Army. The data available provide a number of estimates. If the Alpha register is a guide, then 239 Salvation Army corps are registered, 31% of all corps. However, only 55% of those corps who reported running Alpha in 2002–4 are listed on the register. But it is also evident that many corps who no longer run Alpha are still listed on the register. Earlier research by Escott showed 22% of corps running Alpha in 1996 and 39% in 1998. Salvation Army activity attendance data shows 18% of corps running Alpha in 2002 to 2004 but this under-represents the total because attendance data is collected over an 8-week period each year (see endnote on methodology).

If take up data is imprecise, there is trend data available for 2002 to 2004, see Table 1. This shows a slight decrease both in the proportion of corps taking part and in the average attendance at an Alpha session.

Table 1: Take up of Alpha during the 8-week
attendance-measuring period in 2002–4

Year	Number of Corps	Proportion of all corps	Average attendance per session
2002	73	8.9%	10.3
2003	66	8.3%	13.4
2004	62	7.7%	14.4

*Helen is a member of The Salvation Army and a sociologist but writes here in a personal capacity.

Eighteen corps are listed as having run Alpha in all three years (during the counting period), three with growing attendance, five with static attendance and ten with declining attendance. The range of Alpha weekly session sizes across these eighteen corps is between 5 and 44 people. This compares with the overall range of session sizes between 5–50, suggesting that session size is not a factor in who does Alpha regularly.

The data has limitations, but it looks as if over half of Salvation Army corps have experienced Alpha at some point, but that it is now gradually declining both in terms of numbers of corps involved and size of sessions.

Sixteen telephone interviews were conducted, eight with corps who ran Alpha just in 2002 and eight with corps who had run it in all three years (see endnote for methodology).

Of the eight corps who appear in the 2002 statistics only, three had in fact run it subsequently but outside the counting period. Two of the eight had fixed dates to run it again and another two had intentions to do so. Reasons for stopping Alpha, included a change of commanding officer (minister), the fact it had been seen as a one-off initiative, and insufficient take up. The number of times Alpha had been run varied between once and four times. One corps had used other material with a group of new attenders and was now planning to use Alpha with them. Three of the eight had someone who had received Alpha training. One corps had recruited eight new members as a result of running Alpha, another one member and the rest no new members. Of the eight corps, two had a membership that was slightly increasing, two decreasing and four static membership. Static membership was seen as an achievement given the numbers of elderly members dying and needing to be replaced. The membership size of these corps varied from 18 to 234 with three of the eight being in the largest 10% of corps.

Turning to the eight corps who had run Alpha in 2002–4, five intended to run it again, one was now trying Youth Alpha but two had no plans to run it again. Reasons for stopping Alpha included a change of officer and insufficient take up. Two corps had used the course just with existing members with one feeling it had now served its purpose and the other planning to run it for non-members. The number of times Alpha had been run varied between three and fourteen with an average of seven times. Two corps were planning to use the Willow Creek 'Journeys' course as a precursor to Alpha because they found Alpha assumed too much prior knowledge and lasted too many weeks. Another two were now using Salvation Army material 'Battle Orders' designed to prepare people for soldiership but opening the study group to anyone who was interested. Six of these eight corps had someone who had received Alpha training. Three corps reported an increase in membership and a further two new attenders at worship as a direct result of Alpha. Of these eight corps, two had a membership that was increasing (one of which had discontinued Alpha), three had a decreasing membership and three a static membership. The membership size of these corps varied from 30 to 284 with five of the eight being in the largest 10% of corps.

The impact of Alpha had been greatest in those corps that had run it most frequently but there was no difference between the two groups of corps in their likelihood of membership growth or decline.

Comparisons with other activities

Salvation and Holiness are the twin pillars of Salvation Army belief. From its founding, The Salvation Army was known for innovative methods of evangelism, the most common of which was to hold an outdoor service using a brass band to attract a crowd, with singing, preaching and testimony to hold their attention. This activity continues, see Table 2 below. The proportion of corps holding Open Air Meetings is declining but the average size of these meetings is increasing. Of the sixteen corps I interviewed, two were holding regular open air services and three on an occasional or seasonal basis. However, only one of these reported anyone attending worship as a result of this activity.

Table 2: Open Air Meetings during the 8-week
attendance-measuring period in 200–4

Year	Number of Corps	Proportion of all corps	Average attendance per session
2002	226	28%	28
2003	201	26%	27
2004	178	23%	35

For The Salvation Army, the call to holiness has involved a holistic concern for the person, body, mind and soul, meaning that many corps provide community services knowing that, in serving neighbour and stranger, they are serving Christ. Serving a meal is a key feature of Alpha and so I was interested to look at the outcome of meals served without a direct evangelistic purpose. The 8-week annual count captures data on luncheon clubs which provide a low-cost cooked meal often to older people. This may be done in association with club activities. Table 3 shows that the proportion of corps holding luncheon clubs is increasing but that the average attendance is decreasing, maybe because of their older client group.

Table 3: Luncheon Clubs during the 8-week
attendance-measuring period in 2002–4

Year	Number of Corps	Proportion of all corps	Average attendance per session
2002	303	38%	33
2003	314	40%	30
2004	325	42%	30

Of the sixteen corps I interviewed, ten were running a luncheon club and a further three a community café. Of these thirteen, four had new members and a further five new attenders at worship as a result of this activity. This compares with five that had new members and three new attenders as a result of Alpha.

From such a small interview sample it is hard to be definitive but it seems that Open Air Services are being used by a decreasing number of corps as an evangelistic tool and that where they are being used they do not result in new members or attenders. Given the iconic status of Open Air Meetings in The Salvation Army, Alpha has by contrast grown rapidly and had a measurable evangelistic impact. Luncheon Clubs and Community Cafés are increasing and amongst the interview sample seem to have had a similar impact to Alpha in terms of numbers drawn into membership and worship. However, this statistical comparison doesn't do justice to the way in which Alpha is being used as an evangelistic tool and so the chapter moves in the next section to discuss both practical and evangelistic issues arising from this research.

Issues in Alpha implementation

In a short telephone interview, it is impossible to explore theological issues in depth, and so unsurprisingly many of the issues people reported were practical. However, there were also comments which raised questions about the nature of evangelism.

Practical issues

There appear to be a number of practical barriers to the ongoing rather than episodic use of Alpha. The most significant seems to be the discontinuity that can occur when there is a change of officer (minister). These changes happen less often than in the past with most officers serving a five to seven year term in a corps. Three of the four corps with the most sustained and successful use of Alpha had lay co-oridinators and the programme had continued across the ministry of more than one officer. The moving on of officers can also be an advantage with three officers saying they had implemented or planned to implement Alpha because they had previous positive experience of it. Unsurprisingly, the take up of Alpha training was higher in the group of corps that had made sustained use of Alpha. Despite my selecting corps for telephone interview at random from the list of participants only three of the sixteen were below average size. Three of the four who had made sustained and successful use of Alpha were in the top 10% of size. This suggests that the resources to run Alpha are more likely to be found in larger corps.

Although I want to be cautious given the limited data, there seem to be three main models of implementing Alpha:

- internal – where the Alpha material is used in an existing worship or bible study slot;
- episodic – where Alpha is run when a sufficient group of interested people has been assembled through other activities and networks;
- integrated – where Alpha is an ongoing programme linked into small-group structures such as house groups or cell groups.

Of these three, the last seemed to be most effective but only two corps could be said to have achieved this and both had memberships between 180 and 200.

Evangelistic issues

The data also raises questions about the process of evangelism and whether or not it leads to church membership. The corps that had gained members or attenders whilst running Alpha also had other ways, including community programmes, for drawing people into the life of the corps. Some were using Alpha to introduce Christianity to people who were attending a variety of activities in their building. There seemed to be very few for whom Alpha would be their first point of contact with the corps. Indeed some corps were going as far as to judge when people were 'ready for Alpha' with two implementing a course that people took before they could move on to Alpha. Concerns with the Alpha material seemed to focus on the videos which were felt by some to be too middle class, too long and assuming too much prior knowledge of the Bible. The four corps that had made most consistent use of Alpha all said that it was the turning point for people new to the corps, the thing that facilitated making a commitment to Christ. They were also clear that it needed to be followed up by small groups or other discipling material to enable people to grow in faith. The data on lunch clubs suggests that the Alpha meal may be a significant acknowledgement of the holistic nature of human relating.

Conclusions

The use of Alpha in The Salvation Army grew rapidly in the late 1990s. There is some evidence that its use is starting to wane. Where it has been implemented in an integrated way it is generating new members and worship attenders.

Alpha is being used in a range of ways, some of which reflect practical problems in its implementation, others of which reflect a range of views about the process of evangelism. The corps that made most effective use of Alpha, presented evangelism as a journey that started with belonging to a group, led to believing in Christ and for some led to the additional behavioural requirements of Salvation Army soldiership. The sense of belonging however, could be generated by a range of activities including lunch clubs. Alpha enthusiasts found the course invaluable in moving people from belonging to believing. This journey image of evangelism contrasts with image of the Open Air meeting where the gospel is proclaimed to strangers with the aim of bringing them to belief.

Note on methodology

The statistical data used in this chapter comes form The Salvation Army United Kingdom Territory Corps Diary Project which commenced in 2002. All corps collect attendance data at every activity over an 8-week period in March/April. This is most effective in capturing weekly and monthly activities rather than episodic activity like Alpha. The proportions of corps participating are calculated using the total number of corps open that year and including outposts, outreach centres and church plants which between them account for 10% of the total. This statistical data was supplemented by short telephone interviews with 8 of the 41 corps listed as running Alpha in 2002 only and 8 of the 18 corps listed as running Alpha in 2002, 2003 and 2004. The corps ranged in size between 18 and 284 members (soldiers and adherents) with larger corps being over-represented despite random selection from the list.

Acknowledgements

My thanks go to Major David Pickard, Statistics Officers, The Salvation Army Territorial Headquarters and the sixteen anonymous interviewees.

References

Cameron, H., *The Dynamics of Membership: A Review of Theory, Practice and Policy in the UK*. London: Centre for Civil Society, LSE, 2005.

Davie, G., *Religion in Britain Since 1945: Believing without belonging.* Oxford, Blackwell, 1994.

Escott, P., *Alpha in the Army.* London, THQ, 1997.

Hunt, S., *The Alpha Enterprise: Evangelism in a Post-Christian Era*. Aldershot, Ashgate, 2004.

CHAPTER 13

Alpha and the Kirk

Perspectives on how Alpha has impacted
the life of the Church of Scotland[1]

Rev. David E. P. Currie

Personal Experience

As minister of East Kilbride West Kirk for 17 years (1983–2000) I have
had a reasonable amount of personal experience in running Alpha
courses. Then in my present role as an Adviser in Mission and Evangelism, churches often ask me to recommend good resources for small-
group work, helping people to share their faith, etc.. In this regard,
it has to be said that Alpha is still one such resource which is often
mentioned – by me: recommended as one possible really good starting point; by them: some want help to have a go at it, others are already
doing it because they love it, and some don't want anything to do with
it (for reasons I'll touch on later).

Statistics

What might be helpful is to share some of the results of the research
carried out by Dr. Peter Brierley in his book *Turning the Tide'(the Report
of the 2002 Scottish Church Census)* where, among other things, 'the
Scottish Church Census explored the extent to which it (Alpha) had
been used by churches'.[2] This research revealed that 27% of Scottish
churches overall (i.e. about 1,120 churches) had held the Alpha course
– e.g. more than half, 58%, of Baptist churches, and almost a third
(29%) of Church of Scotland churches.

This figure may be slightly higher than I would have expected from
the figures recently obtained from the Alpha Course Co-ordinator
at Holy Trinity Brompton who shared that 'the number of Church of
Scotland churches presently registered with us as running or having
run Alpha is 222'. The number of Church of Scotland charges in the
2004/2005 Year Book is 1,229, and if 29% of Church of Scotland charges
have run Alpha courses then this gives a total of 356, so there is a bit
of a discrepancy. However, some may have run courses in the past
then stopped for some reason and no longer show up on any central

records, and presumably there will also be a good number of congregations who use the material but don't register officially with HTB.

Research and Reports

In my post as Senior Adviser in Mission I am personally aware that quite a lot of students base their degree dissertation, and indeed postgraduate thesis, on matters relating to the analysis of process evangelism courses, and of Alpha in particular, but time and space do not allow me the luxury of cataloguing or discussing these in any great detail. Suffice it to say as a kind of 'back-handed' compliment to those who market Alpha that this in itself is a sign that there is a recognisable, unique commodity here which students at least deem is worth researching. (In nearly 20 years of Parish Ministry no-one ever asked me about the impact my Membership Course was making on our community – a fairly standard basic 'Christian Belief' course probably very similar to the one most parish ministers would use, and actually not too far removed from Alpha-type teaching).

What has the impact of the Alpha Course been on the Church of Scotland?

However, the one piece of research I do want to refer to is an official report contained in 'The Church of Scotland General Assembly Reports 1999', pages 20/64–20/67 and titled 'What has the impact of the Alpha Course been on the Church of Scotland?'. This report was instigated as a result of a discussion of the Alpha Course at a previous General Assembly when, after a typical Assembly debate with contributions from the 'broad church' we all love to hate (some evangelicals loved it, some anti-charismatics wanted us to be very wary of it – you know the kind of thing!), it was finally decided (surprise, surprise!) that 'The Apologetics Committee is instructed by the General Assembly to report on the impact of the Alpha Course upon the Church of Scotland'.

The main thrust of the Committee's research was via a questionnaire sent to all congregations asking whether they had run one or more Alpha courses; followed by a more detailed questionnaire to the 'Yes' respondents. (Meantime the 'No' respondents were asked to submit any comments on the first questionnaire.)

It may be worth noting that the responses were received during the Spring and Summer of 1998 and therefore before the Autumn 1998 National Alpha Initiative – i.e. the Committee's research pre-dates this Initiative (during which time a number of articles and reports appeared in the daily press and religious media).

It has to be said that the response to the questionnaire was fairly disappointing. Nevertheless, 90 churches confirmed that they had run Alpha, 124 responded 'No' with a comment, and 42 responded 'No' with no comment. Of the 90 'Yes' churches, 58 returned a second questionnaire fully completed, and even although we may suspect that those bothering to fill this in would be on the whole supportive churches, it nevertheless seems fair in this article to summarise some of the findings *of this group of 58.*

- First courses run by churches have averaged less than 10% of non-church members attending. For subsequent courses the average rises to 20%.
- No discernable bias in either geographical or urban/rural distribution is indicated by the locations of the 'Yes' respondent churches. Nor has use of the Alpha course been restricted to congregations of one theological style or ethos.
- Over 500 professions of faith were reported from the 58 churches as a result of Alpha. More than 350 course attendees had joined the church, while almost 700 had become more actively involved in their church, and more than 60 are seeking to become elders. Indications were that those churches which included the meal and the weekend or day away reported better results.
- Most churches commented very favourably when comparing Alpha with existing Enquirers' Courses – e.g. 'Alpha replaces previous courses', 'Easily the best both in content and presentation. All ages respond positively to Nicky Gumbel'.
- Without exception (again, in this group of 58), when asked about the impact on individuals and congregations, the comments were positive –
  - ○ People reaching a new understanding of discipleship and the faith of Christians being deepened.
  - ○ Some attendees admitted that, before Alpha, they had not understood what the church was about and certainly did not know Jesus as their Saviour.
  - ○ Many who were nominal members found their faith came alive.
  - ○ Knowledge, faith and fellowship have all increased.
  - ○ People have been more willing to talk about their faith and to participate enthusiastically in worship.

The report comes to a conclusion with these honest and helpful comments.

> In any survey it is likely that those most motivated to respond will be those with strong views, whether positive or negative. In this regard, very few negative responses have been received and, while recognising that the 'Yes' respondents were a self-selecting group, the responses from the churches that have run the Alpha Course have been predominantly positive about its overall value. This is true even where some churches

have felt it necessary to change the emphasis of, for example, the Holy Spirit teaching. While it could be argued that watching a video of one person speaking for 45 minutes is not an educationally sound approach, and that the central London cultural ethos is inappropriate to a Scottish audience, those who have used the Course have not found this to be a barrier.

Finally, in conclusion, the methods used by Alpha would seem to be very valuable, namely:

- A fellowship meal;
- A clear systematic presentation;
- The opportunity to ask questions and hear other people asking questions;
- A mix of live speaking, video and discussion;
- A day of weekend away together.[3]

An Alpha Plus or An Alpha Minus?

I think it would be fair to say that the Alpha Course is serving our church very well indeed.

Of course, in a 'broad church' there will be church leaders and others who either love the Alpha Course or detest it. Having tried to do justice to the views of those in our denomination who are enthusiastic supporters of Alpha, let me now give expression to some of the reservations voiced by others over the past few years, and even though much of this is anecdotal evidence, it would be unfair not to mention some of these issues.

There are some who say that 45-minute talks by a middle-class London lawyer do not go down very well in parts of Scotland. The more serious criticism here is that some believe the style and length of presentations to be culturally inappropriate with some groups, especially in our post-modern experiential society – 'Don't just tell me what you believe, show me it in action.'

Perhaps the most distressing and challenging situation I have come across is the church who really caught the 'Alpha bug' in its early days. They were one of the first churches in Scotland to run the courses and have tremendous 'success' with them – swelling evening services in what is a fairly small village, etc. But a few years down the line it was becoming increasingly difficult to get any more 'new faces' along out of a small local 'pool'. The initial batch of enthusiastic 'outside visitors' slowly disappeared, and what had been submerged local divisions over the charismatic emphasis (real or imagined, it doesn't really matter) rose to the surface – all leading to a culture of blame, disenchantment, and the eventual breakdown of the minister. Now, let me first of all make it quite clear about what I'm *not* saying: I'm not saying that Alpha is to blame here since there were all sorts of factors involved. But what

I *am saying* is: be well prepared, support local leaders, have plans and strategies in place for effective follow-up, etc.

There is, however, a fairly deep division in our denomination about the emphasis placed on the Holy Spirit material – in particular the teaching on Speaking in Tongues and Healing. Some churches avoid the course altogether simply because of this content, while others omit this material in part or in whole.

Again referring to the Report mentioned previously:[4]

Answers to the question 'How did you respond to the special emphasis on the Holy Spirit?' varied from –

- Not very positively;
- Did not focus on tongues unless asked;
- Did only one study on this issue and did not do the 'Weekend Away' videos;

to –

- What special emphasis?
- A difficult subject well explained. Some want to see the video again;
- Very positively. It was an eye-opener for some. It brought their faith to life.

Some church leaders in our denomination then talk in very positive terms about Alpha and would give it an 'Alpha Plus', while others give it an 'Alpha Minus' –

Of the 124 'No' responses, but with a comment, 7% had a course planned or underway, 27% were actively considering it, 35% had not yet considered it, and 32% had decided against running a course. The 32% who decided against running an Alpha Course break down as follows. Almost 40% of them are using an alternative or have access to Alpha at a nearby church. One third of them did not consider the course to be of sufficient value or interest. Seven churches (18%) were concerned about the way the Holy Spirit and Healing topics are handled by the Course.[5]

By way of showing my appreciation to those who were good enough to respond to my pleas for assistance with research for this article, I now want to share a couple of very positive stories – one from our heavily-populated Central Belt and one from just about as far North as you can go, Orkney.

1. First, David Geddes is the Area Facilitator for the Presbytery of Hamilton with several years' experience of organising and running Alpha courses and he shared the following helpful comments.

- I offer in Lanarkshire a Holy Spirit day away, which groups have found better than – (a) organising their own day away, or (b) organising a weekend away. I have offered this day in November for about 7–8 years and found it useful as a focal point for many groups (numbers will range from 70–120); for clearly presenting a gospel challenge; for offering the opportunity for ministry that many church/alpha leaders are unsure about themselves.
- I think the course is a useful tool. I believe the Church of Scotland is now better taught on the Holy Spirit. We have not been an experiential church in recent years but now in some places it is possible to receive all kinds of experiential ministry in a local church situation.
- The course is certainly one which requires the minister to like the charismatic flavour. Where he/she has not, some ministers have written their own course along similar lines. Others have used 'Christianity Explored' or 'the Y course'. Alpha has in those situations been a catalyst for the use of alternative seeker courses.
- A weakness relating to the course is not Alpha itself (which is not perfect but is really useful), but is the church's view of outreach. We are not a church comfortable with outreach, so when we ask people to invite their friends we and they find that difficult. The result may be guilt or courses fading after one or two being run. If Alpha is to work there needs to be teaching from the pulpit which moves on from the 'You should do mission' to an understanding of the real need for mission – stories of lives changed, what we have in Christ, prayer, and stories of outreach/conversions in other parts of the world. In short, a new focus on mission which touches mind and heart.

2. Tom Clark is the minister of Orphir linked with Stenness, Stromness, Orkney, and kindly replied in these glowing terms.
   - It is one of the most amazing courses around at the present time, to be used across the board, from people with no faith to people with some, yet open to learn more. It has been the greatest encouragement to our congregation, bringing people to a clearer understanding of the Christian message and to new life in Christ. It has given people of all ages and social backgrounds a new confidence to witness and take active part in service.
   - It is used as an outreach to people outside the church who find it easier to meet in a home in an informal setting with open discussion.

- It makes the teaching so relevant in 'bight-size' portions and with a touch of humour.
- It has been an encouragement to the congregations to see young and older members becoming much more bold and confident.
- In almost 20 years in the ministry I have not found any other course coming anywhere near what is available in Alpha.

Conclusion – or Omega!

Finally, then, I want to thank those who have been willing to share their thinking about the Alpha Course. As a result of this, I can say that – while noting some reservations with regard to style of delivery, weighting of content, possible post-Alpha trauma or anything else – for the time being this seems to be *the* Basic Christianity Course which is being used more than any other (in Scotland and around the world). It is serving some churches very well indeed as they try different ways of sharing the faith and has been responsible for helping to shift our thinking in mission terms from event to process and from teaching *expliciter* to fellowship and teaching together.

Notes

[1] This article was completed before Alpha Scotland began its work in the spring of 2005.

[2] Peter Brierley *Turning the Tide*, Christian Research, 2003, p. 109.

[3] *The Church of Scotland General Assembly Reports 1999*, pages 20/64–20/67.

[4] Ibid.

[5] Ibid.

CHAPTER 14

Alpha and Methodism

Charles Freebury

The 'shape' of Methodism

Methodism is currently the second largest protestant denomination in Britain after the Church of England, with which it is now formally in Covenant. Both are mixed tradition denominations with a similar profile: roughly one-third each evangelical, broad/liberal and 'other'.[1] The Methodist Church Life Profile (CLP)[2] reveals in more detail that its two main traditions are 'non-aligned' and evangelical (various groupings). A good number describe themselves as 'moderate' and a small proportion as 'liberal'.

CLP also reveals that Methodists are stronger than other denominations in social activity, welcoming and practical caring, but much less strong on attending devotional groups and undertaking evangelism. These factors have a very marked effect on the impact of Alpha in Methodist churches.

The 'fit' of Alpha with Methodist ethos and theology
Historically

Early Methodists would have been on home ground with both the doctrinal and experiential (including charismatic) sides of Alpha. Michael Green notes the affinity in *I believe in the Holy Spirit*[3] and Andrew Baguley develops this further.[4] Methodism's roots make much of experiential aspects of the faith, following John Wesley's own conversion experience, which he described as 'I felt my heart strangely warmed'. The 'class meeting', a system of structured small groups for study, prayer and oversight, is one of its most quoted aspects. The need for personal salvation and holiness is demonstrated in the 'four alls' that remain a distinguishing characteristic of Methodism today: 'All need to be saved. All may be saved. All may know themselves to be saved. All may be saved to the uttermost'.[5]

Today

In principle, Alpha fits well with Methodist doctrine and aims. The 1932 Deed of Union states that: 'it ever remembers that in the providence of

God Methodism was raised up to spread scriptural holiness through the land by the proclamation of the evangelical faith'. A set of four focus themes, known as 'Our Calling', is now being widely used in British Methodism: Worship, Learning and Caring, Service and Evangelism. All fit well with Alpha although Alpha is very weak in content on issues of social service, action and justice,[6] which are especially important in Methodism. A supplementary set of key Methodist priorities includes a statement that is entirely in harmony with Alpha and reflects the much higher importance that Methodism now places on evangelism: 'Developing confidence in evangelism and in the capacity to speak of God and faith in ways that make sense to all involved'.[7]

In practice, as in any mixed tradition denomination, the fit varies from church to church and person to person: some are fully at home with all aspects of Alpha, others feel acutely uncomfortable.

The impact of Alpha

Since 2000, there has been some research of Alpha specific to Methodist churches,[8] but none has been undertaken centrally, therefore this assessment is based on a mix of research and practitioners' experience. Both reveal a high degree of consistency across Methodism in the outcomes of Alpha. CLP also provides helpful clues to understanding the nature of Alpha's impact.

Usage of Alpha

As in other denominations, those Methodist churches with an evangelical tradition or leadership are likely to be ongoing users of Alpha. Those with a mixed or non-aligned tradition may well try Alpha a couple of times but then either discontinue, or conversely find that the church is changed through Alpha. The more liberal churches would not normally choose Alpha. Many Methodists are not necessarily strongly 'for' or 'against' the charismatic side of Alpha, but simply feel uncomfortable with it, apprehensive of what they might encounter and of consequent change. Some churches therefore omit the more experiential parts of the course.

The level of take-up of Alpha, hard to assess but perhaps up to one in five Methodist churches nationally, appears similar to that in the Church of England, unsurprising given the similarity in churchmanship profile. In many parts of the country, it seems that most churches that are likely to use Alpha have already done so, therefore any significant increase in take-up in these regions seems unlikely.

Where Methodism starts to diverge from others is in its low use of alternative evangelistic courses where, for one reason or another, Alpha is not favoured. The most-used alternative in other churches is *Emmaus*, but while this is well-known to Anglicans it is hardly known at all to Methodists; nor are other widely used courses such as *Christianity Explored* or *Start!*. Some traditional Methodists can be inclined to limit their resources to those with Methodist credentials, and this includes only the niche courses *Essence* (for those attracted to New Age or alternative spiritualities) and *Journey* (whose perspective is derived from liberation theology). Consequently, if a Methodist church does not use Alpha, it may not use an evangelistic course at all, so reducing the total take-up of this important type of evangelism within Methodism.

Because Methodists are more likely than other denominations to be involved in social activities and service,[9] they have a big advantage in the strength and number of their social relationships, with the consequent respect and trust in the community that this brings – which is often considerably higher than the church realises. This means a large number of contacts to invite to an Alpha supper. Methodists are famed for catering well, so the Alpha supper will come naturally!

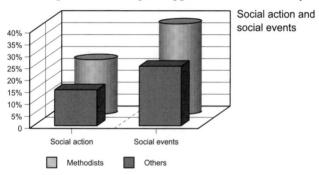

Social action and social events

What does not come naturally, however, is to develop these social contacts to the level that is needed for people to react positively to an invitation to attend Alpha. Methodists are only half as likely as those in other denominations to be involved in local church-based evangelism, are less likely than others to have specific outreach activities in the church and less likely to be active in faith-sharing.[10]

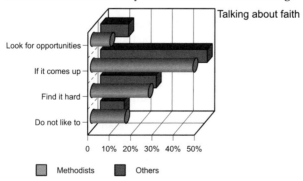

Talking about faith

The net result of this is that Methodists know plenty of people to invite to Alpha, but struggle to make the transition from social encounter to spiritual engagement.

Effectiveness

In terms of helping to bring people to faith, move on in their faith journey, and encounter the Holy Spirit, the impact of Alpha in Methodist churches is similar to elsewhere. Around one in six attenders coming to faith through Alpha is a fairly consistent indicator for both Methodist and other denominations.

Methodist attenders who are already Christians often find themselves much moved on in their faith journey (60% of attenders is not untypical). They also commonly find, perhaps for the first time, that the inherited and acquired fragments of their belief system come together. For Methodists, accustomed to a very mixed diet from a wide variety of ordained and lay preachers, and only about half as likely as others to attend a study group, this is highly significant.

Encountering the Holy Spirit is also experienced somewhat differently in many Methodist churches than elsewhere. As already noted, some shy away from the experiential side of Alpha, so reducing it to an exercise in doctrine and neglecting the opportunity for a life-changing experience of God. Mike Lewis's *Why not the Dove?* looked at a fairly typical Methodist Circuit that had run Alpha for some years and revealed that Alpha attenders started out with certain expectations (sometimes fears) of whether and how they would encounter the Holy Spirit. There was subsequent disappointment at the absence of phenomena such as speaking in tongues and no visible signs of people receiving spiritual gifts.

But when Lewis spoke in depth to past attenders, he found people witnessing to a range of experiences: gentleness, inner peace, joy, confidence, guidance, an inner glow, forgiveness, release, invigoration and especially love. Other ongoing effects included the continuing or constant presence of God and assurance of this, an indescribable inner peace, the fulfilment of hitherto unrecognised needs, and changed lives. In the longer-term, people had become more active in evangelism and prayer, new forms of worship emerged and people had become worship leaders and local preachers.

The gifts and fruit of the Spirit were there in abundance after all. Lewis concluded that Alpha 'did not provide the path for ministry in the power of the Spirit in the way either I or HTB expected. But it enabled God to work....The Dove was not missing. I was just looking in the wrong direction'.

Changing the church

Perhaps the most significant impact of Alpha in Methodism is to change the local church and help get it back to its roots. Research has shown

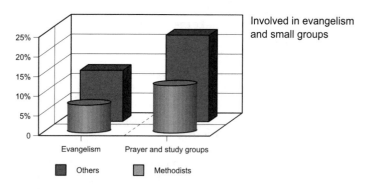

qualitative change to be much more common in Methodist churches than in some others, and to be the single most marked outcome, more than growth in numbers.

Alpha has returned many churches to the environment of small groups that first characterised the Methodist movement through its class meetings, very important for a denomination that is now more characterised by its lack of them.[11] Although Methodism is less involved in the cell church movement than some other denominations, those that use Alpha are more likely also to be using cell church and moving Alpha 'graduates' into cell groups.

Alpha has been regularly found to foster a new vision for church-based evangelism and enabled everyone to be part of this. It has introduced churches to some key characteristics of church health and growth. And Alpha has helped Methodist churches to recover the balance between social action, where it was always strong, and evangelism which in past decades received a much weaker emphasis.

Sustained development

We know that, to achieve the maximum impact, Alpha or similar initiatives need to be embedded into the life of the church and courses run regularly. To run two or three courses and then stop can change the church for the better, but does not yield the sustained impact of a long-term ongoing commitment.

A particularly common problem is that, once Alpha has been run two or three times, all the members and 'regulars' have come, and others would run a mile at the thought of being at the receiving end of an evangelistic programme, even though they are perfectly happy to come to the church's social functions and probably look on the Methodist church as 'my church'. This is a direct outcome of the strong social contacts that Methodists have, combined with the difficulty of moving these relationships towards a more spiritual engagement. Much emphasis is now placed by Methodism on the importance of relation-

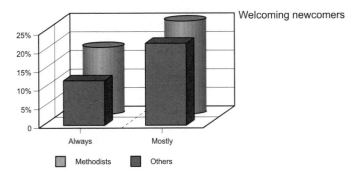

ships in evangelism and at least one new course[12] is aimed at helping Methodists to develop relationships in this way.

However, there are some strengths that Methodist churches can play to, so as to make the outcome of Alpha more sustainable. Methodist churches are strong at welcoming newcomers and on retaining people who have joined. And Alpha in Methodist churches has been found to build on this by helping develop leadership especially for house or cell groups, prayer groups and ministry teams. House and prayer group leadership helps to correct areas where Methodism has been weaker than other denominations. Conversely, twice as many Methodists as in other denominations are already likely to be involved in pastoral care, and ministry team development can add substantive value to this.

Alpha's contribution?

What is likely to be the most important contribution that Alpha can make to Methodism? There are many Methodist churches in good heart, but also large numbers in decline and, as the age profile is higher than in other denominations, time is not on their side. Therefore possibly the main contribution that Alpha offers is to be an instrument or catalyst of renewal and to foster key characteristics of church health and growth.[13]

Vision is strongly associated with congregational vitality, but Methodists are less clear than others about their church's vision and less committed to it. It would be difficult for Methodists to have experienced an effective Alpha initiative without catching a new vision[14] and being drawn into commitment to it, both personally and as a church.

Many in the church experience a personal renewal, maturing in their faith and opening the door to the Holy Spirit, His gifting and fruits. This leads to the revitalisation of small groups for study and prayer, supports leadership formation and every member ministry and engages the church in evangelism with increasing confidence.

It is not simply an afterthought to recognise the vital importance of caring, sensitive and inclusive leadership in any mixed tradition church, to ensure that the vision and all the outcomes of Alpha are carried forward in unity of fellowship rather than divisiveness. Although the Holy Spirit is characterised by love and unity, we are still human and this task should not be underestimated! Methodists, as much as those in other denominations, find the need to work hard and constantly at this.

The following titles by the same author are available without charge via CD-Rom or download from charles.freebury@tesco.net, tel: 01460 78501:

Alpha or Emmaus? (2002, 2005, 103pp. with PowerPoint presentation)

Stepping-stones: from coffee morning to Sunday morning (2005, 31pp. with Power-Point presentation)

FAQs: God and suffering, God and other religions (2004, 10pp., course handouts for two supplementary sessions for use with evangelistic or discipling courses)

Notes

[1] Peter Brierley, 'Churchgoing in England: results of the English church attendance survey', *Quadrant*, January 2000.

[2] Escott and Gelder, *Church life profile 2001: denominational results for the Methodist church*, New Malden: Churches Information for Mission, 2002 (downloadable from www.methodist.org.uk).

[3] Michael Green, *I believe in the Holy Spirit* (Eastbourne: Kingsway, revised edition 2004) pp. 350, 322.

[4] Andrew Baguley, *Alpha in a Methodist context* (prepared for the Methodist Alpha Conference, 1999 (contact andrew.baguley2@btopenworld.com).

[5] *Called by name: being a member in the Methodist Church*, MPH, Peterborough, 2002, p. 8.

[6] But note that Alpha's home church, Holy Trinity Brompton, has strong initiatives in all these areas.

[7] See www.methodist.org.uk.

[8] Charles Freebury, *Alpha or Emmaus?* (2002, 2005, 103pp. with PowerPoint presentation, available without charge via CD-Rom or download from charles. freebury@tiscali.co.uk) and Mike Lewis, *Why not the Dove?*,Cliff College MA dissertation, 2001, (see http://www.cliffcollege.org/college_postgrad.html).

[9] 38% of Methodists are involved in social groups (other denominations 25%) and 23% in community service, social justice or welfare activities of their church (other denominations 15%). Source CLP.

[10] 7% of Methodists are involved in evangelistic or outreach activities (other denominations 13%); 9% do not have outreach activities in the church (other denominations 6%); 43% do not like to, or find it hard to talk about their faith (other denominations 37%). Source CLP.

[11] 12% of Methodists are involved in small prayer, discussion or Bible study groups (other denominations 22%). Source CLP.

[12] Charles Freebury, *Stepping-stones: from coffee morning to Sunday morning* (2005, 31 pages with PowerPoint presentation, contact charles.freebury@tiscali.co.uk).

[13] See, for example, the characteristics identified in Robert Warren, *The healthy churches' handbook* (London: CHP, 2004) and Christian Schwarz, *Natural church development handbook* (Moggerhanger: BCGA, 1999).

[14] *Cf.* Peter Brierley, *Leadership, vision and growing churches* (London: Christian Research, 2003) p.12: 'Churches which had held an Alpha course were twice as likely to have a vision for the future as those which had not (31% to 17%).'

CHAPTER 15

Alpha and Roman Catholicism

Andrew Brookes

Beginnings and Early Support for Alpha for Catholics

The first Catholics to do Alpha did so as guests of Non-Catholic Christians and attended courses run by other denominations in 1996. Their faith benefited hugely from the course and they were encouraged to take the course back to their own Catholic parishes. A few such courses were run and had a big local impact. Around this time other Catholics were beginning to show interest due to the publicity surrounding Alpha and the fact that in the decade of evangelisation, originally called by Pope John Paul II, many Catholics were keen to find useful tools to take up this challenge. At the same time three representatives were sent to an Alpha Conference on behalf of Catholic Charismatic Renewal to investigate. A meeting was held with Sandy Millar and Nicky Gumbel who were very surprised that Roman Catholics were interested in running Alpha but were keen to see what could be done to support the use of the course by Catholics. It soon became evident that the historic, theological and popular mindset gaps between the Catholic and Protestant worlds were such that special efforts and strategies would be required if the course was to have much chance of being used effectively by Catholics.

Three Alpha for Catholics Conferences were held in Westminster in the next two years. These conferences – using the normal Alpha conference talks given by Sandy Millar and Nicky Gumbel – were attended by about 500 people. Support material, notably a booklet written by Catholics addressing the main questions that Catholics tended to ask about the course was produced. The number of courses running in Catholic parishes rose rapidly. An Alpha for Catholics Office (headed by David Payne and with a staff of volunteers) was soon established to support the use of Alpha by Catholics. This had close links with HTB. It was funded in significant part by CREW TRUST, the charitable trust connected with Catholic Charismatic Renewal in England and Wales. This office supplied speakers to give Alpha for Catholics Seminars at main Alpha Conferences. They also organised and ran Alpha for Catholic Training Days and other events around the country. These covered similar material in a shorter time and gave more attention to issues facing Catholics. A more explicitly Catholic context was given to the setting with citations of church teaching on evangelisation etc. Over four years around twelve day-conferences were organised all over the country, attended by many Catholic parishes. Various Bishops have on occasions given written endorsements and encouraged the use of Alpha in other ways too. Some support was also given to help Catholics outside the UK run Alpha too.

Initial impact: Uptake and Fruit

The initial interest shown both by the good attendance at the West-minster Conferences and by a lot of parishes (and some Catholic schools) taking it up. was certainly striking. Quite soon between 400–450 courses were reckoned to be running. However this number then stayed steady before beginning to fall. HTB conducted research in 2003/4 which indicated that around 150 churches were now running or hoped to run again soon. This appears not to have changed notably by the end of 2005. To put these in perspective there are just under 3,000 parishes in England and Wales and around 450 in Scotland.

What lay behind the initial surge of interest? A good deal of interest came from Catholic Charismatics who were well networked in various ways and very much informed of these developments. The Charismatic dimension of the course gave it immediate interest and support from many in this grouping. Probably about half of the courses which ran were started because Charismatics persuaded their parishes to run the course or were given permission to run it themselves within the parish. There is a strong tendency in the UK for there to be a Charismatic Prayer meeting that runs one evening a week and is linked to the parish without the main-stream of the parish being 'charismatic'. Sometimes these prayer groups are highly valued by the wider parish, sometimes they are viewed less positively and feel isolated. Generally this results in Charismatic worship and gifts operating explicitly at the Charismatic prayer meeting but not being used in clear explicit ways in wider church worship or ministry. The leadership of Alpha by Catholic Charismatics has sometimes created problems since the course has then often been viewed as promoting Charismatic Catholicism/Christianity. It has sometimes made it harder to integrate the course and the guests into the wider life of the parish and also to attract guests from beyond the networks of the Charismatics. A better strategy and results tend to happen when the parish priest whole-heartedly backs the course and the leadership team includes a variety of Catholics (only some of whom have experience of Charismatic Renewal) but who are able to work together well as a team. Some familiarity and experience with things charismatic certainly helps the course be under-stood and well implemented.

The other half of the interest and uptake came mainly from parishes with a 'Get up and have a go' attitude, typically well organised with good lay involvement who were willing to have a look at the latest spiritual/pastoral aids and if appropriate give them a try. There was interest from parishes with good ecumenical links who knew of local churches of other denominations who were fruitfully using Alpha. The decade of evangelisation and frequent calls of Pope John Paul II for Catholics to evangelise also stimulated interest.

Most of the guests on the courses have tended to be people who are already Catholics. Often these have been practising Catholics even before the course began. However, Alpha has brought many Catholics to a deeper faith, one marked by a more conscious and clear sense of personal relationship with Jesus. People have had a stronger sense of the love of God for them and of the action of the Holy Spirit in their lives. They have often moved from a duty-based faith to a more freely chosen and actively committed one. Deeper devotion to prayer, scripture and church action has often resulted.[1] Significant numbers have come back to the practice of their faith and some have made a journey into first Christian and then full Catholic faith. However, these are a minority. Some ran Alpha as a pre-RCIA course (i.e. as its pre-cate-chemunate phase). Generally Catholics have struggled to invite people, without an already significant church link, onto the course as guests. This reflects deep-seated attitudes and fears in the Catholic population of this country[2] – and a basic problem in overcoming the sound barrier and talking about faith in terms of a relationship with Jesus and of sharing their testimony. This has meant the course has tended to fizzle out after a few runs in most cases. There are some exceptions including English Martyrs Church, Wakefield, which is now an Alpha Resource Church. This trend has sometimes been aggravated by a difficulty in attracting new team members, a difficulty in establishing suitable follow up (especially small faith-sharing groups) and a general lack of ease with the course by the parish as a whole on grounds that somehow it is not Catholic enough. This may be because of its Protestant origin or its Evangelical and Charismatic tone. When run, most frequently Alpha has been merely allowed alongside other activities or sometimes more consciously bolted on to existing activities but rarely has it been used as part of a cohesive pastoral – let alone missionary – strategy.

Opposition, Reactions and Development of other Courses

The main criticisms of Alpha from Catholic circles focussed on its Protestant (and perceived Evangelical-Charismatic) provenance and linked to this on what was specifically felt to be gaps in the content from what was considered as essential in a proper course on the

Catholic Faith. Arguably this largely missed the point that Alpha is intended as an introduction – and an evangelistic one – that can be followed up by other course material. These criticisms have tended to focus on the lack of teaching on the sacraments, and the role of the church more generally, and especially its magesterium. An assumption of Biblical authority has been pointed out. (Other criticisms about the presentation of the cross, nature of faith, aspects of evil have also been made as has the approach to suffering/healing and the lack of social teaching or reference to Mary and the Saints.) For some it is just too experience-based. Leaving aside the gaps, the early versions of *Questions of Life* did have phrases and material problematic to Catholics. This has now generally been changed, but not before people had publicly pointed the problems out and set many people against the course.

Partly in response to this and partly due to direct encouragement from the Vatican, other video resources were provided that covered these topics. These were produced by Catholic Evangelisation Services (CES – which had evolved out of the Alpha for Catholics Office) sometimes working in conjunction with other organisations. A number of video series have been produced, initially intended as direct follow-up to Alpha and then on other faith topics. There was recognition that there was a lack of such resources for Catholics and there has been a big demand for these.

Examination of what was happening to Alpha by its Catholic promoters pointed to a number of issues that needed addressing to aid Alpha's integration into Catholic parishes and also to help Catholic parishes become more generally active evangelising communities. These included: (1) the need to renew the faith of Catholics, nurturing a personal and experiential faith based on a deeper sense of God's love for them and presence and action in their lives; (2) a need to foster and form small faith-sharing groups; (3) a better understanding of the teaching on evangelisation and the role of all Christians in this; (4) encouraging responsibility and providing training and resources to undertake evangelisation including clear outreach/proclamation.

Building on the resources already produced, further ones were produced (by CES) and developed into a process/programme of different modules (with some flexibility) that it was hoped would lead a parish into a position of being a renewed community with small groups, and able to undertake evangelisation – including Alpha. It was called 'Catholic Faith Exploration' or 'CaFE' for short. Many insights and aspects of Alpha's method and approach were admired and incorporated. Thus, Alpha's relaxed and hospitable style, respectful of guests, providing non-threatening opportunities for people to explore faith issues and the sense of process and journey that ran through this appealed and were seen to be of value. CaFE has been well received and training events run in most dioceses in England and Wales. It has a language, and spirituality permeating it that are clearly more Catholic than Alpha and with which many Catholics are more at ease. By the end of 2005 it is estimated that over 1000 parishes in the UK had started the programme. Not all were moving through it according to the proposed model, it being evident that people are using it as a palette of resources which are accessed flexibly in varied ways. It is difficult to assess its full impact yet. However, despite its wide use, it seems that parishes have struggled to generate long-term small groups and are still struggling to really commit to outreach/proclamation evangelisation. Although it has been offered and suggested, there has been very little further adoption of Alpha as a result so far, though this should only happen well into the process. Evangelism and faith sharing beyond a fairly obvious Catholic fringe is still a challenge to be overcome for most Catholics. The creation of the Catholic Agency to Support Evangelisation (CASE) in 2004 is promoting evangelisation and may have an impact on Alpha too.

Alpha for Catholics within AI and Overseas

Alongside these developments HTB/AI has continued to promote Alpha's use for Catholics in close line with how it promotes Alpha right across all the denominations. In 2003 they created an Alpha for Catholics Department staffed by Catholics employed by AI and working from AI's own offices.[3] This shows an ongoing commitment by AI to getting Alpha to work among Catholics. This has helped AI generate more confidence in some Catholic circles. Networking and link-building with various Catholic organisations has been undertaken. However, it is not yet clear how this will translate into courses being run by Catholics and when this happens how long they will be sustained, how well they will integrate with the local church and how much real outreach to unchurched or even dechurched people will occur.

There has been some uptake of Alpha by Catholics in other parts of the world. Much is made by HTB of the relative success of Alpha in France where a Catholic couple heads up Alpha for the whole country and all denominations. It is not clear if the factors involved here are transferable to other countries. In some other countries and language groups, HTB/AI have effectively impeded the use of Alpha by Catholics because they have selected agencies and publishing houses to promote Alpha who are unsympathetic or have even been openly hostile to Catholics. Some of these situations have now been changed with Catholics taking more prominent roles in the Alpha set up. AI claims Alpha is still attracting interest from very significant numbers of Catholics globally, including some Bishops, and that the relatively low level of interest in the UK is not typical. It remains to be seen how well Alpha will bed down in some of these other countries. Some of the new movements and communities have expressed an interest though some already have similar programmes of their own.

Summary

In conclusion, the interest of Catholics in Alpha was surprising. HTB have done a significant amount to help promote it but have wanted as far as possible to keep this in uniformity with how Alpha operates in other denominations. This means it is generally proposed as the *first* step of a (renewal and then) outreach programme. There are certainly some local situations where Alpha has fitted in with the overall ethos, values and approach of the parish or community, worked long-term and has achieved real outreach. Often the use has been more short-term though. It has had a significant positive influence on the faith of many Catholics and had many other good, if indirect, influences by stimulating and enriching other new approaches and materials for use by Catholics in evangelisation and pastoral care.

More generally it has helped Catholics undergo the 'evangelical shift'[4] seen as part of the work of Vatican II and recent Popes and it or other forms of association with Alpha International may do so still more in the future. If Catholics then start becoming more effective at doing outreach or even reaching their own dechurched population, Alpha or something fairly similar could still be a good tool. Alpha has also given many Christians of other denominations/traditions a much more positive view of Catholics, and changed some Catholic views of Non-Catholics too, and has thus fostered mutual respect with all the fruit that potentially goes with this.

Notes

[1] A large nationwide survey in England and Wales conducted in 2001-2 indicated that 18% of Catholics had had 'a positive contact with the Alpha course or similar'. (*Evangelisation in England and Wales*, P. Knights and A. Murray).

[2] These are linked to the legacy of Catholics being first persecuted and then marginalised after the Reformation, something leaving a long shadow of derision and suspicion, and also the fact that most British Catholics came into this country as immigrants who formed relatively self-contained communities (of ethnic minorities). None of these features have encouraged outward looking evangelisation and bold proclamation.

[3] The staffing of the Alpha for Catholics Department was reduced during the winter of 2005-06 as part of wider staff cuts at AI/HTB.

[4] I think this term is preferable to the relatively common language of describing many Catholics as 'sacramentalised but not evangelised' since this tends to drive a wedge between the sacraments (and by association often the church) and evangelisation, a polarisation that tends to impoverish both church and mission. Such an 'evangelical shift' (See ch. 9 for a characterisation), itself a process, must impact (1) Catholic spirituality, (2) how the faith is understood and articulated

and (3) practical activities and new initiatives. This needs to occur with individuals and also communities (at various levels).

I discuss what Catholics can learn from Evangelicals in the article 'Evangelical Catholics?' in *Changing Evangelisation*, edited by Philip Knights, CTBI, 2007. The book presents a helpful overview of the theory and current practice of Catholic evangelisation in Britain and Ireland.

SECTION 5

Thematic Theological and Pastoral Reflections

If Section 4 examined the width of Alpha's impact in more detail then Section 5 examines the depth of Alpha's impact in more detail. Most, probably all, contributions in this section combine both theological and practical reflections. An attempt was again made to get authors from a wide variety of church backgrounds and also to invite them to bring their own specific theological competence and other expertise to bear on Alpha. In this way, thinking on Alpha is being pushed still further into new ground. Although other subjects could have been included most of the main issues are addressed.

AB

CHAPTER 16

The Spirit, Mission and Alpha

Philip Walker

Spirit-Baptism

The Holy Spirit has an important part to play in the Alpha course. Of the fourteen talks, three are on the Holy Spirit directly given during the Holy Spirit Retreat, whether it is held over a weekend or a day away (as seems to be very common). But the Holy Spirit is mentioned in many more of the talks, than just these three. One critic of the course has suggested that there is more space in the Alpha course devoted to the Holy Spirit than to the Lord Jesus, and while he has another agenda to deal with, there is some truth in what he is saying.

At first sight it would seem strange that the Holy Spirit seems to have more importance than Jesus, but the reality is that the concentration on Jesus comes in the first two talks, and the ones that follow are much more to do with living the Christian life, although at the stage where the transition takes place, people may not have come to faith yet.

I am sure that this division is right, and so is the emphasis on the Spirit. In Acts 1:8 the disciples were instructed to wait in Jerusalem until the Holy Spirit came, so for them and for us today, the issue of empowerment to live the Christian life and serve Christ effectively in the world, is an essential part of the gospel. Until quite recently the Church has downplayed the work of the Holy Spirit at conversion, which has meant that there has been the need for a second and subsequent experience.

There can be no doubt that the Holy Spirit becomes an integral part of a believer's life from salvation onwards. It is commonly the act of water baptism that identifies a person as a believer in Christ and a member of his Body, but the presence of the Holy Spirit truly marks the transition. He is the seal and guarantee (2 Cor 1:22; Eph 1:13), but conversion is the beginning of a process, for it has to do with making disciples. The Church has often been more interested in the beginning rather than the process. Only disciples of Jesus Christ can be true converts, and the Spirit not only begins the work, he completes it too.

I agree with Clark Pinnock who suggests that the doctrine of subsequence has come from bad teaching and bad practice in the Church. The power dimension of the coming of the Spirit has often been overlooked, so the deficit has to be made up later. He argues that baptism and confirmation should be charismatic events, but often they are not, so subsequent encounters must be charismatic in nature. As he puts it, 'The power for effective witness comes better late than never.'[1]

This is an important point. Some scholars suggest that the Holy Spirit can be received without any evidence – that may follow later. This is what Lederle calls the 'sacramental interpretation of Spirit-baptism.'[2] Yet a careful study of the New Testament shows that everyone received the Holy Spirit with a clear knowledge that something had happened. No one had any doubt. This must be the thrust of Paul's question to the Ephesians in Acts 19:2 when he asked them, 'Did you receive the Holy Spirit when you believed?' He expected them to know. While it is certainly true that it is not recorded that all of them spoke in tongues, there were obvious manifestations when the Spirit came upon them. This must also be Paul's meaning when he talks of the Holy Spirit sealing new believers (2 Cor 1:22; Eph 1:13, 4:30). This was their assurance that Christ had accepted them into his Body.

The evidence is clear: Spirit-baptism must be a definite and dramatic experience. Anything else is a contradiction in terms, like saying water baptism can be valid without water. It must be a self-evident event, of which both the receiver and others nearby are fully aware. This must be more than an emotional feeling, for the New Testament often records the outward evidence of unexpected speech spontaneously ejaculated. Sometimes, this was speaking in tongues, which is the most common evidence mentioned, but praise and prophecy are also included.[3]

As the early church spread beyond the Jews, the majority of new converts were coming from a world where active involvement in paganism was the norm, so deliverance and exorcism were essential. The situation in the 21st century is little different; postmodernism, syncretism and outright paganism are becoming the norm, so the need for evangelism to take on the empowerment of the Holy Spirit (which I would see as the norm) must take on an ever greater significance. Even churches that hold a different theological position to Holy Trinity Brompton, must ensure that the essential role of the Holy Spirit in regeneration *and* empowerment for ministry is not missed.

Alpha's teaching on the Holy Spirit

The teaching on the work of the Holy Spirit during the distinctive *Holy Spirit Weekend* or Day Away is therefore very important. A summary of the three talks on the Holy Spirit will assist us in knowing what is covered:

Talk 8: 'Who Is the Holy Spirit?'

The Holy Spirit, who has the characteristics of a Person, was active in creation and with particular people at particular times. The Father promised the Holy Spirit in the new covenant (Jer. 31:33; Ezek. 36:26–7; Joel 2:28–9). Jesus reaffirmed the Spirit's coming (Luke 24:49; Acts 1:8), and the predictions began to be fulfilled at Pentecost for you, your children, and all whom the Lord our God will call (Acts 2:29, 33). He who is Counsellor, Comforter, and Encourager sets the weak free and enables them to fulfil their divine calling.

Talk 9: 'What Does the Holy Spirit Do?'

The Spirit regenerates us (John 3:5–8), indwells us (Rom. 8:9), and makes us mutually related as sons and daughters of God (Rom. 8:14–17). The Spirit helps us develop family likeness, gives security, promotes unity, and bestows gifts on each member. There is an urgent need for spiritual gifts to be exercised. The church cannot operate at maximum effectiveness until each person is playing his or her part.

Talk 10: 'How Can I Be Filled with the Holy Spirit?'

The filling of the Spirit rarely happens imperceptibly, although everyone is different, so a variety of manifestations occur. People will be released in praise, and may be given a new language. This new language can help the Christian to express to God what we really feel in our spirit. Tongues are particularly helpful in praise and worship, when praying under pressure and when praying for other people. The principle difficulties people can have in receiving from God (and he *wants* to give) are doubt, fear and inadequacy. Those who want to be filled should seek someone to pray for them, but it is possible to pray on your own, too.

The first of these three talks is unlikely to cause problems for anyone as the doctrine of the Holy Spirit is presented in orthodox terms and in textbook fashion. The problem may come in the second and third talks, for they will cause some heart-searching and theological consideration, especially for those who have been taught that these things are not for today. Personally, I have no problem with the content, but I can see that others could have.

I see four main areas for consideration of the Holy Spirit, missions and Alpha.

The Evangelical and Charismatic background of Holy Trinity Brompton

Holy Trinity Brompton is within the evangelical, charismatic, Anglican tradition, but surprisingly, perhaps, the Alpha course is being used by a very wide variety of churches with very different theological understandings. The course itself, while always remaining true to this background with a long-time commitment to a ministry of evangelism, is really much wider as the teaching is Trinitarian, and Bible-based.

The church experienced renewal through the ministry of John Wimber in the early 1980s, and was part of the introduction to the new things that were happening in Toronto in the 1990s. It has therefore been a part of the so-called Third Wave of the Holy Spirit, where the first wave was the Pentecostal movement of the early 1900s and the second wave was the Charismatic and House-Church movement of the 1960s and 70s. The church today combines lively worship, a warm-hearted welcome, expository bible teaching, and a hint of Anglican Prayer Book liturgy.

Peter Wagner suggests that this Third Wave is distinct from, but at the same time very similar to the first and second waves. The major variation comes in the meaning of baptism in the Holy Spirit and the role of tongues authenticating this. Each of Jesus' commissions to the church[4] is accompanied by a clear power promise. It is power for witnessing and living a Godly life but it is also power for miracles, deliverance and healing.[5]

I am certain that this is a correct understanding of New Testament mission theology, for a theology of mission cannot be truly evangelical and Trinitarian unless it is also Pentecostal! Nor can a Pentecostal theology be effective in mission without also being Trinitarian in nature. When theology tends to define *church* in terms of it being a historical institution, as an object, it fails to see it as a Pentecost event and its relation to the mission of God to the world. But, the Third Wave movement may have an over-focus on the supernatural; a truly Biblical mission theology which includes the power of God manifest in weakness as well as the miraculous, there is a balance which may have been reached in Alpha.

Much is made by some of the manifestations on an Alpha retreat which can include: shaking uncontrollably; powerful electric shocks; a voice in the head; laughing for no reason; being knocked to the ground; white lights in the head; and unnatural heat. Alpha teaches clearly that the manifestations themselves don't matter, and that we should simply judge by the resulting fruit. Perhaps this is the balance we are thinking about. For the purpose of the Holy Spirit's filling and gifts is to assist Christians to put on the new self 'which is being renewed in knowledge in the image of its Creator' (Col. 3:10); and is 'created to be like God in true righteousness and holiness' (Eph. 4:24).

The Away Day and Its Value

Nicky Gumbel himself confirms the significance of the Holy Spirit weekend. He writes: 'At the end of the course I send out questionnaires....If there is a change I ask when that change occurred. For many the decisive moment is the Saturday evening of the weekend.'[6] It is perhaps no wonder that many people count this time as the moment of their conversion. *Alpha News* records stories regularly of people who have seen God at this time and have never been the same again.

It might be suggested that the strange manifestations which sometime occur, are the main focus, but the prime focus is the sense of the presence of God. It is not about spiritual gifts but it is about the numinous experience of God, which is the main focus of the 'Holy Spirit Weekend-Away'. People doing Alpha are told to expect all manner of things might happen to them. Sometimes, when people are filled, they shake like a leaf in the wind. Others find themselves breathing deeply as if almost physically breathing in the Spirit. It is not restricted to this, however: 'Physical heat sometimes accompanies the filling of the Spirit and people experience it in their hands or some other part of their bodies. One person described a feeling of "glowing all over". Another said she experienced "liquid heat". Still another described "burning in my arms when I was not hot".'[7]

In this day of increasing seeking for spirituality, when young people look everywhere except the Church, this aspect of Christianity seems to have been missed by many. In some senses the Pentecostal Movement of the early years of the 20th century and the Charismatic Movement of the 1960s and 70s, were part of a movement in the Evangelical world, which reacted against the dry formalism of much of it, and sought to meet with God. In the later part of the 20th century, John Wimber and the Third Wave movement, the experiences at the Toronto Airport Fellowship and in Pensacola may be a part of this whole process. The danger may have been the excess which have been well documented down through the years, but my impression is that people are crying out to experience God.

It was a Pentecostal pioneer, Donald Gee, who first used the truism: 'All Word and no Spirit we dry up, all Spirit and no Word we blow up, but Spirit and Word we grow up.' This remains as true as ever, and we always need to seek a balance, but the New Testament describes a situation where people knew that God was at work. Stephen was 'full of God's grace and power, [and] did great wonders and miraculous signs among the people.'[8] The next verse describes the growing opposition to this manifestation of God's power, and Saul was obviously aware of this as he gave his consent to the execution of Stephen, and yet in Acts 19:20 (for example) we see Paul at Ephesus working in a similar way, 'In this way the word of the Lord spread widely and grew in power.'

Paul was not ashamed of this in any way as he records in 1 Corinthians 2:4–5 'My message and my preaching were not with wise and persuasive words, but with a demonstration of the Spirit's power, so that your faith might not rest on men's wisdom, but on God's power.' So I ask myself 'Has much of the Church moved away from this?', for today we would be much more likely to say, 'My message and my preaching were only with wise and persuasive words, without any demonstration of the Spirit's power, so that your faith might rest on men's wisdom, instead of God's power.'

Is this going too far? Perhaps, but with so many looking for reality, and so many feeling God at work on the Away Day, this is one reason for the success of Alpha today.

And yet...a careful reading of the recent *Alpha News* shows that the pattern seems to be changing. A good number of the stories do not record coming to faith in Christ during the Alpha course, but some time after the event. Is this because in the early days this was a Discipleship Course which was helping church-goers towards a deeper faith, whereas today many more are unchurched and need more time to work through the process, part of which is the very real experience of God. Perhaps this needs more research in the months and years ahead!

The Negative Literature Concerning the Holy Spirit and Alpha

As I began to think about this subject I did an Internet search on Alpha and the Holy Spirit. To my great surprise, I found very few positive articles but many more arguing against Alpha because of its teaching on the Holy Spirit. Some of these weighed the course carefully but rejected it because of a cessationist theological understanding of the work of the Holy Spirit. As might be expected, this is especially the case in connection with the Spirit's work and gifts. As one critic wrote, 'This should come as no great surprise for Gumbel is extremely Charismatic in his teaching. His work is therefore filled with charismatic teaching and although the book was prepared prior to the phenomenon known as the Toronto Blessing it is undoubtedly pro Toronto Blessing.'

Nicky Gumbel's Background

The criticism seems to begin with the impact that John Wimber had when he visited HTB. At one point on the video set, Nicky Gumbel dates his call to evangelism to an incident in 1982, when he received prayer from John Wimber. On that occasion, he experienced such supernatural power that he called out for it to stop. It was from that time that Nicky traces his ministry of telling others to that particular time. There is no doubt that I would be 'written off' in the same way, as I was also influenced by the work of John Wimber, but we need to look clearly at the fruit rather than write someone or something off because it doesn't fit our particular theology. After all, we might have got our own theology wrong in the first place! The Bible says that it is the lasting fruit that is important (John 15:16).

John Wimber's doctrine is described as Restorationism, or Dominion Theology – a unique and new form of Pentecostalism which is the basis of the 'Toronto Blessing'. The Alpha Course is accused of showing similar aspects when Nicky Gumbel refers to the preaching of the Kingdom in the same terms as John Wimber, along with the healing of the sick, signs and wonders. This is apparently paving the way for people to experience similar phenomena to the so-called 'Toronto Blessing', which is itself a replica of New Age philosophy and practice in the guise of Christianity.

There is no doubt that the Holy Spirit teaching of the Alpha Course does move people towards the experiential side of Christian life, but even Paul said, 'My message and my preaching were not with wise and persuasive words, but with a demonstration of the Spirit's power, so that your faith might not rest on men's wisdom, but on God's power.' (2 Cor. 2:4–5).

Direct Criticisms

Martyn Percy, director of the Lincoln Theological Institute for the Study of Religion and Society of the University of Sheffield, England, has been quoted as saying 'The Alpha approach has been faulted for pushing an experience-driven approach to evangelism that sidesteps intellectual difficulties.'[9] To my mind this seems to be missing the teaching from the early sessions of the Alpha Course. I would have thought that these sessions were actually describing intellectual difficulties and allowing people to explore them in safe surroundings, rather than ignoring them. To me the more surprising issue is the inclusion of so many aspects of the faith which relate far more to discipleship than finding faith and yet have been instrumental in a changed life for many – the fruit of John 15 maybe?

One criticism found in several places is that the Holy Spirit of Alpha is not the Holy Spirit of the Bible, for the 'Spirit' in Alpha appears to work in ways that lie outside the confines of Scripture. The criticism continues in such a way to leave the authors open to the charge of blasphemy arguing that it cannot be the Holy Spirit to whom people are introduced in Alpha. He is the agent for giving people an 'experience' that is going to make God real to them. I am certain that this is a total misunderstanding of a true Biblical theology of the Holy Spirit and of Alpha, but it does correctly indicate the importance of the Holy Spirit in the course.

The Ecumenical Aspects of Alpha

We have seen that it is the evangelical churches who are far more likely to run an Alpha course (in the survey competed in Scotland, and of these the Evangelical-Charismatics are even more likely to run a course. Stephen Hunt has argued that Alpha has been most effective in those already attending church, and in spreading Evangelical-Charismatic Christianity. He may be right, but Alpha courses and the Holy

Spirit day (or weekend) are not limited to just those churches. Many different types of churches are involved from charismatic/Pentecostal to liberal to Catholic. There are few distinct groups which have refused to use Alpha at all.

Only the Bible Society seems to have a wider impact on the many churches with differing church backgrounds than Alpha. The Bible Society has been established for many years and certainly does have the widest acceptance of any organisation, being able to bring together every aspect of the church background and theology. I am sure this is because of the importance of the Bible for every stream, but it is also the way the Bible Society carefully produces their material, and they are to be congratulated for their work. The surprise, perhaps, is that the 'young upstart' also has such a wide impact in churches of very differing theologies. There are some churches that will not use Alpha, of course, as the criticism noted above would indicate, but by and large it has had an impact on many churches in many streams. This is even more surprising given that the main aim is reaching out, when ecumenical circles struggle to find a common language for evangelism/evangelisation.... Now some churches of different persuasion are even running joint courses!

I don't believe that Alpha set out to be as widely ecumenical in the early days, but there is no doubt that is what they do now, and they are to be honoured for this aspect of their work, for it is revitalising churches of every shade, denomination and stream. There is another aspect to this, however, and that it has also given the opportunity and impetus for other churches and groups to create their own courses, and has brought the need for intentional mission to the local church, involving the people rather than an imported evangelist. All the different gifted people in a church can be (and are) working towards the reaching of the fringe people in the church and beyond.

Final thoughts

A careful reading of *Alpha News*, seems to show that things are changing. Fewer seem to be coming to faith during the course – they seem to need more time to work through the process than the 10 weeks of the course. Is this because the people now attending the course know so much less and therefore need more time to think through and work through the issues? But people are still coming to faith. It is still an effective mission tool, and for me the concentration on the Holy Spirit weekend/day, is an important reason for this.

Every valuable tool for the church (or for business for that matter) needs to be constantly revised. Does Alpha need ongoing revision? Certainly it does! It cannot be left as it is for many years or it will lose its effectiveness and its value. There needs to be constant tweaking as well as major revision from time to time, based on good research to make sure that the Course and all that is involved really does meet the need. I believe that the tweaking does take place, but major revision – that waits to be seen.

I would not want the concentration on the Holy Spirit to be removed or weakened, although a recognition of the need for inculturation in a wider range of churches may be needed, and a recognition that Alpha is not the ONLY way, there are others courses and churches may need to use different methods at different times and with different people.

The greatest challenge however, is the incorporation of people who have come to faith through Alpha into the wider circle of the church. My experience was that the transition was too great for some – and they left and went to another church instead, which is fine, but how many don't make that transition at all? Something is needed to help local churches to become more healthy and reflect some of the values of Alpha in other services, so that a greater percentage of those experiencing the numinous – a real 'God-experience' by the power of the Holy Spirit – will continue to follow him throughout the rest of their lives.

Notes

[1] Clark H. Pinnock, *Flame of Love: A Theology of the Holy Spirit*, Downers Grove: Intervarsity Press, 1996, pp. 167–9.

[2] H. I. Lederle, *Treasures Old and New: Interpretations of 'Spirit-Baptism' in the Charismatic Renewal Movement*, Peabody, MA: Hendrickson Publishers, 1988, pp. 104–36.

[3] David Pawson, *Jesus Baptises in One Spirit,* London: Hodder and Stoughton, 1997, pp. 121–3, 179.

[4] Found in Matthew 28:18–20; Mark 16:15–18; Luke 24:46–19, John 20:21–3, Acts 1:8.

[5] C. Peter Wagner, *The Third Wave*, Vine Books, 1988.

[6] Nicky Gumbel, *Telling Others*, Kingsway, 1994, p. 120.

[7] Nicky Gumbel, *Questions of Life*, 1994, p. 162.

[8] Acts 6:8.

[9] Quoted in *Christianity Today*, Feb. 9, 1998, pp. 37–9.

CHAPTER 17

Eating Alpha

Anne Richards

The Alpha Supper

The Alpha Supper is an essential ingredient in the Alpha phenomenon. It comes in two forms. An Alpha Supper as a one-off event has often been a means of invitation to all comers to find out something about the Alpha course itself. Alpha Suppers can also be organised to fit in with other mission strategies and events. Moreover, an Alpha supper also marks the beginning of each session of the Alpha course and can range from very simple meals of cheese and biscuits, or soup and sandwiches, to complex meals of several courses. One of the largest ever such events was held in a tent on Clapham Common in London and was attended by around 2,400 people. On this occasion, long tables with white tablecloths were served up with coronation chicken with saffron rice and salad, followed by chocolate biscuit cake with cream. Coffee and mints followed. A live jazz band provided entertainment before Nicky Gumbel interviewed people whose lives had been changed by the Alpha course and before giving his talk on 'Christianity: boring, untrue and irrelevant?' In terms of the whole Alpha course, meals are also an essential part of the time spent away together and part of the course's celebratory ending.

Because meals are so closely integrated into the course it is necessary to ask what their role is in the functioning of the course itself. Are meals in fact the primary evangelising context? Or does eating and drinking together 'soften people up' for what is to come? What can we learn by reflecting theologically on the place of the meal in our tradition and in our contemporary society? And what is the relationship between Jesus and acts of eating and drinking?

A Gospel Supper

We can start an investigation of the Alpha supper by reflecting on scripture:

He entered Jericho and was passing through it. A man was there named Zacchaeus; he was a chief tax collector and was rich. He was trying to see who Jesus was, but on account of the crowd he could not, because he was short in stature. So he ran ahead and climbed a sycamore tree to see him, because he was going to pass that way. When Jesus came to the place, he looked up and said to him, 'Zacchaeus, hurry and come down; for I must stay at your house today.' So he hurried down and was happy to welcome him. All who saw it began to grumble and said, 'He has gone to be the guest of one who is a sinner.' Zacchaeus stood there and said to the Lord, 'Look, half of my possessions, Lord, I will give to the poor; and if I have defrauded anyone of anything, I will pay back four times as much.' Then Jesus said to him, 'Today salvation has come to this house, because he too is a son of Abraham. For the Son of Man, came to seek out and to save the lost' (Luke 19:1–10)

This marvellous story from Luke's gospel gives us many clues about why the meal can play such a central role in evangelism and therefore helps us to think about the role of eating together within the Alpha course. More than this, the story contains a number of parallels with the Alpha process itself.

In this story, Zacchaeus is a seeker or a searcher, like many joining an Alpha course. He has heard about Jesus and would very much like to get a glimpse of him for himself. He goes along as part of a crowd, perhaps as much to gauge their reactions as to see Jesus. But for one reason or another, the straight line to Jesus is blocked. In Zacchaeus' case he is too short to see over the crowd. So the seeker looks around to see what is available to let him get a chance of seeing the truth about Jesus for himself. The tree is a good idea – it gets round the obstacles without the seeker being obtrusive or obvious. But something happens, an actual encounter with Jesus takes place. The encounter is personal and carries an invitation to move from passive watching to active doing. Zacchaeus responds. What happens next is especially interesting; Jesus comes not as a host but as a guest. Jesus enters into the context of hospitality as the one who must be welcomed, hosted and fed. It is up to Zacchaeus to decide what such hospitality means for his future life. So making Jesus welcome, eating with him, transfers exactly onto the phrases we use about asking Jesus in, welcoming Jesus into our lives and so on. It is in the context of eating and drinking that real transformation takes place. Zacchaeus opens his heart to the poor and promises to make right any wrongs. It is in that context that Jesus proclaims salvation. The presence of Jesus in the sinner's life, dwelling with him, bears the fruit of conversion. Scripture also makes it clear that Jesus is willing to be a guest in anyone's life: 'behold I stand at the door and knock, if anyone opens the door I will go in to him'.

If we think deeper into what this implies we can understand more about why the meal has an important part in evangelism. Out on the streets of Jericho there is a personal invitation from Jesus to Zacchaeus. He is clearly chosen or selected, hence all the jealous grumbling from others, but what happened next was very unlikely to have been a quiet supper. Zacchaeus would have taken Jesus into his rich man's household of family, friends and servants, while Jesus would surely have brought his own family of disciples and friends. Zacchaeus would therefore make the decision to change his life in the context of his entire household and what it would mean for them. In this he would be encouraged and helped by the example of those Jesus had with him and around him. Eating and drinking in fellowship together would cement that bond and that decision. Within such intimacy, the life-changing decision can be made.

Digesting the Alpha meal

Eating as doing

If we look deeper at the process of sharing a meal, we can identity what elements of eating together enhance evangelism. In the first place, eating requires us to acknowledge our creaturely needs as physical beings who require sustenance to survive and to thrive. We cannot purely theorise or speculate intellectually about eating. We only understand eating by doing it and by comparing those experiences. Eating and drinking require physical activity, forms of doing, so no one can be entirely passive or not participate. So everyone who eats even a little bit of what is on offer at the beginning of an Alpha session is already in some way participating in the course itself. That the meal is followed by a talk or video, sets up a correlation between the satisfaction of physical hunger and the possibility of satisfying any spiritual hunger the guests may experience.

Eating as equality

Secondly, if all the people present share the same food, this offers equality of opportunity that sets all participants on the same level. Irrespective of how or little much a person may already know about Christian faith, equal sharing of food, so that no one deserves more than another, levels the playing field, perhaps especially for those who feel some caution, fear or trepidation about coming to such a course. Such equality of opportunity and sharing is a fundamental feature of Christian life and has to be carefully nurtured. In the New Testament, Paul writes in his first letter to the Corinthians: 'when you come together to eat, wait for one another. If you are hungry, eat at home, so that when you come together, it will not be for your condemnation'(1

Cor 11:33–4). Clearly, in the early church, some Christians arrived early and ate all the food! There are however other factors which may mask this levelling process of equality and sharing, which we will have to address.

Eating as sharing

Thirdly, the process of eating food can make sharing and bonding easier. If someone talks all the time they will not get to finish their food. If someone says nothing all the time, they will finish first and have to look at an empty plate while others finish. The best balance is both to talk and listen, and for people who find either of these difficult, the process of eating and drinking may make it easier to find a balance. Eating gives people an excuse to look away or break eye contact if they feel threatened. Dealing with your plate gives you a legitimate reason to find something else to do if you feel adrift or if there is an awkward silence or if you have said something you didn't quite mean.

Being fed

Being a guest and being fed produces in many, perhaps most, people, a sense of obligation to the host. Having received something, we look to give thanks or to give something back. Eating therefore can create a receptivity, and we may look for a way of showing gratitude or willingness to respond. Placing the meal at the beginning at the evening can therefore prepare participants for evangelism; goodwill has been inculcated and prepared. Further, as any busy parent knows, most adults spend their time doing the cooking and offering it to others. Having food cooked for you and offered to you is a luxury. So most of us understand that cooking and feeding are deeply involved with nurturing those we love. So when we are nurtured in our turn, we may very well respond to that pastoral care of our basic needs. Being fed has the capacity to return us to feelings of childhood wellbeing and can prepare us to learn. Of course, a key issue here is to nurture those feelings without making people feel nannied or babied or that their integrity as adults is being compromised or manipulated. This is of course a potential problem in any course which fits within a timeframe and which runs to a programme, as Alpha does.

The social function of eating together does a lot of the preparatory work for the Alpha course. As the course progresses session by session, the meals permit the chance for people to continue to bond, to catch up on news, chat and indulge in small talk. So if people start to feel that the input of the actual sessions is unhelpful, confusing or simply not for them, they may at least continue to come and stay the course because they are unwilling to give up new friends. One could even go so far as to argue that the course is a mere excuse or framework for a form of friendship evangelism that is unconsciously placed on the group of guests and left to work. Where intimacy and sharing are built up, the beginnings of community are already found.

Problems

One of the criticisms which has been levelled at the Alpha supper is that its design and execution is a particularly middle-class concept which is alien to others who would never dream of either attending or hosting a supper or a dinner party. In today's society a number of sociological factors have driven a wedge through the idea of a family meal. Many people with busy working lives eat fast food on the run or in front of the television. Adults may not necessarily eat with their children, or perhaps ever get to sit down with their children and actually talk or share with them. Even the 'traditional' Sunday lunch may be impossible to keep going in the face of competing needs to shop, take the children to sporting activities or travelling to other family members. Similarly, it is often increasingly difficult for friends to get together to share meals, and intimacy is relayed by telephone chats, emailing or texting. A special meal might be a curry or an evening at Pizza Hut on the odd occasion, or fish and chips on a day out. It has been reported that for some people, the Alpha meal may initially be a daunting experience, where the rules are behaviour and procedure are unknown and nobody knows quite what to expect. In a mixed group therefore, certain people may have an advantage and get more out of the meal environment than others who may feel alienated and estranged. It is interesting therefore to note that as the Alpha process has been rolled out across the country, different churches often advertise something specific about their meals, – 'nothing fancy, just soup', in response perhaps to the idea that attending a 'supper' might be a threat or even an ordeal.

Venues

The Alpha course was and is associated with Holy Trinity, Brompton and is therefore first and foremost identified with Church. Necessarily, of course, many Alpha courses are held in church premises, church buildings or halls, but as the programme has been developed and adapted, course sessions are also held in people's homes. Sometimes different volunteers will take turns in holding a course session in their homes and take turns in providing the meal, so that the guests encounter a series of hosts who both nurture and feed them in their own environment. As successive 'generations' of Alpha take place, Alpha converts may become hosts in turn, adding their positive experience to the mix.

Bonding people together at church or in homes automatically creates community, sometimes in cells of shared belief or understanding that may have something in common with the early church communities.

For many people, this helps to create a sense of family that lasts the length of the course and beyond. Where this occurs, eating together cements that community so that the actual content of the course becomes more like a Pauline epistle confirming and exhorting people who are already bonded by eating in friendship. Or this can work like a monastic model of reading scripture as edification for the mind while the food edifies the body, providing an holistic model of nourishment, – physical and spiritual feeding overlaid on one another. 'One does not live by bread alone, but by every word that comes from the mouth of God' (Matthew 4:4; cf Deuteronomy 8:3).

Church and community

A further question then arises as to what the bonded, meal-sharing community actually is in terms of its ecclesiological identity. Some people, such as the Revd Dr Michael Moynagh, in his research for *Changing World, Changing Church*,[1] have suggested that such a community is *already* a church and the dispersal or absorption of such a tight friendship-group into institutional Church is probably unhelpful. If the only end of Alpha is evangelisation or straightforward conversion then it is clear that some participants may be moved to respond and become part of a church if they are not already part of a congregation. But some others may fall by the wayside. If, however, what is offered is the formation of community, bonded by eating and drinking, then it is likely that every course, whether people come to accept the Christian faith or not, generates a fellowship in which the sceptics and unbelievers are nonetheless supported and nurtured and valued. Needless to say there can be tensions where the members of bonded group feel pressure to end up conforming to an expected model. The desire to stay with the friendship group, but to resist the invitation to commitment can be spiritually and psychologically difficult for some people. The Holy Spirit weekend or whatever equivalent local churches can provide, is often the point for testing this difficulty, where people, removed from their familiar environment but finding familiar friends and food-companions, find it easier to please their bonded group than test the difficulty or misgivings in their hearts.

Theological models and ideas

God as the one who feeds us

Scripture teaches us that God feeds us and Jesus' command to Peter is 'Feed my sheep' (John 21:17). If we love the Lord, this is what we must do in response to him. There is therefore a correlation between the establishment of a community which eats together and which is nurtured by God. The act of eating couples with the intellectual idea that God gives us our food, knows everything that we need, and offers both sustenance and pastoral care. Where such teaching comes into contact with the process of being fed, the understanding of God as the Father who feeds his child and gives us what we need, is reinforced. 'Give us this day our daily bread' makes sense if indeed we have just received our daily bread. If we can know this for ourselves then we can also accept the next part of the Lord's Prayer that acknowledges that God can forgive our sin.

Invitation and welcome

Much evangelism is built around the idea of welcome and invitation and the provision of a safe, friendly space in which people can encounter the gospel and have the opportunity to respond. But what is perhaps often overlooked is that the invitation and welcome to a meal excites all kinds of responses in people. Often these are positive: pleasure, gratitude, the excitement reminiscent of being a child invited to a party. Of course for some people, such invitation also brings trepidation and a sense of unworthiness or ignorance, which can be overcome by sensitive pastoral care, or, as George Herbert puts it:

> Love bade me welcome but my soul drew back
> Guiltie of dust and sinne.
> But quick-ey'd Love, observing me grow slack
> From my first entrance in,
> Drew nearer to me, sweetly questioning,
> If I lack'd any thing.
>
> A guest, I answer'd, worthy to be here:
> Love said, You shall be he.
> I, the unkinde, ungratefull? Ah my deare,
> I cannot look on thee.
> Love took my hand, and smiling did reply,
> Who made the eyes but I?
>
> Truth, Lord, but I have marr'd them: let my shame
> Go where it doth deserve.
> And know you not, says Love, who bore the blame?
> My deare, then I will serve.
> You must sit down, sayes Love, and taste my meat,
> So I did sit and eat.[2]

Herbert's poem teaches us the significance of invitation and welcome in the context of guest at a meal. As host, Love responds to the needs and feelings of the guests and overcomes any sense of concern or unworthiness. More to the point, offering people food addresses the concern that people have that the Church is only interested in the 'dust and sinne'. Love is more than able to address that suspicion by an unconditional giving and this is therefore something which should not be compromised by heavy handed treatment of human sin in the ensuing sessions.

Service

Another important element in the process of receiving people and feeding them is that it demonstrates the service that is at the heart of Christian life. Indeed the sacrificial service demonstrated by Christians towards others is often what people outside the Church admire, even if they feel generally negative or hostile towards the Church itself. Christians who run soup kitchens, hostels, or who work with vulnerable, oppressed and poor people show forth the reality of a God who seeks continually to raise up and save the broken hearted. Often, also, spiritual seekers feel they are not themselves worthy of such service. This suggests that it is not the Nicky Gumbels or the Sandy Millars talking and explaining about Jesus who only make a difference in the way the gospel is offered to people. In fact the catering team, or volunteer hosts are probably just as important, if not more so, in creating a context of hospitality and service to which people can respond. Being Martha without complaint so that others can be released to be Mary is itself important witness to the kind of Christian life on offer.

Eucharist

We can also argue that inviting people to supper, to eat and drink in a new fellowship already brings people into a eucharistic community before many of them have perhaps even heard the word or know what it means. What Jesus did in the company of his disciples at the Last Supper forever binds the notions of eating and drinking to the memory of Jesus's life given unconditionally for human beings. The incarnate Christ, born as one of us, had to eat and drink to survive as we do. Scripture tells us, over and over again, of feasts and meals at which Jesus was present. Jesus provided wine, oversaw a catch of fish, spoke of living water at a well, cooked breakfast. Jesus fed the crowds who came to hear his words and the food never ran out and no one ever went hungry or less than satisfied. That same Christ also nourishes us in the sacrament. Those who would become immersed in the Christian faith and life have to understand the power and mystery of the sacrament, but no one can do this without understanding why we must nourish our bodies and seek to nourish and nurture others as part of our care for human beings. Therefore beginning an Alpha course with an act of eating and drinking with friends foreshadows the full sacramental life of participating in Holy Communion within the fellowship of the Church. There is a sense then that any such meal, celebrated in a Christian context, carries with it the memory of Christ's actions: ''The cup of blessing that we bless, is it not a sharing in the body of Christ? The bread that we break, is it not a sharing in the body of Christ? Because there is one bread, we who are many are one body, for we all partake of the one bread.' (1 Corinthians 10:16–17).

Eschatological glimpses

'When he was at the table with them, he took bread, blessed and broke it, and gave it to them. Then their eyes were opened, and they recognised him; and he vanquished from their sight. They said to each other "Were not our hearts burning within us while he was talking on the road, while he was opening the scriptures to us?"' (Luke 24:30–2).

> When they had gone ashore, they saw a charcoal fire there, with fish on it, and bread...Jesus said to them 'Come and have breakfast'. Now none of the disciples dared to ask him 'Who are you?' because they knew it was the Lord. Jesus came and took the bread and gave it to them, and did the same with the fish. (John 21:9, 12–13)

What is truly amazing about these two incidents from scripture is that they take place after Jesus' death and are resurrection appearances. For both stories, people who might well be unable to cope with the enormity of the resurrection have its reality confirmed to them in the context of a meal. A ghost, spirit, hallucination or phantasm does not break bread or invite people to breakfast. The continuity of relation with the person of Jesus is affirmed. In both stories Jesus gives bread to those with whom he is in relation. He feeds their bodies as well as their minds and hearts, caring for the whole person, as God desires.

The provision of a meal then, and the acts of feeding those who are spiritually searching is therefore not only a eucharistic act but also an eschatological act. This makes sense because the pictures of heaven which Jesus gives to a questioning people in the gospels are pictures of feasting and celebration. The prodigal son returns to the father and is received into his house and family with rejoicing and a great feast. Heaven is like a wedding to which everyone who loves the Lord is invited. Professor David Ford argues that Ephesians 1:10 represents 'a stupendous picture of Jesus Christ as the host of the universe, entertaining everything and everyone.' He goes on to indicate how being part of that opens our minds and hearts to an inclusiveness that is capable of transforming the world:

> Let us stretch our imaginations to begin to conceive the significance of that. It of course embraces the literal hospitality we have been discussing, with feasting as the practice that can most clearly hint at the ultimate destiny to which God is inviting us. That in turn involves healing of relationships, forgiveness of wrongs, justice and all that makes for peace in which people can enjoy each other across all differences.[3]

If an Alpha meal can suggest even a glimpse of this eschatological promise, then it surely points enquirers and those who are already Christian to a vision of the sheer attractiveness and hopefulness of God's promise. This is what the *rest* of the course has to deliver. It is no surprise then, that the end of each course is marked by celebration and affirmation. A wonderful meal with friends is a glimpse of eternity.

Entertaining angels unawares and the hospitality of God

The famous Rublev icon depicts Abraham entertaining the angels unawares. The story is told in Genesis 18 and is a lovely picture of ancient courtesy and hospitality. Abraham offers himself to them as their servant, offers rest and refreshment and spares no expense in giving them good bread and meat. What Abraham does not know, is that he is receiving a visitation from the Lord. In the Rublev icon, the three figures from the story are depicted sitting around a table on which stands a cup. Each of the figures inclines to the others and the icon is therefore also seen as a depiction of God's nature, as the Trinity, eternally involved in *perichoresis*, a dance of mutuality, hospitality and graciousness. This helps us to understand how Jesus is among us as both host and guest, master and servant, and how every fellowship which eats and drinks in mutuality and care for one another reflects not only the hospitality of God but also something of God's own nature, giving and receiving.

The function of the Alpha meal is therefore critical to the success of the enterprise itself. Rather than being simply a matter of function, the meal is perhaps *the* evangelising influence, beyond which the testimonies, videos and talks are (perhaps literally) the icing on the cake. The provision of a meal, no matter how simple, allows a Christian community to make actions speak louder than words, and makes it possible for anyone to begin to participate in a fellowship, no matter how fierce their resistance to the Christian invitation. This is something which is increasingly understood and used in forms of outreach. Café churches and meetings in pubs, fellowship meals in homes and church halls – all these use the principle of serving and feeding others as a way of helping people encounter Jesus as one sitting and serving among them. It is not surprising then that the formula appeals to so many people. With every last supper, new disciples may appear to accompany Jesus to Calvary and the resurrection and the fish and bread that awaits on a further shore.

Notes

[1] Michael Moynagh, *Changing World, Changing Church*, Monarch, 2000

[2] *The English Poems of George Herbert*, edited by C A Patrides, Dent 1974, p. 192.

[3] David F Ford, *The Shape of Living*, HarperCollins (Fount), 1997, pp. 168–9.

CHAPTER 18

Worship, Sacramental Liturgy and Initiation Rites within Evangelism and Alpha

James Heard [1]

Up until the 1990s, evangelism for evangelicals generally involved emotionally charged events, often held in large stadiums, which meant that evangelists were unable to care for those who converted. The unintended result of this was that new converts generally did not make the leap to church and thus remained organically severed from the body of believers where they might have been nourished, discipled, and baptised. Into this situation came the Alpha course. It has revolutionised the way evangelism is conducted, locating evangelism firmly within the body of Christ, and carried out by the whole laity rather than just the 'specialists'. It is largely through the extraordinary generosity of Holy Trinity Brompton (HTB) that the Alpha course has been made available and has made such a huge impact on the church.

This chapter will concentrate on three issues in relation to evangelism and the Alpha course. First is the role of sung worship and the particularly charismatic form that it takes on Alpha. Second is the difficult question of whether traditional liturgy should have a role in evangelism. Is it essential for anything that is remotely 'churchy' to be dropped for the purpose of attempting to engage with the non-churched? Lastly, what exactly is Alpha? Does it attract the type of people it is aiming to attract? And how does it link with the sort of initiation process seen in the early church's catechumenate, which has experienced a revival recently? While a number of churches follow Alpha with their own courses, I shall restrict my analysis to Alpha and its four follow-on courses. To what extent do these courses fulfil Jesus' call to make disciples? (Matt 28:19–20)

Worship on Alpha

In contrast to Willow Creek's ethos of not including worship in its 'services' aimed at enquirers, Alpha encourages the use of worship from the start of the course.[2] AI suggests that courses start with songs that guests might have sung at school: 'Praise to the Lord the Almighty' or

'Amazing Grace'. Over the next few weeks, the time for sung worship gradually becomes longer, with the style and songs increasingly reflecting the influence of John Wimber on HTB and Alpha. This is seen both in the worship and times of 'prayer ministry'. The main characteristic of charismatic worship is intimacy: 'a desire for an intimate encounter with a powerful and transforming God' (Ward 2005: p. 100). As such it is open to the epicletic incoming and indwelling of the Holy Spirit and its concomitant sense of God's presence. James Steven (2002: p. 170) describes the 'cultural backdrop' to charismatic worship as being that of popular culture developed from the 1960s counter-culture with its emphasis on individual participation and expressiveness, impatience with formality and institutional life and willingness to experiment with new forms of community life. The style of such worship involves a flow of uninterrupted worship songs, each taking one more step towards intimacy with God. This is in contrast to the teaching function that hymns have regularly had in Protestant traditions. So by the Alpha weekend, guests are singing: 'Your love is amazing, steady and unchanging... I can feel this love song rising up in me'. Such songs are similar to secular romantic love ballads. Percy has noted the grammar of paternalism and passionate (or quasi-erotic) intimacy in charismatic worship (see Percy 1997: pp. 71–106).

Critics of Alpha view this element of the course as a sort of 'charismatic imperialism', and question the therapeutic and individualistic nature of such worship. But how do Alpha guests find this element of the course? Nicky Gumbel describes how, although guests often find worship difficult to begin with, by the end of the Alpha course, 'they often find it is the part they value most... [and it] helps people to make the step from Alpha to the church' (Gumbel 2001b:62). Because Alpha guests come from a wide range of backgrounds, their response to worship is varied. Those with some church background don't tend to find sung worship too difficult to get into. Indeed, some testify to their faith coming alive through such worship. Worship can also have an overflow in which the non-churched guest discovers that 'God is really among you' (1 Cor 14:25). And yet, for those who remain non-Christian on Alpha, it is difficult to sing many of these songs with honesty and integrity. Hunt (2004) describes how some attendees found that the inclusion of sung worship reminded them of what they most disliked about church. One Alpha guest comments:

> It was all rather curious. You were expected to join in a world that was entirely alien to you. I can't sing, and found myself either miming the words or remaining silent and looking around me at people swaying about and their hands outstretched, thinking they are all rather a strange lot really or what on earth am I doing here? (Hunt 2004: p. 62)

One guest from my research became irritated when worship was introduced:

> I thought, on a course, it wasn't really appropriate, really. I was
> just a bit surprised. I didn't really want to sing songs. I didn't
> know them for a start...And I also felt, they were making a
> little bit of an assumption that we all want to do that...And
> that's when I started to get a little irritated...

So, the inclusion of sung worship has a mixed response from guests:
some positive whilst others negative.

What about the theology of charismatic worship? Steven's (2002)
research into charismatic worship includes a theological critique,
which also relates to Alpha. He found an implicit orthodox understanding of Trinitarian worship, with praise and prayer offered 'in
the Spirit' to each of the three persons of the Trinity. However, he
also found an inadequate theology conveyed by the more charismatic
elements – the sung worship and 'prayer ministry' – that can be traced
back to a failure to locate this worship through the Son, to the Father.
This included an overemphasis on the triumphant ascended Christ,
with a neglect of the incarnate Christ (Steven 2002: p. 208).

On the one hand, Alpha, along with charismatics generally, have
brought a refreshing focus on the dynamic and experiential element
of being a Christian, together with a genuinely optimistic hope that
God's hand is at work in the world today. This is in contrast to what is
often a sober institutional Church (*We Believe in the Holy Spirit*, 1991,
p. 54). On the other hand, the difficulty comes with a subtle group pressure towards expressing constant joy coupled with a strong emphasis
on intimacy. Such worship can all too easily neglect those present who
may be in physical pain, grieving, clinically depressed or simply spiritually numb. There is also a danger of including worship as a 'strategy for
evangelism' in that worship can easily become utilitarian, just a means
to an end, and lacking in integrity. Further, charismatic worship will not
suit everyone, with one vicar protesting, 'We need flexibility if we're to
use [Alpha] at all in our culture. We are not (and don't want to be) Holy
Trinity Brompton – but the assumption is that we should be' (cited in
Ireland 2000: p. 22).

Walker's (1995) remark that charismatic worship eventually
becomes routinised over time is confirmed by the observations of
Pete Ward (2005) and James Steven (2002) that charismatic worship
is carefully constructed. The worship tends to start with up-tempo
songs and then move to appreciably slower songs with ballad melo-
dies. The careful crafting of charismatic worship may lead us to ask
to what extent it has become a form of rite itself. It is surely naïve to
suggest, 'We don't do liturgy'. Rejection of traditional liturgy tends to
be replaced with an implicit liturgy, which inevitably becomes just

as structured as the explicit type. Whilst setting out to not be liturgical, to what extent has charismatic worship become precisely this? To liturgy we now turn.

Liturgy

Is there a place for liturgy in evangelism? The Orthodox Church has highlighted the importance of liturgy not only for mystagogy[3] but also for evangelism. Alexander Schmemann, for example, argues for a return to the ancient and normative practices of the eucharistic liturgy. To a postmodern world, the liturgy can have huge potential. Andrew Walker (1995) writes, 'To come to the liturgy is to penetrate sameness, to discover for the first time transcendence and otherness; to experience words and images, signs and symbols that have a reference point beyond themselves.' Liturgy need not be understood only as a repetition of words. It can include words and images, theologically significant body language, lights and colours, smells and food. It is, in one word, incarnational. This is in stark contrast to Willow Creek's minimalist model of evangelism, in which anything that is remotely 'churchy' is viewed as irrelevant and removed from their seeker sensitive services.

Where are HTB and Alpha located along this spectrum? On the one hand, Alpha's inclusion of sung worship and 'prayer ministry' might suggest that it is qualitatively different from Willow Creek. On the other hand there is Alpha's aim of 'stripping the gospel down to its bare essentials'[4] in order to make it accessible to the non-churched. This includes using simplified language, a simplified theology and a removal of ritual and symbols. Both HTB and Alpha share with many evangelicals a suspicion of set prayers, avoidance of traditional liturgy or creeds, and, unlike the catechumenate, there is no connection with the church's yearly cycle and liturgical calendar, which could actually provide greater breadth and balance to people's journey of faith.

As such, on Alpha and its follow-on courses, there is a lack of *celebrations* or milestones within the ongoing worship of the Church, to affirm people's journey of faith. In the catechumenate, these celebrations are not confined purely to those going through the initiation process. These 'rites on the Way' provide an opportunity for all the baptised to continually explore as a community the riches of baptism and to re-examine and renew their own discipleship (CW: Initiation Services). One of the consequences of a frail ecclesiology is downgrading the importance of the institutional life of the Church. As the Anglican doctrinal report, *We Believe in the Holy Spirit* (1991: p. 55) observes, 'Openness to change, vitality, warmth and surprise all need to be balanced by continuity, regularity, stability and rationality. In other words, structure and form are as important as the living content; both should be understood as the work of the one and the same Spirit.'

HTB is consumed with a passion to make the gospel known to first-time seekers. Therefore, always thinking of the non-churched, their weekly services follow a simple Vineyard liturgy: worship, teaching and prayer ministry. Alpha guests are slowly exposed to this style of worship as the course progresses. HTB recognise, contra Schmemann, that too much can be asked from the liturgy. The wonderful canonical liturgies of the church yield their treasures to those who have been adequately prepared in faith. However, as Abraham notes, the price paid for neglecting these treasures is a liturgy that has been sacrificed on the altar of missional pragmatism. If Schmemann asks too much and expects the uninitiated to grasp what is normally available to the mature believer, does HTB expect too little? Surely there is a way whereby, with adequate catechesis and formation, even the seeker can come to revel in the common life of the church's liturgy. With people coming from further back – with no Christian narrative to build upon and from a situation that can only be described as pagan – this process will be lengthy. Such a situation forces a rethinking of what it is to be a mission-shaped church and how the gospel might be inculturated. While it might be understandable for Alpha to strip the Christian faith down to 'the essentials' to make it accessible, to leave people there robs them of some of the treasures of the Christian tradition.

Perhaps I have been unfair to Schmemann. While many people are still children of the Enlightenment and appreciate a rational presentation of the Christian faith, post-modern spiritual searchers will be turned off by such an approach. To suggest that the Alpha Weekend is the spiritual post-modern bit of the Alpha course is a moot point. We are increasingly in a world which is open to a spirituality that includes symbol and ritual, lights and colours, smells and food. All those spiritual paths that are emerging in the West as serious alternatives to mainline Christian belief incorporate significant elements of the mystical, the numinous, the unpredictable and the non-rational (which, Drane notes, is not the same the irrational). Arguably, the more rationalised everyday life becomes, the more important it is for our lives to be focused on something mysterious (Drane 2000: p. 45). Perhaps the Orthodox Church will appeal to a culture that is more open to mystery, and less convinced by Enlightenment-fuelled deductive or inductive arguments.[5]

The link between worship, liturgy and evangelism may be further reflected upon in the light of traditional practices of the Church – now renewed in Catholic and Anglican traditions – concerning Christian initiation.

Links with traditional liturgical practices for initiation

From Matthew's commissioning passage (28:16–20) it is clear that *making disciples* is the overarching imperative, with baptism and teaching as part of that overall process. The early (Western) Church developed four stages with several passage rites that marked the transition to the next period of growth (see chart below). Drawing on various sources within the tradition, Hippolytus, a bishop of Rome, developed these in the *Apostolic Tradition*, written around 215 CE.[6] This has seen a revival recently, having been taken up in the Rite of Christian Initiation for Adults (RCIA) in the Roman Catholic Church, the Anglican Church[7] and even among some evangelicals.[8] The chart below gives an outline of these four stages.

Phase 1	Pre-catechumenate/evangelism
Passage Rite	Rite of welcome /enrolment
Phase 2	Catechumenate/pre-baptismal teaching
Passage Rite	Election and public scrutiny
Phase 3	Sacramental initiation
Passage Rite	Baptism, confirmation and first communion
Phase 4	Mystagogy ('explanation of the mysteries').
	Post-baptismal nurturing of the faithful into full membership

The process would generally last over three years and was a highly tactile affair, including repeated laying-on of hands; consumption of bread and wine, milk and honey; signings with the cross on the forehead; and oil and new clothing (Kavanagh 1978: p. 65). Whilst a rigid or uniform pattern should be avoided, it is important for both Church and individual that Christian initiation and formation takes place within a clear framework. Interestingly, Alpha shares many of the catechumenate ingredients: *welcoming* people as they are, *accompanied journey, faith sharing* usually through story and dialogue, and *community*, expressed through the involvement of congregation, sponsor and group leaders (*On the Way* 1995: p. 35).

So, where specifically does Alpha fit with the above schema? Alpha is *intended* primarily to be used as a tool for evangelism, as evidenced by the numerous dramatic conversion stories told in the quarterly publication *Alpha News*. Secondarily, Alpha is for new Christians and those wanting to brush up on the faith. In catechumenate terms, Alpha's aim is to do both pre-catechumenate and mystagogy.[9] Yet according to Hunt's (2004) research, what Alpha is *actually* doing, at this present stage in its history, is more of the latter than the former. My research points to another function of the Alpha course: re-initiation of those with some church background into the church community.[10] This is highly significant. Alpha is performing a crucial role in reviving the faith of Christians, re-initiating those who have dropped out of church, and welcoming back prodigals. The same concern was behind Pope

John Paul II's call for a 'new evangelisation'. Brueggemann also sees the evangelising of 'insiders' as being the primary agenda in evangelism (Brueggemann 1993: p. 73). In addition, Alpha has given a forum, often lacking in churches, for Christians to be able to ask questions and express doubt.

Because Alpha sees itself as being an ecumenical course, and presenting the 'basics' of the Christian faith, it shies away from the third phase of the catechumenate: sacramental initiation. I shall come on to ecumenism shortly. Nervousness over the sacraments has been a general feature of evangelicalism.[11] For example, Norman Warren's *Journey to Life* (1964) argued that baptism and confirmation counted for nothing unless you have faith and repent. Anthony Lane has noted the lack of any clear inclusion of baptism in initiation in the evangelism of the last forty years, addressing as it did a mostly nominal Christian audience.[12]

My impression is that while Alpha shies away from sacramental teaching due to its ecumenical stance, a charismatic experience of the Holy Spirit on the Alpha Weekend may (sometimes anyway) act as a sort of surrogate form of initiation. Ritual and rites of passage hold a very important role in initiation, and when baptism is ignored, as it has been within evangelical revival campaigns over the last three centuries, substitutes have been invented or borrowed to take its place. This is seen in Charles Finney's 'new measure' where the 'anxious seat' acts as a public manifestation of becoming a Christian. Finney displays here a weak and pragmatic conception of baptism, but his point is extremely significant. By replacing baptism, evangelists have lost the richness of grace provided by the sacraments of the church (Abraham 1989: p. 131).

There is very little mention (one paragraph) of baptism on either Alpha or the four follow-on courses written by Nicky Gumbel. A critical question here is, 'What part of the Church's traditional liturgical practices is an intrinsic and necessary part of evangelism?' It might be understandable that baptism is not highlighted in the Alpha course itself; in the early church, baptism came after an extended period of spiritual formation. However, looking at the follow-up material, the lack of teaching on baptism or Eucharist suggests that HTB have created an unsacramental form of Christian initiation. For the majority of Roman Catholics, Orthodox and Anglicans, it is inconceivable for a two year programme of evangelism and discipleship not to stress the intrinsic link between baptism and evangelism, or to see baptism, confirmation[13] and eucharist as the goal of the initiation process.

Attempting a course that is accepted and that works ecumenically is frighteningly difficult.

What is viewed as the Christian basics depends on ecclesiology and it is at the level of ecclesiology where much of the criticism around

Alpha lies. There is no ecclesially neutral standpoint. So who decides what the basics of the Christian faith are? Where, or with whom, does authority lie? For the Roman Catholic Church, this is relatively straightforward. People know who the Pope is and where he is. The difficulty with the evangelical tradition is that there are multiple 'popes' and it is not entirely clear who they are! Stephen Brian's (2002) PhD thesis also raises the question of authority and Alpha's 'basics'. He argues that Nicky Gumbel is essentially Alpha's pope and that it is he who decides what the basics are, viz. a charismatic evangelical, ethically conservative form of Christian faith. So it is perhaps not quite accurate for Nicky Gumbel to suggest that the basics on Alpha include those things upon which all Christians agree. That is clearly not the case.

One might argue that since Alpha is mostly attracting people already with some church connection (who are already baptised?) this does not matter. Again, this highlights the difficulty of having a mixed 'audience' and content. For Alpha, this includes the potential clash of agenda between the non-churched and Christians seeking a refresher course. This is not just a problem for churches running Alpha. Some Anglican Churches running a catechumenate found that many enquirers are already baptised, raising the possibility of ignoring their baptism in order to fit them into the rites (*On the Way* 1995: p. 35). On Alpha, it is not uncommon for the few guests that are non-churched to feel totally outnumbered by Christians, and as a result feel inhibited to ask questions. One course I researched 'dissolved' after the fifth week because of this, and other guests whom I interviewed left after just one session for the same reason.

Another difficulty in having a mixed group is how the Eucharist is handled. HTB's Alpha course includes an 'informal Communion' at its weekend away. If Alpha is aiming at the non-churched, who have not been baptised, the placement of the Eucharist before baptism or confirmation is highly irregular. This is a contentious issue which cannot be dealt with fully here. Put briefly, the Eucharist is the sacrament of nourishment of our continuing relationship with Christ, just as baptism marks its beginning. Graham Cray argues that an act of worship made too accessible to post-modern consumers may be at the cost of the very elements that are central to the building up of Christians (Cray 1999). Offering the Eucharist to the unbaptised ends up diluting or even altering the very nature of the sacrament itself, not to mention ignoring centuries of church tradition. Mike Riddell (1999) views the 'fencing of the table' as working against mission and cites John Wesley, who saw the Eucharist as a 'converting ordinance'. He argues that, ironically, while Christ's act of self-giving for the world demonstrates the inclusive nature of gospel grace, the Eucharist has traditionally been exclusive, alienating non-churchgoers. However, it needs to be kept in mind that in Welsey's day, the overwhelming number of people in Britain were baptised as infants, so to speak of the Eucharist as a 'converting ordinance' means in all likelihood the awakening of faith in the *already baptised*.

The last area I want to touch on is the narrow focus that evangelical conversion has taken in contrast to the catechumenate, where there is an integral link between evangelism and discipleship. One of the four attributes Bebbington (1989) assigns to evangelicals is conversionism,[14] and it only takes a cursory review of *Alpha News* to see how significant it is for the course. Such a stress should be applauded. Indeed, despite numerous calls from within the Anglican Church to recognise the changing mission context in the UK, it has mostly been evangelicals, and courses like Alpha, that have acted to any great extent on these challenges. The difficulty is that it has resulted in evangelism taking precedence over all else the church does. As Abraham notes, it ignores the primary horizon of the kingdom of God within which evange-lism, social action, pastoral care and all else the church does must ultimately be set (Abraham 1989: p. 86). And if Alpha is to be run as recommended, three times a year, for most churches this leaves little time or energy for anything else. It also means that with such a focus on evangelism, many converts have not owned the intellectual claims of the Christian faith nor been supported in their spiritual and moral formation. This is not helped by the evangelical suspicion of repetitive liturgy. The early church catechumenate, during the intense period of preparation before baptism, included a 'handing over of the Creed' (*Traditio Symboli*) by the bishop or a deputy. Later the candidate had to come back and repeat it in a ceremony called the 'Giving back of the Creed' (*Redditio Symboli*). The sponsors helped them to learn these prayers (Yarnold 1977: p. 12). An interesting question for those who convert on Alpha is whether, two years after completing the course, they could recite and give a simple explanation of the Apostles Creed? This is where the Emmaus Course, which is essentially a modern cate-chumenate, has an edge over Alpha. Alpha and its follow on courses would certainly gain in breadth and depth by listening to the experi-ences and insights that the revival of the catechumenate has brought. As it stands, churches running Alpha, or thinking about it, would be well advised to think very carefully through the broader context of Christian initiation, bearing in mind that Christ's command is *to make disciples*, and *to baptise* (Matt 28:16–20).

Conclusion

My aim in this chapter has been to attempt a friendly critique of Alpha, in particular its use of sung worship, the role of liturgy and links with the early Church's form of evangelism and discipleship. Whilst I make some criticisms it must be said that much good has come from Alpha.

In contrast to the evangelistic campaigns that were so prevalent up until the 1990s, Alpha has set evangelism firmly within the body of Christ, to be carried out by the whole laity. And contrary to some critics who suggest that Alpha conversions are shallow and short-lived, there are an increasing number of Alpha graduates who have been through theological training and have been ordained. God has transformed many lives on Alpha courses throughout the world, and this should be the cause of great rejoicing.

There are inherent tensions and even confusion between the use of Alpha as a (discipleship) course for Christians and its use as an (evangelistic) course for non-Christians with added tension regarding how many sacraments nominal or lapsed Christians have received prior to going on the course. This may reflect Alpha's history as originally being designed for new Christians and then adapted for the non-churched. Perhaps this makes the course more flexible but it does creates difficulty in how certain elements of the course are received, notably, the Eucharist on the Alpha Weekend. It also complicates how to follow up participants and in ensuring ongoing formation. For the non-Christian guest who converts on Alpha, this must surely lead to sacramental initiation. But even for those already baptised as infants, a rite re-affirmation one's baptismal commitment would also be helpful.[15] In sum, the mixed grouping on Alpha means that its initiation structure tends to be rather untidy and unfocused. Alpha and its follow-on courses cannot stand alone as a holistic model for initiating people into the Christian faith and thus ecclesial life; nor does it fulfil all that Jesus requested in baptising and making disciples (cf Matt 28:19–20). Churches running Alpha have different ecclesiologies but serious thought needs to be given to these issues, and what else is needed for integrating people into the full riches of church life.

Bibliography

Abraham, William, *The Logic of Evangelism* (London: Hodder and Stoughton, 1989); *The Logic of Renewal* (London: SPCK, 2003).

Arnold, Clinton, 'Early Church Catechesis and New Christians' Classes in Contemporary Evangelicalism', *Journal of the Evangelical Theological Society*, Vol. 47, no.1, March 2004, 39–54.

Bebbington, David, *Evangelicalism in Modern Britain: A History from the 1730s to the 1980s* (London: Routledge, 1989).

Booker, Mike and Ireland, Mark, *Evangelism – Which Way Now?* (London: Church House Publishing, 2003).

Brian, Stephen, *The Alpha Course: an analysis of its claim to offer an educational course on 'The Meaning of Life'* (PhD thesis, University of Surrey, 2003).

Brueggemann, Walter, *Biblical Perspectives on Evangelism: Living in a Three-Storied Universe* (Nashville: Abingdon Press, 1993).

Cray, Graham, Ward, Pete (ed), *Mass Culture: Eucharist and Mission in a Post-*

modern World (Oxford: The Bible Reading Fellowship, 1999).

Dearborn, Kerry, 'Recovering a Trinitarian and Sacramental Ecclesiology.' In J. John Stackhouse (ed.), *Evangelical Ecclesiology: Reality or Illusion?* Grand Rapids, Mich.: Baker Academic, 2003.

Drane, John, *The McDonaldization of the Church* (London: Darton Longman and Todd, 2000).

Finney, John, *Finding Faith Today* (Swindon: British and Foreign Bible Society, 1992).

Gumbel, Nicky, *Questions of Life* (Eastbourne, Kingsway, 2001a); *Telling Others* (Eastbourne: Kingsway, 2001b).

Hunt, Stephen, *The Alpha Enterprise: Evangelism in a Post-Christian Era* (Aldershot: Ashgate, 2004).

Ireland, Mark, *A Study of the Effectiveness of Process Evangelism Courses in the Diocese of Lichfield, with Special Reference to Alpha* (Cliff College, MA dissertation, 2000).

Johnson, Maxwell, The Rites of Christian Initiation (Minnesota: Liturgical Press, 1999)

Kavanagh, Aidan, *The Shape of Baptism: The Rite of Christian Initiation* (New York: Pueblo Publishing Company, 1978).

Macquarrie, John, *A Guide to the Sacraments.* (London: SCM Press, 1997).

Percy, Martyn, 'Sweet rapture: subliminal eroticism in contemporary charismatic worship.' *Theology and Sexuality* 6: 71-106, 1997.

Riddell, Mike, 'Bread and Wine, Beer and Pies.' In P. Ward (ed.), *Mass Culture: Eucharist and Mission in a Post-modern World.* (Oxford: The Bible Reading Fellowship, 1999).

Schmenmann, Alexander, *The Eucharist, Sacrament of the Kingdom.* (Crestwood, New York: St Vladimir's Seminary Press, 1988).

Steven, James, *Worship in the Spirit: Charismatic Worship in the Church of England* (Carlisle: Paternoster, 2002)

Walker, Andrew, *Telling the Story* (London: SPCK, 1995).

Ward, Pete (ed), *Mass Culture: Eucharist and Mission in a Post-modern World* (Oxford: The Bible Reading Fellowship, 1999); *Selling Worship* (Milton Keynes: Paternoster, 2005).

Webber, Robert, *Journey to Jesus: The Worship, Evangelism and Nurture Mission of the Church.* (Nashville: Abingdon Press, 2001); *Ancient–Future Evangelism: Making Your Church a Faith-Forming Community* (Grand Rapids, Michigan: Baker Books, 2003).

Yarnold, Edward, *The Awe Inspiring Rites of Initiation* (Slough: St Paul's Publication, 1977).

Church Reports

On the Way: Towards an Integrated Approach to Christian Initiation (London: Church Publishing House, 1995).

We Believe in the Holy Spirit: The Doctrinal Commission of the Church of England. (London: Church House Publishing, 1991).

General Synod Liturgical Commission, *Common Worship: Initiation services, 'Rites on the Way and reconciliation and Restoration'* (London: Church Publishing House, 2003).

Notes

[1] In this chapter I shall make reference to my own doctoral research on Alpha, which has so far included participant–observation in five Alpha courses, including post-course interviews of both Alpha leaders and guests. For full details of references cited in this article, please see list at the end of the article.

[2] Of course, whether sung worship is actually included on Alpha courses outside HTB is questionable. Gumbel suggests that small courses are unlikely to have any singing (Gumbel 2001b:62). In my research, sung worship has rarely been included, apart from on the Alpha Day or Weekend. This has largely been due to a sense of discomfort because of the smallness of the group.

[3] That is, post-baptismal catechesis (see below).

[4] Sandy Millar in Gumbel 2001b: p. 22.

[5] One Orthodox Church in London has recently started a course called 'A Foundation in Orthodox Christianity', and it has generated a substantial amount of interest. *The Way*, Institute for Orthodox Christian Studies, Wesley House, Jesus Lane, Cambridge CB5 8EJ. E-mail: aneste@aol.com.

[6] For a comprehensive treatment of these rites, see Yarnold (1977) and Kavanagh (1978).

[7] See the House of Bishop's report *On the Way* (1995).

[8] See Robert Webber (2001, 2003) and Clinton Arnold (2004).

[9] Peter Hocken sees Alpha as belonging to the pre-RCIA, or pre-catechumenate, stage, and the French Monsignor Pierre d'Ornellas, sees Alpha as being like mystagogy.

[10] Having led a number of Alpha small groups at HTB itself, my impression is that this is largely what is going on there.

[11] Certainly, Karl Barth viewed baptism as being a mere dispensable sign. The outward sign of the water could disappear and leave the inward reality unaffected. Yet as Macquarrie notes, 'Is this not a kind of docetism, a denial that human beings are embodied creatures whose being is a being-in-the-world?' (Macquarrie 1997: pp. 71–2) Such disembodied spirituality is a denial of the incarnation and of God's repeated demonstrations that creation can host the divine (Dearborn 2003: p. 39).

[12] Anthony Lane, 'British Evangelical Identity' conference at King's College London, 30 July 2004.

[13] Or some kind of rite giving symbolic–sacramental expression to the sealing gift of the Holy Spirit (see Johnson 1999).

[14] The other three attributes are biblicism, activism and crucicentrism.

[15] See 'Rites on the Way' (2003).

CHAPTER 19

Alpha and Advertising:
an Evaluation of it's Promotional Campaign

John Griffiths

The Alpha promotional campaign is unique. Since 1998 the Alpha course has been promoted using conventional advertising. Christian organisations and churches have of course used advertising before. But these campaigns have run for perhaps two-three months at most. An exception is the Church Advertising Network's Christmas poster and radio campaign, which has been run annually for a number of years but where the creative approach has regularly changed. What is remarkable about the Alpha campaign is how the campaign has consciously re-used core elements. This means that there is a cumulative effect as later campaigns reprise and build on what has been done before. The second difference from other campaigns is the consistency of the Alpha course itself. In 2005 there are now a number of variants but the basic course is still substantively the same as when it was first made publicly available. It is always easier to advertise a consistent product. The Alpha promotional campaign is worth considering in some detail to see how the application of conventional marketing techniques over eight years has worked. In this chapter I propose to review the creative content of the campaign, to review the ways in which the campaign may be considered to be working and to review the research which has been carried out for Alpha. Some of the material comes from an interview I conducted with Tricia Neill, the worldwide executive director of Alpha, and Mark Elsdon-Dew, the communications director.

Summary of the impact of the
Alpha course and marketing campaign

The number of churches in the UK running at least one Alpha course in 2005 was 5,700 of the 28,000 churches in the UK according to an annual survey run by the Christian Research Association (CRA).[1] There is no centralised roll call mechanism so there is no accurate way of measuring the number of those taking the course, nor is there a mechanism for measuring how many participants subsequently make a Christian commitment, though the CRA asks the proportion who subsequently attend church. The 2005 Alpha Survey report claims that the total number attending an Alpha course during the year ran to 182,000 at an average of 21 per course with 1–2 people (per course) attending church as a consequence.[2] Between 2002 and 2005 656,000 non-churchgoers attended the course.[3] This represents one of the main evangelistic initiatives for the UK church and makes a visible difference to a church congregation. For those churches participating it means that on average 13–15 of those attending their services have come as a result of attending an Alpha course.

Outside of the UK the figures are just as impressive. Worldwide the number of churches running Alpha courses was 27,000 in 2004. Estimates of worldwide participation run to well over a million people a year.[4]

The Alpha course has for a number of years been promoted using 48 sheet posters and posters on the back of buses. In 2005 for the first time a cinema commercial was used. In addition, participating churches put up posters and banners outside their own churches. Leaflets promoting the course are also available using the same brand identity as the posters. In 2001 ITV ran a series based on the Alpha course called *The Alpha course will it change their lives*? And there has been regular coverage of the course in the national press.

Alpha International is cautious about giving out figures of media spend but conservatively estimate the media value of it as running to around £1 million – though this is well in excess of what they spend directly on media buying. The following figures represent the advertising industry published figures on Alpha's media spending. These are based on ratecards and since the space is always sold at a discount the actual media spend is lower. However, the cost of creating and printing the materials isn't included in these figures.

2001	2002	2003	2004	2005
£351,827	£385,645	£210,198	£170,735	£218,234

Source: Register Meal Alpha expenditure 2001–2005

Media spend since 2000 has run to perhaps £200,000 a year. Since the first year when participating churches were invited to contribute to the costs, the finance for the campaign has been raised principally through private donations. The advantage of this is obvious: there is no shareholder body to paralyse decision-making or to lobby for changes in the promotional message.

Review of creative approach[5]

The creative approach has been remarkably consistent since the advertising began in 1998. As a matter of record Alpha have used the same agency throughout which has made a difference. The analysis of the creative content that follows is provided because it illustrates power-fully how consistent the campaign has been.

1998

Even in its first year the poster is breaking new ground for religious advertising because the focus is firmly on the course and not on making assertions about God, the church or the problems of the world and it resists the temptation to shoehorn other messages in! The headline implies that the audience are young – for whom the flat, the car, the girlfriend are important trophies. Even more interestingly, the head-line finished with a question – an unusual approach for a Christian organisation given the conventional perception that the church typi-cally makes absolute and authoritarian claims. The implication of the headline is that those who will find the course useful are those who are dissatisfied with a materialistic lifestyle and want more out of life. The implication is that the Alpha course will provide the solution.

In this first poster there is no clear call to action nor a way of finding out which church near to you is actually running the course. The poster announces that the course is being run by a church nearby. The Alpha team told me they would not consider advertising until they were confident there would be a sufficient number of churches partic-ipating to ensure that anyone seeing a poster would be able to attend a course near them. This principle is still adhered to and strongly recom-mended to churches in other parts of the world thinking of advertising the Alpha course.[6]

On a more technical note – the typography is san serif, which is typical of most UK poster communications (though not religious advertising which tends to use serif fonts). There are a variety of type sizes and colours. The layout is quite crowded and not particularly clear or confident. For example in the line *Still not satisfied?* it is not clear why the font is fainter and italicised.

The Alpha branding is actually quite low key. There is no indication at this stage that the man wrestling with the question mark is a logo – a conventional device for building recognition across different types of media. It could just be a visual to illustrate the headline.

1999

For the second poster the context is the autumn leading up to the millennium. The question format is kept from the previous year. The examples are still aimed at a young audience – though there are topical references to the Millennium Dome and the Millennium Bug, which were talking points at the time. Both were controversial and problematic. But now for the first time there is a claim – *an opportunity to explore the meaning of life*, a message which has appeared on every poster campaign since. There is a clear implication that people will use the context of the millennium to think more deeply about the direction of their lives.

For the first time a telephone number is provided if people want to find the details when and where the Alpha course is being run.

Despite the change in the background colour from red to white, this is clearly a continuation of the previous year's poster. The typography has become quite cartoon like, the font is sans serif but with the use of 2 different colours red and blue matching the colours in the logo. Again there is a range of (5!) type sizes, and bold and italic are used without any particular logic being evident.

The logo is more clearly a logo now – it's bigger, on the right hand side and 'The Alpha course' clearly put underneath it. This is a key stage in the Alpha branding process though the logo never gets bigger than this! But having established the logo, also repeated on church posters and flyers, it can be used as an ongoing element of the campaign to tie in all promotional materials

2000

For the third year there is a major change in the visual treatment. But there is enough continuity with the name of the course, the logo, and the claim that it is being run at a local church to tie it in with the previous years. The format ending with a question has been replaced by the claim that the course will help you explore the meaning of life. From now on 'the Alpha course' takes pride of place in the headline. The cartoon treatment has been replaced by high quality photography. The Alpha team take pains to point out that when they use models in promotional material they are of real people who have taken the Alpha course.[7] The model for the 2000 campaign is aimed firmly at Middle England – young, attractive, casually dressed (for the workplace?). The pose suggests either that she has found the answer or that the course is interesting and engaging. (Is she leaning on a table or desk?)

The now familiar logo is placed sits on the right hand side – smaller than the previous year with the Alpha course shortened to Alpha. This reflects or assumes a certain familiarity of it.

The text is now a cool grey – the urgency and cartoon style has been replaced by a confident open typographical style. The telephone number has been dropped and the website put in its place that also reminds us that Alpha is a course. The campaign ran in the autumn of 2000 after the dot com bubble had burst. It's an interesting historical note that the online audience (running at perhaps a quarter of the population) was seen to be big enough to use this instead of the telephone number. It would have been a lot easier and cheaper to use this as a response function. But it would have skewed response towards those who got on to the internet first – younger, more experimental, more educated and more affluent people.

Again there is a clear family resemblance to previous campaigns in what is said and how the logo is used.

2001

The claim is kept from the previous year but now 'the Alpha course' has been made the dominant statement emphasised by size, putting the headline in red and italicising Alpha.

The high quality photography treatment has been maintained. I suspect the selection of the model was a reaction to criticism that the female model used for the previous year was too WASPish and that the campaign needs to be seen to be more inclusive, reflecting the breadth of people taking the course. It isn't until the following year that a group based course is promoted using a group of people. However the use of the white polo neck – casual wear smart enough for leisure or work use ensures that the campaign continues to be aspirational – the sort of thing that the professional classes would be happy to attend. And the model's expression communicates satisfaction and fulfilment. Alpha is still presenting itself as offering meaning to the individual, the potential for transformation.

The text has reverted to more than one colour. If there is a criticism it must be that the typography has varied in style, colour and size every year for no very good reason. But the consistency of inconsistency is impressive!

2002

The Alpha course is now set in serif block capitals as the dominant feature on the page. Along with the website URL and the logo Alpha is mentioned 3 times and in 3 different typefaces – rather busy for a poster. The now established claim is laid out in two lines with a continuous underline beneath it drawing the eye to no particular purpose.

The aspirational photographic treatments of previous years have been replaced by an abstract group image – blurred, dressed in primary colours and drawn from more than one ethnic group. For the first time the visual dramatises how the Alpha course is run – through

group discussions. This would have been reinforced because of the ITV series presented by Sir David Frost, which ran earlier in the year. So exploring the meaning of life has become a shared experience – less academic and more interactive. Is the figure in orange the group leader? Is this figure carefully placed lower than the others to suggest he is willing to listen?

The website reference has dropped the ubiquitous www. Someone is working to ensure that the layout stays lean and doesn't fill up with text.

This is the fifth year of the campaign and the discipline is remarkable despite the vagaries of typography.

2003

The blurred group image goes but the group visual stays. The Alpha Course branding is as bold and imperious as it was last year. But now the group depicts young people, possibly students but more likely young professionals. The campaign has swung back towards aspiration. Are these the kind of people you would like to discuss the meaning of life with? What was the promise of the transformation of the individual has now become a group exploration. And it is a reminder that one of the reasons a young person might opt to attend a group of this kind might be to meet other young people. It certainly doesn't feel at all like church! This probably wouldn't have been credible in the early years of the campaign. The church is popularly seen as authoritarian and removed. In this visual there isn't even the suggestion that the group may be listening to a group leader – this is a level playing field where opinions are given and received.

Type and layout continues to be rather scattergun with a range of sizes and fonts – but this too is consistent!

2004

And the yuppies have been replaced by a mobile phone! There would always be dangers in clearly showing young professionals in posters emanating from a church in prosperous Knightsbridge. But by using a mobile phone owned by almost the entire adult population and lionised by the young – the campaign continued to communicate that the course is interactive and can answer everybody's questions.

Type and layout are cleaner and tighter here than for a number of years – the website has finished wandering and is tucked beneath the familiar logo.

The question is back after five years absence but more direct than ever before: *Is there more to life than this?* We come full circle.

But this only serves to reinforce the unity of the campaign, which has been remarkably consistent. For seven years the advertising has promoted a course that helps you explore the meaning of life when there are so many other topics Christians would like to address the nation about.

2005

In 2005 the question *Is there more to life than this?* is supported using posters and a cinema commercial. The posters promote a website landing page called istheremoretolifethanthis.com which links in turn to the alpha.org website. The poster is a bricolage of screen elements. The mobile graphic of 2004 has been replaced by a mobile/computer screen. This is perhaps the biggest departure over previous years but the typeface of the Alpha Course Headline stays the same and the logo is the same as ever.

This year for the first time a cinema commercial has been added as well. Again, it features young people who have taken the course. To a thumping trance groove we watch a footballer score a goal in a Premier League match, a model on the catwalk and a mountaineer scale a peak. All of them ask the question to camera – 'Is there more to life than this?' All of them, the Alpha team assure me, have done the course and are members of the Holy Trinity Brompton congregation. They are all at the top of their respective professions. The tone of the

Images © Alpha International

THE ALPHA COURSE
explore the meaning of life

alpha.org

Alpha

cinema commercial is challenging but once again the element of aspiration is back. These young people are role models for the course but would be role models anyway by virtue of what they do for a living. (The 'mountain-top' image was used again as the centrepiece of the 2006 campaign, in which the cinema ad was re-run, but did not include billboard advertising.)

How it works

Advertising is complicated and works at a number of levels. Summarised, here are the levels at which the campaign is operating.

The first way is to encourage churches to run their own Alpha courses. The CRA research makes it clear than as of 2005, awareness of Alpha posters and busbacks is at 69% of participating churches interviewed.[8] A question unfortunately discontinued after 2002 asked why churches opted to take part. For half, the successful running of a previous Alpha course is the primary factor in encouraging them to run it again. The second most important factor to this was the national advertising campaign which 48% had given as a reason. The previous year when the ITV series was running, 48% of the sample had given the ITV series as the reason for participating and 35% also cited the advertising then.[9] So it is clear that awareness of mass publicity is a strong incentive persuading churches to participate and run their own courses. Arguably it is the strongest factor in encouraging new churches to sign up to run courses.

The second way in which the campaign works is to legitimise the course for individual Christians and encourage them to invite their friends. The role of invitation is central to the course. According to the CRA surveys the ratio of church members to non-church members (including leaders) can be as high as 2:1 on the courses themselves.[10] The success of the course depends on the active participation of church members who do not leave it up to the leaflets or the advertising to bring people in. There is no direct survey evidence of the campaign working this way because this audience hasn't been researched. If it were true, there would be a clear difference between those in areas where there had been a heavy weight of advertising inviting their friends and neighbours and those where advertising was lighter weight. But we have no evidence of the impact on individual Christians.

The third way in which the campaign works is to legitimise the campaign for course attendees to reassure them that this is a genuine course that is widely known and accepted. Again we don't have direct evidence for this because no surveys have been carried out with course attendees.

What the advertising may be doing, however, is to attract younger people to the course than churches could normally attract. From the 2004 Alpha survey, the age mix of the course polarises with the average age of non-churchgoers attending Alpha courses set at 39 and the number of churchgoers attending Alpha courses at 45. The age group accounting for the highest proportion of non-churchgoers is the 20–29s with 20%. The only age group of churchgoing attenders which is higher than this is the over 60s![11] In other work that the Christian Research Association have carried out they have drawn attention to the dramatic decline in British young people attending church services and joining churches. Indeed, the drain among the under 20s since 1995 has been running at a net lost of 1000 young people a week.[12] One of the major contributions the Alpha course has made is to give those under the age of 30 an opportunity to hear the Christian message. They aren't coming to conventional church services to hear it.

The last role for the advertising is that the advertising directly influences people to come on Alpha courses. There is no survey evidence of this again because no one attending the course has been asked how they heard of the course and in truth the reporting and attribution of advertising as an influence is not reliable. However, there is still plenty of anecdotal evidence that individuals who are far beyond the churches and who don't know any Christians have on occasion been stirred to try it. However, this is likely to be a minor effect of the advertising relative to personal invitation. The evidence from surveys conducted by organisations such as the Billy Graham Association is that the biggest reason for people being drawn to faith is friendship with Christians. The fundamental design of Alpha – the meals, the church locations and the discussions – are designed to make the most of these friendships and to help those exploring the Christian faith to make new friends.

Measuring the success of Alpha

I have already made considerable use of the CRA's surveys conducted in and outside of the UK. But Alpha also commission MORI to run a national survey twice a year in June and September each year in order to benchmark the progress of the campaign. This makes fascinating reading as it has been run since 1999. This shows the steady increase in awareness of the Alpha course and the correct attribution of Alpha as a course about Christianity. As of September 2005 this reached a new peak of 22% of the adult population from 9% in 2000.[13] Of these people half had either taken the course or knew those who had. This reveals the real achievements of the Alpha course. Church attendance has been falling for several decades in the UK. Currently less than 7% of the population is recorded as attending church on Sundays. So the Alpha course has, it would appear, built a presence in the fringe around the churches to roughly twice the size of the churchgoing population. And despite a fallback during 2004 the 22% figure is the highest yet recorded. There is no evidence that Alpha has peaked or stalled. It may be appropriate to take into account less frequent church goers. According to the most recent church census of 1998 16.2% of the population have been to a church service at least once in the last year.[14] If all such people recognise the logo – which is probably unlikely – Alpha is still recalled by 6% of the population who haven't been to church in the last year – and the figure could well be higher. So Alpha can't be written off as only being about Christian education of well-established churchgoers by another means.

However it is also true that 68% of people surveyed claimed that they had never heard of Alpha and were unable to say what it was. And 9% didn't know/remember. Despite television series, and sustained advertising – three quarters of the adult population would appear to be untouched by it. This is important because within the Alpha organisation there has been talk of a tipping point following the book of the same name by Malcolm Gladwell about word of mouth marketing.[15] The theory goes that once sufficient people have heard about a product a tipping point results in mass trial and adoption. Despite nearly 2 million people taking the course in the UK (and national adverting campaigns for 8 years), Alpha is national news but it is emphatically not a household word. (I saw a poster for the Queen Musical 'We will rock you' recently which announced that 4 million people have now been to see it – which puts the Alpha figures in context even if it is attendance of a course covering some 10 weeks!)

Further analysis of those aware of the Alpha course may provide an indication of the gulf that remains to be crossed. The age profile of those aware of the course is skewed towards those older than 35 reflecting the ageing profile of churchgoers. But something the CRA surveys were unable to analyse is that the demographic skew of the course is firmly middle to upmarket: 31% of ABC1s[16] were aware that Alpha is a Christian course. The higher the income the more likely they are to make the connection: 32% of those whose households have £30,000 a year were able to correctly identify the course (this is the top 25% of all households). Lastly a full 40% of broadsheet readers knew what Alpha was compared with 13% of tabloid readers. Broadsheet readers account for a mere 20% of the population.[17] Now the church in the UK may be predominantly middle class. But the churches of the UK are universally distributed. In principle everyone in these islands is within reach of a local church. And as I have said it was central to the Alpha's initiative that advertising was not run until the course was available across the whole country. The advertising media used for Alpha since the start of the advertising has been outdoor, arguably the most egalitarian of media channels. But despite the widespread communication of the course – those who correctly identify the course are mainly the educated and the affluent.

However the following factors need to be considered: firstly the response function through the internet is only available to perhaps 60% of the population. The digital divide is a real one. It might be worth testing the use of a telephone line and SMS/text communications to see if this opens up a new group of the population – still young, heavy on phone usage but not necessarily online. Secondly, it really does depend on who is doing the inviting: whether Christians are evenly distributed throughout society and what proportion of the population are likely to know a Christian well enough who will invite them on an Alpha course.

The Alpha organisation are utterly clear that an Alpha course is not a quick fix for churches and that the course needs to be run several times to be bedded down in a local context. As Tricia Neill said 'It is vital that as Alpha is used as an ongoing part of a churches outreach so church members continue to invite those around the fringe'.[18] Otherwise the supply of those coming on the courses dries up after 2–3 courses after church members have taken the course (course 1) invited their friends (course 2) then run out of people to invite (course 3 and close down).

Dealing with the criticisms

In this section I wanted to address some of the criticisms made of the Alpha campaign.

The first goes under the heading of McDonaldization.[19] Detractors argue that a standardised approach is inappropriate for evangelism, which needs to take on an authentic form in each neighbourhood. This is an odd criticism – or at least one at odds with many other aspects of church life and practice. Long before the arrival of McDonalds churches opted to use standard Bible translations, to use clergy trained centrally, and to use liturgy and doctrine which was also standardised. Arguably the church has been standardised much longer than your average burger bar. But there is a serious point underlying the criticism, which is that the Alpha course is deploying mass marketing techniques to promote the Christian faith. This would be a just criticism if, like the Billy Graham organisation, Alpha published statistics of converts thereby positioning itself as a technology with measurable outputs. What Alpha has done successfully is to use a standardised course format, which can be taught rapidly to course leaders and rolled out with national advertising support so that ordinary churches can offer a basic introduction to Christianity without the need to write their own course material. The effect of the advertising has been undoubtedly to legitimate attendance of the course, making it easier for people on the fringes to consider. If Alpha was not standardised then this would not be possible to do since there would be no guarantee that the course in the local church was the same as that promised by the advertising. This does mean that the implementation of Alpha is disciplined with pressure being brought on those who want to make radical changes. Apart from the substitution of local speakers for the Nicky Gumbel video teaching there is strong encouragement to use the course as it is offered.

The second objection is that Alpha has become one size fits all. And that the advertising has the effect of making the course the only choice for church outreach over other more relevant alternatives. I would argue that this is unfair. The Alpha course continues to be run and developed out of Holy Trinity Brompton. It is hardly surprising that the content of the course requires abstract thinking and debate – and the format of the Alpha course reveals its origins in one of the most prosperous neighbourhoods in London with a much higher than average proportion of graduates, both students and professionals. There has never been any attempt to dumb down the Alpha course or to 'un-Knightsbridge' it. It has been proven to be a successful format at HTB and this has been refined for local use and offered should it prove useful elsewhere. It is also interesting to look at the extension of the Alpha portfolio. Aside from variants for the workplace and for students etc, the new products such as the marriage course are developed for the HTB congregation and will be offered further afield once the course has been tried and tested. There is no indication that Alpha is offered as the solution for every single church or that courses are being multiplied to cover every lifestyle or demographic. Mark Elsdon-Dew commented 'Alpha makes no claim for ubiquity. This is a product, not a denominational initiative which has to achieve universal coverage and effectiveness.' [20]

Next we need to consider the issue of aspiration. And here I believe there is a case to answer. What is normal in Knightsbridge isn't normal elsewhere – even if Premier League footballers and catwalk models are a commonplace on the Brompton Road! In advertising, celebrities have always been an established tool for creating aspirations around a product – and over a million people a week buy celebrity magazines. The Alpha campaign is not using celebrities – i.e. people familiar to most of the public. But if the invitation to explore the meaning of life is supplemented with the layering of messages about personal success and social mobility then the success of the course in drawing people in may not be entirely because people are attracted to the Christian message. And as the course reaches out to demographic groups further away from middle-aged middle class Christianity – these aspirational associations may become a handicap rather than a motivator.

Lastly there is the fundamental charge that it is inappropriate to treat sinners as consumers. Confront them with the gospel – don't waste time marketing a course. I would argue that the Bible is much more realistic about the motivation of human beings than we are! When in Ephesus the apostle Paul held daily discussions in Tyrannus lecture hall for a period of two years until all the Jews and Greeks in the region had heard the message.[21] If Paul was prepared to use the facilities of the local sophists then who are we to spiritualise the presentation of the faith. If the presentation of the Christian faith begins and ends with the unbeliever as a consumer then indeed it is deficient. But if the evangelist starts with the unbeliever as consumer, then, if this is the way in which most of our society look at the world, then what better place to begin?

Where next for Alpha?

I have already alluded to the development of the product portfolio. There are no less than 7 product variants now: for prisons, for youth, students, the forces, the workplace, for seniors and support materials for use in the Catholic Church. Not only that, importantly, the launch of the marriage course marks the second separate product. The benefits of a second product are that branding elements can be shared between products – leading to faster take-up of the new course. Those who have been on the Alpha course now have a new course to go on – if they are married. It also means that using shared branded elements that it will be possible to have advertising which may promote different courses at different times of the year but has a halo effect awareness of the overall Alpha brand. The Alpha team are very clear that they won't consider advertising the marriage course nationally until they have enough churches will to run it – until then it is not yet formally classified as an initiative – universally available.

But undoubtedly the biggest challenge is going to be deciding at what point the Alpha course has reached its natural limits and whether they continue to develop product variants to reach segments of the audience already within Alpha's reach or whether they develop entirely new products to take them beyond the current fringe of the churches. Arguably the limitation is the churches themselves and their connections to the communities they are in. The danger in producing new courses would be to multiply options without increasing the reach of those courses to the rest of the population. The real challenge is to mobilise local Christians as friends and witnesses.

In Summary: Learnings from Alpha's advertising campaign

1. The power of centralised decision making
It seems to me from analysing the creative work and speaking to the team that Alpha has successfully kept its promotional campaign from the creeping sickness of committees and muddled and politicised decision making. The campaign is a unique example of a consistent offer of the course and as such it is to be commended.

2. Only promise what you can deliver
The Alpha team has been careful to ensure that they only advertise the course when there are enough participating churches to deliver it. Would that more commercial advertisers did the same. In this regard, since they haven't run evaluation research into how satisfied participants are with the course, the advertising ensures that the Alpha course is protected in large part against people feeling that the course has been misrepresented to them. Also, arguably, the mass coverage through advertising and PR helps to discourage local course leaders from taking Alpha too far away from its roots.

3. Continuity of team and agency
It seems to me that the consistency in the client and agency team has made a major contribution to the consistency of the campaign. Personnel changes and new brooms play havoc with marketing strategies: the average length of tenure of a brand manager in the UK is 18 months!

4. The value of consistency
The growing reach of the campaign hasn't been inexorable – there have been periods when awareness has fallen back. However the benefit of advertising regularly and using the same branding elements has

meant that the campaign has been able to build on previous investment in effect ensuring better value for money.

5. The power of cohesion

Makes all promotional activity work together more effectively. As the branding elements are used and reused it does mean that promotional materials work harder (better?) because they remind people of previous campaigns. The use of posters year after year has undoubtedly helped this. Whenever new media channels are used it will take time to develop the branding elements, which work naturally across channels. At present there is little cohesion between the Alpha.org site and the promotional campaign – the landing page where enquirers land when they type in details copied from the posters contains design elements which are also in the posters but the cinema commercial doesn't fit with anything apart from the key question! Stability in the use of media helps to encourage better cohesion.

6. Simplicity

Keeps the course format the same. By ensuring that the basic format of Alpha courses has stayed the same, it is possible for all product variants to benefit from advertising, increasing its value.

7. Value

We have to consider this most sensitive of topics. If a typical year's campaign has cost as much as £300,000 taking into account media spend as well as originating all the material, this might seem a vast sum of money. But it has succeeded in establishing a year round awareness of the Alpha course with over 8 million of the population (14%) for an average cost of just under 4 pence per person. Were you to have the address of every one of those people you could not expect to mail them once for an expenditure of less than £4 million. In the final analysis the Alpha campaign is maintaining a level of awareness, which it would be hard, if not impossible, to replicate by spending the budget any other way. PR couldn't be depended on to deliver the consistency and control of message in the way that advertising has. Advertising is still one of the cheapest ways to build and maintain the awareness of a mass audience.

8. Realism

We must be realistic about what can be achieved. The campaign has built a substantial fringe around the church. But there is no evidence that Alpha is any closer to challenging the current prevailing postmodern orthodoxy outside of the church. Spirituality continues to grow as a mainstream interest in contrast to religion with which Christianity and the church is still firmly associated and where relevance (or rather lack of it) is still a barrier to people seeing the Christian faith as a way of exploring spiritual issues. Alpha has become a dominant channel of church outreach but has yet to touch the mainstream of UK culture. But this depends on the activation of ordinary church members to invite and keep on inviting their friends and neighbours. Arguably one of the most powerful initiatives would be to put in a research metric to measure the extent to which the invitation and re-invitation to Alpha courses is being extended and to whom.

Notes

[1] Page 14 2005 Alpha Invitation and Autumn Course by the Christian Research Association.

[2] Page 19 2005 Alpha Invitation and Autumn Course CRA.

[3] Page 19 2005 Alpha Invitation and Autumn Course CRA.

[4] Page 13 International Alpha Courses in 2004 Christian Research Association.

[5] This analysis was first developed in a workshop run for the Church Advertising Network in January 2005.

[6] Interview with Tricia Neill and Mark Elsdon-Dew, Oct 26th 2005.

[7] Interview with Tricia Neill and Mark Elsdon-Dew, Oct 26th 2005.

[8] Page 30 2005 Alpha Invitation and Autumn Course CRA.

[9] Page 4 2002 Alpha Initiative and Autumn Course CRA.

[10] Page 17 2004 Alpha Invitation and Autumn Course CRA.

[11] Page 21 2004 Alpha Invitation and Autumn Course CRA.

[12] 2.21 Religious Trends 5 2005/2006 CRA.

[13] Alpha Awareness Sept 2005 Post Advertising MORI.

[14] Church Census 1998 Christian Research Association.

[15] *The Tipping Point*, Malcolm Gladwell, Abacus, 2002.

[16] ABC1 is a demographic measure which the advertising business has been unable to move away from because it is still intrinsic to how media is bought. It is a very loose descriptor for levels of household income and education. ABC1s are middle to upmarket. However the term is not a precise one.

[17] *Alpha Awareness* Sept 2005, Post Advertising MORI.

[18] Interview with Tricia Neill and Mark Elsdon-Dew, Oct 26th 2005.

[19] *McDonaldization of Society*, George Ritzer, Sage, 2004 revised.

[20] Interview with Tricia Neill and Mark Elsdon-Dew, Oct 26th 2005.

[21] Acts 19:9–10

CHAPTER 20

Alpha and Evangelism in Modern and Post-Modern Settings

John Drane

Introduction

In the theological colleges of the future, I can imagine someone setting an essay question with a title such as: 'Compare and contrast the approaches to evangelism found in the Alpha course and the emerging church.' That is always supposing that there are theological colleges in the future, or indeed that there is anything left of what we now recognize as church. And, for those who are wondering what sort of answer will command a high grade, it is probably that Alpha is a manifestation of a modernist approach to mission, whereas the reality we know as 'emerging church' is – for all its diversity – rooted in a conviction that, to be intelligible (let alone accepted) the Gospel needs to be contextualized in a very different culture, namely that of post-modernity.

The precise distinction between these different ways of being has been discussed endlessly (and often pointlessly) in recent years. In some church circles, it seems that they talk about nothing else. The ways of describing today's culture are seemingly endless: postmodernism (or post-modernism), postmodernity (also sometimes with a hyphen), post-Christian, secular, post-secular, late modernity, liquid modernity, post-Christendom, and many others. Those who use these terms do not always define them carefully, and in some cases I suspect that people use them without knowing what they mean. In fact, that may be the safest way in which to regard these terms: to admit that in the final analysis we do not know what is going on in the culture, and that any term we apply to try and articulate our understanding is likely to be provisional, even inaccurate. Out of the plethora of terms in current use, I tend to adopt post-modernity (with a hyphen), not so much as a precise definition but rather as a shorthand way of referring to the chaos into which things have descended once the previous worldview ('modernity') began to be questioned and rejected. It will fall to future generations to decide whether post-modernity turns out to be anything more substantial than that, though on the basis of all the available evidence right now it strikes me as unlikely that either 'post-modernity' or any of the other terms in common use represent any sort of coherent worldview. Arguing about words gives the appearance of rationality to discussions about contemporary culture, which no doubt explains why it has become so popular. But to paraphrase Marx's famous dictum, 'post-modernity' has become the opiate of the intelligentsia, a make-believe expression that encourages academics and others to think they understand what is going on in the world – and behind that is the thought that if we are able to name it correctly, we will also be able to control it. This is just wishful thinking: Western civilization is in a bigger mess than most of us care to admit. It may be in a phase of final meltdown.

Practical post-modernity

I will continue to use the term post-modernity as a convenient way of referring to whatever it is that is going on in Western society right now, but without any necessary inference with regard to what this means people may or may not believe in a theoretical sort of way. In terms of effective mission, the reality with which we need to deal has less to do with philosophical discourse, and is more about lifestyles and personal perspectives. The practical impact of post-modernity manifests itself in three ways that are relevant to this discussion. In everyday life, we are conscious of the fact that *nothing seems to work the way it once did*. This includes transient operations such as cooking, cleaning, or washing, as well as more profound matters like exploring the meaning of life. In his novel *Microserfs*, Douglas Coupland spells out how this sense of disconnectedness form the past affects our search for personal identity:

> people without lives like to hang out with other people who don't have lives. Thus they form lives.[1]

They tend not to hang out in churches, though, because the church is perceived as just one more thing that – whatever its usefulness to previous generations – is now well and truly past its sell-by date. George Lings is not being cynical but merely telling it how it is when he writes that for many people

> Church is what some others do. It is noticed sadly, in their terms, not only as an alien and expensive building that I wouldn't know what to do in, worse, it is occupied by people I wouldn't be seen dead with.[2]

The spiritual reality of that in terms of mission was eloquently articulated by a 20-year-old woman in a study carried out by George Barna in the USA (where, remember, church is still more highly valued than in the UK):

I honestly tried the churches, but they just couldn't speak to me ... All I want is reality. Show me God. Help me to understand why life is the way it is, and how I can experience it more fully and with greater joy.[3]

A second mark of everyday post-modernity is the realization that *the way Western people have lived is not the only possible way to be*, nor is it the only one that can lead to a fulfilled and meaningful life. A couple of generations ago, other world faiths were beyond the experience of most people, whereas today they are on our doorstep. But this is only one aspect of the diversity that we now experience. Within the Christian church, there is an awareness that there are many different ways of worshipping, and of doing theology. The rise of Pentecostalism from nothing at the beginning of the 20th century to being one of the major strands of the world church today is just one aspect of that. And within the wider culture, the nature of leadership has changed, not only in the fact that women now share it with men, but in the realization that leadership itself need not be defined by reference to the sort of hierarchical models inherited from the past. Along with that is a change in the ways in which we both exercise and acknowledge authority. Though political and industrial leaders struggle with this as much as the church does, there is a widespread feeling in the culture that power should no longer be something to be exercised 'over' people, but is something to be shared. There is enough power to go round without it all needing to be in the hands of just a few individuals! This is one important distinguishing factor in the rise of New Spirituality, for whereas traditional religions tend to be led by recognized authorities who exercise control over the beliefs and behaviour of their followers, New Spirituality creates a space for us all to explore our own pathway, and assumes that – especially in spiritual matters – there can be no experts who know it all, only pilgrims who can share what they have learned in the course of their own journey through life.

The third notable feature of everyday post-modernity stems directly from that, in *the frequently expressed desire to be 'spiritual' rather than religious*. The reasons why this has come about are complex and contested,[4] but the phenomenon cannot be ignored in relation to the mission of the church. An ethnographic study over a two year period of the spiritual and religious life of Kendal, a small town on the fringe of the English Lake District, demonstrated not only the reality of this shift, but also suggested that the rising interest in what the authors of that report called 'the holistic milieu' had largely occurred at the expense of the local churches.[5] Twenty years ago, Shirley Maclaine intuited the same conclusion, when she claimed that 'Your religions teach religion – not spirituality'.[6] It is certainly the case that, at the same time as the UK churches (of all denominations) have experienced significant decline, there has been a corresponding growth in the popularity of new forms of experiential spirituality, whether that be through the study of arcane texts, involvement in techniques to enhance spiritual awareness, or experimentation with so-called 'complementary' healing therapies and so on. Moreover, a much publicized research project carried out by David Hay at the turn of the millennium revealed that such spiritual experience is apparently not restricted to those with an overt faith commitment, but is widespread within the 'secular' population.[7] George Ritzer succinctly expressed one of the reasons why we are increasingly conscious of the need to find that special experience that will make sense of life:

> Human beings, equipped with a wide array of skills and abilities, are asked to perform a limited number of highly simplified tasks over and over ... [are] forced to deny their humanity and act in a robot-like manner.[8]

When I first came across that statement, I realized that it could just as easily be applied to church life as to any one of the other rationalized systems with which we increasingly struggle in everyday life, which is why I then wrote a book about it – a book which immediately struck a chord with large numbers of other people.[9] It is debatable whether the church really is as 'unspiritual' as some people claim, but whether we like it or not that is a widely held perception among those people who ponder such things. It makes sense to think that individuals who already believe that something spiritual is important for a wholesome life are more likely to be interested in the Gospel than those who are avowed atheists or agnostics, which means that our ability to reach these people will play a key role in creating the church of the future.[10]

A fourth characteristic of everyday life – and one that is growing in importance all the time – is *a consciousness that we live in fearful times.* Martin Rees is no scaremongering fundamentalist (he is Astronomer Royal, and a Cambridge professor), but in his book *Our Final Century* he paints a bleak picture:

> I think the odds are no better than fifty-fifty that our present civilisation on Earth will survive to the end of the present century ... What happens here on Earth, in this century, could conceivably make the difference between a near eternity filled with ever more complex and subtle forms of life and one filled with nothing but base matter.[11]

His book makes depressing reading, as he lists all the possible ways in which the ultimate doomsday scenario might be played out, most of which involve human error rather than deliberate terrorist actions. But the presence of indiscriminate killers on the streets of cities around the world is reminding us of just how fragile human existence is.

To be effective, any evangelistic strategy will need to connect with these concerns, and the church will not be part of the UK future unless we are able to contextualize the Gospel within this frame of reference. If that sounds unduly pessimistic, we need to remember that all the facts known to us point in that direction. Even Peter Brierley, a Christian researcher who wants the church to survive and thrive, has concluded that by 2040 there will – on present trends – be little distinctive Christian witness left in Britain, and that the denominational structures with which we are now familiar will have imploded and disappeared long before then.[12] He is not alone. American researcher George Barna reaches a similar conclusion with regard to the future of mainline denominations in the USA, and documents the rise of new expressions of Christian faith, such as home churches, marketplace ministries, and cyberchurch – all of which he projects will have overtaken regular participation in congregational activity within a very short time, so that even those who consciously model their lives on the Gospel (and also engage in a committed way in activities such as prayer, Bible, and spiritual direction) will be doing this without any formal connection with a local church.[13]

As a Christian believer and a theologian, I have no doubt that the church has a future: my belief in God (as well as my naturally optimistic personality type) allows me to see a future in which the Gospel is still a transformational spiritual force. But my analysis of the cultural trends in Britain also requires me to qualify that by saying that the church of the future may not be in these islands (or indeed in the West more generally), unless we address these serious missional challenges in more creative ways than we have so far been able to do. There are, of course, many signs of hope – not least the out-of-the-box thinking represented by the emerging church, with which this chapter started. The Church of England in particular has made a good start by embracing the insights offered in its *Mission-Shaped Church* report, followed so speedily by the establishment of 'Fresh Expressions' as a vehicle through which some genuinely missional creativity can be exercised.[14] But the real test will come in the next five to ten years, as the system faces radical questions about the continuity of new and old ways of being church. There will be no single answer to that question, but the one thing that is now indisputable is that the inherited patterns of church life no longer have meaning for the majority of Western people. Debates about the legitimacy of change are increasingly irrelevant, because the church has already changed beyond recognition. In my lifetime, it has gone from being a vibrant spiritual community at the centre of civic life to being on the margins, from being an all-age community to being largely the preserve of old people, and from being a place of nurture and spiritual growth for children to being a prison from which they escape as soon as they are old enough to make their own choices. There are of course numerous local exceptions, but the future of the institution as a whole is clearly in jeopardy. The days when the church was the single most dominant force in Western society have long gone. Indeed, the pendulum may even have swung to the opposite end of the scale, with large numbers of people taking it for granted that the church has nothing at all to contribute to today's search for ontological meaning, and significant numbers expressing resentment whenever Christians do venture to voice an opinion on the things that matter.

Alpha and post-modernity

In placing the Alpha course alongside these four marks of practical post-modernity, it might look as if Alpha works quite well in in spite of being developed principally in a modern setting. However, its foundationalist approach to Christian faith is certainly quite different from the more relational and experimental attitudes that I have identified as being central to the ways in which people do things today. In terms of the first mark, Alpha strives hard to avoid being categorized as a hangover from the past that no longer works in today's circumstance. All its advertising is designed to convince the public that not only does it work, but it represents something trendy. It is cool, or hip, to take the Alpha course – an image that is reinforced by the fact that a few celebrities have done so. The marketing suggests that, far from being attached to something outmoded and irrelevant (like the church), Alpha is at the cutting-edge of contemporary reflection on the meaning of life. The only connection with an institution is portrayed as more or less coincidental: the course may be 'coming to a church near you', but in reality it is more likely to be in a home or restaurant than in a place which looks like 'church'. If Alpha is church, it is certainly not church as our grandparents knew it.

This image, however, is more than just marketing hype. For the course itself avoids having to address the question of the church's irrelevance by scarcely mentioning the church at all! Christian discipleship is mainly portrayed (especially in the content of the talks) as a solitary affair between an individual and God, and insofar as it might become communal it is the sort of community created on an *ad hoc* basis by those who happen to be a part of the course. Sandy Millar and others may espouse conversion to Christ's church (as well as to Christ) and the Alpha approach to all this could be defended (I can think of several arguments myself that might be advanced in its favour), but its consequences require further reflection both theologically and culturally. Theologically, in relation to whether one can be a Christian without being a part of a church: this is a big question not only in the UK, but worldwide, with the emergence of indigenous churches in 'the next christendom' which either see no reason to have a connection with historic Christianity, or even reject the notion of 'church' altogether as being an imperialistic Western construct.[15] And culturally, I wonder if it is really possible to engage in effective mission today without acknowledging some sense of accountability for all the past baggage of Christendom (not all of which was negative). Moreover, in relation to a theology of culture, I am not sure that 'relevance' is an appropriate category. Truly effective contextualization will not be about making the Gospel 'relevant', but about being incarnational within the culture.

When we consider the matter of different ways of doing things, I will single out just one issue: leadership. Alpha is highly rationalized, and though to some people the label of 'McDonaldization' is a bad thing, a by-word for oppressive structures, narrow-mindedness, and personal exploitation, Nicky Gumbel repeatedly cites the business model associated with this label as a way of justifying the imposition of a rigid form of control that insists that Alpha must conform to a particular scheme wherever it is delivered, regardless of the local cultural context.[16] Leadership is very tightly controlled: interested non-Christians can only join as guests or possibly helpers, not as leaders. In spite of the fact that discussion and questioning appears to be encouraged, the reality is that Nicky Gumbel always has the right answer. Alpha tries to address this sort of criticism through its informal style, the emphasis on meals, time spent in groups, and going away for weekends. But even though everybody knows how to eat, and how to entertain their friends, local groups are given instructions about how to organize meals, not only in relation to ambience and the use of videos and talks, but also on the sort of food to serve and how to have 'non-religious' conversations! This can all become very manipulative, especially when it takes place in someone's home, because guests are unlikely to offend their hosts by asking awkward questions. To use a communal model effectively, we need to trust the process, and Alpha (at least in its official formulations) fails to do this because it seems that all the outcomes need – or ought – to be tidy. For many of today's spiritual searchers,[17] the way in which Alpha seeks to protect its product by insisting on rigorously regulated ways of doing things is likely to be regarded with some suspicion, and might well be interpreted as a lack of confidence in the power of the Gospel to look after itself.

A similar comment could be made with regard to the third strand in my presentation of popular post-modernity, that is the desire of people to be 'spiritual'. In *Do Christians know how to be Spiritual?* I identified three major aspects to the way in which this term is commonly used today: lifestyle, discipline, and enthusiasm.[18] If I am correct in this analysis, there are many aspects of the Alpha course that different individuals might regard as being, for them, a spiritual experience. For some, the meal itself might be a spiritual experience, while the discipline of

Bible reading and study would be for others. But Alpha locates spirituality only at the 'enthusiasm' end of the spectrum, with its emphasis on a charismatic understanding of spiritual gifts. Here again, in a post-modern context, this is an unhelpful restriction of the spiritual possibilities. Moreover, the way this is introduced is once again open to the claim of over-rationalization and unnecessary control, for it is generally expected to take place in the context of a 'Holy Spirit weekend', which comes around halfway through the course, and is always after the talk on prayer and before the one on healing.[19] This is a time, I suggest, at which many leaders have expectations that are too high and too rigid about getting a sense of who will be 'in' and who will be 'out', depending on what happens in the 'ministry time' when people respond to the promptings of the Spirit through manifestations such as speaking in tongues or being 'slain in the spirit'. The idea that such experiences are the only way in which one can encounter the mystical is taken for granted by most people in charismatic circles, which is itself odd for any group claiming to take Scripture seriously, where the emphasis is on the unpredictability of spiritual experience, and where the work of the Holy Spirit is at times bordering on the anarchic (e.g. John 3:8). Alpha's understanding of spiritual experience strikes me as being at best limited, in cultural as well as in Biblical terms, which also means it will be limited in missional terms, because it will by definition be unable to recognize as genuinely spiritual encounters many of the things which today's spiritual searchers would value.

Finally, when we come to the culture of fearfulness which is one of the emerging traits of post-modern living, Alpha has very little to say. In this, however, it is neither better nor worse than the rest of the church. One of the most pressing needs of our day is for the articulation of a meaningful Christian eschatology that will connect with the situations we now face, global warming and environmental destruction as well as terrorism and all the other things that frighten us. Most of us (and I include myself in this) either have no significant eschatology at all, or else have taken over uncritically a half-baked collection of vague ideas from the 19th and early 20th centuries. Alpha is no exception.

Lastly, in this section: does all this mean that Alpha is a good thing, or a bad thing? The way in which Alpha presents Christian faith undoubtedly deserves some critical theological scrutiny, and I will say more about that below. But in narrow missional terms, this discussion brings both good news and bad news. In *The McDonaldization of the Church*, I identified seven people groups that I believe the church needs to connect with in order to address the challenges we now face. This list has been widely acclaimed and adopted by others, and comprises the desperate poor, hedonists, traditionalists, spiritual searchers, corporate achievers, secularists, and the apathetic. Of these people groups, the ones who seem most consistently to be attracted to Alpha courses are the traditionalists and the corporate achievers, though I am sure that somebody somewhere is bound to have run an Alpha course for the desperate poor, and there is some anecdotal evidence to suggest that in certain contexts (not least Holy Trinity Brompton itself) hedonists – particularly of the upper- or middle-class variety – can also find it attractive. Of course, not everyone within these groups has been to an Alpha course, and even the figures claimed by Alpha are but a drop in the ocean when compared with the population as a whole. But the one thing that unites these particular groups is that they tend to be cognitive, rational people who take in information through reading, discussion, and regimented thinking processes. That is certainly true of the traditionalists and the corporate achievers, and whilst that may not universally be true of working-class hedonists, it tends to be the case with their middle-class counterparts (who when they are not going to parties might well be corporate achievers).

The point I am making is that Alpha, like many other things in church life, does not connect equally with all sections of society, and in particular has less appeal to spiritual searchers than it does for other groups. It may be objected that the relative success of Alpha in prisons challenges that, inasmuch as the prison population represents a microcosm of the whole of society. But I would argue that prison is a special case and that part of the reason for Alpha's success there is to be found in the fact that it fits rather neatly into the norm of what the authorities regard as an appropriate educational experience in that context. In any event, there is a significant number of people to whom Alpha does not appeal, and in view of the cultural trends identified here there is a strong case for suggesting that a presentation of the Gospel that was less prescriptive would stand a better chance of connecting with these other sections of the community.

Contextualization and Culture

Underlying all this is a key theological question regarding the way in which Gospel and culture relate to one another. Richard Niebuhr's classic work on this subject was published in the middle of the 20th century, and still has value as a way of introducing the discussion and identifying possible trends and tendencies.[20] But the intervening half-century has seen developments in both practical theology and missiology which now require us to pose the question in a slightly different way. Gordon Lynch offers four ways in which the interaction of Gospel and culture can be understood:[21]

- The 'applicationist' approach, which begins by identifying core values from the Christian tradition (the Bible and so on) and then applying these as a way of critiquing the culture. This was in essence Niebuhr's own approach.

- The 'correlational' approach, exemplified by the work of a scholar like Paul Tillich,[22] in which the concerns of contemporary culture may be used as a source of new questions to be addressed to the tradition, with the expectation that new answers might then be forthcoming.

- The 'revised correlational' approach, promoted by scholars such as Don Browning.[23] Like Tillich's approach, this one listens to the culture's questions, but goes much further, and whereas Tillich tended to assume that the tradition would always have the 'right' answers, Browning engages in a more open-ended dialogue in which Christians themselves might need to rethink their understandings.

- 'a *praxis* model of conversation' which Lynch finds in liberation theology, where faith and culture are both evaluated on the basis of their ability to promote right action.

The Alpha course clearly operates within the first of these categories, and assumes that straightforward answers to the culture's questions are to be found in the Bible, particularly on matters of personal morality, and especially sexual behaviour. There is nothing distinctive about that, as the same approach characterized Western educational systems for centuries: that the teacher (or some other authority) knew best, and learning was merely a matter of transferring knowledge from teacher to students. With greater understanding of the human personality, as well as new insights into how we receive and process information, that sort of approach has been abandoned in most educational contexts, and personal experience and exploration are now central in subject areas as diverse as medicine, social science, languages, and the study of literature.[24] This shift from what we might call a creedal to a communal approach not only matches the preferences of today's spiritual searchers, but also has significant connections with the ways in which Jesus invited people to follow in faithful discipleship.

Spiritual searchers are individuals who are knowingly engaged in an intentional search for spiritual meaning and purpose in life. They embrace every demographic and socio-economic group, are as likely to be in their seventies or eighties as in their twenties and thirties, and can be found on council housing estates as well as among the British aristocracy. They are likely to be attracted to a highly diverse, if not eclectic, collection of spiritual activities that might include courses in self-improvement or a search for healing along with more obviously 'spiritual' pursuits such as contacting angels or reading tarot cards. The one thing they all have in common, though, is that their spiritual explorations are likely to begin with experience – their own and that of other people. At the same time, these people are not characterized by intellectual laziness, and often become serious students of the most arcane subjects when they seem to offer some potential for feeding their spiritual appetite. Not long after I had completed a PhD on Gnosticism, I was invited to a seminar by people like this, to tell them what I knew about Gnostic gospels. Some thirty or forty people turned up, and every one of them had learned enough Coptic to be able to make sense of the textual complexities of these documents. But they had not done that simply for the intellectual stimulus: they learned the language because they believed it would enhance their experience of using these texts for their own personal development. We are witnessing a similar phenomenon today with the extraordinary success of Dan Brown's novel, *The Da Vinci Code*, and the interest in some obscure historical periods that it has sparked.

If we move from post-modern educationalists and today's spiritual searchers and go back to Jesus, we find some interesting parallels between his practice and what has just been described. For the shift from the creedal to the relational could also be characterized as a move back to Jesus, whose teaching style was likewise based on persons, not texts, and communicated through stories and shared experience rather than abstract philosophical propositions. I have often heard it said that the interactive communal aspects of Alpha are really good, but the packaging of dogma is more problematic. Alpha prides itself on getting 'back to basics', but it is arguably not basic enough. For what has really happened is the sacralizing of a particular cultural form of Christian belief that is firmly contextualized in the world of modernity, and ultimately is the Gospel as seen through the eyes of Christendom, which in turn owed much of its rationale to ancient Greek thinking and Roman organization.[25] Alpha is indeed a traditional message contained in trendy packaging, but the tradition that it perpetuates is not radical enough, in the true sense of that word, because it does not go back to the root of the tradition in Jesus.

It does not require specialized knowledge of the gospels to see that Jesus' attitude to leadership, for example, was quite different from Alpha. Rather than using very specific criteria for selecting people for leadership positions, he was very welcoming, and his open inclusiveness even in choosing his closest disciples was one of the secrets of his success as an evangelist. Even those who turned out to be most foundational for the later life of the church could sometimes hold heterodox views on important topics, and I have often wondered if even Peter would have passed a test on orthodoxy before the episode reported in Mark 8:27–38 – not to mention his behaviour in Mark 14:66–72 or Acts 10:9–43. At the same time, and precisely because of this way of operation, he was able to challenge all those whom he met – whether they were religious types (who wanted their belief systems cut-and-dried in Alpha style), or others who were searching for meaning and healing in the midst of their own fractured and fragmented world.[26] Since Jesus still enjoys 'a good reputation' even among non-Christians,[27] his method of making disciples might just have something we could learn from.

Jesus does feature in Alpha, of course, and there is focus on Jesus as a person to be known and loved because he has first loved and taught us but, also largely as an object of belief. Arguably there is too much emphasis on doctrinal formulations, and too little on the model offered by the person of Jesus as depicted in the New Testament. Jesus' typical *modus operandi* was not to tell people 'how it is' (unless they specifically asked), but rather to ask questions and tell stories. Telling stories opens up spaces for reflection that not only inform and inspire, but also encourage other people to share their own stories. Storytelling with spiritual intentionality is a poetic, if not mystical, device, especially in the way Jesus used it. His stories communicated so well (and still do) because they point hearers to the truth that lies beyond the words, rather than suggesting that the truth can itself be encapsulated in words. In a world of so many competing ideas, the open-endedness of story theology has a significant advantage over highly structured and carefully defined propositional analysis. Not only is it intrinsically faithful to Jesus, but it also creates spaces for discussion that are safe as well as uniquely challenging. If I invite someone to believe in a set of abstract propositions, there is always going to be room for disagreement as to the precise nature of those propositions, their implications and ultimate meanings. If I invite another person to share my story, he or she might find it entirely alien to their own experience, but the one thing they cannot do is argue about its veracity, because it is my story and its authenticity derives not from its content but from who I am judged to be.[28]

In practice, the delivery of most Alpha courses at local level tends to take account of that, and there is generally more sharing of personal stories than can seem to be the case when only the videos and books are reviewed. Few local leaders have the verbal skills of Nicky Gumbel, nor do they always know all the 'right' answers to the questions that may be asked. Most ordinary Christians have their own questions, and are nothing like as certain about it all as perhaps Alpha International would like them to be. Indeed, some would say that, to be real at all, faith must always be the other side of the coin of doubt, and the true source of Alpha's apparent success may well be found more in the honest vulnerability of such people than in all the glossy marketing and presentation.

There is one further question regarding Gospel and culture that takes us back to our starting point in comparing Alpha with the emerging church. As was noted above, Alpha has very little to say about the church, yet there is an underlying assumption that the church (through its use of the Bible) is actually the sole repository of the divine. No doubt some Alpha devotees would wish to qualify that, but however Alpha's understanding of the relationship between Gospel and culture be defined, it clearly stands in a very different place from this statement made by one of Britain's most successful emerging churches:

> We believe that God is already in the world and working in the world. We recognise God's indefinable presence in music, film, arts and other key areas of contemporary culture. We wish to affirm and enjoy the parts of our culture that give a voice to one of the many voices of God and challenge any areas that deafen the call of God and hence constrain human freedom. Experience is vital and experience defines us. We aim to provide an environment is which people can experience 'the other'. In which the vastness of God can be wondered at whilst reflecting on the paradox of the human who was God, Jesus.[29]

One of the most significant missiological insights of the 20th century was the articulation of the concept of the *missio Dei*, the realization that mission is the work of God and not of the church or of individual believers. It follows from this that God must already – and continuously – be at work in the world, and therefore we can expect to meet God in the context of everyday life. The question here is about Biblical faithfulness as well as cultural relevance. For this sort of expression of the relationship between Gospel and culture is based not on wishful thinking, but on a serious exegesis of Genesis 1:26–7, where people – by virtue of being in existence, as humans – are described as made 'in the image of God'. Taking that seriously, and combining it with missiological reflection on the *missio Dei*, leads to a view of culture and of human nature that challenges much that is taken for granted in the Alpha course, not least its dualistic insistence on some absolute disconnection between human nature and divinity, and between the Gospel and the culture. It may be that this dualistic worldview is so deeply embedded within the charismatic mindset that has given birth to Alpha that it would not be possible to address this without radically changing the shape of the entire enterprise. But if the Gospel cannot be authentically contextualized within the culture of post-modernity (however we define or understand it), then the future of Christianity in the West looks even more bleak than we think.

And the essay question with which we started this piece? Answers on a postcard please…time allowed, ten years!

Notes

[1] Douglas Coupland, *Microserfs* (London: Flamingo 1995), p. 313.

[2] George Lings, *Living Proof – a new way of being church?* (Sheffield: Church Army 1999), p. 13.

[3] George Barna, *Baby Busters* (Chicago: Northfield 1994), p. 93

[4] Cf John Drane *Do Christians know how to be Spiritual? The Rise of New Spirituality and the Mission of the Church* (London: Darton Longman and Todd 2005), pp. 1–40.

[5] Paul Heelas and Linda Woodhead, *The Spiritual Revolution: why religion is giving way to spirituality* (Oxford: Blackwell 2005).

[6] Shirley Maclaine, *Out on a Limb* (London: Bantam 1986), p. 198

[7] David Hay and Kate Hunt, *Understanding the Spirituality of People who don't go to Church* (Nottingham: University of Nottingham Centre for the Study of Human Relations 2000).

[8] George Ritzer, *The McDonaldization of Society* (Thousand Oaks CA: Pine Forge Press 1993), p. 26

[9] *The McDonaldization of the Church* (London: Darton Longman and Todd 2000); and in George Ritzer, *McDonaldization: the Reader* (Thousand Oaks: Sage 2002), pp. 71, 151–61.

[10] For more on this, see *Do Christians know how to be Spiritual?*, 90–120.

[11] Martin Rees, *Our Final Century* (London: Heinemann 2003, p. 8.

[12] Peter Brierley (ed), *UK Christian Handbook Religious Trends 5: The Future of the Church* (London: Christian Research 2005), 12:1–14.

[13] George Barna, *Revolution* (Ventura CA: Barna Research 2005).

[14] Church of England General Synod, *Mission-Shaped Church* (London: Church House Publishing 2004). See http://www.freshexpressions.org.uk (*Mission-Shaped Church* can also be downloaded from this site).

[15] See Philip Jenkins, *The Next Christendom: the coming of global Christianity* (New York: Oxford University Press 2002); Timothy C Tennent, 'The Challenge of Churchless Christianity: an evangelical assessment', in *International Bulletin of Missionary Research* 29/4 (2005), pp. 171–7.

[16] Though there is a nod in the direction of local adaptation, the Alpha copyright is as strident a statement as one could imagine, with its insistence that 'This teaching should neither be departed from nor qualitatively altered ... [so as to avoid] ... *causing confusion and ujncertainty as to what the Alpha course really is.*' (original italics and emphasis).

[17] Cf my *McDonaldization of the Church*, pp. 69–73 for a definition of 'spiritual searchers'.

[18] *Do Christians know how to be Spiritual?*, pp. 41–89.

[19] For a description and analysis of this weekend experience, see Stephen Hunt, *The Alpha Enterprise* (Aldershot: Ashgate 2004), pp. 233–47.

[20] Richard Niebuhr, *Christ and Culture*, 50th anniversary edition (San Francisco: HarperSanFrancisco 2001), originally 1951.

[21] Gordon Lynch, *Understanding Theology and Popular Culture* (Oxford: Blackwell 2005), 101–7.

[22] Cf Paul Tillich, *Theology of Culture* (New York: Oxford University Press 1959).

[23] Cf Don Browning, *A Fundamental Practical Theology* (Minneapolis: Fortress Press 1991).

[24] In light of my argument here, perhaps it is not too surprising that the teaching of theology remains largely resistant to experiential interactive learning and teaching.

[25] Cf Stuart Murray, *Post-Christendom* (Carlisle: Paternoster 2004); and for some contemporary theological/cultural implications, my article 'From Creeds to Burgers: religious control, spiritual search, and the future of the world', in James

R Beckford and John Walliss, *Religion and Social Theory* (Aldershot: Ashgate 2006), also in George Ritzer, *McDonaldization: the Reader* 2nd ed (Thousand Oaks: Sage 2006).

[26] Cf Richard V Peace, *Conversion in the New Testament* (Grand Rapids: Eerdmans 1999).

[27] Nick Spencer, *Beyond the Fringe: Researching a Spiritual Age* (Calver: Cliff College Publishing 2005), p. 142.

[28] For more on this, see *McDonaldization of the Church*, pp. 133–54.

[29] http://www.sanctus1.co.uk/whoweare.php.

CHAPTER 21

Alpha and the Challenge of Post-Christendom

Stuart Murray

Singing the Lord's song in a strange land

The long era of 'Christendom' is finally coming to an end in most of western culture. The twenty-first century is witnessing a decisive shift to a new era that as yet we can only call 'post-Christendom'.[1]

Christendom originated in the fateful decision of the fourth-century Roman emperor, Constantine, to adopt Christianity as his own religion and to promote this religion over all others. Constantine's successors confirmed his decision, lavished further favours on the expanding imperial church and, before long, insisted that everyone in the empire should be Christian. Christendom developed over several centuries through a fluctuating but intimate partnership between church and state and the dissemination of Christianity, by persuasion and coercion, until it became empire-wide and penetrated deep into regions beyond the empire. It survived the transition from the ancient world to medieval Europe and later the political and religious upheaval of the Reformation that fractured but did not destroy this remarkable and tenacious system.

Christendom was a sacral society, in which the Christian story and worldview decisively shaped laws, customs and culture; church and society were effectively coterminous. Some historians suggest that the level of Christian faith and commitment throughout this era was often remarkably low; pagan ideas survived and flourished long after Europe was supposedly fully evangelised, and nominality, immorality and absenteeism from church services were rife. Others, recognising that such elements were present, nevertheless emphasise the influence of rituals, architecture, customs and language on the common believing, behaving and belonging that characterised the Christendom era.[2]

Assessments of the validity of Christendom also vary from enthusiastic endorsement of a bold attempt to christianise an entire society, through reluctant acknowledgement that this was an inevitable and valuable (albeit deeply flawed) development, to the claim that the

Christendom shift was illegitimate and deeply damaging to the church and its mission.

But, however we assess Christendom, the twentieth century was the final century of this era, at least in Europe and much of western culture.[3] Decreasing church attendance, the diminishing influence of Christianity in public life, the growing popularity of other forms of religion and spirituality within an otherwise increasingly secular society and profound ignorance of the Christian story (and the language of faith) in the emerging generation provide compelling cumulative evidence of a sea-change in western culture.

There are still many vestiges of Christendom scattered across our society. There may yet be over 70% of the population who, for various reasons, identify themselves on census forms as 'Christian'.[4] There will continue to be thriving churches who assume everything can continue as before and provide connecting points for the last Christendom generation and places of refuge for those who prefer not to face into a disturbing future. But we are witnessing the death throes of Christendom and the advent of a new culture, the contours of which are as yet hazy.

In post-Christendom, we Christians will find ourselves on the margins, one minority faith community among others in a contested environment. We will no longer enjoy erstwhile privileges, and our ambiguous history during the Christendom era will be burdensome as well as sometimes inspiring. Our sacred text and the 'big story' we tell will no longer be accorded respect or special authority. Many commentators have drawn parallels between the exilic experience of the Jews in Babylon in the sixth century BCE and the experience of Christians in post-Christendom. Some have asked the same question the Jewish exiles asked: 'how can we sing the Lord's song in a strange land?'[5]

One important dimension of 'singing the Lord's song' is telling the Christian story, but in post-Christendom we will do this in a society that has changed. In Christendom, almost everyone knew this story and understood the terminology in which the story is couched. Evangelism was regarded either as unnecessary in a 'Christian' culture or as a strategy to revitalise dormant faith and activate passive discipleship. Almost everyone was either an active Christian or a latent Christian. The few exceptions (notably the Jewish community) were regarded as anomalies – and often treated shamefully or coerced into believing.

But during the past two centuries these anomalies have multiplied, recently through the presence and influence in western nations of other religions, but previously through the impact of post-Enlightenment secular philosophies that challenged all religions, but especially the dominant western religion, Christianity. Evangelism in late Christendom, set in the context of secular critiques of faith, required the development of apologetic strategies to present persuasive evidence that Christian faith was reasonable and worth exploring further.

The evangelistic legacy of the Christendom era, then, comprises a mixture of apologetics against secularism and invitations to move from latent to active Christian faith. But what forms of evangelism will post-Christendom require? In the twilight zone between the end of Christendom and the full emergence of post-Christendom several challenges (and opportunities) are already becoming apparent:

- The evangelistic starting point for many people is much further back than we have been accustomed to beginning – we now encounter sheer ignorance of the story, little familiarity with standard terminology to explain the gospel and no inherent respect for biblical authority.

- The journeys of many people towards Christian faith are lengthy, complex and prone to detours and delays, requiring more patience and flexibility than many evangelistic strategies and processes allow.

- Multiple and eclectic worldviews characterise a plural society, which requires of us much more careful and sustained listening than we have deemed necessary in a more monochrome Christendom environment. This is crucial if we are to respond contextually, faithfully and creatively, retelling the story in fresh ways.

- The use of apologetics as an evangelistic strategy is less convincing in a culture that is deeply suspicious of arguments and spin, and our conversation-partners are much more varied. The issue is less often between 'God' and 'no God' (although the challenge of secular atheism remains), than 'which God' or 'what we mean by God'.

- Authoritative pronouncements from institutional spokespersons carry less weight in a more sceptical era, especially in light of the church's chequered history and diminishing strength and influence. Our tone of voice and attitude are crucial, and opportunities for genuine dialogue, rather than monologue, are essential.

Alpha on the threshold of post-Christendom

How appropriate and effective will the Alpha course be for a post-Christendom context? This is not the same question as asking how appropriate and effective Alpha has been in the past decade or may be at present. Other chapters in this book explore these issues. But will Alpha persist beyond the final years of the Christendom era? Will it continue to be a popular means of sharing faith in the transitional period that leads into post-Christendom? Will those responsible for developing the course be prepared to engage with a changing mission environment and reinvent Alpha to address an emerging culture and the different questions this throws up?

There are some reasons to doubt whether Alpha will be able, or indeed willing, to adapt to a post-Christendom context. The course, after all, originated during the final stages of Christendom and may be ineluctably tied to that era and its concerns. It grew out of an introductory course for new Christians in a context where the gap between enquirers from beyond the church and new Christians did not seem that great. The material presented in the first four sessions of the course, summarised in the book *Questions of Life*,[6] already seems very dated in its style, references and mode of argument; it will become even more incongruous over the coming years unless significant revisions are made. And the well-documented, if understandable, reluctance of those who hold the copyright of the course either to adapt its contents (beyond limited revisions) or to allow users significantly to contextualise it does not bode well for its use in an increasingly diverse society.

On the other hand, there are several aspects of Alpha that may have enduring value and may indeed point the way towards an appropriate and effective means of sharing faith in post-Christendom. Whether or not Alpha itself makes the transition into this new culture, these features of the course may help to transform churches into missional communities that grapple with the evangelistic requirements of a changing society. For example:

- The course depends very heavily on church members developing relationships with others who are not yet Christians and who are unlikely to attend church uninvited. While the term 'friendship evangelism' provokes necessary questions about motivation and integrity, raising the spectre of insincerity and manipulation, in post-Christendom friendships between Christians and others who are not yet Christians will surely be critical to effective faith-sharing. The Alpha course may encourage churches to release their members from excessive internal activities so that they can develop friendships beyond the church community, some of which will offer opportunities for faith-sharing. Even if the Alpha course is no longer an appropriate and effective means of such faith-sharing in post-Christendom, its use in the present transitional period may help to prepare our churches to operate in an environment where internal activities must be streamlined and evangelism will depend more than ever on friendships beyond the church.

- The course anticipates and allows for 'belonging' before 'believing' – even if this terminology was unfamiliar when it was taking shape. Alpha (whenever it works properly) creates a hospitable and accepting environment for those interested in Christianity to explore this interest without any prior commitment or guaranteed outcome. Regardless of whether Alpha thrives or even survives, if this relaxed, patient and generous approach to evangelism can permeate our churches, many will be better equipped to walk alongside those in post-Christendom who will be intrigued by the Christian faith but will need time and space to investigate this without undue pressure.

- The course is the leading contemporary example of 'process evangelism', built on the widespread recognition (supported by research findings) that many people become Christians gradually rather than suddenly, through a process of discovery rather than a crisis. Although some urge caution lest this emphasis on process undermines the importance of crises and challenges to take steps of faith[7], most accept that this is likely to be a familiar feature of post-Christendom evangelism. Many people in a sceptical culture and with less initial knowledge of Christianity will take much longer to reach decisions about faith and commitment.

- The course involves dialogue as well as monologue, giving guests opportunities to ask questions, express doubts, voice disagreements and discuss what they have heard. Although the course contains a surprisingly lengthy monologue section (whether live or in pre-recorded format), the authoritative and didactic tone of which may become increasingly problematic in post-Christendom culture, this is set in the context of conversation over a meal and small-group discussion. The power of shared meals to build trust, develop intimacy and help people relax is not only widely recognised but is rooted in deep biblical traditions. This context and the freedom to unpack and dissect the presentations are surely crucial to the impact of Alpha and may be vital for evangelism, with or without Alpha, in post-Christendom.

Whatever the impact of the course on people beyond the churches in post-Christendom or even in the transitional phase between Christendom and this new era, Alpha might make a significant contribution to the task of refocusing and recalibrating churches for mission in a different environment. Wittingly or unwittingly, the course appears to have embraced some key aspects of evangelism that churches on the threshold of post-Christendom must grasp and incorporate into whatever means of faith-sharing they develop.

Alpha after Christendom?

But will the course itself, or even an adapted version, flourish as Christendom fades and post-Christendom arrives? There are other features of Alpha that seem less well suited to evangelism in this changing context:

- Alpha moves rapidly over foundational subjects and much of the curriculum deals with topics and issues that comprise a discipleship course for new Christians, rather than an evangelistic course for not-yet Christians.[8] This is not surprising, since Alpha evolved from a discipleship course that was unexpectedly attracting those who were not yet Christians; but this may pose increasing problems for its use in a post-Christendom culture. The course may simply move too fast and give insufficient attention to foundational issues in a context where guests know far less than at present about basic Christianity. Lengthening the course may not be a viable option (some already find it too long), so a more fundamental rethink may be necessary. Alpha may have pointed the way towards 'process evangelism', but in practice much of the course is 'process discipleship'. In post-Christendom the evangelistic process may take rather longer than Alpha expects or allows.

- Alpha makes assumptions about familiarity with Christian language and concepts, and about the authority of the Bible, which will be less and less sustainable as Christendom fades. The course not only moves quickly over foundational issues, but it does not start at the right place for many people or address questions with which they are wrestling as they search for faith. It assumes that awareness of guilt will precipitate conversion (although guests may be converted at any stage, including the weekend away when the emphasis is on other issues), but there is far less awareness of guilt today than in the Christendom era, so evangelism may need to explore other avenues to faith. The course may continue to connect with the diminishing number of *de-churched* people in contemporary society, but it will be less amenable to the increasing proportion of *non-churched* people. Alpha simply does not offer the resources needed to engage with the ignorance of Christianity in a post-Christendom world. An increasingly common suggestion among users of the course is that a pre-Alpha course is becoming essential.

- Alpha offers a traditional apologetic approach that regards the typical guest as a post-Enlightenment rationalist. It employs arguments that might have been widely persuasive in a previous generation but which now appeal – and seem convincing – only to a limited section of the population.[9] In particular, the course appears to assume a secular mission context; it gives little attention to the truth claims of other faiths or the plural religious environment that will be a highly significant component of post-Christendom. If Alpha is to survive, even as the discipleship course from which it originally sprang, it must help new Christians engage with a plural society and the multiple gods and spiritualities that will comprise post-Christendom. If it is to persist as an evangelistic course, it must surely expect to welcome guests who are religious rather than secular and whose starting-points, questions and responses will be very different from late-Christendom secularists.

- Alpha places considerable emphasis on the work of the Holy Spirit and (especially during the weekend away) encourages spiritual encounters that go beyond mere apologetics. This seems to chime in well with the spiritual openness of many in contemporary post-secular culture, but it is doubtful whether the course engages sufficiently with the past and present spiritual experiences of guests that are not explicitly Christian.[10] Furthermore, some will find this and other aspects of the course rather too prescriptive and inadequately attuned to the element of mystery inherent in genuine Christian faith and increasingly attractive in a society wary of simplistic answers and all-embracing explanations.

- Alpha employs, as we have already noted, a mixture of authoritative proclamation and opportunities for dialogue. This is an attractive combination, allowing careful explanation without interruption and the freedom to investigate issues in an open environment. There are evidently situations where this works well, but some have expressed concern that often the discussion is not genuinely open, with limited freedom to move beyond prescribed lines of discussion. This may indicate that those running the course are not applying its principles properly, rather than a weakness in the course itself, but sensitivity to manipulation and hidden agendas will be even more acute in post-Christendom and will damage the evangelistic efforts of churches who indulge in such behaviour. We might also ask if two-way learning is a possibility in the context of Alpha, or even double conversions, such as occurred in Peter's encounter with Cornelius.[11] Post-Christendom evangelism may require much greater openness and open-endedness than many Alpha courses allow.

- However congenial the atmosphere may be on a well-run Alpha course, this is still essentially an attractional evangelistic strategy, which usually operates on church premises or in situations where Christians are acting as hosts. There is nothing inherently wrong with this, but it may become increasingly problematic as church buildings and church culture appear more and more alien. Incarnational and truly missional approaches may be necessary that operate in contexts where Christians are guests, not hosts, where we are less in control and may feel less comfortable. Excessive reliance on Alpha might discourage churches from grappling with this issue and shifting from the largely centripetal traditional approach to a centrifugal mission strategy.[12]

- While the content and style of (even an unrevised) Alpha may continue to appeal to some people for the foreseeable future, no one approach can possibly suffice in the plural and multi-faceted society that is emerging. Those who promote Alpha will serve the churches best by acknowledging this publicly and by encouraging the development of diverse strategies, rather than maintaining the claim made by some that 'Alpha works everywhere'. As one approach among many, Alpha may continue to play a valuable if more limited evangelistic role; if promoted as omnicompetent, it may hinder effective contextual evangelism and the emergence of strategies that will be more appropriate in post-Christendom.

Whether Alpha persists into post-Christendom may depend on the rigour and flexibility of those responsible for its continuing development. How carefully will they research the impact of the course in diverse cultural and social contexts? How ready will they be to adapt the course – its contents, style, focus and ethos – to a changing society? As some have found who have tried to obtain information to help them analyse and assess Alpha, there is either a dearth of internal research or a surprising lack of candour in making this information available. Others have commented that the selectivity and triumphalism of the stories reported in Alpha publications gives a misleading impression of its impact and may discourage churches whose experiences have been more mixed.

In post-Christendom, such triumphalism will become ever more jarring and any claim to ubiquity for Alpha (or any other evangelistic approach) will hinder creative and diverse responses to the emerging multi-faceted mission environment. Careful ongoing research and honest appraisal will be essential if the course is to thrive. This must include not only reports of wonderful conversions but recognition that some guests are left unmoved and others find the course alienating, pushing them further away from Christian faith.

Despite the criticism, noted above, that those responsible for Alpha are reluctant to relax copyright restrictions or authorise contextual adaptation, there is some evidence that they are receptive to the need for change. Understandably, they have been wary of introducing too many changes or authorising too much diversity in a course that has spread rapidly, is marketed as a distinct and recognisable package and through which significant numbers of people have been coming to faith. However, in response to requests and challenges, they have introduced theological changes or clarifications; they have developed new versions of the course for particular sectors of society; and course contents have slowly evolved over the years.

Whether further slow and incremental changes will be sufficient to enable Alpha to make the transition into a post-Christendom context is an open question. But the undoubted evangelistic passion of those responsible for the course may yet prompt a more radical appraisal and courageous engagement with an evolving mission context.

This might mean engaging in fresh research to discover questions non-churched (rather than de-churched) people are currently asking about issues of faith and introducing new material into the course; or it might mean a more substantial overhaul. It might involve sifting carefully through the current contents, extracting the elements that will be most relevant to not-yet Christians and developing an evangelistic course that does not double as a discipleship course. It might include advocating more strongly that the course should normally operate in (to Christians) less familiar surroundings than church premises.[13] It might mean investigating any negative impact the course makes on those who participate in it – confirming stereotypical views of Christianity and Christians, making it harder to reach them in the future in more appropriate ways. It might mean reviewing their policy on adapting the course to local circumstances; or it might mean advising potential users to think carefully about their context before choosing Alpha from a range of available evangelistic resources.

Hopefully, those responsible for Alpha will rise to this challenge. It is of course possible that, even if they do and revised versions of the course emerge better suited to a post-Christendom context, Alpha as an evangelistic approach (whatever its contents) could quite soon be obsolete in a culture that moves away from Christian faith and any interest in the churches much faster than we anticipate. But a revised and more contextual Alpha might continue to be an effective evangelistic approach after Christendom, if only to a diminishing constituency.

Alpha and the Christendom mindset

There is a further dimension of the relationship between Alpha and the transition from Christendom to post-Christendom to which we should give attention. Might some of the contents – and silences – of the course unwittingly hinder us from engaging with post-Christendom? Might Alpha actually reinforce a Christendom mindset and dissuade us from the fresh thinking needed on various issues in post-Christendom?

- Given that Alpha is as much a course for new Christians as an evangelistic course, what kind of discipleship does it encourage? Such an introductory course cannot, of course, be comprehensive but the choice of contents still reveals much about what the course's designers regard as essential for Christian catechesis. As many have remarked, the emphasis in most sessions is individualistic and pietistic, if not privatised. In post-Christendom, even more than in the post-Enlightenment world we have known, there will be a very strong temptation to retreat into a privatised form of discipleship rather than discovering new ways of engaging with a world we no longer control. Does Alpha challenge or exacerbate this trend?

- Although current versions of the course are more nuanced than earlier versions and many other evangelistic presentations, its emphasis on penal substitution as the normative (though not exclusive) model of atonement may be increasingly problematic in a culture in which this interpretation of the work of Christ appears distasteful and ethically dubious.[14] The emphasis on penal substitution may not only be less potent evangelistically than in the past; it may also discourage fresh engagement with other biblical teaching on the atonement if young Christians assume that this Christendom-shaped doctrine is beyond challenge.

- The course seems to emphasise the divinity of Christ rather than his humanity and his death rather than his life.[15] It pays relatively little attention to the teaching of Jesus on many ethical issues and it gives no indication of the political, economic and social challenges of Jesus that resulted in his death. This is fully compatible with many centuries of teaching in a Christendom context that found the life and teaching of Jesus too radical and uncomfortable. But it may not equip followers of Jesus in post-Christendom to communicate with those who find the human figure of Jesus intriguing. Nor will it encourage young Christians to grapple afresh with the radical life and teaching of Jesus that we have an opportunity to rediscover as the Christendom era draws to a close.

- Some have criticised Alpha for relegating the subject of the church to nearly the end of the course, but from the perspective of the transition to post-Christendom a more significant issue may be its largely uncritical presentation of the church.[16] Surely, for the sake of Christian integrity and evangelistic potency, we need to be more explicit about the chequered history of the church and its capacity to abuse as well as nurture. The story of Augustine converted through the prayers of his mother is heart-warming; however, though he was 'one of the greatest theologians of the church'[17] he was responsible for introducing into Christendom all kinds of deviations from traditional Christian belief and practice, not least the endorsement of violent compulsion in the name of Christ. In post-Christendom we must be more self-critical and less triumphalistic if we are to commend our faith with integrity and winsomeness.

- Of the silences in the Alpha course, perhaps the most glaring omission in light of current geo-political and social issues is any consideration of violence. While the course does grapple with certain moral issues (especially sexual morality), it offers nothing at all to help young Christians engage with the issue of violence or Jesus' summons to his disciples to be peacemakers. In a post-Christendom world wracked by institutional oppression, the threat of terrorism and multiple forms of violence – and in light of many centuries of compromise on this issue during the Christendom era – surely this must be reinstated as a fundamental component of Christian discipleship.

The future of Alpha?

The future of Alpha, like so much in western Christianity at the end of Christendom, is uncertain. There are aspects of the course that may endanger the evangelistic work of the churches if we become locked into these and unable to explore other ways of 'singing the Lord's song'. There are components of its curriculum (or significant silences) that could disable young Christians from encountering the radical Jesus and his teaching. But there are also lessons to learn from its ethos and praxis that may help many churches face the challenges ahead and seize the opportunities of post-Christendom.

Maybe Alpha is a transitional evangelistic strategy, a bridge between traditional and now largely inappropriate Christendom-style methods and new approaches that will emerge in the years ahead. Perhaps, by offering churches a way of engaging in evangelism that is sufficiently familiar for many to embrace enthusiastically but different enough from older methods to provoke questions about future approaches, Alpha might act as a midwife to truly post-Christendom forms of evangelism.

Another possibility is that, while its future *evangelistic* impact may be questionable, its *ecclesiological* impact may be more significant. Alpha might be modelling a way of being church that – if this allowed to transform and revitalise existing churches – could result in the evolution of attractive and hospitable communities better able to respond to the opportunities and challenges of post-Christendom. Some churches grieve that those who are converted through the Alpha courses they run then seem unable to find a home in these churches. The mismatch between the course and the sponsoring church is severe. Others, however, allow the ethos of the course to challenge and reshape their community life.

For example, although most churches have some opportunities for dialogue, most often in small groups that are adjuncts to congregational activities, the virtual absence of this feature in corporate worship means that newcomers from Alpha are confronted by an unfamiliar (and often uncongenial) experience of unchallengeable monologue preaching. Perhaps Alpha can encourage churches and preachers to reassess the dominant role of monologue preaching, reflect on its poor pedagogical results, recognise this dominance as a vestige of the Christendom era[18] and become more effective learning communities – for the sake of both newcomers and established members in a culture where authoritative monologues are increasingly problematic. And what may be true for how churches learn may also be true for other dimensions of church life if the experience of Alpha is allowed to influence these.

The future of Alpha, then, may depend not only on the courage and creativity of those who continue to develop it for the unfolding culture of post-Christendom but on the receptivity and attentiveness of those who use the course in this transitional period and discern what aspects of Alpha can renew church life, inspire faithful discipleship and stimulate fresh evangelistic encounters.

Notes

[1] See Stuart Murray: *Post-Christendom* (Carlisle: Paternoster, 2004).

[2] See, for example, Eamon Duffy: *The Stripping of the Altars: Traditional Religion in England 1400-1580* (Yale: Yale University Press, 1992) and Richard Fletcher: *The Barbarian Conversion* (Berkeley and Los Angeles: University of California Press, 1999), pp508ff.

[3] New forms of Christendom are, however, emerging in the southern continents. See Philip Jenkins: *The Next Christendom* (Oxford: OUP, 2002).

[4] This needs scrutiny and interpretation before we laud it as encouraging evidence of the persistence of Christendom or Christian faith. It may mean little more than 'British' or 'non-Muslim'. See further Steve Bruce: *God is Dead: Secularization in the West* (Oxford: Blackwell, 2002).

[5] Psalm 137:4.

[6] Nicky Gumbel: *Questions of Life* (Eastbourne: Kingsway, 2003).

[7] See, for instance, Robert Warren: *Signs of Life* (London: Church House, 1996).

[8] Only pages 11-65 in *Questions of Life* are evangelistic (concluding with a prayer of faith); pages 67-231 are aimed at those who are already Christians.

[9] For example, Gumbel quotes a common response to Christianity: 'It's great for you but it's not for me' and argues 'this is not a logical position' (*Questions*, p16). Even if the reliance on logic is still regarded as helpful in a post-modern culture, this simplistic dismissal of a position held today by many people, at both academic and popular levels, will not do without a greater appreciation of the changed philosophical and cultural context. Similarly, reliance on C S Lewis' claim that Jesus was either mad, bad or God (pp29 and 37) is less effective now (when more nuanced positions are adopted) than in previous generations.

[10] Unlike, for example, the *Essence* course that builds gently and progressively on spiritual experiences and encourages participants to engage increasingly with Christian spirituality. For information on *Essence*, see www.cpas.org.uk.

[11] See Acts 10. Cornelius was certainly converted, but so too, it seems, was Peter, whose worldview and beliefs were turned upside down by his conversation and the vision that preceded this. Peter's attitude in this incident is worth noting as an example of the humility and openness that transforms evangelism from proselytism to genuine encounter.

[12] For a book-length discussion of this issue, see Michael Frost and Alan Hirsch: *The Shaping of Things to Come* (Peabody: Hendrickson, 2004). See also Stuart Murray: *Church after Christendom* (Milton Keynes: Paternoster, 2005), pp135-164.

[13] The course originated in homes and runs in various places, but church premises appear to have become the norm, despite encouragement to consider alternatives.

[14] See *Questions*, pp19, 40-41, 48-49 for the course's exposition of penal substitution as the primary atonement motif, and see p42 for the equation of justice with punishment. See also the more nuanced statement on God's self-substitution on p43 (but how nuanced will local presentations be?).

[15] See *Questions*, pp. 24, 39.

[16] For one minor criticism, see *Questions*, pp. 215.

[17] See *Questions*, pp. 93.

[18] See further, David Norrington: *To Preach or not to Preach* (Carlisle: Paternoster, 1996).

CHAPTER 22

Alpha as a Technological Phenomenon: Do Churches need Technicians or Mentors for Mission?

Philip R. Meadows

In this chapter, I will argue that the Alpha phenomenon cannot be fully understood apart from the technological culture which characterises our contemporary society. My suggestion is that some of the more ambiguous interpretations of Alpha arise precisely because it is *both* a thoroughgoing product of our technological culture *and yet* cannot be finally contained within it or explained by it.

This is, perhaps, most evident in the sociological critique of the Alpha Course as a sophisticated commodification of the gospel.[1] On the one hand, these studies reveal the extent to which Alpha International has become accommodated to the rationalizing and standardizing techniques of packaging and mass marketing. On the other hand, they clearly cannot account for the various counterclaims that God may take up and use those techniques as a means of authentic evangelism. Of course, it is in the nature of social science to adopt a 'methodological atheism' which inevitably reduces Alpha to a phenomenon that must be accounted for without the reality of God. Theological appeals to divine providence, however, cannot be allowed to conceal the temptation toward 'practical atheism' inherent in the techniques of such a marketing orientation. There is a danger of embracing a programme like Alpha as a technique that will produce the desired results regardless of the faith of those that employ it. In other words, the danger of practical atheism is that we may invest the programme itself with a power that belongs to God alone; thus rendering the spiritual quality and witness of our own lives practically irrelevant. The ambiguity of Alpha as a technological phenomenon, however, lies in the tension between a marketing orientation that brings with it the temptation to practical atheism, and the genuine desire to find a means of grace through which the reality of God's presence and power can be sought.

This ambiguity is specially present when one moves from the 'supply-side' of Alpha International to the 'ground-level' activity of implementing the 'package' in a local church. On the one hand, various sociological approaches have sought to analyse the technical efficiency with which courses are run; evaluating their success against arguably measurable goals, such as levels of uptake, ease of use, patterns of attendance, numbers of converts, growth in membership, and other aspects of consumer satisfaction.[2] Indeed, Alpha International itself uses such evidence as a way of promoting the success of the Alpha Course and its associated materials. On the other hand, it is also clear that the worth of running Alpha at the 'ground-level' cannot be reduced to such findings because people of faith may interpret its spiritual impact in ways which remain incapable of such evaluation. So, the *variety* of conversion experiences, *depth* of spiritual growth, and *extent* of church renewal are really immeasurable by ordinary empirical study. Considered as a marketable technique for evangelism and disciple-making, however, it is reasonable to conclude that Alpha will always remain susceptible to the charge of selling-out or selling-short the Gospel (in one way or another), notwithstanding the robust theological defence by its management and stakeholders.

I suggest that the ambiguity of Alpha arises insofar as the deeply technological commitments of Alpha International are subverted by the very ordinary practices the Alpha Course delivers into the hands of faithful Christians. In other words, the theological importance of Alpha as a programme does not lie in its ability to package the 'one best way' of making converts in a post-Christian era, but in its ability to apprentice those that use it in the kind of corporate practices that constitute the witness of mission-minded congregations. Insofar as it is successful in this regard, however, so far is it also likely to generate dissatisfaction with the prescriptive nature of the course as a technique, and cultivate the desire to improve upon its shortcomings by way of locally developed approaches to evangelism and disciple-making.

In other words, it may be that Alpha is best thought of as a *mentor* rather than a *technician*: as a medium for renewing a sense of missionary vocation throughout a Christian community rather than the supplier of an effective technological solution to any church's evangelistic needs. Yet there remains an uneasy tension between these two realities in the Alpha phenomenon.

Our Technological Culture

Alpha International has made good use of modern technology to disseminate and deliver its programme throughout the world. We might think of the *media technology* used for printing, reproducing and packaging Alpha materials; the *audio-visual technology* used to present the Alpha talks and train course leaders; the *marketing technology* used for 'franchising' the course to churches and 'selling' its value to the un-churched; the *information technology* used in the development, maintenance and interconnection of world-wide Alpha websites; the *transportation technology* used to move the training team from one Alpha conference to another, one country to the next; and the *communications technology* used to broadcast conferences via satellite from anywhere to anywhere. Examined this way, and the list is far from exhaustive, it is clear that Alpha is a technological phenomenon.

The question of technology, however, cannot be reduced to the way we take up our tools or techniques as though they were merely neutral means through which we can advance our desired ends. The technologies we use are inseparable from the culture in which they are embedded and how they shape every aspect of our daily lives. So, in this section, we will survey some of the ways that technology has come to specify the character of contemporary culture, and raise some questions about Alpha to be addressed more directly in the following section.

The Rule of Technology

Martin Heidegger claimed that 'the essence of technology is by no means anything technological.'[3] By this, he meant that our technologies are merely signs of the way we take up with all of reality as a 'standing reserve.' In other words, the essence of technology is manifest in the way our lives have become thoroughly oriented toward 'setting upon', 'entrapping' and 'ordering' all things as resources for ends of our own choosing.[4]

On the whole, we tend to adopt an instrumental view of technology as a mere means to an end, such that 'everything depends on our manipulating technology in the proper manner as a means.' A right relationship to technology, therefore, depends upon the 'will to mastery.'[5] But technology is no mere means. Heidegger explains that it exerts its 'rule' through shaping a culture which orients our thinking toward the idea that all things exist to enrich the kind of life we choose to make for ourselves in the world.

The trouble is, we are blinded to the truth of our own dehumanization by this illusion of mastery, as we ourselves become reduced to manipulable resources in a technologically specified way of life.[6] In the end, it is technology that masters us by shaping our lives to fit the kind of world that it creates. According to Heidegger, the 'rule of technology' will continue to 'hold sway' and 'entrap' us in this way of living so long as its orienting power can be concealed behind our own will to master its tools and techniques as mere means.

Albert Borgmann develops Heidegger's argument by suggesting that the character of contemporary life is shaped by the 'device paradigm', or the way modern technology subjects all of reality to a pattern of commodification.[7] So, the rule of technology is extended through the promise to disburden and enrich our lives by reproducing everything we need or desire in a universe of commodities which can be procured instantly, easily, safely, ubiquitously and, above all, disposably.

For instance, the culture of the table is reduced to the consumption of mere food as the technology of packaging disburdens us of growing, preparing, cooking and presenting real meals. The celebration of community is reduced to the consumption of mere entertainment as the technology of audio-visual equipment disburdens us of learning how to read, tell, sing, play and accompany others in story and song. The practices of care-giving are reduced to the consumption of mere securities as the technology of insurance disburdens us of the need to bear one another's burdens, share our possessions, and give sacrificially. The list could be extended almost indefinitely.

The rule of technology, therefore, is also exerted through its power to conceal that which has been transformed or lost in the extension of the paradigm itself. A life supplied with commodified food, entertainment, and security is not the same as a life sustained by meals around the table, filled with music and story, and surrounded by mutual care. That which once had the power to bring intimacy and mutual engagement to the lives of persons, families and whole communities – in the context of their particular histories, places and aspirations – has been substituted by commodities which tend to disengage us from the very things which grace life with meaning and direction.

How far is the rule of technology extended through the commodification of Alpha as an example of the 'device paradigm'? What may be lost or concealed through the promise of Alpha to disburden and enrich the church's evangelistic ministry? By satisfying our 'will to mastery', how might Alpha actually change the way we think about God, the life of the church, and its mission in the world?

The God of Technique

For Jacques Ellul, it is a captivity to 'technique' that forms the essence of our technological culture. The term 'technique,' as Ellul uses it, 'does not mean machines, technology, or this or that procedure for attaining an end.' Rather, 'in our technological society, *technique* is the *totality of methods rationally arrived at and having absolute efficiency... in every* field of human activity.'[8] Although the machine is 'the most obvious, massive, and impressive example of technique,' our commitment to technical efficiency means that everything tends to be 'reconsidered in terms of the machine.'[9]

Indeed, this is what technique does: it 'integrates the machine into society' by constructing 'the kind of world the machine needs' for it to work perfectly.[10] As the 'calculus of efficiency,' technique promises to analyze, rationalize and standardize every area of life in mechanistic terms, with the promise of ever greater prediction and control. The application of technique is gradually transforming our whole society into a 'technical universe' where every part is adapted to and interfaced with every other in the perfect efficiency of one vast machine.

Ellul defines a *technical operation* as that which is 'carried out in accordance with a certain method in order to attain a particular end,' always marked by the search for greater efficiency and adaptation. The *technical phenomenon* of our time arises from the application of scientific measurement to our technical operations in an attempt to reduce the multiplicity of means to the one most efficiently adapted to any desired end. So, technique can be described as 'the quest for the one best means in every field.'[11]

This 'technical imperative' shapes a culture in which 'technique' makes efficiency an end in itself. First, it is a culture which requires experts, specialists, or technicians, who are capable of carrying out the calculations necessary to choose the 'one best means' in any area of human activity, and demonstrate its superiority over all others. Second, it makes 'effective' action a matter of perfecting the operation of our tools and techniques themselves rather than the kind of people that use them.[12] Third, it strives for a perfection of the 'one best way in the world' rather than the one best way in a particular locality.[13]

Although technique aims at the efficient adaptation of means to a desired end, technical methods themselves are presumed to have a universally rational and standardized operation that transcends the need for local variations. So, once a technique has become established, it tends to adapt us and our particular ends to its own universal means, until it is overthrown by another new and improved technique.

In a manner similar to Heidegger and Borgmann above, Ellul also argues that our commitment to 'technique' has become a total worldview or way of taking up with reality itself.[14] Through the accumulation of technical means, we are creating for ourselves an evermore rational and artificial world in which traditional communities and ways of life are dismantled, adapted, and assimilated to the machinery of a 'technical civilization.'[15] Indeed, he claims that technique is experienced as an autonomous power that gradually extends its influence around the world: deceiving and domesticating us by promising a share in its rule.

How does Alpha satisfy our technological desire to predict, control, and secure the future of the church? To what extent does Alpha present the task of evangelism as a 'technical operation', or the 'one best means', most efficiently adapted to the end of making disciples? How far is the rule of technology extended by making Alpha an end in itself, or adapting the particular mission of local churches to its own universal means?

The State of Technopoly

In our technological culture, however, it would seem that there is no escaping the uneasy tension between controlling and being controlled by our technologies. Neil Postman argues that technological change is neither 'additive' nor 'subtractive' but 'ecological' in the sense that 'one significant change generates total change': new technology does not add or subtract something, 'it changes everything.'[16] There are echoes of Ellul in his claim that our technologies are integrated into life only by reshaping the kind of world they need to operate most efficiently.

Postman traces how modern culture has reduced truth and reality to what is mathematically calculable, scientifically demonstrable, and technologically manipulable. The ideas of objectivity, efficiency, expertise, standardization, measurement, and progress are the virtues of a new 'technocratic' culture in which everything becomes oriented around the development and use of tools and techniques. They are not so much 'integrated' into the culture as they 'attack' it; they 'bid to *become* the culture' and 'as a consequence, tradition, social mores, myth, politics, ritual, and religion have to fight for their lives.'[17]

The logical conclusion of this project is what Postman has called the state of 'technopoly'; that is, a 'totalitarian technocracy' which has as its aim 'a grand reductionism in which human life must find its meaning in machinery and technique' and that 'society is best served when human beings are placed at the disposal of their techniques and technology.' In short, it represents 'the submission of all forms of cultural life to the sovereignty of technique and technology.'[18] Technopoly is both a state of culture and a state of mind. It 'consists in the deification of technology, which means that the culture seeks its authorization in technology, finds its satisfactions in technology, and takes its orders from technology.'[19]

For Postman, our technological culture is shaped by an 'ideology of machines' which has taught us to think that reality is at its best when operating like a machine: *analysable* into interchangeable parts that work together with law-like efficiency; *calculable* as systems of quantifiable processes working with precision toward measurable goals; *manageable* through the techniques of mastery, prediction and control; and *dependable* through the employment of proven, quick, and standardized means. What is important about this way of thinking is that it has become applied to every aspect of natural, material, social, and psychological life; all managed by experts who are 'invested with the charisma of priestliness.'[20]

It is, however, illusory because human life and culture is not finally capable of such rationalization. Notwithstanding the best intentions of social science researchers, Postman argues that there can be no real 'experts' in child-rearing or friend-making or community-building. The 'ideology of the machine' is one of instrumentality and efficiency not moral values or virtues. As such, it brings with it no specific vision of the good life – except the freedom to choose it and the means to pursue it for ourselves – while at the same time rendering irrelevant the moral claims embedded in traditional narratives and communities.

To what extent does Alpha as a tool or technique reshape the life of a church by overruling its historic commitments and traditions? How far does it cause us to think about church life according to the 'ideology of machines', with the promise of proven, quick and dependable results? Are we convinced that evangelism can be reduced to technical 'expertise', or a programme for which we can be trained by 'specialists', irrespective of who we are or where it is used?

The Ambiguity of Alpha

In this section, I want to address some of the foregoing questions and examine how the ambiguities of Alpha may arise from the wider issues of our technological culture. I offer it, not by way of settled conclusion, but as an exploration into the kinds of question that might be required of us as faithful Christians in a world such as ours.

A Commodity?

Thanks to the work of Stephen Hunt, it is not difficult to identify how Alpha has been shaped by the 'marketing orientation' of a consumer culture. Under these conditions, the Christian life gets reduced to a matter of private preference amidst a 'spiritual marketplace' of religious goods. Hunt, therefore, assumes that 'churches are now forced to see themselves as units in a market competing for the time, loyalty and money of a limited clientele'; and, as such, 'they largely behave as secular, commercial units operating in their mass markets: with an eye to mass appeal, advertising...and so forth'. For Hunt, the bottom line is that 'Christianity is forced to adapt or be marginalized in its more sectarian expressions.'[21] Since it would seem that 'sectarian expressions' of Christianity are undesirable (which is an assumption far from self-evident), it would seem the value of Alpha can only be measured in terms of *how well* it actually helps the church to perform in the marketplace, not *whether* it should be located there in the first place.[22]

There is, however, constant ambiguity in Hunt's account. On the one hand, he insists on criticizing Alpha for its worldly accommodation to the marketing orientation; yet, on the other hand, he critically affirms this approach as an appropriate (and perhaps even necessary) adaptation to twenty-first century culture. This is probably all that a fair-minded social scientist can do. It is perhaps unsurprising, then, that the conclusion of his study is merely the suggestion of a new and improved alternative to the Alpha course; but, of course, better adapted to the market as a result of his own social research!

The deeper problem, however, is the degree to which social science itself becomes the servant of technology and the ideology of the machine. As such, it only has something meaningful to say about the organization of human life insofar as it can be rendered mechanistically; i.e., analysable, calculable, manageable, and dependable. There is nothing worse than theological claims about the person and work of the Holy Spirit for upsetting the methodological atheism of social scientists! In striving after some kind of scientific objectivity, the social researcher actually fixes the nature of Alpha as a technological phenomenon in the very act of observation. From a missiological perspective, however, my view is that the benefit of such research begins and ends with their ability to highlight the ambiguous relation that Alpha actually has with our technological culture, and invite a more substantive theological reflection.

It has to be admitted that the Alpha phenomenon does embody a complex pattern of commodification upon which social research can get a clear purchase. On the supply-side, Alpha International markets its programme to churches as an evangelistic 'package' that works, and to the general public as a package 'deal' or free introductory tour of 'basic Christianity'. On the consumer-side, churches themselves can buy into Alpha as a technical solution to evangelism and disciple-making, while those that join the courses do so as a means to satisfy their individual spiritual needs (churched and unchurched). In the middle of this, churches act as both consumer and supplier; or as agencies for the transmission of Alpha-style basic Christianity from the 'mother church' at Holy Trinity Brompton (hereafter, HTB) to the world at large. This may, of course, be judged a good thing.

The programme has a variety of features which indicate this marketing orientation, from standardization and branding of the package (secured by the Alpha copyright) to all the peripheral materials and conferences aimed at training churches how to install, run and manage every aspect of the programme most effectively. At this level, Alpha International's own use of social science methods to develop and demonstrate the popularity, portability, and productivity of the Alpha Course simply invites the critique of social researchers on their own terms. In other words, Alpha plays into the hands of its critics when it resorts to the 'ideology of the machine' in order to advance its own interests in the marketplace.

The picture becomes more complicated, however, when one examines the nature and use of the Alpha Course itself by the churches. Notwithstanding the observation that Alpha has few clearly measurable processes or goals, social researchers typically resort to surveys and opinion polls – the *sine qua non* of social science in our technological culture – as a means of evaluating whether or not the programme actually 'works'! Yet, how can one even measure *claims* to conversion, renewal, and spiritual growth? Attempts to do so typically beg further questions about what people mean by these very things; and this 'hermeneutical circle' can go on indefinitely. Indeed, it has been argued that social research never really discovers anything, but merely uses quantification as a means to give precision to its own ideas; by seeking to demonstrate the truth or falsity of patterns it has already determined to be measurable on their own terms.[23] On the basis of sociological evidence alone, therefore, both the supporters and critics of Alpha will forever be deadlocked in a battle of competing assertions.

I suggest the ambiguity surrounding Alpha as a commodity cannot be understood apart from the history of its own origin and development within the life of HTB. Sociological accounts tend to narrate this history as a way of introducing various numerical trends, and then proceed on the tacit assumption that the whole programme is subject to the exigencies of strategic planning. If one begins with the marketing orientation of Alpha International, it is easy to see how this narrative can construe the whole 'enterprise' as an intentional effort to penetrate the spiritual marketplace.[24]

Such interpretations, however, fail to remember that the shape of the Alpha Course is largely determined by its origins as a programme of catechesis for new converts, and that the basic pattern of meeting/ instruction has remained the same to date. It is a matter of *divine providence* that a course designed to offer instruction about the Christian life was to became an introduction to the Christian faith for enquirers. It is a matter of *technological progress*, however, that a course raised up within a particular context and community was to become abstracted as a commodity made available on the market.

The fact is, Alpha was not developed as an evangelistic method in response to opinion polls about the spiritual longings of a post-Christian culture, or the aspirations of spiritual renewal among declining mainline churches. Rather, it was grown under the influence of gifted Christian leaders within the womb of a lively, mission-minded, charismatic-evangelical church, as means of initiation into its community of faith. As such, it rightly embodies a set of theological commitments and practices that have not been determined by the marketing orientation, and which constantly stand in tension with the technical imperatives of its new existence.

So, from a sociological-marketing perspective, it seems backward not to constantly revise the form and content of the course to make it more 'relevant' to the various 'felt-needs' of churched and unchurched consumers. From a historical-theological perspective, it makes perfect sense to fix the curriculum as Alpha does, in the service of what HTB understands to be 'basic Christianity'. For instance, I don't think it really matters whether truly unchurched people are haunted by questions like, 'Why did Jesus die?' or 'Why and how should I read the bible?' or 'How can I be filled with the Spirit' or 'Why and how should we tell others?' Clearly, they are not! The point is, rather, that these are the kind of questions seekers *should* be asking when confronted with the gospel if they are to understand the promises and claims it makes upon them. Arguably, this constitutes an excellent approach to narrative apologetics.

By answering its own questions, therefore, Alpha was intended to narrate the basics of Christian thought and practice – shaped by the particular commitments of HTB – as an extended invitation for participants to engage with the gospel narrative in a concrete community of faith. As a home grown course turned marketable evangelism package, however, it is not surprising that there should be so much intra-Christian controversy about the form and content of the curriculum. If I am right, the root of our confusion lies in the moment when the machinery of our technological culture seized a locally developed programme of catechesis and commodified it into a globally marketed package for evangelism and disciple-making.

The process of captivity is subtle. Having observed the programme at HTB, other churches were naturally led to ask for a copy of the curriculum with the hope of reproducing its success for themselves; and *Questions of Life* is written.[25] But our modern technology allows for so much more than this! Why not make a film of the book? Why not produce a course manual for participants to guide the group discussions? Why not develop some training materials to equip those leading every aspect of the programme?[26] Indeed, why not go the whole way and stage regional conferences to assist local churches in planning and delivering the course? Furthermore, what about regional officers to promote the course around the country and support the growing number of churches registered as taking it up? Surely, the more churches using the course, and the more help given to those running it, the better? Is this not the way God gets things done today?

Notwithstanding the concerns expressed by different Christian groups, it is generally taken as self-evident that the possibility of marketing such an evangelistic package is a good thing.[27] So, it is not the pattern of commodification that comes under suspicion, but the way it has served to spread HTB's particular form of charismatic-evangelical spirituality throughout the mainline denominations. Indeed, as time goes on, this challenge has been met by other churches and groups who, following the example of Alpha, have introduced their own courses as competitors in the marketplace, with claims to complement or address deficiencies found in the rest.[28]

If we are attentive to Albert Borgmann's critique, however, this pattern of commodification itself deserves to be challenged more thoroughly. The very idea that we might imagine a church could package its success and pass it on to others simply reflects our captivity to the rule of technology and the 'device paradigm' that turns reality into commodity. What we desire is a technical solution to the task of evangelism and disciple-making that can be procured instantly, easily, safely, ubiquitously and disposably. But the question is, what reality has been lost in the extension of this paradigm over church life, or concealed behind the promise of control, liberation and enrichment? Surely it is that which has been overlooked by the social researchers and marketers; namely, the very history out of which Alpha arose, and the lessons we might learn about what it means to exercise authentic Christian leadership in a mission-minded church.

The real issue with commodification of Alpha, therefore, is not revealed by opinion polls and 'customer satisfaction' surveys, but by the growing difference that exists between the kind of gifts and skills necessary for local missionary engagement which can be found at HTB, and the growing lack of these things in the churches that consume its courses. The success of Alpha at HTB grew up through a long history of local outreach to the unchurched and experimentation in the practices of evangelism and disciple-making. At stake is not merely the history of a course, but of the spiritual journey undertaken by a particular community of faith, through which it has learned how to pray and work for the kingdom in its own context of mission and ministry.

This is the reality that gets commodified and packaged by the machinery of our technological culture; not some gospel in the abstract or disembodied essentials of 'basic Christianity' for all times and all places. There is no such thing. The technical imperative, however, presses us to imagine that the charisms associated with the missionary traditions of a church like HTB can be reduced to a set of universal laws and principles which, if reemployed exactly, will reproduce the same effect anywhere. In Heidegger's terms, the rule of technology orients us to rethinking the nature of church as providing 'hardware' resources for such a 'software' package to use in accomplishing its specified end. The hardware needs no virtues of its own except that it slavishly performs the tasks assigned by the programme; and should it do so efficiently, the best results will follow.

The background danger which lurks behind the foreground promise of Alpha, therefore, is that churches may be encouraged to imagine they can share in the success of HTB without having to share in the charisms formed over its long and arduous history. Indeed, as the package becomes an ever more fully specified and self-supporting system of techniques, the more alluring is the promise of being disburdened from the historical reality that builds the kind of community which develops Alpha-like practices for itself.

In other words, among the potential losses which accompany the marketing of packages like Alpha, as a universal technical solution, are the very charisms necessary for the long haul adventure of missionary engagement by particular Christian communities in all its local variations. Without these charisms, all a church can do is trust that social scientists are capable of performing the kind of research that can predict the future of dominant cultural trends and wait for the latest, new and improved packages to keep them under control.

A Technique?

It may appear to some that my argument rules out the possibility of learning from the accumulated wisdom of other churches, but this is not so. The issue is not *that* there are things to be learned, but *what* we have to learn from them.

As we have seen, our technological culture causes us to think of truth and reality according to the ideology of the machine: as that which is analysable, calculable, manageable, and dependable. Under the rule of technology, therefore, we immediately tend to look for the mechanism by which things get done so efficiently. Our scientistic mindset assumes that what we have to learn from other churches is how they organize their life together as a system of interconnected parts, operating a set of clearly defined processes, each carefully managed towards measurable goals, with predictable and law-like regularity. Mechanized in this way, the 'wisdom' of church life can be rendered as a collection of transferable resources and principles capable of being packaged for the marketplace. By turning the lessons to be learned into technical questions about how to get things done, however, we run the risk of absorbing the 'practical atheism' of a technological culture which gets along equally well with or without the reality of God![29]

It is not difficult to see how this applies to the Alpha phenomenon. The device paradigm presents the Alpha Course as a masterpiece of technical efficiency, disencumbered from its moorings in the particular commitments and traditions of a whole church. My argument, however, is that the ambiguity of Alpha arises from this process of technological abstraction, and not with the course itself. In the context of HTB, we might think of Alpha as the reduction of a *practice* to a *technique*. On the one hand, 'practices' are those activities which are located within, and help make sense of, the established charisms and traditions of a particular community. On the other hand, 'techniques' have the more magical quality of being able to accomplish a desired end simply as a matter of right performance, irrespective of who performs it. Our technological culture has a habit of turning practices into techniques, and then packaging them as marketable programmes.[30]

It is in the marketing orientation of Alpha International that the transformation of Alpha into a single highly rationalized and standardized technique has been accomplished. Although it probably would not claim to be 'the one best way' of evangelism and disciple-making, it certainly mirrors what Jacques Ellul describes as a technological 'quest for the one best means' in its field.

First, there is a confidence that the Alpha Course, as a universally applicable tool or technique, is the best adapted means to the end of converting people at any age and in any walk of life. Hence, it has been successfully marketed across churches of every major Christian denomination, and in secular contexts extending across the workplace, universities, prisons and armed forces. Accommodating the programme to these different settings, however, really amounts to minor adjustments in the way elements of the programme are delivered, and not changes to the substance of the course itself. Notwithstanding the creation of special material for 'Youth Alpha', the curriculum remains largely the same; and the recent 'Compact Alpha' amounts to a mere shortening of the standard Alpha videos.

Second, this confidence is supported by a whole cadre of experts and specialists; beginning with the Alpha International team based at HTB, and extending across the world through regional offices. As 'technicians' they continually present a case for the 'superiority' of Alpha as a proven method of evangelism, and run various kinds of training conferences which explain how it can be made to work most efficiently in different settings. Behind all this is a clear appeal to our technologically oriented minds, as we look for ever greater efficiency and tend to measure the worth of any 'means' by the ease, scale and speed with which it can produce the desired 'end'.

Third, the confidence in Alpha as a technique most perfectly adapted to the end of evangelism – and as a brand most effectively marketed to the unchurched – is manifest in the way Alpha International resists the development of local variations, and protects its technology through the use of a trademark and copyright clause. Although some changes to the programme are formally permitted, they are again restricted to fine-tuning aspects of programme delivery rather than significant modifications of, additions to, or omissions from the prescribed course. Indeed, consumers are disburdened of even the need to do such fine-tuning if variations of the programme continue to be developed for different segments of the market.[31] As a result, Alpha exhibits one of the strongest features of a technique; that is, the adaptation of users to its own manner of working and to the ends it has been designed to serve.

Another danger lurking behind the use of Alpha, therefore, is that churches may mistake the acquisition of a 'technique' for the adoption of a 'practice'. In other words, there is a difference between learning how to run a programme and learning the art of evangelism. In general, a technique adapts its users by the reduction of learning to 'training'. You can train a dog to perform new tricks. You can train a parrot to sing the national anthem. You can train a monkey to type its name. If we want to demonstrate the simplicity and ease with which a task can be performed, we might claim that anyone or anything can be trained to do it. This idea fits well with the ideology of the machine, insofar as a complex task can be broken down into simple parts so that each part can be trained to perform efficiently in relation to the rest.

Technicians are not so much concerned with what kind of person you are, just that you have a willingness and determination to get things done. In this sense, being *trained in a technique* is quite different from being *apprenticed in a practice*; whether at the level of individual persons or a whole community. Apprenticeship means standing in a tradition where the transmission of a practice from one to another involves the formation of gifts and skills that sustain received wisdom in the very act of improvising upon it. Well apprenticed craftsmen, musicians, and evangelists will apply their art in recognisable but different ways depending upon the particular persons and contexts concerned.

Good mentors pass on their wisdom by guiding apprentices in their own serious engagement with the 'material' at hand; while celebrating the particular qualities that such a new engagement produces. A serious question to be levelled at Alpha International, then, is the extent to which it sees the Alpha Course as a technician or a mentor; as training churches how to run a programme, or apprenticing them in the art of evangelism. The more it tends towards the technician, the more it may simply encourage churches to be satisfied with a mere simulacrum of real evangelism. The more it tends towards the mentor, however, the more it will encourage churches to be in substantial engagement with the particular contexts of mission in which they are situated.[32]

A Technopoly?

There are numerous ways in which one might interpret the wide-scale uptake of Alpha. It would seem, however, that reasons are likely to include a common malaise around numerical decline, diminishing resources, and loss of missionary nerve among local churches. The sad fact is that many churches simply have neither the tradition nor the imagination necessary to engage in home grown practices of evangelism. Given this reality, the availability of a programme such as Alpha may seem like the best hope for recovering an evangelical spirit or evangelistic impulse within a congregation.

We live in a time when mainstream denominations are suffering a crisis of identity. This has resulted from a failure to catechize members in the distinctive doctrines and practices associated with our historic traditions coupled with the reality of a consumer culture that has made churchgoing more a matter of personal preference than denominational loyalty. It is under these conditions that Alpha has managed to level denominational differences and create the new ecclesial identity of an 'Alpha church'. Interestingly, this new identity may communicate as much (if not more) about the life and commitments of a congregation than being specifically Anglican, Methodist, Baptist, and so on. And this may, of course, be viewed as a positive advantage for evangelism in a postmodern marketplace.

I suggest, however, that the formation of Alpha churches is a phenomenon closely associated with the technological character of the Alpha itself. Jacques Ellul suggested that the integration of any new technique actually entails the reshaping of a whole social reality to become the kind of context in which it can work most efficiently.[33] The power of a technique is experienced in its ability to dismantle, adapt and assimilate traditional communities and different ways of life for its own purposes. Neil Postman put it more starkly when he said that our tools and techniques are not so much integrated into a culture but bid to become the culture at the expense of older traditions. Or, to use another of his images, the introduction of a technique brings about an entire ecological change within any social reality, which would include that of local church life. To speak of an 'Alpha church', then, is to identify the power of an Alpha course to reconfigure the whole life of a congregation around the implementation and maintenance of its own programme.

This is particularly true in smaller churches for whom running the programme is enough to exhaust all its resources. Yet there are always technical solutions to technological problems. Alpha International positively encourages churches to see the programme as their core activity, because the same technique can be used in place of other separate classes for church membership, confirmation, baptism and wedding preparation etc. One might say that the Alpha course has the power to create a kind of 'technopoly' in which the programme comes to reconfigure and authorise many of a church's traditional core practices.

With this in view, it may not be so surprising that there is still no official production of a post-Alpha course. First, if the programme itself is all a church can manage, then appending another similar course is going to be impracticable. Second, to admit that such a course is needed only confirms the technological captivity of Alpha churches. On the one hand, it suggests that there is nothing beyond Alpha into which graduates of the course can be initiated. On the other hand, to look for yet another package merely suggests that Alpha has done little to cultivate the charisms necessary for continuing the disciple-making process. Third, even if a post-Alpha course were developed and taken up, churches would still find themselves in a technological dependence upon the subsequent arrival of a post-post-Alpha course and a post-post-post-Alpha course etc.

This issue also highlights a danger in any kind of technical application; namely, that the efficient running of the means actually becomes an end in itself. Alpha comes closest to this with the suggestion that the course must be run continually for its true effects to be felt, and that 'graduates' should rejoin the course as part of the delivery team. Why produce a post-Alpha course when the end of Alpha is more Alpha? For such persons, the Alpha Course is not only a means of conversion and renewal but the very mode of their continuing discipleship: perhaps advancing, as a consequence of this iterative design, to the role of small-group leader etc. The autonomy of Alpha may also conceal the temptation to settle for ever more participation in the programme as a simulacrum of real Christian discipleship.

It would seem, however, that Alpha brings the possibility of identity and purpose to the life of local churches struggling with both. What is more, marketing it as a standardized package can bring a sense of ecumenical unity via an interdenominational network of Alpha churches. Nevertheless, the portability of Alpha is more likely to stem from the wider crisis of denominational identity, coupled with the ecological triumph of courses in the local church, than bearing the essentials of Christian thought and practice. It is interesting, at a time when Alpha actually seems to be losing some of its earlier momentum, that the idea of an Alpha church may find a new authority – and be given a new lease of life – as a 'fresh expression of church'; thus bringing the technique to its logical conclusion as a method of church planting or replanting.[34]

The relative autonomy of Alpha as a technique, however, also tends to conceal the possibility that it may be run with or without the existence of any substantial Christian community beyond that gathered by the programme itself. The origin of Alpha, as a programme of catechesis was aimed at initiating persons into the wider life of HTB, and the nature of the course naturally reflected the common commitments and core practices of the church itself. It is only in the technological abstraction, commodification, and marketing of the course that Alpha has to present itself as a neutral tool – shaped by the ecumenical essentials of basic Christianity – if it is to retain its character as a method of evangelism and initiation into the life of any local church. Yet, as I have already argued, there is no such thing as a neutral tool.

The question facing any Christian community thinking about taking up Alpha, therefore, is what form of church life are its graduates being prepared for; and does Alpha actually prepare those persons for that kind of life? An even more pointed question would be whether the church actually has a recognisable form of life, shaped by the sort of common commitments and core practices into which graduates of an Alpha course can be initiated. My suspicion is that this form of life is precisely what many churches are lacking, and that Alpha must be taken up for its renewing function in order to make the promise of evangelism intelligible. At issue, then, is the extent to which a church may take up Alpha as means of discovering the richness and particularity of its own life together in the context of evangelistic outreach.

It seems to me, however, that the potential of the course to promote such renewal lies in conflict with the marketing orientation of Alpha International, whose end is more and better run Alpha courses.[35] Elsewhere I have argued that the goal of Alpha should literally be the 'end' of Alpha, since its purpose as a mentor would be to do itself out of a job![36] Unless the goal of Alpha is merely to reproduce carbon copies of itself, then it could act more intentionally to reshape and offer up the programme as an expendable means for cultivating local expressions of mission and ministry. Resistance to this possibility, of course, simply mirrors the captivity of Alpha International to the marketing orientation and the technological promise of a more reliable future secured through the mechanisms of prediction and control. This is, however, the subtle temptation of practical atheism.

Alpha as Medium and Mentor

It would seem, then, that aspirations toward church renewal are more basic and important than the efficacy of Alpha as an evangelistic technique; but only if such renewal is accompanied by catching a vision for the church's missionary vocation by embracing a more deeply-rooted evangelistic culture. My question is, can the uptake of Alpha as a technological phenomenon accomplish this end? Can it be taken up as a mentor rather than a technician? What is it about running the course itself that might subvert the rule of technology, the allure of commodification, and our desire for a technical fix?

Marshall McLuhan famously asserted that 'the medium is the message' because 'it is the medium that shapes and controls the scale and form of human association and action'. He goes on, however, to claim 'it is only too typical that the 'content' of any medium blinds us to the character of the medium' itself.[37] In the case of Alpha, a preoccupation with debates about the form and content of the course may tend to conceal the true power of the programme as a technique to shape the total thought and practice of a congregation. McLuhan also offers an interesting twist on his popular dictum by proclaiming that 'the medium is the *massage*' because 'all media work us over completely'; that is, they don't just extend our capacities, but transform the whole way we think and feel and speak and act.[38] If the Alpha Course is thought of as a medium in this sense, then the issue is not how efficient a congregation can become at running it, but how its life together is transformed in the process. Do our congregations need such a 'work over' and can Alpha accomplish that for the good?

If the answer to these questions is 'yes', then the ambiguity of reading Alpha as a technological phenomenon lies in the possibility that a course marketed as a technical solution to the problem of evangelism may actually serve as a medium for cultivating the kind of common life that naturally engages in locally developed forms of mission activity. In other words, for many churches, it is precisely a 'massage', or whole ecological change, that is necessary; and this is precisely what the adoption of a new technique can accomplish. The question is, whether Alpha as a technique can be intentionally appropriated as a means to that end, or whether it becomes an end in itself. The answer is not likely to be straightforward, given the inescapable tension between using and being used by the technologies we adopt.

In practice, the issue may turn on the extent to which running a course on the ground can subvert the pressures toward technological autonomy authorized by the marketing orientation of Alpha International. I suggest that where this happens, it is because there is nothing technologically remarkable about the content of the course itself! Alpha merely re-engages the church with a whole spectrum of ordinary Christian practices such as offering hospitality, proclamation, prayer, bible study, small-group fellowship and faith sharing. As a technical medium, it can bring a fresh purpose and new energy to these practices by connecting and orienting them toward the goal of evangelism and disciple-making. The charismatic-evangelical ethos of the course, however, is that which keeps the temptation to practical atheism at bay.

If Alpha is to act as a mentor rather than a technician, however, care must be taken not to reduce this range of practices to techniques by imagining that their evangelical virtue depends upon the technical efficiency with which they get done in some merely programmatic manner. The evangelistic culture of a church is not likely to be sustained by those who have simply been 'trained' how to welcome others, pray together, and share their faith in the predictable and controlled environment of an Alpha course. It is, however, more likely to be firmly rooted in a church whose members have been apprenticed in the art of being hospitable and prayerful witnesses in all circumstances and over the long haul of mission and ministry.

Experience of Alpha, however, is that it often fails at this very point. The course only 'works' as a means for evangelising the unchurched if those in the church have the skills and virtues necessary to invite their neighbours to come along. If a church does not already have such a culture, or the seeds of it, then Alpha is unlikely to create it; and the programme struggles to get past the first few cycles which are attended mainly by church members themselves. Of course, it would seem that the commitment of Alpha International to a standardized package coupled with effective national advertising campaigns can offer a technical solution to this technological problem. If, however, brand recognition is offered as a substitute for personal witness, then we are truly captivated to the rule of technology.

In conclusion, I would make some recommendations to Alpha International and to those thinking of taking up the Alpha Course. Social researchers like Hunt typically call for new and improved versions of the course; more inclusive, more basic or more finely-tuned than the original. In my view, these responses are simply doomed to fall upon their own petard. If I am right that the churches need to be apprenticed in the art of evangelism and mentored through the development of a mission-minded culture – and if our technological culture makes us look to programmes like Alpha for that possibility – then two final points must be made.

First, churches taking up the Alpha Course should be very intentional about seeking to discern what kind of common life they want to pursue through it, and how that life might be capable of sustained missionary engagement in their own local contexts. It is probably helpful for such discourse and deliberation to begin prior to adopting the programme and to continue as a means of review each time it is run. If the course is functioning as a mentor, it is likely to raise questions about whether it might be done differently, or whether it needs to be run at all. I suggest that the genius of Alpha will best be continued through imparting a vision for the long haul adventure of missionary experimentation and the desire for more locally developed practices of evangelism.

Second, my challenge to Alpha International is that it should sacrifice those commitments to a marketing orientation which get in the way of Alpha as a mentor. In particular, they might give up the Alpha copyright – for there is no sound *theological* reason to keep it – and perhaps even work on packaging some materials with the programme that can assist churches in the task of spiritual discernment outlined above. Perhaps, then, the charisms of the Holy Spirit can build a church capable of withstanding the practical atheism of our technological culture.

Notes

[1] See Pete Ward, 'Alpha – The McDonaldization of Religion?,' *Anvil*, 15:4 (1998), pp. 279–86. This critique also figures prominently in the work of Stephen Hunt. See, *Anyone for Alpha? Evangelism in a Post-Christian Society* (Darton, Longman and Todd, 2001); and especially, *The Alpha Enterprise: Evangelism in a Post-Christian Era* (Ashgate, 2004), p. 36f and ch. 9.

[2] For a helpful analysis of the surveys to date, see Charles Freebury, *Alpha or Emmaus? Assessing Today's Top Evangelistic Courses* (Charles Freebury, 2005). Available from Higher Severalls House, 89 Hermitage Street, Crewkerne, Somerset TA18 8EX. This is a revision of an MA dissertation submitted to Cliff College in 2001. Freebury also draws on the work of Stephen Hunt cited above, and that of Mark Ireland, *A Study of the Effectiveness of Process Evangelism Courses in the Diocese of Lichfield, with Special Reference to Alpha* (Cliff College, MA dissertation, 2000). See also, Booker and Mark Ireland, *Evangelism – Which Way Now?* (Church House Publishing, 2003); and John Finney, *Emerging Evangelism* (Darton, Longman and Todd, 2004), p. 77f.

[3] Martin Heidegger, 'The Question Concerning Technology,' in *The Question Concerning Technology and Other Essays*, translated by William Lovitt (Harper and Row, 1977), p. 4. See also the accompanying essay, 'Science and Reflection' for an articulation of the scientific view of reality and its relation to technology.

[4] Heidegger, 'The Question Concerning Technology,' pp. 16f. and 23f.

[5] Heidegger, 'The Question Concerning Technology,' p. 5f.

[6] Heidegger, 'The Question Concerning Technology,' p. 26.

[7] Albert Borgmann, *Technology and the Character of Contemporary Life: A Philosophical Enquiry* (Chicago University Press, 1984), pp. 40f and 76f. See also, Albert Borgmann, *Power Failure: Christianity in the Culture of Technology* (Brazos Press, 2003), pp. 17f, 31 and 121f.

[8] Jaques Ellul, *The Technological Society* (Vintage Books, 1964), p. xxv.

[9] Ellul, *The Technological Society*, pp. 3–4.

[10] Ellul, *The Technological Society*, p. 5.

[11] Ellul, *The Technological Society*, pp. 19, 20 and 21.

[12] Ellul, *The Technological Society*, p. 67.

[13] Ellul, *The Technological Society*, p. 70.

[14] Ellul, *The Technological Society*, p. 63.

[15] Ellul, *The Technological Society*, pp. 78f, 128f, 131f.

[16] Neil Postman, *Technopoly: The Surrender of Culture to Technology* (Vintage Books, 1993), p.18.

[17] Postman, *Technopoly*, p. 28.

[18] Postman, *Technopoly*, p. 52.

[19] Postman, *Technopoly*, p. 71.

[20] Postman, *Technopoly*, p. 90.

[21] Hunt, *The Alpha Enterprise*, p. 32–3.

[22] If being 'sectarian' simply means living together with the intention to embody a set of virtues and values different from that of the dominant culture, then there is a case to be made for this as the proper stance of the church as an agent of mission. See Philip Kenneson, *Beyond Sectarianism* (Trinity Press International, 1999). Indeed, some sort of 'sectarian' stance may be the only way forward for the church in a technological culture that proceeds equally well with or without the existence of God. Submitting to the techno-logic of the market is really a kind of theological suicide!

[23] For a critique of social science in our technological culture, see Postman, *Technopoly*, ch. 9.

[24] Note Hunt's careful choice of the word 'enterprise' which can denote any risky venture, but is recast in our technological culture to mean a business venture aimed specifically at growth and profit.

[25] Nicky Gumbel, *Questions of Life* (Kingsway, 2001). This is the 'authorized text' upon which the Alpha talks are based.

[26] There is a whole range of Alpha publications from *Searching Issues* to the *Alpha Administrator's Handbook*; an *Alpha Cookbook*; *Introducing Worship to Alpha* and the *Alpha Worship Pack*; *Prayer on Alpha*; *Maximising the Potential of Your Alpha Course*; and various other resources aimed at training leaders and helpers.

[27] Pete Ward actually upholds 'the commodification of religious product' as one important principle of a more 'liquid' ecclesiological future. See, *Liquid Church* (Paternoster, 2002), p. 47 and ch. 6. It would seem that Ward basically shares Hunt's assessment of the church's inevitable location in the marketplace.

[28] For a comparison of the 'Alpha' and 'Emmaus' courses see Booker and Ireland, *Evangelism: Which Way Now?* and Freebury, *Alpha and Emmaus*. Other contemporary courses include 'Credo', 'Christianity Explored', 'Y Course', 'Start' and 'Essence', etc.

[29] Postman roots our technological culture in a 'scientism' which promotes the 'illusory belief that some standardized set of procedures called 'science' can provide us with an unimpeachable source of moral authority' (*Technopoly*, p. 162). It is a faith in science itself as a belief-system that can give meaning and direction to all of reality. It is a belief that science and technology can be applied to the analysis and control of human behaviour, both psychologically and sociologically. And it is a belief formidably underwritten by a confidence that social science is capable of measuring and organizing our life together on a rational basis towards common ends (*Technopoly*, p. 147).

[30] At the level of particular practices, one can now buy into packaged courses for everything from marriage guidance to youth work to prayer meetings. At the level of whole congregations, there are packages aimed at the fundamental re-organization of church life. For becoming a *Purpose Driven* church, see Rick Warren, *The Purpose Driven Church* (Zondervan, 1995). For becoming a *Willow Creek* church, see Lynne and Bill Hybels, *Rediscovering Church* (Zondervan, 1995). This text is especially interesting because it reveals the pattern of commodification I have described quite clearly: part one tracing the history of Willow Creek Community Church; and part two abstracts from that history a set of strategic principles underlying their success.

[31] Supported variations on the programme include 'Alpha in the Workplace', 'Youth Alpha', and 'Alpha for Students' as well as 'Alpha for Prisons', 'Alpha for Forces', etc.

[32] Those to whom we minister are not some general 'unchurched Harry and Mary' – or the demographically idealized consumer in a spiritual marketplace – but real people with real lives who need to be reached by Christians with the missionary love of God and neighbour.

[33] The truth of this can be seen in the way that our technologies move from the periphery to the centre of our lives – like cars, computer, mobile phones etc. – reconstructing how we think, speak, work, and relate to one another.

[34] For a useful introduction to 'fresh expressions of church' and 'emerging church' see Michael Moynagh, *emergingchurch.intro* (Monarch, 2004).

[35] See the emphasis on 'Alpha Initiatives' which have the threefold aim of raising public awareness of the Alpha course, supporting churches in attracting guests to their Alpha courses, and strengthening Alpha courses through training http://alphacourse.org/runningacourse/initiative.

[36] Philip Meadows, 'The Alpha Course,' in Stephen Gunter and Elaine Robinson (eds.), *Considering the Great Commission* (Abingdon Press, forthcoming).

[37] Marshall McLuhan, *Understanding Media: The Extensions of Man* (Signet, 1964), p. 24.

[38] Marshall McLuhan and Quentin Fiore, *The Medium is the Massage: An Inventory of Effects* (Bantam Books, 1967), p. 26.

CHAPTER 23

Alpha as a Fresh
Ecumenical Opportunity

Simon Barrow

The Range of Reactions to Alpha

Two years ago I carried out a small experiment at an ecumenical conference on mission, which had among its participants a whole spectrum of Christian opinion – from liberal Anglican to evangelical new church, from conservative Catholic and moderate Pentecostal to radical Methodist and Anabaptist. I slipped each of them a piece of paper asking various questions about their reaction to the Alpha Course, and I told them that any comments they gave me would not be used to identify them.

I plan to keep to that deal, but I must say the overall results were fascinating. Among a group of people dedicated, remember, to the development and transmission of the Gospel message, only 30 per cent would wholeheartedly recommend Alpha to local churches or invite neighbours to attend one of the courses.

Among the (often quite harsh) criticisms was 'doctrinal narrowness', a 'simplistic' message, the reduction of Christianity to 'an evangelical agenda', the 'wrong doctrine of the Holy Spirit', a 'lack of connection with social action', alleged 'hostility towards other faiths', a 'lack of emphasis on the Bible', a 'smug middle class approach', 'rejecting of lesbians and gays', 'copyright obsessed', 'theological naiveté', the 'cringe factor', 'spin-doctored faith', 'hostility to scepticism', 'questionable doctrine' and 'fake dialogue'.

On the positive side, others said that Alpha was 'open and inviting', 'clearly scriptural', 'warm and welcoming', 'hospitable', 'surprisingly engaging', 'sincere', 'media savvy', 'open to various Christian traditions', 'simple and direct, 'respectful of participants', 'interesting to people with little religious background', 'not too complicated' and provided 'a good, basic introduction to Christian faith.'

Others suggested that a framework similar to Alpha could be developed for 'different constituencies' (as in Credo for Anglo-Catholics) or replaced by 'a different approach' altogether (as in the Urban Theology Unit course on travelling with radical Jesus).

Of 27 people who replied (out of 40) eight said they knew somebody who had been brought back to faith through attending an Alpha event, 15 said they knew no-one who had attended a course, and one said that she had been 'revived' in her own Christian journey by Alpha, though she would now 'understand the faith journey rather differently to the way it was presented to me that evening.'

Now this survey was entirely unscientific, I should stress, excepting that it embraced a good cross-section of engaged opinion. But it does confirm the very wide range of views about Alpha I have experienced (and sometimes shared myself) in ecumenical circles – that is, in those spaces where Christians of different traditions and temperaments who would not otherwise connect with one another have an opportunity to meet, think, pray, worship, talk and work together.

In one respect it also echoes the research that has been done about the spread and scope of the Alpha Course. A little under two-thirds of those Christians who replied to my short questionnaire had not had any direct programmatic contact with it at all. That is broadly true of the churches in Britain and Ireland overall, and there are two ways of looking at this. On the one hand, the take-up and impact of the course can be seen as extraordinarily wide given that it emanated originally from one London church. On the other hand, there are still a remarkable number of Christians who remain aloof or hostile to Alpha – or simply uninformed – in spite of, or even because of, the extensive publicity it has enjoyed.

The Evangelistic Effectiveness of Alpha

My purpose here is not primarily to enter into the debate about what makes Alpha good for some and problematic for others (though these issues will certainly come up), but specifically to ask what kind of ecumenical opportunity it is, how it might engage more fruitfully with those in its sceptical hinterland, and what challenges the bewildering globalisation of Christianity will offer for Alpha in its next phase of development.

My starting point is an affirmation of Alpha in one central respect. Whatever problems some of us might have with its content (and I have a number), this is a venture which is seeking to create an opportunity for people who have lost touch with Christianity. It enables them to meet faith again (or for the first time), and to do so on the good ground of food, friendship and welcome. Astonishingly, this is something which the majority of churches in Britain and Ireland have shown little interest in over the past forty years – even though sharing food and tables, and meeting Jesus there without regard to religious restrictions, is the very essence of what the Gospels depict.

At the tail-end of Christendom (the long era when Christian faith could assume a 'natural' predominance in 'our' culture and society) the pattern has either been to hide in our fortresses and expect people to beat a path to our front door, or to engage in evangelistic 'raiding parties' which often pay less attention to the many they dissuade than the comparatively few they persuade. Similarly, churches have oscillated between 'big events' and the purely personal in conveying their message, and have seen the task of generating new believers as a matter either of osmosis or drama, slow convergence or instant conversion.

Alpha has been part of changing all that, and in so doing has reflected a number of significant shifts in Western Christianity which are noticeable across the entire theological spectrum. Rather than 'doing religion in secret' or 'foisting it in the public square', Alpha has camped at the threshold of the church window onto the community, inviting people through tables of hospitality. It still mainly operates on church property, of course, occasionally branching into halls and public spaces – and more controversially, given plural and secular sensitivities, schools and prisons. In fact Alpha started in homes and the organisation still encourages it to be run in such settings and in venues like pubs. All this represents the beginning of a shift away from church 'settlement' towards the sometimes uneasy space of 'crossed boundaries' where convictions may be shared and collaborative projects entertained.

Similarly, Alpha has come to view Christian initiation and formation more in terms of 'process' than 'event' (something which has elicited much anxiety from some hard-line Evangelicals). It has also spanned the gap between 'rallies' and one-to-one encounters by bringing people together in significant gatherings and then breaking them up into smaller, more intimate groups. Personal invitations and the development of friendships accompanies the whole process.

Alpha's Ecumenical Approach: Pros and Cons

There is, of course, nothing new in this. But the simple Alpha formula has been to make 'space, places and graces' something regular and organisational – rather than occasional and exceptional – in seeking an interface between the believing cabal and the wider community. In so doing the Course has, in spite of the criticism it has elicited for being 'too narrow', brought together an astonishingly diverse range of people both inside and outside the churches. For the tough truth which 'ecumenical Christians' (those who think of themselves as habitual bridge-builders) must face is this: *far more people of far greater a variety have run Alpha Courses or attended Alpha Conferences together than have ever ventured into a 'Churches Together' event in their lives.*

This illustrates the most truly astonishing change in the interpersonal and institutional face of ecumenism. While ecumenical structures are shrinking and losing funds, entrepreneurial initiative and money have come pouring into and out of an organisation focussed around one church, Holy Trinity Brompton. The 'Alpha industry' (as it is sometimes accused of being) now dwarfs many church development and mission agencies, outweighs the resources available within denominational and ecumenical bodies, and creates conversation between people – like Catholic bishops and Protestant house church leaders – which the formal negotiating mechanisms of ecumenism have failed to achieve.

Alpha is, in fact, very ecumenical, even if it often has a tempered (some would say Baptist-like) Anglican face. Organised ecumenism, on the other hand, frequently attracts a shrinking band of enthusiasts who struggle to maintain proper relations with their grassroots in the churches and rapidly develop a language of their own which actually speaks to fewer and fewer. I should know. I worked for nine years with Churches Together in Britain and Ireland (CTBI). I admire and still support the work CTBI does. But it has a hard job persuading its constituency to move out of a Christendom shell where internal reconfiguration and 'resolutionary Christianity' still reign.

That said, Alpha International remains very much within 'the Christendom mould' when it comes to the way that it runs. Though disaggregated from church structures, it has a disciplined top-down structure of its own. This means that it has been very efficient at getting its message across and at organising events, publicity and publications. But it has been less than responsive to the ground-up impulses of contextual Christianity, the way the Gospel takes shape through local conditions and through the inculturation of its message in particular communities. This breeds criticism and imposes severe limits. Neither the culture nor style of Alpha videos fits well with many situations. In its present form Alpha faces a 'glass ceiling', and though it has broken the evangelical mould in many respects, it remains rather establishment in its ethos. Some have suggested, with justification, that the standardisation of the programme, message and presentation comes across as 'McDonaldized'.

In a sense, this 'top down' approach reflects a certain style of ecumenism too, the sort that occasionally found expression in the 'Council of Churches'. Such bodies became seen (not always fairly) as a kind of 'supra-church structure' which agreed policy statements and promoted additional activities to denominations and local churches. Over the past seventeen years the conciliar approach has given way to a 'Churches Together' model of working, in which the ecumenical partners talk, pray and collaborate on a shared journey, while respecting their own integrity, distinctiveness and autonomy regarding authority and decision-taking. The idea has been to promote more realism, as well as encouraging flexibility in working rather than long-term structures. This approach is less 'top down'. However, what has been gained in accountability and responsibility has sometimes been accompanied by losses in energy and creativity. What is now needed is more trust and risk taking. Perhaps Alpha International could benefit from studying these ecumenical lessons and developments.

Change could come not only through a loosening of the strings (a willingness to allow different range of topics, say) but through a wider range of presentations of the Christian message drawing on the true ecumenicity of the Christian community. There have been moves in this direction as a result of conversations between AI/HTB and the Catholic Church, certainly. But this has largely been a matter of introducing 'small additional elements' or alternative phrasing into an existing framework. In the longer run, many would argue, that framework would benefit being broken open and remoulded.

Breaking the Mould or Branding the Mission?

Let me try and indicate some of the issues and how this might work, along with the tensions it throws up, with the following example. Not that long ago, I was involved in a local 'Churches Together' meeting where two congregations who had run Alpha courses suggested to other Christian partners in the area that it might be a ripe time to share how they had done this, and to invite other churches to follow suit. Someone else immediately got 'the wrong end of the stick', but in a quite helpful and agenda-changing way. She suggested setting up a small ecumenical group of people with gifts in communications, theology and group-work to discuss how the Christian Gospel might come across best to non-church goers in the neighbourhood. Her idea was that six weekly talks and a weekend could then be devised around basic Christian themes, but bearing in mind the particular culture, needs, demography and make-up of those the churches in the area were trying to reach and work with.

There was a slight embarrassed silence. Then someone from one of the Alpha-running congregations responded, slightly sniffily, that this was not a 'pick and mix' course; that the talks by Nicky Gumbel were 'non-negotiable'; and that the whole point was that 'this package is proven to be the best one for getting across the core Christian message.'

A lively discussion broke out. Someone who had read Alpha materials and Nicky Gumbel's books began criticising aspects of them, saying that to run the Course at his church the message would need to change. Someone else said that she was unhappy with the superficial apologetic ploys overheard on one of the Courses she attended – such as the C. S. Lewis 'Jesus must be mad, bad – or God' gambit, or the idea that 'the world must have been made by God, because to believe otherwise would be like expecting the works of Shakespeare to emerge fully-formed from an explosion in a printing factory.' Brief discussions of psychology ('he could just have been wrong') and astrophysics ('a series of explosions in the right conditions could do that') followed! More substantial theological objections came in the shape of regrets that the Course as a whole seemed to many to presuppose a split between conversion and discipleship, with 'knowing Jesus' being seen as prior, conditional and separable from 'following Jesus' – which barely seemed to feature in Alpha at all.[1] The absence of social witness, peace and justice was particularly noted.

It was interesting, and perhaps also a difficulty, that a majority in the room *wanted* to run an 'Alpha-style' series. They just *didn't want* it pre-packaged on a basis that seemed to them far too 'take it or leave it'. Responsive talk of 'scope for improvisation, as well as fixed elements, within the overall event' was not convincing to them.

Is Alpha Subversive Enough?

All this points to a key issue from an ecumenical perspective. The whole point of the 'ecumenical movement' is not that curious structures are set up to promote unity, but that people walk together, learning and growing (and arguing) as they do so. One person in this particular discussion made the point that the young people she was in touch with would respond well to Jesus' message to be peacemakers, to welcome the stranger, to feed the hungry, to stand up for justice, to question the control of the religious and political authorities over who gets blessed. So why not start there? A shared commitment out of which questions of faith and fraternity could emerge. This would also involve recognising that, for many people today, the test for true religion is not just intellectual credibility (believing) and communal feeling (belonging) but neighbourly integrity (behaving).

In the midst of this exchange, an idea for a different approach to the course seemed to be emerging. But for those involved it didn't look as if the 'inherited framework', would make such a move possible. In my view, it ought to be. Alpha is an inspired idea, and those who want to go on running it in the 'traditional way' should be able to do so. But there are others who hear, receive and practice the Gospel of Jesus differently. Shouldn't they be encouraged to spread the word too, to use the resources that have been developed so far in new and exciting ways? When this was raised, it was responded to in terms of 'branding'. In order to 'benefit from the name and image' of Alpha, you needed to 'buy into the package' (that word again) it was said. And pay into the pot. Otherwise how would it survive and maintain its identity?

The same question, of course, could be asked of Christianity – where the historical and spatial span extends from Eastern Orthodoxy and black African Initiated Churches to the European charismatic movement and radical base communities in Latin America. The fact is, the Gospel is diverse, characterised by both family likeness and deep differences in the matter of the transforming impact of Jesus Christ in our world. Proclaiming and practising the Gospel also requires sustaining and developing in a whole variety of different ways, not just through fixed-term courses.

If Alpha International is to move forward and to gain credibility in parts of the Christian world which have so far rejected it, it needs to be more responsive to the dynamism and diversity of lived Christianity across the globe. And it also needs to recognise that to become a follower of Jesus is to be received into a community with a counter-cultural edge, one that does not (or, at least, should not) accept or adapt to the divisions, injustices, conflicts and prejudices it has to negotiate in the world – but challenges and confronts them. That was one of the questions asked from the back of the room in the particular local Churches Together discussion about Alpha that I recall most vividly: 'Where's the subversive Jesus in all this?'

Alpha to Omega: Dreaming Dreams & Embracing the Earth

This leads to one final (but fundamental) ecumenical opportunity and question. Ecumenism is not, as some suppose, a matter either of ecclesiastical joinery (trying to unite church structures) or of flaccid accommodation (papering over our differences in the interests of peace-and-quiet). In its New Testament origins, the word *oikumene* is about the loving purposes of God for 'the household', by which is meant the whole human household, as well as the people called out to be *ekklesia* – a Jesus-shaped gathering whose life witnesses to the power of love, forgiveness, peace, hope, joy, justice and faith for people-in-community. From this word we also get *oikonomia*, the economy (or household purse). And we get the major missionary question of the Acts of the Apostles: 'where, in the Spirit-impelled movement of God's people to the margins, are 'the ends of the earth'?' How far can and should we go. It's about risk, not caution.

The Gospel, in other words, is not just about 'me and God', it is about the personal vision of a healed creation reordered around right relations, the triumph of life-giving over death dealing, the victory of healing (wholeness that restores) over sin (being cut off in selfishness). Someone who I met recently, and who benefited in a number of ways from Alpha, ended up in an Anabaptist-related congregation where this breadth of ecumenical, discipleship-based vision is foundational. It has changed his life. What he says now is, 'At Alpha I got a glimpse of what was on offer... and many questions. With this church I have seen that Christian faith is the kind of global movement which can turn me and the world upside-down. But I got virtually no whiff of this when I started out.'

The 'missing link', he suggested to me, is that an introduction to Christianity shouldn't just be about Alpha (a more of less prescribed telling of the Christian story to be believed), it should be an invitation to *Omega* – a biblically-shaped space for our young and old people to see visions, to dream dreams…and to be invited into God's movement for a renewed creation. That's a pretty large idea. But it suggests that what has been Alpha so far could look fruitfully different in the future – more local, more experimental, more diverse, more questioning, more practical, more rooted in the lives of those who want to make the world a better place…because they realise that this is what the redemption signalled and embodied by Jesus means. This would be a truer and fuller ecumenism, one that embraces not just an ever-widening Christian household, but (as in the Gospels) meeting Jesus in the broader human struggle for personal, social, economic, political and spiritual transformation. Doing this would involve some letting go. But the gains could be considerable.

Notes

[1] However, please see Chapter 6 of this book for a fuller discussion of the nature of conversion on Alpha and its link with discipleship.

PART TWO

SECTION 6

Drawing Things Together

Section 6 rounds off the book. It consists firstly of the initial reactions of Nicky Gumbel to issues raised by the first five sections of the book, that I put to him in an interview. Then there are some thoughts of mine, drawing together in very general and extremely brief terms the key themes, insights and suggestions of the book as it has developed, focussing on how the Alpha Phenomenon may progress from here. This is not a formal conclusion, since that would run the risk of simplifying, and thus impoverishing, the richness of what is on offer to those that have read the book so far, with its multiplicity of contributing voices. Looking at this section is thus not a substitute for reading the whole book. Furthermore, the book and the wider project that birthed it were constructed as a conversation and dialogue and that needs to continue …

AB

CHAPTER 24

Initial Responses and Reactions from Nicky Gumbel

An Interview given by Nicky Gumbel to Andrew Brookes

I was keen to include in the book the thoughts and reactions of Nicky Gumbel to what others had written. He was willing to co-operate and, since he is a busy man, an interview format, rather than a written article, was suggested. I am grateful to him for giving the time for a 25-minute interview which I was given permission to print in full. As explained in the introduction, he chose not to see the text of the book in advance and left the choice of questions to me though I very briefly indicated the topics to him in advance. I tried to gather together the main issues raised by the book within the time constraints and to get his first reactions to these.

When Nicky reads the whole book, he may, of course, think about these topics more deeply and prefer to have answered in more nuanced, full or different terms. Or he may not. These comments should thus be taken as what they are: only first reactions to my summary questions. It will be interesting to see what further responses, if any, Nicky Gumbel and Alpha International later make.

Notations:
NG = Nicky Gumbel.
AB = Andrew Brookes.
I have used *italics* to indicate a few words that Nicky particularly stressed.
[ ] have been used to indicate occasional words added for clarity only.
A few explanatory footnotes by AB are included.

The interview was conducted and taped at HTB, 15th February, 2006.

The text has been left very much as originally transcribed and thus is very much the authentic original conversation we had – even if this does at times strain the conventions of English grammar and the requirements of good written style!

AB: Thank you for taking the time for this interview, Nicky. The first issue that we'll look at is the insight that Alpha highlights that evangelisation is a journey, a process, and obviously giving people ten weeks in the context of coming to belong as well as believe is vital to how God is working with people. However, commentators are saying that as we move from working with people on the fringe of church to the dechurched and even nonchurched, we will have to apply this principle more thoroughly. Do we have to take longer, change the content or change our assumptions about people Christian background? Do you care to comment on these ideas for the present and the future of Alpha?

NG: Well, there are two different sort of critiques. One is that it is too short and needs to be longer because people need longer in a post-Christian society. The other is that it is too long and no-one can cope with a ten week (15 session) course and it should be shorter, for instance, six weeks or four weeks or eight weeks. There are both those arguments and I can see the force of both of them. It is true that at the end of the course some people say: 'Oh, is it finished already?' The answer to that is 'No, it is not. You have just started on a life-long process called being a Christian, it is discipleship and it will go on till you die.' The next step is join a pastorate or do 'A Life Worth Living' or do RCIA[1] or whatever is the appropriate follow-up within that person's context where they have come to faith. Alpha is just a practical introduction to the Christian faith. Alpha is the first letter of the Greek alphabet it is not the whole alphabet. It is only an introduction.

For those who think it should be shorter, it is my experience that it needs to be that long for the reasons that you have given. Should you have a pre-Alpha course along the lines of suffering, other religions, all those sorts of things that a person who is miles away might be asking? We used to have it – we had it for a number of years, it was called 'agnostics anonymous' or something and we used to get six people coming on it and sometimes one or two became Christians. When we combined it with Alpha, Alpha took off. We used to say to people who weren't Christians, 'Go on Agnostics Anonymous' and to Christians 'Go on Alpha'. And we had a hundred people on Alpha and six on Agnostics Anonymous. Then we designed Alpha for people who weren't Christians and shut down Agnostics Anonymous and then it [Alpha] took off. And far more people responded to Alpha than to the pre-Alpha course.

AB: Why do you think that is?

NG: I think there are a number of reasons. I think it is because the process operates at different levels. One level is an intellectual level which is answering their questions which they get an opportunity to do in the groups anyway. The kind of questions that people want to address in their pre-Alpha course group don't actually take you any further forward, even if you answer them. For example is you take the question 'Why does God allow suffering?' which for some people is a very big question. If you have a talk on that, what you do is you raise it for everybody – so for the person for whom it is not a question, it becomes a question. Since there is no satisfactory answer anyway to the whole question you are not going to satisfy the ones that did have problem with it – or you are very unlikely to. If you do, all you've done is keep the ball out. It is like a defensive shot in cricket. You don't score any runs but you keep the ball out. Whereas every talk on Alpha takes people further forward. If they understand who Jesus is, they move forward. If they understand the cross, they move forward. If they understand faith, they move forward. If they start reading the Bible or they start praying, they move forward. It is an attacking shot. And it is not as if we are ducking the other issues. They will come up in the small groups if they are a problem and people want them to, but not if they don't. And we can deal with it there and we can discuss it and that is the best forum I think for doing it. So that is the first reason, the intellectual level.

Secondly, evangelism is more than just an intellectual approach it is about experiencing community for a start, Christian community. And if you just put a bunch of people on an Agnostics Anonymous course, they are probably not going to experience Christian community. Part of it is experiencing worship, experiencing community over a meal, community in small groups, friendships that emerge and it is that aspect of it that is one of the key factors.

Thirdly, they are observing what Christian are like, they are observing small-group leaders and building trust and they see a model of life that they probably don't see out in the world very often.

I think it is all those kind of processes that are going on in people's lives [during Alpha]. They are not above the surface but are beneath the surface and they are as important, if not more important than some of the intellectual processes.

AB: The original material was a discipleship course that was expanded. If we are moving towards a seriously unchurched situation then even allowing for what you say about the importance of community, does the material, especially in the first two to three weeks, perhaps make too many assumptions about prior Christian knowledge?

NG: Absolutely! I would never have written the course as it is for people who are not Christians. There is hardly anything in the course I would have written if I had come up with a course for evangelism. It just would not have been like that; it would have been something completely different. It certainly would not have had all the stuff about the Holy

Spirit, about healing, about the church; probably we would not have been going so deep into things or we would not be moving beyond the first three weeks after three weeks. But that's not how it worked. We had a course that we thought was for Christians that we found was working for hundreds of people outside of the church and it works as well or better now than when that process first started happening. I don't see any difference. If I did I would change it, because I am there at every course in a small group, watching people who are totally outside of the church responding. It probably has changed subtly over the years as I've observed them. But if they weren't responding I would change it. Fundamentally I don't see any difference now from how it was. But I agree with you. It is not the obvious thing. What we were brought up with is the obvious thing and it didn't work.

AB: O.K. I suppose the time might come when you could take all that methodological insight and it might be interesting or appropriate to stretch or change some of the content?

NG: Yeah! A lot of people have tried it. Just to say – if someone does come up with a better course, we'll do it. If someone does come up with a better course we'd love it; it would be wonderful! We are looking for more effective ways of reaching people with the Good News about Jesus.

AB: Great! Building on your comments and the insight that Alpha is a very church centred form of evangelism – it takes people into community – how important is it, not just for the local church to run Alpha, but to adopt similar sorts of strategies as HTB regarding small groups or pastorates, some of the core values of the church – for example, all people engaged in ministry, and doing this by recognising people's gifts and developing them. So Alpha is not just a bolt-on course but also something that emerges from the whole church. Do you think more attention needs to be given to that and, if so, how? I realise that's a huge challenge.

NG: People can use Alpha in whichever way they want to use Alpha. For some people it may just be a bolt-on but if it's a bolt-on that helps people, that's great! Other people say: 'Well, we've had a lot of people coming to faith on Alpha. We want to look after them afterwards. We are finding it hard to hold them. Maybe we need to develop small groups which we didn't have before.' Other people say: 'Well, look at all these people coming, they are young, and they find what we do on Sunday difficult. We may have to adjust what we do on Sunday to try and hold on to these people.' So it affects different churches in different ways. Some churches just literally use it as an evangelistic course and that is the only way they use it. Others are interested in some of the ways we've developed as follow-up. But it depends on which part of the church they come from. As you know, the Catholic church have their own follow-up material and we want people to join whatever church they do Alpha in. So if it's in a Catholic church we hope they'll join the Catholic church. If it's in an Anglican church we hope they'll join the Anglican church or in the Salvation Army they'll join the Salvation Army.

AB: So you don't feel there is a need to look more at the whole area of integration of Alpha into the church? Or do you think it's best not to do too much and to leave people free?

NG: Well, all we are trying to do is provide resources for churches that want them. And if people want an evangelistic course, we hope that Alpha is a help to them. If people want help to integrate Alpha into the church we have resources to help with that. If people want follow-up material we have resources available, but they don't have to take the whole lot. They can take just Alpha, or Alpha and a Life Worth Living or Alpha and Integrating Alpha. They can take anything, but the only thing we ask as far as Alpha is concerned, please don't change it. Whatever they do after that or before Alpha is up to them. Of course, if they want to run a pre-Alpha course, that's fine; if they want a post Alpha course for Russian Orthodox or Catholics or the Salvation Army or whoever they can run their own courses.

AB: Thanks. Alpha has been standardised – and good reasons can be given for this. Put in the briefest way, it is important to 'follow the recipe' to understand how the course really works. But with standardisation you have the opportunity for advertising and for the national campaigns. But set against that, this puts limits on flexibility in changing the course and, some would say, really addressing local mission issues regarding the local culture. Any comments on the balance of all this?

NG: Yeah! You understand the reason why we have it the same – so that we can go out to the country and say it is an opportunity to explore the meaning of life at a church near you and it is the same thing. You couldn't do that if it was different things because no-one would know what they were getting.

As far as local flexibility is concerned – every church can run it. They can have their own speakers; be giving their own talks and they have their own small-group leaders – so the questions in the small groups will be different. The worship will be different, the food will be different, context will be different, the décor will be different. It's going to be *completely* different and every church has the possibility of adapting it to the local culture.

The only thing we say is please keep the essential character of the course if you are going to call it Alpha. If you want to do something that is essentially different please do not call it Alpha. But, of course, any church can run any course they want. They don't have to run Alpha – they can run any course they want. All we are saying is if you are going to *call* it Alpha it is a bit misleading for people who are sending their friends if you are running something that is *essentially* different. That is the only thing we say – 'to keep the essential character of the course'. But the worship, the small group, the speaker, everything else can be different.

AB: Thanks for that. Again some people have commented, building on this, that Alpha, particularly post 1993, has made very good use of business insights and been very professional and all the rest of it. The question comes up in a consumer society, 'What is the balance between taking advantage and making good use of consumerism to promote and proclaim the gospel and to what extent do we end up making God into some sort of provider and conforming him to our image and consumer mentality?' Arguably this has connections and overlaps with issues such as God's option for the poor and other deep issues of justice.

NG: Yeah – well, Alpha is the answer to consumerism. Consumerism is a form of hedonism that says life is about pleasure. What Alpha is saying is that that is not what life is all about. Life is about Jesus. It is about a relationship with God for which we were created. Alpha's message is the opposite of consumerism – that is not what life is all about. So it is speaking into a culture which is quite often caught up in materialism and consumerism and saying that there is an alternative.

Jesus said: 'Go and make disciples of all nations.' People need to hear about Jesus – we want as many people as possible to have that opportunity to hear so we want to make it available to them and that means we try and to things as well as we possibly can. So we do try to get things out there as effectively as we can and use people's God given gifts of excellence and management and whatever skills there are to get the message of Jesus out. There seems to be a Gospel imperative to do the best we can, not to do it in a sort of slipshod inefficient way but to do it as efficiently and effectively as we can.

AB: Building on that, I know that you work with Besom and that kind of project. Do you sense, through your work in proclaiming the gospel and bringing people to Jesus, an extra challenge or development to move into social concerns and other crucial issues both within this country and I suppose, through Alpha International, globally?

NG: Yeah, we are deeply concerned. The vision for Alpha is the re-evangelisation of the UK – or wherever we are – and the transformation of society. It is not just about the conversion of individuals, it is about the transformation of society. It's about the *kingdom*, the Kingdom of God. Jesus said, 'The Spirit of the Lord is upon me because he has anointed me to preach the good news to the poor, release for the prisoners and all the rest'. So we are concerned with the poor and a huge number of people who come through Alpha then get involved with poverty issues of one kind or another. We do this as a church with 'Making Poverty History', in social action projects of which there are *numerous* official ones coming out of the church, and there are also *loads* of unofficial ones. These are just individuals who have a vision for things and are going for it. So poverty is a big concern for us as a church. Justice is a big concern, [so are] the voiceless in our society and the future genera-tions. That is why we are doing this present series [of teachings] on poverty, the environment and prisons trying to address some of those issues. Yeah, it is a very key part of the mission of the church, it is part of Jesus' manifesto, his mandate, of what we feel called to do.

AB: So you see environment as being an issue as well?

NG: Yeah, because it affects the poor and it affects the future, the voiceless, it affects our children's children who do not yet have a vote.

AB: And the whole ecological side of environment as well?

NG: Yeah! God loves the world, he loves the cosmos and the whole world was created by Jesus and for Jesus. We have a responsibility. We are to enjoy it, to take care of it and to develop it in a sustainable way.

AB: Alpha has had a long history and has proved itself to have great longevity so far. You have commented before on how it combines elements of modern and post-modern culture. What other issues are out there concerning our changing culture? For example, the post Christian thing, New Age, other spiritualities, paganism, ecological issues? I mean, what are the challenges we need to face as a church – not just Alpha?

NG: Well, I think we have to face, well here in the UK, the rise of secular humanism. And that's the big thing. That's why I think the big chal-lenges facing the church now are not so much from the things that divided the church over the years. The battle is about Jesus. If there is any change that I have noticed in the Alpha small groups in the last fifteen years, it is the fact that God is not a stumbling block now, the Holy Spirit is not so much a stumbling block; it's Jesus, the uniqueness of Jesus that is the biggest stumbling block now, that Jesus is a univer-sal Saviour. I think Fr. Raniero Cantalamessa has put his finger on it, by saying that 'the battle is about the King'[2] and it's the same issue they faced in the first centuries. It is not the battles of the eleventh century, or the battles of the Reformation;[3] it is the battles of the first centuries. It's Jesus the universal Saviour. That's what our society is now finding very difficult to cope with. It's the claims of Jesus. They are happy to have Jesus as one of many, but not as the universal Saviour. That's the issue facing us now. That's what all Christians can unite around. I think that's what we need to do, we need to unite and declare that Jesus is the universal Saviour.

AB: Linked to that and following on, obviously Alpha has had huge ecumenical appeal, much more than I think you would have anticipated at the beginning? Why is that? What is the heart of Alpha's ecumenical secret and dynamism?

NG: Well I think it is, again as Fr. Raniero says, 'what unites us is infinitely greater than what divides us' and Alpha has always been about the things that unites us. It's been about Jesus, the cross, the Resurrection, faith, the Bible, prayer, guidance, the Holy Spirit, the church. These are things that basically – and of course there are variations at the margins – but at the heart these issues are ones about which all Christians are agreed and therefore it is something that we can all unite around. As you know, we did not set out to run an ecumenical course, we set out to run a course for the people who were coming on the course here but then we discovered that the people coming on the course here are no different to people anywhere else in the world. Their needs are the same. There is a hunger for meaning, purpose, a need for forgiveness and they are looking for something beyond this life. You know, these basic core questions are the same worldwide. The Christian answer actually, when you come down to the heart of these churches, is the same. Now, of course, there are different ways of doing things, at the margins there are different doctrines but at the heart is the same message: that Jesus is Lord, Jesus died for us, Jesus rose from the dead and we need to have faith in Jesus; that the Bible is important, that prayer is important, that we have a God who guides us, that the Holy Spirit can come and live within the individual believer; that we have a message to take out there that will change the world, that it will not all be easy – there are battles, and that Jesus came to form a community, so you can't be a Christian on your own and the church is vital. So that in a nutshell is what the Alpha course says and that's what Christians agree about.

AB: And about the Kingdom of God?

NG: Yeah!

AB: Is there anything else you would like to say?

NG: Not at the moment, thanks.

AB: Thank you for your time.

NG: Thank you very much. I hope the book goes really well.

Notes

[1] Editor's comment: 'The Rite for the Christian Initiation of Adults', used in the Roman Catholic Church as the process by which people become Catholic Christians.

[2] Editor's comment. Fr Raniero Cantalamessa is an Italian Fransiscan priest, who is 'Preacher to the Papal Household', an international speaker and retreat giver and the author of many books. He has taken up this theme of the battle being about the King (Jesus) on a number of occasions. One such occasion was at an event organised by HTB in 2005. This talk was recently published by Alpha Publications in a booklet called 'Faith that Overcomes the World'.

[3] Editor's comment: It was the theological 'battles' – and other issues – that split the Western Roman Catholic Church from the Eastern Orthodox Churches in the Eleventh Century. Again, it was the theological disagreements – along with other factors and battles – that split the European church into many national churches, denominations and other groupings in the Reformation period in the Sixteenth century.

CHAPTER 25

Closing Remarks
– and a look to the Future

Andrew Brookes

There is no doubting the impact of the Alpha Course. The statistics speak for themselves. It has made a positive contribution to the life of many churches from right across the church spectrum and on huge numbers of people, millions in fact, at various stages in their spiritual journey. This is the direct and most obviously intended impact of Alpha but there are others that follow in its wake.

A very significant part of these is that it has brought changes to how Christians look at mission and church and the relationship between them. (In part this may be in taking insights that were already being articulated and applied elsewhere and making them much better known.) Thus the role of the church in mission is being rediscovered – and this has a host of practical and pastoral applications and challenges, as well as being a source for useful theological reflection. The nature of how people come to believe and also participate in church and mission are other areas that are being seriously rethought in the light of the impact of Alpha. More work and reflection could still profitably be done here as well. Useful reflection is also being stimulated on the very content of what we present as the Gospel, and how we do it, not least as culture changes. This includes the place of the Holy Spirit though, as I have indicated in this book, reflection on Alpha has implications for how we understand and communicate other areas of God's revelation and salvation in Christ as well. (This may sometimes be less as a result of inherent strengths in Alpha but because it has triggered concerns and thus stimulated further reflection, such as in the link between proclamation and commitment to social justice.) We are rediscovering the importance and significance of hospitality, of conversion as journey and belonging, and much else. Alpha is making many think about the potential for using the media in proclamation of the Gospel. It is also helping to stimulate debate on the contextualisation/inculturation of the Gospel and its appropriate proclamation in different settings, even if AI's sensitivity in this area is disputed.

Alpha's ecumenical appeal is highly significant as well. It has accelerated the melting of many long standing suspicions and the dismantling of dividing walls between Christians. At a deeper level, there is increased respect and co-operation and mutual enrichment. Analysis of the course itself and how it works suggests that in Alpha there is, whether intended or not, synergistic coming together of the graced riches of different Christian traditions and streams. All of this makes the work of mission more effective – and may point to further coming together in the future. Even where other courses have been established, sometimes because of perceived problems or deficiencies with aspects of Alpha, they are in a way a fruit of its impact.

 All of these are really important and are things for the church in general to be grateful for to Alpha, AI/HTB and all the volunteers who have supported its use. It has changed the landscape of church and mission in this country in permanent ways, and continues to have an impact. I, for one, would also affirm the presence of God in the Alpha phenomenon and I have no doubt that the church should be grateful to God for the graces he has given to the church as a whole through the Alpha phenomenon.

However, rather than repeat or heap on further plaudits here, I wish to take some space to highlight and summarise issues of concern, that, if attended to, may help AI or the church more widely, develop fruitfully in the future. Alpha is not an end point. God is constantly at work, seeking to reconcile the world to himself in Christ, and Christians need to constantly move forward with him. I thus hope what follows will be read constructively.

My view, is that the different contributors, writing quite independently of each other, generally agree or at least complement each other. Alpha has been, and is, good – but it is not about to solve all our problems. Just rolling out more courses, undertaking national advertising (however good) and getting more people to do them will not take us beyond a tipping point leading to the conversion of the whole country. I think it is fair to say it is now clear that it is not 'a one size fits all' solution. However, as people become aware of its limitations they may also find the most realistic and effective ways of using it. Its impact on those already at church and its potential for changing – if slowly – the way a church operates should not be undervalued. Much can be learned from it, especially its method and deeper principles, and applied to other forms of mission and emerging church. Nonetheless, ongoing cultural shifts and the emergence of generations less and less influenced by Christianity, suggest the course by itself will become less effective in purely outreach terms over time. The content is most likely to date most rapidly.

But the course does not have to be viewed by itself – and perhaps this is the key to future development around Alpha. As Alpha needs to be seen and its story told in the context of the wider story of HTB, so the use of Alpha in any church needs to be linked to the wider life, vision, values and ethos of that church. If Alpha is to achieve much in evangelistic terms – and clearly it is currently only having limited success in this regard – then it is the whole church, not just the course, that has to become more effective at evangelisation. That means looking at developing small groups, be they cell groups, house groups, pastorates or basic ecclesial communities or some other variation. It means identifying and developing the gifts of everyone and encouraging all to take an appropriate active part in the life and mission of the church. It means being (much) more hospitable. Prayer and worship and overall programmes and processes of Christian initiation may well also need attention, as may Pre- and Post-Alpha formation and courses. Though Alpha Conferences do mention these features on the 'Integrating Alpha into the Church' session I think still more needs to be done.

It is clear from Nicky Gumbel's interview that AI is reluctant to be seen to impose things on other churches, indicating a respect for the autonomy of each local church. This suggests a desire to serve the wider church, rather than build an eccelsial empire of its own. Neither does AI want to expect too much response from other churches. However, the analysis of this book suggests that it would be helpful to have more explicit and developed ways of helping churches become missionary. Relatively few local churches achieve this by themselves at present. AI seems reluctant to undertake new initiatives until they have good, tried and tested resources available. It has helped AI build a reputation for providing high quality professional resources, something which NG's interview points out that they think is important. If anything it means AI is relatively slow to respond to some valid criticisms and this may help explain why so much effort has been focussed on Alpha for so long. It was the only resource available. More resources, looking at more aspects of integrating Alpha into church life, are increasingly becoming available so hopefully more can be done in this direction.

However, it is not just about resources in the sense of programmes etc. Training and really educating local church leaders (clerical and lay) so that they grasp the deeper principles and core values involved and can then apply them flexibly in their own context matters. Finding ways of linking and integrating Alpha with an awareness of what makes a healthy church (following Schwarz, Warren or alternatives) may prove very beneficial. It is commendable that AI is sensitive about not being heavy handed but this may mean they unintentionally leave local churches floundering. Finding a sensitive way of getting alongside local churches and really communicating with them may be necessary. Developing some form of mission accompaniment, which again can be combined with the use of healthy church indicators, may be very worthwhile. This specifically fosters ways of getting alongside local or emerging churches and ministries and helping them, while respecting their autonomy and character. Ironically, concentrating in these ways on the whole church and not just on a tool for outreach may result in more outreach – and sustained outreach at that!

This may prove a more fruitful use of limited finances than advertising, even if this is a good form of communication with a large audience. It appears that this, however successful, can only have a limited impact in evangelising the nation. Less stress on advertising would potentially allow still more flexibility, creativity and local adaptation, and thus more effective contextualisation/inculturation could be achieved.

It would also be helpful to build up and train local regional teams to a higher degree. These teams can then help still more people locally. Importantly they also provide a means for AI to know what is happening at ground level beyond HTB and discover and hopefully respond to the real diversity of local issues. Though this happens to a degree, it could be developed more. The regional offices may be significant in this regard too. Certainly there is evidence of a more localised response and set of supportive strategies beginning to emerge from 'Alpha Scotland' including adaptation to aspects of the Scottish situation.

Such training needs as I am articulating here, which need to go beyond just teaching people to be 'technicians' who put on a programme, may be easier to develop and deliver with the emergence of the Alpha International Campus (AIC). In fact, the range of ministry areas that it is proposed that AIC will develop is encouraging and suggests that a more holistic and integrated approach to the development of church and mission is possible and even, perhaps, already on the agenda. Hints are emerging from AI/HTB that AIC was part of its original vision. It certainly seems to me to give a more rounded and balanced feel to the whole project and potentially provide significantly more chance of effectively helping AI to deliver their vision of (re)-evangelising the nation(s) and transforming society. Initiatives linked to social care and transformation, commitment to the poor, urban mission, and also support for the family are, amongst others, all welcome. Though I did not know about AIC until the very end of this writing project, it could enable AI/HTB to respond to many of the issues, concerns and suggestions put forward in this book.

All this points to the development of AIC as a major new phase in the Alpha phenomenon. To see this in perspective I will outline the 'history of Alpha', which I am inclined to consider in different phases even though it is a simplification. I would outline these thus:

- *Phase 1:* The development of Alpha within a developing HTB until 1992 (*c.*1977–92 [or earlier regarding HTB]);

- *Phase 2:* The initial offering of Alpha with its resources and conference training to the wider church and the rapid uptake of this accompanied by the 'move of God' at HTB (1993–7);

- *Phase 3:* The support and development of use of Alpha with national advertising along with the creation and development of Alpha International (1998–2006);

- *Phase 4:* The Development of Alpha International Campus (2006–).

Clearly, subdivisions can be suggested and other features are import-ant, including the expansion of Alpha overseas as seen in Phase 3. Each phase has built on the previous one and flowed out of it. During each phase the beginning of developments, resources and the identifica-tion and emergence of key personnel, all important for the next phase have happened. Further concrete evidence points to a new phase and strategies. New personnel capable of taking forward new ministries and training have already been identified and HTB or associates already now have experience with many of the proposed ministry develop-ments. Also, billboard advertising has not being undertaken in 2006–7. It will be interesting to see how this new phase develops.

Will AI still see itself as mainly a service and resource provider to the wider church? It is certainly that, but these developments will add new dimensions and energy to the wider 'Alpha Movement', or the 'Alpha Family' as it is sometimes called. Will these different ministries cohere or will they be relatively independent and disparate? They will most probably cohere within HTB and its most closely associated churches. Other churches can choose to take them up on a piece meal basis if they prefer. Nonetheless I suspect that along with this a clearer sense of an 'Alpha Movement' will develop, though I am not convinced that deliberately forming such a movement is a primary intention of AI. However, I expect that around all these ministries and training a more coherent and explicit sense of what connects and holds everything together will emerge. By this I do not mean a sinister plot but that the values, attitudes, and if you like spirituality and even theology of this wider 'Alpha movement' will emerge, be reflected on and be articulated more clearly. The Alpha Movement will become better defined and have more self-understanding. It will be interesting to see how all this will be expressed and some of the reflections in this book may give some useful clues and pointers and may even contribute explicit elements of this. Nor is it yet clear whether the Alpha Movement will be relatively tightly bound and uniform and theologically and spiritually 'monochrome' or whether it will be a looser and more plural set of expressions (possibly reflecting different denominations or traditions) held together in a looser federation/ fellowship. If the latter, it will be possible for a person or church to feel they are part of the Alpha Movement and also adhere by other forms of belonging to other groups and networks. As I have argued, I do not think it is appropriate to see it as just Evangelical-Charismatic Christianity (as that is typically understood) writ large. Whatever happens, the issues and challenges of contextualisation/inculturation need to be engaged with in an ongoing way. How the Alpha Movement develops in part also depends on how the rest of Christianity in these islands, and especially the denominations and other agencies that support it, change. There are likely to be major changes in the years ahead. The future development of Alpha, AI and AIC is inevitably bound up with all these too.

All these developments will take the pressure off Alpha as such. It may receive less of the limelight (within and beyond AI) but this, with the less intense scrutiny that it entails, may increase its shelf life. That said, there was much agreement from various contributors that the content could still do with an update. In a visit I made in February 2006, NG again noted to the HTB Alpha team and gathered advisors the extent to which small-group conversation goes all over the place during the first three weeks. Interestingly, this is when the talks or videos focus most on the presentation of who Jesus is and the main purpose of his life, death and resurrection. NG also observed in his interview (Chapter 24) that it is precisely in grasping the identity and saving mission of Jesus that biggest changes have occurred over the years for guests, and where the biggest challenges now lie for churches. It was also these areas that I highlighted in Chapter 8 as probably being of the most concern. Having pondered things some more, I am inclined to think some significant development could be achieved within the scope of a ten-week course, a useful time period. How similar to Alpha such a course would be remains to be seen (since I have not developed these rudimentary thoughts) and also changing the content significantly might be resisted for a whole range of other reasons.

Whether or not Alpha stays the same, and even though it may well end up with a lower profile over the next years, it will continue to have an impact for the foreseeable future. However, it may turn out that the humble discipleship course that has given its name to a huge global organisation – Alpha International – and to a major training base – AIC – one day will cease to be a major part of the work of these. In short, it may have to decrease that mission may increase. NG has always said they (HTB) will move on from Alpha when it is clear there are better alternatives. Yet Alpha and its huge impact are reasons why AI, and soon AIC, exist and it rightly gives them its name! Even if the Alpha Course itself was to stop running completely, the Alpha phenomenon is likely to continue!

It may prove helpful to more sharply distinguish the future work of HTB, Alpha and Alpha International. Alpha is largely fixed to its existing form by copyright and branding and its own inner coherence. HTB has more freedom but is a specific local church within the Church of England, though this and the wider Anglican Communion are facing very unsettling times and issues. AI may have the most freedom and scope of all for development, since its mission statement gives it a very broad brief. It also has world wide considerations to address beyond the UK. Alpha too may have very different histories in other parts of the world. International variations will probably occur with Alpha increasing in use in some places as it decreases in others. In practice, HTB may want to go on and look at other approaches to evangelism – while other churches still run Alpha. AI will increasingly promote other courses and ministries to support 'evangelisation and the transformation of society'. Its mission statement allows for this. Although most of these have emerged out of HTB perhaps in the future these may also come form other parts of the church. All of this may appear to marginalise Alpha itself. However, in reality, some use of Alpha is likely to persist even if it becomes less significant – even at HTB perhaps – and proportionately less significant within AI.

So there is good reason to think that there is a future for the Alpha Course in the UK and probably a bigger one still for the Alpha phenomenon. Many courses are still being run. Overall these still attract large numbers of guests, and a significant number of these become more involved with Jesus, church and mission as a result. In the final analysis, if Alpha decreases in the future it is not important if mission and church increase. Few things last forever. It has already served a very useful purpose. At the end of the day Jesus Christ is the real Alpha. He is also the Omega and everything in between (Rev 1:8, 21:6, 22:14). It is he who calls people to mission, because he, with the Father and Spirit, are a Missionary God. Let people look to him, giving thanks for the past, committed to the present and confident in the future he is bringing. Abide in him, follow and obey him and people will be fruitful! And the fruit will last (Jn 15:1–8)!

Let the last words be those of Jesus, words that assign Christians their task but also assure them, that challenge and also comfort them always.

> 'All authority in heaven and earth has been given to me. Go, therefore, make disciples of all nations; baptise them in the name of the Father and of the Son and of the Holy Spirit, and teach them to observe all the commands I gave you. And look, I am with you always; yes, to the end of time.'
>
> (Mt 28:19–20)

APPENDIX

Information on other Process Courses and healthy Church resources

Process Courses

The Alpha Course

15 sessions over 10 weeks with weekend away. Materials published by Alpha Publications or Kingsway. Plenty of other courses available too. www.alphacourse.org.

Catholic Faith Exploration (CaFE)

Based on videos and then sharing groups in a relaxed setting. Comes in several modules of around 7 weeks each. Mostly aimed at churched/ fringe/dechurched Catholics. Produced at various dates since around 2000. Videos, training materials and course booklets available from Catholic Evangelisation Services. www.catholicevangel.org.

Christianity Explored

15 sessions over 10 weeks with weekend away. Generally considered more attractive to conservative Protestants than Alpha. Materials are by Rico Tice with others. Published by Paternoster Press in 2001. Updated recently and with a follow up Course 'Discipleship Explored' now available. www.christianityexplored.com.

Emmaus

Comes in several modules, the Nurture module (15 sessions, no weekend required) corresponding most closely with Alpha. Designed by the Church of England but for broad church appeal. Published by Church House Publishing. Updated since turn of millenium. www.e-mmaus.org.uk.

Essence

A 6-week course with an experiential and exploratory (less didactic) feel, focusing on spirituality and prayer. Connects with New Age issues. Developed by Rob Frost. Kingsway, 2002. A children's version is now available. Other resources available. www.sharejesusinternational. com.

Start!

A 6-week course using video clips. Less academic and more interactive presentations than Alpha etc. Aimed at more working class audience. Published by Church pastoral Aid Society in 2003. www.cpas.org.uk

Y Course

8-week enquirer course consisting of 30-minute talks followd by discussion groups. A more intellectual emphasis with more focus on traditional apologetics than Alpha. Published in 1999 by Agape. (Book of course-talks is *Beyond Belief* by Peter Meadows *et al*).

Many of these courses have specially designed youth versions and materials too.

Other process courses:

Credo (1996). Considered to be Anglo-Catholic.

Good News Down Your Street. Originally produced in1982.

Saints Alive! (revised in 2001)

Charles Freebury makes various 'supplements' available:
    charles.freebury@tiscali.co.uk

Home-grown courses work very well locally – so writing your own course is a good option!

Resources for developing Church Life using indicators of healthy Church Life

Christian Schwarz, *Natural Church Development Handbook* p. 34. (British Church Growth Association, 3rd edition, 1998 Website: www.healthychurch.co.uk.

Robert Warren, *The Healthy Churches Handbook* (Church House Publishing, 2004)

Centre for Mission Accompaniment Writing Group (ed Terry Tennens), *Journey into Growth (Introducing Mission Accompaniment and its Core Values)*, Churches Together in Britain and Ireland, 2006. Website: www.missionaccompaniment.com